The Authors of *Get Into Any College: Secrets Of Harvard Students*

"*Get Into Any College: Secrets Of Harvard Students* delivers 243 pages of invaluable information ranging from the elimination of admission myths to successfully tapping into scholarship funds. From start to finish, (the authors) provide informative step-by-step information combined with their experiences at Harvard, as well as ... the world of other Ivy Leaguers who have traveled down similar paths."

—Leonard Banks, *The Journal Press*

"*Get Into Any College: Secrets Of Harvard Students* is the first college admissions strategy book that actually shows you how to get into college. Authored by recent Harvard graduates Gen and Kelly Tanabe, *Get Into Any College* is the first book to feature the strategies and stories of real students who have been accepted to the country's top colleges. ... The book is filled with student-tested strategies to help applicants write better essays that stand out from the pile, promote themselves during college interviews, ace the SAT and ACT, and find free cash for college."

—Pam Costa, *Santa Clara Vision*

"When you consider the costs of a four year college or university education nowadays, think about forking out (the price) for this little gem written and produced by two who know."

—Don Denevi, *Palo Alto Daily News*

"What's even better than all the top-notch tips is that the book is written in a cool, conversational way and even offers anecdotal bits in their *Stories From Real Life* section."

—*College Bound Magazine*

"The Tanabes literally wrote the book on the topic, having authored the award-winning book, *Get Into Any College: Secrets Of Harvard Students*. The husband-and-wife team also pen the column *Ask the College Experts* appearing in over 200 newspapers nationwide."

—*Bull & Bear Financial Report*

"The Reading List: Offers advice on writing a good entrance essay, taking exams and applying for scholarships, and other information on the college experience—start to finish."

—*Town & Country Magazine*

"*Get Into Any College: Secrets Of Harvard Students* is the first college admissions strategy book that actually shows one how to get into college. (It) is the first book to feature the strategies and stories of real students who have been accepted to the country's top colleges."

—*New Jersey Spectator Leader*

"College applicants need real strategies they can use today, not condescending, common sense theories from so-called 'experts' who applied to college 20 years ago. The authors' goal is to connect students struggling with admissions with the lessons learned by those who have done it before to improve their chances of success."
—Robin R. Plasterer, *The Post & Mail*

"Tanabe, an expert on the application process, can discuss such topics as how to get into the college of your choice, ways to finance your college education, applying online and what universities are looking for in a student."
—*Asbury Park Press*

"Applying for college can be a drag for high school seniors who don't always know exactly what admissions officers are looking for. Now there is a book that can help. *Get Into Any College: Secrets Of Harvard Students* is filled with student-tested strategies to help college applicants write better essays, perform better in interviews, and score higher on entrance exams."
—*The Daily News*

"Gen and Kelly collected college admissions essays—both successful and unsuccessful ... and reproduced them as guidelines for high school students. They interviewed admissions officials, high school teachers and, of course, students."
—Sarah Weld, *San Mateo County Times*

"The Tanabes spent three years researching and writing the how-to book on college admissions, test-taking and essay writing. They wrote the book after recognizing high school students' need for concrete advice on how to beat the admissions game. They used real-life essays from students admitted to top universities."
—Sherri Eng, *The San Jose Mercury News*

Benjamin Franklin Award Finalist. Named in honor of America's most cherished publisher/printer, the Benjamin Franklin Award recognizes excellence in independent publishing. Publications, grouped by genre, are judged on editorial and design merit by top practitioners in each field. *Get Into Any College: Secrets Of Harvard Students* is a Benjamin Franklin Award Finalist.

GET FREE CASH FOR COLLEGE

Scholarship Secrets Of Harvard Students

- BONUS: Comprehensive Scholarship Directory in addition to Scholarship Strategy Guide

- Step-by-step instructions on how to find, apply for, and win scholarships

- Learn from the successes and failures of real students

- The only resource you will ever need on scholarships, including special chapters for graduate students and parents

Gen S. Tanabe • **Kelly Y. Tanabe**

Harvard graduates and authors of the award-winning book
Get Into Any College: Secrets Of Harvard Students

Get Free Cash For College: Scholarship Secrets Of Harvard Students
By Gen S. Tanabe and Kelly Y. Tanabe

Published by SuperCollege, LLC
4546 B10 El Camino Real, #281
Los Altos, CA 94022
650-618-2221
www.supercollege.com

Credits: Cover photo courtesy of George Tanabe. Cover design by Rey Serrano. Edited by Bob Drews. All essays in this book are used by permission of their authors.

Scholarship Data: Provided by Wintergreen/Orchard House, an imprint of Riverside Publishing. Copyright © 2000 by The Riverside Publishing Company. Reproduced with permission. All rights reserved.

Trademarks: All brand names, product names, and services used in this book are trademarks, registered trademarks, or tradenames of their respective holders. SuperCollege is not associated with any college, university, product, service, or vendor.

Disclaimers: This book and SuperCollege are not affiliated with Harvard University and the information in this book is not endorsed by Harvard University. The authors and publisher have used their best efforts in preparing this book. It is intended to provide helpful and informative material on the subject matter. Some narratives and names have been modified for illustrative purposes. SuperCollege and the authors make no representations or warranties with respect to the accuracy or completeness of the contents of the book and specifically disclaim any implied warranties or merchantability or fitness for a particular purpose. There are no warranties which extend beyond the descriptions contained in this paragraph. The accuracy and completeness of the information provided herein and the opinions stated herein are not guaranteed or warranted to produce any particular results. It is sold with the understanding that neither the publisher nor the authors are engaged in rendering legal, accounting, or other professional services. If legal advice or other expert assistance is required, the services of a competent professional person should be sought. SuperCollege and the authors specifically disclaim any responsibility for any liability, loss or risk, personal or otherwise, which is incurred as a consequence, directly or indirectly, of the use and application of any of the contents of this book.

Special Sales: For information on using SuperCollege books in the classroom or special prices for bulk quantities, please contact our Special Sales department at 650-618-2221 or write to the address above.

ISBN 0-9657556-4-9

Manufactured in the United States of America
10 9 8 7 6 5 4 3 2 1

Cataloging-in-Publication Data
Gen S. Tanabe, Kelly Y. Tanabe
     Get Free Cash For College: Scholarship Secrets Of Harvard Students / by Gen S. Tanabe and Kelly Y. Tanabe. –1st ed.
          p.   cm.
     Includes appendices and index.
     ISBN 0-9657556-4-9
     1. College Guides   I. Title
     2. Personal Finance   3. Reference

About SuperCollege
Our mission is to provide the best resources to help you get into and pay for college. We approach college admissions and financial aid from a practical, hands-on point of view. Drawing on the collective knowledge and experiences of students at America's top colleges, we provide real strategies that you can use to increase your chances of getting into your dream school and paying for your education. Please visit our companion website SuperCollege.com (www.supercollege.com) to access more financial aid and scholarship tips and strategies and apply for the SuperCollege.com Scholarship awarded to both parents and students.

Contents At A Glance

Table Of Contents

Part I. Scholarship Strategy Guide

Chapter 8. Strategies For Specific Scholarships / 99

Chapter 9. Free Cash For Graduate School / 115

Chapter 10. Financial Aid Workshop / 127

21 Scholarship Indexes / 363

Special Features

Stories From Real Life

These stories about the successes and failures of real students are entertaining and enlightening. They serve as valuable lessons about how the scholarship process really works!

Tanabe Philosophies

Each chapter includes a Tanabe Philosophy, a brief but important summary of our overall approach. Knowing the larger picture first will help you understand how the rest of the strategies fit together.

Special Highlights

As a step-by-step strategy guide, we have created easy-to-follow practical methods for key areas of the scholarship process.

Quotables

Throughout each chapter are highlights from students, parents, and scholarship judges about their experiences with the financial aid and scholarship process. Many offer interesting insights on how you can improve your search for financial aid.

To our families for shaping who we are.

To Harvard for four of the best years of our lives.

To the many students and friends who made this book possible by
sharing their scholarship experiences, secrets, successes, and failures.

To all the students and parents who understand that paying for college
is a challenging but worthwhile endeavor.

Discover The Key To Free Cash For College

• •

In this chapter, you'll learn:

- Why we're your best personal guides through the scholarship process

- Why not all financial aid is made equal

- The seven urban legends of scholarships

- Why scholarships are financial aid jackpots

- How scholarships are judged & how to beat the system

• •

How This Book Will Help You Get Free Cash For College

We vividly remember the day we received the thick envelope from Harvard. Elated, we read the acceptance letter with disbelief and screamed with excitement. Our parents congratulated us, their faces lit with pride. Then they asked the question that every parent fears from their child's birth, "How are we going to pay the tuition?"

If you're lucky, your last name is Trump, Gates, or Rockefeller. Or, (and this is even less likely!) your parents started saving for your college education since you were a proverbial twinkle in their eyes. But, since you're reading this book, chances are you're like the rest of us, your parents may have some college savings, but you'll also need to do your part and try to win as much free cash as possible from scholarships and financial aid.

Winning over $100,000 in merit-based scholarships allowed us to leave Harvard debt-free and our parents guilt-free. In this book, we will personally guide you step-by-step through every stage of the scholarship process and share the secrets of how we and other students did it!

In our cases we knew that no trust funds bore our names and that we would have to rely on scholarships and financial aid to help foot the bills and save our parents from taking out multiple mortgages. As we researched the scholarship and financial aid opportunities open to us, we made some startling discoveries.

First, we quickly learned that our parents and our friends' parents really didn't know where to go to learn about the financial aid options open to them. With glazed eyes and clenched fists, our parents admitted that they didn't know where to start and the information that they were able to find was about as clear as fog.

Our second discovery was that there were a lot of scholarship directories that were as fat as phone books but provided no hands-on tips or strategies on how to actually win the scholarships. We would rather write five knockout scholarship applications and actually win those five awards than apply to a dozen and win none.

Most importantly, through researching and speaking with students who had already gone through the scholarship and financial aid process, we discovered some extremely effective methods of applying for and winning scholarships. In fact, we won over $100,000 in merit-based awards, ranging from small one-time awards from the local Lions Club to national four-year renewable awards. We left Harvard debt-free and our parents guilt-free. The students we interviewed in researching this book won many, many times more this amount. Some even paid for all four years of their education with nothing more than merit-based scholarships.

What you will find in the first half of this book is our Scholarship Strategy Guide, everything we know and have learned about how to win scholarships and get financial aid. You will learn all of the ins and outs of scholarships, grants, federal financial aid, and more. We guarantee that the glazed look and clenched fists that tormented our parents will not afflict you.

The second half of the book is where you actually get to put what you learned into action. We have put together the most comprehensive Scholarship Directory where there are billions of dollars waiting to be won—by you, of course!

The Cost Of A Good Education

The best strategy is one that you know works. Through the experiences of real students, we show you how to build a complete scholarship strategy to help you win a share of the over $64 billion that is awarded in scholarships and financial aid each year.

College costs often invoke simultaneous feelings of fright, shock, and apprehension. The price tag is staggering–an average of $8,086 per year for tuition and room and board at four-year public schools and $21,339 at private schools.* These costs have grown approximately 30% over the past 10 years, and we all know that the costs will continue to grow.

That is the bad news. The good news is that there was over $64 billion awarded in scholarships and financial aid in 1998-99. Your challenge is to get your slice of this scholarship and financial aid pie.

Tackling scholarships and financial aid on your own can be difficult. There is a mind-numbing vocabulary of new acronyms and confusing financial terms. Information is dispersed across books, newspapers, websites, government documents, and other sources, many of which seem to be aimed at financial experts. Misconceptions also flourish about what it takes to get financial aid and earn scholarship dollars. How can you wade through all of the information (and potentially harmful misinformation) to find what you really need?

The answer is here in your hands. The sole purpose of this book is to show you how to win scholarships and get financial aid. We will share all that we have learned from not only our own experiences but also those of dozens of other students. We want you to emulate our collective triumphs and avoid our most tragic blunders. In short we want you to leave college debt-free and your parents guilt-free.

The Tanabe Philosophy

The "Tanabe" what? We know you didn't buy this book to learn Eastern philosophy, and don't worry you won't. However, in each chapter we offer what we call the Tanabe Philosophy, a brief but important summary of our overall approach. Knowing the large picture will help you understand how all of the smaller points fit.

To begin, we will share with you our view of scholarships in general. We have found that the biggest myth about scholarships is that you have to be an academic, athletic, or extracurricular superstar to win. This is utterly false.

You don't have to be an academic, athletic, or extracurricular superstar to win scholarships.

We don't believe winning is easy. There is tough competition because scholarships are essentially cash prizes with few, if any, strings attached. However, like everything, you can learn how to take your strengths and package them in a way that will increase your chances of winning. Matched with the right scholarships (and there are thousands out there–just check out how many we have in this book alone!) nearly any student regardless of how unacademic, unathletic, or un-extracurricular oriented can win. The secret to winning is to pick scholarships that reward your strengths and then craft an application that makes a nuclear bomb sized impression on the judges.

The truth is that regardless of what kind of student you are, whether or not you win will come down to whether you have a solid strategy.

* *Trends In College Pricing 1999* by The College Board

What You Will Learn From This Book

We will be your personal navigators through the financial aid and scholarship process. Incorporating intensive research and interviews with dozens of students, parents, and scholarship judges, our approach is to use the real-life examples and experiences of those who have achieved the greatest success in funding their college educations. These are proven strategies you can use immediately to improve your chances of winning aid.

Here are some of the insights you'll gain from reading this book. You will learn how to:

● Use a variety of sources to find scholarships and select those that you have the highest chances of winning (Chapter 2, *Find Scholarships You Can Win*)

● Prevent being deceived by tempting and costly scholarship scams (Chapter 3, *Avoid Scholarship Scams*)

● Create powerful scholarship applications that stand out from the rest of the pile (Chapter 4, *Create Stunning Scholarship Applications*)

● Insure you receive supportive recommendations from your teachers and professors (Chapter 5, *Get The Right Recommendations*)

● Craft irresistible scholarship essays that grasp the attention of scholarship committees (Chapter 6, *Secrets To Writing Winning Essays*)

● Take command of the scholarship interview (Chapter 7, *Ace The Interviews*)

● Tweak your application for scholarships in common, specific categories such as academics, leadership, athletics, public service, career field, and more (Chapter 8, *Strategies For Specific Scholarships*)

● Apply many of these tactics toward winning money for graduate school (Chapter 9, *Free Cash For Graduate School*)

● Successfully navigate your way through the federal financial aid process with easy to understand descriptions of federal aid eligibility, requirements, and proven strategies for applying (Chapter 10, *Financial Aid Workshop*)

● As parents, understand financial aid and income tax principles and learn how to provide the help that your student needs to succeed (Chapter 11, *Parents' Guide To Scholarships & Financial Aid*)

● Maximize the potential of the Internet as a free method for finding and applying for scholarships (Chapter 12, *Unleash The Power Of The Internet*)

● Make sense of the financial aid jargon with our easy-to-understand glossary of terms (Appendix A)

● Get additional help with our financial aid and scholarship resource guide (Appendix B)

In addition you will also be able to search our massive Scholarship Directory to find scholarships that fit your financial status, education, goals, and background. To help you locate the most appropriate scholarships, the directory is organized and indexed by category.

In this book, we cover every phase of the scholarship process from finding scholarships to creating winning applications and essays to keeping the money you win.

Seven Scholarship Urban Legends Debunked

You don't have to be financially destitute or an academic or athletic superstar to win scholarships. However, you do need a solid strategy.

You may have heard rumors about scholarships like: You have to have near zero dinero in order to qualify or you have to be the record holder for three-point shots to win. The truth is that many rumors you hear are not true. To help you sort the truth from the tall tale, here are some common scholarship myths and the truth behind them.

Myth #1: Only the most financially destitute are eligible.

The Truth: The most common myth is that you need to be financially destitute in order to win scholarships. While it is true that financial need is a consideration for some scholarships, the definition of "need" varies considerably. Given the cost of a college education, many families who consider themselves to be "middle class" actually qualify for need-based scholarships. Plus, keep in mind that there are many scholarships where financial need is not even a factor. There merit-based scholarships are based on achievements, skills, and talents.

Myth #2: Only star athletes get scholarships, especially full tuition scholarships.

The Truth: The reality is that athletics are a source of revenue for colleges. What better way to maintain ties with alumni's wallets than to have a victorious football team for them to cheer on? There are significant numbers of full tuition and part tuition scholarships that are awarded to these revenue generators, er, athletes. However, this doesn't mean that you have to be the next Michael Jordan to win a scholarship. Colleges are under tremendous pressure to compete academically and have many awards for talented, motivated students who are entirely inept in all ball- or net-based interactions. You will see in this book's Scholarship Directory that there are literally thousands of scholarships for the athletically challenged. Of course if you are an athlete, nothing will help you win that scholarship more than combining your stellar performance on the field with a superbly crafted application using the strategies in Chapter 8.

Myth #3: You need straight A's to win money for college.

The Truth: There's a reason why your parents and teachers have been urging you to hit the books ever since you can remember. They've known that good grades are your key to getting into a good college and winning scholarships. Straight A's certainly don't hurt your chances of winning, as grades are a factor in many scholarships. However, you don't have to have a perfect record. Many scholarships are based on criteria other than grades and awarded for specific skills or talents such as linguistic, athletic, or artistic ability to name a few. Even for scholarships in which grades are considered, oftentimes grades are not the most important factor. For many scholarships, there is a minimum grade point average (GPA) required, but once the minimum is met, the specific GPA is not a consideration. For others, grades are often one of many measures the judges weigh. This all means that you don't need a perfect or even near-perfect transcript to win scholarships.

Myth #4: You should get involved in as many extracurricular activities as possible to win.

The Truth: Scholarship competitions are not pie eating contests where you win through volume. They are like baking contests in which you create an exquisite desert with an appearance and flavor that matches the tastes of the judges. Scholarships are won by quality not quantity.

"I thought that applying for scholarships would be a piece of cake because I was pretty successful at applying to colleges. At first I tried to apply for scholarships in the same way I applied for colleges, but I soon realized that the two were very different. Scholarship applications require much more focus on the individual award and what it's trying to achieve."

—Patrick

Selection committees are looking for students who have made quality contributions that fit the mission of the awards. For example, for a public service scholarship, the judges would be more impressed if you organized and led a school-wide volunteer day than if you were a member of 20 volunteer organizations but did little to distinguish yourself in them. Scholarship judges are looking for meaningful involvement, not a laundry list of clubs that you've joined.

Myth #5: You can and should apply to every scholarship for which you are eligible.

The Truth: When you turn 35, you technically are eligible to become President of the United States. This hardly means that you should start packing your bags for the White House. Similarly, just because you are technically eligible for a scholarship does not mean that you should apply for it. The reason why? You have a limited amount of time to spend on scholarship applications. It is necessary to allocate your time to those in which you have the best chance of winning. You may find that you are technically eligible for 500 scholarships. Unless you're willing to make applying to scholarships your full time avocation, it's unlikely that you can apply to more than a dozen awards. Thus, you need to be selective about which scholarships you fit the best and focus your attention on those. You'll learn how to narrow down your list of scholarships to apply to in Chapter 2. One caveat: This does not mean that you should only apply to the two or three scholarships that fit you best. You should still apply to as many scholarships as you can—just make sure you have them prioritized correctly.

Myth #6: You can use the same strategies for college applications and scholarship applications.

The Truth: College applications and scholarship applications are like twins in some ways. They look alike because they both have application forms, essays, recommendation letters, and interviews. Some strategies for applying are similar and can be transferred from college applications to scholarship applications. However, as twins have separate and distinct personalities, so do college and scholarship applications. The main difference is that your goal with college applications is to demonstrate why you would be a good fit with the entering class of students. Your goal with scholarship applications is to show how you and your accomplishments fulfill the mission of the scholarship, which is oftentimes very different from the mission of a college.

For example, if you were applying for a sculpting scholarship, your application would be very different from your college application. Your college application would include general information about your education and all of your major accomplishments. Your scholarship application would focus on your sculpting skills. There may be material that you can use in both types of applications, but only if it fits. For different goals, you need different approaches to applying.

Myth #7: There's nothing you can do to increase your chances of winning.

The Truth: The crux of our approach as you read in the Tanabe Philosophy is that there are many concrete steps you can take to improve your chances of winning scholarships. In the following chapters you will learn how to select scholarships that best fit you and your background, create a powerful application, write winning essays, and successfully present yourself in interviews. Our approach is to teach you what the most successful students have found to work. There is no secret formula that guarantees that you will win, but we know that our strategies have worked for others and can work for you too.

What The Heck Is Financial Aid?

Before delving into strategies for winning aid, you should understand what you are trying to win. There are different types of aid available, each with its own requirements, advantages, and disadvantages. The types of financial aid available are:

Grants: Money with no strings attached–meaning you don't have to pay it back. This is really the equivalent of hitting the financial aid jackpot. Grants are often awarded by the government and based on financial need.
Advantages: Grants do not need to be repaid.
Disadvantages: Often limited to those with substantial financial need.

Loans: Money you borrow and are required to pay back with interest. In most cases the terms are more generous than other types of loans such as home or auto loans. Loans are based on financial need.
Advantages: Loans are often the easiest form of financial aid to obtain. Often you do not need to repay them until after you graduate or leave school.
Disadvantages: Unlike the other forms of financial aid, loans need to be repaid.

Work-Study: Money you earn the old-fashioned way–by working. This federal program subsidizes your on-campus employment while you are enrolled in school. The program is based on financial need.
Advantages: Allows you to gain valuable work experience while in school. Opens up employment opportunities that are not available to students who are not eligible for work-study.
Disadvantages: You will need to balance your schoolwork with your part-time job. Limited to those with financial need.

Scholarships: Money with no strings attached–meaning you don't have to pay it back. Like grants, scholarships are financial aid jackpots. They are awarded based on a variety of criteria including academics, financial need, leadership, special talents, or academic or career field.

Financial aid comes in many forms. We focus on scholarships in this book because they are the only form of aid that comes with virtually no strings attached and that you can significantly affect your chances of winning.

Advantages: Many are open to students of all financial backgrounds. There are scholarships available that fit your background and accomplishments. You have the ability to affect your chances of winning by the application you create. *Disadvantages:* There is tough competition. Hundreds if not thousands of students may compete for the same scholarship awards.

In this book, we focus mostly on scholarships. Of course this does not mean that you should not apply for the other kinds of financial aid. To the contrary, the majority of financial aid dollars are awarded through loans, work-study, and grants provided by the government. However, there are some advantages that scholarships offer over other forms of financial aid.

• **First, you don't have to hold down a job to win them**. For work-study, you need to work part-time and for loans, you need to toil after graduating to pay them off.

• **Scholarships are also open to students from all financial backgrounds**. The other types of financial aid are based almost exclusively on your parents' and your financial background, something that you have little control over. There are some scholarships that are based on financial need, but there are many that are not.

• **Most importantly, unlike other types of financial aid available, scholarships allow you the greatest opportunity to determine your chances of winning**. Because you create your application and write your essay, you control how you present yourself to the selection committee.

Why Scholarships Are The Financial Aid Jackpots

Scholarships truly are jackpots. With few, if any, strings attached to the money, scholarships can range in size from $100 to over $50,000. They can be awarded from one year to four years.

Scholarships are provided by diverse organizations including schools, colleges, churches, state and local governments, companies, and civic, political, service, and athletic organizations—just to name a few. Often, these groups provide awards to promote their cause. For businesses, the cause may be to contribute to the communities in which they operate or to build relationships with future potential employees. For colleges, the motive may be to recruit the best students, to create a diverse student population by attracting those with different backgrounds, or to encourage students to enter nontraditional fields. Local and civic organizations often promote the missions of their organizations. For example, an equestrian club might sponsor a scholarship to promote horseback riding among students.

For practically every cause, occupation, hobby, and passion that exists, there is a scholarship. It's no wonder that with a little bit of detective work you can find many awards that match your particular skills, talents, achievements, and background. However, nearly all scholarships can be divided into two major categories:

There are scholarships for practically every cause, talent, or interest in existence. Some are based on your financial background (need-based), and others are based on your skills and experience (merit-based).

Need-based: Scholarships in which financial need is a criterion. The importance of financial need and the definition of financial need in the selection process vary by scholarship. For some scholarships, it may be the most important

Story From Real Life: How I Judge Scholarships

Get into the mind of a judge from a national technology company's scholarship. Understanding what happens once your application is received is key to learning how to create a winning application. Read on—you may be surprised.
—Gen and Kelly

The first thing you should understand about national scholarships like ours is the magnitude. We don't just get a box of applications for our scholarship. We get truckloads of applications. I am on the small team of people who sift through this mountain of paperwork.

Our first step is to make a quick first pass. We spend about 10 to 20 seconds taking a brief look at the applications. Even though we don't spend much time on each application, we quickly eliminate applications that don't meet the basic requirements. We purge applications that are not complete, missing information or materials, illegible, or sloppily completed. We're pretty rigid in our decisions because we've found that if students don't even follow our award's simple directions, they probably aren't that attentive to their studies either.

After this first pass, we separate the applications into two piles. One is the pile of students we send thank you notes for entering. The other is the pile with potential. We spend on average between one and three minutes per application, hitting the highlights of the application form and reading the first few paragraphs of the essay. If we are impressed, we place the application in a separate pile.

Our last step is to separate the truly outstanding applications from the merely great ones. This is always the most difficult part. There are always so many more students with superb qualifications than we have scholarships to give. It's not easy to point out exactly what makes an application rise above the rest, but here are some qualities I've found common to our winners:

Academics. There are some scholarships in which academics is not the most important factor. For us, academic excellence is a prerequisite. Students don't have to have perfect grade point averages, but they do have to be committed to their schoolwork and take challenging courses. This should be reflected in the application.

Leadership. We look for students who have made a difference by being leaders in their activities. You don't have to be student body president to be a leader. You can show leadership by serving your community, speaking out for what you believe in, or being an example for other students. We want students who will make a difference both in college and beyond.

Originality. Students with an original approach to their essays rise to the top. Creativity shows intelligence and a readiness to think differently, which is something our company values.

Results. In the students' activities, we seek students who have demonstrated that they can deliver results. We don't care what area these results are in (i.e., music, service, science, sports) but we do want to see that there are actions that support the applicants' words.

Personality. One of the most important things we want are students who we feel like we know after reading their applications. It's important that students convey a piece of who they really are and that we feel like we've gotten to know them a little better through their applications.

Some scholarship judges have the luxury of being able to interview their finalists. Personally, I think it would help to meet the person behind the application. However, I think we do a great job relying on the applications, essays, and recommendations. It's amazing how well you can get to know someone just through their written words.

—Mary, a scholarship judge

factor or may be required for eligibility. For others, it may be one of many factors that are used to pick a winner.

Merit-based: Scholarships in which financial need is not a requirement to apply. These scholarships are based on other qualities such as skills, talents, or accomplishments often with no consideration to your financial status.

How Scholarships Are Judged & How To Beat The System

To beat the system you must understand that organizations provide scholarships to fulfill a specific goal or mission. It's crucial that you understand the mission of the scholarship and craft an application that demonstrates beyond a shadow of a doubt that you best fulfill it.

Unlike a lottery jackpot, scholarships are not based entirely on luck. To win scholarships, you need to show the selection committee how you fit the award. The vehicle is often the scholarship application, essay, and interview. The most important factors in selecting winners may include:

Overall fit with the scholarship's mission: How you fit the goal that the scholarship is trying to achieve. This is the most important criterion.

Application: Your official stats sheet which summarizes your grades, scores, coursework, and achievements.

Recommendations: Letters from teachers, professors, or others about you and your accomplishments.

Essay or Project: The essay is usually on a topic provided by the scholarship committee and projects can range from art work to science experiments.

Interview: Personal interview with members of the selection committee.

Financial need: This may or may not be a factor. How much importance it plays varies by scholarship.

Of these six factors, there are three that you can directly affect: applications, essays, and interviews. We present tips and strategies for creating applications and essays that stand out in Chapters 4 and 6 and for presenting yourself in the most positive way possible in interviews in Chapter 7.

You also have influence in the three remaining factors, perhaps more than you think. Through what you choose to highlight (and ignore) in your scholarship application, you are able to demonstrate your fit with the scholarship's mission. You are also able to influence the information conveyed in recommendation letters through whom you select and what you communicate to them. If financial need is a factor for the scholarship, you may also be able to present your financial background in a way that underscores your need.

In the following chapters you will learn how to use these factors to maximize your chances of winning.

Now let's get started!

Chapter 1 Summary: Discover The Key To Free Cash For College

Not a superstar? Not a problem. Remember that you don't have to be an academic, athletic, or extracurricular superstar to win scholarships. Different scholarships award different strengths. However, you do need a solid strategy for applying for scholarships. Discover the in's and out's of creating a winning strategy in the next chapters from selecting scholarships that fit to creating outstanding applications to keeping the money you win.

Benefit from the experiences of others. The best way to learn is from the experiences of those who have already been through it. We will share the successes (and a few disasters) of students who have been through the scholarship process. Emulate their feats and avoid their failures.

Not all money is the same. Financial aid comes in a number of different forms, each with its own advantages and disadvantages. Loans are repaid while grants and scholarships are not. Work-study allows you to hold a part-time job while attending college.

Debunk scholarship urban legends. Separate the truth from the tall tale about scholarships. Among the truths in this chapter: You don't have to be financially destitute, participate in every extracurricular activity, or apply for every scholarship for which you remotely qualify.

Scholarships for everyone. Okay, not everyone wins scholarship money, but there are scholarships for almost every skill, experience, career aspiration, and field of study you can imagine. Find those that fit you best in our massive Scholarship Directory.

Take advantage of your influence. Scholarships are based on factors such as your fit with the mission, applications, essays, interviews, recommendations, and financial need. Understand that you can positively affect nearly all of these.

Know what the judges want. In the first round, superficial factors are important such as neatness and completeness. After, judges divide applications between good and excellent based on factors such as academics, leadership, originality, strength, results, maturity, and personality.

Judging criteria. One of the most important things to remember when applying for scholarships is that you must show how you fulfill the mission of the award. In the following chapters, you will learn more about defining the mission and using it to your advantage throughout your applications, essays, and interviews.

Find Scholarships
You Can Win

• •

In this chapter, you'll learn:

- The best places to find scholarships
- Strategies to determine which scholarships you have the best chance of winning
- How to get into the minds of the judges
- The magic number of scholarships to target

• •

CHAPTER 2

How To Find The Best Scholarships

We're going to let you in on a little secret. You probably bought this book because it has over 400,000 of the best scholarships, which will hopefully go a long way toward paying those tuition bills. However, as much as we hate to admit it, there is no way any book can contain all of the thousands of scholarships available–especially extremely local awards. Plus, new scholarships are created each and every day.

Our solution is to show you how to find even more scholarships outside of those found in this book. We are going to teach you the techniques that we used to find scholarships. Together with the awards listed in this book, you will have more scholarships to apply for than you ever thought possible.

As important as finding scholarships is, deciding which to apply for is even more important. Because there are thousands of scholarships out there and only one of you to complete their applications, you must be selective about to which scholarships you dedicate the many hours it will take to complete the application. In this chapter, we will also help you decide which scholarships are worth the time and which you should pass on.

Because there are thousands of scholarships and only one you, you need to be selective about which scholarships you enter. The general rule is start with awards that best match your background and experience.

The Tanabe Philosophy

Our approach to selecting scholarships is two pronged:

First, scan through as many scholarships as possible to create a list of every scholarship you are eligible for. Our Scholarship Directory is the best place to start. You will find many scholarships that you can apply to. However, don't stop here. Use our tips to seek out other scholarships–especially local awards given in your community. Compile as large a list as possible from as many sources as possible.

Second, once you have your list, prioritize the scholarships that you will actually apply to. Here is where you will need to do some detective work. Learn enough about the criteria of the scholarship and the goal of the awarding organization to be able to match it to your own background, skills, and experience. This is actually easier than it sounds and we'll show you how to do it quickly.

Once you have your short list of scholarships, you're ready to apply, using the information that you have gathered to create that winning application.

Best Places To Find Scholarships – Besides This Book, Of Course!

One of the best places to find scholarships is right in your own community. Think about all of the groups, clubs, businesses, churches, and organizations

One of the best places to find scholarships is right in your own backyard. Think about all of the groups, clubs, businesses, churches, and organizations in your community. Each of these is a potential source for scholarships.

in your community. Each of these is a potential source for scholarships. In this book, we have provided the most comprehensive directory of scholarships possible, but there are always new scholarships established and local scholarships that are too numerous to be included in a national directory. So there are probably some great local scholarships not in our book (or any national directory for that matter) that are just waiting for you to discover. Here's how to find them:

Counselor Or Financial Aid Office. If you are a high school student, start with your school counselor. Make an appointment to discuss financial aid. Before your appointment, prepare information about your family's financial background and think about what kind of college you want to attend and what special interests or talents you have that would make you eligible for special scholarships. Explain your background to your counselor and ask for suggestions of where to find scholarships that match your experience. Ask if there are any scholarships for which your counselor can nominate you.

It's never too early to speak to your high school counselor. Even if you are a freshman, it will help you later on to understand what opportunities may be open to you. You'll also get a preview of what organizations you may want to join or what activities you may want to participate in that offer scholarships for their members.

If you are an entering freshman or a current college student, make an appointment with your school's financial aid advisor. For your appointment, think about what interests and talents you have and what field you may want to enter after graduation. If you have one, take a copy of your Federal Financial Aid application as background. Mention any special circumstances about your family's financial situation. Ask your advisor for recommendations of scholarships offered by the college or by community organizations. Inquire about being nominated for scholarships that fit your background.

"I made an appointment to speak with my financial aid advisor just to get some information. What a great idea! Not only did we discuss my academic and career goals, but afterward she decided to nominate me for a scholarship for students who want to work in business, and I won! I never would have been nominated if I hadn't taken the time to meet with her."

—Sarah

It's important whenever you speak to a counselor (either in high school or college) that you inquire about any scholarships that require nomination. Often these scholarships are easier to win since the applicant pool is smaller. The largest hurdle is getting nominated. You have nothing to lose by asking, and if anything, it shows how serious you are about financing your education.

School Activities. One fringe benefit of participating in activities might be a scholarship sponsored by the organization. Inquire with the officers or advisors of the organization about scholarship funds. Bands, newspapers, academic clubs, athletic organizations, and service organizations often have scholarships that are awarded to outstanding members.

Community Organizations. If you think about what you do outside of school as well, you will also find another potential source of scholarships. Community organizations that you are involved in may provide scholarships.

Don't limit yourself to only organizations that you belong to. Community groups will often sponsor scholarships that are open to all students who live in the community. For example, local Rotary and Lions clubs often offer scholarships for outstanding students in the community whether or not their parents are members. They view their scholarship programs as part of the way

"I spent a few hours on a Saturday morning looking through back issues of our local newspaper to find previous scholarships awarded. Then, I contacted some of the organizations that gave the awards and entered. I won $2,000 from the scholarships I found through my detective work."

—Richard

they serve their community. Open a phone book and call the five largest organizations in your area. Chances are that at least one will offer a scholarship.

Employer. Many businesses that employ young people offer scholarships as a way to reward students like you who both study and work. Ask your manager if your employer has a scholarship fund and how you can apply.

Parents' Employer. Companies often award scholarships to the children of their employees as a benefit for their employment. Your parents should speak with someone in their Human Resources department about scholarships and other educational programs offered by their company.

Parents' Union. Some unions sponsor scholarships for the children of their members. Your parents should speak with the union officers about scholarships and other educational programs sponsored by the union.

Parents' Organizations. Are your parents involved in civic or other local organizations? These organizations may offer scholarships for members. Ask your parents to find out.

Church Or Religious Organizations. Religious organizations may provide scholarships for members. If you or your parents are members of a religious organization, check with the leaders to see if a scholarship is offered.

Local Government. Some cities and counties provide scholarships specifically designated for local students. Often, local city council members and state representatives have a scholarship fund. Even if you didn't vote for them, call their offices and ask if they offer a scholarship.

Local Businesses. Local business owners who want to see students in their community succeed often set up scholarship funds as a way to thank their customers. Contact your local chamber of commerce to see if there are local businesses that offer scholarships for students in the community.

Local Newspaper. Some local newspapers make announcements about local students who win scholarships. Keep a record of the scholarships printed or go to your library and look at back issues of the newspaper. Check last year's spring issues (between March and June) and you'll probably find announcements of scholarship recipients. Contact the sponsoring organizations to see if you're eligible to enter the next competition.

Internet. One of the benefits of online scholarship directories is that they can be updated at any time. Thus, if you search an online scholarship directory you can find up-to-date information on new scholarships. Check out the free scholarship search on our website, www.supercollege.com, for updates on new scholarships.

How To Choose Scholarships You Can Win

It would save you a lot of time if you knew beforehand which scholarships you'd win and which you wouldn't. With this information, you'd only have to spend your time applying for the scholarships you knew you'd win.

While there's no way to perfectly predict if you'll win, there are some ways you can select scholarships that fit you best and therefore offer you the best chance of winning.

Heed The Words From The Sponsors

Think from the perspective of the scholarship committee: What is it trying to accomplish by awarding the scholarship? What kind of student is it seeking? What is the organization's goal and mission?

When you're watching television, it's perfectly acceptable to get up and grab a soda or munchies during the commercial. Advertisers certainly don't like it, but there are no negative repercussions for ignoring the sponsors' messages. This is not the case for scholarships.

Scholarships of course don't have commercial breaks, but they do have missions. Organizations or sponsors award scholarships for a reason. The mission is like their sponsor message. It is a goal they are trying to achieve or ideology they are trying to promote. For example, a teachers' organization might sponsor a scholarship with the mission of promoting the teaching profession. To fulfill this mission, it could give awards to students who plan to become teachers. An environmental group might sponsor a scholarship with the mission of promoting environmental awareness. It might reward students who have done environmental work.

Scholarship missions are important because they tell you exactly what kind of student the selection committee is seeking. In our example of the teachers' organization scholarship, you know that the organization would like to reward a student who has qualifications such as an education major, student teaching or tutoring, or volunteer work for an educational organization. A student who enjoys interacting with young people and who values education would be a strong fit.

By knowing and understanding what the mission of the scholarship is, you comprehend what kind of student the selection committee would like to honor. The mission is the greatest clue about what the selection committee wants. Therefore, you first task in choosing which scholarships to apply to is to uncover which kind of student each one is looking to reward.

Read The Minds Of The Scholarship Committee

By understanding what the scholarship judges are looking for and by examining how your qualifications fit with the awards, you can make qualified decisions about selecting which scholarship competitions to enter.

If you could have any superpower, here's where flying faster than a speeding bullet and climbing buildings with arachnid-like agility would not help. In understanding which kinds of scholarships you are most fit to win, the superpower of mind reading would be your greatest asset. You want to understand what the scholarship committee wants out of its winners. You need to know what kind of student they are seeking so you can determine if you fit the description. Since none of us have yet discovered how to read minds here's one way we mortals can do it:

To begin, carefully read the scholarship criteria. Sometimes the answer is clearly stated in the award description. You should also look at the application requirements to see what kind of questions they are asking. Is there a GPA requirement? If there is and it's relatively high, then grades are probably important. Does the application provide you with half a page to list your extracurricular activities? If so then they are probably a fairly significant part of the selection criteria. Do you need to submit an essay on a specific topic or a project to demonstrate your proficiency in a field of study? All of these requirements are clues about what the scholarship committee thinks is (and isn't) important.

For example, a public service scholarship may be based only on your philanthropic acts and the entire application focused around describing your selfless deeds. On the other hand, a scholarship given by a major corporation may be based on grades, leadership, and personal integrity.

After you have scanned the application requirements, ask yourself: What is the purpose of the awarding organization? Whether it's helping students who dream of becoming circus performers or rewarding students for their religious fervor, every scholarship has a goal. Again, sometimes the goal is clearly stated in the scholarship description but sometimes you need to look at the organization itself. For example, even if the scholarship description does not directly state it, you can be sure that an award given by an organization that is composed of local physicians will probably prefer that the winner have a connection to or intend to enter the medical field.

> "I found out a lot about one of the organizations that was sponsoring a scholarship by attending one of their meetings. At the meeting, I learned what activities they had planned and even got to speak with some members about what they do. That really helped when it came time for me to apply because I really understood the organization."
>
> —Susan

All things being equal, most clubs and organizations want to reach students who are most similar to their membership. If you don't know much about the organization, contact them to find out more. Check out their homepage to get a sense of their mission and membership. Read their brochures or publications. The more you know about why the organization is giving the award, the better you'll be able to understand how you may or may not fit.

Once you have an idea of what the scholarship committee is looking for, determine if you can convince them that you are that person, which brings us to the next section.

Be Realistic About How Great You Are

Here's where you need to separate reality in your mom's eyes from the rest of the world's reality. From mom's perspective, you are the next Bill Gates, Einstein, or Margaret Thatcher. Mom may be right, but as you are applying for scholarships, take a realistic, un-momlike look at yourself. You know what your strengths are and aren't.

Don't be too hard on yourself. Remember you definitely won't win if you don't apply. But you should (as much as possible) evaluate how well you match the various scholarships on your list. For those that match best, apply first and spend the greatest effort. Set aside those for which you are not as well suited for later.

For example, if you are your school's star journalist, naturally you should apply for journalism scholarships. If you wrote a single editorial for the newspaper, spend your time applying to scholarships that better match what you have done. You can still apply for a journalism scholarship, but don't spend time on it when there are other awards that fits you better.

Size Up The Competition

Size up the competition—both past and present—to get an idea of your prospects and to see what the scholarship committee seeks in the winner.

Knowing how tough your competition is will also help you choose which scholarships to apply to first. Your competition can be as broad as every student in America or as limited as the members of your school's Delta Phi Epsilon. As you can guess, the larger your competition, the more outstanding you need to be to win. Look at your accomplishments and think about how they compare to others at your school, in your city, and in your state. Select scholarships accordingly. If you are a piano player and the highest honor you've won is your school's talent show, you probably have a decent chance of winning a musical scholarship provided by your school. If your highest honor is winning a state competition, then apply for state and national level scholarships. By understanding how you match up to others who will apply, you can spend your time on scholarships that you are most likely to win.

Size Up The Competition From The Past

To really see what the selection committee is looking for and to evaluate if you have what it takes to win the award, check out the competition from previous years. You can usually find out about previous winners through the scholarship organization's website or publications or by contacting the organization. Ask to see sample winning applications and essays. Also, get a list of previous winners. Contact them to learn about their background and achievements. Dig for information on their strategy in applying for the scholarship and for any helpful hints they can provide. Through this detective work, you will see how your background stacks up and gain invaluable insights.

Tick Tock

You can narrow down the scholarships you should apply for by understanding what the scholarship committee is looking for, having a realistic view of how

Story From Real Life: Get Smart About Scholarships

This story shows how important it is to build a scholarship strategy that matches your background and experience. If you are realistic about your achievements, you will have the most success in finding and winning scholarships that match you.
—Gen and Kelly

I had two friends who were determined to beat each other at scholarships. One decided to apply for only the top national scholarships and spent his time crafting a handful of great applications. My other friend, who knew that he would not be able to compete on a national level, concentrated only on local scholarships and entered as many as he could.

At first it looked like my friend who applied to the big nationwide scholarships would win. He made the semifinals in several competitions and won a couple $1,000 prizes.

However, his glory was short lived. My other friend was constantly winning small $100 - $250 prizes. When everything was finally totaled, his collection of small but plentiful loot was $500 more! We learned it's better to go for the awards that fit best, not just the awards with the largest payouts.

—John

When deciding how many scholarships to apply for, create a balance between the quality and quantity of your applications. Don't apply for 75 awards sending in the same application to each. At the same time, don't apply to one or two scholarships and spend four weeks building each application.

your accomplishments match up, and sizing up the competition. A last way to eliminate is practicality–how much time you have before the application is due. Sandwiched among studying, sleeping, and everything else in your busy life, there is limited time to spend on applying to scholarships. If you find a great scholarship with a deadline in one week, which requires a yet-to-be-written original composition and for you to drop out of school to work on it full time, then you should probably pass on the competition. If you know that given the time you have you won't be able to do a decent job on the application requirements then it's better to pass (you may be able to apply for it next year) and move on to awards in which you know have the time to put together a winning application.

The Magic Number Of Scholarships To Apply For

Okay, the truth is there is no magic number of scholarships for which you should apply. However, there is a magical rule: Prioritize your scholarships with the ones you feel you are most likely to win at the top. Then apply to as many on your list as you can given the time you have.

Some students think that they should select only a couple scholarships to apply for so they can focus their efforts on crafting the perfect applications for them. It is true that to have any hope of winning you need to turn in quality applications. However, you should balance between the quality and quantity of your applications. Don't apply for 75 awards sending in the same application to each. You'll just be wasting your time. At the same time, don't apply to one or two scholarships and spend four weeks building each application. Remember, the more scholarships you apply for, the more chances you have to win. And, using the strategies in this chapter, you now know how to select and spend your time on scholarships to maximize your chances of winning.

Chapter 2 Summary: Find Scholarships You Can Win

Use the two prong approach to select scholarships. First, find as many as you can. Then screen and prioritize them based on whether or not you can present yourself as the ideal candidate.

Find scholarships all around you. To find more scholarships, investigate your surroundings such as your school, community organizations, the Internet, your and your parents' employers, local and state governments, and local newspapers and publications.

Choose scholarships you can win. Some tips: Try to understand what the judges are trying to achieve by awarding the scholarship and what they are looking for in the winner. Survey your qualifications, and be realistic about how well you fit the awards. Size up the competition both past and present.

Apply to as many as time allows. There are two factors that limit the number of scholarships you apply for: the amount of time you have to apply and your fit with the scholarship criteria. Apply for as many as you can that are appropriate and for which you have the time to develop quality applications.

Avoid Scholarship Scams

• •

In this chapter, you'll learn:

• The false promises of scholarship scam artists & their motivations

• How to recognize the telltale signs of a scholarship scam

• How one student got taken by a guarantee that was too good to be true

• •

CHAPTER 3

Where To Not Find Scholarships

Now that you have some strategies on where to find scholarships, you need also be aware of where you should NOT find scholarships. While the great majority of scholarship providers and scholarship services have philanthropic intentions, not all do. There are scholarship services and scholarships themselves that you need to avoid. According to the Federal Trade Commission, there were over 175,000 cases reported of scholarship scams, costing consumers $22 million in 1999. In this section, we will explain what to be cautious of and how to avoid wasting money on financial aid scams.

The Tanabe Philosophy

One of the first things to understand about scholarship and financial aid scams is the motivation of those behind them. Those who operate financial aid rip-offs know that paying for college is something that makes parents and students nervous. They know that most parents don't have a complete picture of the financial aid opportunities that are available to them. Because parents don't have all of this information, college financial aid is not only stressful but confusing. Those behind financial aid scams take advantage of parents' fears and discomfort by offering advice and "secret" sources of scholarships for what seems to be a small price to pay.

Common Scholarship Scam Red Flags

The great majority of scholarship providers have philanthropic intentions. Unfortunately, not all do. According to the Federal Trade Commission, there were over 175,000 reported cases of scholarship scams, costing consumers $22 million in 1999.

You may have already received an offer similar to the following. Your parents receive a letter from a very official sounding organization offering a personalized analysis of your financial aid opportunities and expert recommendations of scholarships you should apply for. All for the low cost of a few hundred dollars. Your parents may think that a few hundred dollars is not much considering the cost of your education could run into six digits. That's exactly what these companies want you to think. The truth is that the information they provide is free public information (like descriptions of various loan programs) and none of it is truly personalized–unless you call typing your name on top of a photocopy personalized. Now none of this is technically illegal–but it sure is a waste of money. Our advice is to save your money, and invest a little time in researching financial aid opportunities.

Here are some more examples of "tempting" offers that you should avoid. Remember while the words may change, the message is still the same: Pay us and you won't have to worry about how to pay for tuition.

"Pay us $$$ and we will create a personalized financial aid plan for your child. We have a library of hundreds of resources that we will use to create an individualized financial aid plan for you." What they don't tell you is that the resources they use can easily be found for free on the Internet or in your library. In fact, the scholarships listed in this book are probably their "resources." Save yourself hundreds of dollars and find the scholarships yourself. Plus, you'll do a much more thorough job and actually be able to find scholarships that you can win.

In general, you can detect a scholarship scam if the promise is too good to be true, if you are "guaranteed" to win, or if payment is required to enter.

"Pay us $$$ and we will research and identify the 20 scholarships that fit you best. Why spend weeks researching scholarships when our specialized researchers can do it for you? We have scholarship sources that no one else does. Plus, you are guaranteed to win at least one." You would receive a list of 20 scholarships you could have found on your own for free. Plus, any scholarship that is a "guaranteed" win is a scam, as you'll see later.

"Each year millions of dollars in scholarships are not awarded. Pay us $$$ and we will locate unclaimed scholarship dollars that your son or daughter can win." The reality is that you can find thousands of scholarships on your own in books and on the Internet without paying a search fee. You'll also do a much better job.

"You're a finalist in our scholarship. Pay us $$$ for your registration fee. You're guaranteed to win!" The truth is that you are not guaranteed to win, or if you did win, the prize would be less than the registration fee. Real scholarships never require any fee from applicants.

"You've won our scholarship, guaranteed! All we need is your credit card number to verify your eligibility." Instead of winning a "guaranteed" scholarship, you would get some surprise charges on your credit card.

"You qualify for our exclusive, incredibly low interest loan program. All you need to do is pay us $$$ to lock in the rate." The truth is that you

---

Story From Real Life: I Lost $500 From A Scholarship Scam

Scholarship programs are meant to add dollars to your college fund, not subtract them. Unfortunately, even the most savvy consumers can be taken by scholarship scams. Learn what to look out for from the experiences of this student.
—Gen and Kelly

My parents and I attended a free seminar sponsored by a college financial aid service company. During the seminar, the speaker explained how competitive it was to win scholarships and how many dollars aren't awarded each year because students just don't know about the scholarships. He said that his company would use its comprehensive national database to produce a personalized scholarship program for me. Even better, if I didn't win $2,500 in scholarships from their program, they would refund the fee of $495. My parents and I thought that because we could get our money back, there was no risk in trying the program. Along with most of the other families at the seminar, we signed up for the program.

A week later, we received a packet in the mail. It contained some articles about scholarships and financial aid and a one-page document with scholarships listed. I applied for each of the scholarships. Within the next few months, I won none of them.

My parents remembered the guarantee and we wrote a letter requesting our refund of the $495. Were we surprised when our request was refused. The company said we needed to read the small print of the contract we signed. The guarantee was that I would either win $2,500 in scholarships or that the company's program would provide opportunities that could be worth $2,500. In our excitement on the night of the seminar, we never bothered to read the small print. We were out almost $500. We definitely could have used the money toward my tuition instead of toward a bogus scholarship scam.

—Steven

would pay the fee but not get the loan. Or you may get the loan but the interest rate may be far worse than if you shopped around.

"Come to our very informative financial aid seminar, where you'll learn our secret strategies for scholarships found nowhere else in the world." Seminars like these may actually be sales pitches for any combination of the above. Not all seminars are scams or rip-offs so you'll have to use your own judgment. However, one giveaway is if the seminar sounds like a sales pitch or contains promises that sound too good to be true. If you feel like the marketing copy was written by the same people who produce those late-night infomercials, then you are probably looking at a seminar where you will be asked to part with your money for what may be totally worthless information.

In general the major telltale sign that you are about to be taken by a dubious offer is if you are asked to pay any significant amount of money. Particularly if you are applying for a scholarship, never part with your money. Scholarships are meant to pay you money not the other way around.

Here are some common red flags to watch out for:

● **Registration, entry, or administrative fee:** Legitimate scholarship and financial aid programs do not require an upfront fee. Do not pay for anything more than the cost of postage. Remember, real scholarships are about giving you money, not the other way around.

● **Soliciting your credit card number:** Never give out this kind of financial information to anyone who contacts you without your requesting them to.

● **Refusal to reveal name, address, or phone number:** You know that something is wrong when the person on the telephone won't reveal his or her name or contact information.

● **Guarantee:** Remember, there is no such thing as a guaranteed scholarship. Legitimate scholarships are based on merit or need, not your willingness to pay a registration fee.

If you discover that you have been the victim of one of the scams above, don't be embarrassed. This happens to thousands of parents and students every year. Report it to the Better Business Bureau and Federal Trade Commission (www.ftc.gov) to help prevent it from happening to students in the future. Also, be sure to write to us about it. We maintain lists of dishonest and worthless programs and would like to know if you encounter any.

In general, the old adage of consumer protection applies to scholarships: If an offer sounds too good to be true, it probably is.

Chapter 3 Summary: Avoid Scholarship Scams

Know when a guarantee is not a guarantee. What is tempting about scholarship scams is that they promise guaranteed money or a money-back guarantee. Read the small print—there is no such thing as a guaranteed scholarship.

Keep your wallet closed. Scholarship services and applications should always be free. If a service sounds too good to be true, it probably is.

Create Stunning Scholarship Applications

· ·

In this chapter, you'll learn:

- To create an application plan of attack

- How to present your achievements to captivate the attention of the judges

- Which accomplishments to highlight & which to hide

- How to develop a scholarship resume

- The top 10 scholarship application do's & don'ts

· ·

CHAPTER 4

Scholarship Applications: Your Entry Ticket

At first glance, scholarship applications appear easy. Most ask only a handful of questions and are not longer than a single page. Piece of cake, right?

Don't let their size fool you. Despite their lack of girth, the application is a vital part of winning any scholarship. Scholarship selection committees weed through thousands of applications and use them as their first screen to determine which applicants will continue to the next stage. It's crucial that you make this first cut. To do so you need to craft an application that portrays you in the best light possible.

In this chapter, we'll look at strategies that will transform an ordinary scholarship application form into a screaming testament of why you deserve to win free cash for college. Along the way you'll meet some students who have used well crafted applications to win some incredible awards as well as a few who made some common (and avoidable) application blunders.

The Tanabe Philosophy

Our philosophy for the application form is simple. Although you can't control the questions that are asked or the activities and achievements you already have, you can control how you describe each accomplishment, whether to include or omit information, and the order in which you present each item. In short, you can control how you portray yourself on paper.

This is precisely what makes the application form deceptively simple. Most students rush through the application since they believe that it's nothing more than a place to list their activities, honors, and awards. Big mistake! Even though there is limited real estate on applications, there are strategies you can employ to maximize impact. Our approach requires more work, but we guarantee that you will vastly improve your chances of winning.

"I had six scholarships to apply to, and I had no idea where to begin. Then I gathered all the applications and laid out what needed to be done and by when. I also figured out what information I could re-use in multiple applications. Without this plan there is no way I could have finished everything on time!"

—Michelle

How To Create A Plan Of Attack

With thousands of scholarships on the loose and only one you, it makes sense to develop a strategic plan for tackling scholarships. Before you move into the tactical phase of applying, let's start with some planning. Here are some tips for creating your personal scholarship strategy plan:

Prioritize the scholarships you want to apply to. In the previous chapter, you learned how to select and prioritize scholarships that best match your background and experience. Be sure you have your list prioritized so that you know in which order to apply. If time runs out and you can't get to all of the awards on your list, at least you are sure that you have applied to those in which you have the best chance of winning.

Build a timeline. After you have your prioritized list of scholarships, look at their deadlines and design a schedule for applying.

Recycling means re-using information from one application for another. Recycling saves you time and allows you the opportunity to improve your work each time you re-use it.

Look for recycling opportunities. The second scholarship you apply for will be quicker and easier than the first, and the third will be quicker and easier than the second. This is because for each successive application, you will be able to draw on the materials you've developed for the previous. For example, when you complete your first application, you need to research information you've forgotten, think about your answers, and craft articulate responses. When you complete your second application, you can benefit from the work you've already done for the first. As you're building your timeline, look for scholarships in which you can recycle information from one application for another. Recycling will save you time. In addition, it will also allow you to improve on your work each time you use it. For example, the second time you answer a question about your plans after graduation you can craft your response more effectively than the first. As you recycle information, don't just reuse it, improve it!

Before You Start

Before you fire up your computer or typewriter, here are a few more tips to keep in mind both before and while you are filling out your applications.

Make Application Form Triplets

The first thing to do when you receive scholarship applications is to make two photocopies of them. Why do you need two copies? Your goal is to craft the perfect application. As unlikely as it seems, you probably won't achieve flawlessness the first time around. A spare copy is your insurance should you make a mistake. It's not uncommon to discover that only four out of your five most important life accomplishments fit within the two-inch space on the form.

Regardless of how many copies you make, you should never use your last clean copy of the application form. Trust us—and every student who has ruined their original at 2 a.m. on the day their application was due—it's well worth the investment of a few dimes to have plenty of extra copies.

Be A Neat Freak

You may have dirty laundry strewn across your room and a pile of papers large enough to be classified as its own life form, but you don't want the scholarship committee to know that. When it comes to applications, be incredibly neat.

We would not ordinarily be neatness zealots—we admit to having our own mountains of life-imbibed papers—but submitting an application with globs of correction fluid, scratched out words, or illegible hieroglyphics will severely diminish your message. Think about how much less impressive the Mona Lisa would be if Da Vinci had painted it on a dirty old bed sheet?

You may have the most incredible thoughts to convey in your applications, but if your form is filled with errors none of it will matter. In a sea of hundreds and even thousands of other applications, you don't want yours to be penalized by sloppy presentation. While some applications don't require that you type them, unless you have outstanding penmanship, we recommend that you use a typewriter or computer.

Remember The Application Is You

A scholarship application is more than a couple pieces of paper. In the eyes of the selection committee, it is you. It may not be fair, but in many cases the application is the only thing that the judges will have to measure you by. The last thing you want to be is a dry list of academic and extracurricular achievements. You are a living, breathing person. Throughout the application, try to show who you really are. Show your passion and commitment. The application is your time to demonstrate why you should win.

Five Steps To Crafting A Winning Application
Step 1: Give Them What They Want To Hear

Politicians are notorious for telling their constituents what they want to hear. Good politicians never lie, but they do put a flattering spin on their speeches depending on who they're addressing. We are not suggesting that you lie on your applications–NEVER lie–but we are recommending that you present yourself in the best possible way to appeal to your audience. In short, never lie on an application, but do employ a little spin.

You can't change the facts about your accomplishments, but you can change how you describe them. Employ a different spin for each scholarship. Remember, you can spin, but NEVER lie.

Some politicians have a difficult time with distinguishing between lying and spinning. Here's an example to illustrate the difference. Let's say you are applying for a scholarship that rewards students who are interested in promoting literacy in America. You have been a volunteer for a reading program for children at your local library. Each week you read stories to a dozen children.

No-spin description:
Reading program volunteer.

Lie:
Reading program founder. Started a national program that reaches thousands of children each day to promote literacy.

Spin:
Reading program volunteer. Promote youth literacy among local children through weekly afterschool reading program at public library.

At one extreme, you can see that a lie exaggerates well beyond the truth. At the other extreme, the non-spin description is not very impressive because it does not explain how the program relates to the purpose of the scholarship. (Remember as a scholarship judge looking to reward students involved with promoting literacy, finding an applicant who is doing just that in their community will attract your attention.) The spin version does not stretch the truth, but it does make clear how this activity fits within the context of the goal of the scholarship. To take this example one step further, let's say that now you are applying for a scholarship that rewards student leaders. One of your jobs as a reading program volunteer is to maintain the schedule for other volunteers and help with the recruitment of new volunteers. Your description for this scholarship might read:

Reading program volunteer. Coordinated volunteer schedule and recruited new members for local public library afterschool reading program.

Notice how you have "spun" your activity so that it highlights a different aspect of what you did and better shows the judges how you fit their criteria.

To be able to spin effectively you need to know your audience. A key principle to understanding your audience is: In general, sponsor organizations want to give money to students who are reflections of themselves. In other words, the Future Teachers Of America provides funds for students who plan on pursuing a teaching career. The American Congress of Surveying and Mapping gives money to students who have an interest in cartography.

To determine who your audience is, ask the following questions. Use your answers to each to guide your decisions on how much detail to provide, what to include or omit, and how to prioritize your achievements. You'll find that just thinking about these questions and looking from the perspective of the selection committee will instantly enable you to craft a better application.

Q: What is the mission of the organization giving the scholarship?

Organizations don't just give away scholarships and expect nothing in return. Behind their philanthropic motives lies an ulterior motive: To promote their organization's vision.

Behind every awarding organization's philanthropic motives lies an ulterior motive: To promote their organization's vision. Your job is to uncover what the vision is and spin your application accordingly.

Visit the organization's website, call its offices to ask for more information, or request some materials to read. If it's a local group, meet some of its members or attend a meeting.

Once you know what the organization is about you can better decide which parts of your life and achievements are important and which you can gloss over or omit.

For example, let's imagine that you are applying for an award given by an organization of professional journalists. In conducting your research you learn that print and broadcast journalists join this group because they are passionate about the profession of journalism and want to encourage public awareness about the importance of a free press. Immediately, you know that you need to highlight those experiences that demonstrate your zeal for journalism and, if possible, your belief in the value of a free press. First, simply list all related activities you've done:

```
Columnist for your high school newspaper
Vice-president of the Writers' Club
Participated in a rally in support of free speech on campus

Won an English essay contest
Summer internship at a radio station
```

Among these activities you remember that in the Writers' Club you participated in a workshop that helped a local elementary school start its own school newspaper. Since this achievement matches almost perfectly the mission of our hypothetical journalism organization, use your limited space in the application to list it first and to expand on it.

You might write something like this:

Central High Writers' Club, Vice-President—Helped to organize "Writing Counts" workshop at Whitman Elementary School, which resulted in the launch of the school's first student run newspaper.

Story From Real Life: How My Support Of Legalizing Marijuana Cost Me

Understanding the awarding organization and who is likely to ready your application can give you insight on what to focus on and what to avoid. If this student had asked some questions about the judges, he probably would have won.
—Gen and Kelly

I went to high school in what I thought was a liberal-minded city. Our school principal seemed to be a hippy, straight out of the 1960s, with long hair and even wearing tie-dyed shirts on Fridays. The mayor of our city was constantly in the newspaper for his liberal stands on everything from funding for the homeless to gay rights.

In my senior year I applied for a scholarship for students in my high school. When asked about my leadership in extracurricular activities, I thought nothing of putting down that I was president of our school's Advocate Club. Our club promoted political activism, and we had made local headlines for rallies we held for increasing funding for education, keeping large chain corporations out of our downtown, and legalizing the medicinal use of marijuana. There was a photo of me in the local newspaper holding a marijuana plant at a sit-in.

My friends told me they thought I had a really good chance of winning because I had the highest grades in our class and I was one of a handful of students admitted to Berkeley. I hate to brag, but my teachers really liked me because I took the time to get to know them, and they wrote great recommendation letters. I wrote an essay about my experiences with the Advocate Club and my fight to legalize marijuana.

When the winners were announced at our senior banquet, I was disappointed that I did not win any of the three prizes. I was pretty cocky and thought I should have been a shoo-in. I was so distraught that the next day at school I spoke with my counselor, who was one of the judges, and asked her why she thought I didn't win.

At first she was hesitant to give me any information about what happened behind closed doors. After reassuring her that I wasn't going to tell anyone and that I only wanted to know so I could improve my applications in the future, she let me in on the judges' thoughts. She said that everyone knew that I was qualified, but there were three judges who voted against me because while they admired my devotion to causes, they disagreed with my lobbying for the legalization of medicinal uses for marijuana. I couldn't believe what I was hearing—that my political views prevented me from winning.

After I found out who the judges were, it was easy to understand why they voted against me. They were members of our local government who were very conservative compared to the rest of the city's political leaders. The ironic thing was that I could have found out who the judges were before turning in my application. If I had, I might have given less attention my most controversial belief.

—Mike

Think of the impact this would have on the scholarship committee. "Look here, Fred" one journalist on the committee would say, "This students does what we do! Definitely someone we should interview!"

The bottom line is that before you can even begin to evaluate which activities to list and how to describe them, you need to know as much as you can about the scholarship organization. By understanding the purpose of the organization, you can select achievements and spin them in ways that will be sure to attract the attention of the judges.

Q: Who is reading your application?

Let's imagine for a moment that you need to give a speech to two groups of people. Without knowing who your audience is, you would have a difficult time composing a speech that would appeal to them.

It makes a big difference if one was a group of mathematicians, and the other a group of fashion designers. To grab the attention of each of these audiences, you'd need to shape your speech accordingly. References to mathematical theorems would hardly go over well with the designers just as the mathematicians could probably care less about this spring's hot colors.

It's not always possible to know who your audience is, but you should try to find out who is likely to be on the selection committee. In rare instances you may actually know the people by name—such as an administrator at your school, a local congressman, or business leader. More often, however, you will just have a sense of what kind of people will most likely be judging. Most groups have identifiable traits among their membership: The Veterans of Foreign Wars (VFW) and ACLU, for example, have members who share similar beliefs or experiences.

In the same way that understanding the mission of an organization helps you to decide how to present certain information, so too does knowing the composition of the selection committee. For example, if you know that members of the community who are committed to public service are on the committee, then stress your contributions in that area.

Also, be sure to omit things that might be offensive to the organization's members. Just imagine what would happen if you thoughtlessly included that you were the author of an economic project entitled "How Labor Unions Make the U.S. Unable to Compete & Lower Our Standard of Living" to an award with judges who are members of the Teamsters labor union.

Q: Who is your competition?

Think of the scholarship competition as a reverse police lineup where you want to stand out and be picked by the people behind the one-way mirror. You want the judge to say without hesitation, "That's the one!" The only way this will happen is if your application stands out and doesn't get lost in the crowd. One of the best ways to accomplish this is to know what you're up against, who else will be in the lineup with you.

Try to anticipate who your competition will be—even if it's just a best guess. Depending on who the scholarship is open to, you may have a very specific or very broad pool of people to compete against. If the award is limited to your school you may know everyone who will enter on a first-name basis. If it's national, all you may know is that the applicants are students interested in becoming doctors.

More important than the scope of the competition is the type of students who will apply. One of the biggest challenges in any competition is to distance yourself from the pack. If 5,000 pre-med students are applying for a $10,000 scholarship from a medical association, you need to make sure that your application stands out from those of the 4,999 other applicants. If you are lucky, you may have done something that few have done. Inventing a new vaccine in your spare time would certainly set you apart. Unfortunately, more often than not you will have to distinguish yourself in more subtle ways, through the explanation of your activities and accomplishments.

Let's look at an example. You are applying for a scholarship given by a national medical association that seeks to promote interest in the medical sciences. It just so happens that you are considering a pre-med major and you have even interned at a local hospital. If you hadn't read this book you might have listed under activities:

Summer Internship at Beth Israel Children's Hospital

But you did read this book! So you know that this is a great activity to list first since it demonstrates your commitment to medicine and shows that you truly are interested in becoming a doctor. More importantly, since you have thought about the competition, you realize that a lot of other applicants will also have volunteered at a hospital. So instead of simply listing the internship, you add an explanation to make the experience more unique. You could write:

Summer Internship at Beth Israel Children's Hospital—assisted with clinical trial of new allergy medication.

This is much more unique and memorable. Adding this brief description would provide details that give the judges an illustration of your volunteer work that is different from that of other students. Remember that you can add short descriptions anywhere in the application even if the instructions do not explicitly ask for them.

Here is another example: If you know that many applicants for a local public service scholarship have participated in your school's annual canned food drive, then you need to highlight contributions that go beyond this program. You'd probably want to highlight the other public service activities you did besides the canned food drive because you know that describing the canned food drive would not set you apart from the others.

The key is to first anticipate who your competition will be and what they might write in their applications. Then, figure out how you can go one step farther to distinguish yourself from the rest of the lineup.

"When I was a high school senior, I applied for a scholarship for students at my school who contributed to the community. I was a member of the Key Club, a public service group, but so was 50% of the senior class. I decided I needed to focus on my service outside of Key Club to set me apart from the other students. It was a good decision—I won the scholarship."

—Rachel

Step 2: Go For The Gusto (Quickly)

In movies, the most daredevil-ish car chase, the most harrowing showdown between good and evil, and the most poignant romantic revelations are usually saved until the end. While this works for Hollywood, it does not for scholarship applications. Since selection committees pore through so many applications and often the space on the form is limited, you need to feature your most impressive points first.

Be strategic about what information you choose to include by evaluating how it fits with the mission of the scholarship and its magnitude. Prioritize all of the information so that you include only the most important.

If you have listed four extracurricular activities, assume that some judges won't even read beyond the first two. This doesn't mean that all judges will be this limited, but there are always some who are. Therefore, it's extremely important that you prioritize the information that you present, and rank your accomplishments according to the following–which if you read Step 1 should not come as too much of a surprise.

Fit with scholarship organization's goal. The most important factor in prioritizing your achievements is how they fit with the goal of the scholarship. This is after all why these kind people want to hand you some free dough. Emphasize your feats that match the purpose of the scholarship. If you are applying for an award that rewards athleticism, stress how well you've done in a particular sport before you list your volunteer activities.

Scope. Prioritize your accomplishments by their scope, or how much of an impact they have made. How many people have been affected by your work? To what extent has your accomplishment affected your community? Did your contribution produce measurable results? In simple terms, put the big stuff before the small stuff.

Uniqueness. Since your application will be compared to that of perhaps thousands of others, include accomplishments that are uncommon. Give priority to those that are unique or the most difficult to win. For example, being on your school's honor roll is certainly an achievement, but it is an honor that many others have received as well. Try to select honors that fewer students have received. Remember the reverse police line up idea–you want to standout in order to be selected from the lineup!

Timeliness. This is the least important criterion, but if you get stuck, put the more recent achievements first. Having won an election in the past year conveys more freshness than having won three years ago. We sometimes get questions about listing junior high or even elementary school achievements. Generally, stick to accomplishments from high school if you're a high school student and to college if you're a college student. An exception is if your accomplishment is extremely impressive and relevant–such as publishing your own book in the 8th grade. Of course, if you run out of recent achievements and there is still space on the form, go ahead and reach back to the past–but try to limit yourself to one or two items.

You want your application to be as remarkable and unforgettable as the best Hollywood movies. The only difference between your work and Spielberg's is that you need to place the grand finale first.

Step 3: Write To Impress

The poetic words of Martin Luther King's "I have a dream" speech were punctuated with his dramatic, emotion-filled voice, hopeful expression, and confident motion of his hands. His delivery would not have been as poignant had he spoken in an unexcited, monotone voice with hands stuffed into his pockets and eyes lowered to avoid eye contact. Nor would his dramatic presentation have been as effective if his message had been unimportant. The point? Both content and delivery count.

While you don't have the option for person-to-person delivery with your scholarship applications, you do have the opportunity to present information in a compelling way. Here are some winning writing strategies for presenting yourself through your applications.

Use Your Smarts

Remember that for most scholarships it's important to demonstrate that you will succeed academically in college. Do this by describing academic honors and interests both in the classroom and out.

There's a reason why parents across the country prefer that kids study over almost every other activity. In addition to the correlation between studying and success in school, almost all scholarships (even those that are athletic in nature) require some level of academic achievement. College is, after all, about academics (at least that's what you want your parents to believe).

As you are completing your applications, keep in mind that while you may be applying for a public service scholarship you should also include at least a few academic achievements. For example, it does not hurt to list in an athletic scholarship that you also came in second place at the science fair. This should not be the first thing you list but it certainly should be included to show the committee that you have brains in addition to brawn.

When you describe your intellectual activities, explain how they match the scholarship's goal most closely. For example, if you are applying for a science scholarship, focus on the awards you've won at science fairs and the advanced courses you've taken in the sciences rather than writing awards or advanced literature courses. Use your academic achievements to illustrate why you see your future in the sciences. Scholarship committees ideally want to see that your academic talents are in line with the scholarship's purpose.

Leadership Is Always Better Than Membership

If you've ever tried to motivate a group of peers to do anything without taking the easy way out—bribery—you know that it takes courage, intelligence, and creativity to be a leader. Because of this, many scholarships give extra points to reward leadership. Regardless of the subject, scholarship judges want to know that the dollars will be awarded to someone who will not only make a difference in the future but who will also be a leader and motivate others to do so as well. If you were a successful businessperson trying to encourage entrepreneurship, wouldn't you want to award aid to a young person who is not only an entrepreneur but also one who will motivate others? (Your return on investment [ROI] would be much higher if you can put your money behind leaders rather than followers.)

To show scholarship committees that you are a leader, list any activities in which you held an elected office. Realize that you don't need to be president to be a leader. Many students have organized fundraisers for specific causes or helped run events. These are all examples of leadership. Use active verbs when describing your work:

Organized band fundraiser to purchase new instruments
Led a week long nature tour in Yosemite Valley
Founded Central High's first website to list volunteer activities
Directed independent musical performance

All of these words convey your leadership ability even if you were not an officially elected officer. When describing your leadership, include both formal and informal ways you have led groups. Show the scholarship committee that you are a worthy investment.

Extracurricular Activities & Hobbies

Describe extracurricular activities with values and skills that match those of the objectives of the scholarship.

If your only activity were studying, your life would be severely lacking in the neighborhood of excitement. Scholarship organizers recognize this and thus the criteria for some scholarships include extracurricular activities or hobbies. Scholarship committees want to see evidence that you do more than read textbooks and take exams. They want to know that you have a variety of interests.

As always, when completing your applications, select extracurricular activities and hobbies that fit with the scholarship's mission. For example, if you are applying for a music scholarship, describe how you've been involved in your school's orchestra or how you've taught violin lessons. By showing that you not only have taken classes in music theory but have also been involved with music outside of your studies, the scholarship committee will get a more complete picture of your love for music.

It's also important that you use this opportunity to display your leadership. Try to show how you have been a leader in your activities. Describe leadership positions you've held and what your responsibilities were. Include informal leadership roles you've played so that even if you didn't have an official title, you can include projects or teams you've led. Here's an example:

`Environmental Action Committee Member`, spearheaded report recommendations for reducing waste and increasing recycling on campus.

Describing leadership in your activities or hobbies will help set you apart from the other applicants. There are many who are involved with environmental groups, but only you have actually helped increase recycling on your campus!

Overall, remember that your goal is to use your activities and hobbies to illustrate how passionate you are about a subject and that within these activities you have demonstrated leadership either formally or informally.

Honors & Awards

Don't expect the selection committee to know the in's and out's of the honors or awards you've won. Provide descriptions that illustrate how prestigious the honor is and how it fits with the purpose of the scholarship.

There's a reason why all trophies are gold and gaudy: They shout to the world in a deafening roar, "Yes, this glittery gold miniature man means I am the best!" For applications that ask for your honors and awards, impart some of that victorious roar and attitude. In no way are we recommending that you ship your golden statuettes off with your applications. We are suggesting that you highlight honors and awards in a way that gets the scholarship committee to pay attention to your application.

What makes an award impressive is scope. Besides being a minty mouthwash, scope, in this case, is the impact and influence of the award. You worked for the award and earned every gold inch of it. Show the committee that they don't just hand these statuettes out to anybody. Describe how many awards are given:

English Achievement Award – awarded to two outstanding juniors each year.

By itself, the English Achievement Award does not tell the scholarship committee very much. Maybe half the people in your class were given the award. By revealing the scope of the award (particularly if it was given to only a few) it now becomes much more impressive.

In competitions that reach beyond your school, it is important to qualify your awards. For example, while everyone at your school may know that the Left Brain Achievement Award is given to creative arts students, the rest of the world does not.

Don't write:

Received Left Brain Achievement Award.

Do Write:

Received Left Brain Achievement Award—recognized as an outstanding creative talent in art as conferred upon by vote of art department faculty.

Step 4: Make Sure The Pants Fit

You'd never buy a pair of pants without trying them on. Treat your applications the same way. You have limited space in which to cram a lot of information. You will need to do a lot of editing and may even have to omit many of your accomplishments. Of course by now you know what is crucial and what can be safely omitted. To make sure that everything fits, start completing one of the practice copies of your application. Here's where you'll appreciate having those extra backup copies.

As you fill out the application, you may find that you are trying to squeeze in too many details or that you have more room and can expand on your most impressive achievements. Don't forget to adjust font sizes and line spacing if necessary—just don't sacrifice readability (i.e., don't go below 10 point fonts).

Only by trying on your applications will you get a sense if what you have in mind will fit properly.

Step 5: Some Final Application Tips

When To Leave It Blank

An official Mom canon from childhood is: If you don't have anything nice to say, don't say it. While this is a good lesson on self-restraint, it does not always hold true for scholarship applications. In general, it is not a good idea to leave any area blank. You don't need to fill the entire space, but you should make an effort to list something in every section. However, before you try to explain how the handmade certificate that your mom presented you for being Offspring of the Year qualifies as an "award," recognize that there are limits. If you've never held a job, then don't list anything under work experience. If, however, you painted your grandmother's house one summer and got paid for it, consider listing it if you don't have any other options.

Create a finished product with only the most relevant information in language that is easy to understand. Provide explanations when it is not obvious what your achievement is to a general audience.

Use your judgment and common sense when trying to decide whether or not to leave an area blank. Ask yourself if what you are including will strengthen or weaken your application. Think like a judge. Is the information relevant? Or, does it seem like a stretch? If you cannot convince yourself that what you are listing is justified, then it will certainly not go over well with the actual judges. Recall Mom's advice, leave it blank, and move on to the areas where you have something great to say.

Nip & Tuck

Succinct and terse, scholarship applications bear the well-earned reputation for having less space than you need. Often affording a page or less, scholarship applications leave little room for much other than just the facts. As you are completing your applications, remember to abbreviate where appropriate and keep your sentences short. Often judges are scanning the application form. If they want an essay they will ask for one.

Give More Than You're Asked

If the instructions say: please list your awards in this area, don't feel like you can't add explanation if you need to. If you have three great awards, it is better to use your space to list those three with short explanations rather than cram in all 15 awards that you've won in your life. You are trying to present the most relevant information that shows the scholarship committee why you deserve their money. Use the space to explain how each award, job, or activity relates to the scholarship rather than feel compelled to list everything.

Also, feel free to interpret some instructions broadly. Work experience does not have to be limited to traditional jobs. Maybe you started your own freelance design firm or cut people's lawns on the weekends. The same goes for leadership positions. Who said that leadership has to be an elected position within an organization? Just be sure to explain if the relationship is not totally clear. For example:

```
Volunteer Wilderness Guide—Led clients through seven-day trek
in Catskills. Responsible for all aspects of the trip including
group safety.
```

Scholarship Resumes: One-Page Autobiographies

A resume is your opportunity to tout your greatest achievements and life's accomplishments. Plus, you have an entire page of real estate rather than two-inch boxes on an application form. Some selection committees request resumes to get a quick overview of your achievements. Others don't, but you shouldn't let that stop you from submitting one with the application anyway!

A scholarship resume is not the same as one that you would use to get a job. It's unlikely that your work experience will be the focus. However, the principles and format are the same. A good resume that scores you a job shows employers that you have the right combination of previous work experience and skills to be their next hire. Similarly, your scholarship resume should show the committee why you are the most qualified student to win their award.

Here are the main components of an effective scholarship resume:

● **Contact information**. Your vital statistics, including name, address, phone number, email.

● **Objective**. Purpose of the resume.

● **Education**. Schools you've attended beginning with high school, expected or actual graduation dates.

● **Academic achievements**. Relevant coursework, awards, and honors received.

● **Extracurricular experience**. Relevant extracurricular activities, locations and dates of participation, job titles, responsibilities, and accomplishments.

● **Work experience**. Where and when you've worked, job titles, responsibilities, and accomplishments on the job.

● **Skills and interests**. Additional relevant technical, lingual, or other skills or talents that do not fit in the categories above.

Your resume should be descriptive enough for the selection committee to understand but not so wordy that they can't find what they need. It should be neatly organized and easy to follow. Having reviewed hundreds of resumes, here are some simple strategies we've developed:

Don't worry if your resume presents the same information that's in the application form. Some judges will read only the application or your resume so it's important your key points are in both. However, in the resume, try to expand on areas that you were not able to cover fully in the application.

> A scholarship resume is a one-page overview of your most important achievements. It shows the selection committee why you are the most qualified student to win their scholarship.

Include only the important information. Remember to incorporate only the most relevant items and use what you know about the scholarship organization to guide how you prioritize this information. For each piece of information, ask yourself: Will including this information aid the selection committee in seeing my fit with the award? Is this information necessary to convince them that I should receive the award? Only include that which builds your case for being a fit with the scholarship's mission.

Focus on responsibilities and achievements. In describing your experiences in work and activities, focus on the accountabilities you held and the measurable or unique successes you had. Successes could include starting a project, reaching goals, or implementing one of your ideas. For example, if you were the treasurer of the Literary Club, you would want to include that you were responsible for managing a $10,000 annual budget.

Demonstrate in your resume how you showed leadership. Leadership could include leading a project or team, instructing others, or mentoring your peers. What's more important than your title or where you worked is the quality of your involvement. Explaining your successes and your role as a leader will provide concrete evidence of your contribution.

"I asked my manager at work to edit my scholarship resume. Because she normally receives a dozen resumes a week from job-seekers, she's practically an expert. She helped me learn to use active language and improve the descriptions of what I've done."

—Nick

Be proud. Your resume is your time to shine. Don't be afraid to draw attention to all that you've accomplished. If you played a key role in a project, say so. If you exceeded your goals, advertise it. No one else is going to do your bragging for you.

Don't tell tall stories. On the flip side of being proud is being untruthful. It's important that you describe yourself in the most glowing way possible, but stay connected with the truth. If you developed a new filing system at your job, don't claim that you single-handedly led a corporate-wide reorganization. With your complete scholarship application, selection committees can see through a resume that is exaggerated and doesn't match the rest of the application, essay, and recommendations.

Get editors. After the 103rd time reading your resume, you'll probably not notice an error that someone reading it for the first time will catch. Get others to read and edit your resume. Editors can let you know if something doesn't make sense, offer you alternative wording, and help correct your boo-boos. Some good choices for editors may be teachers or professors, work supervisors, or parents. Work supervisors may be especially helpful since part of their job is to review resumes of job applicants. Your school may also offer resume help in the counseling department.

When creating a scholarship resume, strive for ease of legibility. Your resume should not be an eye exam.

Avoid an eye test. In trying to squeeze all the information on a single page, don't make your font size so small that the words are illegible. The selection committee can have tired, weary eyes from reading all those applications. Don't strain them even more.

Strive for perfection. It's a given that your resume should be error-free. There's no excuse for mistakes on a one-page document that is meant to exemplify your life's works.

To see these resume-building strategies in action, here is an example of one way to create a great resume:

Some points to note about this resume:

Concise. Fitting on a single page, it is concise, to the point, and legible.

Shows leadership. By describing her responsibilities at work and with extracurricular activities, Melissa demonstrates her leadership ability.

Results oriented. Melissa conveys the impact of her work by pointing out concrete results.

To make this resume even more powerful, Melissa could have listed separately the honors and awards that she won.

Melissa Lee
1000 University Drive
San Francisco, CA 94134
(415) 555-5555

Objective
To obtain funding for college through the SuperCollege.com Scholarship.

Education
University of San Francisco   San Francisco, CA
B.A. candidate in sociology. Expected graduation in 2004. Honor roll.

Lowell High School   San Francisco, CA
Graduated in 2000 with highest honors. Principal's Honor Roll, 4 years.

Leadership Experience
SF Educational Project   San Francisco, CA
Program Assistant. Recruit and train 120 students for various community service projects in semester long program. Manage and evaluate student journals, lesson plans, and program participation. 2000-present.

Lowell High School Newspaper   San Francisco, CA
Editor-In-Chief. Recruited and managed staff of 50. Oversaw all editorial and business functions. Newspaper was a finalist for the prestigious Examiner Award for excellence in student journalism. 1997-2000.

Palo Alto Daily News   Palo Alto, CA
Editorial Assistant. Researched and wrote 8 feature articles on such topics as education reform, teen suicide, and summer fashion. Led series of teen reader response panels. Summer 1999.

Evangelical Church   San Francisco, CA
Teacher. Prepared and taught weekly lessons for third grade Sunday School class. Received dedication to service award from congregation. 1996-1998.

Asian Dance Troupe   San Francisco, CA
Member. Perform at community functions and special events. 1999-present.

Skills & Interests
Fluent in Mandarin and HTML. Interests include journal-writing, creative writing, photography, swimming and aerobics.

Top 10 Application Do's & Don'ts

When money is on the table, it's much better that you learn from others' successes and mistakes when applying for scholarships. From interviews with students and scholarship judges and firsthand experience reviewing scholarship applications, we've developed our top ten list of scholarship application do's and don'ts.

Don'ts

1. DON'T prioritize quantity over quality. It's not the quantity of your accomplishments that's important. It's the quality of your contributions.

2. DON'T stretch the truth. Tall tales are prohibited.

3. DON'T squeeze to the point of illegibility. Scholarship applications afford minimal space. It's impossible to fit everything you want. Don't try by sacrificing legibility.

4. DON'T write when you have nothing to say. If you don't have something meaningful to write, leave it blank.

5. DON'T create white out globs. If it's that sloppy, start over.

6. DON'T procrastinate. Don't think you can finish them the night before they're due.

Story From Real Life: My Midnight Scholarship Application

This is why you shouldn't wait until the last minute to do your applications. This story speaks for itself.
—Gen and Kelly

I've always considered myself a fast person. I speak, walk, and move quickly. That's why I didn't think it was out of the question to complete my scholarship application the night before it was due. It was a one-page document with about a dozen questions on it. How difficult could it be?

At about 9 p.m., I whipped out the application. It was a scholarship given by my department, which was sociology. The questions seemed easy enough. They asked about the classes I had taken, my involvement in activities on campus, and what I planned to do after graduation.

Boy, did I underestimate the amount of time it would take to answer those dozen questions. I didn't anticipate spending two hours searching for my transcript because I couldn't remember the exact classes and grades that I received in the two previous years. By 11 p.m., I found a copy of my transcript in the very back of a file box I kept in the corner of my closet. I also didn't think I would make so many errors completing the application. It took forever to white out each mistake, wait for the white out to dry, and then re-align the application to re-type my corrected answer.

By 6 a.m., I finished completing the application. Full of poorly worded sentences, it certainly wasn't one of my best pieces of work. I hand-delivered the completed application to the assistant in my department at 9 a.m. She took one look at me and asked, "Pulled an all-nighter, eh?" I nodded lethargically. After crashing, I awoke in the afternoon to look at a copy of what I submitted. There were mistakes everywhere including incomplete sentences and incoherent thoughts.

As expected, I didn't win the scholarship. I knew I would have had a decent chance if I had spent some quality time on the application. My advice: Don't wait until the night before. You may think you can do it, but I am proof that you can't.

—Charlene

There are a lot of points to remember about scholarship applications. It's almost impossible to follow every Do and Don't. Most importantly, remember that your applications are your time to show the selection committee why they should choose you. Keeping this and the mission of the award in mind will insure that you create a solid application.

7. DON'T be less than perfect. You can have imperfections. Just don't let the selection committee know.

8. DON'T miss deadlines.

9. DON'T turn in incomplete applications. Make sure you have everything you need before sending your applications.

10. DON'T underestimate what you can convey. Scholarship applications may appear to be short and simple. Don't undervalue them. In a small space, you can create a powerful story of why you should win.

Do's

1. DO understand the scholarship's mission. Know why they're giving out the dough.

2. DO remember who your audience is. You need to address animal rights activists and retired dentists differently.

3. DO show how you fit with the scholarship's mission. You're not going to win unless you have what the selection committee wants.

4. DO be proud of your accomplishments. Don't be afraid to brag.

5. DO focus on leadership and contributions. Make your contributions known.

6. DO make your application stand out. Set yours apart with unique accomplishments.

7. DO practice to make sure everything fits. Use your spare copies of the application for practice.

8. DO get editors. They'll help you create the best, error-free applications you can.

9. DO include a resume. Whether they ask for it or not, make sure you include a tailored scholarship resume.

10. DO make copies of your finished applications for reference. Save them for next year when you do this all over again.

Finishing Touches

Once you've completed your applications, check and double-check for accuracy and to make sure that you've filled out all of the information. Remember that presentation affects how scholarship committees view applications. You want to convey that you are serious about winning the scholarship by submitting an application that is complete and error-free.

Make sure that you have all of the pieces that are required. When applicable, don't forget:

- **Application—sign if required.**
- **Recommendation letters**
- **Transcript**
- **Essays**
- **Resume**

Finally, before handing your applications off to the post office, make application twins. Photocopy all of your application materials. If for some reason they are lost in the mail, you have a copy you can resend. Plus, you will have a great starting place for when you apply for scholarships next year.

Chapter 4 Summary: Create Stunning Scholarship Applications

Create an application plan of attack by prioritizing the scholarships you want to apply to, building a timeline and schedule for applying, and determining recycling opportunities, or what information you can re-use for multiple applications.

Do application pre-work. Before you start, make three copies of the forms for practice, remember to be neat, and realize that the application is a reflection of you.

Step 1: Give them what they want to hear. Don't lie, but present the truth in a way that matches the mission of the award. Keep in mind why the organization is providing the award and who your audience is as you are completing your applications.

Step 2: Go for the gusto quickly. This means don't bury your main point. Concentrate on how your accomplishments match the scholarship's goal and the scope, uniqueness, and recentness of your achievements.

Step 3: Write to impress, focusing on academics, leadership, extracurricular achievements, honors, and awards.

Step 4: Make sure the pants fit, meaning make sure the most important information fits in your application forms.

Step 5: Put on those finishing touches. Every question should be answered and all information requested should be provided.

Your one-page autobiography. A resume presents the main highlights of your education and achievements in an easy-to-read format and provides scholarship judges with a brief overview of you.

Get The Right Recommendations

In this chapter, you'll learn:

- How to control your recommendations

- Who makes the best recommenders

- The essential information you must provide to guarantee great recommendations

- How to insure that your recommenders meet important scholarship deadlines

Recommendations: Praise Seeking In Its Highest Form

If you need another reason to kiss up to your teachers or professors, here's one: recommendations. Many scholarships require that you submit recommendations from teachers, professors, school administrators, or others who can vouch for your accomplishments. Scholarship committees use recommendations to get another perspective on your character and accomplishments. Along with what you write in your application, this helps to create a more complete picture of who you are.

Many students believe there is nothing you can do to influence recommendations. This is simply not true. You actually have a lot of control over the kind of letter that your recommenders write. In this chapter we will explore what you can do to insure that you get great recommendations.

The Tanabe Philosophy

We view recommendations as an important opportunity for someone else to convey to scholarship committees why you are the best fit for their scholarship. You may think that because others do the actual writing that the content of recommendations is completely out of your control. Let us provide you with a surprising and powerful insight. You have the power to influence what is written! Through the selection of your recommenders, what you supply to help them write the recommendations, and what you do to follow up, you can shape the direction of your own recommendations. These are very important strategies that most applicants overlook. But not you! Armed with superb recommendations, your scholarship application is sure to rise to the top.

Finding People To Say Nice Things About You

The first step toward getting recommendations is finding recommenders. Unfortunately, mom, dad, and all others related to you are excluded. So, how do you get those without familial ties to sing your praises?

First, think about all the people in your life who can speak meaningfully about you and your accomplishments. Your list may include teachers, professors, advisors, school administrators, employers, religious leaders, leaders of organizations and activities you are involved in, or coaches. While some scholarships require recommendations from specific people (like a teacher or professor), most are pretty liberal and allow you to select anyone who knows you.

Second, now that you have a mental list of all potential recommenders, analyze which of these people could present you in a way that best matches the goals of the scholarships. If you apply for an academic scholarship, you'll want at least one teacher or professor to write a recommendation. If you apply for an athletic scholarship, a coach would be a good choice. Select people who are able to write about the things that are most important to the scholar-

As a general rule, select recommenders who can speak meaningfully about your skills and experiences that match the goal of the scholarship. In other words, choose those who can write about why you should win.

ship selection committees. A good exercise is to imagine what your potential recommender would write and whether or not this would enhance your case for winning the scholarship.

Hopefully, you have several people to choose from. If you can't decide between two equally qualified people, choose the one who knows you the best as a person. For example, if you got A's in three classes and you are trying to decide which professor to ask for a recommendation, pick the one who can write more than a testament to your academic ability. This is important because a recommendation that contains something beyond the expected is extremely memorable. Maybe one of the professors knows you well enough to comment on your character or family background. Ideally, your recommender is able to describe not only your performance in the class but also your values, interests, and character.

"I asked my economics professor to write a recommendation letter even though I didn't know him very well. I got an A in his class and thought I would get a positive letter. What a mistake! He showed me the letter that he wrote, and it was an actual form letter, where he filled in the blanks with my name and grade in his class. Next time I'll ask someone who will give me a little more personal attention!"

—Rebecca

Once you've selected who you'd like to write your recommendations, ask them to do so—early. A general rule of thumb is to allow them at least three weeks before the recommendation is due. Explain that you are applying for scholarships and are required to submit recommendations from people who know you well and who can vouch for your achievements.

A good question to ask is, "Do you feel comfortable writing a recommendation letter for me?" This allows the person the opportunity to decline your request if he or she doesn't feel comfortable or doesn't have the time. If you get a negative or hesitant response, don't assume that it's because he or she has a low opinion of you. It could simply be that the person doesn't know you well enough or has too many things to do. In most cases, potential recommenders are flattered and happy to oblige. Thank your recommender and tell him or her that you will provide more information on the scholarship and your resume.

The Name Game

From being recognized by strangers to getting preferential reservations at the hottest restaurants, there are a lot of perks to being famous or having a fancy title. You would think that this special treatment for name recognition would carry over to recommendations, that scholarship judges would be star-struck by a letter from someone with a fancy title. However, don't think that just because you ask someone well known to write your recommendations that you are a shoo-in for the scholarship. In fact, you might be surprised to learn that doing this could hurt your chances.

What's more important than the name recognition of your recommenders is how well they know you. If they can't write a personalized letter, don't ask them.

We are often asked if it's a good idea to have a well-known person or someone with a fancy title write a recommendation. The answer always comes down to the principles outlined above: How well does the person know you, and can he or she write about you in a way that supports your case for winning the scholarship? If the answer is yes, then by all means, ask the person. However, if you don't know the person very well or if what he or she will write will be totally unrelated to the qualities that the scholarship committee is looking for, then it's better to forgo the value of high name recognition and ask someone who can write about what's most important.

For example, if you work as a summer intern for your state senator, you may think that a letter from someone so widely known could give your application star power to set it apart from others with recommendations from mere mortals. However, if you spent more time photocopying or stuffing envelopes than you did developing keen political strategies and saw the senator as many times as you have fingers on one hand, chances are that he or she would have very few meaningful things to say about your performance. "A skilled photocopier" and "brewed a mean cup of coffee" are not ways you want to be described to the scholarship committee.

If you ask someone well known to write your recommendations, make sure that he or she really knows you and can speak about your accomplishments personally and meaningfully. The quality of what is said in the recommendations is much more important than whose signature is at the end.

Do The Grunt Work

Make the job easy for your recommenders by giving them everything they need. They'll appreciate your effort and you'll appreciate the positive letters they write.

Once you've selected your recommenders and they've agreed to write your recommendations, deliver everything they need to get the job done. Since they are doing you a favor, make the process as easy as possible for them. Plus, this is where you can most influence what they write and actually direct what accomplishments they highlight. But before we delve into the specifics, here is an overview of what you need to provide each and every recommender:

● **Cover letter**. This describes the scholarships you are applying for and their deadlines and gives the recommenders direct guidance on what to write. More on this in a bit.

● **Resume**. A resume provides a quick overview of your most important achievements in an easy to follow one-page format. It is also what your recommenders will use as they cite your important achievements.

● **Recommendation form**. Some scholarships provide an actual form that your recommenders need to complete. Fill in the parts that you can complete, such as your name and address, and include all forms along with any background material that goes with them.

● **Pre-addressed, stamped envelopes**. Read the application materials to find out if you need to submit your recommendations separately or with the rest of your application. If you are to submit them separately, provide your recommenders with envelopes that are stamped and have the scholarship's mailing address on them. If you are to submit them with the rest of your application, provide your recommenders with envelopes that are stamped and have your mailing address on them, unless you plan to pick up the letters in person. Many recommenders prefer to write letters that are private and that you don't review.

Once you have everything, place it in a folder or envelope and label it with your recommender's name.

Give Your Recommenders A Script

Now for the good stuff. Because you know yourself the best and have the most to gain, you might receive the best recommendations if you sat down and wrote them yourself. Unfortunately because scholarship committees are seeking opinions outside of yours, you can't do this. You can, however, help guide the direction of your recommendations through an invaluable tool called the cover letter.

This letter provides your recommenders with all of the information that they need to write your letters, including details about the scholarships and suggestions for what you'd like the recommendations to cover. Since the cover letter also includes other essentials like deadlines, mailing instructions, and a thank you, you will not sound as if you are giving orders, but you will come across as merely providing helpful assistance. In fact, most recommenders will appreciate your help, reminding them what's important and what they should include.

Here are the elements to include in your cover letter:

● **Details on the scholarships**. List the scholarships for which you will use their letters. Give a brief one-paragraph description of the mission of each of the awards and what qualities the scholarship committee seeks. This information will help your recommenders understand how you want to portray yourself and who will read the letters.

● **How you fit the scholarship**. This is the most important element of your cover letter because it's your chance to remind your recommenders of your accomplishments and to offer suggestions for what to write. Make sure that you highlight how you match the goals of the scholarships. For example, if you are applying for a scholarship for future teachers, include information about your student teaching experience and the coursework you've taken in education. Leave out the fact that you were on the tennis team.

● **Deadlines**. Inform your recommenders of how long they have to compose the letters. If you have given them their packets far in advance you may want to suggest that they mail the letters a week before the actual deadlines.

● **What to do with them when done**. Give your recommenders instructions about what to do with the completed letters.

● **Thank you**. Recommendations can take several hours to complete and often your recommenders are very busy people. Don't forget to say thank you in advance for the work that they will put into writing you a great letter of recommendation.

To illustrate the power of a good cover letter, read the example on the following page as if you were a recommender. Remember that this is only one example and your cover letter may be different. However, regardless of your own individual writing style your cover letter should include the same points as this example.

A well-written cover letter is a powerful tool. It allows you to suggest what to write and provides guidance for your recommenders. Craft your cover letters carefully and include all important information.

"I was a little hesitant about giving my professor a cover letter because I thought she might think I was too pushy for giving suggestions about what she might write. I was surprised when she actually thanked me for the letter and said she wished more students did the same. She told me that the information I gave her made mine the easiest to write."

—Jeffrey

Some notes about this cover letter:

Beth describes each scholarship she is applying for, its goal and deadline and why she feels she is a fit with the award.

She gives a quick summary of information she suggests her professor include in the letter.

Beth provides instructions about what to do with the letters when completed.

This is a well-written cover letter that is brief and easy to understand.

Dear Dr. Louis,

Thank you again for writing my scholarship recommendations. These awards are very important for my family and me to be able to pay for my education. Here are the scholarships I am applying for:

SuperCollege.com Scholarship   Deadline: May 31

This is a national scholarship based on academic and non-academic achievement, including extracurricular activities and honors. I believe I'm a match for this scholarship because of my commitment to academics (I currently have a 3.85 grade point average) and because of the volunteer work I do outside of the classroom.

Quill & Scroll Scholarship   Deadline: February 5

This scholarship is for students who want to pursue a career in journalism. Journalism is the field I want to enter after graduation. As you may remember, I am an active editor for our campus newspaper, contributing a column each week on issues that affect our student body.

Community scholarship   Deadline: August 5

This scholarship is for students who have served their community through public service. I have always been committed to public service. Outside of class, I have not only formed the youth literacy project but have also volunteered with the PLUS program.

I've enclosed a resume to help remind you of my background and accomplishments. Here are some highlights you may want to mention:

* The essay I wrote for your class that won the Young Hemingway competition

* How I formed the youth literacy project with you as the project's advisor

* My three years of volunteer work with the PLUS program

* The weekly column I've written for the newspaper on school issues

After you've finished, please return the recommendations to me in the envelopes I've enclosed. If you have any questions, please feel free to contact me at 555-5555. Again, thank you very much for taking the time to help me.

Sincerely,

Beth

"After my teacher wrote a recommendation letter for me, I sent her a nice thank you letter explaining how she was helping me fulfill my dream of going to college. She told me that over the years I was only one of a handful of students to thank her so kindly. I think too many students expect too much of their teachers and don't stop to say thank you. It means a lot to them."
—Katherine

Tie A String Around Your Recommenders' Fingers

All recommenders have one thing in common: They have too much to do and not enough time. Because of this, check in a couple of weeks before the recommendations are due. Monitor the progress of your recommendations. You may find that they're complete and already in the mail. A more common discovery is that they won't have been touched. Be polite yet diligent when you ask about the progress. It's crucial that you work with your recommenders to get the letters in on time.

The "You Can't Spell Success Without U" Mug

You now have everything you need to ask for and receive stellar recommendations. An important thing to keep in mind is that, even if it is a part of their job description, your recommenders are spending their time to help you. Remember this as you ask others to write recommendation letters.

Story From Real Life: Follow Up Or Fall Down

Marla learned how important it is to follow up. While recommenders have the best intentions to help you, they are human and can also forget. Make sure that yours don't.
—Gen and Kelly

Last year I applied for a scholarship for women who are planning to go into business. In addition to the application, I needed to get three recommendation letters from previous employers and professors. An obvious choices was my manager from the previous summer. I had interned in the product development department of a national software company. For the other two recommendations, I asked a professor and advisor at school.

I did everything right, providing all three with my resume, pre-addressed envelopes, and information on the scholarship and its deadline. I let them know that they were supposed to send the letters in directly to the organization. In the meantime, I worked on my part of the application, writing an essay about my summer internship and getting my transcript and other materials together. Amazingly, I completed the application a few days before the deadline and sent it off early. I was feeling pretty good about myself for being so put together. I had to admit that even I felt it was a pretty strong application.

A couple months later, I received a letter from the women's organization. It said that while I had a very high quality application, regretfully because my application was incomplete, the organization was unable to award me a scholarship and instead offered the non-paying distinction of honorable mention. I racked my brain trying to think of what was missing. Over and over I replayed my trip to the post office and knew that I hadn't left anything out.

The next day I contacted the organization to find out what was missing. I was able to speak with someone who was on the selection committee. She looked up my file and said that I only had two recommendations on file, one from my professor and the other from my advisor. My previous manager had not submitted my third recommendation! She said that had all of my materials been submitted, I probably would have won an award.

I learned my lesson. I had assumed that the three people I asked would be responsible enough to remember to submit the recommendation letters, but I was wrong. Two out of three is not good enough. Had I just reminded them, I probably would have won the scholarship.

—Marla

Every time my (Kelly) mother wants to say thank you to a friend or acquaintance, she writes a note and gives a small token gift. My favorite is the "You Can't Spell Success Without U" mug because of its campy play on words.

Whether or not you select an equally campy token gift, it's important that you thank your recommenders. After all, they are dedicating their free time to help you win funds for college.

Chapter 5 Summary: Get The Right Recommendations

You have more influence than you think. You can affect what your recommenders write by whom you select, what materials you provide, and how you follow up.

Familiar faces. Select people who can write meaningfully about your abilities and experience and who can convey how you fit the mission of the award. Try to choose teachers, professors, or others who know you beyond how well you perform on tests.

Do the grunt work. Provide everything they need to get the job done including cover letter, resume, recommendation paperwork, and pre-addressed, stamped envelopes.

A script. You can't write your own recommendation letters, but you can offer reminders to assist your recommenders as they are writing the letters. Include descriptions of the awards, information about accomplishments that they may want to mention, and what they should do once they have completed the letters.

Be a watchdog. It's your job to make sure that the letters are submitted on time. Check in with your recommenders and make sure they meet the deadlines.

Say thank you. After all, your recommenders are trying to help you win money!

Secrets To Writing Winning Essays

In this chapter, you'll learn:

- The real question behind every scholarship essay question

- 20 essential strategies to create a winning scholarship essay

- How to write an essay that will grab the attention of the judges

- The secrets of two students whose essays won them thousands of dollars

- How to choose an original topic

- Which topics to avoid

- How to add life & depth to your work

- Strategies for introductions & conclusions

- The 7 most important essay writing don'ts

Scholarship Essays: Your Ticket To The Finals

Offering greater depth into who you are, scholarship essays are a key factor in the selection of a winner. Your application form can give you entry into the semifinals, but it is the essay and interview that carry you into the finals. For many scholarships, the final decision-making factor is the essay alone because interviews are not required.

Because of their importance, you don't want to fall into the same trap that most applicants do and hastily bang out an essay putting little thought into what you write. The essay is your chance to convince the scholarship committee that the award should be yours. Here is where you put a stake in the ground and tell them why you are the best fit.

In this chapter, we help you take advantage of this opportunity by developing a solid strategy for crafting a winning essay. We will also look at some examples of successful scholarship essays that won their writers over $150,000 in scholarships. (Now that should motivate you to start applying for all those scholarships!) By the time you finish this chapter, you will know everything you need to write a winning scholarship essay.

The Tanabe Philosophy

Regardless of the specific wording, the underlying question and the one you must answer for almost all essay questions is the same: Why do you deserve to win? (Your answer should not be, "Because I need the money!")

Think about these questions: The Future Teachers Of America scholarship asks you to write about the future of education. The Veterans of Foreign Wars asks you to define "patriotism." The National Sculpture Society asks you to "describe your extracurricular passions." All of these questions are driving at the same thing: Why do you deserve to win?

Your answers to each should really answer the underlying question. When writing the Future Teachers Of America essay, you can discuss the general state of education and quote a few facts and figures, but you'd better be sure to cover how you fit into the future of education. If you are planning to be a teacher, you might segue into how you have and will continue to shape the future of education through your work. Similarly use the topic of patriotism to blow away the VFW judges with not only what you believe patriotism to be but also how you have actually acted upon those beliefs. And if you answer the National Sculpture Society question with an essay on how much you love to play the guitar, then you really don't deserve to win!

Our approach when it comes to the essay is to use the question to prove to the scholarship committee that you are the worthiest applicant for the award. Often the question will lead you in the right direction. (Would it surprise you to learn that the Amelia Earhart award asks about your interest in aerospace?) But even if the question is not obvious or is general in nature you should still be answering the same question: Why do you deserve to win?

20 Essential Strategies To Create A Winning Scholarship Essay

If you consider the application as your introduction to the scholarship judges in which they get the basic facts about you, think of the essay as when they silently observe a day in your life. Scholarship essays afford you an opportunity to go beyond the facts and numbers of the application to distinguish yourself from all of the other applicants and share with the judges who you really are. They offer you a time to shine.

Let's look at some concrete strategies that you can apply to your essays. Remember you are always striving to impress upon the scholarship committee why you deserve to win.

1. Brainstorm Topics

Often you will be provided with a topic, but sometimes you will have the freedom to choose your own, which can be even more difficult. If you're having trouble choosing a subject, brainstorm. Set aside some time to develop a list of possible themes. Ask yourself questions like:

- What was a significant event in my life?
- What teacher, relative, friend, or other person has influenced who I am?
- What have I learned from my experiences?
- What are my goals for the future?

When brainstorming, don't be critical of the topics you unearth—just let the creativity flow. Ask parents and friends for suggestions. Then, select the topic that is most appropriate for the scholarship and most interesting to you.

2. Choose A Topic You Like

It seems self-evident, but surprisingly, many students do not select topics that they like. Why do you need to choose a topic that you are fond of? You will be more passionate about the subject, making your essay easier to write. Plus, the judges will be able to sense your enthusiasm when reading your work.

3. Commence Writing

The most challenging step of writing a scholarship essay is getting started. Our advice: Just start writing. The first words you put down on paper may not be a brilliant bit of literature, but don't worry about it. You can always return to edit your work. It's easier to edit words you've already written than words that don't yet exist. The best cure for writer's block is to just start writing.

4. Write For The Scholarship Committee

Let's pretend you're a standup comedian who has two performances booked: one at the trendiest club in town where all the coolest college students congre-

"The most difficult part for me of writing the scholarship essay was learning how to brag. Since I usually don't like to publicize my accomplishments, it felt really awkward spending so much time writing why I was the most deserving candidate to win the award. I wanted so much to shift the focus away from my accomplishments and me. But, of course, after many revisions I had a perfectly nice and egotistical essay."

—Holly

gate on weekends and the other at a retirement home. As a skilled comedian, you would prepare different material aimed at the different audiences. The college audience would be able to relate better to jokes about picking up members of the opposite sex at a bar while your jokes about dentures and arthritis would probably—and this is a hunch—go over better with the senior citizens.

The same goes for writing your essays. Since many are given by specific organizations or for specific purposes, you need to write an essay that is appropriate for the audience. Think about who is going to be reading your essay. Is your audience natural science professors, circus performers, or used car salesmen? Write your essay so it appeals to that audience. This should guide not only your selection of topics but also your word choice, language, and tone.

5. Be Yourself

While you want to present yourself in a way that attracts the attention of the scholarship committee, you don't want to portray yourself as someone that you are not. It's okay to present selected highlights from your life that fit with the award, but it's not okay to exaggerate or to try to be someone you're not. For example, if you apply for a scholarship to promote the protection of animals, don't write about your deep compassion for helping animals when you've never ventured closer than 10 feet to one because of your allergies.

Feel comfortable about everything you write, and don't go overboard trying to mold yourself into being the student the scholarship committee wants.

6. Be An Original

There are two ways of writing an original essay: Write about an original topic, or write about an unoriginal topic originally. Writing about an original topic means forgoing what other applicants will commonly write about such as how your summer trip to Europe made you realize how similar we all are, how your mom or dad has been your role model, or how you scored the winning touchdown/goal/point. To make your essay different, you need a unique topic. Some we've seen include how a student founded the first un-beauty pageant at her college, the friendship between a student and his school's custodian, and a student's protest against inedible dorm food.

In some cases it may not be possible to select an original topic or you may not feel comfortable with a potentially risky topic. Your other option then is to take an unoriginal topic but approach it in an original way. For example, let's say you choose to write about how your mom has been your role model. Moms are one of the most popular role models for essays. How do you make your mom distinct from all the other applicants writing about their moms? Describe a trait that is unique to her like her omnipresent laughter, practical jokes, or obsession with banana splits. It is possible to turn a very popular topic—mom—into an entirely original essay.

Whichever route you choose, know that submitting an original essay (through either topic or approach) is essential in a process that pits you against hundreds or even thousands of other gifted students.

"For one scholarship I had to write about the person who had the greatest influence on my life. I chose to write about my mom because she became a single parent when she left my father, who abused her. When she read my essay, she cried. I knew then that I had written a powerful essay."

—Kate

Story From Real Life: How I Tackled Writer's Block

We've all experienced writer's block at some time. Often the most effective cure is sitting right in front of us.
—Gen and Kelly

When I first started writing my scholarship essay it was like a scene from TV, where I looked at a single sentence on a piece of paper, didn't like what I saw, crumpled the paper and tossed it into the trash can. I repeated this process many times until the crumpled paper started overflowing and I wanted to stop.

Finally, I told myself that I should just start writing and not stop until I had a complete page. It really worked. It wasn't a masterpiece—I didn't come up with the final version of my essay in a single sitting. But I did get two whole pages written at one time.

After that it was much easier because I had something to work with instead of crumpled pieces of paper.

—Kevin

The essay is about you—your opinions, experiences, and thoughts. For every scholarship essay that you write, remember to tie it in some way, directly or indirectly, to yourself.

7. Personalize Your Essay

Think of the scholarship committee members as an audience. The show that they have all come to see stars you. To keep them satisfied, give them what they want.

In other words, the scholarship committee wants to know about your life and experiences. When you write your essay, write about what has happened to you *personally* or about how you *personally* have been affected. If you are writing about drug abuse for an essay about a problem that faces college students today, do more than recite the latest national drug use statistics and the benefits of drug rehabilitation programs. If you do this, your essay might be informative, but it wouldn't be interesting. Instead, write about how a friend nearly overdosed on drugs, how others tried to peer pressure you into trying drugs, or about your volunteer work at a rehabilitation clinic. Instantly, your essay will be more interesting and memorable. Bring your essay to a personal level to share something about you with the selection committee.

8. Make Your Point

You may think that this is obvious, but many students' essays don't have a main point. Use that most basic lesson from Writing Composition 101: Have a statement that embraces the idea or subject of your work.

Try this exercise. See if you can encapsulate your essay into a single sentence that summarizes its main point. If you can't, you don't have a point. And, you'd better get one!

Let's say you are writing about growing up in the countryside. You can describe all the flat land and brush you like, but unless the land and brush add up to something, you don't have a quality essay. You might structure your essay around the idea that growing up in the country gave you a strong work ethic.

9. Support Your Statement

Once you put your statement out there, you can't abandon it. Like a baby, you have to support it because it can't stand on its own. This means you have to provide reasons for why your statement is true. The best way to do this is to give some vivid examples from your own personal experience and accomplishments.

10. Show Activity

If you were forced to sit in a room with nothing in it and nothing but a bare wall to stare at, you would probably be extremely bored. The same thing goes for an essay. Don't force the scholarship committee to read an essay that does nothing. Your essay needs activity and movement to bring it to life. This can consist of dialogue, action, stories, and thoughts. The last thing you want to do is bore your readers. With action, you won't have to worry about that!

11. Write From What You Know

Chances are you could write a better essay about what it's like to be a student than about being an 80-year-old grandparent in a nursing home. Why? Because you write best when you write from your own experience. Your essay will be more meaningful and easier to write if you know the topic first hand. Writing from experience also makes your essay more colorful and genuine since you will be able to include details and examples in a way that you can't with something you haven't experienced.

12. Highlight Your Growth

You may not have grown an inch since the day you hit seventh grade, but scholarship committees will be looking for your growth in other ways. They want to see evidence of emotional and intellectual growth, what your strengths are and how you have developed them. Strengths can include, but aren't limited to, mastery of an academic course, musical talent, helping others, athletic ability, leading a group, and more. Overcoming adversity or facing a challenge can also demonstrate your growth.

Being positive does not mean you have to break out the pompoms but you should strive to give your essay—whatever the subject—a positive tone and outlook.

13. Be Positive

You don't need to break out the pompoms and do a cheer, but you need to reflect a positive attitude in your essay. Scholarship committees want to see optimism, excitement, and confidence. They prefer not to read essays that are overly pessimistic, antagonistic, or critical. This doesn't mean that you have to put a happy spin on every word that you write or that you can't write about a serious topic or problem. Let's look at an example using the very serious topic of teen pregnancy. Which author of the following thesis statements would you rather give your money to?

Thesis 1: We could reduce the number of pregnant teens by one-half if we shifted our reliance away from scare tactics to providing responsible sex education combined with frank discussions on the responsibilities of caring for a child.

Thesis 2: Teen pregnancy is incurable. Teenagers will always act irresponsibly and it would be futile for us to believe that we can control this behavior.

Scholarship committees favor authors who not only recognize problems but also present potential solutions. Leave being pessimistic to adults. You are young, with your entire future ahead of you. Your optimism is what makes your generation so exciting and why organizations want to give you money to pursue your passion for changing the world. Don't shy away from this fact.

14. Use Examples & Illustrations

Anything the scholarship committee can use to visualize what you are writing about helps. Anecdotes and stories help convey your experiences. Examples and illustrations also make your ideas clearer. If you want to be a doctor, then explain how you became interested in becoming a doctor. You might write about the impact of your father giving you a stethoscope when you were 5. Or maybe he took you to his office and introduced you to the patients. If you expanded on some of these influences, you could create a great essay. Examples help readers picture what you are saying and relate to your experiences better.

The best way you can improve your essay is to find good editors. Good editors provide a different perspective, help you see your work in a fresh light, and enhance the message of your writing. Parents, teachers or professors, and friends make convenient editors.

15. Be Concise

The scholarship essay may not have the strict limits of a college admissions essay, but that does not give you a license to be verbose. Keep your essay tight and focused and within the recommended length of the scholarship guidelines. If none are given, then two or three pages should suffice. You certainly want the readers to get through the entirety of your masterpiece. Remember that most scholarship selection committees are composed of volunteers, who are under no obligation to even read all of your essay. Make your main points quickly and keep your essay concise.

16. Edit

Despite what you may think, you aren't infallible. Stop gasping—it's true. Re-read your work and edit it as many times as you can. Try to get someone else to edit your work as well. Roommates, friends, family members, teachers, professors, or advisors make great potential editors. When you get another person to read your essay, he or she will find errors that eluded you as well as parts that are unclear to someone reading your essay for the first time. Ask your editors to make sure your ideas are articulate, that you answer the question appropriately, and that your essay is interesting. Take their suggestions seriously. The more input you get from others and the more times you rewrite your work, the better.

17. Be Smooth: Use Transitions

You want your essay to be like silk: smooth and elegant. When you read your work, make sure your connections between ideas are logical and the flow of your essay is understandable. (This is where editors can be extremely helpful.) Also make sure that you have not included any unnecessary details that might obscure the main point of your essay or left out any information that is vital to it. Your goal is to produce an essay with clear points and supports that logically flow together.

18. Check Spelling & Grammar

The best way to do this is to have someone else do it. If you don't have time to ask someone, then do it yourself carefully. Read your essay at least once with the sole purpose of looking for spelling and grammatical mistakes. (Your computer's spell check is not 100% reliable and won't catch when you accidentally describe how you baked the bread with one cup of "flower" instead of "flour.") Try reading your work out loud to listen for grammatical mistakes.

19. Recycle

This has no relation to aluminum cans or newspapers. What we mean is that you should reuse essays that you have written for college applications, classes, or even other scholarships. Because colleges and scholarship committees usually ask very broad questions, this is generally doable and it saves you a tremendous amount of time.

You will read an example essay in this chapter. You may be surprised to learn that the author, Cynthia, recycled her essay with minimal changes, to answer such differing questions as: "Tell us about one of your dreams," "What is something you believe in strongly?" and "What past experience continues to influence you today?"

However, be careful not to try to recycle an essay when it just doesn't fit. It's better to spend the extra time to write an appropriate essay than to submit one that doesn't match the scholarship.

20. Keys To Ace The Introduction & Conclusion

Studies have found that the most important parts of a speech are the first minute and the last minute. In between, listeners fade in and out of paying attention, but it is the introduction and conclusion that really make a lasting impact. This holds true for scholarship essays as well. Spend extra time making sure these two parts deliver the message you want. Here are some tips to create knockout introductions and conclusions.

Introductions

Create action or movement. Think of the introduction as the high-speed car chase at the beginning of a movie that catches the audiences', or in this case, the readers' attention.

"I wanted to apply for five scholarships but each of them had a different essay topic. After spending weeks on college applications, I knew I didn't have five new essays in me. That's when I started recycling. I was able to apply to all five scholarships because of it."

—Luis

"I love recycling my essays. I've used essays I wrote for English and History classes and even parts of a speech I wrote a year ago. I think it's really cool to be able to use these essays, which would otherwise just be thrown away, to actually win some money!"

—Jenny

Pose a question. Questions draw attention because the readers think about how they would answer them and are curious to see how you will answer them in your essay.

Describe. If you can create a vivid image for readers, they will be more likely to want to read on.

Conclusions

Be thoughtful. Your conclusion should make the second most powerful statement in your essay because this is what your readers will remember. (The most powerful statement should be in your introduction.)

Don't just summarize. The scholarship committee members have already read your essay (we hope), so you don't need to rehash what you have already said. It's okay to summarize in one sentence, but do more than just summarize by adding an extra point or consideration.

Don't be too quick to end. Too many students tack on a meaningless conclusion or even worse, don't have one at all. Have a decent conclusion that goes with the rest of your essay and that doesn't consist of two words, "The End."

Answering Why You Deserve To Win

Theory is great, but we're ready to see it in action in a real essay. Jonathan, a college junior, applied for an award from a foundation for students who major in any field in the social sciences. From his research, Jonathan learned that the scholarship committee was composed of social science professors who often gave special consideration to those who planned to use the social sciences in their future careers.

The topic the scholarship committee asked each applicant to write on was: "Describe one encounter you have had with an area of knowledge in the social sciences and tell us how you might use this experience in your future." The topic was broad and could be answered in many ways. However, given the nature of the foundation and the probable composition of its selection committee—social science professors—the question was probably intended to determine the commitment level of the applicants to the liberal arts.

Remember, most private foundations are started and funded by an individual or group that has a particular interest. Most foundations see scholarships as a way to encourage and support young people who might be interested in their causes, occupations, or activities. An environmental protection group would rather give money to a student who is interested in studying forestry or ecology than poetry. Get into the habit of doing a little detective work on all of the scholarships you are applying to. In particular, be sure to find out the source of the money. If it is a group, try to get its literature to learn its purpose, goals, and who makes up its membership.

Jonathan certainly knew how to appeal to this particular scholarship committee. You can see right away from the tone and content that he knew to whom he was writing and what they wanted to hear. In the margins we offer some

Studies have found that in a speech people only really listen to the first minute and last minute. The same is true for essays. Give the judges introductions and conclusions that are unforgettable.

notes and call attention to points we think are worth remembering when you write your own essay.

As with any example essay, please remember that this is not necessarily the way your essay should be written. Use this example essay simply as an illustration of how a good essay might look.

A Diary Of Influence

—Jonathan

When I was eight I started keeping a diary. Every night I would scribble a short paragraph about the day's events, or when I didn't feel like writing, would draw a picture. I gave up my diary at age twelve when I became too busy with school, little league, and play. I never thought much about my brief experience with diary writing until last year when I read the diary of a man who not only diligently recorded the day's events but did so under some of the most trying circumstances.

Joseph C. Grew, a Harvard man, was the American Ambassador to Japan during the turbulent years from 1932 to 1942. As the point man for American diplomacy during the period leading up to war, Grew was in a unique position to see events unfolding. And he wrote it all down with unflagging dedication. When published in condensed form after the war it stood, I believe, as one of the most fascinating accounts of this period. Like the beginnings of so many works of history, the accidental discovery of his diaries became the basis for my junior history project.

After spending a semester in the world of Joseph Grew, acquainting myself with his disposition toward the Japanese leadership as well as the patterns of his daily life, I began to be able to see the state of Japanese politics through his eyes. While my research culminated in a report which traced the events precipitating the war from Grew's point of view, the effect of having worked with such a personal and at the same time self-consciously historical work left a deep impression on me.

One thing which I could never quite figure out and which I can see will become a life-long pursuit is how to interpret a primary source such as a diary in which the writer not only recorded the present but did so aware of the fact that it might be read in the future.

To help myself understand the complexities of such a historical document, I dug out my own childhood diary. As I flipped through the entries I began to recall my reasons for writing certain entries. Some I had written simply because nothing else special happened: "Today I went to the supermarket. I played a video game while Mom shopped." Similarly I found that Grew also recorded many events of no particular significance. When analyzing, I had to resist the temptation to take as important an event that actually had as little significance as my own entry about going shopping. Realizing this gave me a profound respect for the care that is exercised by historians in identifying the truly significant portions of a body of evidence.

Yet not all entries were insignificant. On other pages I had written clearly under the notion and even intention that someone else or I might read my writings later: "To the older Jonathan, when you get old enough, be sure to get a motorcycle." This was one of the most difficult types of entries to discriminate in Grew's diary since he was naturally reflective and almost always seemed conscious that what he wrote might be scrutinized by others. In fact some of his most interesting writing was done with the future in mind, which made me very suspicious of its veracity. There were several pages where Grew justified his reason for believing that Japan would not go to war because of the moderating influence of liberal and pro-western statesmen. Yet, each passage ended with a caveat as if he were afraid to commit himself too firmly on paper in case history as it did proved him wrong.

Finally, the last kind of entry was plain, uncensored truth: "I hate Bobby Campbell. He stinks and I will never talk to him ever again 'cause he broke my game. Die Bobby Die!" Grew didn't make these kinds of entries too often. But when I thought I found one I would place far more importance on it than on others. Because they were so rare, finding one of these spontaneous passages felt like discovering gold.

Analyzing Grew's diaries and learning how history is written from primary sources was a truly challenging experience. It taught me much about the difficulties of writing good history as well as the dangers of misinterpretation. It made me realize very clearly why I love history so much: The challenge of recovering the past through filtering raw, primary sources is exciting. And being able to catch a glimpse of yesterday felt like an enormous privilege.

After this experience, I resurrected my old diary. I try not to think this as I write, although I cannot help but wish that maybe, just maybe, some day my diary will be the focus of study of another inquisitive student.

These passages where Jonathan compares Grew's diaries with his own are great because they allow the committee members to relate to his experiences.

Jonathan is careful not to stray too far from his objective, which is to show the committee how he has encountered and dealt with the study of history through Grew's diaries. It's important that Jonathan remains focused and not get sidetracked by his interesting examples from his own diary.

Here is a great example of humor that is not contrived. This is a very funny passage but its humor comes not from Jonathan trying to be funny but from the natural humor of the diary entry itself.

This summary of Jonathan's main points reinforces the purpose of his essay. It reiterates very clearly the effect of his encounter with history.

Jonathan ends with a memorable comment on what his studies have led him to do. Members of the scholarship committee probably shared his sentiments. It also gives the essay a nice sense of closure.

How This Essay Won

There are several reasons why this essay is a winner: First, the scholarship was for social science majors, making someone studying history a perfect match. But, just because Jonathan was interested in history did not mean that he was the "best" candidate. To show that he was, Jonathan needed to demonstrate with vivid examples why he was committed to history. Rather than just list reasons, Jonathan uses his encounter with Grew's diary to illustrate why he is excited by history. This is certainly not the kind of essay that a pre-med could write or someone who only had a superficial interest. By bringing the essay to

No topic is totally taboo. Use common sense and avoid topics that are too radical or risque. The scholarship committee might admire your openness or conviction, but if your essay makes them feel uncomfortable they will probably not select you as the winner.

a personal level, Jonathan conveys a sense of who he is beyond his course work and grades.

It is also important to note what Jonathan did not write. He did not include his grades or refer to all of the courses that he took. Jonathan focused on one project and explored it deeply, which is much more powerful and interesting than if he had tried to overwhelm the reader with sheer volume.

The tone of Jonathan's essay is also very contemplative and intellectual. This is not always the best tone to have. But given that the judges were professors, his approach was both appropriate and effective and certainly appealed to this particular committee.

Finally, notice that we learn a little about Jonathan as an individual through his use of his own diary. This might not seem like much, but after you have read 500 essays about the value of history, philosophy, and such, it certainly helps to find a jewel like Jonathan's, a personal and memorable work.

Another Winning Scholarship Essay

Not all scholarships are given by organizations with a cause to further. Some groups just want to develop a relationship with the community or their future employee pool–students. These organizations offer scholarships with the goal of helping students with their education, not to reward students with specific majors or career goals. Often these scholarships ask a general essay question that can be answered by a broad group of students.

Don't be fooled by these questions. You still need to answer the underlying question: Why do you deserve to win? If the scholarship organization does not have a clear type of student it wants to reward (such as a budding astronaut or future journalist) then you should put your best side forward and show the scholarship committee why you are the kind of person they would want to win. It is important that your essay makes a powerful impression on the readers to separate you from the rest of the applicants. Let's take a look at an example of this type of essay:

The question was, "What book has had a significant influence on your life?" The scholarship was sponsored by–you guessed it–a local library. The author, Cynthia, knew that to stand out she had to write about something original. Forget Twain, Hawthorne, or Emerson–everyone would be writing about them. She also knew that while she had to write about a unique book she also needed to show how it had affected her life, and she wanted to show the scholarship committee a part of her personality that would demonstrate her future potential. Although the library scholarship committee was not interested in supporting future librarians, it did want to give money to young people who would go on to do something to improve the community. Since she knew that the readers would be librarians volunteering their time after work, Cynthia was determined to keep the essay within the 500-word limit. No overworked librarian would be able to get through a 10-page tome. Here is her essay–you can see for yourself how memorable it is:

As with any example essay, please remember that this is not necessarily the way your essay should be written. Use this example essay simply as an illustration of how a good essay might look.

`Bet You Can't`

—Cynthia

The book offered a simple challenge: "Bet you can't evenly fold a paper more than eight times." So I tried. But, even after constructing a large piece of paper out of four newspaper sheets taped together, I still could make no more than eight even folds. Although this might seem like proof that indeed a paper cannot be folded more than eight times, I still believe that it can be done. In fact I believe that every impossible task listed in the book titled appropriately *Bet You Can't* is possible.

I bought *Bet You Can't,* a short paperback printed on cheap newsprint paper, when I was in elementary school. Yet, it still sits on my bookshelf between *Shakespeare's Greatest Works* and *The History of the American Revolution.* I could never get myself to pack it away with my other childhood books because I could never accept the fact that there were things that could not be done. After all, if we could discover how to split an atom with a laser and perfect a way to bake cheese inside pizza crust, surely we could find a way to fold a paper more than eight times.

I am a firm believer that there are no limits to what men and women can achieve. I truly feel that the only barriers are those that we impose upon ourselves. And this is precisely why I find *Bet You Can't* so frustrating and why I refuse to accept what it claims is impossible.

Some might say that I am ignoring reality, that I am naive to believe that human beings are capable of everything. I imagine that these same people take great pleasure in reading a book like *Bet You Can't* because it emphasizes the limits, reveals man's weakness, and validates their pessimistic view of the world. They must love taunting someone like me with such a book. Be that as it may, I refuse to accept their outlook and refuse to let a book like *Bet You Can't* exist uncontested.

Where would we be today if we had listened to those who make words like "impossible," "undoable," and "utterly futile" their mantra? How much poorer would we be if people like Newton, Roosevelt, or King had heeded the advice of their contemporaries and abandoned what they were told could not be done?

I know that it may be mathematically true that you cannot fold a paper evenly more than eight times, but that does not keep me

---

Some comments from the judges' point of view:

First of all, who else would choose a book called Bet You Can't? *This is a unique and memorable beginning. Even though she has the scholarship committee's attention, Cynthia must still deliver an interesting and unique message if they are to remember her essay beyond the first paragraph.*

This paragraph justifies Cynthia's choice of the book as legitimate. Notice the subtle comparison to other "real" books.

Here is the main point of the essay and the side of her personality that Cynthia wants to highlight.

Notice the conviction in her writing. Taking a definite stand is something that will help your essay be memorable.

Cynthia knows that some will not agree with her and she addresses their criticisms early.

Cynthia draws on well-known examples and uses rhetorical questions to support her argument.

Notice that the conclusion is extremely memorable. "If anyone can fold a paper more than eight times it will be Cynthia," was probably how the committee felt when it awarded her the grand prize.

from trying. And I know that one day I will achieve that elusive ninth fold.

Three Reasons Why This Essay Is A Winner

Cynthia's essay has three key strengths: First, she makes her essay stand out from the rest by selecting a book that most likely no other student selected. (Other students probably chose books they read in school.) When you are writing your essay, remember to write about a unique topic or approach the topic in a creative way.

Second, Cynthia passionately presents her conviction that there is nothing that people can't accomplish. This kind of optimism and belief in the strength of humanity are traits that scholarship committees like. It is always a good idea to write your essay in a way that highlights your positive characteristics. Plus, taking a stand and being resolute in your ideas will make your essay stand above the many others that stick to vague generalizations and lack conviction.

Third, even though the topic of this essay is a book, Cynthia keeps her work focused on herself. She spotlights how her life has been affected by the book and does not waste any space with a book report or summary. Remember: you can't answer why you deserve to win if you don't write about you.

The Seven Most Important Don'ts For The Scholarship Essay

Since we've just finished showing you what to do to create a knockout essay, it's time to look at a few things you shouldn't do. Most of these lessons were learned the hard way–through actual experience. So take them to heart and don't repeat these common mistakes.

Story From Real Life: Essays In No Time Mean No Money

Stan had the unfortunate experience of falling prey to another Scholarship Don't: Don't wait until the last minute to complete your application. He knows that if he would have spent the time to write his essays, he would have had much greater success.
—Gen and Kelly

I have first hand experience with the importance of starting early and editing your scholarship essay. I found five scholarships that asked virtually the same question so I procrastinated on writing my essay until a few days before. I quickly wrote the essay while watching *Baywatch* and sent it to the five scholarship committees. I also applied for one other scholarship because I could use an essay that I wrote in my AP English class. I had spent weeks on that essay and it was pretty good. Well you can guess what happened. I lost five and won the one with my AP English essay. But what really killed me was that the five I lost were all for awards over $1,000 while the one I won was for a measly 50 bucks!

—Stan

1. DON'T Be Afraid To Get Words On The Paper.

One common cause of writer's block is the fear of beginning. When you sit down to write, don't be afraid to write a draft, or even ideas for a draft, that are not perfect. You will have time to later revise your work. What you want to do first is get words on paper. They can be wonderfully intelligent words or they can be vague concepts. The point is that you should just write. Too many students wait until the last minute and get stuck at the starting line.

2. DON'T Settle For A Weak Introduction Or Conclusion.

There's a reason why the big explosion or high-speed car chase is always during the first five minutes or the last five minutes of blockbuster movies—audiences remember best the start and finish. The same thing goes for your essay. You need to have a memorable introduction and conclusion. If you don't, the readers may not make it past your introductory paragraph or may discount your quality essay after reading a lackluster conclusion.

3. DON'T Try To Be Someone Else.

This is one of the biggest mistakes that students make. Because you want to be the one the scholarship committees are seeking, you want to highlight achievements and strengths that match the criteria of the scholarship. You don't want to lie about yourself. Besides being dishonest, the scholarship committee will probably pick up on your affectation and hold it against you.

4. DON'T Write What Every Other Student Will Write.

Or at least don't write about it in the same way. You may be thinking to yourself, "How am I supposed to know what other students are going to write?" Well, you don't need ESP to make an educated guess. For example, if the topic is to write about someone who has been influential in your life, you can guess that probably many students will write about their mom, dad, teacher, or professor. While you can certainly write about these influential people too, you will need to think of a creative approach.

5. DON'T Try Too Hard To Impress.

By this, we mean that you won't get any bonus points for overusing cliches, quotes, or words you don't understand. Too many students think that quotes and cliches will impress scholarship committees. Unless they are used sparingly and appropriately, they will win you no favors. (Remember that quotes and cliches are not your words, say nothing about you, and are entirely unoriginal.) The same thing goes for overusing the thesaurus. Yes, do experiment with words that are less familiar to you, but do not make the thesaurus your co-author. It's better to use simple words correctly than to make stark blunders with complicated ones.

6. DON'T Stray Too Far From The Topic.

A mistake that many students make is that they don't actually answer the question. This is especially true with recycled essays. Make sure that your essays, whether written from scratch or recycled from others, address the question asked.

"I am going to be a senior in college and I am still applying for scholarships. I have almost completely paid for my whole college education by winning merit-based awards. I started when I was a senior in high school and have not stopped since. I have saved my parents so much money that last Christmas they bought me a new car. As I was driving one day I realized that while they bought this car with their money it was really the scholarships that I had won which paid for it."

—Karen

7. DON'T Give Up If You Don't Win.

Even if you match the criteria of the scholarship perfectly, you still may not win the big prize. There is a certain amount of luck involved in this whole process. If you don't win this year, then enter again next year. You have no chance of winning without trying!

Chapter 6 Summary: Secrets To Writing Winning Essays

The real question. There are many questions you may be asked for a scholarship essay. Whatever question you are asked, remember that you need in some way to convey in your answer why you should win the award.

Write for your audience. Keep in mind who is likely to read your essay and what viewpoint or information you can share to convince them that you are a fit with the award.

Your essay is you. Show who you are through your essay by describing an experience, opinion, accomplishment, or goal. Paint a more complete portrait of yourself that expands beyond the facts and figures of your application.

Be an original. Don't write about what you think every other student will write about. Or, if you do, take an original approach to the topic. Scholarship essays offer the opportunity for you to set yourself apart from the other applicants.

It's alive! Use examples, illustrations, dialogue, and description to inject life into your essay. Create a narration and develop sights, sounds, and emotions that the judges can relate to and envision. Draw them into your work.

Show your strengths and growth. Demonstrate to the selection committee that you have developed the intellectual maturity to take on college and the real world. Describe experiences or traits that show personal growth.

Get editors. The best way to enhance your work is to have others read it and help you improve it. They can help make content, structural, and technical improvements.

Recycle. Whenever possible, save time and sanity by re-using an essay that you've written before. Remember to modify it to fit the new topic.

The two most important paragraphs are the introduction and conclusion. Open with something that will catch the attention of the judges, and close with what you want them to take away from your essay.

Ace The Interviews

In this chapter, you'll learn:

- The important role interviews play in the scholarship process
- The best way to prepare for the interview
- How to remain calm during a stressful interview
- What homework you must do before every interview
- Secrets of creating interactive interviews
- What to wear & how to speak confidently
- The most common interview questions
- Strategies for phone or group interviews

CHAPTER 7

The Face-To-Face Encounter

If your heart beats faster or your palms moisten when you think about the prospect of an interview, you are not alone. While the other parts of scholarship applications take time and effort, they are pieces you can complete in the privacy of your home. Unlike interviews, they don't require interaction with—gasp—a real live human.

The interview is usually the final step in the scholarship application process and if you make it that far then you're a serious contender. In this chapter, we show you what most scholarship committees are looking for and how you should prepare and practice to deliver a winning interview. We also show you how to make the most of your nervousness, how to turn it into an asset rather than a liability.

The Tanabe Philosophy

There are two secrets for doing well in scholarship interviews. The first is: Scholarship interviewers are real people. As such, your goal is to have as normal a conversation with them as possible, considering that the future of thousands of dollars may hang in the balance. It's important that you treat them as real people, interact with them, and ask them questions.

The second secret is: The best way to have successful interviews is to practice. The more you practice interviewing, the more comfortable you'll be. In this chapter, we'll tell you what kinds of questions to expect and how to practice.

Why Human Interaction Is Needed

The first step to delivering a knock-out interview is to understand why some scholarships require interviews in the first place. With the popularity of technology like the Internet, there seems to be less and less need for human interaction. (You may remember when telephones used to be answered by a live person instead of a maze of touchtone options.)

For some scholarship committees, however, a few pieces of paper with scores and autobiographical writing are not enough to get a full picture of who the applicants really are. Remember they are giving away a lot of cash and the members of the selection committee hold the important responsibility of making sure they are giving it to the most deserving students possible.

Scholarship committees use interviews as a way of learning more about who you are and how you compare in person versus on paper. Having been on both sides of the interview table, we can attest to the fact that the person you expect based on the written application is not always the person you meet at the interview.

Interviews play an important role in the scholarship selection process. Selection committees use interviews to see who you are beyond what you write in your application and essay and to select a winner among highly qualified finalists.

Understand that the purpose of interviews is not to interrogate you but rather for the scholarship committee to get to know you better and probe deeper into the reason why you deserve their money.

Interviewers Are Real People Too

If you've ever met a celebrity, you've probably realized that while their face may grace the covers of magazines and they have houses big enough to merit their own zip code, they are still real people. When you strip away the wealth and fame, they eat, drink, and sleep and have likes and dislikes just like any other person (One difference: they eat things with strange names like foie gras. Trust us, you're not missing anything). The same thing holds true for interviewers–they are real people.

You don't have to picture your interviewers in their underwear to relax. Just keep reminding yourself that they are real people. They may be well known in their field or leaders in the community, but they are still just people.

Interviewers can be high profile professors or high-powered businesspeople, but when you strip away the pomp and circumstance, they are real people. They are passionate about some topics and bored with others. They enjoy speaking about themselves and getting to know more about you. Acknowledging this will help keep your nerves under control. Throughout your interview, remind yourself that your interviewer is human, and strive to make the interview a conversation.

Interview Homework

You'd never walk into a test and expect to do well without studying the material. The same is true for interviews. Don't attempt them cold without doing your homework. There is basic information you need to know before starting your interviews so that you appear informed and knowledgeable. It's not difficult information to obtain, and it goes a long way in demonstrating that you care enough about winning to have put in some effort. Here are some things you should know before any interview:

Purpose of the scholarship. What is the organization hoping to accomplish by awarding the scholarship? Whether it's promoting students to enter a certain career area, encouraging a hobby or interest, or rewarding students for leadership, every scholarship has a mission.

Criteria for selecting the winner. From the scholarship materials, you can get information about what the selection committee is looking for when choosing the winner. From the kinds of information they request in the application to the topic of the essay question, each piece is a clue about what is important to the scholarship committee. Scholarships can be based on academic achievement, non-academic achievement, or leadership to name a few criteria. Understand what kind of student the organization is seeking and stress that side of you during the interview.

Background of the awarding organization. Do a little digging on the organization itself. Check out its website or publications. Attend a meeting or speak with someone who's a member. From this detective work, you will get a better idea of who the organization's members are and what they are trying to achieve. It can also be a great topic of conversation during the interview.

Background of your interviewer. If possible, find out as much as you can about who will be interviewing you. In many cases, you may know little more than their name and occupation, but if you can, find out more. You already have one piece of important information about your interviewers: You know that they are passionate about the organization and its mission. They wouldn't be volunteering their time to interview if they weren't.

How To Use This Detective Work To Your Advantage

Once you've done your detective work on the above topics, use the information both to practice for the interview as well as during the interview itself. For example, if you are in front of a group of doctors and they ask you about your activities, you would be better off discussing your work at the local hospital rather than your success on the baseball diamond. As much as possible, focus the conversation on areas where your activities, goals, interests, and achievements match the goal of the awarding organization. Because you will be discussing what matters most to the scholarship committee (and therefore interviewer), you can be sure that this will be a memorable conversation.

By knowing something about your interviewers beforehand, you can think of topics and questions that will be of interest to them. Most interviewers allow some time for you to ask a few questions. Here again your detective work will come in handy since you can ask them more about the organization or their background. By asking intelligent questions (i.e., not the ones that can be answered by simply reading the group's mission statement), you will demonstrate that you've done your homework. You'll also give interviewers something interesting to talk about—either themselves or their organization.

Basically, the more information you can get before the interview, the better you will actually perform in the interview. Having this background information will also allow you to answer unexpected questions better or come up with thoughtful questions on the spot.

You Are Not The Center Of The Universe

Despite what mom or dad says, the earth revolves around the sun, not you. It helps to remember this in your interviews. Your life may be the most interesting ever had, but this is still no excuse for speaking only about you for the duration of the interview.

The secret to successful interviews is: They should be interactive. The surest way to bore your interviewers is to spend the entire time speaking only about yourself. You may have had the unfortunate experience of being on the receiving end of a conversation like this if you have a friend who speaks nonstop about herself and who never seems to be interested in your life or what you have to say. Don't you just hate this kind of conversation? So will your interviewers.

Therefore, to prevent a self-centered monologue, constantly look for ways to interact with your interviewers. In addition to answering questions, ask some

"When I found out I was going to be interviewed by one of our school's deans, I dug up the dirt on him. I found out as much as I could about his academic work and his contributions to the college. He was really impressed that I knew so much about his track record, and we had a great conversation. I won—and I know that my research was one of the reasons why."

—Jeanette

Strive for interactive interviews. Do not do all of the speaking. Pose questions, ask for advice, and have fun.

yourself. Ask about their experiences in school or with the organization. Inquire about their thoughts on some of the questions they pose to you. Take time to learn about your interviewers' experiences and perspectives.

Also, speak about topics that interest your interviewers. You can tell which topics intrigue them by their reactions and body language. From the detective work that you've done, you also have an idea of what they are passionate about.

Try to make your interviews a two-way conversation instead of a one-way monologue. Engage your interviewers and keep them interested in the conversation. If you do this, they will remember your interview as a great conversation and you as a wonderful, intelligent person deserving of their award.

Look & Sound The Part

"For all of my scholarship interviews I wore a coat and tie. My friends said I dressed too formally, but I wanted to make sure that I was taken seriously. The last thing I wanted a judge to think was that I wasn't mature enough to merit the award. My friends may have poked fun, but I was pretty successful at winning."

—Jon

Studies have shown that in speeches what's more important than what you say is how you sound and how you look when you say it. Your interviews are not speeches—at least they shouldn't be—but there are some lessons you can learn from studies on speechmaking. Here are some tips to make sure that you look and sound your best, an important complement to what you actually say:

Dress appropriately. A backward-turned baseball cap and baggy jeans slung down to your thighs may be standard fare for the mall (at least they were last season), but they are not appropriate for interviews. You probably don't have to wear a suit, unless you find out through your research that the organization is very conservative, but you should dress appropriately. No-no's include: hats, bare midriffs, short skirts or shorts, open-toe shoes, and wrinkles. Think about covering obtrusive tattoos or removing extra ear/nose/tongue/eyebrow rings. Don't dress so formally that you feel uncomfortable, but dress nicely. It may not seem fair, but your dress will affect the impression you make and influence the judgment of the committee. Save making a statement of your individuality for a time when money is not in question.

Sit up straight. During interviews, you should not slouch. Sitting up straight conveys confidence, leadership, and intelligence. It communicates that you are interested in the conversation. Plus, it makes you look taller.

Speak in a positive tone of voice. One thing that keeps interviewers engaged is your tone. Make sure to speak in a positive one. This will not only maintain your interviewers' interest but will also suggest that you have an optimistic outlook toward life. Of course, don't try so hard that you sound fake.

Don't be monotonous. Speaking at the same rate and tone of voice without variation is a good way to give your interviewers heavy eyelids. Tape record yourself and pay attention to your tone of voice. There should be natural variation in your timbre.

Speak at a natural pace. If you're like most people, the more nervous you are the faster you speak. Combat this by speaking on the slower side of your

Story From Real Life: The Only Thing In Life That Matters Is Calculus

Following is the experience that I had interviewing an applicant for a scholarship based on academic achievement and contributions to extracurricular activities. Mark, the college sophomore I interviewed, is mathematically gifted but lacked in his presentation an attempt to keep the conversation interactive. Learn from his mistakes.
—Kelly Tanabe

The student is sitting at the table with his hands covering his face. His mop of stringy brown hair dangles around his face. I greet him with a warm and cheery, "Hi. How are you?" Absent of enthusiasm, he mumbles under his breath with his hands still partially covering his face, "Fine." He resists making eye contact of any kind and tilts his head even farther down. My intuition tells me that this is going to be one very long hour.

With that promising start, I notice what Mark is wearing. I can't help it. I'm human. He is wearing jeans with an orange sweater over a faded green t-shirt. His sweater even has a few holes in it. I have nothing against his holey sweater. I too wear clothes with extra ventilation. The thing that bothers me is: Why did he choose to wear mismatching, worn clothes to such an important interview? I'm giving up five hours on a Saturday to interview finalists for this scholarship, and Mark can't even find a decent shirt to wear?

Our conversation is hardly better than his color coordination. When I ask him a question, he replies with short and mumbled single sentence answers. What gets him mildly excited is calculus. Pretty much everything he says relates back to the subject of calculus. His father is a calculus professor. He tutors other students in calculus. He even named his twin Golden Retrievers Sine and Cosine. His knowledge and the graduate level coursework he has taken impress me.

After he finishes listing all of the calculus classes he has taken and calculus awards he has won, I try to direct the conversation in a different route. I want to find out what more there is to him besides a love of calculus. I ask him about what he likes to do outside of schoolwork. He continues to tell me how to prove a calculus theory and how he dreams of calculus formulas in his sleep. His calculus barrage is unrelenting.

To again try to get him to change the subject I mention that I was a sociology major, which, by the way, is about the farthest removed from calculus as possible. It has been several years since I've done a calculus problem. I understand that he is very talented in mathematics, but why don't we talk about something else he enjoys? After all, this is not a scholarship for mathematical achievement. It's a scholarship for overall academic and extracurricular achievement.

He doesn't get the hint and continues to carry on about calculus. As I tune out his math lesson, I can't get over the fact that he never makes eye contact, speaks under his breath whenever he talks, and never puts together more than two sentences at a time. Getting him to speak about anything other than calculus is virtually impossible. When I ask him what his greatest strength and greatest weakness are, he tells me his strength is (surprise, surprise) his mathematical ability and his weakness is his social skills. At least he is honest!

In the end I give up trying to direct the conversation beyond calculus. My overall impression of him is that he may be a mathematical wizard, but he lacks the ability to hold a normal conversation. At the end of an hour, he has not smiled, made eye contact, or asked a single question. As we end the interview I thank Mark for coming in. He does not reply and shuffles out of the room. His head hangs low, and again his stringy brown hair drapes his hidden face.

In spite of his mathematical talents, I find the other applicants to be much more pleasurable and interesting even if they cannot prove a complex theorem as quickly as Mark. The other interviewers agree and we award the scholarship to a student who is not only academically strong but can also hold a conversation.

natural pace. If during your interview you think you are speaking too slowly, in reality you are speaking at just the right pace.

Make natural gestures. Let your hands and face convey action and emotions. Use them as tools to illustrate anecdotes and punctuate important points.

Make eye contact. Eye contact engages interviewers and conveys self-assurance and honesty. If it is a group interview, make eye contact with all of your interviewers—don't just focus on one. Maintaining good eye contact can be difficult, but just imagine little dollar signs in your interviewers' eyes and you shouldn't have any trouble. Ka-ching!

Smile. There's nothing more depressing than having a conversation with someone who never smiles. Don't smile nonstop, but show some teeth at least once in a while.

If you use these tips, you will have a flawless look and sound to match what you're saying. All of these attributes together create a powerful portrait of who you are. Unfortunately, not all of these things come naturally, and you'll need to practice before they become unconscious actions.

The Interview Before Your Interview

One of the best ways to prepare for an interview is to do a dress rehearsal before the real thing. This allows you to run through answering questions you might be asked, practice honing your demeanor, and feel more comfortable when it comes time for the actual interview. If anything will help you deliver a winning interview, it's practice. It may be difficult, but force yourself to set aside some time to run through a practice session at least once. Here's how:

Find a mock interviewer. Bribe or coerce a friend or family member to be your mock interviewer. Parents or teachers often make the best interviewers because they are closest in age and perspective to most actual scholarship interviewers.

Prep your mock interviewer. Share with them highlights from this chapter such as the purpose of scholarship interviews, what skills you want to practice, and typical interview questions, which are described later in this chapter. If you're having trouble with eye contact, for example, ask them to take special notice of where you are looking when you speak.

Set up a video camera. If you have access to a tape recorder or video recorder, set it up to tape yourself so that you can review your mock interview afterward. Position the camera behind your interviewer so you can observe how you appear from their perspective.

Do the dress rehearsal. Grab two chairs and go for it. Answer questions and interact with your mock interviewer as if you were at the real thing.

Get feedback. After you are finished, get constructive criticism from your mock interviewer. Find out what you did well and what you need to work on.

When you speak, be animated, using gestures and making eye contact. These visual cues tell your interviewer that you are confident, charismatic, and interested in the conversation.

"I asked my mom to practice interviewing me. It was a little strange at first, but I got more comfortable as she asked me more questions. When it came time for my real interview, I was much more relaxed than I thought I'd be, and they even asked some of the same questions my mom did!"

—Brittany

What were the best parts of the interview? Which of your answers were strong, and which were weak? When did you capture or lose your mock interviewer's attention? Was your conversation one-way or two-way?

Review the tape. Evaluate your performance. If you can, watch or listen with your mock interviewer so you can get additional feedback. Listen carefully to how you answer questions so you can improve on them. Pay attention to your tone of voice. Watch your body language to see how it communicates.

Do it again. If you have the time and your mock interviewer has the energy or you can find another mock interviewer, do a second interview. If you can't find anyone, do it solo. Practice your answers, and focus on making some of the weaker ones more interesting.

The bottom line is the more you practice, the better you'll do.

Answers To The Most Common Interview Questions

The best way to take a test would be to know the questions beforehand. While we can't help you with test questions, we can give you a preview of questions that you are likely to be asked in scholarship interviews. There are several general questions that come up time and again in scholarship interviews.

From interviewing dozens of interviewers and applicants, we've developed a list of commonly asked questions and suggestions for answering them. This list is by no means comprehensive. There is no way to predict every question you will be asked. Also, in your actual interviews, the questions may not be worded in exactly the same way. However, the answer that interviewers are seeking is often the same.

Before your interviews, take the time to review this list. Add more questions particular to the specific scholarship you are applying for. Practice answering these questions to yourself and in your mock interviews.

You will find that many of the answers you prepare to these questions will be invaluable during your real interviews. Often you'll use pieces from the answers you've practiced in response to other questions you're asked. To the interviewer, you will sound incredibly articulate and thoughtful.

Why did you choose your major?

● For major-based scholarships, interviewers want to know what motivated you to select the major. Make sure that you have reasons for your decision. An anecdote will provide color to your answer.

● Have an answer for what you intend to do with the major in the future.

Why do want to enter this career field?

● For scholarships that promote a specific career field, interviewers want to know your inspiration for entering the field. Articulate your rationale.

In addition to the questions detailed in this section, here are some more common questions for scholarships based on major:

What do you think you personally can contribute to this field of study?

How do you plan to use what you have studied after graduation?

Do you plan to continue your studies in graduate school?

What do you want to specifically focus on within this field of study?

Do you plan to do a thesis or senior project?

Who are your role models in the field?

● Be prepared to discuss your plans for after graduation in the field. You may be asked what kind of job you plan to have and why you would like it.

What are your plans for after graduation?

● You are not expected to know precisely what you'll do after graduation. But you do need to be able to respond to this common question. Speak about what you are thinking about doing. The more specific you can be the better.

● Provide reasons for your plans. Explain the process in which you developed your plans and what your motivation is.

● It's okay to discuss a couple possible paths you may take, but don't bring up six very different options. Even if you are deciding among investment banking, the Peace Corps, banana farming, and seminary, don't say so. The interviewer will think that you don't have a clear direction of what you want to do. This may very well be true, but it's not something you want to convey.

Why do you think you should win this scholarship?

● Focus your answer on characteristics and achievements that match the mission of the scholarship. For example, if the scholarship is for biology majors, discuss your accomplishments in the field of biology. Your answer can include personal qualities (i.e., I have always been attentive to details) as well as accomplishments you've made.

● Be confident but not arrogant. For this type of question, be careful about balancing pride and modesty in your answer. You want to be confident enough to have reasons why you should win the scholarship but you don't want to sound boastful. To avoid sounding pompous, don't say that you are better than all of the other applicants or put down your competition. Instead, focus on your strengths independent of the other people who are applying.

● Have three reasons. Three is the magic number that is not too many or too little. To answer this question just right, offer three explanations for why you fulfill the mission of the scholarship.

Tell me about times when you've been a leader.

● Interviewers ask this to gauge your leadership ability and your accomplishments as a leader. They want to award scholarships to students who will be leaders in the future. When you answer, try to discuss leadership that you've shown that matches what the scholarship is meant to achieve.

● Don't just list off all of the leadership positions you've held. Instead, give qualitative descriptions of what you accomplished as a leader. Did your group meet its goals? Did you start something new? How did you shape the morale of the group you led? For this kind of question, anecdotes are a good way to illustrate how you've been effective as a leader.

● Remember that leadership doesn't have to be a formally elected position. You can describe how you've informally led a special project or group.

Here are some additional commonly asked questions for scholarships based on career goal:

What do you see as the future of this field?

Where do you see yourself in this field in ten years?

What can you add to this field?

What do you think are the most challenging aspects of this field?

What is your ideal job after graduating from college?

Story From Real Life: Don't Hate Me Because I'm Beautiful & Faultless

Here is an interview I had with a student who really needed to learn how to do an interview.
—Kelly Tanabe

From my first impression, she seems promising. I say "hello" to her, and she responds with a smile, eye contact, and a friendly "hello." I notice she is fashionably dressed in a blue color coordinated pantsuit. She is strikingly beautiful, with long blond hair and deep blue eyes. Her makeup is perfectly in place.

Maria tells me that her dream is to travel the world. Why? She finds other cultures "interesting." A generic answer. At this point, I envision her on stage in a Miss America pageant. I ask her to explain. *Miss California comes out of the soundproof room dressed in her blue sequined evening gown. It's her turn to answer the question that will show the judges her ability to demonstrate grace and composure while being beautiful and holding up under the pressure.*

She says, "I think it's so neat to be able to learn about other cultures. We are so different. I just want to learn about cultures around the world." *The judges wince at how generic her answer is. Nine points for composure, but five points for content and zero for creativity.*

Miss California, err Maria, also tells me she is an aspiring model. "It was so incredible. I was sitting at a cafe when a woman came up to me and gave me her business card. She told me she wanted me to model." That explains the perfect makeup. I can almost hear the theme song, *Here she comes, Miss America.*

At this point I admit to myself that I am a little envious of this college freshman who has spent her life turning the heads of the opposite sex. To make up for my bias, however, I purposely give her the benefit of the doubt. I think that there must be more to her than her good looks and Miss America answers. Throughout the remainder of the interview, however, I find no evidence of this. I ask her what leadership experience she has. She says she is the leader among her friends. Because of her they all now aspire to become models. Ugh. Just what the world needs—a whole slew of teenage girls starving themselves with noble aspirations of appearing on magazine covers.

I resort to an easy question. What are her grade point average and test scores? She says she can't remember. I wonder if she is telling the truth. Or, if they are so bad that she doesn't want me to know.

I also ask her a standard job interview question, what her greatest strength and weakness are. She replies, "My greatest strength is my ability to get along with my friends. I am good at getting along with pretty much anyone." *Her greatest strength is that she is popular?!?* "My weakness. Hmm. Well. Um. I can't think of a weakness." *What kind of answer is this? Everyone has a weakness!* I try to coach her, "Isn't there something that is more challenging for you or that you want to work on?" She answers, "Well, I can't really think of anything I want to work on. If something is more challenging I just work harder." *Ladies and gentlemen, not only is Maria perfect looking, but in her mind she is also perfect.*

I am tempted to ask her one of the more difficult job interview questions. One that recruiters from those high paying consulting and investment banking firms ask to understand candidates' thought process and to see how they hold up under pressure. If you have a stack of quarters as high as the Empire State Building, how many quarters will you have? How would you figure out how many psychiatrists there are in the Chicago area? I envision the serious look on her perfectly matted face and the furrow of her delicately plucked eyebrows in thought. Then, her head slowly bloating into an oversized perfectly blonde beach ball, and KABOOM! an explosion from brain overexertion.

I return to reality and end the interview asking if she has any questions. Usually students ask at minimum two or three questions. For many, this is one of their best opportunities to learn about the organization that is awarding the scholarship. Maria has not even one question. *Not only is she beautiful folks, but she has all the answers. The host places the sparkling crown on her head. The newly crowned Miss America starts crying the requisite tears and waves to the cheering audience.*

I bid farewell to Maria. Bad luck. I wonder if the outcome would have been different had she had a male interviewer. One flash of her pearly-toothed smile probably would have won her the scholarship.

● Be prepared to discuss what kind of leader you are. Your interviewer may ask what your approach to leadership is or your philosophy on leadership. Have examples to explain how you like to lead. For example, do you lead by example? Do you focus on motivating others and getting their buy in?

What are your strengths? Weaknesses?

● As you are applying for jobs, you will answer this question more times than you will shake hands. It is a common job interview question that you may also get in scholarship interviews. Be prepared with three strengths and three weaknesses.

● Your strengths should match the mission of the scholarship and should highlight skills and accomplishments that match the characteristics the selection committee is seeking.

● You should be able to put a positive spin on your weaknesses. (And you'd better say you have some!) For example, your perfectionism could make you frustrated when things don't go the way you plan but could also make you a very motivated person. Your love of sports could detract from your studies but could provide a needed break and be representative of your belief in balance in your life. Just make sure that the spin you put on your weakness is not too stretched and that your weakness is really a weakness.

Where do you see yourself in ten years?

● We all know that nobody knows exactly what he or she is going to be doing in ten years. The interviewers don't need specific details. They just want to get a general idea of what your long-term goals are, what you aspire to be. If you have several possibilities, at least one should be in line with the goals of the scholarship.

● Try to be as specific as possible without sounding unrealistic. For example, you can say that you would like to be working at an Internet company in marketing, but leave out that you plan to have a daughter Rita, son Tom, and dog Skip. Too much detail will make your dreams sound too naive.

Tell me about yourself. Or, is there anything you want to add?

● The most difficult questions are often the most open-ended. You have the freedom to say anything. For these kinds of questions, go back to the mission of the scholarship, and shape your answer to reflect the characteristics that the selection committee is looking for in the winner. Practice answering this question several times because it is the one with which applicants have the most trouble.

● Have three things to say about yourself that match the goal of the scholarship. For example, you could discuss three personal traits you have like your motivation, leadership skills, and interpersonal skills. You could discuss three skills applicable to academics you have like your analytical skills, problem-solving skills, and your love of a good challenge.

In addition to the questions reviewed in this section, here are some additional commonly asked questions:

Tell me about a time that you've overcome adversity.

What are your opinions about (fill in political issue)?

Tell me about your family.

What do you hope to gain from college?

Who is a role model for you?

What is your favorite book?

What is the most challenging thing you have done?

● The alternative, "Is there anything else you want to add?" is typically asked at the end of the interview. In this case, make your response brief but meaningful. Highlight the most important thing you want your interviewer to remember.

Remember that with all of these questions your goal is to demonstrate that you are the best fit for the scholarship. Keep that in the back of your mind. Be sure to practice these with your mock interviewer. The more comfortable and confident you feel answering these questions, the better you'll do in your interviews.

Questions For The Questioner

An interview should not be an interrogation, with the interviewer firing all of the questions and you answering. Ask some questions to make the interview interactive. It will be more interesting for both of you.

The difference between an interview and an interrogation is that in an interview, you also ask questions. Make certain that your interview does not become an interrogation by asking questions throughout your conversation. Remember that you want to keep the conversation two-way.

Toward the end of your interview, you will probably have the opportunity to ask additional questions. Take this opportunity. If you don't ask any questions, it will appear that you are uninterested in the conversation or you haven't put much thought into your interview. Beforehand, develop a list of questions you may want to ask. Of course you don't have to ask all of your questions, but you need to be prepared to ask a few.

To get you started, we've developed some suggestions. Adapt these questions to the specific scholarship you are applying for, and personalize them.

● How did you get involved with this organization?
● How did you enter this field? What was your motivation for entering this field?
● Who do you see as your mentors in this field?
● What do you think is the most exciting things about this field?
● What personal or professional advice do you have for someone starting out?
● What do you see as the greatest challenges for this field?
● What do you think will be the greatest advancements in the next 10 years?
● What affect do you think technology will have on this field?

Timing Is Everything

If you have more than one scholarship interview, time them strategically if you can. Schedule less important and less demanding interviews first. This will allow you the opportunity to practice before your more difficult interviews. You will improve your skills as you do more interviews. It makes sense to hone your skills on the less important meetings.

If you are one of a series of applicants who will be interviewed, choose the order that fits you best. If you like to get things over with, try to be interviewed in the beginning. If you need more time to prepare yourself mentally, select a time near the end. We recommend that you don't choose to go first because the selection committee will use your interview as a benchmark for the rest. They may not recognize you as the best applicant because it's difficult for them to believe that even though they have many more applicants to interview they've already met with the best.

The Long Distance Interview

There's a reason why most long distance relationships fall apart in a matter of months. You simply can't communicate over the telephone in the same way that you can in person. Scholarship interviews are similar. Most likely you will apply to scholarships with organizations that are based farther than a bus ride away. You may find that an interview will not be face-to-face but over the telephone instead. If this happens, here are some strategies to help bridge the distance:

Find a quiet place to do the interview where you won't be interrupted. You need to be able to pay full attention to the conversation you are having.

Know who's on the other end of the line. You may interview with a panel of people. Write down each of their names and positions when they first introduce themselves to you. They will be impressed when you are able to respond to them individually and thank each of them by name.

Use notes from your practice interviews. One of the advantages of doing an interview over the telephone is that you can refer to notes without your interviewers knowing. Take advantage of this.

Look and sound like you would in person. Pretend like your interviewers are in the room with you, and use the same gestures and facial expressions that you would if you were meeting in person. It may sound strange, but your interviewers will actually be able to hear through your voice when you are smiling, when you are paying attention, and when you are enthusiastic about what you're saying. Don't do your interview lying down in your bed or slouched back in a recliner.

Don't use a speaker phone, cordless phone, or cell phone. Speakerphones often echo and pick up distracting surrounding noise. Cordless and cell phones can generate static and the battery can die at the worst possible moment.

Turn off call waiting. Nothing is more annoying than hearing the call waiting beep while you are trying to focus and deliver an important thought. (And, this may sound obvious, but never click over to take a second call.)

Use the techniques for regular interviews. You'd be surprised how much is translated over the telephone. Don't neglect good speaking and delivery points just because the interviewers can't see you!

The Group Session

So it's you on one side of the table and a panel of six on the other side. It's certainly not the most natural way to have a conversation. How do you stay calm when you are interviewed by a council of judges? Here's how:

"I just had the worst telephone interview. I forgot to tell my roommates that I was on a very important call, and right in the middle of the interview, they decided to start a water balloon fight with the guys downstairs. I couldn't hear anything the judges said, and they said all they could hear was screaming and laughing on my end."

—Janine

Think of the group as individuals. Instead of thinking it's you versus the team, think of each of the interviewers as an individual. Try to connect with each separately.

Try to get everyone's name if you can. Have a piece of paper to jot down everyone's name and role so that you can refer to them in the conversation and be able to target your answers to appeal to each of the constituents. For example, if you are interviewing with a panel of employees from a company and you know that Sue works in accounting while Joe works in human resources, you can speak about your analytical skills to appeal to Sue and your people skills to appeal to Joe.

Make eye contact. Look into the eyes of each of the panelists. Don't stare, but show them that you are confident. Be careful not to focus on only one or two panelists.

Respect the hierarchy. You may find that there is a leader in the group like the scholarship chair or the CEO of the company. Pay a little more attention to stroke the ego of the head. A little kissing up never hurt anyone.

Try to include everyone. In any group situation, there is usually one or two more vocal members who take the lead. Don't focus all of your attention only on the loud ones. Spread your attention as evenly as possible.

The Disaster Interview

Even if you do your interview homework and diligently practice mock interviewing, you may still find that you and your interviewer just don't connect or that you just don't seem to have the right answers. For students who spend some time preparing, this is a very rare occurrence. Interviewers are not trying to trick you or make you feel bad. They are simply trying to find out more about you and your fit with the award. Still, if you think that you've bombed, here are some things to keep in mind:

Avoid should have, would have, could have. Don't replay the interview in your head again and again, thinking of all the things you should have said. It's too easy to look back and have the best answers. Instead use what you've learned to avoid making the same mistakes in your next interview.

No right answers. Remember that in reality there really are no right answers. Your answers may have not been perfect, but that doesn't mean that they were wrong. There are countless ways to answer the same question.

Other pieces count. Recall that interviews are only one part of what determines if you win a scholarship. There are other components to the scholarship application that the selection committee takes into account.

The toughest judge is you. Realize that you are your own greatest critic. While you may think that you completely bombed an interview, your interviewer will most likely not have as harsh an opinion.

"I had what I thought was a terrible interview. My interviewer asked me what I thought of the quality of public education, and when I expressed my opinion, we actually got into a 30-minute debate about the issue. I left feeling frustrated and disappointed that I had been so outspoken. Was I surprised when I actually won the award! At the awards dinner, I met my interviewer again, and he said he was impressed by my willingness to stand up for what I believe in and that our debate was such a refreshing change from the other interviews. My terrible interview turned out to be terrific!"

—Tammy

The Post-Interview

After you complete your interviews, follow up with a thank you note. Remember that interviewers are typically volunteers and have made the time to meet with you. If you feel that there is very important information that you forgot to share in your interview, mention it briefly in your thank you note. If not, a simple thank you note will suffice. You will leave a polite, lasting impression on your interviewer.

Chapter 7 Summary: Ace The Interviews

For some scholarships, you will be interviewed by members of the selection committee. This allows the committee to get to know you beyond what you write in your applications and essays, to see if you are a reflection of what you've written, and to distinguish among highly qualified finalists.

Scholarship interviewers are real people. Remember this during interviews to calm your nerves and to be able to be yourself.

Do your interview homework. Before the big day, know the purpose of the scholarship, the criteria for selection, the background of the awarding organization, and the background of your interviewer.

Don't just react. Interact! Create a two-way conversation with your interviewer so that you are not just answering questions but asking them too.

Appearances count. Look and act the part by dressing appropriately, sitting up straight, and speaking with interest in your voice.

Do a mock interview. The best way to prepare for scholarship interviews is to practice for them. Get a friend or family member to practice interviewing you. The more practice you get, the more you'll know what to expect and the more comfortable you'll be in the real situation.

Get familiar with the questions that you are most likely to be asked and practice answering these questions. (See the section in this chapter on the answers to the most common interview questions.)

Because of distance, some interviews may not be face-to-face. For telephone interviews, use the same strategies you use for in-person interviews. The person on the other end of the line may not be able to see you but can hear in your voice excitement or interest.

Some interviews may be group sessions with you and more than one interviewer. Remember to direct attention to everyone in the group and to try to connect with each person individually by using first names and making eye contact.

If you feel like you've blown an interview, remember that you are your own toughest judge. Understand that the other pieces of your application count and that you probably did better than you think.

Strategies For Specific Scholarships

CHAPTER 8

In this chapter, you'll learn winning strategies to apply for scholarships based on:

- Major or academic field
- Career goal
- Leadership
- Athletics
- Community service
- Ethnic background
- Religious background
- Financial need

Specific Scholarships & How To Win Them

Here's where you can finally reap financial gain for your delight for dogs or your gusto for golf. From automobile aficionados to zephyr zealots, there exists an organization for the love of almost everything you can imagine. And where there are enthusiast organizations, there are often scholarships to promote that interest to future generations.

Add to this organizations that want to promote specific academic fields, industries, sports, public service, religions, political agendas, and education at large and you get a large body of scholarships with very specific goals and objectives. This means that the majority of scholarships you apply for will reward students with specific backgrounds, skills, or achievements. To take the same approach to all of these scholarships, which have disparate aims, would be a mistake. Each has its own requirements, judging criteria, and competition. Each demands an individualized, well-developed plan of attack.

In this chapter, we provide strategies for specific types of scholarships. Depending on the scholarship, there are different twists you can give your application to insure that it fits the goals of the award.

The Tanabe Philosophy

In our Scholarship Directory, you will find scholarships for nearly every talent, hobby, and interest imaginable. There are scholarships for linguistic majors, soccer players, and future museum curators. On the surface, there may not seem to be many common threads that run among these diverse awards. However, there are two:

First, as we've already discussed in previous chapters, each award has a goal, and you will win only if you craft an application that demonstrates how you fulfill that goal.

Second, although the awards are diverse, there are a handful of qualities that show up over and over again. For example, many scholarships reward talent in academics, leadership, or athletics. Your challenge becomes how to showcase your aptitude in these areas. In this chapter, we discuss the most common qualities that scholarships reward and show you how you can spin your application to address each. For example, scholarships for history majors and polo superstars may both value academic achievement and therefore you will need to present these strengths. While these awards appear different, you can use a similar strategy to win both.

Major In Your Major

Whether you're majoring in Taisho-period Japanese history or Sanskrit, there are scholarships open to you. Scholarships based on academic major or concentration are some of the most commonly available. Colleges and independent organizations provide the scholarships to encourage study in these academic areas. The difficult question is: How do you make your application stand out from those of other students who by definition have similar goals and training as you? Here are some strategies we've developed to help you set your application apart from others in your academic field:

Emphasize your passion for the field. Show the scholarship committee that you are not only a good student of Asian history but that it is a passion and source of intellectual curiosity that you will pursue for the rest of your life. This does not mean that you need to become a professor of history after you graduate. However, finding some way to tie the skills of the discipline with your future career is essential. In all elements—the application, essay, recommendations, and interview—provide evidence of your commitment to your major and how it will influence the rest of your life.

To prevent essays from being a listing of all of the coursework you've taken or plan to take in the field, one possibility is to focus on your inspiration for selecting the major. Again, reveal a passion for the subject that goes beyond the fact (true as it may be) that you picked the major because all your roommates did too! Ask yourself: What motivated you to select this field of study? Do you have an interesting anecdote to illustrate how you made your decision? This is something that differs from student to student and that will add human interest in your application. Think about how you plan to use the skills from this major in your future. Do you plan to make this major a career? What contributions to the field have you made or are you planning to make? Remember, the goal is to show your commitment to the field.

For the essay, do not just reiterate your qualifications as listed in your application or resume. Use the space to add color to your application and to illustrate in a creative way your commitment to the academic field. Think about describing your first interaction with the area of study, a mentor who has influenced your decision, your vision of the future of the field. Anecdotes and dialogue go a long way since most essays focus solely on the purely academic pursuits of their authors.

Although your focus throughout the application should be on academics, you can also discuss how you have developed skills or interests outside of the classroom that relate to the field. For example, if you are studying the sciences, maybe you also volunteer with an organization that helps encourage girls to study the sciences. Weaving in non-academic experiences that support your academic goals is very powerful.

In interviews, don't just list off all of the facts that are in your application. Try to add a personal dimension to your academic interests. Explain how you came to select your major and what your plans are for utilizing your knowledge. Describe in detail your passion for the field and why it is important. Ask your interviewer about his or her commitment to the field and thoughts on its future. Asking a roomful of professors about the state of their field and where it's headed is sure to generate a stimulating and memorable conversation. You already know that this is an area of great interest for your interviewers. Use the topic to relate to them.

For scholarships based on major, the selection committee wants to see evidence of your commitment to your field and your potential for contributing to it while you are in college and afterward.

One of the best ways to find out about scholarships for your field of study is through the department of your major. Check with your department office and with your academic advisor about opportunities.

Recommendations should be from teachers or professors who can vouch for your dedication. Select those who have worked with you in your studies or in developing skills needed in the field. If you apply for a history-related scholarship, you could ask your history teacher for a recommendation. You could also ask a librarian with whom you've worked closely on research, since this is a highly desirable skill for the study of history.

Overall, remember that there will be many other students who have taken similar coursework and received similar grades. Be sure that your application presents your qualifications, your devotion to the field, and your plans for contributing to its advancement.

Your Pre-Paycheck Paycheck

There's the usual: Scholarships for future accountants, doctors, and businesspeople. Then, there's the unusual: Scholarships for those who want to seek answers about the existence of God or work underwater. In nearly every career field you can imagine–both the expected and unexpected–there are scholarships available.

Companies and organizations award career-based scholarships to encourage talented young people to enter their fields. They want to create a relationship with the most promising future leaders in their industries. Your challenge is: How do you convince the selection committee that you are the applicant with the most promise? Since these scholarships attract others interested in the industry, you can bet that many will have similar academic backgrounds as you do. Also, many will say that they intend to enter this career after graduation. These two facts alone will not guarantee a win. You need to distinguish yourself from the pack. Here's how:

As you are completing your applications, keep in mind that you want to show how much promise you have for succeeding in the career field. Describe related work experience, coursework, and honors or awards. Relate experiences in which you've developed the skills needed in the career. Even if you aren't absolutely certain that you will enter the field, it's okay to apply for scholarships. Nobody expects you to sign away your life at this point.

Concentrate on what contributions you plan to make within the industry. If you plan to be a graphic designer, what kind of design do you plan to do? What kind of innovative projects would you like to tackle? Sharing this with the selection committee will make your future contributions to the field more real.

To differentiate your application from the others, discuss how your interest in the career started. Did you have a mentor who piqued your curiosity? Did your studies influence your interest? Your background will be different from that of other students.

Essays offer you the opportunity to go beyond the facts to your personal or emotional dedication to the career. Utilize the space to illustrate your commitment with an anecdote or example. Share your personal opinions and motivations, what attracts you to the field. If you are applying for an

"I applied for a scholarship for students who want to work in business after graduating. Unfortunately, I didn't win the scholarship, but I did meet my future employer. She was one of the judges that I clicked with in my interview, and now I have a great job. I highly recommend networking with the people you meet through scholarship competitions. They're well connected in the industry."

—Miriam

accounting scholarship, don't restate the information in your application about the accounting coursework you've taken and internships you've held. Write about how you first became interested in the field or about the most valuable experience you had while interning. Or, you may want to write about your analytical ability, a skill that is required for accounting. Be sure to connect how the analytical skill you are writing about is related and will contribute to your future as an accountant.

Convey to interviewers information about you that they can't find in your application. Share why you plan to enter the field, highlights from your experience, and your plans for the future. Recognize that your plans may change, but outline where you see yourself in the career in the next five or ten years. Describe your goals and how you hope to make inventive contributions to the field. Also take the time to learn more about the industry from your interviewers. Most likely they have a number of years of experience. Ask them about their background, the positive and negative aspects they've found, and their views on where the industry is headed. This is a great opportunity for you to learn from someone with experience and to gain insights about how to succeed.

Get recommendations from employers if you've had experience in the field. If you haven't, your employers may be able to describe skills that you've developed that are necessary for the career. Ask teachers or professors who have taught related subjects.

Remember that your overall objective is to demonstrate your devotion to the career and your ability to excel and make useful contributions to it.

Leadership & Influencing Others

When you were a child, being a leader meant you decided which schoolyard game to play during recess. Now, it may mean leading an organization, heralding a cause, or influencing the establishment. In the future, it will mean managing and motivating a team of people or making a difference in your community. Scholarship committees recognize the value of supporting students who are promising leaders–in fact this is a quality that almost all scholarships will reward. They want to back those who will move and shake their world.

When you apply for scholarships based on leadership, it's not enough to say that you are a leader. You need to prove it to the scholarship committee with your experiences and illustrations. Here are some strategies for applying for leadership-based scholarships:

To demonstrate your leadership ability, *show* the scholarship committees how you've been a leader. Describe leadership positions you've held and your responsibilities in each, but don't stop here. In addition, use examples to illustrate how you've successfully led a group, how you've directed or motivated your peers. Give the scholarship committee the most shining example of your leadership in action.

> *"It's not enough for students to say that they are leaders. They have to prove it with tangible results. Whether the results are starting a business, directing a play, or recruiting volunteers, I want to see the consequences of their efforts. In the real world, the quality of your leadership is measured by what you produce."*
>
> *—Veronica, a scholarship judge*

Provide concrete examples of the effects of your leadership. Did your team meet its goals? Did you lead a new or innovative project? Did you increase membership or participation? Were there changes as a result of your efforts? This provides solid evidence of the influence of your leadership and your ability to effect change.

Recognize that being a leader doesn't just mean being the president of a class or organization. Leaders are people who are passionate about their cause and who influence other people. Leadership can take many forms from writing an editorial column to leading a Girl Scout troop. Include both formal and informal leadership roles you've played. This may consist of official positions you've held as well as special projects you've led in which you didn't have an official title. The important thing about leadership is that you have influenced other people and rallied them to take action.

In applications, highlight your main responsibilities and achievements as a leader. This will provide a quick overview of your accomplishments. Select those that best fit the mission of the scholarship.

In essays, do not just repeat the information that is in your applications. Provide insight into who you are as a leader. Share an anecdote of one of your experiences leading. Describe your philosophy of being a leader. Explain when you first realized the power of leadership. Talk about a leader you admire.

For interviews, again go beyond your applications. Don't recount information that your interviewers can easily find in your applications or essays. Instead, provide personal information about your leadership experience or approach to leadership. Practice sharing examples of times you've been a leader. Try to exude confidence in your interview. Since you'll be in the company of other leaders on the scholarship committee, ask them about their philosophy of leadership, what they did as students, and what they find challenging about being a leader in their fields.

Ask recommenders to describe examples of your leadership ability. Remind them of projects and events in which you were a leader so that they can complete the portrait of you as a strong leader.

Athletic Scholarships

You're the best dribbler, server, runner, pitcher, or sprinter at your school. How do you use that talent to pay for college? With an athletic scholarship.

Athletic scholarships are the holy grail of scholarships. At their best, they can cover tuition and fees, room and board, and books. That's not bad for doing something that you enjoy.

There are two types of athletic scholarships. This section describes the first, which are awarded by colleges to the best college-bound high school athletes. The next section covers the second, which are from organizations that reward high school or college students who participate in athletics but that may or may not be based on talent.

You don't have to be the next Tiger Woods to receive an athletic scholarship. There are opportunities for strong athletes, who are not necessarily superstars, in sports other than the Big Three of football, basketball, and baseball. Plus, there are scholarships for participating in sports, in which performance is not a factor.

For College-Bound High School Athletes

College athletic scholarships are funded by membership revenue from the National Collegiate Athletic Association (NCAA), which encompasses over 950 colleges. The colleges are divided into three divisions, with athletic scholarships awarded for Division I and Division II schools, which are the most competitive. At Division III schools, student athletes receive scholarships based on financial need but not based on athletic talent.

However, don't think that every talented athlete is instantly showered with a full-ride scholarship. It takes more than talent to win and keep one of these awards. Here are some strategies for winning and managing an athletic scholarship:

Academics rule. You can be the number one player in the country, but if you don't have the grades or tests scores, you won't play competitively in college. The minimum academic requirements for eligibility are that you must:

For athletic scholarships, your scores on the field are important but not as important as your scores in the classroom. To qualify, you must meet minimum academic requirements.

- Graduate from high school.
- Complete a core curriculum of at least 13 academic courses including:
    English: Four years.
    Mathematics: One year of algebra and one year of geometry (or a higher-level mathematics course for which geometry is a prerequisite).
    Natural or physical science (including at least one laboratory course, if offered by the high school): Two years.
    Additional courses: English, mathematics, or natural or physical science: One year.
    Social science: Two years.
    Additional academic courses: in any of the above subject areas or foreign language, computer science, philosophy or nondoctrinal religion courses: Two years.
- Have a core-course grade-point average and a combined score on the SAT verbal and math sections or a sum score on the ACT based on the NCAA qualifier index scale.

You don't have to be a football or basketball star to win athletic scholarships. In fact, you may have better opportunities to win scholarships for less publicized sports like crew, rugby, volleyball, or field hockey. Competition is often less intense for these less popular sports.

Find schools that match both your athletic and academic goals. Don't choose a college solely because of its athletic program. The great majority of student athletes don't go professional after graduating. They go to graduate school or find jobs. Select a college that fulfills your academic needs so that you will be prepared for the next step.

They will not find you. You need to find them. Unless you are a true superstar, the reality is that coaches don't have the resources to do national searches for student athletes. If you want to be noticed, you are going to need to start the conversation. Do this by writing a letter to coaches at prospective colleges. Build a portfolio as evidence of your athletic ability. Your portfolio should include the following:

- Athletic statistics such as win-loss record, times, averages, etc.
- Records set
- Honors or awards won
- Newspaper clips
- Videotapes
- Letters of recommendation from coaches

Keep in touch with the coaches. Follow up to make sure they received your letter and portfolio. Ask if they need additional information. Get your high school coach to call on your behalf. Try to keep yourself at the top of their list of who they want on next year's team.

If you are fortunate enough to receive an athletic scholarship, realize that you are not guaranteed a free ride for the rest of your academic career. There are no guaranteed four-year athletic scholarships in Division I, II or III. Athletic scholarships are awarded for a maximum of one academic year and may be renewed each year for a maximum of five years within a six-year period.

Don't count on that $7 million contract yet. For a very, very small minority, college segues into professional athletics. According to the NCAA, the odds of a high school football player making it to a professional team are about 6,000 to 1, and the odds for a high school basketball player are 10,000 to 1. Do your best, but keep focused on academics, too.

Get more information. The more information you have, the better equipped you'll be for facing the stiff competition for athletic scholarships. Speak with your coach and guidance counselors. Also, get more detailed information on eligibility and a directory of schools that have scholarships for each sport from the NCAA (www.ncaa.org). Contact information for the NCAA can also be foound in Appendix B.

For High School & College Student Athletes

There are also scholarships for high school and college athletic competitors and enthusiasts. These awards are given by aficionado organizations and athletic associations like your school's booster club.

For these scholarships, the level of athletic talent can vary. For some, athletic ability is the key measurement while others equally weigh additional qualities like leadership, academic achievement, or public service. Depending on what you will be judged on, adapt your application accordingly. Here are some strategies to help:

In your application, concentrate on how you meet the mission of the scholarship. For example, if you are applying for a scholarship that is based on both athletic and academic achievement, outline your accomplishments both on the field and in the classroom.

Submit a sports portfolio. Your portfolio brings the selection committee to the sidelines of your game and enables them to see evidence of your athletic ability. Include in your portfolio:

"In high school, I was a track star, winning meets and setting school records. I thought that once my senior year rolled around I would receive dozens of calls from college recruiters. After the fall quarter passed and the phone didn't ring, I realized I needed to do some self promotion. I contacted several coaches and sent them my portfolio. Through these connections, I was able to earn a scholarship. My coach told me that if I hadn't contacted him, I probably wouldn't have been recruited because the school just didn't have the resources to recruit nationwide."

—Ken

- Athletic statistics such as win-loss record, times, averages, etc.
- Records set
- Honors or awards won
- Newspaper clips
- Videotapes
- Letters of recommendation from coaches

Try to go beyond your statistics, records, and times. Describe your motivation for participating in the sport to provide background for your interest. Outline your goals for the future as well to let the scholarship committee know where you are headed. While going off to play in the NFL or NBA may be your goal, consider mentioning alternatives to demonstrate that you understand how difficult going professional is and how much you value a solid education.

Try to make your essays different from what the scholarship committee will expect. Many athletes will write about the time they scored the winning touchdown or the winning homerun. Take a different approach. Depict the first time you recognized your passion for the sport. Describe an unexpected mentor or role model who has shaped who you are as an athlete. Explain why the sport is important besides scoring points and the prospect of becoming a professional athlete. Use the essay to share something about yourself, not to just glorify your accomplishments. The scholarship committee will know by your portfolio that you are a talented player. What you need to show them is that your talent extends to off the field as well.

In interviews, go beyond the information that is in your applications and essays. Again, don't just recount the winning game or match. Provide insight into your personal motivation and goals. Have anecdotes and examples besides those from game time to illustrate your commitment to the sport. Be ready to discuss your major and classes you'd like to take.

It's natural to ask coaches to write recommendations. Encourage your coaches to write not only about your athletic statistics but also to speak about you as a person. You may want to ask a teacher or professor who knows you in a different capacity to write a recommendation as well. Request that he or she comments on your integrity and dedication to academics. This will provide a more complete picture of who you are behind the athletic jersey.

> *"When my students are speaking with recruiters I remind them to explain that they are not only committed to athletics but are committed to their schoolwork as well. Recruiters are impressed that they understand that very few athletes actually make it into the pros and that they will need to rely on more than their athletic abilities to get ahead."*
>
> *—Dan, a high school coach*

Scholarships For Service

It's a rare occurrence, but some scholarships offer the opportunity for philanthropy to actually pay off in cold hard cash. Of course, this should not be your motivation for volunteering, but it is a nice perk of donating your time and service for a worthy cause. Many organizations provide scholarships to encourage public service among youth. Your challenge becomes how you distinguish your application from those of all the other do-gooders.

As with other types of scholarships, what's most important for service-based scholarships is fulfilling the mission. Before you start your applications, understand what the organization is trying to achieve. What is the

"When I started volunteering to help restore public trails near my college, I expected absolutely nothing in return besides the satisfaction of beautifying my community. My advisor suggested I apply for scholarships for public service. I did and won $1,000! What a great surprise. I got rewarded for doing something I enjoyed."

—Phil

organization's purpose? Why is it awarding the scholarship? Once you understand this, mold your application to show how you fit the mission. Highlight service experience that matches the scholarship's mission.

When completing the application, include details that define the quality of the contributions that you made. List the number of hours and periods of time you've contributed. Include any responsibilities you held. Most importantly note the effects of your contributions. Give concrete evidence of how your service has produced results. For example, if you volunteered for an adult literacy program, describe how your students improved their scores on a reading test after working with you. If you volunteered for a voter registration drive, recount how many voters you registered. By providing specific examples of the results of your work, scholarship committees will see that you not only volunteer but you make a difference that is measurable and material.

In essays, extend beyond the information that you present in your application. Discuss your motivation for serving and why the causes you have been helping are important to you. Bring your inspiration to a personal level so that the scholarship committee can understand you better as a person. Be illustrative in your essay, providing lively examples, dialogue, or anecdotes. Don't be afraid to be creative.

Take a similar approach with interviews. Go beyond what you have included in your application and essay. Use this time to show interviewers why your volunteer work is important to you personally. Practice sharing experiences and information to illustrate your points. Also take the time to learn about your interviewers' link to public service. Ask them how they got involved and what motivates them to continue.

In all, don't just state the facts about your public service. Make your service personal by conveying how it has affected the lives of those you have helped and you.

Ethnic Background

Ethnicity-based scholarships are awarded to promote education among groups that are underrepresented. They are also awarded to encourage the preservation of heritage or success of members of ethnic groups. For ethnicity-based scholarships in particular, pay attention to the requirements. Some scholarships seek students who will preserve their ethnic heritage while others seek students who will blend their ethnic background with American culture. Depending on what the mission of the scholarship is, you may or may not be a fit, and you will need to shape your application accordingly.

If the scholarship is for students who are traditionally underrepresented in higher education, the scholarship committee will select students who do well academically and show promise of becoming leaders and role models for other students of the same ethnic background. When applying for one of these kinds of scholarships, highlight your commitment to education and your leadership ability. Show your commitment to helping others who share your ethnic background by describing activities in which you promoted your heritage.

For scholarships that promote the preservation of heritage, highlight related cultural or educational activities. Examples are performing traditional dances or music, attending cultural school to learn the language, participating in religious programs, or volunteering at organizations to help those who share your ethnic background.

If the scholarship supports successful assimilation into American culture, the scholarship committee seeks students who will be successful and be role models. Focus on academics and achievements, which point to your future success.

For each of these kinds of scholarships, in essays and in interviews speak about the significance of your ethnicity to you personally. Don't generalize or speak about other people. Have examples and illustrations to emphasize your points.

Spreading The Gospel: Religious Scholarships

When applying for scholarships, be honest about how committed you are. If you are not truly devoted to the interest or hobby that you say you are, the selection committee will see through you.

When you think of money, religion is probably not the first thing to pop into mind. However, many religious organizations award scholarships to encourage young people to get involved and to promote the growth of the religion. We have a few words of advice for applying for religious-based scholarships.

Most importantly, only apply for the scholarship if you are a true believer of the religion. We don't suspect that you would do this, but some students have been known to apply for such scholarships even though the only time they attend church is when their parents drag them out of bed on Christmas and Easter morning. If you are not truly dedicated to the religion, don't pretend to be.

With that said, emphasize your participation in religious activities in your application. This may include participating in missionary campaigns, teaching, volunteering, or studying religious traditions. These descriptions will help show the selection committee your dedication to the religion. Also emphasize how religious teaching and faith have helped you in the past and what it means to your future.

Money-Making Hobbies

You probably don't think you can earn money from amateur radio operation, bowling, or knowing Latin, but you can. For almost every hobby there is a scholarship. Organizations composed of enthusiasts want to encourage the growth and popularity of the objects of their affection, and thus have established scholarships for students who partake in them. If you are a hobbyist, figure out how to make a distinction between all of the other amateur radio operators and you. Here are some strategies for accomplishing this:

The first step is to ensure that you fit the mission of the scholarship. If the scholarship is for true enthusiasts of the hobby, make sure that you really are. Don't apply for a philatelic scholarship if the only stamps you touch are those you use to send letters.

"I never imagined that my interest in photography would pay off, but I won a $500 scholarship from a local photography store. My winning photograph was of my grandparents."

—Ben

In applications, highlight any honors or awards you have won in the hobby. If you haven't won any, provide other evidence of your skill level. If you are applying for a sewing scholarship and have never won an award in sewing, describe instead how you started a business in which you sold your sewn products. Convey to the scholarship committee your skill level in the hobby whether it's through awards you've won or other personal accomplishments you've made.

Use essays as an opportunity to discuss the personal significance of your hobby in your life. Explain your motivation for becoming involved or role models in the hobby. Make your essay personal with anecdotes, dialogues, or active experiences. Don't be afraid to be creative. Convey how the hobby has affected you personally.

Try to demonstrate that you are committed to continuing your hobby in essays or interviews. Discuss your goals for the future so that the selection committee will understand that by awarding the scholarship to you, they will meet their goal of maintaining the hobby in the future.

In interviews, again provide insight into how the hobby has affected you personally. Ask interviewers how they got their start in the hobby and about their experiences as well. You know in advance that this is a topic of conversation that they will enjoy.

Get recommendations from those who can vouch for your skill level. If you are applying for a sewing scholarship, get a recommendation from your sewing teacher or from a frequent recipient of some of your projects.

The Mom & Dad Scholarship

No, this isn't the scholarship where Mom and Dad write you a check! One perk that employers often provide is a scholarship fund for the sons and daugh-

---

Story From Real Life: My Hobbies Paid For College

Did you ever think that your hobbies would help put you through college? This student didn't think so until he made it happen. Read how he cashed in on his hobbies with scholarships.
—Gen and Kelly

When I was a freshman in college, my parents asked me to apply for scholarships to help pay my tuition bills. I made a list of all of my hobbies and interests. I cross-referenced them with scholarships and found three awards that matched my hobbies: writing, singing, and public speaking.

In the spring I applied for all three. For the writing scholarship, I described how I wrote for our school's literary magazine and included clips from pieces I had gotten published. When I applied for the singing scholarship, I included audio and videotapes of performances I'd made in high school and college. For the public speaking scholarship, I actually had to give a speech as a part of the competition.

It turns out that I won two scholarships, the public speaking and singing scholarship. I never thought that what I love to do in my free time could help me pay for college, but I won $3000!

—Russell

ters of their employees. The great thing about employer scholarships is that the children of employees often have good chances of winning. Because it is a requirement to be the child of an employee, there are a limited number of people who can apply. This does not mean that employer scholarships are easy to win, but it does mean that unlike scholarships in which every student in the country can apply, the competition in these will be significantly less. Here are some strategies to help improve your chances even more.

Ask your parents to find out who the selection committee will be. If they feel it's appropriate, they should informally speak with members of the selection committee to get more information on what qualities they are looking for in students and what kind of students have won in the past. Warn them not to try and lobby for you since this can easily backfire. If your parents are able to gather more information about what the selection committee is looking for beyond the written guidelines, you will have a better idea of how to shape your application and essay.

In the application and essay, focus on conveying how you fulfill the mission of the scholarship. Often the mission will be general, rewarding students for academic achievement and leadership. Review the information in this chapter on applying for scholarships based on academics and leadership.

For the interview, be aware that while it's inappropriate and shouldn't happen, what you say could get back to your mom or dad's manager. While you shouldn't do this in any interview, in employer interviews especially, be careful about how you describe your parents. Do not be critical or relate information that could be used against them. For example, do not say that your parents dislike their managers or express their beliefs about what changes should be made to the company. Chances are that the selection committee will not reveal what they learn, but it's better to be cautious.

Need-Based Awards

Because the purpose of financial aid is to assist those who need help to attend college, it makes sense that financial need is a requirement for many scholarships. To make a case for your need, it's not enough to submit the Free Application for Federal Student Aid (FAFSA) or tax forms. Here is some guidance for applying for need-based scholarships.

Don't count yourself out of need-based scholarships without first understanding how the scholarship committee defines financial need. For some, there are specific guidelines while for others a level of need is preferred but not required.

First, try to find out how the organization defines need and how much of a role it plays in the selection. Different scholarships define need differently. You may find that while you are needy according to the guidelines of one scholarship, you may not be according to another. If you are on the borderline of being needy for a specific scholarship but you find out that financial need does not play the largest role in selection, you may still have a good chance of winning. However, if you discover that it is the largest factor, you may choose to spend your time applying to a different scholarship that fits your background better.

Tell the truth about how much you really need. Most need-based scholarships require documentation of your need anyway so the selection committee will be able to verify your finances.

Build a case that demonstrates your financial need. Concisely highlight the main reasons for your need. By showing that your income and assets are X and you anticipate that your college education will cost Y, you can quickly show the difference between the two. Briefly explain special circumstances that affect your need such as the costs of a sibling's education, medical costs, or the support of an elderly or ailing relative. This helps the selection committee understand your situation.

Money should not be the entire premise of all of your application. Include information about your financial background, but spend the rest of the application making a case for why you're qualified to win. Your financial situation is just one consideration. Once you've established that you need financial help, you need to prove that you meet the mission of the scholarship. Your application, essay, interview, and recommendations should be focused on how you fit the scholarship, not on why you need money.

For additional help, Chapter 10 will give you specifics on qualifying for another whole facet of assistance—financial aid from the U.S. government. And Chapter 11 will provide all you need to know about college costs and estimating how much aid you qualify for.

Recurring Themes

In this chapter, we have outlined strategies that you should use when applying for specific scholarships. Because each is judged by a different group of people and has different qualifications, you need to take an individualized approach to applying. However, throughout these very different types of scholarships, you'll find some recurring themes to take away. In sum, remember:

- Build a case for why you fit the mission of the scholarship.
- Tell the truth.
- Use essays and interviews to go beyond facts and scores to share something personal about you.

By following these guidelines, you will create the strongest application possible.

Chapter 8 Summary: Strategies For Specific Scholarships

There are scholarships for nearly every talent, hobby, or interest imaginable. Your job is to find those that best match your skills and experience. Then, create an application that builds a case for why you should win.

For scholarships based on major, demonstrate your passion for the field and plans to use it after graduating either directly or indirectly.

When applying for scholarships based on career goals, show how much promise you have for contributing to the field in the future and describe your motivation for entering the field and your goals for the future.

For scholarships based on leadership, demonstrate how you've been a leader through examples and illustrations, including the results of your work. Remember that you don't have to hold an official position to be a leader.

If you are a college-bound high school athlete, keep in mind that your scores on the field are important but not as important as the scores you get in the classroom. Academic achievement is a must for athletic scholarships. With a few exceptions for nationally recognized athletes, the coaches will not find you. You will need to build a portfolio to showcase your talents and start the communication with them.

Be realistic about athletic scholarships. Know that there are many more student athletes than there are scholarships available and that your chances of making it into the professional leagues are about 6,000 to 1 for football and 10,000 to 1 for basketball.

For scholarships based on service, highlight the results of your service work and any responsibilities you held. Explain your motivation for participating in service work.

When applying for scholarships based on ethnic background, highlight your contributions to your ethnic community and the role you plan to play in the future.

For awards based on religious belief, focus on your contributions to the community and the responsibilities you held.

For scholarships based on a hobby or interest, showcase awards or honors you've won for the hobby and evidence of your skill in the hobby.

Need-based awards are provided for those students with financial need. Realize that the definition of what financial need is varies by award, which means that you may qualify for awards even if you think you don't. Build a case that illustrates why you need aid by showing the costs of your education and your family's ability to contribute.

Free Cash For Graduate School

....

In this chapter, you'll learn:

- How to adjust your strategy to win graduate financial aid

- Why not all graduate aid is made equal

- Step-by-step strategies for completing applications, essays, & grant proposals

- A sneak peek at the interview questions & how to ace them

- How to keep the money you've won

....

CHAPTER 9

The Long & Expensive Path Of Graduate School

Typically spanning two to eight years, graduate school can be a long and arduous path. With the stresses of dissertations, oral exams, board exams, research, and the quest to publish, the less you need to worry about funding your education the better. While grad student life is hardly equated with luxury, there are a lot of financial aid resources available from graduate schools, the government, and private organizations. The challenge becomes how to find these resources, and because they are limited, how to make your work in your particular field stand out.

Your approach to graduate financial aid should be different than it was to undergraduate financial aid. While undergraduate scholarships are oftentimes based on involvement in activities, leadership, or special skills, the majority of graduate scholarships and fellowships are based primarily on academics and research. Crafting your applications for graduate school aid will require its own set of strategies.

Another difference is that you will find that the community of applicants and judges is often smaller in graduate studies. Graduate students who apply will have more similar backgrounds than undergraduate students. This means that you will need to be particularly strategic about how to set your application apart from those of other students. Because you know that the selection committee will probably be professors or other specialists in your field of study, you need to craft your application materials to impress this very demanding crowd.

The strategies in this chapter are specifically designed for graduate school scholarships and fellowships. Hopefully we can help ease the stress of at least one aspect of graduate school life. As for the dissertation, we're sorry–you're on your own.

Your approach to graduate financial aid should be different than it was to undergraduate financial aid. The majority of graduate scholarships and fellowships are based primarily on academics and research. Therefore, crafting your applications for graduate school aid will require its own set of strategies.

The Tanabe Philosophy

As you move from undergraduate to graduate school, the intensity of academics increases. The same holds true for financial aid. For graduate school, financial aid is not based on leadership or extracurricular activities. Research and academics are the priorities.

Our approach to graduate financial aid is to focus on demonstrating your long-term commitment to academics and research. Judges are no longer casual members of clubs or volunteers. They are the small circle of leaders in your future career field—professors, deans, and academic institutional heads. To win you must show them the intensity of your passion for your field and your ability to contribute to its advancement. You must demonstrate your ability to think critically and innovatively.

Aid In All Shapes & Sizes

The first step to approaching graduate school financial aid is to learn about all of the options that are open to you. There are several forms of financial aid, each with its own requirements and benefits. Here is a brief overview to get you started.

Scholarships: Often given by private organizations, scholarships are typically awarded in general fields of study. They are usually open to both undergraduate and graduate students. Scholarships are based on merit, with some based on financial need as well. They do not need to be repaid.

Grants: Unfortunately, under most circumstances only undergraduate students are eligible for Pell Grants or Federal Supplemental Educational Opportunity Grants (FSEOG) from the government. However, there are special federal grants for students entering the health and medical fields from the National Health Services Corps and the Armed Forces.

In addition, there are research grants for graduate students. Provided by the federal and state governments, graduate schools, or private organizations, this form of aid does not need to be repaid. For graduate students, grants oftentimes fund a specific project, research study, or dissertation. These grants can pay for the costs of materials and sometimes even travel to research centers. They can also provide students with the right to use facilities and libraries that they might not normally have access to.

Fellowships: Provided by graduate school departments, private organizations, and states, fellowships support graduate and post-graduate study, research, or work placement. They typically fund research or study in a specific area at a specific university. Only open to graduate students, fellowships are based on academic merit, with a minority based on financial need, too. They do not need to be repaid and can fund tuition and/or research expenses, with many providing stipends for living expenses. However, don't expect to start living a life of luxury–the stipends are still not enough to raise you above the poverty line. Some require recipients to work as Teaching or Research Assistants.

Federal aid: Funded by the government, federal financial aid includes loans and grants. These are based entirely on financial need. For more information, see Chapter 10, *Financial Aid Workshop.*

Employment: Many graduate schools supplement students' education with employment opportunities to research or teach. For some schools, such employment is a requirement to graduate or a part of the financial aid package.

"With the possible exception of business students, grad school is about having the most education and the least disposable income. Fortunately, financial aid has kept me from starving, but in two years I have eaten 268 packages of ramen."

—Mark

More Than Money

In addition to providing financial relief, scholarships, grants, fellowships, and teaching assistantships can assist you in your career and add prestige to your curriculum vitae. As you apply for these programs, you may need to complete an application or make an in-person case for your research to a committee. In doing this, you gain experience presenting your research proposal, and you hone your skills of persuasion, both necessary skills in academia. These financial aid programs also help you build the foundation of your academic reputation and expose those in your field to your work. You have the prospect to network with professors and other academics who will be your supporters or detractors in the future. Keep in mind these additional opportunities as you apply for these aid programs.

It's All About Academics

The most important thing to remember when applying for graduate aid is that unlike undergraduate aid, it is almost exclusively focused on academics—your contributions to the field, both past and present.

One of the factors that differentiates graduate school grant, scholarship, and fellowship awards from undergraduate awards is the emphasis on academics. Undergraduate awards may be based on criteria like leadership, activities, hobbies, talents, or athletic ability. Graduate awards are almost entirely based on academics and achievement in a particular field of study. They are less about activities, hobbies, or other talents and more about your potential contribution to the academic field.

Keep this focus on academics in mind when applying for graduate awards. Throughout applications, proposals, essays, and interviews, emphasize your contribution to and passion for the academic field. Other factors such as leadership and interpersonal skills are important in how they equip you to succeed in the field, but the main emphasis should be on your ability to contribute to the world's collective knowledge in a specific area.

When applying to graduate programs, check websites and catalogues to find out who the professors are in the department you wish to join. Familiarize yourself with their books and articles and explain how your plans fit in with their academic interests. If you are not able to visit a campus, call individual professors to discuss your plans and their program. They will appreciate your attempts to introduce yourself, your knowledge of their work, and your efforts to find out more about the department's program.

Another area to concentrate on is the mission of financial aid awards. The mission may be simple: to advance a field by supporting those who study it. Or, the mission may be more complex, furthering a specific agenda or encouraging study of specific areas. The government, for example, funds the study of certain languages that are considered to be strategically important. Even if you were studying economics in 17th century Russia, you could qualify for a FLAS award since part of your coursework would include the study of the Russian language.

Learn more about an award's mission by reading the literature of the organization, viewing its website, or speaking with the award administrator. A great way to see the mission in action is to find out information about previous winners. Ask the organization for a list of previous winners. There are probably some winners in your department who are a few years ahead of you. Contact them to find out details on their background, their approach to applying, and any helpful hints they can provide about the award's purpose.

By understanding the mission of the award and the awarding organization, you will know how well you fit what it is trying to achieve. You will also be able to shape the application, proposal, essay, and interview to reflect the mission of the award, making you a stronger fit in the eyes of the selection committee.

Applications: Your Stats Sheet

Applications are like baseball cards. Flip over a baseball card and you'll find the most important statistics about the player such as his hitting averages, speed, and runs. Similarly applications are the place for the most important statistics about your achievements. Selection committees use them as a quick way to learn the key facts about you. Because you are vying for both the limited space provided and the limited attention span of selection committees, follow these strategies to make the most of your applications.

Make application triplets. Before starting, make at least three photocopies of each application. Use one copy for practice to make sure the most important information you need to convey fits in the space given. Keep the other spare copies in case you make an egregious error and need to start over, something which will most likely happen at 3 a.m. the morning the application is due.

Build a case for how you fit the mission of the award. Always keep in mind the mission of the award so that you can provide evidence and examples of how you fit. If the award's objective is to support students who show promise in your academic field, highlight your classes, awards, and accomplishments in the field.

Know who the audience is. Try to find out as much information as you can about the selection committee. You will complete an application differently if the selection committee is professors in your department than if it is employers at a biomedical company trying to build relationships for future recruitment. For a selection committee of professors, focus on research, teaching, and publishing. On the other hand, for employers at a biomedical company, highlight how your research has commercial applications and any similar work experience. By knowing who your audience is, you can shape your application accordingly.

Use applications as a vehicle for building a case for why you should win the award. Present information that demonstrates your academic commitment and achievements.

Focus on your key achievements. With the limited space that applications provide, concentrate on only the most important information. Prioritize information that shows direct contributions or achievements in the field including classes, awards, lectures given, teaching experience, published works, current unpublished projects, and related work experience. Give secondary priority to information that demonstrates skills that are not direct achievements but that are still important to the field.

Neatness counts. Remember that a sloppy application conveys that you don't take the award seriously. Committee members may also think that if you are careless in completing your application, you may be equally careless in your studies. Neither of these are impressions you want to make. If the error is noticeable enough, use the extra copy you made of your application and start over. It will take extra time, but it's worth it.

Make copies after completing. For your records, make a photocopy of your application. The next time you are completing an application, you can use the copy as a cheat sheet since you've already taken the time to prioritize and write descriptions of your accomplishments.

Check to make sure you have everything. Before mailing your applications, ensure that you have included everything. You can be disqualified for missing a single piece.

For more information on applications, refer to Chapter 4, *Create Stunning Scholarship Applications*.

Recommendations: Getting Professorial Praise

Throughout your applications you have the opportunity to praise yourself and your accomplishments in glowing words of admiration. Recommendations offer professors and others the opportunity to do the same and to confirm that you are as great as you say you are. To get the most powerful recommendations possible, follow these strategies for selecting and preparing your recommenders.

Be strategic about who you ask. The most important principle for selecting recommenders is how well they know you. You may have received the highest grade in class, but if your professor couldn't pick you out from a crowd, he or she is not the best person to ask. Select those with whom you've worked closely and who can speak meaningfully about your abilities. An equally important measure is their ability to vouch for your talent and achievements in the academic field. Choose professors and others who can describe first-hand how competent you are in your studies. If you are new to graduate work, don't hesitate to ask your former undergraduate professors to write a recommendation. This is perfectly acceptable.

Do the grunt work for your recommenders. To make writing recommendations easier, provide all of the background information and forms that they need:

● Cover letter: A brief letter describing the awards you are applying for, their deadlines, and helpful reminders of information they may want to include in the recommendations.

● Curriculum vitae: A concise overview of your academic honors, coursework, and achievements.

● Recommendation paperwork: Any forms that your recommenders need to complete with your personal information pre-filled.

Give this information to your recommenders neatly in a folder or envelope so that they have everything they need to get started.

Finally, write a thank you note for their help. Even though writing recommendations is a part of the job for professors, recognize that they have taken time from their busy schedules to help you.

> *When asking professors and others to write recommendation letters, make their job easy by providing everything they need to get the job done.*

> *"I used to think that the reputation that professors had for being absent-minded was unfair. After my professor forgot to send in a recommendation letter for me despite numerous reminders, I now think differently."*
>
> —Joe

For more recommendation strategies, refer to Chapter 5, *Get The Right Recommendations.*

Essays: Getting Personal

If the application is your formal introduction to the selection committee, then the essay is the part of the conversation in which you get more personal. You can use the essay to describe in more detail your academic interests, goals, and contributions. Because essays allow you to get more personal beyond the application form, they offer your best occasion to set your entry apart from the others. The following strategies will help you create an essay with impact.

Focus on the progress you have made in your field. The best essay is one that gets the selection committee excited about your work and makes them want to fund your education so you can complete it. Tempt them with what you have done, reveal some early results even if they are only preliminary, or describe the plans for your research. You may be a history major who is breaking new ground with a project on colonial America. If appropriate, highlight some of your research and early findings. Give the selection committee a tantalizing view into what you are learning. Know who is on the committee and what their interests are. Don't go into technical detail if the committee members won't understand it.

Give them something they can't get anywhere else. Don't just restate what's in your application or curriculum vitae. If you do this, you will simply waste the space afforded to you. Essays should provide information and insight about you that is not included in the applications.

Get personal. Reveal something about yourself. What motivated you to choose this area of study? What do you feel is the most exciting thing about the field? Who has been a mentor for you? What do you hope to accomplish in the field? Answering a question like one of these would give the selection committee an insight into your thoughts and help to distinguish you beyond your achievements.

Remember who the audience is. Adjust your message and level of formality based on who will be reading your work. Your essay should be more formal and academic in nature if the intended audience is professors than if it is community leaders. Write thinking about who will read your essay.

Get editors. Don't rely on yourself for the entire direction of your essays. Professors, colleagues, and family members make great editors. They can offer suggestions for improvement, expand on ideas you have, and make sure you don't have any mistakes. The more help you can get from others, the better your essays will be.

Be creative. When it comes to describing your coursework and achievements in the application, there isn't much room for creativity. Not so for essays. Be as ingenious as you can be and as is appropriate. Use anecdotes, dialogue, and action to make your essay come alive. If appropriate, innovatively discuss your approach or your start in the field. Use illustrations to show you have the skills needed for the field or to reflect your dedication to it. After reading

Selection committees use essays to learn more about you on a personal and professional level beyond the straight facts of your application. They view essays as their opportunity to understand your motivations and goals and how you view your field of study. Essays are your best opportunity to set your application apart from the others.

many essays that are alike, the selection committee will probably appreciate one that takes chances with a little inventiveness. If you are worried about being too imaginative, ask a professor for feedback.

Address intellectual issues. Graduate school is a world of specialists who devote themselves to certain technical and intellectual issues in their field. Demonstrate your knowledge of these issues, and your ability to discuss the latest developments. You need not be longwinded about this; be brief and to the point. It is important to let your readers know that you know the field in which you too will become a specialist.

Be yourself. Most importantly, make sure that your essay echoes who you really are. Only write what is comfortable for you. In trying to make your essay different from the others, don't do so by adopting a strange alter ego. Be yourself and use your accomplishments in the field to make you stand out.

Refer to Chapter 6, *Secrets To Writing Winning Essays*, for more help with essays.

Research Grant Proposals: Application Heavies

Research grant proposals require more details than regular essays. Impress the selection committee by showing them that you've thought through all of the steps and potential obstacles to successfully complete the project.

If scholarship essays are the featherweights of graduate financial aid, then grant proposals are the heavyweights. Unlike normal scholarship essays, research grant proposals require outlining specific academic objectives and implementation plans. Provided by the government, graduate schools, and private organizations, most graduate grants award aid for a specific project, study, or dissertation. Because the awarding organizations have limited funds, their objective is to get the most academic mileage out of the least amount of money. When applying for grants, follow the strategies for essays above, but keep these additional strategies in mind:

How will your research benefit the field? Awarding grants is not a selfless task. The committee wants the bragging rights for backing research that advances the field. To fulfill this need, explain the potential significance of your research on the field. Show why your research is meaningful. Include specific applications of your research if it is not immediately apparent.

Your plan of action. It's important to convey that you have goals for your research, but it's equally important to explain how you're going to get there. An essential component of a grant proposal is an outline of your plan of action. Include measurable objectives to reach along the way, a timeline, and budget. Make it clear that you have an organized, thoughtful approach and plan for accomplishing your objectives. Everyone knows that research takes more time than you think and costs more than you budget. Show the committee an aggressive but realistic plan and they will be impressed. It is also important to indicate the limits of your project—what you will not be addressing as well as what you propose to accomplish.

Fit with the future you. The selection committee realizes that few people do research for philanthropic reasons. They want to know what's in it for you, your reasons for being interested in the research and how it fits with your future career plans. Explain how you hope to use what you learn in the future and what your future plans are.

Offer specifics. Be as specific as possible to show the seriousness of your efforts. For example, don't just offer your hypothesis, describe the line of reasoning that you have taken to reach it. Offer an excerpt of the sources you plan to use. Explain who your advisors will be and their roles. You must show the committee how committed you are to the project. Giving them a taste of what you have found so far is a great way to demonstrate your seriousness.

Interviews: Interaction With A Purpose

For some awards, the interaction gets even more personal than essays or proposals. Some require interviews with one or more members of the selection committee. The selection committee uses interviews as a way to get to know you beyond your application as well as to delve deeper into your academic interests. The most important rule is to never go to an interview without having done your homework. Here are your assignments:

Know the purpose cold. Understand the purpose of the award and the awarding organization. Research both by speaking with members of the organization, reading the group's literature, and talking to past recipients.

Practice. Practice doing mock interviews before the real thing. Ask a friend or family member to ask you questions and practice answering them. To get even more out of mock interview tape them and review afterward.

Have an interactive conversation. Don't just speak about you and your accomplishments. Interviewers have most likely worked in the field for a number of years. Use this time to find out more about how they got to where they are and to discuss their thoughts on the future of the field. Try to engage them in your project. Ask their opinions on what they think the results might be. Be sure to prepare questions in advance so that you have an arsenal of thoughtful and provocative questions ready.

Be ready for anything. Most interviews are straightforward, with interviewers asking questions you can generally anticipate. However, especially for graduate awards, interviewers have been known to throw in a curveball or two. Some professors treat interviews as a time to bolster their egos and ask esoteric questions about their fields. If you are surprised with one of these questions, take a second to think and do your best. You can always say that you don't know the answer now but would be happy to get back to the professor. After the interview, find the answer and email it that day to the professor. Chances are, if you were stumped, so were the other applicants. To prepare for this kind of question, ask your mock interviewer to toss in a few outlandish questions as well.

Remind yourself to overlook the prestige of your interviewers. Professors can be intimidating. Remember that they are real people. Treat them with deserved respect, but don't be intimidated by them. If you don't have a lot of experience speaking with professors or if you find yourself extremely nervous around them, set up some office hours with professors on your campus to talk about the field and to ask about the award. Get used to talking one-on-one with professors before you walk into your first interview.

Interviews require homework. Practice for them so you aren't surprised by the questions. Do some research on the awarding organizations and your interviewers.

"I'm a great researcher but not so great at interpersonal skills. I knew that the interview for my fellowship would be a challenge. To prepare myself, I set up meetings with my advisor to practice. It helped. The interview was still stressful, but I got funded."

—Kim

"I had what you'd call a nightmare interview. Everything was going fine until my interviewer asked me to name and summarize ten of his most significant published works. When I admitted that I only knew of five, he started yelling at me. He said that his works were the foundations of the field and how dare I apply for a fellowship without knowing every detail of his writing. His question was absolutely out of left field because contrary to what he believed, his works are not very well regarded in the field. My advice: Be prepared for anything."

—Ed

Get to know your award, its requirements and restrictions so that you can keep what you've earned and use it to its fullest potential. Read the small print when you receive an award so there are no surprises.

Know their publications. If you know who your interviewers will be, read their publications and be conversant about their work. The opinions presented in their published work will be a very useful clue to predict how they might react to your work and opinions.

You can find more interview strategies in Chapter 7, *Ace The Interviews.*

Get Paid To Step Into A Classroom Or Lab

After you've exhausted the resources for winning money for your education, you can always resort to the traditional method: Working for it. Many schools offer opportunities to earn money through on-campus employment. For some schools and fellowships, it's a requirement.

Typical employment opportunities are teaching or researching. Grad students offer schools an additional pool of young and enthusiastic instructors for undergraduate courses. Grad students also assist professors with conducting research. In the sciences, lab work is a staple of the graduate school education.

To find out about opportunities for employment at your school, go to your department or your school's career services office. Be prepared with a curriculum vitae that outlines your desired type of work and qualifications. If that doesn't work, approach individual professors and ask about opportunities directly. You may even be able to create a position for yourself.

Caring For Your Aid

Despite your wishes, once you win a research grant, fellowship, or scholarship, you can't take the money and run. You don't need to pay the money back, but you still have some responsibilities for maintaining your award. Here are some tips for caring for your award:

Get to know your grant, fellowship, or scholarship administrators. Along with assisting with the administrative paperwork, they will also be able to answer your questions about the details of your award as well as offer advice on how to maximize the benefits of it.

Be aware of your award's term and requirements. How long does the award last? What happens if you take a leave of absence, study part-time, or quit your studies? Is the award renewable? If it is, what do you need to do to renew it?

Learn about restrictions for spending the dough. Some awards are limited to tuition only. Others can be used for books, travel, or even living expenses. Some provide the money directly to your school while others provide a check made out to you. Make sure you understand what you can spend it on and what sort of records you need to keep.

Know what happens once you're finished with your studies. Understand who owns the equipment that you purchase and if the awarding organization has any kind of ownership of your work. Keep records of your expenditures including receipts and purpose of the purchase.

Learn the tax implications of your award. Speak with the award administrator or the IRS (www.irs.gov or 800-829-1040).

Keep the awarding organization up to date on your progress. Provide the organization with a summary report or copy of the finished product after you have finished your work. In your work be sure to credit the various groups that have given you awards. This is not only good manners, but it will help insure that the award is around in the future.

Getting More Help

Now that you are now armed with strategies for winning scholarships and fellowships, don't stop here. Investigate these additional resources to lighten the burden of being a poor grad student. Here are some:

The best way to get money for graduate school is to find out as much information as you can. Look around you—there are resources in your department, on the Internet, and on campus. Use them!

Your department. Inquire about awards and employment opportunities. Read newsletters distributed by your department and check the department bulletin board.

Your peers. It's probably a small circle of people who study your field. Ask fellow students about awards you might be interested in.

Award administrators. Speak with award administrators to see if they know of other awards that may be applicable to you.

Professors. Communicate your goals for the future so that if your professors come across an appropriate program or award they will think of you. Share ideas for research and employment. Your professors may be able to help you develop proposals to fund your ideas.

Financial aid office. Make sure you have the most up to date information on programs offered by your school's financial aid office. Meet at least twice per year with a financial aid advisor to review your situation.

Career services office. Use this office to investigate potential employment opportunities.

Internet. Search websites that offer information and scholarship databases for graduate students. Our site, SuperCollege.com (www.supercollege.com) has a free searchable database of thousands of scholarships.

Your surroundings. On-campus organizations, employers, and community groups often award scholarships and fellowships. Wherever you are, keep an eye out for opportunities.

Chapter 9 Summary: Free Cash For Graduate School

Priorities change. While undergraduate awards are often based on a combination of academics, leadership, and activities, graduate awards are almost always based solely on academics and research. You will need to adjust your strategy to highlight your commitment to your field.

Different types of money. Graduate financial aid comes in several formats: Federal loans need to be repaid while scholarships, grants, and fellowships do not. Some graduate programs require teaching or research as a part of their financial aid packages.

Prestige and money. Graduate financial aid not only provides financial reward but enhances your curriculum vitae as well.

Applications: your time to shine. Applications offer you the opportunity to build a case for how you fit the mission of the award. Know who your audience will most likely be and present the information that will show them that you are the best fit.

Help your recommenders help you. When asking others to write your recommendation letters, provide everything they need including a cover letter, curriculum vitae, and accompanying paperwork. Make their job as easy as possible.

Show your academic might in essays. Address academic issues and demonstrate how through your research or projects you fit the requirements for the award.

Research grant proposals are the application heavies. You must provide detailed information about the project you propose, your plan of action, and the potential benefits to your field of study.

Practice for interviews by predicting what questions you might be asked and practicing responses for them. Learn as much as you can about the awarding organization and the interviewers themselves.

Keep what you've won. Each award has its own requirements and restrictions. Get to know them so you hold onto your winnings and use the award to its fullest extent.

Don't be afraid to ask for help. If you look around your department, there are many resources for you to use from professors to the financial aid office to fellow students. Take advantage of them all when finding money for grad school.

Financial Aid Workshop

• •

In this chapter, you'll learn:

- How to get your share of $46 billion in federal financial aid

- What you need to qualify for "financial need" & how to apply

- Eligibility requirements, deadlines, & amounts of each financial aid program

- Proven strategies for negotiating for more aid from your college

• •

CHAPTER 10

$46 Billion In Federal Financial Aid

Each year, the federal government awards over $46 billion in educational financial aid. Your mission: To make sure some of that money comes to you. In this chapter, we show you how.

First, we provide a quick, easy to understand overview of the various kinds of financial aid that are available and the advantages and disadvantages of each. Then, we explain how to complete the necessary paperwork to apply and how to avoid costly mistakes.

The Tanabe Philosophy

This is probably the simplest philosophy we have: Just apply! Take advantage of the fact that you don't need to compete to get financial aid. Funded by the government, federal financial aid is awarded to applicants who meet certain objective financial criteria. This is different from scholarships, for which students must compete to win dollars from private organizations and colleges that use subjective criteria for selecting winners.

For example, of 10 qualified students who meet the government's criteria to receive a Stafford loan (you'll learn more about this in a minute), 10 will receive it. But of the 10 qualified students who apply for a Rotary Club Scholarship, only one may receive it.

Don't second-guess yourself – many students mistakenly don't apply thinking: "I don't understand how the financial aid process works" or "My family's income is too high for me to get financial aid." Just apply—you may be surprised at what you get!

Federal Financial Aid: What Is It?

It's not enough to know that financial aid is money. You need to understand what kind of money it is. (Keep in mind that not all money is created equal!) The government awards three distinct types of financial aid, each with its own benefits and eligibility requirements:

Grants: Money with no strings attached—meaning you don't have to pay it back. This is really the equivalent of hitting the financial aid jackpot.

Loans: Money you borrow and are required to pay back with interest. In most cases the terms are more generous than other types of loans such as home equity loans.

Work-Study: Money you earn the old-fashioned way—by working. Through work-study, you may be eligible for part-time jobs on-campus or near campus that other students are not because the government subsidizes your pay.

These are the three types of financial aid the government provides. Most financial aid packages are a combination of the above. Depending on the package you receive, you may need to pay back the funds, work for the funds, or not do anything except go to class. In the following sections, we provide more information on the specific types of grants, loans, and work-study programs the government offers.

Unless you enjoy reading loan agreements in your spare time, you will probably not be able to decipher all of the terms and acronyms in this chapter. To help, refer to our glossary in Appendix A. In addition, consult Appendix B for the contact information for financial aid-related organizations that can provide additional help.

The Federal Financial Aid Programs

Federal Pell Grants

"In 1998-99, the average Pell award was $1,869. The Pell Grant now manages to cover slightly over one-third the average cost of attendance at a four-year college and one-seventh that of a private four-year college."

—The College Board

To apply: Complete the Free Application for Federal Student Aid (FAFSA), which is described in detail in the section, "What You Need To Do: The FAFSA," in this chapter.

Eligibility: See the "How Can I Get My Hands On The Cash?" section in this chapter for federal financial aid eligibility requirements. For undergraduate study, with the exception of post-baccalaureate teacher certification programs. You can be enrolled less than half time. Provides every eligible student with funds.

Based on: Financial need as determined by your Estimated Family Contribution and Cost Of Attendance, full-time or part-time status, length of enrollment, i.e., full academic year or less.

Amount: Varies based on funding. The maximum amount for the 1999-2000 school year was $3,125.

Cost: None.

How you get the money: Your school can credit the grant to your school account, pay you directly, or do a combination of both.

Stafford Loans

To apply: Complete the Free Application for Federal Student Aid (FAFSA), which is described in detail in the section, "What You Need To Do: The FAFSA," in this chapter.

Details: There are two types of Stafford Loans: Direct Stafford Loans and FFEL Stafford Loans. Direct Stafford Loans are available through the William D. Ford Federal Direct Loan Program, with the U.S. government as the lender. FFEL Stafford Loans are available through the Federal Family Education Loan Program with participating banks, credit unions, or other lenders as the lenders. For FFEL Stafford Loans, you will locate a lender by contacting your school or the Federal Student Aid Information Center. See the end of this chapter for the Information Center's contact information.

Eligibility: See the "How Can I Get My Hands On The Cash?" section in this chapter for federal financial aid eligibility requirements. You must be enrolled at least half time.

Based on: Subsidized loans are based on financial need. The government subsidizes the interest payments so that you are not charged interest before you begin repayment or in approved periods of deferment. Unsubsidized loans are not based on financial need. You are charged interest from the time the loan is disbursed until it is paid off. In one school year, you can have a Subsidized Stafford Loan, Unsubsidized Stafford Loan, or both.

Amount: For dependent undergraduate students, you can borrow a maximum of $2,625 if you're a first-year student in a full academic year program, $3,500 if you have completed your first year of study and are enrolled in a full academic year program, or $5,500 a year if you've completed two years of study and are enrolled in a full academic year program. For independent undergraduate students or dependent students whose parents are not able to get a PLUS loan, you can borrow a maximum of $6,625 if you're a first-year student in a full academic year program ($2,625 of this amount can be subsidized), $7,500 if you've completed your first year of study and are enrolled in a full academic year program ($3,500 of this amount can be subsidized), or $10,500 a year if you've completed two years of study and are enrolled in a full academic year program ($5,500 of this amount can be subsidized). For graduate students, you can borrow a maximum of $18,500 each year ($8,500 of this amount can be subsidized).

Cost: The interest rate varies from year to year but will never exceed 8.25 percent. There is also a fee of up to 4 percent of the loan.

How you get the money: The money will be disbursed to your school either by the Department of Education for Direct Stafford Loans or by the lender for FFEL Stafford Loans. The money must first be used for tuition, fees, and room and board. After these expenses are paid, you will receive the remaining amount in a check.

How you repay the money: You will begin to repay your loan after you graduate, leave school, or drop below half-time enrollment. For Direct Stafford Loans, you can pay using one of four methods: the Standard Repayment Plan of a fixed amount per month for up to 10 years; the Extended Repayment Plan, which extends the repayment period to generally between 12 and 30 years; the Graduated Repayment Plan, in which your payments start lower and increase generally every two years; or the Income Contingent Plan, in which your income affects the amount of your monthly payments.

For FFEL Stafford Loans, you can pay using one of three methods: Standard Repayment Plan, Graduated Repayment Plan, or the Income-Sensitive Repayment Plan, in which your income affects the amount of your monthly payments. All loans must be repaid within 10 years.

"I thought that there was no way that I would qualify for financial aid. Was I shocked when I learned that at my school over 80% of students receive financial aid! That made me turn in my financial aid application. I was pleased to receive a low interest loan, which allowed me to afford going to school here."

—Steven

Under certain circumstances, you can receive a deferment to temporarily postpone payments on your loan. For subsidized loans, you do not pay interest during the deferment period. For unsubsidized loans, you do. Under certain circumstances you can receive forbearance, a limited and temporary postponement or reduction of your payments if you are unable to meet your repayment schedule and are not eligible for a deferment. These circumstances may include poor health, serving in a medical or dental internship or residency, or if the payments exceed 20 percent of your monthly gross income. For both subsidized and unsubsidized loans, you pay interest during the forbearance period. Deferments and forbearance must be approved by the Direct Loan Servicing Center if you have a Direct Stafford Loan or with the lender if you have an FFEL Stafford Loan. Contact information for the Direct Loan Servicing Center is in Appendix B.

PLUS Loans

To apply: Complete a Direct PLUS Loan application for Direct PLUS Loans or a PLUS Loan application for FFEL PLUS Loans.

Details: Loans for parents with good credit histories to pay for their dependent undergraduate students' educations. Available through both the Direct PLUS Loan and FFEL PLUS Loan Program. For FFEL PLUS Loans, you will locate a lender by contacting your school or the Federal Student Aid Information Center. See the end of the chapter for contact information.

Eligibility: See the "How Can I Get My Hands On The Cash?" section in this chapter for federal financial aid eligibility requirements. Students must meet these requirements, and parents must meet some of the requirements as well. This program is available for undergraduate students who are enrolled at least half time.

Based on: Not based on financial need.

Amount: Maximum is the Cost of Attendance minus any other financial aid you receive. For example, if your Cost of Attendance is $10,000 and you receive $6,000 in financial aid, the maximum amount your parents could borrow is $4,000.

Cost: The interest rate varies from year to year but will never exceed 9 percent. There is also a fee of up to 4 percent of the loan.

How you get the money: The money will be disbursed to your school either by the Department of Education for Direct PLUS Loans or by the lender for FFEL PLUS Loans. The money must first be used for tuition, fees, and room and board. After these expenses are paid, your parents will receive the remaining amount in a check.

How you repay the money: Repayment begins within 60 days after the first loan disbursement, and interest starts to accumulate from the first disbursement.

For Direct PLUS Loans, you can pay using one of three methods: the Standard Repayment Plan of a fixed amount per month; the Extended Repay-

"I never knew that my credit history could affect the kinds of loans that we could get for my son's education. Because I have a couple of rough spots in my credit history, we weren't able to get a PLUS loan. Fortunately, we were still able to make ends meet with the rest of the financial aid package, but I highly recommend that you fix your credit early on to keep all options open."

—Anne, a parent

ment Plan, which extends the repayment period; or the Graduated Repayment Plan, in which your payments start lower and increase every two years.

For FFEL PLUS Loans, your parents will follow a repayment schedule provided by the lender that is a minimum of $600 per month for a maximum period of 10 years.

Under certain circumstances, you can receive a deferment to temporarily postpone payments on your loan. Under certain circumstances you can receive forbearance, a limited and temporary postponement or reduction of your payments if you are unable to meet your repayment schedule and are not eligible for a deferment. These circumstances may include poor health, serving in a medical or dental internship or residency, or if the payments exceed 20 percent of your monthly gross income. Deferments and forbearance must be approved by the Direct Loan Servicing Center if you have a Direct PLUS Loan or with the lender if you have an FFEL PLUS Loan. Contact information for the Direct Loan Servicing Center is in Appendix B.

Consolidation Loans

To apply: Contact the Loan Origination Center's Consolidation Department at 800-557-7392 or the consolidation department of a participating lender.

Story From Real Life: I Assumed I Wouldn't Get Aid, But I Was Wrong

Jeffrey assumed that because he received an underwhelming financial aid package one year that he didn't need to apply in following years. His assumption cost him perhaps thousands of dollars, which taught him to not make assumptions and just apply!
—Gen and Kelly

Before my freshman year I spent an entire weekend dutifully completing all of the financial aid forms. After spending all that time on the forms, I thought that I would get a sweet financial aid package. My family certainly wasn't at the poverty level, but it wasn't unheard of for students in similar financial situations as mine to get some significant grants.

I was pretty disappointed that after spending all that time gathering financial information and getting my parents to do their taxes early just to apply, I only received a medium-sized loan. Because my parents were doing okay financially—they own a travel agency—we decided not to take the loan and to squeeze by on what we had.

After my experience in my first year, I decided not to waste my time applying for financial aid for my sophomore or junior years. I assumed that I would only be offered a loan anyway, so why waste my time? During those couple of years, business for my parents went up and down as usual depending on how much people wanted to travel.

Before my senior year, one of my roommates asked how I was doing with my financial aid applications. I said that I don't usually apply. He was shocked and told me I should apply. After some badgering, I obliged and applied just to get him to stop bugging me.

I didn't see a whole lot of difference in my family's financial situation between my first year and my last, but I received an offer for a loan and a grant. A grant? That's money I don't have to repay. After getting the grant, I realized I should have taken the time to apply before. Even though my family's financial situation didn't change dramatically over the years, it changed enough to make the difference between a loan and grant. What I learned: Apply even if you don't think you should.

—Jeffrey

Details: Allows students and parents to consolidate a number of federal financial aid loans into a single loan to simplify repayment. This allows the borrowers to make one payment per month and in some cases obtain a lower interest rate. All of the federal loans described in this chapter can be consolidated.

Direct Consolidation Loans are provided by the U.S. Department of Education. They can be one of three types: Direct Subsidized Consolidation Loans, Direct Unsubsidized Consolidation Loans, or Direct PLUS Consolidation Loans.

FFEL Consolidation Loans are provided by participating banks, credit unions, savings and loans, and other lenders as either a Subsidized FFEL Consolidation Loan or an Unsubsidized FFEL Consolidation Loan.

More than half of the students who attend four-year institutions pay tuition and fees of less than $4,000. Almost 75% attend schools with tuition and fees of less than $8,000 while 7% attend schools that charge $20,000 or more.
—The College Board

Eligibility: See the "How Can I Get My Hands On The Cash?" section in this chapter for federal financial aid eligibility requirements. You can get a Consolidated Loan once you've started repayment or during deferment or forbearance. If you are in school, you can apply for a Direct Consolidation Loan if you are attending at least half time and have at least one Direct Loan or FFEL Loan in an in-school period. You may be eligible for a Consolidated Loan if you are in default on a Direct Loan.

Cost: The interest rate is fixed throughout the repayment period and is the weighted average of the loans being consolidated. It will never exceed 8.25 percent.

Federal Supplemental Educational Opportunity Grants (FSEOGs)

To apply: Contact your school to find out if additional information is required other than the Free Application for Federal Student Aid (FAFSA). The FAFSA is described in detail in the section, "What You Need To Do: The FAFSA," in this chapter. Deadlines are determined by each school and may be earlier than the FAFSA deadline.

Details: Grants for undergraduates with the most financial need, i.e., the lowest Expected Family Contributions. FSEOG Grants do not need to be repaid. The government provides limited funds for individual schools to administer this program. This means that there is no guarantee that every eligible student will receive an FSEOG Grant.

Eligibility: See the "How Can I Get My Hands On The Cash?" section in this chapter for federal financial aid eligibility requirements.

Based on: Financial need, other aid you receive, and the availability of funds at your school. Priority is given to those who receive Federal Pell Grants.

Amount: $100-$4,000 per year.

Cost: None.

How you get the money: The school will credit your account, pay you by check, or both.

Federal Work-Study

To apply: Contact your school to find out if additional information is required other than the Free Application for Federal Student Aid (FAFSA), which is described in detail in the section, "What You Need To Do: The FAFSA," in this chapter. Deadlines are determined by each school and may be earlier than the FAFSA deadline.

Details: Provides jobs for undergraduate and graduate students with financial need allowing them to earn money while attending school. The focus is on providing work experience in your area of study. Generally, you will work for your school on campus or for a nonprofit organization or public agency if you work off campus. You will have a limit on the hours you can work in this program. The government provides limited funds for individual schools to administer this program.

Eligibility: See the "How Can I Get My Hands On The Cash?" section in this chapter for federal financial aid eligibility requirements.

Based on: Financial need, other aid you receive, and the availability of funds at your school.

Amount: Federal minimum wage or higher.

Cost: None.

How you get the money: Paid by the hour if you're an undergraduate. Paid by the hour or a salary if you're a graduate school student.

Federal Perkins Loans

To apply: Contact your school to find out if additional information is required other than the Free Application for Federal Student Aid (FAFSA), which is described in detail in the section, "What You Need To Do: The FAFSA," in this chapter. Deadlines are determined by each school and may be earlier than the FAFSA deadline.

Details: Low-interest loans for undergraduate and graduate students with extreme financial need. Your school provides the loan from funds provided by the government and its own funds. You must repay the loan.

Eligibility: See the "How Can I Get My Hands On The Cash?" section in this chapter for federal financial aid eligibility requirements.

Based on: Financial need, other aid you receive, and availability of funds.

Amount: You can borrow up to $4,000 per year as an undergraduate or $6,000 per year as a graduate student.

Cost: 5 percent interest. There are no additional fees.

How you get the money: Your school will either pay you directly or credit your school account.

How you repay the money: Nine months after you graduate, leave school, or drop below half-time enrollment, you will begin repayment.

Under certain circumstances, you can receive a deferment to temporarily postpone payments on your loan. You do not pay interest during the deferment period. Under certain circumstances you can receive forbearance, a limited and temporary postponement or reduction of your payments if you are unable to meet your repayment schedule and are not eligible for a deferment. These circumstances may include poor health, serving in a medical or dental internship or residency, or if the payments exceed 20 percent of your monthly gross income. Interest is accrued during the forbearance period. Deferments and forbearance must be approved by your school.

How Can I Get My Hands On The Cash?

Unless your last name is Gates (as in father Bill), the $46 billion the government awards in financial aid is a large sum of money. However, remember that this amount is spread among millions of college and graduate students each year. Thus, even though $46 billion is more money than most of us can imagine, it is still limited. This means there are restrictions on who is eligible to receive aid.

To qualify for federal financial aid, you must:

● Have financial need. While some loans do not require financial need, most federal aid is based in some part on this qualification. Financial need is determined by the following formula:

Unlike applying for scholarships, applying for financial aid is not a competition that is based on your skills and experience. However, you still need to qualify based on your financial need.

Cost Of Attendance – Expected Family Contribution = Financial Need

Cost Of Attendance (COA) is the cost of attending your college or university for one year. These costs includes: tuition and other fees, room and board, transportation between your home and the college, books and other supplies, and estimated personal expenses.

Expected Family Contribution (EFC) is what the government has determined your family can afford to pay for your education. It is based on a formula established by the U.S. Congress and it applies equally to all applicants for financial aid. The formula is complex and by completing the Free Application for Federal Student Aid (FAFSA) you will give the government what it needs to calculate this number. When you receive your federal financial aid offer you will be told exactly what the government believes you and your family can contribute toward your education.

● Graduate from high school or receive a General Educational Development (GED) certificate.

● Be a student working toward an eligible degree or certificate program. Eligibility requirements are determined by the U.S. Department of Education.

● Be a U.S. citizen, U.S. national, or U.S. permanent resident who has an I-151, I-551, or I-551C. Or, have an Arrival-Departure Record (I-94) from the

U.S. Immigration and Naturalization Service designating your status as Refugee, Asylum Granted, Indefinite Parole and/or Humanitarian Parole, Cuban-Haitian Entrant Status Pending, or Conditional Entrant (if issued before April 1, 1980).

● Have a valid Social Security Number.

● Meet satisfactory academic standards set by your school.

● Agree to use the funds only for educational purposes.

● Certify that you are not in default on a federal student loan and that you do not owe money from a federal student grant.

● Register with the Selective Service if required. All males ages 18 or over need to register with the Selective Service. You can do this at any U.S. Post Office.

"I left college with over $15,000 in student loans, but I know that it's worth it. I'm one of the first people in my family to attend college, and even though there's nothing wrong with it, I'm not going to be a lifetime food server like my father and grandfather. I'm going to be a doctor."

—Maria, a recent graduate

While there are a number of requirements, the great majority of students in the U.S. are eligible for the government's programs. If you have questions about your eligibility, use the contact information at the end of this chapter to get in touch with the Department of Education.

Declaring Your Independence

At a certain point in life, it becomes time to cut the ties that bind you to Mom and Dad. For some, it's after graduating from college when you get a job of your own. For others, it's before college. In most cases, you will be considered dependent on your parents to support you in your college education, and their income and assets will be considered when determining your financial aid package. Under certain circumstances, you will be evaluated independently of your parents, and only you and your spouse's (if you have one) income and assets will be taken into account. You're considered to be independent if one of the following is true:

● You were born before January 1, 1977 (for the 2000-2001 school year).
● You're married.
● You're enrolled in a graduate or professional degree program.
● You have legal dependents other than a spouse.
● You're an orphan or ward of the court.
● You're a veteran of the U.S. Armed Forces.

There may be other circumstances in which you'll be considered independent. Discuss your situation with the Financial Aid Administrator at your school.

What You Need To Do: The FAFSA

Because it's the government that's awarding the dollars, naturally there is a form to complete. This application form is the Free Application for Federal Student Aid (FAFSA). You will need to provide information on your family and your employment, income, and assets. With the exception of Direct or FFEL PLUS Loans, the FAFSA is the only form you'll need to complete for federal financial aid. Here's how to get and complete the form:

• Online at www.fafsa.ed.gov

• By using the FAFSA Express software, which you can download from the Internet by clicking on the FAFSA link at www.ed.gov/finaid.html or which you can get on diskette by calling 800-801-0576.

• By submitting the form electronically through your school, if it offers the service.

• By mail. Get an application from your school or use the contact information at the end of this chapter to get it from the Federal Student Aid Information Center.

For each school year, forms must be completed as soon as possible AFTER January 1. The deadline for submission is typically in July, and there are no extensions or exceptions. Note that individual schools may have earlier deadlines for the FAFSA and for their own financial aid forms to apply for school-specific financial aid. Pay attention to these important deadlines.

> *"At first glance, the FAFSA was pretty complex. There is a lot of information that you need to give, and it can be kind of frustrating, like doing your taxes. But of course it must be done. Once it was in the mail, I felt satisfied knowing that I had done my part to help my daughter finance her education."*
>
> *—David, a parent*

If you have applied for federal financial aid before, you may be eligible to complete the Renewal FAFSA, which has information pre-filled from your previous application. Check with your school or the Federal Student Aid Information Center for more information.

As with all forms, at first glance the FAFSA can seem intimidating. However, if you spend some time working on it, you'll find that the information is relatively straightforward. To help, here are some tips for completing the form.

File the form as soon as possible after January 1. This is an important form. Don't procrastinate.

Complete your income tax forms early. Unless you're an accountant, there are many more enjoyable things you'd probably rather do, but information from your income tax forms will be very helpful for completing the FAFSA. Plus, while others are stressed and panic-stricken around April 15, you'll already be done with your taxes.

Follow directions. The Department of Education reports that delays are caused most often because students or parents don't follow directions when completing the FAFSA. Spend the time to read the directions and follow them completely.

Be thorough. Answer questions completely. Take the time to find the answers to all of the information requested.

Realize that the FAFSA takes time. Set aside a couple afternoons or evenings to be able to concentrate on completing the form. Don't think that you can complete it during the commercials of your favorite sitcom.

Save time with the Renewal FAFSA. If you've applied for federal financial aid before, you can usually use the Renewal FAFSA. This form will save you time because it will be pre-filled with your prior information. Ask your counselor or financial aid office for more information.

Check with your school, scholarship programs, and fellowship programs to see if any additional forms are required. With the exception of Direct or FFEL PLUS Loans, the FAFSA is the only form you need to complete for federal aid. However, for individual schools, scholarship programs, and fellowship programs, you may need to complete additional forms. Ask them.

If you transfer schools, check with your new school to see what forms you should complete. Your financial aid package does not automatically transfer with you.

Don't think you're on your own. Use the help provided by your school and by the government. The Department of Education has an entire staff of people dedicated to assisting you with completing the necessary forms and answering your questions about financial aid. Use the information at the end of the chapter to contact the Federal Student Aid Information Center.

It's In The Bag: The SAR & What's Next

In case the acronyms are a bit confusing, here's a quick review. You submit the Free Application for Federal Student Aid (FAFSA) to the government. In return, you get the Student Aid Report (SAR), which determines your Estimated Family Contribution (EFC). The EFC is used by your school to develop a financial aid package.

Once you've submitted the FAFSA, the Department of Education will process your application and in two to four weeks provide you with the Student Aid Report (SAR). The SAR reflects the information that you submitted in the FAFSA and provides your Estimated Family Contribution (EFC). Your responsibility is to review the SAR and, if necessary, submit any corrections to the Department of Education.

Using your SAR and EFC, your school will develop a financial aid package. The school's goal is to meet your Financial Need, which is the difference between the Cost of Attendance and EFC. Because it has limited resources, the school may or may not be able to meet your entire Financial Need.

The Effect Of Scholarships: Exchanging One Kind Of Money To Another

In an ideal world, you would receive a financial aid package from your school, and any scholarships you won would be a bonus on top of the package. Unfortunately, scholarship dollars you win are subtracted from your Cost of Attendance. This means that as your school creates a financial aid package for you, your scholarship dollars will be counted as a part of the package and may decrease the amount of other financial aid you receive. For example, if you received a $1,000 scholarship, you might receive a loan for $1,000 less. If this happens, it is not necessarily a bad thing. It's better for you to receive financial aid in the form of scholarships, which you do not need to repay, than as loans, which naturally need to be repaid.

Negotiating For More Money

Financial aid is not exactly like buying a car where you haggle with a salesperson over the cost of floor mats and how much below the sticker price you will pay. Nevertheless, in some cases there may be some flexibility in the financial aid package you are offered.

Once you've received the Student Aid Report (SAR), your school's Financial Aid Administrator will try to build a package that meets your Financial Need. Know that there is flexibility in the two numbers that determine your Financial Need: the Cost of Attendance and the Expected Family Contribution. They may be adjusted if you have special circumstances such as:

● Unusual medical or dental expenses
● Tuition for a sibling's private secondary or elementary school education
● Unemployment of a spouse or parent

If your financial situation has changed significantly or if you have one of the circumstances above, contact your school's financial aid office to discuss your package. We recommend first writing a letter that outlines your special circumstances in quick, easy to understand bullet points. Your Financial Aid Administrator will then have all the information he or she needs. Follow up with a telephone call to see if he or she needs any additional information and check on the status of your inquiry.

In some cases there is also flexibility when you have been admitted to more than one school and are selecting which to attend. For example, if you are accepted to College A and College B, but College B offers a significantly more generous financial aid package, you could try to work with College A to raise or match College B's package. First, write a letter to College A, stating that you would like very much to attend the college but that you may not be able to because of the financial aid package offered. Outline in quick bullet points the financial aid package offered by College B. Provide brief reasons why you need a package like that offered by College B. Reiterate that you would prefer to attend College A and would like to know if there is anything the financial aid office can do to increase the package. Follow up with a phone call. It does not always work, but in many cases the college will attempt to adjust their aid package.

In both of these cases, only ask for more aid if you think that you have strong reasons to, if your financial situation has really changed significantly, or if there is a significant difference between the financial aid packages offered between schools. There often is flexibility, but unlike buying a car, it is more difficult to walk away from the purchase. Still, it is better to inquire if there is flexibility. The college may surprise you.

A Negotiation Success Story With Harvard

If you find it hard to believe that a single letter can result in a larger financial aid package, here is the proof. The following is an actual letter one student wrote to the Harvard financial aid office. Before writing the letter, the student

"In my freshman year my sister became ill. My parents thought that I might have to take a leave of absence because her medical costs were so high. I explained my situation to my financial aid office, and they adjusted my financial aid package so I didn't have to leave school. That was fortunate but not as fortunate as my sister's recovery."

—Edward

There is no guarantee that your school will be able to adjust your financial aid package, but it doesn't hurt to ask. Write a brief letter that contains the most important points about the change in your family's economic situation. Be ready to provide additional information if asked.

had received only a small loan from Harvard despite the fact that her father had been laid off for over a year. The student composed this letter to explain her family's extenuating circumstances, describing their actual income and expenses. Her letter paid off—she got a $6,500 grant for the semester!

Letter To Harvard

Dear Sir or Madam:

I am writing to request that my financial aid package for the fall semester be reconsidered. My family and I were disappointed with the amount we were offered because in addition to my father having been unemployed for over a year, my older sister will be a sophomore in college; and my mother, a part-time teacher, has received no income since June because of summer break.

We understand that nearly every family must undergo an amount of hardship to send its members to college. However, because my parents wish to continue financing my sister's and my education, they are worried about how they will pay for their own expenses. They have been using my mother's income to basically cover their mortgage payments, and their savings to pay for everything else. In February, my parents had $33,000 in savings. In the last six months, their savings has decreased by about $15,000. They now have about $18,000 to contribute to my sister's and my college expenses as well as to spend on their and my younger brother's food and basic necessities. They don't know how long their savings will last without a change in the amount of aid I will receive.

At the end of this month, my sister will begin her sophomore year at USC. The cost will be $26,998, and she has received $18,758 in financial aid. This makes my parents' contribution amount to $8,240, of which they will borrow $2,625. One of the things you might be able to address is why my sister's financial aid package was dramatically higher than mine.

Since July of last year my father has been unemployed. His severance pay ended in October, and his unemployment benefits have been depleted since February. Although he has applied for over a dozen positions, his prospects for finding a job in his specialty are slim.

My parents and I have discussed the possibility of having me take a year off so that I may work to help pay for tuition, but we'd much rather that I finish school now and work after I have received my degree.

Please contact my parents or me with any further questions you may have. Thank you very much for your time and consideration. I hope that this information is helpful in your review of my application.

Sincerely,

"When I applied for financial aid, I got all the help I could get. I contacted the Student Aid Information Center, my school's financial aid office, and my parents' accountant. There's a lot of help if you look for it. If I had tried to apply on my own, I would have been lost."

—Jon

There's no guarantee that a letter like this will work every time, but if the situation for your family changes, get in touch with your financial aid office. They want to be able to help you afford the bills.

Help!

In this chapter, we have provided you with a solid foundation of information on financial aid programs offered by the government and which provide over $46 billion in aid each year. To make the most of these programs and to find out more, refer to the Department of Education's literature, website, and Federal Student Aid Information Center. In addition, refer to the appendices at the end of this book. You'll find contact information for additional organizations that can help you. Also, read Chapter 11 *Parents' Guide To Scholarships & Financial Aid* for information on educational tax benefits.

Realize that you are not on your own when it comes to funding your education. In addition to scholarship providers, the government wants to help you make ends meet.

U.S. Department of Education
Federal Student Aid Information Center
P.O. Box 84
Washington, DC 20044-0084
800-4-FED-AID
www.ed.gov

Chapter 10 Summary: Financial Aid Workshop

Each year the government awards over $46 billion in financial aid. Your mission is to make sure some of that money comes to you. Unlike scholarships in which you need to compete for the funds, in most cases, if you qualify for federal financial aid, you will receive it. Your responsibility is to learn about the different options open to you and to apply.

There are three types of federal financial aid: Grants, which do not need to be repaid; loans, which allow you to borrow money and must be repaid; and work-study, which allows you to work at a part-time job while attending school.

To qualify for federal financial aid, you need to have financial need, which is determined by the cost of attending your college (Cost of Attendance) and the amount that the government determines your family can contribute toward your education (Estimated Family Contribution). There are additional requirements including: graduating from high school, working toward an eligible degree program, and being a U.S. citizen, U.S. national, or U.S. permanent resident.

To apply, you must complete the Free Application for Federal Student Aid (FAFSA). You can do this online, using your computer, or using old-fashioned paper.

After submitting the FAFSA, you will receive a Student Aid Report (SAR) from the government which determines your Estimated Family Contribution (EFC), or the amount that your family is expected to contribute. Your school's financial aid office will develop a financial aid package using this information that may be a combination of scholarships, loans, grants, and/or work-study.

The scholarship dollars you win may affect your financial aid package because they reduce your Cost of Attendance. Realize that this may not be bad if your package is composed of more scholarship dollars, which do not need to be repaid, and less loan dollars, which of course do need to be repaid.

There is room for negotiation once you've received the financial aid package from your college, especially if there are extenuating circumstances such as medical or dental expenses, tuition for a sibling, or a change in your parents' employment situation. In some cases, there is also flexibility when you are deciding between two colleges with differences in their financial aid packages.

For more information, refer to the appendices at the end of the book.

Parents' Guide To Scholarships & Financial Aid

······································

In this chapter, you'll learn:

- Your two main responsibilities as a parent

- How to develop a savings strategy with the five steps to saving for college

- How much your child's education will cost & how much you need to save to pay for it

- Why it's never too late to start saving

- How you can take advantage of invaluable educational tax breaks

- What you can do to help your child find & win scholarships

······································

CHAPTER 11

How Am I Going To Put My Baby Through College?

If you think back to when your son or daughter was born, your first thought was probably, "What a beautiful baby!" And your second was likely, "How am I going to put my baby through college?" In an ideal world, after your son or daughter's birth, you would have immediately begun saving and by now you have enough socked away to foot the bill.

Now back to reality.

Seventeen years later, maybe you saved here and there but not enough to keep up with the rising costs of education. Have you taken a look at tuition costs recently?

The good news is that there was over $64 billion awarded in scholarships and financial aid in 1998-99. To successfully get a share of this money, you need to work with your child. In this chapter we offer hands-on strategies that you as parents can use to help your student.

The Tanabe Philosophy

In the years we've spent helping parents with college, the one piece of advice that helps more than anything else is: It's never too late to save. It doesn't matter if you have six months or six years before your child goes off to school (or even if your child is already in college), the best thing you can do is learn about financial aid options and start an aggressive savings plan now.

Your child's college education will probably be one of his or her most important and influential experiences—next to being raised by you of course. Your student will expand his or her knowledge base, make the transition from adolescent to adult, and figure out how to be self-supportive after graduation (and that's not easy!). In turn you want to do whatever it takes to help pay for it. So again, the most important thing you can do is stop putting it off, educate yourself on financial aid opportunities, and work out a savings plan today. Even compared to tuition, there is no price that can be attached to the benefits of a good education.

"When I saw the tuition costs and I looked at how much we had in savings, I thought we'd never make it. Fortunately, with loans and scholarships, we've been able to make ends meet. It has meant not taking that vacation to Europe, but it's been worth it. My daughter is planning to become an architect."

—Renee, a parent

Five Steps To Saving For College

According to the College Board, the average costs for tuition and room and board at four-year public schools for the 1999-2000 school year were $8,086, a 31 percent increase over the past 10 years. For four-year private schools, the costs were $21,339, a 29 percent increase. And, we all know that the costs will continue to grow.

All those numbers probably make you wonder how you could possibly save enough to send your student to college. Is it too late to start saving after your child's first birthday? With college costs rising, how much will it be when it's your child's time to go? What if your child is heading off to college in the next 12 months and you haven't even started saving yet? Or, what if your child is already in college?

We have developed a method for answering these questions, the Five Steps to Saving for College.

Step 1: How Much Will College Cost?

How much college costs today will not be how much college costs in the future. If it is more than a year until your child starts college, unfortunately, college costs will most likely rise. And, if your child is already in college, you are likely to face increases each year. Read on to learn how you can develop a savings strategy that compensates for these increases.

The first step in evaluating how much to save is to estimate how much your child's education will cost. The calculation becomes difficult because rising costs make the amount you need to save a moving target. To help, we've included the following Estimated College Costs Table, which outlines estimates of how much your student's total education will cost now and in the future. The costs are based on the 1999-2000 average costs from the College Board and assume a 5 percent increase each year.

To use the table, select which type of college you think your child will attend: two-year public, two-year private, four-year public, or four-year private. Then, using the second column, select the number of years until your student begins college. Look at the corresponding amount in the third column to find your estimated future total costs. This is the estimated cost of your child's entire two or four-year education.

For example, if your child will attend a two-year private college and it is seven years until he or she begins college, your estimated future total cost for the two-year education is $33,938. If your child will attend a four-year public college and it is two years until he or she starts, your estimated future total cost for the four-year education is $38,425.

	Years until student begins college	Total estimated cost of education
Two-year public	1	$3,501
	2	$3,676
	3	$3,860
	4	$4,053
	5	$4,256
	7	$4,692
	10	$5,430
	12	$5,986
	15	$6,929

Based on $1,627, the current average annual cost for two-year public colleges. Assumes a 5 percent increase per year.

	Years until student begins college	Total estimated cost of education
Two-year private	1	$25,324
	2	$26,591
	3	$27,921
	4	$29,317

Two-year private	5	$30,783
	7	$33,938
	10	$39,288
	12	$43,314
	15	$50,141

Based on $11,765, the current average annual cost for two-year private colleges. Assumes a 5 percent increase per year.

Four-year public	1	$36,595
	2	$38,425
	3	$40,346
	4	$42,363
	5	$44,481
	7	$49,040
	10	$56,771
	12	$62,591
	15	$72,460

Based on $8,086, the current average annual cost for four-year public colleges. Assumes a 5 percent increase per year.

Four-year private	1	$96,571
	2	$101,339
	3	$106,469
	4	$111,793
	5	$117,383
	7	$129,414
	10	$149,812
	12	$165,168
	15	$191,201

Based on $21,339, the current average annual cost for four-year private colleges. Assumes a 5 percent increase per year.

Step 2: How Much You've Already Squirreled Away

Now that you know roughly how much you will need, it's time to look at what you already have and how much it will be worth when your child goes to college. To help, here's a table that shows an estimate of how much your college savings will be worth when your child goes to college.

To use the table, locate how much you've saved in the first column. Move horizontally along this line until you reach the number of years until your child starts college. The number you stop at is an estimate of how much the money you currently have will grow. For example, if you've saved $5,000 and college is five years away, you will have an estimated $6,381 when your child starts college.

This table is based on a conservative 5 percent return rate. If the returns on your investments are not as high, the value of your savings will be less. And, of course, if your investments have better returns, you will see even better results and you will make a sizable donation to Gen and Kelly Tanabe. (Okay, we had to see if you were paying attention.)

"For the five years before our son started college, we had socked some money away for his education. When it came time to pay the tuition, we suddenly realized we hadn't saved enough. Fortunately, we took stock of our other savings and came up with an extra pool of money we had inherited that helped us come up with a solution. My advice: Review your finances early to make sure you know what you have."

—Michael, a parent

Savings	Years until student starts college								
	1	2	3	4	5	7	10	12	15
1,000	1,050	1,103	1,158	1,216	1,276	1,407	1,629	1,796	2,079
2,000	2,100	2,205	2,315	2,431	2,553	2,814	3,258	3,592	4,158
3,000	3,150	3,308	3,473	3,647	3,829	4,221	4,887	5,388	6,237
4,000	4,200	4,410	4,631	4,862	5,105	5,628	6,516	7,183	8,316
5,000	5,250	5,513	5,788	6,078	6,381	7,036	8,144	8,979	10,395
6,000	6,300	6,615	6,946	7,293	7,658	8,443	9,773	10,775	12,474
7,000	7,350	7,718	8,103	8,509	8,934	9,850	11,402	12,571	14,552
8,000	8,400	8,820	9,261	9,724	10,210	11,257	13,031	14,367	16,631
9,000	9,450	9,923	10,419	10,940	11,487	12,664	14,660	16,163	18,710
10,000	10,500	11,025	11,576	12,155	12,763	14,071	16,289	17,959	20,789
15,000	15,750	16,538	17,364	18,233	19,144	21,107	24,433	26,938	31,184
20,000	21,000	22,050	23,153	24,310	25,526	28,142	32,578	35,917	41,579
25,000	26,250	27,563	28,941	30,388	31,907	35,178	40,722	44,896	51,973

Step 3: How Much Can Financial Aid Help?

Don't think that you're on your own when it comes time to pay for college. Uncle Sam, colleges and universities, community organizations, and businesses provide loans, grants, and scholarships for college. According to the College Board, over $64 billion in financial aid was awarded in the 1998-99 school year. Dividing this number by the total number of equivalent full-time students results in an average of just over $6,000 per student.

Of course, you shouldn't assume that you'll receive the average amount. Many financial aid programs are based on financial need. Many scholarships are based on academic achievement. It's difficult to predict how much aid you'll receive until you actually start crunching the numbers on your family's assets and income.

Here's what you can do to prepare: Use this book to learn as much as you can about scholarships and financial aid. We offer hands-on strategies you can use when applying for scholarships and financial aid. Also, if you need additional information on scholarships and financial aid, contact the organizations listed in Appendix B. Take comfort in knowing that the government and other organizations are trying to help.

Step 4: How Much Do You Need To Save?

Now comes the part where you start to ask yourself if you really need that designer pair of shoes or that daily dose of double espresso. Saving means cutting down on those extra perks, but it also means having enough to send your child to a great college, which makes it all worth it. Plus, think of who's going to care for you in your retirement.

The best way to succeed in saving for college is to know how much you need to save and have a plan for doing it. You've already done the main calculations you need for determining how much you need to save.

(a) Calculate the estimated cost of your child's education from Step 1. Divide it by the number of years of school (usually either two or four years):

_____

As early as possible, figure out how much you need to save so you have a goal in mind and can develop a strategy for meeting your goal.

(b) Estimate the future value of what you have already saved from Step 2. Subtract this value. Divide by the number of years in school.

-_____

(c) Subtract the estimated amount of financial aid you will receive from Step 3. (This is extremely difficult to do, but you can use a percentage of the average per equivalent full time student $6,085 as a guess.)

-_____

(d) Total

_____

The total is how much you need to save each year. Here's an example:

Let's assume your child is a junior and plans to attend a four-year public college. You have two years until your first tuition bill is due.

(a) Estimate the cost of your child's education from Step 1. Divide by 4:
$38,425 / 4 years of education = $9,606 per year.

(b) You've saved $4,000 toward her education. From Step 2, you estimate that in two years, this will be worth an estimated $4,410.

Divide the estimated future value of your savings in two years by the number of years of education:
$4,410 / 4 years of education = $1,102 available per year.

Subtract this value:
- $1,102

(c) You believe that your income and assets will qualify you for receiving the average amount in financial aid for an equivalent full-time student.

Subtract the estimated financial aid:
- $6,085

(d) Total
$9,606   (a)
- $1,102   (b)
- $6,085   (c)
= $2,419 per year for 4 years

Now that you have an estimate of how much you need to save, develop a plan for how you will accomplish this. Use the chart below to see how much to save per month and an estimate of the value of your savings when your child goes to college. This chart shows the benefits of saving between $50 and $500 per month. Select the number of years you will save before you need the money. Then match the total amount needed from your calculations to the amount saved in the last column of the chart.

In our example, you have two years until your child goes to college and you need to save $2,419 per year. If you save $100 per month, your estimated savings would be $2529 in two years. This would cover the first year of tuition. Then you need to save about $200 per month in order to pay the $2,419 you'll need for each of the next three years.

As you can see, the amount you can save even with a limited budget and in a short amount of time can add up. Keep in mind, however, that if the tuition of your child's school is higher or your financial aid package lower, you will have to save more. This table is based on a 5 percent growth rate.

Number of years saved	Amount saved per month	Total amount saved
1	50	616
1	100	1,233
1	250	3,082
1	500	6,165
2	50	1,264
2	100	2,529
2	250	6,322
2	500	12,645
3	50	1,945
3	100	3,891
3	250	9,728
3	500	19,457
4	50	2,661
4	100	5,323
4	250	13,308
4	500	26,617
5	50	3,414
5	100	6,828
5	250	17,072
5	500	34,144
7	50	5,037
7	100	10,074
7	250	25,186
7	500	50,373
10	50	7,796
10	100	15,592
10	250	38,982
10	500	77,964
12	50	9,879
12	100	19,758
12	250	49,395
12	500	98,791
15	50	13,420
15	100	26,840
15	250	67,100
15	500	134,201

"Saving was difficult for us at first because we thought that we only spent money on basic necessities. When we really started to look at how much we saved, we realized we weren't saving anything and there were some really easy ways to cut expenses. We now have a family policy of saving 10 percent of every paycheck. It works!"

—Edward

Step 5: Develop An Investment Strategy

An investment strategy does not mean taking all of your college savings and dumping it into a stock based on a hot tip from your Uncle Leo. To develop an investment strategy, work with a financial planner. Almost every brokerage or mutual fund company has a department devoted to assisting you with your college planning. When deciding what to do, here are some tips.

Do your own research. Don't rely on television commercials, glossy brochures from a company, or fast-talking sales pitches to make your investment decisions. Do your own research by reading prospectuses and by studying other publications' analysis of your potential investments.

It's important to be comfortable with your investment strategy. Whether you are developing it on your own or with the help of a financial planner, create a strategy that matches your personal tolerance for risk.

Take into account the amount of time until your child goes to college. If your son or daughter is heading off to college in the fall, you probably want to make conservative investments so that the money is accessible when you need it. However, if you have several years before your child goes to college, you might consider investments with higher risk and higher potential for gains such as equities.

Recognize your propensity for risk. More important than what a financial planner says is whether or not you are comfortable with your investments. Do not invest unless you are comfortable.

Don't be afraid to ask questions. If you don't understand terms that a financial planner uses, don't be afraid to ask. It's your financial planner's job to answer questions.

The It's Too Late To Save Myth

You may think that the Five Steps To Saving For College plan is wonderful—in theory. But what if your child starts college this fall, and you haven't started saving? What if your child is already in college? Is it too late? Will your child need to forgo higher education?

We will repeat our mantra: It is never too late to save.

If you find yourself both short on time and short on college savings, there are strategies you can use to jump-start your saving. They will require work and sacrifice, but they will put you on the right track toward sending your son or daughter to college.

Even if your child starts college in the fall or if he or she is already a student, it's not too late to save. You can start using these strategies today to save for your child's education.

1. Take stock of your savings. Make a record of all of your financial accounts and investments and the amount that you have in each. You may not have saved for the purpose of college, but when you look at your assets, you may have savings you can use toward college. Regardless, know what your assets are.

2. Research financial aid and scholarship options. Use this book to learn about the opportunities you may have for financial aid from your child's college, the government, and scholarships.

3. **Get help**. Speak with your child's high school counselor or college financial aid office. Explain your situation and work with them to develop strategies for saving.

4. **Make sure you are credit-worthy**. Some student loans are based on your credit-worthiness. Ensure that credit reports are accurate, and try to reduce your debt as much as possible. This will offer you the best opportunity for obtaining student loans.

5. **Be supportive when your child applies for financial aid and scholarships**. Your child will need your assistance when completing applications for financial aid and scholarships. Dedicate time to helping. See the rest of this chapter for specific suggestions on how you can help.

6. **Reduce costs**. Forgo the unnecessary extras in your spending and figure out ways to reduce costs on essential items as well.

7. **Remember that college is four years**. Even if you haven't saved for your child's first year of college, you can start saving now for his or her second, third, and fourth year.

8. **Start using the Five Steps To Saving For College plan described in this chapter now**. It's not too late to start.

9. **Know that you are not the only one in this situation**. There are many other parents who for their own reasons have not been able to save for their children's college education. Don't be embarrassed to discuss your situation with high school counselors or college financial aid officers who can help.

Federal Financial Aid: Get Your Tax Dollars Back

Applying for financial aid takes time, but it's well worth the effort. For many students, it makes the difference between being able to afford or not afford going to college. Spend the time to complete the forms thoroughly and provide information that gives a complete picture of your family's situation.

Your tax dollars allow the federal government to award almost $50 billion in financial aid each school year. It makes sense that you'd want to get some of those tax dollars back in the form of student financial aid. To do this, we have developed strategies that you can use to learn about financial aid and to help your child apply.

Study up on financial aid. Read Chapter 10, *Financial Aid Workshop* to learn about the various grants, loans, and work-study programs that the government provides. Know and understand what your options are.

Meet the deadlines. You can apply for federal aid as soon as possible AFTER January 1. For something this important, don't procrastinate. Set aside time to spend with your child to complete the application.

Help your child complete the application. The application that you will need to complete with your child is the Free Application for Federal Student Aid (FAFSA). For the FAFSA you will need to provide information on your family's income and assets. Spend time gathering this information for your child.

Story From Real Life: How Our Meddling Cost Us Thousands

These parents learned the hard way when to get involved and when to give their daughter space. It's a difficult balance to strike, but it must to maintain your son or daughter's and your sanity.
—Gen and Kelly

I have a true nightmare to share. My wife and I have a tendency to want to really get involved in everything that's going on in our daughter's life. It was difficult for us to realize that our little girl was growing up and becoming an adult. It really cost us.

The night before our daughter's financial aid forms for her college's aid programs were due, we sat down as a family to discuss applying for financial aid. We told her that because we were very interested in figuring out how to pay for her education, we were going to apply for financial aid as a family. That was a mistake.

Seventeen arguments, four slammed doors, and two crying fits later, we reached our goal of completing the financial aid forms as a family. With three of us working on the forms, it seemed like every question brought an argument. Answering questions about our savings caused our daughter to accuse us of having not been good parents by spending too much. Listing our incomes resulted in an argument between my wife and me about whose job was more dead-end.

There were simply too many of us working on something that one of us should have taken the lead on. And, we should have known we couldn't wait until the last minute. We finally finished what could have been relatively easy but what turned into a painstaking process. Our daughter said she would drop the application in the mail after school that day.

In the next few weeks, the parents of other students started to share with us the financial aid packages their colleges put together. As the days passed, we grew anxious because we hadn't heard anything from our daughter's college. Finally, I contacted the financial aid office directly and asked when we would get an answer back. They said that they had never received our daughter's application!

After interrogating our daughter, she admitted that because she was so angry, she never mailed the application in. My wife and I couldn't believe it! We grounded our daughter for pulling a stunt like that.

It was too late to apply for aid from the college. Fortunately, we were not too late to apply for aid from the government. My guess is that we probably missed out on a few hundred or even thousand dollars. We've forgiven our daughter, but we've also learned that we need to let her do some things on her own.

—Pat, a parent

Do your taxes. Information from your taxes will be used in the FAFSA. Sure you have until April 15 to do your taxes, but it's worth it to do them earlier and receive financial aid.

Make sure you are credit-worthy. Some loan programs are based on your credit-worthiness as parents. Review your credit report and correct any errors. Reduce debt as much as possible. Close unused credit card accounts.

Get help. You can get free help from your child's high school counselor, college financial aid officer, and the Department of Education's Federal Student Aid Information Center. See Appendix B for the contact information for the Federal Student Aid Information Center.

Don't get scammed. You will probably receive very official looking letters from very official sounding organizations offering assistance with federal financial aid for a fee. Be very wary of these organizations. In most cases, they are scams. Use the information in Appendix B to contact the Federal Student Aid Information Center for free information. Or, get it from banks and other lenders, who provide free guidance with the hope that you will take out a student loan with them. (You can take advantage of the information they offer, but you are in no way obligated to select them as your lender.)

Don't be afraid to ask questions. Most importantly, realize that it is your right to ask questions. There is a lot of information to absorb. Don't be embarrassed if something doesn't make sense or if you don't understand one of the numerous acronyms tossed about. Ask!

Tax Breaks

There are tax benefits you can take advantage of that allow you to save for your child's education or deduct educational expenses from your income. Read more about the opportunities here and consult with the IRS or your accountant for more information.

Money doesn't always flow out of your wallet when it comes to your child's education. There are some major tax benefits when saving and paying for your child's education. While the following is an overview of some of the more important tax breaks, check with an accountant to confirm that these programs fit your individual situation.

Education IRA: Allows you to accumulate interest tax-free and to withdraw money from the IRA without penalty for educational expenses. All earnings accumulate tax-free and there are no taxes due upon withdrawal if the money is used for education, books, or room and board. If you withdraw funds before 59 ° years old for non-educational purposes, you would normally pay a 10 percent tax penalty. This penalty is waived when the money is used for educational purposes. Unfortunately, there are limits to how much you can put into this IRA. For each child under 18, families may deposit $500 per year into their education IRA.

State-sponsored tuition plans: These plans allow you to save for tuition and room and board. You do not pay taxes until you withdraw the money, and funds withdrawn are eligible for the Hope tax credit or the Lifetime Learning tax credit. Refer to Appendix B for the contact information for your State Agency for Student Financial Assistance.

To encourage career or personal development, some employers pay for or subsidize their employees' educations. You can exclude some of the expenses from your income. For example, for undergraduate classes you started before June 1, 2000, you could exclude up to $5,250 from your income. Speak with your company's human resources department and with your tax professional for more information.

Hope and Lifetime Learning tax credit: These are tuition tax credits of up to $1,500 in 2001 for the Hope tax credit and up to $1,000 for the Lifetime Learning tax credit until 2002. Only one credit can be claimed per student each year. The credit is subtracted from your income tax on a dollar-for-dollar basis. This is more beneficial than a deduction, which is subtracted from your income before you calculate your tax. The Hope tax credit can be used for your child's first two years of school. The Lifetime Learning credit can be used for any postsecondary education including graduate school. Qualified expenses that can be credited include tuition and related fees, minus any tax-free grants or scholarships received. The credits are open to single filers with incomes of up to $40,000 and joint tax filers with incomes of up to $80,000. The credit is phased out for single filers with incomes between $40,000 and $50,000 and joint tax filers between $80,000 and $100,000.

Interest from student loans after your child has graduated: You can deduct interest you pay on student loans from your taxes. If loans have been forgiven because of community service, the amount forgiven is tax exempt.

Scholarship dollars your child wins may not be free from taxes. Scholarships and fellowships are tax-free if all of the following criteria are met:

● He or she is enrolled as a full-time or part-time student pursuing a degree at a primary, secondary, or postsecondary school.
● The award pays for tuition and fees.
● The award pays for books and supplies needed for his or her classes.

Fellowships or scholarships are taxable if they pay for:

● Room and board
● Travel
● Research

For more information, consult with an accountant, call the IRS hotline at 800-829-1040, or read the IRS publication 970, Tax Benefits for Higher Education. This publication is available from the IRS hotline or on the Internet at www.irs.gov.

Scholarships: Free Cash For College

Unlike loans, scholarships do not need to be repaid. They are awarded to students based on their skills and experiences. While your son or daughter needs to apply for the awards, you can offer assistance and support. Scholarship applications often require multiple pieces including the application forms, essays, recommendation letters, and interviews.

Scholarships are at the top of the financial aid food chain. Unlike loans, they don't need to be repaid and unlike work-study, your child doesn't have to hold a job to receive the money. However, this does not mean that scholarships are easy to find or win. Since they come with few, if any, strings attached, your child will face tough competition and will have to spend time to create a winning application. It's not an easy task, but fortunately, there are some things you can do to help.

Learn as much as you can, and encourage your child to learn too. The first thing you should do is learn about scholarships, where to find them, how they work and how to win. If you haven't already, look at some of the earlier chapters in this book. In particular, read Chapter 2 for an introduction to scholarships and how to find them. Most importantly, make sure your child reads these chapters.

Help find scholarships. In this book you'll find a comprehensive directory of thousands of scholarships, but that doesn't mean that there aren't more for you to find. Look at Chapter 2 to see how you can use guidance counselors, the college's financial aid office, and the Internet to expand your search.

Some of the best scholarships are those given locally. Your employer or community organization may offer scholarships. These are great to apply to since the competition is often limited making it more likely that your child will win. Don't overlook organizations that you are involved in such as clubs, churches, and professional organizations.

Assist your child in selecting appropriate scholarships. Your child will have the best chance of winning the scholarships that most closely fit his or her achievements and in which your child can stand out from the other applicants. Help your student review the missions of the scholarships that he or she wants to apply for and see how they fit with their own accomplishments.

Help your child develop a strategy for applying. Your child may need help prioritizing the scholarships, allotting time to apply for them, and meeting deadlines. Make sure that your child has a plan and schedule for applying.

Avoid scholarship scams. You will probably receive letters from very official-sounding agencies that promise to provide you with secret unclaimed scholarships or scholarships that perfectly match your child's background for a fee. Do not use any scholarship services that make promises that sound too good to be true or that charge a huge upfront fee. There are plenty of free resources available, and these paid services will provide you with the same information that you can get on your own.

Scholarship Applications: Your Child's Vital Statistics

Scholarship committees use the application forms to get a quick glance at your child's skills and accomplishments. Often these forms are the first thing that the judges look at when separating the candidates into those with potential and those who will be thanked for entering. It's important that your son or daughter completes every question and follows the directions.

Your child has about two pages to describe his or her coursework, grades, awards, honors, work, and other experience. These few pages make up the scholarship application, which is a basic requirement of most scholarships. Scholarship selection committees use applications to quickly see your child's achievements and measure his or her fit with the scholarship. Because selection committees often have a limited amount of time to review hundreds or even thousands of applications, your child needs to make sure that he or she writes an application that truly stands out. While your child should complete the applications, and not you, there are some ways you can help.

Make sure your child understands the scholarship's mission. Ensure that your child understands what the goal of the scholarship is so that he or she can highlight the accomplishments that best fit the scholarship.

Help your child prioritize. There will be many more scholarships that your child can apply for than he or she has time to. Make certain that your child is spending the most time on those scholarships that are the best fit. For example, if your child is applying for a music scholarship and has won awards from his or her school but not on a national level, he or she will probably want to focus on local and statewide music scholarships rather than national music scholarships.

Be added memory for your child. When your son or daughter is completing the applications, he or she may not remember every accomplishment. Help him or her list achievements, honors, and awards. You may remember something important that your child has forgotten.

Edit your child's applications. First impressions count. A sloppy application or one filled with mistakes does not make a good first impression. Even before the selection committee reads the application they'll assume that your son or daughter is just as sloppy in life as he or she is in filling out the application. To avoid this, offer to edit your child's work, proofreading it and offering suggestions for improvement.

Don't do the work for your child. It may be tempting to write your child's applications. After all, it is your bottom line that the scholarships will be saving. However, applications should be completed by the applicants. They will give your child experience that will be useful in the future as he or she applies for jobs. Your child should understand the importance of and have a vested interest in winning scholarships.

Recommendations: Praise For Your Child From Someone Other Than You

Recommendations provide scholarship committees with feedback from others about your son or daughter. We all know that you could provide the best recommendations—after all you've known your child since birth. Unfortunately, relatives are excluded.

If you're a typical parent, you've probably praised your child's crayon drawings as Picasso-like and intelligence as Einstein-ian. Recommendations offer the opportunity for others to praise your prodigy. Your child will ask teachers, professors, employers, or others to write letters vouching for his or her accomplishments. Scholarship committees view recommendations as a way to learn more about your child and to get unbiased confirmation of his or her accomplishments. Although you know your child better than anyone, you are unfortunately out of the pool of potential recommenders. Still, there are ways you can help your child get outstanding recommendations.

Work with your child to select the best recommenders. What's most important in selecting recommenders is how well they know your child. Work with your child to choose people who can describe traits and accomplishments that match the scholarship for which your child is applying.

Assist your child in preparing materials for the recommenders. In Chapter 5, *Get The Right Recommendations* we describe all of the materials that your child needs to provide: cover letter describing the recommendations that your child needs and suggestions for what to write in them, resume to remind recommenders of accomplishments, recommendation forms, and pre-addressed, stamped envelopes. Help your student gather this information and put it together.

Remind your child to say thank you. Recommenders spend time from their busy schedules to help your child win scholarships. They will appreciate a thank you note or small thank you gift.

Scholarship Essays: Your Child's Life In 500 Words Or Less

From scholarship applications, selection committees get a quick overview on your child's coursework and achievements. From recommendations, they get other people's thoughts about your child's potential. From scholarship essays, they want to grasp something about your child that is not easily conveyed in applications or recommendations. Essays offer your child the opportunity to use anecdotes and illustrations to express his or her motivations, goals, and character. Of course your child needs to write his or her own essay, but you can help as an editor.

Brainstorm. One of the most difficult parts about writing essays is selecting a topic. Help your child by brainstorming topics. Topics should fit with the mission of the scholarship and your child should be excited about the subject.

Be an editor. Being an editor does not mean writing your child's essay. It means offering praise and constructive criticism to help improve the work that your child has done. It also means checking for spelling, syntax, and grammatical errors.

Focus on the fit with the mission. As you are editing your child's work, make sure that it conveys how your child fits with the mission of the scholarship. Your child can produce an incredibly well-written essay, but if it doesn't show why he or she should win the scholarship, it won't be a winner.

Concentrate on your child. The essay should also reveal something about your child that is not found in the application or recommendations. If your child is applying for an engineering scholarship, a listing of coursework will be in the application and his or her recommenders will praise his or her ability. For the essay, your student could write about why he or she has decided to study engineering or what he or she hopes to accomplish as an engineer. An essay like this would provide insight not found in the other elements of his application.

Most scholarship applications require an essay. This is your child's opportunity to describe an element of his or her life beyond the brief facts of the application. The best scholarship essays exhibit how the student fits with the mission of the scholarships.

Story From Real Life: I Was Too Friendly With The Scholarship Judges

This parent tried to help her son by influencing the judges but discovered it was better to let him stand on his own merits.
—Gen and Kelly

Please learn from my mistake. When my son was a freshman in college, he applied for a scholarship from our local museum's support club. Because I was a previous president of the club and an active member, I knew every member, including all of the judges for the scholarship.

Having been a judge before for a number of years, I knew what typical applicants had to offer and that my son was very qualified for the scholarship. Still, I decided to start a mini-campaign for him with each of the judges. One by one, I took each judge aside and reminded her of my son's accomplishments. I explained how intelligent he was and how the money would help him pursue his dream of working in the government. I also mentioned how much I had contributed to the club and how great it would be to reward someone who had served the club so loyally.

Well, my son didn't win the scholarship. I can't be certain that it was because of my campaigning, but I'm pretty sure it was. The student who won was not nearly as good a student as my son and her parents weren't even members of the supporter club. This year, when my son applies, I'm going to let his application speak for itself. My campaigning days are over.

—Marilyn, a parent

"I was honored to help edit my son's scholarship essay. He wrote about a time he went fishing with his grandfather. What a beautiful piece. He had never expressed to me verbally the emotions he felt while spending time with his grandfather, but it was all in his essay. I felt shivers as I read his thoughts and feelings. I'll cherish his words always."

—Kimberly

"My daughter and I had a great time practicing for her scholarship interviews. I got to ask her questions that I normally wouldn't, like what her career goals are and what she expects out of college. On a day to day basis it's difficult to connect with her because she's a typical teenager, but this gave me the opportunity to get to know her better."

—John, a parent

Be sure to read Chapter 6, *Secrets To Writing Winning Essays* so you know what to look for in a good essay.

Interview Skills

Scholarship interviews offer a tangible justification for the countless times you have told your child to look people in the eye when speaking with them and to shake hands firmly and confidently. In interviews, your child will spend about an hour interacting with a member of the scholarship selection committee. This is the time for the selection committee to ask follow up questions to your child's application, learn more about your child, and measure his or her social skills. While you can't accompany your child to the interviews, you can help him or her prepare beforehand.

We suggest that you and your child review Chapter 7, *Ace The Interviews* for more information on what your child can expect in interviews and detailed advice on approaching them. Here are a couple of key tips to keep in mind:

Practice with your child. The most important thing you can do is offer to practice mock interviewing with your child. Get ideas for questions from Chapter 7, sit down with your child and start asking. Pay attention to what your child says. Is he or she answering with information that pertains to the scholarship? Watch how he or she answers the questions. Does his or her body language convey confidence? Does he or she display enthusiasm? Does he or she respond with questions to make the interview interactive? Offer your child both praise and constructive criticism after completing your mock interview.

In mock interviews, encourage your child to interact with the interviewer. Offer suggestions for questions to ask. Have him or her practice not just answering questions but asking questions as well. This two-way, interactive conversation will be the most interesting and impressive for the interviewer.

Give your child room. The last thing you want the interviewer to think is that your child is entirely dependent on you. That may be true, but don't let it be for the interview. He or she needs to do the interview independently of you to show that he or she is mature enough for college and its rigors.

Parental Encouragement

We've described a number of ways you can help your child apply for financial aid and scholarships. The most important thing you can do is offer positive encouragement. With the numerous forms and information requested, figuring out how to pay for college can be stressful and complicated. Try to keep an open mind about where your child wants to go to school, knowing that there are a number of different ways to finance his or her education. What your child needs most are patience, understanding, and encouragement.

Chapter 11 Summary: Parents' Guide To Scholarships & Financial Aid

You have two main responsibilities as parents: First, absorb as much information as possible about how the financial aid and scholarship processes work. By learning more, you will know which opportunities are open to you and how to take advantage of them. Second, offer your child support as he or she applies for aid.

Develop a savings strategy with the Five Steps To Saving For College:

Step 1: Estimate the future cost of your child's education, based on the current cost and an estimate for inflation.

Step 2: Take stock of how much you've already squirreled away so you know how much you have to work with. Estimate how much you think your savings will grow by the time your child is ready for college.

Step 3: Estimate how much you may receive in federal financial aid.

Step 4: Estimate how much you need to save, which is the difference between the cost of your child's education and how much you've already saved and an estimate of how much you'll receive in financial aid.

Step 5: Develop an investment strategy that coincides with the amount of time you have until your child starts college, how much risk you are willing to take, and how much you want to save.

Realize that it's never too late to save. Even if your child has already started college, you can start saving now and take steps to help pay for his or her education.

When applying for financial aid, provide assistance for your child. Don't be afraid to ask questions and seek help. Use the information in Appendix B to contact the Federal Student Aid Information Center.

Understand the different tax breaks you may be able to benefit from: Education IRAs, which allow you to accumulate interest tax-free and withdraw money without penalty for educational expenses; state-sponsored tuition plans, in which you don't pay taxes until you withdraw the money; and the Hope and Lifetime Learning tax credits, which are subtracted from your income tax.

Assist your child in applying for scholarships by acting as an editor and advisor. Help your child develop a strategy for selecting and applying for scholarships. Scout out scholarships from your employer and organizations in which you are involved.

For scholarship applications, help your child prioritize his or her achievements and edit the application.

Discuss the best possible recommenders with your child and assist him or her with preparing the materials for recommenders, but let your child actually ask for the letter of support.

Edit, but do not write, your child's essays. Offer advice to improve the structure, content, and mechanics of his or her work. Help your child demonstrate personal qualities that show the selection committee his or her fit with the mission of the award.

Practice with mock interviews with your child so that he or she gets comfortable in interview situations. Offer constructive criticism to help your student improve his or her interpersonal skills.

Most importantly, offer support and understanding for your child. Try to strike a balance between helping and taking the lead.

Unleash The Power Of The Internet

· ·

In this chapter, you'll learn:

- How to find more scholarships online

- Strategies for applying for scholarships via the Internet

- The importance of researching awarding organizations & past winners online

- How to avoid costly scholarship scams on the Internet

· ·

CHAPTER 12

Opening Access With The Internet

In the pre-Internet days, the only way to find out about scholarships was through books, the only way to research the background of awarding organizations was to write or call, and the only way to apply was with typewriter and paper. The Internet has helped open up the possibilities for scholarships by providing more access to scholarships, an easy method to find out about awarding organizations, and a means for applying with your computer. In this chapter, we show you how to take advantage of it all.

The Tanabe Philosophy

Our approach to scholarships is to find and apply to them wherever they are. The Internet has a wealth of information waiting to be found, and best of all, it's free! Use traditional sources for finding and applying for scholarships like this book, college counselors, and financial aid advisors, but take advantage of the power of the Internet. Here's how to make the most of this new media.

How To Find Scholarships Online

You will find the most comprehensive directory of scholarships in the second half of this book. However, no directory has every scholarship available. New scholarships are formed every day. One of the benefits of using the Internet in your search is that website databases can be updated very quickly. Here are some tips for using the Internet:

Look for databases of scholarships that you can search for free. We have one on our site at **www.supercollege.com**. Here's how our database works. You answer questions about your education, academic goals, career goals, activities, parents' activities and employment, religion, talents, ethnicity, and additional background information. Our database uses your answers to the questions to search thousands of awards and provide matches for scholarships that fit your individual background.

When you use online scholarship databases, keep the following advice in mind:

Searches should always be free. Never pay for a scholarship search.

Before you begin your search, prepare a list of your parents' employers and activities and your activities, talents, and interests ahead of time. This will save you time when you are actually using the website to search and help insure that you don't miss out on anything.

Spend time to complete the questions about your background. There may be a lot of questions, but the more specific and accurate you can be about your background, the better your results.

In addition, you can use links to find additional resources. For example, on our site SuperCollege.com, we link to hundreds of other websites that you may find helpful. Many sites do this as a way of helping you find more information that's related and useful.

Zap! Applying For Scholarships Online

In the old days, you used to have to lug out the typewriter and correction fluid every time you wanted to complete an application. It's much easier now. Fire up your computer and connect to the Internet. No correction fluid needed!

You can now apply for some scholarships over the Internet. The benefits of doing this are that you can easily correct typos and you don't have to make a trip to the Post Office. However, for even the most tech-savvy students, applying for scholarships online can be a new and challenging experience. To help, here are some tips for applying electronically:

Preview the application. Before you start completing the application, take a sneak peek at it so you know what questions are asked and what information you'll need to provide.

If you don't feel comfortable completing the application online, then use the old-fashioned method. It's better to spend time perfecting your essay than to spend time figuring out how to use the Internet to apply.

Prepare your materials and answers in advance. Because you know what the questions are, you can compose and organize the information in advance. Spend time on your answers. Just because you can apply instantly with the click of a button doesn't mean that you should craft your answers as speedily.

Read the directions to see if you need to complete the entire application in a single sitting or if you can save it, return at another time, and complete it. In most cases, you will need to submit all of your information at one time.

Compose your essay in a word processing program first, then upload it. Don't try to write your essay at the time that you are submitting your application. When submitting your essays online, follow the same strategies as when you submit them offline. Brainstorm topics, write with passion, and get editors to review your work. Don't take shortcuts. Review Chapter 6 for strategies for writing essays.

Be careful about typos or mistakes. It's easy to make careless mistakes when you submit your applications online. Take time to review your work.

Print out what you submit so you have a hard copy. You can refer to the hard copy when applying to other scholarships, and you will have a spare in case your electronic copy gets lost.

Read the instructions for any information you need to submit offline. For some scholarships, you will complete your application online and then print it out and send it. For others, you will submit your application online

> *"Whenever I'm given the option, I apply for scholarships online. It saves me time because all I have to do is cut and paste my essays and information, and I'm done. I don't have the extra hassle of running to the Post Office any more."*
>
> —Diane

but send additional information like letters of recommendation or transcripts by regular mail. Follow the directions carefully.

Get confirmation. When you submit your application online, most organizations will send you confirmation that they have received your application. If they do not, get confirmation by sending an email.

Do Some Detective Work Online

"Through the Internet I was able to get in touch with the previous winners of a local scholarship. What a find! They happily shared with me the applications they used to win and tips on the interview. Thanks to the Internet I won $2,000!"

—Phillip

There's a reason why the Internet was once nicknamed the "Information Superhighway." You can find out the dirt on pretty much anything, including scholarship organizations. In addition to finding scholarships and applying to them online, use the Internet to research the sponsor organizations and awards. Here are some tips:

Search for the sponsor organization's website to read more about the mission of the organization and the award. This will help you understand what the organization is trying to accomplish by awarding the scholarship.

Request additional information, newsletters, or other literature if it's available. Or, read the literature online. Many organizations have their literature and newsletters accessible on their websites.

Get information on past winners. Some organizations list past winners on their websites and often include brief biographical information. Again, this will help you understand what kind of student the organization seeks.

The more you can learn about the organization, the award, and their missions, the better you can craft your application to fit.

Be Cautious Of Scams

Both offline and online there are a small minority of people who try to take advantage of students' and parents' fears of the high costs of college. Here are some red flags to watch for:

Registration, entry, or administrative fee: Legitimate scholarship and financial aid programs do not require an upfront fee. Never pay to search a scholarship database on the Internet.

Soliciting your credit card number: Never give out this kind of financial information to anyone who contacts you without your requesting them to.

No name, address, or phone number: Legitimate online businesses post their contact information on their websites.

Guarantee: Remember, there is no such thing as a guaranteed scholarship. Legitimate scholarships are based on merit or need, not your willingness to pay a registration fee.

Read Chapter 3, *Avoid Scholarship Scams* for more information on scholarship scams. While there are a small group of people who try to take advantage of students and parents, there are a number of great services that can provide scholarship and financial aid guidance—for free. We welcome you to visit our website SuperCollege.com and to use search engines and other financial aid websites to complete your scholarship strategy.

Chapter 12 Summary: Unleash The Power Of The Internet

The Internet is a great tool for finding scholarships, applying for scholarships, and learning more about the sponsoring organizations. The information can be updated very quickly, and best of all, it's free! Use it in combination with traditional resources like this book and your high school counselor or financial aid officer.

Find scholarships online through websites with free, searchable scholarship databases and through search engines.

Some scholarships allow you to apply online. Take advantage of this opportunity to save time and headaches. Be as diligent about the quality of your work when you apply online as when you apply on paper.

Do online detective work. Learn more about scholarship sponsors and past winners as research to improve your application.

Avoid online scholarship scams. Be wary of any scholarship services that require a fee, solicit your credit card number, have no contact information, or make "guarantees" that sound good to be true.

You are welcome to visit our website, SuperCollege.com (www.supercollege.com) to search our free database of thousands of scholarships, learn more scholarship and financial aid tips and strategies, and enter our own SuperCollege.com scholarship.

How To Keep The Money You Win

In this chapter, you'll learn:

- What you need to do to insure that you keep the financial aid & scholarship dollars you win

- Our advice for approaching & winning scholarships

- A special request from Gen & Kelly

CHAPTER 13

You're There!

When you learn to skydive, your first lesson does not start with you jumping out the side of an airplane. First you go through training in which you learn techniques and safety measures–on the ground. Then you can take to the sky.

You've learned step-by-step strategies for every piece of the scholarship process from finding scholarships to writing winning applications to using the Internet to expand your search. Now it's time to move on to our comprehensive Scholarship Directory and find awards that specifically match your background and experience.

In your scholarship education, you have just completed the ground training and are ready to take the plunge (groan). As you move from the strategies for applying for scholarships to actually applying, we have a few words of advice on how to keep the dollars you earn and how to stay motivated.

Keeping The Dollars That Are Yours

We're jumping ahead to after you win a cache of scholarship dollars. It would be nice if once the scholarship checks were written you could run off for that well-deserved trip to the Bahamas, but alas there are restrictions on how you can spend the cash and how to maintain your scholarship. Besides, everyone knows that Hawaii is the place to go. Here are some tips to keep in mind:

Get to know your scholarship and financial aid administrators. This duo will be able to answer questions about your award and make sure that you are spending it the way you should.

Give them proof if they want it. Some awards require that you provide proof of enrollment or transcripts. Send it to them.

Be aware of your award's requirements and what happens if something changes. How long does the award last? What happens if you take a leave of absence, study part-time, study abroad, transfer schools, or quit your studies? College is full of possibilities! Do you have to maintain a minimum grade point average or take courses in a certain field?

It would be a total waste to win an award, only to be unable to renew it the following year simply because you forgot to put in the effort required.

Know if there are special requirements for athletic scholarships. If you've won an athletic scholarship, you are most likely required to play. (You didn't get that full ride scholarship for nothing!) Understand the implications of what would happen if you were not able to play because of circumstances such as an injury or not meeting academic requirements.

Find out if the award is a cash cow (renewable). If an award is renewable, you are eligible to extend it. Some renewable awards can be extended to cover the length of your entire education. If the award is renewable, find out what you need to do and when you need to do it to renew. Some awards just require a copy of your transcript while others require you to submit an entirely new application.

Understand restrictions for spending the dough. Some awards are limited to tuition only. Others can be used for books, travel, or even living expenses. Some provide the money directly to your school while others provide a check made out to you. Make sure you understand what you can spend it on and what sort of records you need to keep.

Learn the tax implications of your award. Speak with the award administrator or your pals at the IRS (www.irs.gov or 800-829-1040).

Be aware of requirements after you graduate. Some awards such as ROTC scholarships require employment after graduation. Because these arrangements can drastically affect your future, learn about the requirements now.

Keep the awarding organization up to date on your progress. Write the organization a thank you note, and keep them updated on your progress at the end of the year. This is not only good manners, but it will help insure that the award is around in the future.

Our Inspiring Parting Words

Applying for scholarships is not easy. They require time, patience, and self reflection. The competition is tough. As you are applying, remind yourself that the reward is even greater. As you receive your college diploma, you will feel deep satisfaction from knowing that you played a significant role in paying for this education.

I (Gen) remember when I won the Sterling Scholarship, one of the highest honors for students in Hawaii. The awards ceremony was televised live throughout the state. For weeks, I prepared for the competition, compiling a 50-page application book, practicing for the eight hours of interviews, and enlisting the help of no less than three teachers from my high school. Even though the scholarship was only $1,000, my parents still keep the trophy on display and share with unwitting visitors the videotape of my triumph. I realize now that I was able to put in such extensive effort because of my outlook on the award. I knew whether I won or lost, I would gain the experience of building a portfolio, becoming a skilled interviewee, working closely with my teachers, and meeting some incredible students.

While scholarships are primarily a source of funding for your education, approach them in the same way that you do your favorite sport or hobby. I also played for my school's tennis team—and lost just about every match. Yet, I continued because I enjoyed the sport and found the skills a challenge. If you approach your scholarships in this manner, you'll not only win more but have more fun as well. Treat them like a chore, and you'll hate every minute, neglecting to put in the effort required to win.

The bottom line is that if you are going to take the time to apply, you should take the time to win. The secrets, tips, and strategies in this book will put you within striking distance. Follow them and you'll win more and more often.

This book is unique in that it really is two books in one. Now that you know how to win, it's time to begin finding scholarships for which to put these strategies to use. The second half of this book is a complete listing of scholarships and awards and is indexed by various criteria so you can quickly find those that match your interests and qualifications. And, because we know you just can't get enough of us, we also encourage you to visit our website, SuperCollege.com, (www.supercollege.com), for the most up-to-date information on scholarships and financial aid.

We both wish you the best of luck.

A Special Request

Our books are grounded on the experiences of other students—both good and bad. Help us help more students by sharing your experiences.

Before you jump headlong into the wonderful world of scholarships we have a special request. We would love to hear about your experiences with scholarships and how this book has helped you. Please send us a note after you've finished raking in all of your free cash for college:

Gen and Kelly Tanabe
c/o SuperCollege.com
4546 B10 El Camino Real, #281
Los Altos, CA 94022

gen@supercollege.com
kelly@supercollege.com

Onward!

Let's fly! Flip the page and start finding scholarships to apply to and put all of the strategies and tips you've just learned to work for you!

Scholarship Directory

•••

A comprehensive directory to thousands of scholarships, grants, & contests. Includes:

- Over 400,000 awards
- Over $1.1 billion in prize money
- Awards for high school, undergraduate, & graduate students
- Complete index to help you find the scholarships that are right for you

•••

DIRECTORY

Welcome To Our Scholarship Directory

Our Scholarship Directory contains over 400,000 individual awards worth over $1.1 billion in prize money. Happy hunting!

It's time to employ all of the secrets, tips, and strategies that you learned in the first half of this book to help you actually apply for and win scholarships.

We've put together one of the most extensive directories of scholarships anywhere. In the pages that follow you will find over 400,000 individual awards that together add up to more than $1.1 billion in prize money.

To help you find the best scholarships, we have organized all awards by 77 general categories. As you browse these categories, keep in mind that scholarships often have detailed eligibility requirements. To help in your search, we have specified contact information, type of award, eligibility requirements, fields of study, deadlines, award amounts, number of awards, applications received, and odds of winning. If any information is missing, it was not provided by the awarding organization.

The Scholarship Indexes, which follow the Directory, group the awards by additional categories and criteria, giving you more ways to find scholarships that are right for you.

Use the Scholarship Indexes at the end of this Directory to search for scholarships that match your specific talents, interests, and background. The scholarships are organized into 21 different indexes.

The general scholarship categories are:

Academic/Leadership Ability
Accounting
Aerospace/Aeronautical Engineering
Agriculture
Allied Health
Animal Science/Veterinary Medicine
Architecture/Landscape Architecture
Athletic Ability
Automotive Studies
Biology
Business Administration/Management
Business/Corporate/Professional Affiliation
Chemistry
City/County of Residence
Civil/Environmental Engineering
Club Affiliation
Communications
Computer Science
Culinary Arts/Baking
Cultural Studies
Dentistry
Dietetics/Food Science/Nutrition
Disability
Drama/Theatre
Education-General
Engineering-General
English/Literature/Writing
Environmental Science
Fashion Design/Interior Decorating
Fine Arts
Fire Science
Foreign Languages
Forestry

Gender/Marital Status
Graphic Arts
History
Home Economics
Horticulture/Plant Sciences
Hospitality/Hospitality Administration
Humanities
Industrial/Manufacturing Engineering
Instrumental Music
Insurance
Journalism
Law
Library Science
Marine Science
Mechanical Engineering
Medicine
Military Affiliation
Military Science/ROTC
Mining/Metallurgical/Materials Engineering
Multiple Majors
Music-General
National Merit
Nuclear Engineering
Nursing
Optometry
Other
Pharmacy
Physical Sciences
Physical/Occupational Therapy
Psychology
Race/Ethnicity
Radio/TV Broadcasting
Real Estate
Religion/Theology/Philosophy
Religious Affiliation
Respiratory Therapy
Sciences-General
Speech/Forensics
State/Country of Residence
Transportation/Traffic Management
Union Affiliation
Vocational/Technical
Voice
Wildlife Resources/Management

Don't forget to use what you've learned in the first half of this book to prioritize the awards and select those that fit you and your background best. Spend the most time on those awards that you are most likely to win.

When using the Scholarship Indexes, once you find scholarships that match your interests, skills, and talents, go to the listings. Depending on the data provided by the awarding organization, you will find such useful information as the eligibility criteria, deadlines, number of awards given, amounts, and percentage of applicants who won an award.

Use the strategies in Chapter 2 to prioritize these awards and use the contact information to request an application. Wherever possible, we have tried to include website and email addresses to make your search easier and faster.

Happy hunting!

Academic/Leadership Ability

AMERICAN BOARD OF FUNERAL SERVICE EDUCATION (ABFSE)

38 Florida Avenue
Portland, ME 04103

#1 • ABFSE Scholarship

Type: Scholarship. Not renewable.
Eligibility: Applicant must have completed at least one semester of funeral service education in an ABFSE-accredited program and must be a U.S. citizen. This award must be used in the following years of study: • Junior • Senior
Field(s) Of Study: Funeral service.
Deadline: March 15; September 15.
Award Amount: $ 250 - $ 500.
Number Of Awards: 25 - 50.
Applications Received: 100.
Odds Of Winning: 50% of applicants on average receive an award each year.
Contact: Scholarships
Phone: 207-878-6530
Fax: 207-797-7686

ARKANSAS DEPARTMENT OF HIGHER EDUCATION

114 East Capitol
Little Rock, AR 72201
Phone: 501-371-2000
Fax: 501-371-2001
Email: finaid@adhe.arknet.edu
Website: http://www.adhe.arknet.edu

#2 • Arkansas Student Assistance Grant

Type: Grant. Not renewable.
Eligibility: Awarded by individual institutions based upon financial need. Applicant must attend an institution in Arkansas and complete FAFSA as application. This award must be used in the following years of study: • Freshman • Sophomore • Junior • Senior
Deadline: Determined by each institution.
Award Amount: $ 100 - $ 600.
Number Of Awards: 7,300.
Applications Received: 25,000.
Odds Of Winning: 30% of applicants on average receive an award each year.
Contact: Philip Axelroth, Assistant Coordinator of Financial Aid
Phone: 501-371-2052
Email: phila@adhe.arknet.edu

BARRY M. GOLDWATER SCHOLARSHIP AND EXCELLENCE IN EDUCATION FOUNDATION

6225 Brandon Avenue Suite 315
Springfield, VA 22150-2519
Phone: 703-756-6012
Fax: 703-756-6015
Email: goldh2o@erols.com
Website: http://www.act.org/goldwater

#3 • Barry M. Goldwater Scholarship and Excellence in Education Program

Type: Scholarship. Renewable.
Eligibility: Applicant must be a U.S. citizen, permanent resident, or resident alien who submits letter of intent to obtain U.S. citizenship, have a minimum "B" grade average, and rank in top quarter of class. Selection is based upon merit, outstanding potential, and intent to pursue career in mathematics, natural sciences, or engineering. This award must be used in the following years of study: • Junior • Senior
Field(s) Of Study: Engineering, mathematics, natural sciences.
Deadline: February 1.
Award Amount: $ 7,500.
Number Of Awards: 250.
Applications Received: 1,200.
Odds Of Winning: 22% of applicants on average receive an award each year.
Contact: Goldwater Faculty Representative on campus

BETA SIGMA PHI

1800 West 91st Place
P.O. Box 8500
Kansas City, MO 64114-0500
Phone: 816-444-6800
Fax: 816-333-6206
Email: service@betasigmaphi.org
Website: http://www.betasigmaphi.org

#4 • Walter and Dorothy Ross Memorial Scholarship

Type: Scholarship. Not renewable.
Eligibility: Applicant must be a child of a member or member of Beta Sigma Phi. Selection is based upon academic qualifications and civic involvement. Essay and letters of recommendation required. This award must be used in the following years of study: • Freshman • Sophomore • Junior • Senior • Masters • Doctoral • Other postgraduate level
Deadline: January 31.
Award Amount: $ 1,000.
Number Of Awards: 33.
Applications Received: 670.
Odds Of Winning: 5% of applicants on average receive an award each year.

Contact: Barbara Champion, Scholarship Coordinator

BOYS AND GIRLS CLUBS OF AMERICA

1230 West Peachtree Street, NW
Atlanta, GA 30309
Phone: 404-815-5762
Fax: 404-815-5789
Website: http://www.b&gca.org

#5 • National Youth of the Year Scholarship

Type: Scholarship. Not renewable.
Eligibility: Applicant must be a Boys and Girls Club member between the ages of 14 and 19. This award must be used in the following years of study: • Freshman
Deadline: Varies.
Award Amount: $ 2,000 - $ 8,000.
Number Of Awards: 5.
Applications Received: 750.
Odds Of Winning: Less than 1% of applicants on average receive an award each year.
Contact: Scholarship Committee

BRESCIA UNIVERSITY

717 Frederica Street
Owensboro, KY 42301-3023
Phone: 270-686-4290 or 800-264-1234
Fax: 270-686-4266
Email: vivianp@brescia.edu
Website: http://www.brescia.edu

#6 • Dean's Scholarship

Type: Scholarship. Renewable for four years if recipient maintains minimum 3.0 GPA and full-time enrollment.
Eligibility: Applicant must have a minimum 3.0 GPA, rank in the top quarter of secondary school class, and have a minimum ACT composite score of 21 (combined SAT I score of 970). This award must be used in the following years of study: • Freshman
Deadline: March 15.
Award Amount: $ 1,798. Partial Tuition. (One-fifth tuition).
Number Of Awards: 38.
Contact: Vivian J. Pearson, Director of Financial Aid

BUREAU OF HIGHER EDUCATION OPPORTUNITY PROGRAM/UTEA/ SCHOLARSHIPS

Room 1071 EBD
Albany, NY 12234
Phone: 518-486-1319
Fax: 518-486-5346

Email: heop1@higher.nysed.gov
Website: http://www.higher.nysed.gov/

#7 • Regents Professional Opportunity Scholarship

Type: Scholarship. Renewable.
Eligibility: Applicant must major in one of the licensed professions in New York state. Recipient must serve as a licensed professional in New York one year for each year award is received. This award must be used in the following years of study: • Freshman • Sophomore • Junior • Senior • Masters • Doctoral
Deadline: May 1.
Award Amount: $ 1,000 - $ 5,000.
Number Of Awards: 220.
Applications Received: 2,000.
Odds Of Winning: 9% of applicants on average receive an award each year.
Contact: See above.

CHINESE HISTORICAL SOCIETY OF SOUTHERN CALIFORNIA

ATTN: Scholarship Chair
P.O. Box 862647
Los Angeles, CA 90086-2647
Phone: 323-222-0856
Website: http://www.chssc.org

#8 • CHSSC Scholarship

Type: Scholarship. Not renewable.
Eligibility: Applicant must have a minimum 3.0 GPA and attend a school in Southern California. This award must be used in the following years of study: • Sophomore • Junior
Field(s) Of Study: Chinese-American studies in the humanities or social sciences.
Deadline: March 10.
Award Amount: $ 1,000.
Number Of Awards: 1.
Applications Received: 3.
Odds Of Winning: 33% of applicants on average receive an award each year.
Contact: Winifred L. Lew, Scholarship Chair

CITY UNIVERSITY OF NEW YORK, BARUCH COLLEGE

Undergraduate Admissions Office
Box 279, 17 Lexington Avenue
New York, NY 10010
Phone: 212-447-3750
Website: http://www.baruch.cuny.edu

#9 • Baruch Incentive Grant

Type: Scholarship. Renewable if recipient maintains minimum 3.3 GPA.

Eligibility: Applicant must have a minimum "85" grade average and a minimum combined SAT I score of 1200. Selection is based upon interview and two letters of recommendation. This award must be used in the following years of study: • Freshman • Sophomore • Junior • Senior
Deadline: Varies.
Award Amount: $ 500 - $ 1,000.
Number Of Awards: 80.
Odds Of Winning: 50% of applicants on average receive an award each year.
Contact: Hugo Morales, Scholarship Coordinator
Phone: 212-447-3753

COCA-COLA SCHOLARS FOUNDATION, INC.

P.O. Box 442
Atlanta, GA   30301-0442
Phone: 404-733-5420
Fax: 404-733-5439
Email: scholars@na.ko.com
Website: http://www.thecoca-colacompany.com

#10 • Coca-Cola Scholarship

Type: Scholarship. Renewable.
Eligibility: Applicant must be a U.S. citizen, U.S. national, U.S. permanent resident, temporary resident, refugee, asylee, Cuban-Haitian entrant, or a humanitarian parolee planning to pursue a degree at an accredited U.S. post-secondary institution, must have a minimum 3.0 GPA, and must be a high school senior who is graduating in the year of application. Selection is based upon leadership, character, and merit. Children and grandchildren of employees, officers, or owners of Coca-Cola bottling companies, divisions, or subsidiaries are not eligible. This award must be used in the following years of study: • Freshman
Deadline: Postmarked by October 31.
Award Amount: $ 4,000 - $20,000.
Number Of Awards: 250.
Applications Received: 137,000.
Contact: High School Guidance Counselor

COLLEGENET

Universal Algorithms, Inc.
One S.W. Columbia, Suite 100
Portland, OR   97258
Phone: 503-973-5200
Fax: 503-973-5252
Website: http://www.collegenet.com

#11 • CollegeNET Scholarship

Type: Scholarship. Not renewable.
Eligibility: Applicant must submit application for admission via CollegeNET and be accepted for full-time enrollment at one of the selected schools (List of schools can be found at http://www.collegenet.com). This award must be used in the following years of study: • Freshman • Sophomore • Junior • Senior • Masters • Doctoral • Other postgraduate level
Deadline: March 31.
Award Amount: $ 1,000 - $10,000.
Number Of Awards: 5.
Contact: Betty Chapman, Administration Manager
Email: bett@unival.com

COLORADO COMMISSION ON HIGHER EDUCATION

1300 Broadway 2nd Floor
Denver, CO   80203
Phone: 303-866-2723
Fax: 303-860-9750
Website: http://www.co.us/cche_dir/hecche.html

#12 • Colorado Student Incentive Grant

Type: Grant. Renewable.
Eligibility: Applicant must demonstrate substancial financial need. This award must be used in the following years of study: • Freshman • Sophomore • Junior • Senior
Deadline: Varies.
Award Amount: Varies.
Number Of Awards: Varies.
Contact: College Financial Aid Office

COMMUNITY FOUNDATION SERVING RICHMOND AND CENTRAL VIRGINIA

7325 Beaufort Springs Drive, Suite 210
Richmond, VA   23225-8470
Phone: 804-330-7400
Fax: 804-330-5992
Email: sdavis@tcfrichmond.org
Website: http://www.tcfrichmond.org

#13 • Raymond F. Burmester Endowment for Scholastic Achievement

Type: Scholarship. Not renewable.
Eligibility: Applicant must be a U.S. citizen, graduating from Northumberland High School (Heathsville, Va.), planning to enroll in a two- or four-year college or university in the continental U.S., and must demonstrate academic achievement and leadership or community service. This award must be used in the following years of study: • Freshman
Deadline: March 10.
Award Amount: $ 500 - $ 5,000.
Number Of Awards: 3.
Contact: Susan Brown Davis, Senior Program Officer
Email: sdavis@tcfrichmond.org

#14 • Mark Smith Neale II "Cross of Life" Scholarship

Type: Scholarship. Not renewable.
Eligibility: Applicant must be a male, U.S. citizen, graduating from West Point High School (Va.), planning to enroll in a two- or four-year college or university in the continental U.S., who is multitalented athlete participating in an average of three sports (at least two varsity sports during senior year) and an enthusiastic outdoorsman who has achieved a balance of love, work, play, and worship, and must demonstrate academic achievement, leadership, community service, and a commitment to school and worship. This award must be used in the following years of study: • Freshman
Deadline: March 10.
Award Amount: $ 500 - $ 5,000.
Number Of Awards: Varies.
Contact: Susan Brown Davis, Senior Program Officer
Email: sdavis@tcfrichmond.org

CONSTRUCTION EDUCATION FOUNDATION

1300 North Seventeenth Street
Rosslyn, VA 22209
Phone: 703-812-2000
Fax: 703-812-8235
Email: mccray@abc.org
Website: http://www.abc.org

#15 • Associated Builders and Contractors Scholarship

Type: Scholarship. Not renewable.
Eligibility: Applicant must have successfully completed at least one year of schooling in an associate or baccalaureate degree program in construction (other than a design discipline) by August 31, and be an active member of their school's ABC student chapter, if the school has one. Scholarships are awarded on the basis of financial need, academic performance, extracurricular activities, and employment experience. This award must be used in the following years of study: • Sophomore • Junior • Senior • Associate of Arts candidates who have completed their first year.
Field(s) Of Study: Construction education and research.
Deadline: June 1.
Award Amount: $ 500 - $ 2,000.
Number Of Awards: 14.
Applications Received: 180.
Odds Of Winning: 8% of applicants on average receive an award each year.
Contact: Deanna McCray, College Relations Manager

EAA AVIATION FOUNDATION, INC.

P.O. Box 3065
Oshkosh, WI 54903-3065
Phone: 920-426-4815
Fax: 920-426-6865
Email: education@eaa.org
Website: http://www.eaa.org

#16 • Friendship One Flight Training Scholarship

Type: Scholarship. Not renewable.
Eligibility: Applicant must have attended at least one resident aviation experiences for youth at the EAA Air Academy. This award must be used in the following years of study: • Freshman • Sophomore • Junior • Senior • Masters • Doctoral • Other postgraduate level
Field(s) Of Study: Commercial flight training, flight training, private pilot training.
Deadline: May 1.
Award Amount: $ 2,500 - $ 5,000.
Number Of Awards: 1 - 2.
Contact: Scholarship Coordinator
Phone: 920-426-6815

EDDIE G. ROBINSON FOUNDATION

P.O. Box 50609
Atlanta, GA 30302
Phone: 877-284-EGRF
Fax: 404-346-3292
Email: info@eddierobinson.com
Website: http://www.eddierobinson.com

#17 • Eddie G. Robinson Foundation High School Senior Scholarship

Type: Scholarship. Renewable for up to four years if recipient maintains good academic standing and remains chemically free.
Eligibility: Applicant must make a commitment to remain chemically free. Essay, letters of recommendation, standardized test scores, and transcript required. This award must be used in the following years of study: • Freshman
Deadline: February 16.
Award Amount: $ 5,000.
Number Of Awards: 2 - 4.
Contact: Cherie Kirkland, Associate Director

EDMUND F. MAXWELL FOUNDATION

P.O. Box 22537
Seattle, WA 98122-0537
Email: admin@maxwell.org
Website: http://www.maxwell.org

#18 • Edmund F. Maxwell Scholarship

Type: Scholarship. Renewable up to four years if recipient maintains a high level of academic achievement and has continued financial need.
Eligibility: Applicant must have a minimum combined SAT I score of 1200 and demonstrate financial need. Applicant must file FAFSA. Essay, official transcript, and employment history required. Applicants from Western Washington given preference. This award must be used in the following years of study: • Freshman • Sophomore • Junior • Senior
Deadline: April 30.
Award Amount: $ 900 - $ 3,500.
Number Of Awards: 35.
Applications Received: 180.
Odds Of Winning: 20% of applicants on average receive an award each year.
Contact: Jane Thomas, Administrator

EDUCATIONAL COMMUNICATIONS SCHOLARSHIP FOUNDATION

721 North McKinley Road
Lake Forest, IL 60045-5002
Phone: 847-295-6650   *512-440-2300*
Fax: 847-295-3972
Email: scholar@ecsf.org

#19 • Educational Communications Scholarship

Type: Scholarship. Not renewable.
Eligibility: Applicant must be a U.S. citizen, have a minimum grade average of "B," and have taken the ACT or SAT I. Selection is based upon GPA, test scores, leadership qualifications, work experience, and essay evaluation. Some consideration is given to financial need. Request for application, including the applicant's year in school, name of school, and approximate GPA, must be made by March 15. This award must be used in the following years of study: • Freshman
Deadline: May 31.
Award Amount: $ 1,000.
Number Of Awards: 200.
Contact: Assistant to the Chairman
721 North McKinley Road
Lake Forest, IL 60045
Email: scholar@ecsf.org

ELKS NATIONAL FOUNDATION

2750 North Lake View Avenue
Chicago, IL 60614-1889
Email: scholarship@elks.org
Website: http://www.elks.org

#20 • Elks National Foundation Most Valuable Student Award

Type: Scholarship. Not renewable.
Eligibility: Applicant must be a U.S. citizen, be a high school senior, reside within the jurisdiction of the B.P.O. Elks of the U.S.A., have a scholarship rating of 90%, and rank in top 5% of his or her class. Selection is based upon scholarship, leadership, and financial need. Applications are available on the internet in mid-October and from local lodges or the Elks National Foundation after November 1. This award must be used in the following years of study: • Freshman • Sophomore • Junior • Senior
Deadline: in January.
Award Amount: $ 1,000 - $ 7,500.
Number Of Awards: 500.
Contact: Jeannine Kunz, Scholarship Coordinator
Phone: 773-755-4732

Leadership & scholarship more heavily weighted than financial need.

ELON COLLEGE

2700 Campus Box
Elon College, NC 27244
Phone: 800-334-8448, extension 1
Fax: 336-538-3986
Website: http://www.elon.edu

#21 • Honors Fellow Scholarship

Type: Scholarship. Renewable for up to four years if recipient maintains satisfactory academic progress and participation in Honors Program.
Eligibility: Interview required of selected applicant. Recipient must participate in Honors Program. Selection is based upon GPA, class rank, standardized test scores, and course selection. This award must be used in the following years of study: • Freshman
Deadline: February 1.
Award Amount: $ 2,000 - $ 5,000.
Number Of Awards: 24.
Applications Received: 258.
Odds Of Winning: 9% of applicants on average receive an award each year.
Contact: Office of Admissions and Financial Planning

#22 • Isabella Cannon Leadership Fellows Scholarship

Type: Scholarship. Renewable for up to four years if recipient maintains satisfactory academic progress and participation in Isabella Cannon Leadership Program.
Eligibility: Applicant must be accepted for full-time enrollment. Selection is based upon exceptional high school leadership experience, academic achievement, and standardized test scores. Recipient must participate in leadership development program. This award must be used in the following years of study: • Freshman

Deadline: February 1.
Award Amount: $ 2,000.
Number Of Awards: 4.
Applications Received: 221.
Odds Of Winning: 2% of applicants on average receive an award each year.
Contact: Office of Admissions and Financial Planning

FEDERATION OF AMERICAN CONSUMERS AND TRAVELERS (FACT)

ATTN: Scholarship Program
P.O. Box 104
Edwardsville, IL 62025
Phone: 800-872-3228
Fax: 618-656-5369
Email: gmsfact@aol.com
Website: http://www.fact-org.org

#23 • FACT Continuing Education Scholarship

Type: Scholarship. Not renewable.
Eligibility: Applicant must be a FACT member or child or grandchild of a member. Award open to high school seniors, people who have graduated from high school four or more years ago and are now planning to enroll in an undergraduate college, university, or trade school program, and students currently enrolled in an undergraduate college, university, or trade school program. Selection is based upon academic involvement, student involvement, community involvement, and essay. This award must be used in the following years of study: • Freshman • Sophomore • Junior • Senior
Deadline: January 15.
Award Amount: $ 2,500 - $10,000.
Number Of Awards: 6 - 7.
Applications Received: 750.
Odds Of Winning: 1% of applicants on average receive an award each year.
Contact: Vicki Rolens, Managing Director

GEORGIA STUDENT FINANCE COMMISSION

2082 East Exchange Place Suite 200
Tucker, GA 30084
Phone: 770-724-9004 or 800-776-6878
Website: http://www.gsfc.org

#24 • Helping Outstanding Pupils Educationally (HOPE) Scholarship

Type: Scholarship. Renewable if recipient maintains minimum 3.0 GPA.
Eligibility: Applicant must have a minimum 3.0 GPA in core curriculum courses. This award must be used in the following years of study: • Freshman •

Sophomore • Junior • Senior
Deadline: Varies.
Award Amount: Full-tuition. Partial Tuition. Full tuition at public institutions, $3,000 at private institutions.
Number Of Awards: 140,000.
Contact: See above.

GOUGH SCHOLARSHIP FUND

ATTN: J. David Gough, Fund Administrator
CMR 443, Box 655
APO AE, TN 09096
Phone: 011-49 6122 935424 (Germany)
Email: goughd@wiesbaden.vistec.net

#25 • Gough Family Scholarship

Type: Scholarship. Renewable. Recipient must reapply for renewal.
Eligibility: Applicants must submit an essay of no longer than three typed pages on why they deserve the scholarship and for what they intend to use their education in the future. This award must be used in the following years of study: • Freshman • Sophomore • Junior • Senior • Masters • Doctoral • Other postgraduate level • technical programs beyond high school
Deadline: March 20; June 20; September 20; December 20.
Award Amount: $ 1,000.
Number Of Awards: 2 - 4.
Contact: Dave Gough, Fund Administrator

HUMANE SOCIETY OF THE UNITED STATES

New England Regional Office
P.O. Box 619
Jacksonville, VT 05342
Phone: 802-368-2790
Fax: 802-368-2756
Website: http://www.hsus.org

#26 • Shaw-Worth Memorial Scholarship

Type: Scholarship. Not renewable.
Eligibility: Applicant must have made a meaningful contribution to animal protection over a significant period of time. Applications are in essay format. This award must be used in the following years of study: • Freshman
Deadline: March 15.
Award Amount: $ 1,000.
Number Of Awards: 1.
Applications Received: 50.
Contact: Hillary Twining, Program Specialist

ILLINOIS STUDENT ASSISTANCE COMMISSION/CLIENT SUPPORT SERVICES

1755 Lake Cook Road
Deerfield, IL 60015-5209
Phone: 800-899-ISAC or 847-948-8550
Website: http://www.isac1.org

#27 • Illinois Incentive for Access

Type: Grant. Not renewable.
Eligibility: Applicant must demonstrate financial need, complete FAFSA, and attend an approved Illinois school. This award must be used in the following years of study: • Freshman
Deadline: October 1.
Award Amount: $ 500.
Number Of Awards: 20,200.
Applications Received: 46,000.
Odds Of Winning: 41% of applicants on average receive an award each year.
Contact: Client Relations

#28 • Student to Student Program of Matching Grants

Type: Grant. Not renewable.
Eligibility: Applicant must attend a participating Illinois school and demonstrate financial need. This award must be used in the following years of study: • Freshman • Sophomore • Junior • Senior
Deadline: October 1.
Award Amount: $ 1,000.
Number Of Awards: 3,300.
Contact: Client Relations

#29 • Higher Education License Plate Program (HELP)

Type: Grant. Not renewable.
Eligibility: Applicant must attend a participating school and demonstrate financial need. This award must be used in the following years of study: • Freshman • Sophomore • Junior • Senior
Deadline: October 1.
Award Amount: $ 2,000.
Number Of Awards: Varies.
Contact: Client Relations

#30 • Illinois College Savings Bond Bonus Incentive Grant (BIG)

Type: Grant. Not renewable.
Eligibility: Applicant must hold an Illinois College Savings Bond and attend an approved Illinois school. This award must be used in the following years of study: • Freshman • Sophomore • Junior • Senior • Masters • Doctoral • Other postgraduate level
Deadline: May 30.
Award Amount: $ 260.
Number Of Awards: 1,300.

#31 • Grant Program for Descendents of Police, Fire, or Correctional Officers

Type: Grant. Renewable.
Eligibility: Applicant must be the descendent of a police, fire, or correctional officer killed or disabled in the line of duty and attend an approved Illinois school. This award must be used in the following years of study: • Freshman • Sophomore • Junior • Senior • Masters • Doctoral • Other postgraduate level
Deadline: Varies.
Award Amount: Varies.
Number Of Awards: 30.
Contact: Client Relations

JOHN F. KENNEDY UNIVERSITY

12 Altarinda Road
Orinda, CA 94563
Phone: 925-254-0200
Website: http://www.jfku.edu

#32 • John F. Kennedy University Scholarship

Type: Scholarship. Renewable. Reapplication and satisfactory academic progress required for renewal.
Eligibility: Applicant must prove financial need. This award must be used in the following years of study: • Junior • Senior • Masters • Doctoral
Deadline: March 2.
Award Amount: $ 250 - $ 2,000.
Number Of Awards: 25 - 40.
Applications Received: 400.
Odds Of Winning: 10% of applicants on average receive an award each year.
Contact: Mindy Bergeron, Director of Financial Aid
Phone: 925-258-2385
Fax: 925-258-2266
Email: finaid@jfku.edu

LYNCHBURG COLLEGE

1501 Lakeside Drive
Lynchburg, VA 24501
Phone: 804-544-8228
Fax: 804-544-8653
Email: snow_s@mail.lynchburg.edu
Website: http://www.lynchburg.edu

#33 • Academic Merit Award

Type: Scholarship. Renewable if required GPA is maintained.
Eligibility: Selection based upon applicant's academic ability. This award must be used in the following years of study: • Freshman • Sophomore • Junior • Senior
Deadline: Varies.
Award Amount: $ 3,000 - $10,000.
Number Of Awards: Varies.
Contact: Sarah Snow, Coordinator of Financial Aid

MANPOWER FOUNDATION INCORPORATED

Program Scholarship Coordinator
5301 North Ironwood Road
Milwaukee, WI 53201
Phone: 414-906-6355
Fax: 414-906-7951
Email: carolyn.cockroft-smith@na.manpower.com
Website: http://www.manpower.com

#34 • Manpower Foundation Scholarship

Type: Scholarship. Not renewable.
Eligibility: High school senior applicants must be under age 21, enrolling in an accredited institution, and have a minimum 3.0 GPA. Undergraduate applicants must be under age 25, enrolled full time at an accredited institution, and have a minimum 3.0 GPA. All applicants must be children of full-time staff employees of Manpower or its subsidiaries or franchises. This award must be used in the following years of study: • Freshman • Sophomore • Junior • Senior
Deadline: March 15.
Award Amount: $ 2,000.
Number Of Awards: 35.
Contact: Carolyn Cockroft-Smith, Human Resources Coordinator/Scholarship Coordinator

MARY BALDWIN COLLEGE

Staunton, VA 24401
Phone: 540-887-7022
Website: http://www.mbc.edu

#35 • Wilson Grant

Type: Grant. Renewable if recipient maintains satisfactory academic progress.
Eligibility: Contact for details. This award must be used in the following years of study: • Freshman
Deadline: Varies.
Award Amount: $ 2,000 - $ 7,000.
Number Of Awards: Varies.
Contact: Jacquelyn D. Elliott-Wonderly, Associate Dean of Admission
Phone: 540-887-7019
Fax: 540-886-6634
Email: jelliott@mbc.edu

MASSACHUSETTS COLLEGE OF LIBERAL ARTS

375 Church Street
North Adams, MA 01247
Phone: 413-662-5410 or 800-292-6632
Fax: 413-662-5179
Email: admissions@mcla.mass.edu
Website: http://www.mcla.mass.edu

#36 • Academic Recognition Scholarship

Type: Scholarship. Renewable if recipient maintains a minimum 3.0 GPA.
Eligibility: Selection is based upon GPA and standardized test scores. Transfer applicants must have at least 45 credit hours with a minimum 3.25 GPA. This award must be used in the following years of study: • Freshman • transfers
Deadline: Varies.
Award Amount: $ 500 - $ 3,500.
Number Of Awards: 82.
Applications Received: 943.
Odds Of Winning: 9% of applicants on average receive an award each year.
Contact: Denise Richardello, Dean of Enrollment Management
Fax: 413-662-5179
Email: admissions@mcla.mass.edu

MISS OUTSTANDING TEENAGER SCHOLARSHIP PROGRAM

P.O. Box 9267
Helena, MT 59604
Phone: 406-442-7035
Fax: 406-443-7322
Email: teenscholarship@missoutstandingteen.com
Website: http://www.missoutstandingteen.com

#37 • Miss Outstanding Teenager

Type: Contest. Renewable for up to four years.
Eligibility: Applicant must be a girl aged 13-18 with at least a 3.0 GPA. This award must be used in the following years of study: • Freshman • Sophomore • Junior • Senior
Deadline: Varies.
Award Amount: $ 500 - $10,000.
Number Of Awards: 1 - 8.
Applications Received: 200.
Odds Of Winning: 10% of applicants on average receive an award each year.
Contact: Mark M. Budak, Director/Founder
Phone: 406-442-7035
Fax: 406-443-7322
Email: teenscholarship@missoutstandingteen.com

NATIONAL ACADEMY OF AMERICAN SCHOLARS (NAAS)

1249 S. Diamond Bar Boulevard
PMB #325
Diamond Bar, CA 91765-4122
Phone: 909-621-6856
Email: staff@naas.org
Website: http://www.naas.org

#38 • Easley National Scholarship

Type: Scholarship. Renewable. Minimum 3.0 GPA or grade average of "B" and full-time enrollment are required to retain scholarship.
Eligibility: Applicant must be a U.S. citizen or permanent resident with a minimum 2.0 GPA who plans to attend an accredited four-year institution. Applicant must take SAT I or ACT. Home-schooled applicants may be accepted on a case-by-case basis. Selection is based upon scholastic excellence and outstanding character. Send self-addressed stamped envelope (#10) with a $2.00 handling fee for application and information packet. This award must be used in the following years of study: • Freshman
Deadline: February 1.
Award Amount: $ 200 - $10,000.
Number Of Awards: 13.
Contact: Scholarship Committee

#39 • NAAS II National Scholarship

Type: Scholarship. Renewable if recipient maintains full-time enrollment and a minimum 3.0 GPA or grade average of "B".
Eligibility: Applicant must be a U.S. citizen or permanent resident pursuing a four-year degree full time at an accredited four-year institution and must have a minimum grade average of "C." Selection is based upon scholastic excellence and outstanding character. Send self-addressed stamped envelope (#10) with a $2.00 handling fee for application and information packet. This award must be used in the following years of study: • Sophomore • Junior
Deadline: March 1.
Award Amount: $ 1,000 - $ 3,000.
Number Of Awards: 1.
Contact: Merit Committee

NATIONAL ALLIANCE FOR EXCELLENCE, INC.

20 Thomas Avenue
Shrewsbury, NJ 07702
Phone: 732-747-0028
Fax: 732-842-2962
Email: info@excellence.org
Website: http://www.excellence.org

#40 • Honored Scholars and Artists Program

Type: Scholarship. Not renewable.
Eligibility: Applicant must be a U.S. citizen, have a minimum 3.7 GPA, have taken the SAT I and received written results prior to application (minimum combined SAT I score of 1300, demonstrate outstanding academic achievement or excel in the visual/performing arts, and pursue full-time study at an accredited U.S. institution or participate in an approved foreign exchange program. Financial need is not considered.

SAT I scores are not considered in visual/performing arts categories. Send self-addressed, stamped envelope with application request. This award must be used in the following years of study: • Freshman • Sophomore • Junior • Senior • Masters • Doctoral • returning students
Deadline: None.
Award Amount: $ 1,000 - $ 5,000.
Number Of Awards: 50.
Applications Received: 7,000.
Odds Of Winning: 1% of applicants on average receive an award each year.
Contact: Linda Paras, President

NATIONAL ASSOCIATION OF SECONDARY SCHOOL PRINCIPALS (NASSP)

1904 Association Drive
Reston, VA 20191

#41 • National Honor Society Scholarship

Type: Scholarship. Not renewable.
Eligibility: Applicant must be a high school senior who has been nominated by his or her local chapter. Each National Honor Society chapter may nominate two applicants based on leadership, scholarship, character, and service. Contact your local National Honor Society advisor for further information. This award must be used in the following years of study: • Freshman
Deadline: January 29.
Award Amount: $ 1,000.
Number Of Awards: 250.
Contact: Local Chapter Advisor

#42 • Principal's Leadership Award

Type: Scholarship. Not renewable.
Eligibility: Applicant must be a student leader and rank in the top fifth of his or her class. This award must be used in the following years of study: • Freshman
Deadline: December 11.
Award Amount: $ 1,000.
Number Of Awards: 150.
Contact: Principal or Guidance Counselor

NATIONAL BLACK POLICE ASSOCIATION

3251 Mount Pleasant Street, NW
Washington, DC 20010-2103
Phone: 202-986-2070
Fax: 202-986-0410

#43 • Alphonso Deal Scholarship

Type: Scholarship. Not renewable.
Eligibility: Contact for details. This award must be used in the following years of study: • Freshman
Deadline: June 1.
Award Amount: $ 500.
Number Of Awards: 2.
Applications Received: 700.
Odds Of Winning: Less than 1% of applicants on average receive an award each year.
Contact: Scholarship Committee

NATIONAL TOURISM FOUNDATION (NTF)

546 East Main Street
Lexington, KY 40508
Phone: 800-682-8886
Fax: 606-226-4414
Email: scudderb@mgtserv.com
Website: http://www.ntaonline.com

#44 • Eric and Bette Friedheim Scholarship

Type: Scholarship. Not renewable.
Eligibility: Applicant must have at least a 3.0 GPA. Applicants must submit an NTF scholarship application, two recommendation letters (one from a tourism-related faculty member and the other from a professional in the tourism industry), a resume, college transcripts, and an essay. This award must be used in the following years of study: • Junior • Senior
Field(s) Of Study: Travel/tourism.
Deadline: April 15.
Award Amount: $ 500.
Number Of Awards: 1.
Contact: Brooks A. Scudder, Assistant Executive Director

NEWMAN UNIVERSITY

3100 McCormick Avenue
Wichita, KS 67213
Phone: 316-942-4291
Website: http://www.ksnewman.edu

#45 • Dean's Scholarship

Type: Scholarship. Renewable if recipient maintains a minimum 3.25 GPA and full-time enrollment.
Eligibility: Applicant must have a minimum 3.0 GPA and minimum composite ACT score of 21 (combined SAT 1 score of 1100). This award must be used in the following years of study: • Freshman
Deadline: Varies.
Award Amount: $ 2,500.
Number Of Awards: Varies.
Contact: Marla McClure, Director of Financial Aid
Phone: 316-942-4291, extension 103
Fax: 316-942-4483
Email: mcclurem@ksnewman.edu

OHIO NORTHERN UNIVERSITY

525 South Main Street
Ada, OH 45810
Phone: 419-772-2272
Fax: 419-772-2313
Email: financial-aid@onu.edu
Website: http://www.onu.edu

#46 • Dean's Scholarship

Type: Scholarship. Renewable if recipient maintains a minimum 3.0 GPA after freshman year (3.3 GPA thereafter).
Eligibility: Applicant must have a minimum 3.3 GPA and a minimum composite ACT score of 25 (combined SAT I score of 1150). This award must be used in the following years of study: • Freshman
Deadline: April 15.
Award Amount: $ 4,000 - $10,000.
Number Of Awards: 290.
Applications Received: 1,400.
Odds Of Winning: 21% of applicants on average receive an award each year.
Contact: Wendell A. Schick, Director of Financial Aid

OLIN L. LIVESEY SCHOLARSHIP FUND

3538 Central Avenue, Suite 2A
Riverside, CA 92506
Phone: 909-684-6778
Email: scholars@urs2.net
Website: http://www.scholarshipsite.org

#47 • Olin L. Livesey Scholarship

Type: Scholarship. Not renewable.
Eligibility: Applicant must have a minimum 2.0 GPA and a minimum combined SAT I score of 850. Applicant must submit a completed application, letters of recommendation, and a resume (optional). Finalists (who are the top 5% of the preliminary group) are chosen in each category and notified by July 1 of each year. Finalists are then requested to submit further materials which include IRS forms, transcripts, a letter of acceptance, a processing fee, and a statement of financial need. This award must be used in the following years of study: • Freshman
Deadline: June 1 (preliminary applications), July 10 (finalists).
Award Amount: $ 100 - $10,000.
Number Of Awards: 100 - 500.
Applications Received: 67,473.
Odds Of Winning: 1% of applicants on average receive an award each year.
Contact: Executive Director

PUBLIC EMPLOYEES ROUNDTABLE

P.O. Box 75248
Washington, DC 20013-5248

Phone: 202-927-4926
Fax: 202-927-4920
Email: per@theroundtable.org
Website: http:www.theroundtable.org/

#48 • Public Employees Public Service Scholarship

Type: Scholarship. Not renewable.
Eligibility: Applicant must plan to enter public service and be enrolled in a four-year program with a minimum 3.5 GPA. Self-addressed, stamped envelope must be included to receive an application. Application may be downloaded from webpage. This award must be used in the following years of study: • Sophomore • Junior • Senior • Masters • Doctoral
Deadline: May 19.
Award Amount: $ 500 - $ 1,000.
Number Of Awards: 12.
Applications Received: 200.
Odds Of Winning: 4% of applicants on average receive an award each year.
Contact: Irma D. Salley, Program Coordinator

SOCIETY FOR RANGE MANAGEMENT

Office of the Executive Vice President
445 Union Boulevard, Suite 230
Lakewood, CO 80228-1259
Phone: 303-986-3309
Email: srmden@ix.netcom.com
Website: http://www.srm.org

#49 • Masonic Range Science Scholarship

Type: Scholarship. Not renewable.
Eligibility: Applicant must be sponsored by a member of the Society for Range Management, the National Association of Soil and Water Consevation Districts, or the Soil and Water Conservation committee, and submit two referral letters, transcripts, and standardized test scores. This award must be used in the following years of study: • Freshman • Sophomore
Field(s) Of Study: Range science.
Deadline: January 15.
Award Amount: $ 1,400.
Number Of Awards: 1.
Contact: Scholarship Committee

SOUTH DAKOTA RETAILERS ASSOCIATION (SDRA)

P.O. Box 638
Pierre, SD 57501
Phone: 800-658-5545
Fax: 605-224-2059
Email: dleslie@sdra.org
Website: http://www.sdra.org

#50 • SDRA Scholarship

Type: Scholarship. Renewable. Recipient must reapply for renewal.
Eligibility: Applicant must attend an institution in South Dakota and submit an essay, employment history, and letters of recomendation. This award must be used in the following years of study: • Sophomore • Junior • Senior • Other postgraduate level
Field(s) Of Study: Retail.
Deadline: May 10.
Award Amount: $ 500 - $ 1,000.
Number Of Awards: 5.
Applications Received: 30.
Odds Of Winning: 16% of applicants on average receive an award each year.
Contact: Donna Leslie, Communications Director

ST. DAVID'S SOCIETY OF THE STATE OF NEW YORK

47 Fifth Avenue
New York, NY 10003
Phone: 212-397-1346

#51 • St. David's Society of the State of New York Scholarship

Type: Grant. Renewable.
Eligibility: Applicant must be from a Welsh background or in Welsh studies. This award must be used in the following years of study: • Sophomore • Junior • Senior • Masters • Doctoral • Other postgraduate level
Deadline: May 30.
Award Amount: $ 250 - $ 1,500.
Number Of Awards: 12.
Contact: See above.

ST. JOHN'S UNIVERSITY

8000 Utopia Parkway
Jamaica, NY 11439
Phone: 718-990-6161
Fax: 718-990-5945
Website: http://www.stjohns.edu

#52 • Academic Merit Scholarship

Type: Scholarship. Renewable if recipient maintains a minimum 3.0 GPA through freshman year, a minimum 3.1 GPA through sophomore year, and a minimum 3.2 GPA through junior year.
Eligibility: Contact for details. This award must be used in the following years of study: • Freshman
Deadline: Varies.
Award Amount: $ 4,083.
Number Of Awards: 1,023.
Contact: Jorge L. Rodriguez, Assistant Vice President and Executive Director of Financial Aid

Phone: 718-990-6403
Fax: 718-990-5945

TELACU EDUCATION FOUNDATION

5400 East Olympic Boulevard, Suite 300
Los Angeles, CA 90022
Phone: 323-721-1655
Fax: 323-724-3372
Website: http://www.telacu.com

#53 • TELACU/Cesar Chavez Award

Type: Scholarship. Not renewable.
Eligibility: Applicant must come from a low-income household, be a first-generation college student, have a minimum 2.5 GPA, and must be a U.S. citizen or permanent resident and a permanent resident of unincorporated East Los Angeles, City of Los Angeles, Bell Gardens, Commerce, Huntington Park, Montebello, Monterey Park, or South Gate. This award must be used in the following years of study: • Freshman • Sophomore • Junior • Senior
Deadline: April 1.
Award Amount: $ 2,500.
Number Of Awards: 1.
Applications Received: 20.
Odds Of Winning: 5% of applicants on average receive an award each year.
Contact: Michael E. Alvarado, Scholarship Program Director

U.S. JAYCEE WAR MEMORIAL FUND (JWMF)

P.O. Box 7
Tulsa, OK 74102-0007

#54 • U.S. Jaycee War Memorial Fund Scholarship

Type: Scholarship. Not renewable.
Eligibility: Applicant must be a U.S. citizen and demonstrate leadership, potential for academic success, and financial need. Request application by February 1 with a $5 application fee and self-addressed, business-sized stamped envelope. This award must be used in the following years of study: • Freshman • Sophomore • Junior • Senior • Masters • Doctoral
Deadline: February 1 (priority).
Award Amount: $ 1,000 - $ 5,000.
Number Of Awards: 26.
Applications Received: 3,800.
Odds Of Winning: Less than 1% of applicants on average receive an award each year.
Contact: JWMF Scholarship Administrator
Department 94922
Tulsa, OK 74194-0001

Phone: 918-584-2481
Fax: 918-584-4422

U.S. JUNIOR CHAMBER OF COMMERCE

4 West 21st Street
Tulsa, OK 74114-1116

#55 • Jaycee War Memorial Fund Scholarship (JWMF)

Type: Scholarship. Not renewable.
Eligibility: Applicant must be a U.S. citizen, possess academic potential and leadership traits, and show financial need. Enclose a self-addressed, business-sized, stamped envelope and a $5 application fee (check or money order made payable to JWMF) with request between July 1 and February 1. This award must be used in the following years of study: • Freshman • Sophomore • Junior • Senior • Masters • Doctoral
Deadline: March 1.
Award Amount: $ 1,000.
Number Of Awards: 25.
Contact: Jaycee War Memorial Fund (JWMF) Scholarship
Department 94922
Tulsa, OK 77194-0001

VENTURA COUNTY COMMUNITY FOUNDATION

1317 Del Norte Road, Suite 150
Camarillo, CA 93010
Phone: 805-988-0196
Fax: 805-485-5537

#56 • Vicky Howard Community Service Award

Type: Scholarship. Not renewable.
Eligibility: Applicant must show high dedication to community service. This award must be used in the following years of study: • Freshman
Deadline: Varies.
Award Amount: $ 500.
Number Of Awards: 1.
Applications Received: 9.
Odds Of Winning: 11% of applicants on average receive an award each year.
Contact: Gail Brown, Program Director

#57 • Sage Scholarship

Type: Scholarship. Not renewable.
Eligibility: Award must be used at a Ventura County, Calif. school. This award must be used in the following years of study: • Freshman
Deadline: Varies.
Award Amount: $ 1,000 - $ 1,500.
Number Of Awards: 3.

Applications Received: 37.
Contact: Gail Brown, Program Director

#58 • Salik Omar Shah Scholarship

Type: Scholarship. Not renewable.
Eligibility: Applicant must be a graduate from the Oxnard, Calif., school district. This award must be used in the following years of study: • Freshman
Deadline: March 9.
Award Amount: $ 1,000.
Number Of Awards: 1.
Applications Received: 4.
Odds Of Winning: 25% of applicants on average receive an award each year.
Contact: Gail Brown, Program Director

#59 • Laura Duval Toomey Saticoy Poinsettia Club Scholarship

Type: Scholarship. Renewable.
Eligibility: Applicant must have attended a Ventura County, Calif., high school and college. This award must be used in the following years of study: • Freshman • Sophomore
Deadline: March 9.
Award Amount: $ 500 - $ 1,400.
Number Of Awards: 1.
Applications Received: 26.
Odds Of Winning: 4% of applicants on average receive an award each year.
Contact: Gail Brown, Program Director

WAL-MART FOUNDATION

702 South West Eighth Street
Bentonville, AR 72716
Phone: 800-530-9925
Fax: 501-273-6850
Website: http://www.wal-mart.com

#60 • Sam Walton Community Scholarship

Type: Scholarship. Not renewable.
Eligibility: Selection is based upon community involvement, academic record, test scores, transcript, personal interview, and essay. This award must be used in the following years of study: • Freshman
Deadline: February.
Award Amount: $ 1,000.
Number Of Awards: 1,500 - 2,000.
Contact: Counselor or personnel manager at local Wal-Mart store

WASHINGTON AND JEFFERSON COLLEGE

60 South Lincoln Street
Washington, PA 15301
Phone: 724-223-6019
Email: nsninsky@washjeff.edu
Website: http://www.washjeff.edu

#61 • Dean's Award

Type: Scholarship. Renewable if recipient maintains a minimum 2.8 GPA.
Eligibility: Selection is based upon academic promise, extracurricular activities, and good citizenship. This award must be used in the following years of study: • Freshman
Deadline: Varies.
Award Amount: $ 3,000.
Number Of Awards: 15.
Contact: Nancy R. Sninsky, Director of Financial Aid

WISCONSIN HIGHER EDUCATIONAL AIDS BOARD

P.O. Box 7885
Madison, WI 53707
Phone: 608-267-2206
Fax: 608-267-2808
Email: HEABmail@heab.state.wi.us
Website: http://heab.state.wi.us

#62 • Academic Excellence Scholarship

Type: Scholarship. Renewable.
Eligibility: Applicant must be a Wisconsin resident enrolled full-time at a University of Wisconsin campus, Wisconsin Technical College, or independent Wisconsin institution. Applicant must have the highest GPA in his or her class. This award must be used in the following years of study: • Freshman • Sophomore • Junior • Senior
Deadline: Varies.
Award Amount: $ 2,250.
Number Of Awards: 2,586.
Contact: Alice Winters, Program Coordinator
Phone: 608-267-2213
Email: alice.winters@heab.state.wi.us

Accounting

AMERICAN SOCIETY OF WOMEN ACCOUNTANTS (ASWA)

60 Revere Drive Suite 500
Northbrook, IL 60062
Phone: 847-205-1029
Fax: 847-480-9282
Email: aswa@aswa.org
Website: http://www.aswa.org

#63 • ASWA Scholarship

Type: Scholarship. Not renewable.
Eligibility: Applicant must be a female, have a minimum 3.0 GPA, have completed at least 60 semester

hours, and demonstrate financial need. This award must be used in the following years of study: • Junior • Senior • Masters • Doctoral
Field(s) Of Study: Accounting.
Deadline: March 15.
Award Amount: $ 2,000 - $ 4,500.
Number Of Awards: 3 - 6.
Applications Received: 53.
Odds Of Winning: 11% of applicants on average receive an award each year.
Contact: Local Chapter Scholarships

EDUCATION FOUNDATION FOR WOMEN IN ACCOUNTING

60 Revere Drive, Suite 500
Northbrook, IL 60062
Phone: 800-326-2163
Fax: 847-480-9282
Email: aswa@aswa.org
Website: http://www.aswa.org

#64 • American Society of Woman Accountants Scholarship

Type: Scholarship. Not renewable.
Eligibility: Applicant must be a woman and have completed a minimum of 60 semester hours or 90 quarter hours. Career goals, communication skills, financial need, GPA, and personal circumstances are considered. This award must be used in the following years of study: • Senior • Masters • Doctoral • Other postgraduate level
Field(s) Of Study: Accounting.
Deadline: March 1.
Award Amount: $ 2,500.
Number Of Awards: 6.
Contact: See above.

KENTUCKY SOCIETY OF CERTIFIED PUBLIC ACCOUNTANTS

ATTN: Educational Foundation
1735 Alliant Avenue
Louisville, KY 40299-6326
Phone: 502-266-5272
Fax: 502-261-9512
Email: kycpa@kycpa.org
Website: http://www.kycpa.org

#65 • KSCPA High School Scholarship

Type: Scholarship. Not renewable.
Eligibility: Award may be used at Kentucky colleges or universities only. This award must be used in the following years of study: • Freshman
Field(s) Of Study: Accounting.
Deadline: March 1.
Award Amount: $ 500 - $ 500.
Number Of Awards: 10.

Applications Received: 200.
Odds Of Winning: 5% of applicants on average receive an award each year.
Contact: Dianna Ott, Public Relations Manager

MARYLAND ASSOCIATION OF CERTIFIED PUBLIC ACCOUNTANTS EDUCATIONAL FOUNDATION

P.O. Box 4417
Lutherville, MD 21094-4417
Phone: 410-296-6250
Fax: 410-296-8713
Website: http://www.macpa.org

#66 • Maryland Association of Certified Public Accountants Educational Foundation Scholarship

Type: Scholarship. Renewable. Recipient must reapply for renewal.
Eligibility: Applicant must be a Maryland resident with a minimum 3.0 GPA, must have completed courses in accounting principles I and II, plan to take the CPA exam, and show financial need. Student aid report and transcripts required This award must be used in the following years of study: • Junior • Senior • Masters
Field(s) Of Study: Accounting.
Deadline: April 15.
Award Amount: $ 1,000.
Number Of Awards: 23.
Applications Received: 40.
Odds Of Winning: 58% of applicants on average receive an award each year.
Contact: Margaret DeRoose, Accounts Clerk
Email: mderoose@mcpa.org

NATIONAL SOCIETY OF ACCOUNTANTS (NSA) SCHOLARSHIP FOUNDATION

1010 North Fairfax Street
Alexandria, VA 22314-1574
Phone: 703-549-6400
Fax: 703-549-2984
Website: http://www.nsacct.org

#67 • NSA Scholarship Award

Type: Scholarship. Not renewable.
Eligibility: Applicant must be a U.S. or Canadian citizen with a minimum grade average of "B" in a degree program at an accredited U.S. college or university. This award must be used in the following years of study: • Sophomore • Junior • Senior
Field(s) Of Study: Accounting.
Deadline: March 10.
Award Amount: $ 500 - $ 1,000.
Number Of Awards: 40.
Applications Received: 1,430.

Odds Of Winning: 3% of applicants on average receive an award each year.
Contact: Susan E. Noell, Foundation Director

NEW YORK STATE SOCIETY OF CERTIFIED PUBLIC ACCOUNTANTS

ATTN: Foundation for Accounting Information
530 Fifth Avenue, Fifth Floor
New York, NY 10036
Phone: 212-719-8300
Fax: 212-719-3364
Email: sparanandi@nysscpa.org
Website: http://www.nysscpa.org

#68 • Excellence in Accounting Scholarship

Type: Scholarship. Renewable if recipient maintains a minimum 3.0 GPA.
Eligibility: Contact for details. This award must be used in the following years of study: • Sophomore • students who have completed at least 60 credits
Field(s) Of Study: Accounting.
Deadline: April 1.
Award Amount: $ 1,500.
Number Of Awards: 70.
Applications Received: 100.
Odds Of Winning: 75% of applicants on average receive an award each year.
Contact: Joyce Lewis, Education Manager
Phone: 212-719-8379
Fax: 212-719-3364
Email: jlewis@nysscpa.org

Aerospace/Aeronautical Engineering

AIR TRAFFIC CONTROL ASSOCIATION, INC.

2300 Clarendon Boulevard Suite 711
Arlington, VA 22201
Phone: 703-522-5717
Fax: 703-527-7251
Email: atca@worldnet.att.net
Website: http://www.afca.org

#69 • Half to Full-time Student Scholarship

Type: Scholarship. Not renewable.
Eligibility: Applicant must be a U.S. citizen. Selection based on academic performance and financial need. This award must be used in the following years of study: • Freshman • Sophomore • Junior • Senior • Masters • Doctoral
Field(s) Of Study: Aerospace, aviation.

Deadline: May 1.
Award Amount: $ 1,500 - $ 2,500.
Number Of Awards: 6.
Applications Received: 350.
Odds Of Winning: Less than 1% of applicants on average receive an award each year.
Contact: Vice President of Operations and Training, James L. Crook

AIRCRAFT ELECTRONICS ASSOCIATION (AEA) EDUCATIONAL FOUNDATION

4217 S. Hocker Drive
Independence, MO 64055
Phone: 816-373-6565
Fax: 816-478-3100
Email: info@aea.net
Website: http://www.aea.net

#70 • Garmin Scholarship

Type: Scholarship. Not renewable.
Eligibility: Contact for details. This award must be used in the following years of study: • Freshman • Sophomore • Junior • Senior
Field(s) Of Study: Avionics, aircraft repair.
Deadline: February 15.
Award Amount: $ 2,000.
Number Of Awards: 1.
Applications Received: 150.
Odds Of Winning: 1% of applicants on average receive an award each year.
Contact: Mike Adamson, AEA Educational Foundation Executive Director

AMERICAN INSTITUTE OF AERONAUTICS AND ASTRONAUTICS (AIAA)

Student Programs Department
1801 Alexander Bell Drive Suite 500
Reston, VA 22091
Phone: 703-264-7500
Fax: 703-264-7551
Email: custserv@aiaa.org
Website: http://www.aiaa.org

#71 • AIAA Undergraduate Scholarship

Type: Scholarship. Renewable. Reapplication and minimum 3.0 GPA required to retain scholarship.
Eligibility: Selection is based upon academic credentials, career goals, recommendations, and extracurricular activities. Applicant must be a U.S. citizen or permanent resident, have a minimum 3.0 GPA, and major in some field of science or engineering encompassed by the technical activities of the AIAA. This award must be used in the following years of study: • Sophomore • Junior • Senior

Field(s) Of Study: Aeronautical engineering, aerospace engineering, engineering.
Deadline: January 31.
Award Amount: $ 2,000.
Number Of Awards: 30.
Applications Received: 100.
Odds Of Winning: 33% of applicants on average receive an award each year.
Contact: Student Programs Department

AVIATION COUNCIL OF PENNSYLVANIA (ACP)

ATTN: Executive Secretary
3111 Arcadia Avenue
Allentown, PA 18103
Phone: 610-797-1133
Fax: 610-797-8238
Website: http://www.acpfly.com

#72 • Professional Pilot, Aviation Management, Aviation Technology Scholarship

Type: Scholarship. Not renewable.
Eligibility: Applicant must be a resident of Pennsylvania. This award must be used in the following years of study: • Freshman • Sophomore • Junior • Senior • Masters • Doctoral • Other postgraduate level
Field(s) Of Study: Aviation.
Deadline: June 30.
Award Amount: $ 1,000.
Number Of Awards: 3.
Applications Received: 45.
Odds Of Winning: 7% of applicants on average receive an award each year.
Contact: Scholarship Committee

MOONEY AIRCRAFT PILOT ASSOCIATION (MAPA)

Safety Foundation
P.O. 460607
San Antonio, TX 78246
Phone: 210-525-8008
Fax: 210-525-8085
Website: http://www.mooneyapa.com

#73 • MAPA Safety Foundation Scholarship

Type: Scholarship. Not renewable.
Eligibility: Applicant must be an MAPA member or be sponsored by a member and have a minimum 3.0 GPA. Essay, transcripts, and two letters of recommendation required. This award must be used in the following years of study: • Junior • Senior
Field(s) Of Study: Aviation.
Deadline: July 15.
Award Amount: $ 2,500.

Number Of Awards: 1.
Applications Received: 1.
Contact: Lela Hughes, Scholarship

NEBRASKA SPACE GRANT CONSORTIUM

Allwine Hall 422-UNO
Omaha, NE 68182-0406
Phone: 402-554-3772
Fax: 402-554-3781
Email: nasa@unomaha.edu
Website: http://cid.unomaha.edu

#74 • Nebraska Space Grant and EPSCOR College and Fellowship Program

Type: Scholarship. Renewable. Recipient must reapply for renewal.
Eligibility: Applicant must be a U.S.citizen studying in an affiliate school in Nebraska. This award must be used in the following years of study: • Freshman • Sophomore • Junior • Senior • Masters • Doctoral • Other postgraduate level
Field(s) Of Study: Aeronautics, aviation, mathematics, science, technology, and related fields.
Deadline: Varies.
Award Amount: $ 250 - $ 7,500.
Number Of Awards: Varies.
Odds Of Winning: 50% of applicants on average receive an award each year.
Contact: Mary Schaffart, Coordinator

Agriculture

AMERICAN ASSOCIATION OF CEREAL CHEMISTS (AACC)

3340 Pilot Knob Road
St. Paul, MN 55121-2097

#75 • AACC Undergraduate Scholarships

Type: Scholarship. Renewable. Recipient must reapply on same basis as new applicants.
Eligibility: Applicant must be a full-time student with a minimum 3.0 GPA, have already completed at least one quarter or semester at the college level, and be enrolled in a program emphasizing cereal science/ technology, and recommended by department head or faculty advisor. Selection is based upon academic record, career interest, courses taken, jobs held (part- or full-time), active participation in student science club, and grades in science classes. This award must be used in the following years of study: • Sophomore • Junior • Senior
Field(s) Of Study: Cereal science.

Deadline: April 1.
Award Amount: $ 1,000 - $ 2,000.
Number Of Awards: 15.
Applications Received: 33.
Odds Of Winning: 50% of applicants on average receive an award each year.
Contact: Dr. Elwood Caldwell, Scholarship Jury

BOCES GENESEO MIGRANT CENTER

Scholarship Coordinator
27 Lackawanna Avenue
Mt. Morris, NY 14510
Phone: 716-658-7960
Fax: 716-658-7969
Email: gmigrant@frontiernet.net
Website: http://www.migrant.net

#76 • Migrant Farmworker Baccalaureate Scholarship

Type: Scholarship. Renewable up to five years.
Eligibility: Applicant must be a member of a family that has a history of movement to obtain work in agriculture, has completed one year of college, demonstrates financial need and academic achievement, and submits a 500-word personal essay, college transcript, tax forms, and three letters of recommendation. This award must be used in the following years of study: • Freshman • Sophomore • Junior • Senior • Masters
Deadline: July 1.
Award Amount: $ 2,000.
Number Of Awards: Varies.

#77 • Gloria and Joseph Mattera National Scholarship for Migrant Children

Type: Scholarship. Not renewable.
Eligibility: Applicant must be a child of a migratory farm worker or a migrant farm worker, enrolled in or accepted to an accredited institution or a dropout or potential dropout from high school who shows academic promise, and must be recommended by a representative of the community, school, or other educational agency able to vouch for the educational and financial status and financial need of the applicant. This award must be used in the following years of study: • Freshman • Sophomore • Junior • Senior
Deadline: Varies.
Award Amount: Varies.
Number Of Awards: Varies.

FREEHOLD SOIL CONSERVATION DISTRICT

Education Coordinator
211 Freehold Road
Manalapan, NJ 07726
Phone: 732-446-2300

Fax: 732-446-9140
Email: fscd@webspan.net
Website: http://www.webspan.net/~fscd/fsmain.htm

#78 • Munch & Clark Scholarship

Type: Scholarship. Not renewable.
Eligibility: Applicant must be a resident of Middlesex or Monmouth County in N.J. This award must be used in the following years of study: • Junior • Senior • Masters
Field(s) Of Study: Agriculture, conservation, environmental studies, or related fields of study.
Deadline: June 5.
Award Amount: $ 1,000.
Number Of Awards: 3.
Contact: Karen Rowe, Education Coordinator

#79 • FSCD Scholarship

Type: Scholarship. Not renewable.
Eligibility: Applicant must be a resident of Middlesex or Monmouth County in N.J. This award must be used in the following years of study: • Junior • Senior • Masters
Field(s) Of Study: Agriculture, conservation, environmental studies, or related fields of study.
Deadline: June 5.
Award Amount: $ 1,000.
Number Of Awards: 3.
Contact: Karen Rowe, Education Coordinator

HEART OF AMERICA RESTAURANTS AND INNS

The Machine Shed Scholarships
1501 River Drive
Moline, IL 61265
Phone: 309-797-9300
Fax: 309-797-8700
Website: http://www.hoari.com

#80 • WOC/JR Underwood Scholarship

Type: Scholarship. Not renewable.
Eligibility: Contact for details. This award must be used in the following years of study: • Freshman • Sophomore • Junior • Senior
Field(s) Of Study: Agriculture/agricultural sciences.
Deadline: Varies.
Award Amount: $ 1,000.
Number Of Awards: 2.
Contact: Max Molleston, Farm Director
WOC Radio 3535 East Kimberly Road
Davenport, IA 52807
Phone: 319-344-7000

#81 • KOEL/Dave Sylvester Scholarship

Type: Scholarship. Not renewable.
Eligibility: Contact for details. This award must be

used in the following years of study: • Freshman •
Sophomore • Junior • Senior
Field(s) Of Study: Agriculture/agricultural sciences.
Deadline: Varies.
Award Amount: $ 1,000.
Number Of Awards: 1.
Contact: KOEL Radio
2502 South Frederick P.O. Box 391
Oelwein, IA 50662
Phone: 319-283-1234
Fax: 319-283-3615

#82 • KGLO/Al Heinz Scholarship

Type: Scholarship. Not renewable.
Eligibility: Contact for details. This award must be
used in the following years of study: • Freshman •
Sophomore • Junior • Senior
Field(s) Of Study: Agriculture/agricultural sciences.
Deadline: Varies.
Award Amount: $ 1,000.
Number Of Awards: 1.
Contact: KGLO Radio
341 Yorktown Pike Box 1300
Mason City, IA 50401

UNITED AGRIBUSINESS LEAGUE (UAL) SCHOLARSHIP PROGRAM

54 Corporate Park
Irvine, CA 92606
Phone: 949-975-1424
Fax: 949-975-1671
Email: info@ual.org
Website: http://www.ual.org

#83 • UAL Scholarship

Type: Scholarship. Renewable. Reapplication
required for renewal.
Eligibility: Contact for details. This award must be
used in the following years of study: • Freshman •
Sophomore • Junior • Senior • Masters
Field(s) Of Study: Agriculture.
Deadline: March 31.
Award Amount: $ 1,000 - $ 6,000.
Number Of Awards: 7.
Applications Received: 35.
Odds Of Winning: 25% of applicants on average
receive an award each year.
Contact: Christiane Steele, Executive Secretary
Fax: 949-975-1573
Email: csteele@ual.org

VENTURA COUNTY COMMUNITY FOUNDATION

1317 Del Norte Road, Suite 150
Camarillo, CA 93010

Phone: 805-988-0196
Fax: 805-485-5537

#84 • Calavo Scholarship

Type: Scholarship. Renewable.
Eligibility: Contact for details. This award must be
used in the following years of study: • Freshman •
Sophomore • Junior • Senior
Field(s) Of Study: Agriculture.
Deadline: March 9.
Award Amount: $ 625.
Number Of Awards: 1.
Applications Received: 1.
Odds Of Winning: 100% of applicants on average
receive an award each year.
Contact: Gail Brown, Program Director

#85 • Milton McKevett Teague Scholarship

Type: Scholarship. Renewable.
Eligibility: Applicant must attend a school in Ventura
County, Calif. This award must be used in the following
years of study: • Freshman • Sophomore • Junior
Field(s) Of Study: Agriculture.
Deadline: March 9.
Award Amount: $ 2,500.
Number Of Awards: 2.
Applications Received: 5.
Odds Of Winning: 40% of applicants on average
receive an award each year.
Contact: Gail Brown, Program Director

#86 • Ventura County Agriculture Scholarship

Type: Scholarship. Not renewable.
Eligibility: Applicant must be the child of an
agriculture worker. This award must be used in the
following years of study: • Freshman
Deadline: Varies.
Award Amount: $ 750.
Number Of Awards: 2.
Applications Received: 5.
Odds Of Winning: 20% of applicants on average
receive an award each year.
Contact: Gail Brown, Program Director

Allied Health

AMBUCS

P.O. Box 5127
High Point, NC 27262
Phone: 336-869-2166
Fax: 336-887-8451
Email: ambucs@ambucs.com
Website: http://www.ambucs.com

#87 • National AMBUCS Scholarship for Therapists

Type: Scholarship. Renewable. Recipient must reapply for renewal.
Eligibility: Applicant must be U.S. citizen, have a minimum 3.0 GPA, and be accepted into an accredited program. Assistant programs are not eligible. Selection is based upon financial need, academic record, motivation, application form, and IRS Form 1040. Send self-addressed, stamped envelope for application. This award must be used in the following years of study: • Junior • Senior • Masters • Doctoral
Field(s) Of Study: Hearing audiology, occupational therapy, physical therapy, recreational therapy, speech language pathology.
Deadline: April 15.
Award Amount: $ 500 - $ 6,000.
Number Of Awards: 435.
Applications Received: 1,600.
Contact: Joe Copeland or April Quick, Scholarship Coordinator

AMERICAN COLLEGE OF MEDICAL PRACTICE EXECUTIVES (ACMPE)

104 Inverness Terrace East
Englewood, CO 80112-5306
Phone: 303-643-9573

#88 • Constance L. Lloyd/ACMPE Scholarship

Type: Scholarship. Not renewable.
Eligibility: Applicant must be a woman enrolled at an accredited college or university in Georgia. Applicant must submit a letter stating career goals and objectives, a resume showing employment history with a brief narrative describing specific employment responsibilities in health care field, and three letters of recommendation. Reference letters should address performance, character, potential to succeed, and need for scholarship support. Send for an application with a self-addressed, stamped, business size envelope. This award must be used in the following years of study: • Freshman • Sophomore • Junior • Senior • Masters • Doctoral
Field(s) Of Study: Heath care.
Deadline: June 1.
Award Amount: $ 1,500.
Number Of Awards: 1.
Contact: See above.

FOUNDATION OF RESEARCH & EDUCATION IN HEALTH INFORMATION MANAGEMENT

Attn: Scholarships and Loans
919 Michigan Ave., Suite 1400

Chicago, IL 60611-1683
Phone: 312-573-8556
Fax: 312-787-5926

#89 • Anthony Scholarship

Type: Scholarship. Not renewable.
Eligibility: Applicant must show financial need and attend a Committee on Allied Health Education and Accreditation (CAHEA) school. Applicant must submit transcripts and three letters of reference. This award must be used in the following years of study: • Sophomore • Junior • Senior • Masters • Doctoral
Field(s) Of Study: Health information management.
Deadline: April 30 / May 30.
Award Amount: $ 1,500.
Number Of Awards: 2.
Applications Received: 200.
Contact: See above.

#90 • Aspen Scholarship

Type: Scholarship. Not renewable.
Eligibility: Selection is based upon academic achievement, communication skills, and financial need. Volunteer experience is also taken into consideration. Applicant must be an active or associate member of the American Health Information Management Association (AHIMA). Applicant must submit transcripts and three letters of reference. This award must be used in the following years of study: • Senior • Masters • Doctoral
Deadline: May 30.
Award Amount: $ 1,000.
Number Of Awards: 1.
Applications Received: 200.
Contact: See above.

#91 • Foundation of Research & Education in Health Information Management Scholarship

Type: Scholarship. Not renewable.
Eligibility: Selection is based upon financial need and academic achievement. Applicant must be an active or associate member of AHIMA. Applicant must submit transcripts and three letters of reference. This award must be used in the following years of study: • Sophomore • Junior • Senior • Masters • Doctoral
Field(s) Of Study: Health information management.
Deadline: April 30/May 30.
Award Amount: $ 1,000 - $ 5,000.
Number Of Awards: Varies.
Contact: See above.

#92 • Smart Scholarship

Type: Scholarship. Not renewable.
Eligibility: Applicant must submit transcripts and three letters of reference. This award must be used in the following years of study: • Freshman • Sophomore • Junior • Senior • Masters

Field(s) Of Study: Health information management, health information technology.
Deadline: April 30.
Award Amount: $ 1,000.
Number Of Awards: 1.
Applications Received: 200.
Contact: See above.

#93 • Thomas Scholarship

Type: Scholarship. Not renewable.
Eligibility: Selection is based upon academic achievement, communication skills, financial need, references, and experience. Applicant must be a single parent attending a CAHEA-accredited school. Applicants must submit transcripts and three letters of reference. This award must be used in the following years of study: • Freshman • Sophomore • Junior • Senior • Masters
Field(s) Of Study: Health information management, health information technology.
Deadline: May 30.
Award Amount: $ 5,000.
Number Of Awards: 1.
Applications Received: 50.
Odds Of Winning: 2% of applicants on average receive an award each year.
Contact: See above.

#94 • Transcript Scholarship

Type: Scholarship. Not renewable.
Eligibility: Selection is based upon academic achievement, communication skills, financial need, references, and experience. Recipients are asked to write an essay addressing an aspect of HIM. Applicant must submit transcripts and three letters of reference and attend a CAHEA-accredited school. This award must be used in the following years of study: • Freshman • Sophomore • Junior • Senior • Masters
Field(s) Of Study: Health information management, health information technology.
Deadline: Graduate May 30th, Undergraduate April 30th.
Award Amount: $ 1,000 - $ 2,000.
Number Of Awards: 3.
Applications Received: 2,000.
Contact: See above.

INTERNATIONAL ORDER OF THE KING'S DAUGHTERS AND SONS

P.O. Box 1310
Brookhaven, MS 39602
Phone: 601-883-5418

#95 • Health Careers Scholarship

Type: Scholarship. Renewable if recipient reapplies and submits financial statement and transcript.

Eligibility: Applicant must be a U.S. or Canadian citizen enrolled full time in an accredited school of study in the U.S. or Canada and submit resume, official transcripts, an itemized budget endorsed by the school's finanical aid officer, and two letters of recommendation. Pre-med students are not eligible. Enclose two stamped, self-addressed, business-sized envelopes with inquiry. This award must be used in the following years of study: • Junior • R.N. students
Field(s) Of Study: Dentistry, medical technology, medicine, nursing, occupational therapy, pharmacy, physical therapy.
Deadline: April 1.
Award Amount: $ 1,000.
Number Of Awards: 50.
Contact: Mrs. Fred Cannon, Health Careers Director
P.O. Box 1310
Brookhaven, MS 39602

MARYLAND HIGHER EDUCATION COMMISSION

State Scholarship Administration
16 Francis Street
Annapolis, MD 21401-1781
Phone: 410-974-5370 or 800-974-1024
Fax: 410-974-5994
Email: ssamail@mhec.state.md.us
Website: http://www.mhec.state.md.us

#96 • Professional School Scholarship

Type: Scholarship. Renewable up to three years if recipient continues to meet eligibility requirements; applicant must file SSA and FAFSA by March 1 each year.
Eligibility: Applicant must be a Maryland resident and be enrolled full-time. Selection is based upon financial need. Applicant must submit FAFSA and SSA. Award may be used at eligible Maryland schools only. This award must be used in the following years of study: • Sophomore • Junior • Senior • Masters • Doctoral
Field(s) Of Study: Dentistry, law, medicine, nursing, pharmacy, social work.
Deadline: March 1.
Award Amount: $ 200 - $ 1,000.
Number Of Awards: 200.
Applications Received: 600.
Odds Of Winning: 33% of applicants on average receive an award each year.
Contact: Cis Whittington, Program Adminstrator

NATIONAL ENVIRONMENTAL HEALTH ASSOCIATION SCHOLARSHIP

Veronica White, Member Liaison
720 South Colorado Boulevard, Suite #970
Denver, CO 80246
Phone: 303-756-9090

Fax: 303-691-9490
Email: staff @neha.org
Website: www.neha.org

#97 • NEHA Scholarship

Type: Scholarship. Renewable. All renewal applications will be viewed as new.
Eligibility: Applicant must be pursuing a career in environmental health sciences and/or public health. Undergraduates must be enrolled in an NEHSPAC accredited school or NEHA Institutional/Educational or Sustaining member school. Applicants must submit an official application form, an academic transcript, one letter of recommendation from an active NEHA member, and two faculty letters of recommendation. Selection is based upon demonstrable need and academic record. This award must be used in the following years of study: • Freshman • Sophomore • Junior • Senior • Masters • Doctoral • Other postgraduate level
Field(s) Of Study: Environmental health sciences and/or public health.
Deadline: February 1.
Award Amount: $ 500 - $ 2,000.
Number Of Awards: 3 - 4.
Applications Received: 26.
Odds Of Winning: 15% of applicants on average receive an award each year.
Contact: Veronica White, NEHA liason
Email: veronica.white@juno.com

SUBURBAN HOSPITAL SCHOLARSHIP PROGRAM

Human Resources
8600 Old Georgetown Road
Bethesda, MD 20814
Phone: 301-896-3830
Fax: 301-897-1339
Website: http://www.suburbanhospital.org

#98 • Suburban Hospital Scholarship

Type: Scholarship. Renewable.
Eligibility: Applicant must reside in the metropolitan Washington, D.C. area, have a minimum 2.5 GPA, and enrolled in a nursing, radiology technology, respiratory therapy, medical technology, physical therapy, physical therapy assistant, occupational therapy, or physician assistant undergraduate program. Applicant must submit two letters of recommendation, transcript, and letter of acceptance or good standing. This award must be used in the following years of study: • Sophomore • Junior • Senior
Field(s) Of Study: Medical technology, nursing, occupational therapy, physical therapy, physical therapy assistant, physician assistant, radiology technology, respiratory therapy.
Deadline: April 30.

Award Amount: $ 5,000.
Number Of Awards: 8.
Contact: Charmaine Williams, Human Resources Specialist
Phone: 301-896-3795
Email: cwilliams@suburbanhospital.org

Animal Science/Veterinary Medicine

ARABIAN HORSE TRUST

12000 Zuni Street
Westminster, CO 80234-2300
Phone: 303-450-4710
Fax: 303-450-4707

#99 • William Zekan Memorial Scholarship

Type: Scholarship. Not renewable.
Eligibility: Applicant must have an ongoing interest in and commitment to Arabian horses. Applicant must also demonstrate financial need. This award must be used in the following years of study: • Freshman
Deadline: January 31.
Award Amount: $ 2,500.
Number Of Awards: 1.
Contact: Janet Kamischke, Office Manager

NATIONAL DAIRY SHRINE

1224 Alton-Darby Creek Road
Columbus, OH 43228-9792
Phone: 614-878-5333
Fax: 614-870-2622
Email: ndairyshrine@hotmail.com
Website: htttp://www.dairyshrine.org

#100 • McCullough Scholarship

Type: Scholarship. Not renewable.
Eligibility: Contact for details. This award must be used in the following years of study: • Freshman
Deadline: March 15.
Award Amount: $ 1,000 - $ 2,500.
Number Of Awards: 2.
Applications Received: 8.
Odds Of Winning: 25% of applicants on average receive an award each year.
Contact: See above.

Architecture/Landscape Architecture

AMERICAN ARCHITECTURAL FOUNDATION (AAF)

1735 New York Avenue, NW
Washington, DC 20006

#101 • AIA Minority/Disadvantaged Scholarship Program

Type: Scholarship. Renewable. Recipient must maintain a satisfactory GPA and demonstrate continued financial need to retain scholarship.
Eligibility: Applicant must be a financially-disadvantaged U.S. resident nominated by an individual architect or firm, an AIA chapter, a community design center, a guidance counselor, a teacher, a dean or administrative head of an accredited school of architecture, or director of a community, civic, or religious organization. Applicant must attend a NAAB-accredited school. This award must be used in the following years of study: • Freshman • Sophomore
Field(s) Of Study: Architecture.
Deadline: January 15.
Award Amount: $ 500 - $ 2,500.
Number Of Awards: 20.
Applications Received: 135.
Odds Of Winning: 20% of applicants on average receive an award each year.
Contact: Mary Felber, Director of AIA/AAF Scholarship Program

Athletic Ability

AMERICAN WATER SKI EDUCATION FOUNDATION (AWSEF)

799 Overlook Drive, SE
Winter Haven, FL 33884-1671
Phone: 941-324-2472
Fax: 941-324-3996
Email: 102726,2751@compuserve.com
Website: http://www.usawaterski.org

#102 • AWSEF Scholarship

Type: Scholarship. Not renewable.
Eligibility: Applicant must be a U.S. citizen who is a current American Water Ski Association member. Selection is based upon academic qualifications, leadership, extracurricular involvement,

recommendations, and financial need. This award must be used in the following years of study: • Sophomore • Junior • Senior
Deadline: April 1.
Award Amount: $ 1,500.
Number Of Awards: 6.
Applications Received: 45.
Contact: Carole Lowe, Executive Director
P.O. Box 2957
Winter Haven, FL 33883-2957
Phone: 941-324-2472
Fax: 941-324-3996
Email: 102726,2751@compuserve.com

FINA, INC.

Public Affairs Department
P.O. Box 2159
Dallas, TX 75221-2159
Phone: 800-555-FINA, extension 4
Email: scholar.athlete.program@fina.com

#103 • FINA/*Dallas Morning News* All-State Scholar-Athlete Team Scholarship

Type: Scholarship. Not renewable.
Eligibility: Applicant must be a Texas high school graduate with a minimum grade average of 90 and rank in the top tenth of class. Applicant must have lettered in a UIL-recognized varsity sport. Selection is based upon academic achievement and leadership in varsity athletics. This award must be used in the following years of study: • Freshman
Deadline: December 13.
Award Amount: $ 500 - $ 4,000.
Number Of Awards: 44.
Applications Received: 2,500.
Odds Of Winning: 2% of applicants on average receive an award each year.
Contact: Scholarship Committee

NEW JERSEY STATE GOLF ASSOCIATION

1000 Broad Street
Bloomfield, NJ 07003
Phone: 973-338-8334
Fax: 973-338-5525
Email: njsga@usga.org
Website: http://www.njsga.org

#104 • New Jersey State Golf Association (NJSGA) Caddie Scholarship

Type: Scholarship. Renewable if recipient maintains satisfactory grades and demonstrates financial need.
Eligibility: Applicant must have caddied at least one year at a member NJSGA club and enroll as a full-time student at an accredited college or university. Selection is based upon scholastic achievement, SAT I

scores, character and leadership qualities, length and quality of caddie service, and financial need. This award must be used in the following years of study: • Freshman • Sophomore • Junior • Senior
Deadline: May 1.
Award Amount: $ 1,000 - $ 2,500.
Number Of Awards: 45.
Applications Received: 132.
Odds Of Winning: 34% of applicants on average receive an award each year.
Contact: Education Director
P.O. Box 6947
Freehold, NJ 07728
Phone: 732-780-3562

PETER A. MCKERNAN SCHOLARSHIP FUND

P.O. Box 5601
Augusta, ME 04332-5601
Phone: 207-582-2729
Email: cyndi@gwi.net

#105 • Peter A. McKernan Scholarship

Type: Scholarship. Not renewable.
Eligibility: Applicant must be a Maine resident attending a Maine high school, have a minimum "C" grade average, have earned a varsity letter or its equivalent in a high school sport, submit an essay "What Friendship Means to Me," be nominated by high school, and demonstrate financial need. Each Maine high school may nominate two students, one who will be attending a four-year school and one for a vocational/technical college. Applications available only through high school guidance office. This award must be used in the following years of study: • Freshman
Deadline: April 15.
Award Amount: $ 2,000.
Number Of Awards: 3.
Applications Received: 160.
Odds Of Winning: 2% of applicants on average receive an award each year.
Contact: High school guidance counselor

PRO BOWLERS ASSOCIATION

1720 Merriman Road
P.O. Box 5118
Akron, OH 44334-0118
Phone: 330-836-5568
Fax: 330-836-2107
Website: http://www.pbatour.com

#106 • Billy Welu Memorial Scholarship

Type: Scholarship. Not renewable.
Eligibility: Applicant must be actively involved in bowling (college team, coaching, etc.) and maintain a minimum 2.5 GPA. This award must be used in the following years of study: • Sophomore • Junior • Senior • Masters • Doctoral
Deadline: May 31.
Award Amount: $ 500.
Number Of Awards: 1.
Contact: Pro Bowlers Association

#107 • John Jowdy Scholarship

Type: Scholarship. Renewable if recipient maintains minimum 2.5 GPA.
Eligibility: Applicant must be actively involved in bowling and have a minimum 2.5 GPA. This award must be used in the following years of study: • Freshman
Deadline: April 1.
Award Amount: $ 500.
Number Of Awards: 1.
Contact: Pro Bowlers Assocation

UNITED STATES SKI AND SNOWBOARD TEAM EDUCATION FOUNDATION

P.O. Box 100
Park City, UT 84060
Phone: 435-647-2023
Fax: 435-647-2656
Website: http://www.usskiteam.com

#108 • United States Ski and Snowboard Team Foundation Scholarship

Type: Scholarship. Renewable. Recipient must reapply for renewal.
Eligibility: Applicant must be a current or retired member of the U.S. Ski and Snowboard Team. This award must be used in the following years of study: • Freshman • Sophomore • Junior • Senior • Masters • Doctoral
Deadline: May 1.
Award Amount: $ 1,000.
Number Of Awards: Varies.
Applications Received: 33.
Odds Of Winning: 98% of applicants on average receive an award each year.
Contact: Bridgett Bourgault, Assistant, Athlete and Donor Relations
Email: bridgettb@ussa.org

Automotive Studies

AUTOMOTIVE HALL OF FAME

21400 Oakwood Boulevard
Dearborn, MI 48124-4078
Phone: 313-240-4000

#109 • Charles V. Hagler Memorial Scholarship

Type: Scholarship. Not renewable.
Eligibility: Applicant must show a sincere interest in an automotive career, be enrolled full time at an accredited college or university, and maintain satisfactory academic progress. Financial need is considered. This award must be used in the following years of study: • Freshman • Sophomore • Junior • Senior • Doctoral
Field(s) Of Study: Automotive studies.
Deadline: May 30.
Award Amount: $ 800 - $ 1,000.
Number Of Awards: 1.
Contact: Scholarship Coordinator

#110 • Larry H. Averill Memorial Scholarship

Type: Scholarship. Not renewable.
Eligibility: Applicant must show a sincere interest in an automotive career, be enrolled full time at an accredited college or university, and maintain satisfactory academic progress. Financial need is considered. This award must be used in the following years of study: • Sophomore • Junior • Senior • Doctoral
Field(s) Of Study: Automotive studies.
Deadline: May 30.
Award Amount: $ 500 - $ 1,500.
Number Of Awards: 1.
Contact: Scholarship Coordinator

#111 • Dr. Dorothy M. Ross Scholarship

Type: Scholarship. Not renewable.
Eligibility: Applicant must show a sincere interest in an automotive career, be enrolled full time at an accredited college or university, and maintain satisfactory academic progress. Financial need is considered. This award must be used in the following years of study: • Freshman • Sophomore • Junior • Senior • Doctoral
Field(s) Of Study: Automotive studies.
Deadline: May 30.
Award Amount: $ 300 - $ 500.
Number Of Awards: 1.
Contact: Scholarship Coordinator

#112 • Ken Krum-Bud Kouts Memorial Scholarship

Type: Scholarship. Not renewable.
Eligibility: Applicant must show a sincere interest in an automotive career, be enrolled full time at an accredited college or university, and maintain satisfactory academic progress. Financial need is considered. This award must be used in the following years of study: • Sophomore • Junior • Senior
Field(s) Of Study: Automotive studies.
Deadline: May 30.

Award Amount: $ 250.
Number Of Awards: 1.
Contact: Scholarship Coordinator

#113 • John E. Echlin Memorial Scholarship

Type: Scholarship. Renewable. Recipient must reapply for renewal.
Eligibility: Applicant must be a full-time student, have a sincere interest in pursuing an automotive career upon graduation, regardless of major, and demonstrate satisfactory academic performance. Financial need is considered but not necessary. This award must be used in the following years of study: • Sophomore • Junior • Senior • Doctoral
Deadline: May 30.
Award Amount: $ 500 - $ 1,300.
Number Of Awards: 1.
Contact: Scholarship Coordinator

#114 • TRW Foundation Scholarship

Type: Scholarship. Not renewable.
Eligibility: Applicant must show a sincere interest in an automotive career, be enrolled full time at an accredited college or university, and maintain satisfactory academic progress. Financial need is considered. This award must be used in the following years of study: • Sophomore • Junior • Senior • Doctoral
Deadline: May 30.
Award Amount: $ 250.
Number Of Awards: 1.
Contact: Scholarship Coordinator

SPECIALTY EQUIPMENT MARKET ASSOCIATION (SEMA)

P.O. Box 4910
Diamond Bar, CA 91765-0910
Phone: 909-396-0289

#115 • SEMA Scholarship Fund

Type: Scholarship. Not renewable.
Eligibility: Applicant must intend to enter the automotive aftermarket field. This award must be used in the following years of study: • Sophomore • Junior • Senior • Masters • Doctoral
Field(s) Of Study: Automotive.
Deadline: April 15.
Award Amount: $ 1,000 - $ 2,500.
Number Of Awards: 10 - 15.
Odds Of Winning: 13% of applicants on average receive an award each year.
Contact: Diane Guerena, Foundation Director
Phone: 909-396-0289, extension 125

Biology

MANOMET CENTER FOR CONSERVATION SCIENCES

Kathleen S. Anderson Award
Box 1770
Manomet, MA 02345
Phone: 508-224-6521
Fax: 508-224-9220

#116 • Kathleen S. Anderson Award

Type: Grant. Not renewable.
Eligibility: Award is to encourage projects in avian research and to help promising biologists in their work. Applicant must submit a resume, proposal, budget, and two letters of recommendation. Enrollment in an academic program is desirable, but not required. This award must be used in the following years of study: • Junior • Senior • Masters • Doctoral • Other postgraduate level
Field(s) Of Study: Biology.
Deadline: December 1.
Award Amount: $ 500 - $ 1,000.
Number Of Awards: 1 - 2.
Applications Received: 12.
Odds Of Winning: 17% of applicants on average receive an award each year.
Contact: Jeannie Robbins, Administrative Assistant

Business Administration/ Management

AMERICAN PRODUCTION & INVENTORY CONTROL SOCIETY (APICS), INC./EDUCATION & RESEARCH (E&R) FOUNDATION, INC.

5301 Shawnee Road
Alexandria, VA 22312
Phone: 703-354-8851 or 800-444-2742
Fax: 703-354-8106
Email: m_lythgoe@apics-hq.org
Website: http://www.apics.org

#117 • Donald W. Fogarty International Student Paper Competition

Type: Contest. Renewable. Recipient must submit a new paper to retain scholarship.
Eligibility: Applicant must be enrolled as either a part- or full-time graduate or undergraduate student at a college or university at time of submission. Prospective applicants are encouraged to use the 800 number listed above to request a manual (item #01002) and the name of the local APICS chapter. High school students are not eligible. This award must be used in the following years of study: • Freshman • Sophomore • Junior • Senior • Masters • Doctoral
Field(s) Of Study: Production and operations management.
Deadline: May 15.
Award Amount: $ 100 - $ 1,750.
Number Of Awards: 162.
Contact: Michael H. Lythgoe, E&R Foundation Associate
Phone: 703-354-8851, extension 2202
Fax: 703-354-8794
Email: m_lythgoe@apics-hq.org

AMERICAN WELDING SOCIETY FOUNDATION, INC. (AWS)

550 N.W. LeJeune Road
Miami, FL 33126
Phone: 800-443-9353, extension 293 or 305-445-6628
Fax: 305-443-7559
Email: found@aws.org
Website: http://www.aws.org

#118 • James A. Turner, Jr. Scholarship

Type: Scholarship. Renewable. Recipient must reapply for renewal.
Eligibility: Applicant must be planning a career in management of welding store operations or welding distributorship, be at least 18 years old, be a U.S. citizen attending an institution in the U.S., and be employed at least 10 hours per week at a welding distributor. This award must be used in the following years of study: • Sophomore • Junior • Senior
Field(s) Of Study: Business.
Deadline: January 15.
Award Amount: $ 3,000.
Number Of Awards: 1.
Applications Received: 6.
Odds Of Winning: 16% of applicants on average receive an award each year.
Contact: Vicki Pinsky, Scholarship Coordinator
Phone: 800-443-9353, extension 461
Email: vpinsky@aws.org

COMMUNITY FOUNDATION SERVING RICHMOND AND CENTRAL VIRGINIA

7325 Beaufort Springs Drive, Suite 210
Richmond, VA 23225-8470
Phone: 804-330-7400
Fax: 804-330-5992
Email: sdavis@tcfrichmond.org
Website: http://www.tcfrichmond.org

#119 • Lori Ann Robinson Memorial Scholarship

Type: Scholarship. Not renewable.
Eligibility: Applicant must be a U.S. citizen from central Virginia planning to enroll in a two- or four-year college or university in the continental U.S., and must demonstrate academic achievement and leadership or community service. Special consideration given to applicants from King and Queen Central High School (King and Queen Court House, Va.). This award must be used in the following years of study: • Freshman
Field(s) Of Study: Accounting, business administration, economic administration, finance.
Deadline: March 10.
Award Amount: $ 500 - $ 5,000.
Number Of Awards: Varies.
Contact: Susan Brown Davis, Senior Program Officer
Email: sdavis@tcfrichmond.org

GOLDEN STATE MINORITY FOUNDATION

333 South Beaudry Avenue, Suite 216-C
Los Angeles, CA 90017
Phone: 213-482-6300
Fax: 213-482-6305
Email: gsmf@earthlink.net
Website: http://www.gsmf.org

#120 • Golden State Minority Foundation Scholarship

Type: Scholarship. Renewable. Reapplication required for renewal.
Eligibility: Applicant must attend school in Southern California, be African-American, Latino, Native American, or other underrepresented ethnic minority, and be a U.S. citizen or permanent legal resident. Applicant must be enrolled full-time, be employed no more than 25 hours per week, and have a minimum 3.0 GPA. This award must be used in the following years of study: • Junior • Senior • Masters • Doctoral
Deadline: April 1.
Award Amount: $ 2,000.
Number Of Awards: 35.
Applications Received: 150.
Contact: Jay C. Johnson, Scholarship Coordinator

MAINE EDUCATION SERVICES FOUNDATION

P.O. Box 549
Augusta, ME 04332
Phone: 207-623-2600
Fax: 207-623-1493
Website: http://www.mesfoundation.com

#121 • Peoples Promise Scholarship

Type: Scholarship. Not renewable.

Eligibility: Selection is based upon academic ability, extracurricular activities, and financial need. Essay and letters of recommendation required. Award includes a three-month internship at Peoples Heritage Bank. This award must be used in the following years of study: • Freshman
Deadline: March 26.
Award Amount: $ 2,500.
Number Of Awards: 10.
Contact: Betty Ryder, Scheduling Coordinator
Phone: 207-623-2600, extension 645
Fax: 207-623-1493
Email: eryder@mesfoundation.com

MEXICAN AMERICAN GROCERS ASSOCIATION

405 North San Fernando Road
Los Angeles, CA 90031
Phone: 213-227-1565
Fax: 213-227-6935
Website: http://www.maga.org

#122 • Mexican American Grocers Association Foundation Scholarship

Type: Scholarship. Renewable. Recipient must reapply for renewal.
Eligibility: Applicant must be Hispanic and a full-time student, have a minimum 2.5 GPA, and demonstrate financial need. Applicant must submit official transcripts. Recipient must be able to attend the Scholarship Awards Banquet. This award must be used in the following years of study: • Sophomore • Junior • Senior
Field(s) Of Study: Business.
Deadline: July 31.
Award Amount: $ 500 - $ 1,000.
Number Of Awards: 20.
Applications Received: 500.
Odds Of Winning: 4% of applicants on average receive an award each year.
Contact: Jacqueline Solis

TRUSTEES OF FUKUNAGA FOUNDATION SCHOLARSHIP

P.O. Box 2788
Honolulu, HI 96803
Phone: 808-521-6511
Fax: 808-523-3937

#123 • Fukunaga Foundation Scholarship

Type: Scholarship. Renewable. Applicant must maintain a minimum 3.0 GPA and full-time status to retain award.
Eligibility: Applicant must be a permanent resident of Hawaii (at least one year), rank in top quarter of class, have a minimum 3.0 GPA, and demonstrate

financial need. He or she must also demonstrate the ability, industriousness, dependability, and determination needed to succeed in business within the Pacific Basin area. This award must be used in the following years of study: • Freshman • Sophomore • Junior • Senior
Field(s) Of Study: Business administration.
Deadline: February 15.
Award Amount: $ 2,000.
Number Of Awards: 10 - 16.
Applications Received: 90.
Odds Of Winning: 18% of applicants on average receive an award each year.
Contact: Evie Kobayashi, Administration Manager
Email: eviek@servco.com

UNIVERSITY OF SOUTH ALABAMA (USA)

260 Administration Building
Mobile, AL 36688-0002
Phone: 334-460-6231
Website: http://www.usouthal.edu

#124 • Abraham Mitchell Business Scholarship

Type: Scholarship. Renewable. Recipient must maintain a minimum 3.0 to retain $7,000 and a minimum 3.5 GPA to retain $8,000
Eligibility: Award is based upon academic achievement. Applicant must have a minimum 23 ACT score. This award must be used in the following years of study: • Freshman
Field(s) Of Study: Business.
Deadline: January 1.
Award Amount: $ 8,000.
Number Of Awards: 5.
Contact: Director of Admissions
182 Administration Building
Mobile, AL 36688
Phone: 334-460-6141
Fax: 334-460-7876
Email: admiss@usamail.usouthal.edu

Business/Corporate/Professional Affiliation

AMERICAN AIRLINES/AMR MANAGEMENT CLUB

4200 Amon-Carter Boulevard
P.O. Box 2526 CP2
Fort Worth, TX 76155
Phone: 817-963-6189

#125 • American Airlines/AMR Management Club Merit Scholarship

Type: Scholarship. Not renewable.
Eligibility: Applicant must be the dependent of an AMR Corporation employee who works in the Dallas-Fort Worth metroplex area. This award must be used in the following years of study: • Freshman
Deadline: March 17.
Award Amount: $ 1,500.
Number Of Awards: 4.
Contact: Chris Thomas, Scholarship Committee Chairperson

#126 • American Airlines/AMR Management Club Community/Leadership Scholarship

Type: Scholarship. Not renewable.
Eligibility: Applicant must be the dependent of an AMR Corporation employee who works in the Dallas-Fort Worth metroplex area. This award must be used in the following years of study: • Freshman
Deadline: March 17.
Award Amount: $ 1,500.
Number Of Awards: 4.
Contact: Chris Thomas, Scholarship Committee Chairperson

AMERICAN FLINT GLASS WORKERS UNION

ATTN: Assistant Secretary Ernest Inzana
1440 South Byrne Road
Toledo, OH 43614
Phone: 419-385-6687
Fax: 419-385-8839

#127 • AIL/Lawrence Bankowski AFGWU Scholarship Award

Type: Scholarship. Not renewable.
Eligibility: Applicant must be a high school senior and the child, stepchild, or legally adopted child of a member of the American Flint Glass Workers Union with continuous membership for at least one year. If parent is not in good standing, applicant is eligible if one of the following applies: member died within the last year and at the time of death had continuous good standing for at least one year; member is on sick leave or layoff with contractual rights to return to work and at the beginning of such sick leave or layoff had continuous good standing of one year. Applicant must submit essay of at least 500 words on a topic selected by the National President. Children of national officers, national representatives, or employees of the national union are not eligible. This award must be used in the following years of study: • Freshman
Deadline: August 1.
Award Amount: $ 1,000.

Number Of Awards: 5.
Applications Received: 29.
Contact: Ernest Inzana, Assistant Secretary

ARMSTRONG WORLD INDUSTRIES, INC.

P.O. Box 3231
Lancaster, PA 17604
Phone: 717-397-0611
Website: http://www.armstrong.com

#128 • Armstrong Foundation Award

Type: Scholarship. Renewable up to four years in accordance with the rules set forth by National Merit Scholarship Corp.
Eligibility: Applicant must be the son or daughter of an Armstrong employee or retiree and have National Merit Scholarship status. This award must be used in the following years of study: • Freshman • Sophomore • Junior • Senior
Deadline: Varies.
Award Amount: $ 2,000 - $ 4,000.
Number Of Awards: 15 - 18.
Applications Received: 100.
Contact: Karen J. Harnish, Coordinator
Phone: 717-396-2212
Email: kjharnish@armstrong.com

BAPTIST LIFE ASSOCIATION SCHOLARSHIP GRANTS

Baptist Life Association, Scholarship Committee
8555 Main Street
Buffalo, NY 14221-7494
Phone: 800-227-8543, extension 14
Fax: 716-633-4916
Website: http://www.baptistlife.org

#129 • Baptist Life Association Scholarship Grant

Type: Scholarship. Not renewable.
Eligibility: Applicant must have had an insurance policy with Baptist Life for at least two years prior to the May 31 deadline. Selection is based upon academic ability, financial need, goals, and good character. This award must be used in the following years of study: • Freshman • Sophomore • Junior • Senior • Masters • Doctoral
Deadline: May 31.
Award Amount: $ 250 - $ 700.
Number Of Awards: Varies.
Applications Received: 65.
Odds Of Winning: 30% of applicants on average receive an award each year.
Contact: Laurice A. Vance, Scholarship Coordinator

BIOMET FOUNDATION, INC.

P.O. Box 587
Warsaw, IN 46581

#130 • Biomet Foundation Scholarship

Type: Scholarship. Renewable. Recipient must reapply and show satisfactory academic progress to retain scholarship.
Eligibility: Applicant must be the dependent child of an employee of Biomet, Inc., or its subsidiaries. This award must be used in the following years of study: • Freshman • Sophomore • Junior • Senior
Deadline: April 1.
Award Amount: $ 2,000.
Number Of Awards: 10.
Applications Received: 25.
Odds Of Winning: 40% of applicants on average receive an award each year.
Contact: Darlene Whaley, Board Member

BOEING EMPLOYEES' CREDIT UNION

P.O. Box 97050
Seattle, WA 98124-9750
Phone: 800-233-2328, extension 5939

#131 • BECU Foundation Scholarship

Type: Scholarship. Not renewable.
Eligibility: Applicant must be eligible for membership in the Boeing Employees' Credit Union. This award must be used in the following years of study: • Freshman • Sophomore • Junior • Senior
Deadline: Varies.
Award Amount: $ 2,000.
Number Of Awards: 25.
Applications Received: 320.
Odds Of Winning: 10% of applicants on average receive an award each year.
Contact: Tara Cramer, Community Relations Manager

BUTLER MANUFACTURING COMPANY FOUNDATION

BMA Tower, 31st and Southwest Trafficway
P.O. Box 419917
Kansas City, MO 64141-0917
Phone: 816-968-3208
Fax: 816-968-3211
Email: blfay@butlermfg.org

#132 • Butler Manufacturing Company Foundation Scholarship

Type: Scholarship. Renewable. Minimum 2.0 GPA is required to retain scholarship.
Eligibility: Applicant must be a U.S. citizen, the child of an employee of Butler Manufacturing, Co.,

and demonstrate financial need. This award must be used in the following years of study: • Freshman
Deadline: February 19.
Award Amount: $ 2,500.
Number Of Awards: 8.
Applications Received: 52.
Contact: Barbara L. Fay, Foundation Administrator
Fax: 816-968-3211

CLARA ABBOTT FOUNDATION

200 Abbott Park Road
Abbott Park, IL 60064-3537
Phone: 847-937-1090
Fax: 847-938-6511
Website: http://www.clara.abbott.com

#133 • Clara Abbott Foundation Educational Grant Program

Type: Grant. Renewable.
Eligibility: Applicant must be a child or dependent of an Abbott Laboratories employee or retiree. Selection is based upon financial need. This award must be used in the following years of study: • Freshman • Sophomore • Junior • Senior
Deadline: March 13.
Award Amount: $ 1,100 - $13,000.
Number Of Awards: 3,500.
Applications Received: 4,100.
Contact: Jeriann Dosemagen, Manager, Educational Grant Programs
Phone: 847-937-3294
Email: jeriann.dosemagen@abbott.com

DRUG, CHEMICAL, AND ALLIED TRADES ASSOCIATION (DCAT)

510 Route 130 Suite B1
East Windsor, NJ 08520
Phone: 800-640-DCAT
Fax: 609-448-1944
Email: info@dcat.edu
Website: http://www.dcat.org

#134 • DCAT Scholarship

Type: Scholarship. Renewable if student maintains acceptable GPA.
Eligibility: Applicant must be the child of a full-time employee of a DCAT-member company. Selection is based upon academic achievement, SAT I or ACT scores, essay, and leadership qualities. This award must be used in the following years of study: • Freshman • Sophomore • Junior • Senior
Deadline: January 21.
Award Amount: $ 1,000.
Number Of Awards: 11.
Applications Received: 2,000.
Contact: Executive Director

DUKE ENERGY CORPORATION

422 South Church Street
Charlotte, NC 28201-1244
Website: http://www.duke-energy.com

#135 • Duke Energy Scholars Program

Type: Scholarship. Renewable if recipient maintains a minimum 3.0 semester GPA and full-time status.
Eligibility: Applicant must be the child or ward of an employee of Duke Energy who has had one year of continuous employment with the company by February 1 of the award year. Selection is based upon academic qualifications, essay, letters of recommendation, and financial need. SAT I scores required. This award must be used in the following years of study: • Freshman
Deadline: December 1.
Award Amount: $ 1,000 - $ 5,000.
Number Of Awards: 15.
Contact: Dianne S. Wilson, Scholarship Admin. Duke Energy Scholars Program P.O. Box 1642
Houston, TX 77251-1642
Fax: 713-627-4061

FEDERAL EMPLOYEE EDUCATION AND ASSISTANCE FUND

8441 W. Bowles, Suite 200
Littleton, CO 80123-9501
Phone: 800-323-4140
Fax: 303-933-7587
Email: FEEAHQ@aol.com
Website: http:www.feea.org

#136 • FEEA Scholarship

Type: Scholarship. Not renewable.
Eligibility: Applicant must have been a civilian federal employee for at least three years or the legal dependent of one. Selection is based upon merit. To receive an application, send a self-addressed, stamped envelope (#10). This award must be used in the following years of study: • Freshman • Sophomore • Junior • Senior • Masters • Doctoral
Deadline: March 31.
Award Amount: $ 300 - $ 2,000.
Number Of Awards: 400.
Applications Received: 5,000.
Odds Of Winning: 8% of applicants on average receive an award each year.
Contact: Scholarships

HORACE MANN INSURANCE COMPANIES

Scholarship Program
P.O. Box 20490

Springfield, IL 62708
Website: http://www.horacemann.com

#137 • Horace Mann Scholarship

Type: Scholarship. Renewable. Some awards are renewable for up to four years. Recipient must maintain a minimum 2.0 GPA and satisfactory academic progress to retain scholarship.
Eligibility: Applicant must be the child of a U.S. public school, college, or university employee and must have a minimum 3.0 GPA and a minimum combined SAT I score of 1100 (composite ACT score of 23). This award must be used in the following years of study: • Freshman
Deadline: February 12.
Award Amount: $ 1,000 - $25,000.
Number Of Awards: 16.
Applications Received: 11,000.
Odds Of Winning: Less than 1% of applicants on average receive an award each year.
Contact: Scholarship Coordinator

HORMEL FOODS CORPORATION

1 Hormel Place
Austin, MN 55912
Phone: 507-437-5611

#138 • Hormel Foods Scholarship

Type: Scholarship. Renewable.
Eligibility: Applicant must be a high school student who is the child of an employee of Hormel Foods Corporation and its subsidiaries. Selection is by the National Merit Scholarship Corp. and is based upon test scores, academic records, leadership, and extracurricular accomplishments. Applicant must take the PSAT/NMSQT exam during junior year of high school and attend a regionally accredited U.S. college. This award must be used in the following years of study: • Freshman
Deadline: January 11.
Award Amount: $ 750 - $ 3,000.
Number Of Awards: 5.
Contact: V. Allen Krejci, Scholarship Program Director

JOHNSON CONTROLS FOUNDATION

5757 North Green Bay Avenue, M.S. X-46
Milwaukee, WI 53209
Phone: 414-228-2296

#139 • Johnson Controls, Inc. Foundation Scholarship

Type: Scholarship. Renewable. Satisfactory academic progress is required to retain scholarship.
Eligibility: Applicant must be the child of a full-time Johnson Controls employee, rank in top 30% of class

after first semester of senior year, plan to be a full-time student at a four-year college or university in an accredited program leading to a college degree, and demonstrate leadership. Standardized test scores required. Selection is based upon academic, leadership, and civic achievements. This award must be used in the following years of study: • Freshman • Sophomore • Junior • Senior
Deadline: February 11.
Award Amount: $ 2,000.
Number Of Awards: 1 - 16.
Contact: Valerie Adisek, Foundation Coordinator
Phone: 414-228-1200 or 888-524-0752

KOHLER COMPANY

Communications Department
444 Highland Drive
Kohler, WI 53044
Phone: 920-457-4441
Fax: 920-457-9064

#140 • Kohler, Co. College Scholarship

Type: Scholarship. Renewable. Good academic standing, full-time enrollment, and continuing employment or parental employment are required to retain scholarship.
Eligibility: Applicant must be an employee or the child of an employee of Kohler (or U.S. or Canadian subsidiary). rank in the top tenth of class, have a near-perfect GPA, and have a minimum combined SAT I score of 1150. This award must be used in the following years of study: • Freshman • Sophomore • Junior • Senior
Deadline: February 15.
Award Amount: $ 1,200 - $ 1,500.
Number Of Awards: 15.
Applications Received: 170.
Odds Of Winning: 9% of applicants on average receive an award each year.
Contact: Peter J. Fetterer, Manager of Civic Services
Email: pete.fetterer@kohlerco.com

MAYTAG CORPORATION FOUNDATION

P.O. Box 39 403 West 4th Street N
Newton, IA 50208-0039
Phone: 515-787-6357
Fax: 515-787-8676

#141 • Maytag Scholarship Program

Type: Scholarship. Renewable, based on grades.
Eligibility: Applicant must be the child of a Maytag Corp. employee and take the PSAT in the fall of his or her junior year in high school. This award must be used in the following years of study: • Freshman
Deadline: January 2.

Award Amount: $ 500 - $ 2,000.
Number Of Awards: 25 - 35.
Applications Received: 150.
Odds Of Winning: 23% of applicants on average receive an award each year.
Contact: Janis C. Cooper, Director, Foundation Programs

MEDTRONIC, INC.

Corporate Human Resources
7000 Central Avenue, NE
Minneapolis, MN 55432
Phone: 612-514-3367
Fax: 612-514-3123
Website: http://www.medtronic.com

#142 • Palmer J. Hermunslie Scholarship

Type: Scholarship. Renewable.
Eligibility: Applicant must be the dependent child of a Medtronic employee. This award must be used in the following years of study: • Freshman • Sophomore • Junior • Senior
Deadline: January 15.
Award Amount: $ 500 - $ 3,000.
Number Of Awards: 52.
Applications Received: 150.
Odds Of Winning: 25% of applicants on average receive an award each year.
Contact: Citizen's Scholarship Foundation of America, Inc.
1505 Riverview Road P.O. Box 297
St. Peter, MN 56002
Phone: 800-537-4180

NATIONAL ASSOCIATION OF LETTER CARRIERS

100 Indiana Avenue, NW
Washington, DC 20001
Phone: 202-393-4695

#143 • Wm. C. Doherty Scholarship

Type: Scholarship. Renewable. Transcript submittal required for renewal.
Eligibility: Applicant must be the child of an active, retired, or deceased letter carrier. This award must be used in the following years of study: • Freshman
Deadline: December 31.
Award Amount: $ 800.
Number Of Awards: 15.
Contact: Scholarship

NEW HAMPSHIRE FOOD INDUSTRIES EDUCATION FOUNDATION

110 Stark Street
Manchester, NH 03101

Phone: 603-669-9333
Fax: 603-623-1137
Email: scholarships@grocers.org

#144 • New Hampshire Food Industry Scholarship

Type: Scholarship. Renewable.
Eligibility: Applicant must be an employee or the child of an employee of a New Hampshire Grocer's Association (NHGA)-member company. This award must be used in the following years of study: • Freshman • Sophomore • Junior • Senior
Deadline: March 31.
Award Amount: $ 1,000.
Number Of Awards: 10.
Applications Received: 150.
Odds Of Winning: 13% of applicants on average receive an award each year.
Contact: John Dumais, Treasurer

PITNEY-BOWES INC.

One Elmcroft (52-11)
Stamford, CT 06926-0700
Phone: 203-351-6161

#145 • Pitney-Bowes Scholarship

Type: Scholarship. Not renewable.
Eligibility: Applicant must be a graduating high school senior, rank in top third of class, and be the dependent of a Pitney-Bowes employee. Selection is based upon high school class rank, SAT I scores, potential accomplishments, and financial need. This award must be used in the following years of study: • Freshman • Sophomore • Junior • Senior
Deadline: December 31.
Award Amount: $ 2,500.
Number Of Awards: 30.
Contact: Scholarships
One Elmcroft (52-11)
Stamford, CT 06926-0700
Phone: 203-351-6161

RAHR FOUNDATION

567 Grain Exchange Building
P.O. Box 15186
Minneapolis, MN 55414
Phone: 612-332-5161
Fax: 612-332-6841

#146 • Rahr Foundation Scholarship

Type: Scholarship. Renewable. Satisfactory GPA and full-time status are required to retain scholarship.
Eligibility: Applicant must be the child of a current or retired Rahr Malting, Co. employee. This award must be used in the following years of study: • Freshman • Sophomore • Junior • Senior

Deadline: March 15.
Award Amount: $ 3,000.
Number Of Awards: 7.
Contact: Mary Gresham, Secretary and Director
Phone: 612-332-5161

RHODE ISLAND GOLF ASSOCIATION, BURKE MEMORIAL FUND

Charles Orms Building
10 Orms Street, Suite 326
Providence, RI 02904
Phone: 401-272-1350

#147 • John P. Burke Memorial Scholarship

Type: Scholarship. Renewable. Recipient must maintain a minimum 2.0 GPA for renewal.
Eligibility: Applicant must have worked for at least three years as a caddie, pro shop worker, or grounds personnel at a golf club affiliated with Rhode Island Golf Association. This award must be used in the following years of study: • Freshman • Sophomore • Junior • Senior
Deadline: May 15.
Award Amount: $ 750 - $ 2,000.
Number Of Awards: 26.
Contact: Kathrina McCurry, Administrator

SID RICHARDSON MEMORIAL FUND

309 Main Street
Fort Worth, TX 76102
Phone: 817-336-0494
Fax: 817-332-2176
Email: jhrosacker@sidrichardson.org

#148 • Sid Richardson Memorial Fund Scholarship

Type: Scholarship. Renewable. Recipient may reapply if he or she maintains a minimum 2.0 GPA.
Eligibility: Applicant must be the child or grandchild of a current or retired employee (with at least three years of full-time service) of one of the following companies: Bass Brothers Enterprises, Bass Enterprises Production, City Center Development, Leapartners, L.P. (dba Sid Richardson Gasoline Co.-Jal), Perry R. Bass, Inc., Richardson Aviation, Richardson Oils, Richardson Products II, San Jose Cattle Co., Sid Richardson Carbon, Sid Richardson Gasoline, Sid W. Richardson Foundation, SRGC Aviation. Selection is competitive and is based upon academic achievement and financial need. This award must be used in the following years of study: • Freshman • Sophomore • Junior • Senior • Masters • Doctoral • Other postgraduate level
Deadline: March 31.
Award Amount: $ 1,000 - $ 6,000.
Number Of Awards: 15.

Applications Received: 62.
Odds Of Winning: 25% of applicants on average receive an award each year.
Contact: Jo Helen Rosacker, Administrator

STONE FOUNDATION SCHOLARSHIP

150 North Michigan Avenue
Chicago, IL 60601-7568

#149 • Stone Foundation Scholarship

Type: Scholarship. Renewable. Scholarship is renewable at the discretion of the scholarship committee if recipient maintains a minimum 2.0 GPA.
Eligibility: Applicant must be the child of a full-time Stone Container, Corp. employee who has worked at the company for at least two years. Selection is based upon scholarship, character, community, and student activities. This award must be used in the following years of study: • Freshman
Deadline: April 1.
Award Amount: $ 2,000.
Number Of Awards: 10.
Contact: Nicole Stevens, Compensation Analyst
Phone: 312-649-4253

THE GERBER FOUNDATION

4747 West 48th Street, Suite 153
Fremont, MI 49412
Phone: 231-924-3175
Fax: 231-924-7906

#150 • Gerber Foundation Scholarship

Type: Scholarship. Renewable. Minimum 2.0 GPA is required to retain scholarship.
Eligibility: Applicant must be the dependent of an employee of Gerber Products, Co. This award must be used in the following years of study: • Freshman • Sophomore • Junior • Senior
Deadline: February 28.
Award Amount: $ 1,500.
Number Of Awards: 205.
Applications Received: 48.
Odds Of Winning: 68% of applicants on average receive an award each year.
Contact: Catherine Obits, Program Assistant
Phone: 231-924-3175
Fax: 231-924-7906

TUITION EXCHANGE

1308 19th Street, NW
Washington, DC 20036
Phone: 202-462-9100
Fax: 202-785-1540
Website: http://www.tuitionexchange.org

#151 • Tuition Exchange Scholarship

Type: Scholarship. Renewable.
Eligibility: Applicant must be a family member or dependent of an employee at one of the approximately 430 participating Tuition Exchange colleges and universities. This award must be used in the following years of study: • Freshman • Sophomore • Junior • Senior • Masters • Doctoral • Other postgraduate level • study abroad, special programs
Deadline: None.
Award Amount: Varies.
Number Of Awards: 2,700.
Contact: Tuition Exchange liaison officer where parent is employed

ULTRAMAR DIAMOND SHAMROCK CORPORATION

P.O. Box 696000
San Antonio, TX 78269-6000
Phone: 210-592-2000
Fax: 210-592-2195
Website: http://www.udscorp.com

#152 • Ultramar Diamond Shamrock Scholarship

Type: Scholarship. Renewable.
Eligibility: Applicant must be the child of an Ultramar Diamond Shamrock, Corp. employee. This award must be used in the following years of study: • Freshman
Deadline: January 1.
Award Amount: $ 500 - $ 2,000.
Number Of Awards: 8.
Applications Received: 50.
Odds Of Winning: 16% of applicants on average receive an award each year.
Contact: Jodie Carlson, PR Coordinator
Phone: 210-592-4163
Fax: 210-592-2195
Email: jodie_carlson@udscorp.com

UNION PACIFIC RAILROAD

Scholarship Administrator
1700 Farnam Street, 10th Floor North
Omaha, NE 68102
Phone: 402-997-4000 or 877-275-8747

#153 • Employee Dependent Scholarship

Type: Scholarship. Renewable.
Eligibility: Applicant must be a dependent of a Union Pacific Railroad employee and a National Merit finalist. This award must be used in the following years of study: • Freshman • Sophomore • Junior • Senior
Deadline: Varies.
Award Amount: $ 1,500.

Number Of Awards: 51.
Contact: UP Benefits Center

US AIRWAYS

Public and Community Relations
Crystal Park Four
2345 Crystal Drive
Arlington, VA 22227
Phone: 703-872-5100
Fax: 703-872-5134

#154 • L.O. Barnes Scholarship

Type: Scholarship. Not renewable.
Eligibility: Applicant must be a child of a US Airways employee who has at least two years of full-time service and must submit SAT I scores, a brief description of school/community activities, and a personal statement. This award must be used in the following years of study: • Freshman
Deadline: April.
Award Amount: $ 1,000.
Number Of Awards: 5.
Contact: Sharon Taylor, Director of Public Affairs
Email: sharontaylor@usairways.com

VENTURA COUNTY COMMUNITY FOUNDATION

1317 Del Norte Road, Suite 150
Camarillo, CA 93010
Phone: 805-988-0196
Fax: 805-485-5537

#155 • Saticoy Lemon Association Employee Scholarhip

Type: Scholarship. Not renewable.
Eligibility: Applicant must be the legal ward of an employee of Saticoy Lemon Association. This award must be used in the following years of study: • Freshman
Field(s) Of Study: Agriculture.
Deadline: March 9.
Award Amount: $ 600.
Number Of Awards: 2.
Applications Received: 3.
Odds Of Winning: 66% of applicants on average receive an award each year.
Contact: Gail Brown, Program Director

WASHINGTON POST

Thomas Ewing Memorial Carrier Scholarship
1150 15th Street, NW
Washington, DC 20079
Phone: 202-334-6060
Fax: 202-334-4319

#156 • *Washington Post* Thomas Ewing Memorial Education Grant

Type: Grant. Renewable.
Eligibility: Applicant must be a *Washington Post* carrier who has been on the route at least 18 months. This award must be used in the following years of study: • Freshman • Sophomore • Junior • Senior • Masters • Doctoral • technical or vocational school students
Deadline: January 29.
Award Amount: $ 1,000 - $ 2,000.
Number Of Awards: 35.
Odds Of Winning: 80% of applicants on average receive an award each year.
Contact: Jay O'Hare or Terry Lyn Johnson, Sales Development Managers
Fax: 202-496-3947

WOMEN GROCERS OF AMERICA

1825 Samuel Morse Drive
Reston, VA 20190-5317
Phone: 703-437-5300
Fax: 703-437-7768
Email: wga@nationalgrocers.org
Website: http://www.nationalgrocers.org

#157 • Mary Macey Scholarship

Type: Scholarship. Renewable. Reapplication is required for renewal.
Eligibility: Applicant must be planning a career in the grocery industry. This award must be used in the following years of study: • Sophomore • Junior • Senior • Masters
Deadline: June 1.
Award Amount: $ 1,000.
Number Of Awards: 2.
Applications Received: 31.
Odds Of Winning: 23% of applicants on average receive an award each year.
Contact: Anne Wintersteen, N.G.A. Liaison

Chemistry

AMERICAN CHEMICAL SOCIETY (ACS)

1155 16th Street, NW
Washington, DC 20036

#158 • ACS Scholars Program

Type: Scholarship. Renewable. Partially renewable if recipient maintains 3.0 GPA, remains in chemical science program, and continues to demonstrate financial need.

Eligibility: Applicant must be an African-American, Hispanic/Latino, or Native American (including Native Hawaiian and Alaskan Native) with a minimum 3.0 GPA. This award must be used in the following years of study: • Freshman • Sophomore • Junior • Senior
Field(s) Of Study: Chemistry, chemical-related science.
Deadline: February 15.
Award Amount: $ 600 - $ 2,500.
Number Of Awards: 50 - 300.
Applications Received: 1,000.
Odds Of Winning: 30% of applicants on average receive an award each year.
Contact: Robert J. Hughes, Program Manager
Phone: 202-872-6048 or 800-227-5558
Fax: 202-776-8003

#159 • ACS/PPG Scholars Plus Program

Type: Scholarship. Renewable.
Eligibility: Applicant must be a high school senior entering a full-time four-year undergraduate program with a major in chemistry or chemical engineering. Applicant must be African-American, Hispanic/Latino, or American Indian, demonstrate financial need, be a U.S. citizen or permanent resident, and be from one of the following locations: Lake Charles, La; Shelby and Lexington, N.C.; Cleveland, Ohio; Pittsburgh, Penn; Oak Creek, Wis.; Houston, Tex.; Natrium or New Martinsville, W.Va. This award must be used in the following years of study: • Freshman
Field(s) Of Study: Chemical engineering, chemistry.
Deadline: Varies.
Award Amount: Varies.
Number Of Awards: Varies.
Contact: Robert J. Hughes, Program Manager
Phone: 202-872-6048 or 800-227-5558
Fax: 202-776-8003

City/County of Residence

50 MEN AND WOMEN OF TOLEDO, INC.

P.O. Box 80056
Toledo, OH 43608
Phone: 419-729-4654
Fax: 419-729-4004

#160 • James B. Simmons Memorial Scholarship

Type: Scholarship. Renewable.
Eligibility: Contact for details. This award must be used in the following years of study: • Freshman
Deadline: March 15.
Award Amount: $ 1,500.

Number Of Awards: Varies.
Contact: James C. Caldwell, President

AMARILLO AREA FOUNDATION, INC. (AAF)

801 South Fillmore, #700
Amarillo, TX 79101
Phone: 806-376-4521
Fax: 806-373-3656
Email: sylvia@aaf-hf.org

#161 • AAF Scholarship

Type: Scholarship. Not renewable.
Eligibility: Applicant must be a resident of Armstrong, Briscoe, Carson, Castro, Collingsworth, Childress, Dallam, Deaf Smith, Donley, Gray, Hall, Hansford, Hartley, Hemphill, Hutchinson, Lipscomb, Moore, Ochiltree, Oldham, Parmer, Potter, Randall, Roberts, Sherman, Swisher, or Wheeler county in the northernmost Texas Panhandle. This award must be used in the following years of study: • Freshman
Deadline: April 1.
Award Amount: $ 500 - $ 1,000.
Number Of Awards: 75 - 219.
Applications Received: 700.
Contact: Sylvia Artho, Scholarship Coordinator

BAILEY FOUNDATION

P.O. Box 494
Clinton, SC 29325
Phone: 864-938-2632
Fax: 864-938-2669

#162 • Mercer Silas Bailey Memorial Scholarship

Type: Scholarship. Renewable.
Eligibility: Applicant must have attended either Clinton High School or Laurens District #55 Consolidated High School (S.C.). Selection is based upon academic standing, SAT I scores, extracurricular activities, and financial need. This award must be used in the following years of study: • Freshman • Sophomore • Junior • Senior
Deadline: April 15.
Award Amount: $ 4,000.
Number Of Awards: 2.
Applications Received: 28.
Contact: Cheryl Allen, Trust Officer

BERTELSMANN'S WORLD OF EXPRESSION SCHOLARSHIP PROGRAM

1540 Broadway, 23rd Floor
New York, NY 10036-4098
Phone: 212-930-4978

Fax: 212-782-0349
Email: bwoesp@bmge.com
Website: http://www.worldofexpression.org

#163 • World of Expressions Scholarship

Type: Scholarship. Not renewable.
Eligibility: Applicant must attend a public secondary school in New York City and submit an original composition in music, literature, or new media. Selection is based upon creative expression and originality. This award must be used in the following years of study: • Freshman • Sophomore • Junior • Senior
Deadline: February 1.
Award Amount: $ 500 - $10,000.
Number Of Awards: 68.
Applications Received: 2,363.
Odds Of Winning: 3% of applicants on average receive an award each year.
Contact: Yamira Fret, Administrative Assistant
Phone: 212-930-5899
Fax: 212-982-0349
Email: yamira.fret@bmge.com

BERYL BUCK INSTITUTE FOR EDUCATION

18 Commercial Boulevard
Novato, CA 94949
Phone: 415-883-0122
Fax: 415-883-0260

#164 • Marin County American Revolution Bicentennial Scholarship

Type: Scholarship. Not renewable.
Eligibility: Applicant must have been a resident of Marin County (CA) since September 1 of the prior year and plan to attend an approved institution. This award must be used in the following years of study: • Sophomore • Junior • Senior • Masters • Doctoral • Other postgraduate level
Deadline: March 31.
Award Amount: $ 500 - $ 3,500.
Number Of Awards: 1 - 3.
Applications Received: 125.
Odds Of Winning: 2% of applicants on average receive an award each year.
Contact: Marie Kanarr

BLACKHAWK STATE BANK

P.O. Box 719
Beloit, WI 53512-0719
Phone: 608-364-8914

#165 • George E. Andrews Scholarship

Type: Scholarship. Renewable.
Eligibility: Applicant must be a graduate of a Beloit,

Wis., high school. Selection is based upon financial need, moral character, industriousness, and scholastic standing. Applicant must rank in top 3rd of class. Award must be used in the following years of study: Freshman
Deadline: March 15.
Award Amount: $ 3,000.
Number Of Awards: 1 - 2.
Applications Received: 50.
Odds Of Winning: 4% of applicants on average receive an award each year.
Contact: Jan Ruster, Trust Officer

CHEMFIRST FOUNDATION, INC.

700 North Street
P.O. Box 1249
Jackson, MS 39215-1249
Phone: 601-948-7550
Fax: 601-960-6832

#166 • ChemFirst Foundation Scholarship

Type: Scholarship. Not renewable.
Eligibility: Applicant must be a resident of Dayton, Ohio, Hayward, Calif., Jackson, Miss., Tyrone, Penn., or the Mississippi Gulf Coast, and have the recommendation of his or her high school guidance counselor. This award must be used in the following years of study: • Freshman
Deadline: in Spring.
Award Amount: $ 1,300.
Number Of Awards: 23.
Applications Received: 23.
Odds Of Winning: 100% of applicants on average receive an award each year.
Contact: Your high school guidance counselor

COLLINS PINE COMPANY

Almanor Scholarship Fund
P.O. Box 796
Chester, CA 96020
Phone: 916-258-2111

#167 • Almanor Scholarship

Type: Scholarship. Renewable if recipient is enrolled full-time and maintains a minimum 3.0 GPA.
Eligibility: Applicant must be a graduate of Chester High School in California. This award must be used in the following years of study: • Freshman • Sophomore • Junior • Senior • Masters • Doctoral • Other postgraduate level
Deadline: August 1.
Award Amount: $ 1,800 - $ 2,400.
Number Of Awards: 60 - 70.
Applications Received: 50.
Odds Of Winning: 95% of applicants on average receive an award each year.
Contact: Dede Rame, Bookkeeper

COMMUNITY FOUNDATION OF GREATER CHATTANOOGA, INC.

1220 Market Street
Chattanooga, TN 37402
Phone: 423-265-0586
Fax: 423-265-0587

#168 • Together We Can Scholarship

Type: Scholarship. Renewable. Normal progress towards degree required to retain scholarship.
Eligibility: Applicant must be enrolled in Hamilton County school and be a resident of Chattanooga, Tenn. For further information, contact high school guidance counselor. This award must be used in the following years of study: • Freshman • Sophomore • Junior • Senior
Deadline: March 28.
Award Amount: $ 1,330 - $ 2,660.
Number Of Awards: 50.
Applications Received: 150.
Contact: Sandra Visher, Scholarship Administrator

COMMUNITY FOUNDATION OF GREATER LORAIN COUNTY

1865 N. Ridge Road, East Suite A
Lorain, OH 44055
Phone: 440-277-0142
Fax: 440-277-6955

#169 • Walter and Virginia Nord Scholarship

Type: Scholarship. Renewable.
Eligibility: Contact for details. This award must be used in the following years of study: • Freshman
Deadline: Varies.
Award Amount: $ 1,000.
Number Of Awards: 4.
Applications Received: 167.
Odds Of Winning: 3% of applicants on average receive an award each year.
Contact: See above.

COMMUNITY FOUNDATION SERVING RICHMOND AND CENTRAL VIRGINIA

7325 Beaufort Springs Drive, Suite 210
Richmond, VA 23225-8470
Phone: 804-330-7400
Fax: 804-330-5992
Email: sdavis@tcfrichmond.org
Website: http://www.tcfrichmond.org

#170 • Cental Virginia Scholarship

Type: Scholarship. Not renewable.
Eligibility: Applicant must be a U.S. citizen attending a high school in metropolitan Richmond, Va.,

planning to enroll in a two- or four-year college or university in the continental U.S., and must demonstrate academic achievement and leadership or community service. Preference is given to applicants enrolling in private postsecondary institutions. This award must be used in the following years of study: • Freshman
Deadline: March 10.
Award Amount: $ 500 - $ 5,000.
Number Of Awards: Varies.
Contact: Susan Brown Davis, Senior Program Officer
Email: sdavis@tcfrichmond.org

#171 • Kristin Elaine Dickerson Scholarship

Type: Scholarship. Not renewable.
Eligibility: Applicant must be a U.S. citizen planning to enroll in a two- or four-year college or university in the continental U.S., graduating from Atlee High School (Hanover County, Va.), and must demonstrate academic achievement and leadership or community service. This award must be used in the following years of study: • Freshman
Deadline: March 10.
Award Amount: $ 500 - $ 5,000.
Number Of Awards: Varies.
Contact: Susan Brown Davis, Senior Program Officer
Email: sdavis@tcfrichmond.org

#172 • Dollars for Scholars

Type: Scholarship. Not renewable.
Eligibility: Applicant must be a U.S. citizen planning to enroll in a two- or four-year college or university in the continental U.S., graduating from Northumberland High School (Heathsville, Va.), and must demonstrate academic achievement, financial need, and leadership or community service. This award must be used in the following years of study: • Freshman
Deadline: March 10.
Award Amount: $ 500 - $ 5,000.
Number Of Awards: Varies.
Contact: Susan Brown Davis, Senior Program Officer
Email: sdavis@tcfrichmond.org

#173 • Matthew Anthony Grappone Memorial Scholarship

Type: Scholarship. Not renewable.
Eligibility: Applicant must be a U.S. citizen planning to enroll in a two- or four-year college or university in the continental U.S., graduating from Atlee High Schoo (Hanover County, Va.) or other public high schools in Hanover County, and must demonstrate academic achievement and leadership or community service. This award must be used in the following years of study: • Freshman
Deadline: March 10.
Award Amount: $ 500 - $ 5,000.

Number Of Awards: Varies.
Contact: Susan Brown Davis, Senior Program Officer
Email: sdavis@tcfrichmond.org

#174 • Joseph H. Jones, Sr. Scholarship

Type: Scholarship. Not renewable.
Eligibility: Applicant must be a U.S. citizen planning to enroll in a two- or four-year college or university in the continental U.S., graduating from Charles City High School (Charles City, Va.), and must demonstrate academic achievement and leadership or community service. This award must be used in the following years of study: • Freshman
Deadline: March 10.
Award Amount: $ 500 - $ 5,000.
Number Of Awards: Varies.
Contact: Susan Brown Davis, Senior Program Officer
Email: sdavis@tcfrichmond.org

#175 • Christopher Gray and George Chancellor Memorial Scholarships

Type: Scholarship. Not renewable.
Eligibility: Applicant must be a U.S. citizen planning to enroll in a two- or four-year college or university in the continental U.S., graduating from James Monroe High School (Fredericksburg, Va.), and must demonstrate academic achievement, financial need, and leadership or community service. This award must be used in the following years of study: • Freshman
Deadline: March 10.
Award Amount: $ 500 - $ 5,000.
Number Of Awards: 2.
Contact: Susan Brown Davis, Senior Program Officer
Email: sdavis@tcfrichmond.org

#176 • Frederic Scott Reed Scholarship

Type: Scholarship. Not renewable.
Eligibility: Applicant must be a U.S. citizen planning to enroll in a two- or four-year college or university in the continental U.S., graduating from Goochland High School (Goochland, Va.), and must demonstrate academic achievement, civic contributions to Goochland County, and leadership or community service. This award must be used in the following years of study: • Freshman
Deadline: March 10.
Award Amount: $ 500 - $ 5,000.
Number Of Awards: Varies.
Contact: Susan Brown Davis, Senior Program Officer
Email: sdavis@tcfrichmond.org

DONNA REED FOUNDATION FOR THE PERFORMING ARTS

1305 Broadway
P.O. Box 122
Denison, IA 51442

Phone: 712-263-3334
Fax: 712-263-8026
Email: info@donnareed.org
Website: http://www.frii.com/~fujii/home.html

#177 • Donna Reed Performing Arts Scholarships - Crawford County

Type: Scholarship. Not renewable.
Eligibility: Applicant must be a resident of Crawford County, Iowa, or a Crawford County high school graduate, be a citizen or permanent resident of the U.S. or one of its official territories, and graduate or have graduated from high school between September 1 of the previous year and August 31 of the current year. Scholarships will be awarded in each of the following divisions: Actiing, Musical Theatre, Vocal, Instrumental, and Dance. Applicant must submit audiotape, videotape, or CD of his or her performance, depending on category. This award must be used in the following years of study: • Freshman
Deadline: March 15 (early entries); April 1 (late entries).
Award Amount: $ 500. Partial Tuition. Tuition-free scholarships to Annual Donna Reed Festival and Workshops for the Performing Arts.
Number Of Awards: 10.
Contact: Sandy Scott, Director

FULLER E. CALLAWAY FOUNDATION

209 Broome Street
P.O. Box 790
LaGrange, GA 30241
Phone: 706-884-7348
Fax: 706-884-0201

#178 • Hatton Lovejoy Scholarship

Type: Scholarship. Renewable. Applicant must rank in the top half of college class to retain scholarship.
Eligibility: Applicant must have been a resident of Troup County, Ga., for at least two years, must graduate from an accredited high school, and must rank in the top quarter of graduating class. This award must be used in the following years of study: • Freshman
Deadline: February 15.
Award Amount: $ 3,600.
Number Of Awards: 10.
Contact: J. T. Gresham, General Manager
209 Broome Street P.O. Box 790
LaGrange, GA 30241
Phone: 706-884-7348

GEORGE J. RECORD SCHOOL FOUNDATION

P.O. Box 581
365 Main Street

Conneaut, OH 44030
Phone: 440-599-8283

#179 • George J. Record School Foundation Scholarship

Type: Scholarship. Renewable. Six semesters or nine quarters of religion over the four years of college are required to retain scholarship.
Eligibility: Applicant must be a legal resident of Ashtabula County, Ohio, plan to attend on a full-time basis a private, Protestant-based college approved by the Foundation, and demonstrate financial need. This award must be used in the following years of study: • Freshman • Sophomore • Junior • Senior
Deadline: May 20 (freshmen); June 20 (others).
Award Amount: $ 500 - $ 3,000.
Number Of Awards: 64 - 82.
Applications Received: 50.
Odds Of Winning: 25% of applicants on average receive an award each year.
Contact: Charles N. Lafferty, Executive Director

H.T. EWALD FOUNDATION

15175 East Jefferson Avenue
Grosse Point, MI 48230
Phone: 313-821-1278
Fax: 313-821-3299
Email: ewaldfndtn@aol.com

#180 • H.T. Ewald Scholarship

Type: Scholarship. Renewable if recipient provides current grades and schedules an interview with a board member.
Eligibility: Applicant must be a resident of metropolitan Detroit and submit grades, test scores, and letters of recommendation. This award must be used in the following years of study: • Freshman
Deadline: April 1.
Award Amount: $ 2,000.
Number Of Awards: 12.
Applications Received: 350.
Odds Of Winning: 3% of applicants on average receive an award each year.
Contact: Shelagh Czuprenski, Secretary

HAUSS-HELMS FOUNDATION, INC.

P.O. Box 25
Wapakoneta, OH 45895
Phone: 419-738-4911

#181 • Hauss-Helms Foundation, Inc. Scholarship

Type: Grant. Not renewable.
Eligibility: Applicant must be a resident of Allen County or Auglaize County, Ohio, demonstrate financial need, and rank in the top half of graduating

class or have a minimum 2.0 GPA. This award must be used in the following years of study: • Freshman • Sophomore • Junior • Senior • Masters • Doctoral
Deadline: April 15.
Award Amount: $ 400 - $ 5,000.
Number Of Awards: 200.
Contact: James E. Weger, President

ITALIAN AMERICAN CHAMBER OF COMMERCE

30 South Michigan Avenue Suite 504
Chicago, IL 60603
Phone: 312-553-9137
Fax: 312-553-9142

#182 • Italian American Chamber of Commerce Scholarship

Type: Scholarship. Not renewable.
Eligibility: Applicant must be a resident of Cook, DuPage, Kane, Lake, McHenry, or Will counties, Ill., be of Italian ancestry, and have a minimum 3.5 GPA (4.5 on 5.0 scale). Applicant must submit a letter including biographical sketch, explanation of Italian ancestry, and reason for wanting the award, two letters of recommendation, transcripts, photo, and a self-addressed, stamped envelope. This award must be used in the following years of study: • Freshman • Sophomore • Junior • Senior
Deadline: May 31.
Award Amount: $ 1,000.
Number Of Awards: 2.
Applications Received: 40.
Contact: Italian American Chamber of Commerce Scholarship

JEWISH FAMILY AND CHILDREN'S SERVICES (JFCS)

2245 Post Street
San Francisco, CA 94115
Phone: 415-561-1226
Fax: 415-561-1242
Email: lag@jfcs.org

#183 • Vivienne Camp College Scholarship

Type: Scholarship. Renewable. Recipient must reapply to retain scholarship.
Eligibility: Applicant must be Jewish, have a minimum 3.0 GPA, be a resident of Marin, San Francisco, San Mateo, northern Santa Clara, or Sonoma Counties, Calif., and demonstrate academic achievement, promise, and financial need This award must be used in the following years of study: • Freshman • Sophomore • Junior • Senior • vocational school
Deadline: None.
Award Amount: $ 4,350.

Number Of Awards: 4.
Contact: Val Steinberg, JFCS Financial Aid Center

#184 • Jacob Rassen Memorial Scholarship Fund

Type: Scholarship. Not renewable.
Eligibility: Applicant must be Jewish, be under age 22, have a minimum 3.0 GPA, demonstrate financial need, and be a resident of Marin, San Francisco, San Mateo, northern Santa Clara, or Sonoma Counties, Calif. Award is for a study trip to Israel. This award must be used in the following years of study: • Freshman • Sophomore • Junior • Senior • Masters
Deadline: none.
Award Amount: $ 1,900.
Number Of Awards: 1.
Odds Of Winning: 50% of applicants on average receive an award each year.
Contact: Val Steinberg, JFCS Financial Aid Center

#185 • Stanley Olson Youth Scholarship

Type: Grant. Renewable. Reapplication required.
Eligibility: Applicant must be Jewish, be under age 26, have a minimum 3.0 GPA, demonstrate financial need, and be a resident of Marin, San Francisco, San Mateo, northern Santa Clara, or Sonoma Counties, Calif. This award must be used in the following years of study: • Freshman • Sophomore • Junior • Senior • Masters • Doctoral
Field(s) Of Study: Liberal arts.
Deadline: None.
Award Amount: $ 2,500.
Number Of Awards: Varies.
Odds Of Winning: 5% of applicants on average receive an award each year.
Contact: Val Steinberg, JFCS Financial Aid Center

#186 • Rozsi & Jeno Zisovich Jewish Studies Scholarship Fund to Teach the Holocaust

Type: Scholarship. Not renewable.
Eligibility: Applicant must be a resident of Marin, San Francisco, San Mateo, northern Santa Clara, or Sonoma Counties, Calif., have a minimum 3.0 GPA, demonstrate financial need, and be pursuing a career that will involve teaching the Holocaust to future generations. This award must be used in the following years of study: • Freshman • Sophomore • Junior • Senior • Masters • Doctoral • Other postgraduate level
Field(s) Of Study: Holocaust-related studies.
Deadline: None.
Award Amount: $ 3,200.
Number Of Awards: 1.
Contact: Val Steinberg, JFCS Financial Aid Center

LAWRENCE COUNTY CONSERVATION DISTRICT

Attn: Scholarship Committee
430 Court Street

New Castle, PA 16101
Phone: 724-652-4512
Fax: 724-657-2008
Email: lawcon@pathway.net
Website: http://www.pathway.net/lawcon/

#187 • Lawrence Conservation District Scholarship

Type: Scholarship. Not renewable.
Eligibility: Applicant must be a resident of Lawrence County (PA) who is attending a U.S. school. This award must be used in the following years of study: • Sophomore • Junior • Senior
Field(s) Of Study: Agriculture, agriculture education, conservation, conservation education, environmental resource management, environmental resource management education, forestry, forestry education.
Deadline: December 31.
Award Amount: $ 500.
Number Of Awards: 1 - 2.
Applications Received: 2.
Odds Of Winning: 50% of applicants on average receive an award each year.
Contact: Jo Ann McCready, District Manager

LEOLA W. AND CHARLES H. HUGG TRUST

Chase Bank of Texas
P.O. Box 6033 SU Station
Georgetown, TX 78626
Phone: 512-863-1259

#188 • Trust Scholarship

Type: Scholarship. Renewable if recipient maintains minimum 2.5 GPA and shows financial need.
Eligibility: Applicant must graduate from Williamson County High School and have resided in Williamson County at least two years prior to graduation. Applicant must rank in the top quarter of class and show financial need. This award must be used in the following years of study: • Freshman • Sophomore • Junior • Senior
Deadline: May 1.
Award Amount: Varies.
Number Of Awards: Varies.
Applications Received: 350.
Contact: Debbie Sanderfer, Hugg Trust Scholarship Consultant

LEONARD H. BULKELEY SCHOLARSHIP FUND

P.O. Box 1426
New London, CT 06320
Phone: 203-447-1461

#189 • Leonard H. Bulkeley Scholarship

Type: Scholarship. Renewable. Reapplication is required to retain scholarship.
Eligibility: Applicant must be an undergraduate student between the ages of 16 and 25, who is a resident of New London, Conn. Selection is based upon academic standing, financial need, school and community activities, and a personal interview. This award must be used in the following years of study: • Freshman • Sophomore • Junior • Senior
Deadline: April 1.
Award Amount: $ 1,000.
Number Of Awards: 48.
Applications Received: 80.
Odds Of Winning: 75% of applicants on average receive an award each year.
Contact: Saun Murallo, Secretary

MARIN COUNTY AMERICAN REVOLUTION BICENTENNIAL COMMITTEE

Buck Institute for Education
18 Commercial Boulevard
Novato, CA 94949
Phone: 415-883-0122
Fax: 415-883-0260
Email: buck@bie.org
Website: http://www.bie.org

#190 • Marin County American Revolution Bicentennial Scholarship

Type: Scholarship. Not renewable.
Eligibility: Applicant must be a resident of Marin County, Calif., since September 1 of the year prior to application. Applicant must plan to attend an approved institution of higher learning. This award must be used in the following years of study: • Freshman
Deadline: on or before March 31.
Award Amount: $ 500 - $ 3,500.
Number Of Awards: 1.
Contact: Marie Kanarr
Email: marie@bie.org

MOUNT VERNON URBAN RENEWAL AGENCY

City Hall, Roosevelt Square Second Floor
Mount Vernon, NY 10550
Phone: 914-699-7230

#191 • Thomas E. Sharpe Memorial Scholarship

Type: Scholarship. Renewable. Reapplication is required to retain scholarship.
Eligibility: Applicant must be a Mount Vernon, N.Y., resident, have a minimum 2.0 GPA, be enrolled on a

full-time basis, and meet the income criteria. This award must be used in the following years of study: • Freshman • Sophomore • Junior • Senior
Deadline: Early June.
Award Amount: $ 300 - $ 1,000.
Number Of Awards: 156.
Contact: Mrs. Donna Fulco, Scholarship Program Manager

NELLIE MARTIN CARMAN SCHOLARSHIP COMMITTEE

P.O. Box 60052
Shoreline, WA 98160-0052
Phone: 206-542-9357

#192 • Nellie Martin Carman Scholarship

Type: Scholarship. Renewable for up to four years in the state of Washington if recipient maintains minimum 3.0 GPA.
Eligibility: Applicant must be nominated by his/her high school to become a candidate for this scholarship. Applicant must be attending a public high school in the county of King, Pierce or Snohomish in the state of Washington, be a U.S. citizen, and be planning to attend college in the state of Washington. Applicants majoring in music, sculpture art, interior decorating, and domestic science are not eligible. Selection based on financial need, academic record, college test scores, school and community activity. This award must be used in the following years of study: • Freshman
Deadline: March 15.
Award Amount: $ 1,000.
Number Of Awards: 30 - 40.
Applications Received: 85.
Contact: High school guidance counselor

NEW YORK TRI-STATE OWNERS & OPERATORS

Valley Stream, NY 11580
Phone: 800-537-4180
Website: http://www.mcdonaldsnymetro.com

#193 • McDonald's Golden Arches Scholarship

Type: Scholarship. Not renewable.
Eligibility: Applicant must be a resident of the New York tri-state area, have a minimum 3.0 GPA, and demonstrate financial need. Selection is based upon community service or employment. This award must be used in the following years of study: • Freshman
Deadline: March 1.
Award Amount: $ 1,000 - $ 5,000.
Number Of Awards: 92.
Applications Received: 1,800.
Odds Of Winning: 5% of applicants on average

receive an award each year.
Contact: Your high school guidance office.

PSYCHOLOGICAL SERVICES FOR YOUTH

Dr. Patricia Carpenter
121 West North Street
Brighton, MI 48116
Phone: 810-227-9333

#194 • Phoenix Scholarship

Type: Scholarship. Not renewable.
Eligibility: Applicant must be a resident of Livingston County, MI. Based on exceptional creativity and financial need. This award must be used in the following years of study: • Freshman • Sophomore • Junior
Field(s) Of Study: Acting, creative writing, dance, drawing, music performance or composition, painting, sculpture, singing.
Deadline: May 8.
Award Amount: $ 100 - $ 1,000.
Number Of Awards: 1 - 4.
Applications Received: 12.
Odds Of Winning: 60% of applicants on average receive an award each year.
Contact: Dr. Patricia Carpenter

ROSALIE TILLES NONSECTARIAN CHARITY FUND

P.O. Box 387
St. Louis, MO 63166
Phone: 314-418-2992

#195 • Rosalie Tilles Scholarship Award

Type: Scholarship. Renewable. Recipient must maintain a minimum 2.75 GPA to renew the award.
Eligibility: Applicant must be a resident of St. Louis or St. Louis County, Mo. and be attending a college or university in Missouri. This award must be used in the following years of study: • Freshman
Deadline: May 1.
Award Amount: Varies.
Number Of Awards: 5 - 15.
Contact: Your college financial aid office

SAN JOSE PEACE CENTER

48 South Seventh Street
San Jose, CA 95112
Phone: 408-297-2299
Fax: 408-297-2299

#196 • Charles Walton Peace Essay Contest

Type: Contest. Not renewable.
Eligibility: Applicant must be a high school student

(grade 9-12), be a resident of Santa Clara County, Calif., and submit essay. Contact above address for application form and essay theme. This award must be used in the following years of study: • Freshman
Deadline: February 22.
Award Amount: $ 25 - $ 1,000.
Number Of Awards: 15.
Applications Received: 30.
Odds Of Winning: 50% of applicants on average receive an award each year.
Contact: Ann Beaudet, Peace Essay Coordinator

VAN WERT COUNTY FOUNDATION

138 East Main Street
Van Wert, OH 45891
Phone: 419-238-1743
Fax: 419-238-3374
Email: vwcf@bright.net
Website: http://www.vanwert.com

#197 • General Scholarship

Type: Scholarship. Renewable if recipient maintains a minimum 3.0 GPA and proves financial need.
Eligibility: Applicant must be a resident of Allen, Van Wert, or Paulding counties, Ohio, with a minimum 3.0 GPA who can prove financial need. This award must be used in the following years of study: • Sophomore • Junior • Senior
Deadline: June 1.
Award Amount: $ 350 - $ 3,000.
Number Of Awards: 270.
Applications Received: 300.
Odds Of Winning: 90% of applicants on average receive an award each year.
Contact: Larry L. Wendel, Executive Secretary

VENTURA COUNTY COMMUNITY FOUNDATION

1317 Del Norte Road, Suite 150
Camarillo, CA 93010
Phone: 805-988-0196
Fax: 805-485-5537

#198 • Charles K. Gose Scholarship

Type: Scholarship. Not renewable.
Eligibility: Applicant must be a graduate of Channel Islands, Calif. high school and have an interest in government and civic activities. This award must be used in the following years of study: • Freshman
Deadline: March 9.
Award Amount: $ 2,000.
Number Of Awards: 1.
Contact: Gail Brown, Program Director

#199 • Gary W. Chism Memorial Award

Type: Scholarship. Not renewable.

Eligibility: Applicant must be a Ventura County, Calif., student. This award must be used in the following years of study: • Freshman • Sophomore • Junior
Field(s) Of Study: Business/medical research.
Deadline: Varies.
Award Amount: $ 1,000.
Number Of Awards: 1.
Contact: Gail Brown, Program Officer

#200 • Jean Weber Memorial Scholarship

Type: Scholarship. Not renewable.
Eligibility: Applicant must be a Ventura County, Calif., student who has contributed to safe schools, improved school attendance, and encouraged good citizenship. This award must be used in the following years of study: • Freshman • Sophomore • Junior
Deadline: Varies.
Award Amount: $ 500.
Number Of Awards: 2.
Contact: Gail Brown, Program Officer

Civil/Environmental Engineering

ACI INTERNATIONAL/CONREF

P.O. Box 9094
Farmington Hills, MI 48333
Phone: 248-848-3713
Fax: 248-848-3720
Email: dlepping@aci-int.org

#201 • Peter D. Courtois Concrete Construction Scholarship

Type: Scholarship. Not renewable.
Eligibility: Applicant must demonstrate interest and ability in the field of concrete construction and attend school in the U.S. or Canada. Applicant must submit transcripts, recommendations, and essay. This award must be used in the following years of study: • Senior
Field(s) Of Study: Concrete construction, engineering, technology.
Deadline: January 11.
Award Amount: $ 1,000.
Number Of Awards: 2.
Applications Received: 25.
Odds Of Winning: 12% of applicants on average receive an award each year.
Contact: Dot Lepping, Scholarship Coordinator

AMERICAN SOCIETY OF HIGHWAY ENGINEERS - CAROLINA TRIANGLE SECTION

5800 Faringdon Place
Suite 105

Raleigh, NC 27609
Phone: 919-878-9560

#202 • American Society of Highway Engineers - Carolina Triangle Section Scholarship

Type: Scholarship. Not renewable.
Eligibility: Applicant must be a U.S. citizen and North Carolina resident. Applicant must submit transcripts and short statement on achievements and academic interests. This award must be used in the following years of study: • Sophomore • Junior • Senior
Field(s) Of Study: Civil engineering/transportation.
Deadline: March 31.
Award Amount: $ 1,000.
Number Of Awards: 3.
Applications Received: 12.
Odds Of Winning: 25% of applicants on average receive an award each year.
Contact: Lubin V. Prevatt, Scholarship Chairman
Phone: 919-733-7842

AMERICAN WATER WORKS ASSOCIATION NEW YORK SECTION

Department of Civil Engineering
University at Buffalo
Buffalo, NY 14260
Phone: 716-645-2409

#203 • John C. Robbins Scholarship

Type: Scholarship. Not renewable.
Eligibility: Applicant must have a major that is considered beneficial to the New York State water works. Selection is based upon academic achievement and extracurricular activities. This award must be used in the following years of study: • Junior • Senior
Deadline: November 30.
Award Amount: $ 1,000.
Number Of Awards: 1.
Contact: John E. Van Benschoten, Associate Professor

ASSOCIATED GENERAL CONTRACTORS (AGC) EDUCATION AND RESEARCH FOUNDATION

1957 E Street, NW
Washington, DC 20006
Phone: 202-393-2040

#204 • AGC Education and Research Foundation Undergraduate Scholarship

Type: Scholarship. Renewable for up to four years if recipient maintains satisfactory GPA.
Eligibility: Applicant must plan to pursue a career in the construction industry, enroll in a four- or five-year program, and be a U.S. citizen or permanent resident alien. Selection is based upon grades, extracurricular activities, employment experience, financial need, and desire for a construction career. This award must be used in the following years of study: • Sophomore • Junior • Senior
Field(s) Of Study: Civil engineering, construction.
Deadline: November 1.
Award Amount: $ 1,500 - $ 6,000.
Number Of Awards: Varies.
Contact: Floretta D. Slade, Program Coordinator
Fax: 202-347-4004

ASSOCIATION OF STATE DAM SAFETY OFFICIALS (ASDSO)

450 Old Vine Street 2nd Floor
Lexington, KY 40507-1544
Phone: 606-257-5140
Fax: 606-323-1958
Email: damsafety@aol.com, info@damsafety.org
Website: http://members.aol.com/damsafety/homepage.htm

#205 • ASDSO Scholarship

Type: Scholarship. Renewable. Junior scholarship may be renewed; reapplication required to renew scholarship.
Eligibility: Applicant must be a U.S. citizen enrolled in an accredited program, have a minimum 3.0 GPA for the first two years of college, and demonstrate an interest in pursuing a career in hydraulics, hydrology, or geotechnical disciplines, or another discipline related to the design, construction, and operation of dams. Applicant must be recommended by his or her academic advisor and must submit a typewritten essay describing his or her goals and purpose for applying. Selection is based upon academic scholarship, financial need, work experience/activities, and essay. This award must be used in the following years of study: • Junior • Senior
Field(s) Of Study: Civil engineering or other field of study relating to dam safety.
Deadline: February 15.
Award Amount: $ 500 - $ 5,000.
Number Of Awards: 1 - 2.
Applications Received: 50.
Odds Of Winning: 1% of applicants on average receive an award each year.
Contact: Sarah Mayfield, Information Specialist
Email: smayfield@damsafety.org

NATIONAL ASSOCIATION OF WOMEN IN CONSTRUCTION (NAWIC)

327 Adams Street
Fort Worth, TX 76104
Phone: 817-877-5551 or 800-552-3506
Fax: 817-877-0324

Email: nawic@onramp.net
Website: http://www.nawic.org

#206 • NAWIC Founders' Scholarship Foundation

Type: Scholarship. Renewable. Recipient must reapply for renewal.
Eligibility: Selection is based upon applicant's grades, extracurricular activities, employment experience, interest in construction, evaluations, and financial need. This award must be used in the following years of study: • Sophomore • Junior • Senior
Field(s) Of Study: Construction.
Deadline: February 1.
Award Amount: $ 500 - $ 2,000.
Number Of Awards: 35.
Odds Of Winning: 12% of applicants on average receive an award each year.
Contact: D'Ann Sard, Scholarships
327 Adams Street
Fort Worth, TX 76104
Phone: 817-877-5551 or 800-552-3506
Fax: 817-877-0324
Email: nawic@onramp.net

NATIONAL ROOFING FOUNDATION (NRF)

10255 West Higgins Road
Suite 600
Rosemont, IL 60018-5607
Phone: 847-299-9070

#207 • Roofing Industry Scholarship/Grant

Type: Scholarship. Renewable if recipient maintains minimum "C+" grade average.
Eligibility: Applicant must be an employee, the immediate family member of an employee, or an immediate family member of a regular contractor member of National Roofing Contractors Association. This award must be used in the following years of study: • Freshman • Sophomore • Junior • Senior
Deadline: January 31.
Award Amount: $ 1,000.
Number Of Awards: 3.
Applications Received: 195.
Odds Of Winning: 2% of applicants on average receive an award each year.
Contact: Scholarship Coordinator

Club Affiliation

A.R.A. SCHOLARSHIP FOUNDATION, INC.

3975 Fair Ridge Drive, Suite 20

Terrace Level North
Fairfax, VA 22033-2924
Phone: 703-385-1001
Fax: 703-385-1494
Website: http://www.autorecyc.org

#208 • A.R.A. Scholarship

Type: Scholarship. Renewable. Recipient must reapply for renewal.
Eligibility: Applicant must be a child of employees of direct member companies belonging to the Automotive Recyclers Association. This award must be used in the following years of study: • Freshman • Sophomore • Junior • Senior • Trade students
Deadline: March 15.
Award Amount: $ 1,000.
Number Of Awards: 35.
Odds Of Winning: 35% of applicants on average receive an award each year.
Contact: Kelly Badillo, Foundation Manager

AIRCRAFT ELECTRONICS ASSOCIATION (AEA) EDUCATIONAL FOUNDATION

4217 S. Hocker Drive
Independence, MO 64055
Phone: 816-373-6565
Fax: 816-478-3100
Email: info@aea.net
Website: http://www.aea.net

#209 • Lee Tarbox Scholarship

Type: Scholarship. Not renewable.
Eligibility: Contact for details. This award must be used in the following years of study: • Freshman • Sophomore • Junior • Senior
Field(s) Of Study: Avionics/aircraft repair.
Deadline: February 15.
Award Amount: $ 2,500.
Number Of Awards: 1.
Applications Received: 150.
Odds Of Winning: 1% of applicants on average receive an award each year.
Contact: Mike Adamson, AEA Educational Foundation Executive Director

AMERICAL DIVISION VETERANS ASSOCIATION

P.O. Box 1381
Boston, MA 02104
Phone: 314-631-4106

#210 • ADVA Scholarship Fund

Type: Scholarship. Not renewable.
Eligibility: Applicant must be a relative of a dues-

paying Americal Association member. This award must be used in the following years of study: • Freshman • Sophomore • Junior • Senior
Deadline: May 1.
Award Amount: $ 1,000 - $ 3,000.
Number Of Awards: 3.
Applications Received: 19.
Odds Of Winning: 20% of applicants on average receive an award each year.
Contact: R. Ward, Chairman, ADVA Scholarship Fund

AMERICAN ANGUS ASSOCIATION

ATTN: Junior Activities
3201 Frederick Avenue
St. Joseph, MO 64506
Phone: 816-383-5100
Fax: 816-233-9703
Email: angus@angus.org
Website: http://www.angus.org

#211 • Angus Foundation Scholarship

Type: Scholarship. Not renewable.
Eligibility: Applicant must be a regular, life, or junior member of the American Angus Association. This award must be used in the following years of study: • Freshman • Sophomore • Junior • Senior
Deadline: May 15.
Award Amount: $ 1,000 - $ 2,500.
Number Of Awards: 17.
Applications Received: 70.
Odds Of Winning: 24% of applicants on average receive an award each year.
Contact: James Fisher, Director of Junior Activities

AMERICAN ASSOCIATION OF BIOANALYSTS (AAB)

917 Locust Street
Suite 1100
St. Louis, MO 63101-1419
Phone: 314-241-1445
Fax: 314-241-1449
Email: aab1445@primary.net

#212 • David Birenbaum Scholarship

Type: Scholarship. Not renewable.
Eligibility: Applicant must be an AAB member in good standing or the child or spouse of an AAB member. This award must be used in the following years of study: • Freshman • Sophomore • Junior • Senior • Masters • Doctoral • Other postgraduate level
Deadline: April 15.
Award Amount: $ 500 - $ 1,000.
Number Of Awards: 3.
Applications Received: 15.
Odds Of Winning: 20% of applicants on average

receive an award each year.
Contact: Scholarships

AMERICAN CRIMINAL JUSTICE ASSOCIATION/LAMBDA ALPHA EPSILON (ACJA/LAE)

P.O. Box 601047
Sacramento, CA 95860
Phone: 916-484-6553
Fax: 916-488-2227
Email: acjalae@aol.com
Website: http://www.acjalae.org

#213 • ACJA/LAE National Student Paper Competition

Type: Contest. Not renewable.
Eligibility: Applicant must be a member of ACJA/LAE in good standing and submit an original paper dealing with issues concerning the criminal justice field. This award must be used in the following years of study: • Sophomore • Junior • Senior • Masters • Doctoral
Field(s) Of Study: Criminal justice.
Deadline: January 31.
Award Amount: $ 50 - $ 150.
Number Of Awards: 9.
Applications Received: 6.
Odds Of Winning: 100% of applicants on average receive an award each year.
Contact: Karen K. Campbell, Executive Secretary

AMERICAN LEGION - KANSAS

1314 Topeka Avenue
Topeka, KS 66612
Phone: 913-232-9315

#214 • Albert M. Lappin Scholarship

Type: Scholarship. Not renewable.
Eligibility: Applicant must be the child of an American Legion or Auxiliary member. Scholarship must be used at an approved Kansas college, university, or trade school. This award must be used in the following years of study: • Freshman • Sophomore • Junior
Deadline: Febuary 15.
Award Amount: $ 1,000.
Number Of Awards: 1.
Contact: Scholarships

#215 • Charles W. and Annette Hill Scholarship

Type: Scholarship. Not renewable.
Eligibility: Applicant must be a descendant of an American Legion member. This award must be used in the following years of study: • Freshman

Deadline: February 15.
Award Amount: $ 1,000.
Number Of Awards: 1.
Contact: Scholarships

AMERICAN LEGION - SOUTH CAROLINA

P.O. Box 11355
Columbia, SC 29211
Phone: 803-799-1992
Fax: 803-771-9831

#216 • American Legion Robert E. David Scholarship

Type: Scholarship. Renewable. Recipient must reapply to retain scholarship.
Eligibility: Applicant must be a relative of a South Carolina Legionnaire. Selection is based upon academics and financial need. Award may be used at South Carolina schools only. This award must be used in the following years of study: • Freshman • Sophomore • Junior • Senior
Deadline: May 1.
Award Amount: $ 500.
Number Of Awards: 5 - 20.
Applications Received: 50.
Odds Of Winning: 10% of applicants on average receive an award each year.
Contact: Jim Hawk, Department Adjutant

AMERICAN LEGION - WASHINGTON

P.O. Box 3917
Lacey, WA 98509-3917
Phone: 360-491-4373
Fax: 360-491-7442

#217 • Children and Youth Scholarship

Type: Scholarship. Not renewable.
Eligibility: Applicant must be the child of an American Legion member or its auxiliary and live in Washington. This award must be used in the following years of study: • Freshman
Deadline: April 1.
Award Amount: $ 1,000 - $ 1,500.
Number Of Awards: 2.
Contact:
P.O. Box 3917
Lacey, WA 98509-3917
Phone: 360-491-4373
Fax: 360-491-7442

AMERICAN LEGION AUXILIARY (ALA), NATIONAL HEADQUARTERS

777 North Meridian Street
Third Floor
Indianapolis, IN 46204
Phone: 317-635-6291
Fax: 317-636-5590

#218 • Spirit of Youth Scholarship

Type: Scholarship. Renewable. Applicant must maintain a minimum 3.0 GPA and continue membership in ALA to retain scholarship.
Eligibility: Applicant must be a junior member of the ALA and have paid dues for the three preceding years. This award must be used in the following years of study: • Freshman • Sophomore • Junior • Senior
Deadline: March 10.
Award Amount: $ 1,000.
Number Of Awards: 5.
Contact: National Secretary, Accounting Manager, or Secretary to National President, Scholarships

#219 • Girl Scout Achievement Award

Type: Scholarship. Not renewable.
Eligibility: Applicant must have received the Girl Scout Gold Award, be an active member of her religious institution and received the appropriate religious emblem (cadet or senior scout level), must have demonstrated practical citizenship, and submit four recommendations. This award must be used in the following years of study: • Freshman
Deadline: March 10.
Award Amount: $ 1,000.
Number Of Awards: 1.
Contact: National Secretary, National Treasurer, or Youth Programs Coordinator, Scholarships

AMERICAN QUARTER HORSE YOUTH ASSOCIATION (AQHYA)

P.O. Box 200
Amarillo, TX 79168
Phone: 806-376-4811
Fax: 806-349-6409

#220 • AQHYA Scholarship

Type: Scholarship. Renewable if minimum requirements are met.
Eligibility: Applicant must have been a member of AQHYA for at least three years, meet academic qualifications, and submit letters of recommendation. Selection is based upon civic involvement and financial need. This award must be used in the following years of study: • Freshman
Deadline: May 15.
Award Amount: $ 1,000.
Number Of Awards: 25.
Applications Received: 100.
Odds Of Winning: 25% of applicants on average receive an award each year.
Contact: Lori Pearson, Youth Secretary

AMERICAN SOCIETY OF MECHANICAL ENGINEERS (ASME)

Education Services Department
Three Park Avenue
New York, NY 10016-5990
Phone: 212-591-8131
Fax: 212-591-7143
Website: http://www.asme.org/educate/aid

#221 • Melvin R. Green Scholarship

Type: Scholarship. Not renewable.
Eligibility: Applicant must be a student member of ASME. Selection is based upon leadership, potential contribution to the mechanical engineering profession, and academic ability. This award must be used in the following years of study: • Junior • Senior
Field(s) Of Study: Mechanical engineering or a related program.
Deadline: April 15.
Award Amount: $ 3,000.
Number Of Awards: 2.
Contact: Theresa Oluwanifise, Admin. Assistant
Email: oluwanifiset@asme.org

AMERICAN SOCIETY OF TRAVEL AGENTS (ASTA) FOUNDATION, INC.

1101 King Street
Alexandria, VA 22314
Phone: 703-739-2782
Fax: 703-684-8319
Email: astasysop@astanet.com
Website: http://www.astanet.com

#222 • Arizona Chapter Dependent/ Employee Membership Scholarship

Type: Scholarship. Renewable. Reapplication required.
Eligibility: Applicant must be the dependent of an active ASTA Arizona Chapter agency member or associate member or be an employee or the dependent of an employee of an Arizona ASTA member agency. Applicant must be enrolled in a school in Arizona and submit a 500-word essay on career goals. Send a self-addressed, stamped envelope for information and application. This award must be used in the following years of study: • Sophomore • Junior • Senior • last year in junior college
Deadline: July 28.
Award Amount: $ 1,500.
Number Of Awards: 1.
Contact: Myriam Lechuga or Mary Kate Koehl

ASSOCIATION OF THE SONS OF POLAND

333 Hackensack Street
Carlstadt, NJ 07072-1043
Phone: 201-935-2807
Fax: 201-935-2752
Email: dkwasop@aol.com

#223 • Association of the Sons of Poland Achievement Award

Type: Scholarship. Not renewable.
Eligibility: Applicant must be a member of the Association of the Sons of Poland for at least two years and be insured by the association. Selection is based upon high school transcript, letter of application, character, and leadership qualities. This award must be used in the following years of study: • Freshman
Deadline: May 14.
Award Amount: $ 50.
Number Of Awards: 16.
Applications Received: 16.
Odds Of Winning: 100% of applicants on average receive an award each year.
Contact: Dorothy Kostecka-Wieczerzak, Secretary

BIG BROTHERS BIG SISTERS OF AMERICA/ARBY'S

230 North 13th Street
Philadelphia, PA 19107
Phone: 215-567-7000
Fax: 215-567-0394
Website: http://www.bbbsa.org

#224 • Big Brothers Big Sisters of America/ Arby's Scholarship

Type: Scholarship. Renewable up to four years.
Eligibility: Applicant must have participated in a Big Brothers Big Sisters program as a "Little Brother or Sister" only with an affiliated Big Brothers Big Sisters program. High school "Big Brothers or Sisters" are not eligible. This award must be used in the following years of study: • Freshman • Sophomore • Junior
Deadline: March 31.
Award Amount: $ 5,000.
Number Of Awards: 2.
Contact: Gina P. Jones, Fund Development Office Manager
Email: gjones@bbbsa.org

BOY SCOUTS OF AMERICA DEL-MAR-VA COUNCIL

Scholarship Administrator
801 Washington Street
Wilmington, DE 19801-4319
Phone: 302-622-3325
Fax: 302-622-3308

#225 • Del-Mar-Va Council, Inc. Boy Scouts of America Educational Scholarship

Type: Scholarship. Renewable. Reapplication required.

Eligibility: Applicant must be a registered Del-Mar-Va Scout or Explorer. This award must be used in the following years of study: • Freshman
Deadline: June 30 (fall semester); December 31 (spring semester).
Award Amount: $ 500 - $ 1,000.
Number Of Awards: 4.
Contact: Martin J. Tuohy, Exploring Executive

BOYS AND GIRLS CLUBS OF CHICAGO

820 North Orleans, Suite 235
Chicago, IL 60610
Phone: 312-627-2700
Fax: 312-258-0005

#226 • Nichols Scholarship

Type: Scholarship. Renewable.
Eligibility: Applicant must be a member of the Boys and Girls Clubs of Chicago with a minimum 2.5 GPA. Applications must be submitted by the club director. Selection is based upon financial need and grades. This award must be used in the following years of study: • Freshman
Deadline: May 1.
Award Amount: $ 200 - $ 2,000.
Number Of Awards: 20.
Contact: Mary Ann Mahon-Huels, VP of Operations

CALIFORNIA TEACHERS ASSOCIATION (CTA)

1705 Murchison Drive
P.O. Box 921
Burlingame, CA 94011-0921
Phone: 650-697-1400
Email: scholarships@cta.org
Website: http://www.cta.org

#227 • CTA Scholarship for Members

Type: Scholarship. Renewable.
Eligibility: Applicant must be an active member of CTA. This award must be used in the following years of study: • Masters • Doctoral • Other postgraduate level
Deadline: February 15.
Award Amount: $ 2,000.
Number Of Awards: 5.
Applications Received: 140.
Odds Of Winning: 4% of applicants on average receive an award each year.
Contact: Human Rights Department

CATHOLIC AID ASSOCIATION

3499 Lexington Avenue North
St. Paul, MN 55126-8098
Phone: 651-490-0170
Fax: 651-490-0746
Website: http://www.catholicaid.qpg.com

#228 • Catholic Aid Association College Tuition Scholarship

Type: Scholarship. Not renewable.
Eligibility: Applicant must be a member of Catholic Aid for at least two years at time of application. Applicant must submit current transcript, letter describing vocational goals and interests, letters of recommendation from his or her pastor and principal or counselor, and recent photograph. This award must be used in the following years of study: • Freshman • Sophomore
Deadline: March 15.
Award Amount: $ 300 - $ 500.
Number Of Awards: 150.
Applications Received: 200.
Odds Of Winning: 75% of applicants on average receive an award each year.
Contact: Bonnie M. Volpe, Executive Secretary

CATHOLIC WORKMAN

ATTN: Scholarships
111 West Main P.O. Box 47
New Prague, MN 56071
Phone: 612-758-2229
Fax: 612-758-6221
Email: catholicwk@aol.com

#229 • Catholic Workman College Scholarship

Type: Scholarship. Not renewable.
Eligibility: Applicant must be a Catholic Workman member for at least 12 months. Freshman applicant must submit most recent ACT/SAT I scores. Other applicants must submit most recent college transcript and two letters of recommendation. Submission of record of Catholic Workman/school/community/church involvement is optional. This award must be used in the following years of study: • Freshman • Sophomore • Junior • Senior • Masters • Doctoral • Other postgraduate level
Deadline: July 1.
Award Amount: $ 500 - $ 1,000.
Number Of Awards: 14.
Applications Received: 50.
Odds Of Winning: 28% of applicants on average receive an award each year.
Contact: Lenore Krava

COMMUNITY FOUNDATION SERVING RICHMOND AND CENTRAL VIRGINIA

7325 Beaufort Springs Drive, Suite 210
Richmond, VA 23225-8470

Phone: 804-330-7400
Fax: 804-330-5992
Email: sdavis@tcfrichmond.org
Website: http://www.tcfrichmond.org

#230 • Becky Briggs Memorial Scholarship

Type: Scholarship. Not renewable.
Eligibility: Applicant must be a U.S. citizen planning to enroll in a two- or four-year college or university in the continental U.S., and must demonstrate academic achievement, leadership or community service, and commitment to community service, scholarship, school, and Interact (Rotary-sponsored) activities. This award must be used in the following years of study: • Freshman
Deadline: March 10.
Award Amount: $ 500 - $ 5,000.
Number Of Awards: Varies.
Contact: Susan Brown Davis, Senior Program Officer
Email: sdavis@tcfrichmond.org

COSTUME SOCIETY OF AMERICA (CSA)

55 Edgewater Drive
P.O. Box 73
Earleville, MD 21919
Phone: 410-275-1619
Fax: 410-275-8936
Website: http://www.costumesocietyamerica.com

#231 • Stella Blum Research Grant

Type: Grant. Not renewable.
Eligibility: Applicant must be participating in a degree program at an accredited institution, is a Costume Society of America member, and has research projects in the field of North American costume that are part of the degree requirements. Selection is based upon creativity and innovation, specific awareness of and attention to costume matters, impact on the broad field of costume, awareness of interdisciplinarity of the field, ability to successfully implement the proposed project in a timely manner, and faculty advisor recommendation. This award must be used in the following years of study: • Sophomore • Junior • Senior • Masters • Doctoral • Other postgraduate level
Deadline: February 1.
Award Amount: $ 3,000.
Number Of Awards: 1.
Applications Received: 3.
Odds Of Winning: 33% of applicants on average receive an award each year.
Contact: Chair, Stella Blum Research Grant

#232 • Adele Filene Travel Award

Type: Contest. Not renewable.
Eligibility: Applicant must be a member of CSA. Award is to assist travel to CSA National Symposia to present either a juried paper or a poster. This award must be used in the following years of study: • Freshman • Sophomore • Junior • Senior • Masters • Doctoral • Other postgraduate level
Field(s) Of Study: Costume.
Deadline: March 15.
Award Amount: $ 500.
Number Of Awards: 1.
Applications Received: 3.
Odds Of Winning: 33% of applicants on average receive an award each year.
Contact: Scholarship Committee

DANISH SISTERHOOD OF AMERICA

7326 Lehigh Court
Zephyrhills, FL 33540-1014
Phone: 813-715-0642

#233 • Danish Sisterhood of America Scholarship

Type: Scholarship. Not renewable.
Eligibility: Applicant must be a Danish Sisterhood of America member or the child of a member. Selection is based upon academic achievement. This award must be used in the following years of study: • Freshman • Sophomore • Junior • Senior • Vocational/technical students
Deadline: February 28.
Award Amount: $ 1,000.
Number Of Awards: 5.
Contact: Joyce G. Houck, National Vice President and Scholarship Chairperson

DELTA GAMMA FOUNDATION

3250 Riverside Drive
P.O. Box 21397
Columbus, OH 43221-0397
Phone: 614-481-8169
Fax: 614-481-0133
Website: http://www.deltagamma.org

#234 • Delta Gamma Foundation Scholarship

Type: Scholarship. Not renewable.
Eligibility: Applicant must be a member of Delta Gamma fraternity. This award must be used in the following years of study: • Sophomore • Junior • Senior
Deadline: February 1.
Award Amount: $ 1,000.
Number Of Awards: 100.
Odds Of Winning: 50% of applicants on average receive an award each year.
Contact: Kathy Kessler, Scholarships, Fellowships, and Loans Chairman
Email: kathyd@deltagamma.org

DELTA PHI EPSILON EDUCATIONAL FOUNDATION

734 West Port Plaza, Suite 271
St. Louis, MO 63146
Phone: 314-275-2626
Fax: 314-275-2655
Email: info@dphie.org
Website: http://www.dphie.org

#235 • Delta Phi Epsilon Scholarship

Type: Scholarship. Not renewable.
Eligibility: Applicant must be a member of Delta Phi Epsilon or the child or grandchild of a member. This award must be used in the following years of study: • Sophomore • Junior • Senior • Masters • Doctoral • Other postgraduate level
Deadline: April 1.
Award Amount: $ 500.
Number Of Awards: 4 - 8.
Contact: Ellen Alper, Executive Director

EASTERN ORTHODOX COMMITTEE ON SCOUTING

862 Guy Lombardo Avenue
Freeport, NY 11520
Phone: 516-868-4050
Fax: 516-868-4052

#236 • Eastern Orthodox Committee on Scouting Scholarship

Type: Scholarship. Not renewable.
Eligibility: Applicant must be of the Eastern Orthodox faith, be a Boy Scout or Girl Scout, and have earned Eagle Award or Gold Award. This award must be used in the following years of study: • Freshman
Deadline: March 15.
Award Amount: $ 500 - $ 1,000.
Number Of Awards: Varies.
Applications Received: 600.
Odds Of Winning: Less than 1% of applicants on average receive an award each year.
Contact: George H. Boulukos, National Chairman

EXPLORERS CLUB

46 East 70th Street
New York, NY 10021
Phone: 212-628-8383
Fax: 212-288-4449
Website: http://www.explorers.org

#237 • Youth Activity Grant

Type: Grant. Not renewable.
Eligibility: Applicant must submit two letters of recommendation. This award must be used in the

following years of study: • Freshman • Sophomore • Junior • Senior • Masters
Deadline: April 30.
Award Amount: $ 700 - $ 1,000.
Number Of Awards: 30.
Applications Received: 1,500.
Odds Of Winning: 2% of applicants on average receive an award each year.
Contact: Youth Activity Fund

FEDERATION LIFE INSURANCE OF AMERICA

ATTN: President
6011 South 27th Street
Greenfield, WI 53221
Phone: 414-281-6281
Fax: 414-281-6405

#238 • Federation Life Insurance of America Scholarship

Type: Scholarship. Renewable.
Eligibility: Applicant must be a member of Federation Life Insurance for at least five years. This award must be used in the following years of study: • Freshman • Sophomore • Junior • Senior
Deadline: May 31.
Award Amount: $ 350.
Number Of Awards: 20 - 30.
Applications Received: 22.
Odds Of Winning: 100% of applicants on average receive an award each year.
Contact: Sandy King
Phone: 414-281-6281

FIRST CATHOLIC SLOVAK LADIES ASSOCIATION (FCSLA)

Director of Fraternal Scholarship Aid
24950 Chagrin Boulevard
Beachwood, OH 44122
Phone: 216-464-8015
Fax: 216-464-8717

#239 • First Catholic Slovak Ladies Association Scholarship

Type: Scholarship. Not renewable.
Eligibility: Applicant must have had an annuity, $5,000 term insurance, or $1,000 legal reserve policy with the FCSLA for at least three years prior to application. Applicant must be a full-time student, submit transcript, 500-word essay on career goals and objectives, and demonstrate financial need. Award may be used toward tuition only. This award must be used in the following years of study: • Freshman • Sophomore • Junior • Senior • Masters • Doctoral • Other postgraduate level
Deadline: March 1.

Award Amount: $ 1,000.
Number Of Awards: 80.
Applications Received: 200.
Odds Of Winning: 40% of applicants on average receive an award each year.
Contact: Scholarship Committee

GOLF COURSE SUPERINTENDENTS ASSOCIATION OF AMERICA FOUNDATION

1421 Research Park Drive
Lawrence, KS 66049
Phone: 785-832-3678
Fax: 785-832-3665
Website: http://www.gcsaa.org

#240 • GCSAA Legacy Awards

Type: Scholarship. Not renewable.
Eligibility: Applicant must be the child or grandchild of a member of the Golf Course Superintendents Association of America. Selection is based upon academic excellence, extracurricular activities, and a brief essay. This award must be used in the following years of study: • Freshman • Sophomore • Junior • Senior • Masters • Doctoral
Deadline: April 15.
Award Amount: $ 1,500.
Number Of Awards: 10.
Applications Received: 50.
Odds Of Winning: 20% of applicants on average receive an award each year.
Contact: Pam Smith, Scholarship Coordinator
Email: psmith@gscaa.org

INTERNATIONAL BUCKSKIN HORSE ASSOCIATION (IBHA)

P.O. Box 268
Shelby, IN 46377
Phone: 219-552-1013
Fax: 219-552-1013
Email: ibha@netnit.co.net
Website: http://www.ibha.org

#241 • Youth Scholarship Fund of IBHA, Inc.

Type: Scholarship. Renewable. Minimum "B" grade average is required to maintain scholarship.
Eligibility: Applicant must hold membership in IBHA, participate in IBHA Youth events for at least two years, be 22 or younger with excellent test scores and strong recommendations, and participate in school and community activities. This award must be used in the following years of study: • Freshman • Sophomore • Junior • Senior
Deadline: February 1.
Award Amount: $ 500 - $ 1,500.

Number Of Awards: 8.
Applications Received: 12.
Odds Of Winning: 75% of applicants on average receive an award each year.
Contact: Richard E. Kurzeja, Secretary
3517 West 231st Avenue
Lowell, IN 46356
Phone: 219-552-1013

JAPANESE AMERICAN CITIZENS LEAGUE (JACL)

National Headquarters
1765 Sutter Street
San Francisco, CA 94115
Phone: 415-921-5225
Fax: 415-931-4671
Email: jacl@jacl.org
Website: http://www.jacl.org

#242 • Patricia & Gail Ishimoto Memorial Scholarship

Type: Scholarship. Not renewable.
Eligibility: Applicant must be a member or the child of a member of JACL. Selection is based upon personal statement, letters of recommendation, transcripts, work experience, and community involvement. This award must be used in the following years of study: • Freshman
Deadline: March 1.
Award Amount: $ 1,000 - $ 5,000.
Number Of Awards: Varies.
Contact: Scholarship Administrator

#243 • Kyataro & Yasuo Abiko Memorial Scholarship

Type: Scholarship. Not renewable.
Eligibility: Applicant must be a member or the child of a member of JACL. Selection is based upon personal statement, letters of recommendation, transcripts, work experience, and community involvement. This award must be used in the following years of study: • Sophomore • Junior • Senior
Field(s) Of Study: Preference is given to applicants interested in journalism or agriculture.
Deadline: April 1.
Award Amount: $ 1,000 - $ 5,000.
Number Of Awards: Varies.
Contact: Scholarship Administrator

#244 • Masao & Sumako Itano Memorial Scholarship

Type: Scholarship. Not renewable.
Eligibility: Applicant must be a member or the child of a member of JACL. Selection is based upon personal statement, letters of recommendation, transcripts, work experience, and community

involvement. This award must be used in the following years of study: • Freshman
Deadline: March 1.
Award Amount: $ 1,000 - $ 5,000.
Number Of Awards: Varies.
Contact: Scholarship Administrator

#245 • Kenji Kasai Memorial Scholarship

Type: Scholarship. Not renewable.
Eligibility: Applicant must be a member or the child of a member of JACL. Selection is based upon personal statement, letters of recommendation, transcripts, work experience, and community involvement. This award must be used in the following years of study: • Freshman
Deadline: March 1.
Award Amount: $ 1,000 - $ 5,000.
Number Of Awards: Varies.
Contact: Scholarship Administrator

#246 • Henry & Chiyo Kuwahara Memorial Scholarship for Entering Freshmen

Type: Scholarship. Not renewable.
Eligibility: Applicant must be a member or the child of a member of JACL. Selection is based upon personal statement, letters of recommendation, transcripts, work experience, and community involvement. This award must be used in the following years of study: • Freshman
Deadline: March 1.
Award Amount: $ 1,000 - $ 5,000.
Number Of Awards: Varies.
Contact: Scholarship Administrator

#247 • Sam S. Kuwahara Memorial Scholarship for Entering Freshmen

Type: Scholarship. Not renewable.
Eligibility: Applicant must be a member or the child of a member of JACL. Selection is based upon personal statement, letters of recommendation, transcripts, work experience, and community involvement. This award must be used in the following years of study: • Freshman
Field(s) Of Study: Preference is given to applicants with an interest in agriculture or related fields.
Deadline: March 1.
Award Amount: $ 1,000 - $ 5,000.
Number Of Awards: Varies.
Contact: Scholarship Administrator

#248 • Mr. & Mrs. Takashi Moriuchi Scholarship

Type: Scholarship. Not renewable.
Eligibility: Applicant must be a member or the child of a member of JACL. Selection is based upon personal statement, letters of recommendation, transcripts, work experience, and community involvement. This award must be used in the

following years of study: • Freshman
Deadline: March 1.
Award Amount: $ 1,000 - $ 5,000.
Number Of Awards: Varies.
Contact: Scholarship Administrator

#249 • Gongoro Nakamura Memorial Scholarship

Type: Scholarship. Not renewable.
Eligibility: Applicant must be a member or the child of a member of JACL. Selection is based upon personal statement, letters of recommendation, transcripts, work experience, and community involvement. Preference is given to applicants with an interest in public speaking or debate. This award must be used in the following years of study: • Freshman
Deadline: March 1.
Award Amount: $ 1,000 - $ 5,000.
Number Of Awards: Varies.
Contact: Scholarship Administrator

#250 • Yutaka Nakazawa Memorial Scholarship

Type: Scholarship. Not renewable.
Eligibility: Applicant must be a member or the child of a member of JACL. Selection is based upon personal statement, letters of recommendation, transcripts, work experience, and community involvement. This award must be used in the following years of study: • Freshman
Deadline: March 1.
Award Amount: $ 1,000 - $ 5,000.
Number Of Awards: Varies.
Contact: Scholarship Administrator

#251 • South Park Japanese Community Scholarship

Type: Scholarship. Not renewable.
Eligibility: Applicant must be a member or the child of a member of JACL. Selection is based upon personal statement, letters of recommendation, transcripts, work experience, and community involvement. This award must be used in the following years of study: • Freshman
Deadline: March 1.
Award Amount: $ 1,000 - $ 5,000.
Number Of Awards: Varies.
Contact: Scholarship Administrator

#252 • Mr. & Mrs. Uyesugi Memorial Scholarship

Type: Scholarship. Not renewable.
Eligibility: Applicant must be a member or the child of a member of JACL. Selection is based upon personal statement, letters of recommendation, transcripts, work experience, and community involvement. This award must be used in the

following years of study: • Freshman
Deadline: March 1.
Award Amount: $ 1,000 - $ 5,000.
Number Of Awards: Varies.
Contact: Scholarship Administrator

#253 • Mitsuyuki Yonemura Memorial Scholarship

Type: Scholarship. Not renewable.
Eligibility: Applicant must be a member or the child of a member of JACL. Selection is based upon personal statement, letters of recommendation, transcripts, work experience, and community involvement. This award must be used in the following years of study: • Freshman
Deadline: March 1.
Award Amount: $ 1,000 - $ 5,000.
Number Of Awards: Varies.
Contact: Scholarship Administrator

#254 • Alice Yuriko Endo Memorial Scholarship

Type: Scholarship. Not renewable.
Eligibility: Applicant must be a member or the child of a member of JACL. Selection is based upon personal statement, letters of recommendation, transcripts, work experience, and community involvement. Preference is given to residents of the Eastern District Council and to applicants interested in public or social service. This award must be used in the following years of study: • Sophomore • Junior • Senior
Deadline: April 1.
Award Amount: $ 1,000 - $ 5,000.
Number Of Awards: Varies.
Contact: Scholarship Administrator

#255 • Nobuko R. Kodama Fong Memorial Scholarship

Type: Scholarship. Not renewable.
Eligibility: Applicant must be a member or the child of a member of JACL and must be solely provided for by a single parent. Selection is based upon personal statement, letters of recommendation, transcripts, work experience, and community involvement. Preference is given to applicants from the Pacific Northwest District. This award must be used in the following years of study: • Sophomore • Junior • Senior
Deadline: April 1.
Award Amount: $ 1,000 - $ 5,000.
Number Of Awards: Varies.
Contact: Scholarship Administrator

#256 • Saburo Kido Memorial Scholarship

Type: Scholarship. Not renewable.
Eligibility: Applicant must be a member or the child of a member of JACL. Selection is based upon

personal statement, letters of recommendation, transcripts, work experience, and community involvement. This award must be used in the following years of study: • Sophomore • Junior • Senior
Deadline: April 1.
Award Amount: $ 1,000 - $ 5,000.
Number Of Awards: Varies.
Contact: Scholarship Administrator

#257 • Henry & Chiyo Kuwahara Memorial Scholarship for Undergraduates

Type: Scholarship. Not renewable.
Eligibility: Applicant must be a member or the child of a member of JACL. Selection is based upon personal statement, letters of recommendation, transcripts, work experience, and community involvement. This award must be used in the following years of study: • Sophomore • Junior • Senior
Deadline: April 1.
Award Amount: $ 1,000 - $ 5,000.
Number Of Awards: Varies.
Contact: Scholarship Administrator

#258 • Sam S. Kuwahara Memorial Scholarship for Undergraduates

Type: Scholarship. Not renewable.
Eligibility: Applicant must be a member or the child of a member of JACL. Selection is based upon personal statement, letters of recommendation, transcripts, work experience, and community involvement. Preference is given to applicants interested in agriculture or a related field. This award must be used in the following years of study: • Sophomore • Junior • Senior
Deadline: April 1.
Award Amount: $ 1,000 - $ 5,000.
Number Of Awards: Varies.
Contact: Scholarship Administrator

#259 • Mari & James Michener Scholarship

Type: Scholarship. Not renewable.
Eligibility: Applicant must be a member or the child of a member of JACL. Selection is based upon personal statement, letters of recommendation, transcripts, work experience, and community involvement. This award must be used in the following years of study: • Sophomore • Junior • Senior
Deadline: April 1.
Award Amount: $ 1,000 - $ 5,000.
Number Of Awards: Varies.
Contact: Scholarship Administrator

#260 • Yoshiko Tanaka Memorial Scholarship

Type: Scholarship. Not renewable.

Eligibility: Applicant must be a member or the child of a member of JACL. Selection is based upon personal statement, letters of recommendation, transcripts, work experience, and community involvement. Preference is given to applicants interested in Japanese language/culture or in enhancing U.S./Japanese relations. This award must be used in the following years of study: • Sophomore • Junior • Senior
Deadline: April 1.
Award Amount: $ 1,000 - $ 5,000.
Number Of Awards: Varies.
Contact: Scholarship Administrator

#261 • Dr. Thomas T. Yatabe Memorial Scholarship

Type: Scholarship. Not renewable.
Eligibility: Applicant must be a member or the child of a member of JACL. Selection is based upon personal statement, letters of recommendation, transcripts, work experience, and community involvement. This award must be used in the following years of study: • Sophomore • Junior • Senior
Deadline: April 1.
Award Amount: $ 1,000 - $ 5,000.
Number Of Awards: Varies.
Contact: Scholarship Administrator

#262 • Abe & Esther Hagiwara Student Aid Award

Type: Scholarship. Not renewable.
Eligibility: Applicant must be a member or the child of a member of JACL and must exhibit severe financial need. Selection is based upon financial need, personal statement, letters of recommendation, transcripts, work experience, and community involvement. This award must be used in the following years of study: • Freshman • Sophomore • Junior • Senior • Masters • Doctoral
Deadline: April 1.
Award Amount: $ 1,000 - $ 5,000.
Number Of Awards: Varies.
Contact: Scholarship Administrator

#263 • Aiko Susanna Tashiro Hiratsuka Memorial Scholarship

Type: Scholarship. Not renewable.
Eligibility: Applicant must be a member or the child of a member of JACL. Selection is based upon personal statement, letters of recommendation, transcripts, work experience, and community involvement. Professional artists are not eligible. This award must be used in the following years of study: • Freshman • Sophomore • Junior • Senior • Masters • Doctoral
Field(s) Of Study: Performing arts.
Deadline: April 1.

Award Amount: $ 1,000 - $ 5,000.
Number Of Awards: Varies.
Contact: Scholarship Administrator

JAYCEE WAR MEMORIAL FUND

Department 94922
Tulsa, OK 74194-0001
Phone: 918-584-2481
Fax: 918-584-4422

#264 • Scholarship Program

Type: Scholarship. Not renewable.
Eligibility: Applicant must be a U.S. citizen and nominated by the state Jaycee organization (one per state). Selection is based upon the applicant's potential for academic success, financial need, and leadership traits. To request an application, send a self-addressed, stamped #10 envelope, and a $5 application fee. The check or money order should be made payable to JWMF. Requests are taken between July 1 and February 1 only. This award must be used in the following years of study: • Freshman • Sophomore • Junior • Senior • Masters
Deadline: Varies.
Award Amount: $ 1,000 - $ 5,000.
Number Of Awards: 26.
Contact: Scholarship Coordinator
Phone: 918-584-2481, extension 2989

KIWANIS CLUB OF KIRTLAND

Memorial Scholarship Fund
c/o M.G. Winchell, M.D.
9179 Chillicothe Road
Kirtland, OH 44094
Phone: 440-256-1128
Fax: 440-256-8677

#265 • Kirtland Kiwanis Memorial Scholarship

Type: Scholarship. Renewable. Recipient must reapply for renewal.
Eligibility: Applicant must be be a resident in the Kirtland, Ohio, School District and have a minimum 2.5 GPA. This award must be used in the following years of study: • Freshman • Sophomore • Junior • Senior • Masters • Doctoral • Other postgraduate level • Postsecondary students
Deadline: May 9.
Award Amount: $ 1,000.
Number Of Awards: 3 - 4.
Applications Received: 33.
Odds Of Winning: 9% of applicants on average receive an award each year.
Contact: Murray G. Winchell, M.D

KNIGHTS OF COLUMBUS

P.O. Box 1670
Department of Scholarships
New Haven, CT 06507-0901
Phone: 203-772-2130, extension 332
Fax: 203-772-2696

#266 • Matthews & Swift Educational Trust Scholarship

Type: Scholarship. Renewable.
Eligibility: Applicant must be the child of a Knights of Columbus member who was killed or permanently disabled during the conflicts of war or by criminal violence during law enforcement or firefighter duties. Parents must have been members in good standing at the time of their death or disablement. Award may be used at Catholic colleges only. This award must be used in the following years of study: • Freshman • Sophomore • Junior • Senior
Deadline: Varies.
Award Amount: Varies.
Number Of Awards: 2 - 6.
Contact: Rev. Donald Barry, S.J., Dir. of Scholarships

LAMBDA ALPHA NATIONAL COLLEGIATE HONORS SOCIETY FOR ANTHROPOLOGY

Department of Anthropology
Ball State University
Muncie, IN 47306-1099
Phone: 765-285-1577
Fax: 765-285-2163

#267 • Dean's List Scholarship

Type: Scholarship. Not renewable.
Eligibility: Applicant must be Lambda Alpha lifetime member. Applicant must contact the faculty sponsor of his/her chapter to apply. All application materials are submitted by the chapter's faculty sponsor. Selection is based upon academic achievement, commitment to the discipline, and the applicant's future plans. This award must be used in the following years of study: • Senior
Field(s) Of Study: Anthropology.
Deadline: March 1.
Award Amount: $ 1,000.
Number Of Awards: 1.
Applications Received: 8.
Odds Of Winning: 13% of applicants on average receive an award each year.
Contact: See above.

LAMBDA IOTA TAU (LIT)

Prof. Bruce W. Hozeski, Executive Secretary
Department of English

Ball State University
2000 West University Avenue
Munice, IN 47306-0460
Phone: 765-285-8456, 765 285-8580
Fax: 765-285-3765
Email: 00bwhozeski@bsuvc.bsu.edu
Website: http://www.bsu.edu/english/

#268 • LIT Scholarship for Excellence

Type: Scholarship. Not renewable.
Eligibility: Applicants must be a current student member of LIT (which requires being in the top 35% of class, having a minimum 3.5 GPA in at least 12 semester hours of literature, having a 3.0 cumulative GPA, and being in the fifth college semester). Applicants must be sponsored by an active chapter. Selection is based upon the quality of the applicant's scholarly or creative writing as evaluated by a committee. Recipients should demonstrate academic excellence, and should submit an application and a writing sample. This award must be used in the following years of study: • Senior • Masters • Doctoral
Field(s) Of Study: Literature.
Deadline: May 31.
Award Amount: $ 1,000.
Number Of Awards: 3.
Applications Received: 20.
Contact: Bruce W. Hozeski, Executive Secretary

MENOMINEE INDIAN TRIBE OF WISCONSIN

Menominee Tribal Education Office
P.O. Box 910
Keshana, WI 54135
Phone: 715-799-5118
Fax: 715-799-1364
Email: vnuske@mail.wiscnet.net

#269 • Menominee Tribal Higher Education/Adult Vocational Grant

Type: Grant. Renewable if recipient maintains a minimum 2.0 GPA.
Eligibility: Applicant must be a member of the Menominee Indian Tribe of Wisconsin. This award must be used in the following years of study: • Freshman • Sophomore • Junior • Senior
Deadline: Varies.
Award Amount: $ 100 - $ 2,200.
Number Of Awards: Varies.
Contact: Grants

MERCANTILE TRUST, CO. N.A.

P.O. Box 192
Topeka, KS 66601-0192
Phone: 913-291-1000

#270 • Claude and Ina Brey Memorial Endowment Fund Scholarship

Type: Scholarship. Not renewable.
Eligibility: Applicant must be a Fourth Degree Kansas Grange member. This award must be used in the following years of study: • Freshman • Sophomore • Junior • Senior • Masters • Doctoral • Other postgraduate level • trade school
Deadline: April 15.
Award Amount: $ 800.
Number Of Awards: 8.
Contact: Your Local Kansas Grange Chapter

MINERALS, METALS, AND MATERIALS SOCIETY (TMS)

TMS Scholarship Committee
184 Thorn Hill Road
Warrendale, PA 15086
Phone: 724-776-9000, extension 213
Fax: 724-776-3770
Website: http://www.tms.org

#271 • J. Keith Brimacombe Presidential Scholarship

Type: Scholarship. Not renewable.
Eligibility: Applicant must be a member of TMS. This award must be used in the following years of study: • Senior
Field(s) Of Study: Engineering, materials science, metallurgical engineering, minerals processing/extraction.
Deadline: May 1.
Award Amount: $ 5,000.
Number Of Awards: 1.
Contact: Member and Educational Services Department, TMS Student Awards Program

#272 • SMD Scholarship

Type: Scholarship. Not renewable.
Eligibility: Applicant must be enrolled full time and be a member of TMS. Preference is given to seniors enrolled full time in an engineering program related to the structure, property, and processing of materials. This award must be used in the following years of study: • Sophomore • Junior • Senior • Masters
Field(s) Of Study: Materials science/engineering, physical metallurgy.
Deadline: May 1.
Award Amount: $ 2,500.
Number Of Awards: 2.
Contact: Member and Educational Services Department, TMS Student Awards Program

#273 • International Symposium on Superalloys Scholarship

Type: Scholarship. Not renewable.
Eligibility: Applicant must be a member of TMS. Preference is given to an applicant planning a career in superalloys. This award must be used in the following years of study: • Sophomore • Junior • Senior • Masters
Field(s) Of Study: Engineering, materials processing/extraction, materials science, metallurgy.
Deadline: May 1.
Award Amount: $ 1,000.
Number Of Awards: 4.
Contact: Member and Educational Services Department, TMS Student Awards Program

NASA FEDERAL CREDIT UNION

Mitchell-Beall Scholarship
P.O. Box 1588
Bowie, MD 20717-1588
Phone: 301-248-1800, extension 235 or 271
Fax: 301-390-4531
Email: webmaster@nfcu.org
Website: http://www.nfcu.org

#274 • Mitchell-Beall Scholarship

Type: Scholarship. Not renewable.
Eligibility: Applicant must be a member of the NASA Federal Credit Union under age 21. Essay, questionnaire, and interview required. This award must be used in the following years of study: • Freshman
Deadline: in February.
Award Amount: $ 1,000 - $ 5,000.
Number Of Awards: 5 - 7.
Contact: Mitchell-Beall Scholarship

NATIONAL ASSOCIATION OF BLACK ACCOUNTANTS, INC. (NABA)

Program Coordinator
7249-A Hanover Parkway
Greenbelt, MD 20770
Phone: 301-474-6222
Fax: 301-474-3114
Email: cquinn@primanet.com
Website: http://www.nabainc.org

#275 • NABA National Scholarship Program

Type: Scholarship. Renewable. Reapplication is required for renewal.
Eligibility: Applicant must be a current or potential member of NABA of ethnic minority and have a minimum 2.5 GPA. Applicant must submit personal statement, resume, and essay. This award must be used in the following years of study: • Sophomore • Junior • Senior • Doctoral
Field(s) Of Study: Accounting, business administration, economics, finance.
Deadline: December 31.
Award Amount: $ 6,000.

Number Of Awards: 40.
Applications Received: 120.
Odds Of Winning: 33% of applicants on average receive an award each year.
Contact: Charles Quinn, Program Coordinator
Phone: 301-474-6222, extension 114

NATIONAL BETA CLUB

151 West Lee Street
Spartanburg, SC 29306
Phone: 864-583-4553
Fax: 864-542-9300
Email: betaclub@betaclub.org
Website: http://www.betaclub.org

#276 • National Beta Club Scholarship

Type: Scholarship. Not renewable.
Eligibility: Applicant must be a member of National Beta Club and nominated by his or her school. Applicant should contact his or her school's Beta Club for more information. This award must be used in the following years of study: • Freshman
Deadline: December 10.
Award Amount: $ 1,000 - $ 2,500.
Number Of Awards: 206.
Applications Received: 846.
Odds Of Winning: 21% of applicants on average receive an award each year.
Contact: School Beta Club Sponsor (Advisor)

NATIONAL COURT REPORTERS ASSOCIATION

8224 Old Courthouse Road
Vienna, VA 22182-3808
Phone: 703-556-6272
Email: dgaede@ncrahq.org

#277 • CASE Scholarship

Type: Scholarship. Not renewable.
Eligibility: Applicant must be an NCRA member in an NCRA-approved court program and must have a machine shorthand speed of 140-180 words per minute. This award must be used in the following years of study: • Sophomore • Junior
Field(s) Of Study: Court reporting.
Deadline: April 1.
Award Amount: $ 500 - $ 1,500.
Number Of Awards: 3.
Applications Received: 16.
Odds Of Winning: 19% of applicants on average receive an award each year.
Contact: Donna M. Gaede, Approval Program Specialist
Phone: 703-556-6272, extension 171

NATIONAL FRATERNAL SOCIETY OF THE DEAF

1118 South Sixth Street
Springfield, IL 62703
Phone: 217-789-7429
Fax: 217-789-7489
Email: thefrat@nfsd.com
Website: http://www.nfsd.com

#278 • Deaf Scholarship

Type: Scholarship. Renewable if recipient does not receive more than two scholarships from the National Fraternal Society of the Deaf and is a member of the society for one full year.
Eligibility: Applicant must be a member of the National Fraternal Society of the Deaf in good standing for one year prior to application. This award must be used in the following years of study: • Freshman • Sophomore • Junior • Senior
Deadline: July 1.
Award Amount: $ 1,000.
Number Of Awards: 1 - 10.
Applications Received: 7.
Contact: Al Van Nevel, Grand President

NATIONAL SOCIETY OF THE SONS OF THE AMERICAN REVOLUTION

Eagle Scout Scholarship
1000 South Fourth Street
Louisville, KY 40203
Phone: 502-589-1776
Website: http://www.sar.com

#279 • Eagle Scout Scholarship

Type: Scholarship. Not renewable.
Eligibility: Applicant must be in the current class of Eagle scouts (class year runs from July 1 to June 30 of each year). This award must be used in the following years of study: • Freshman
Deadline: December 31.
Award Amount: $ 1,000 - $ 5,000.
Number Of Awards: 2.
Applications Received: 1,500.
Odds Of Winning: Less than 1% of applicants on average receive an award each year.
Contact: National Chairman, Eagle Scout Committee

NATIONAL WOMAN'S RELIEF CORPS

P.O. Box 165
New Durham, NH 03855-0165
Phone: 603-859-2861

#280 • National Woman's Relief Corps Scholarship

Type: Scholarship. Not renewable.

Eligibility: Applicant must be a member or a relative of a member of the National Woman's Relief Corps, Auxiliary to the Grand Army of the Republic, Inc. This award must be used in the following years of study: • Freshman • Sophomore • Junior • Senior
Deadline: June 30.
Award Amount: $ 200 - $ 350.
Number Of Awards: 2 - 12.
Applications Received: 12.
Odds Of Winning: 66% of applicants on average receive an award each year.
Contact: National Woman's Relief Corps

NORTHEASTERN LOGGERS' ASSOCIATION (NELA)

P.O. Box 69
Old Forge, NY 13420
Phone: 315-369-3078
Fax: 315-369-3736
Email: nela@telenet.net

#281 • NELA Scholarship Contest

Type: Scholarship. Not renewable.
Eligibility: Applicant must be a member of the immediate family of a member of NELA or an immediate family member of an employee of an industrial or associate member of NELA. Applicant must submit transcripts and an 1,000-word essay. This award must be used in the following years of study: • Freshman • Sophomore • Junior • Senior • Masters • Technical school students
Deadline: March 31.
Award Amount: $ 500.
Number Of Awards: 3.
Applications Received: 14.
Odds Of Winning: 14% of applicants on average receive an award each year.
Contact: Mona Lincoln, Scholarship Contest
Email: nela@telenet.net

PARENTS WITHOUT PARTNERS

International Scholarship Program
1737 Ridgemont Drive
Tuscaloosa, AL 35404
Phone: 205-553-3974
Email: gaewtrtl@aol.com

#282 • Parents Without Partners Scholarship

Type: Scholarship. Not renewable.
Eligibility: Applicant must be a child of a member in good standing of Parents Without Partners. This award must be used in the following years of study: • Freshman
Deadline: March 15.
Award Amount: $ 500.

Number Of Awards: 14.
Contact: Ann Willard, Scholarship Chairman

PHI SIGMA IOTA

Office of the Executive Director
5211 Essan Lane, Suite 2
Baton Rouge, LA 70809
Phone: 225-769-7100
Fax: 225-769-7105

#283 • Phi Sigma Iota Scholarship

Type: Scholarship. Not renewable.
Eligibility: Applicant must be a member of Phi Sigma Iota and be sponsored by the Faculty Advisor. This award must be used in the following years of study: • Senior • Masters • Doctoral
Field(s) Of Study: Foreign languages.
Deadline: February 1.
Award Amount: $ 500.
Number Of Awards: 6 - 13.
Applications Received: 10.
Contact: Dr. Marie-France Hilgar, President Department of Modern Languages University of Nevada, Las Vegas
Las Vegas, NV 89154
Phone: 702-895-3545
Fax: 702-895-1226
Email: mfhilgar@ccmail.nevada.edu

PHI SIGMA KAPPA INTERNATIONAL HEADQUARTERS

2925 East 96th Street
Indianapolis, IN 46240
Phone: 317-573-5420
Fax: 317-573-5430
Website: http://www.phisigmakappa.org/

#284 • Wenderoth Undergraduate Scholarship

Type: Scholarship. Not renewable.
Eligibility: Applicant must be a member of Phi Sigma Kappa and have a minimum "B" grade average. Selection is based upon academic criteria and essay competition. This award must be used in the following years of study: • Sophomore • Junior • Senior
Deadline: January 31.
Award Amount: $ 1,000 - $ 2,000.
Number Of Awards: 4.
Contact: Patty Adams, Conference Coordinator
Email: patty@phisigmakappa.org

PHI SIGMA PI NATIONAL HONOR FRATERNITY

2119 Ambassador Circle
Lancaster, PA 17603

Phone: 717-299-4710
Fax: 717-390-3054
Email: pspoffice@aol.com
Website: http://www.phisigmapi.org/

#285 • Richard C. Todd & Claude P. Todd Tripod Scholarship

Type: Scholarship. Not renewable.
Eligibility: Applicant must be a member of Phi Sigma Pi National Honor Fraternity. This award must be used in the following years of study: • Junior • Senior • Masters • Doctoral • Other postgraduate level
Deadline: Varies.
Award Amount: $ 1,400.
Number Of Awards: 1.
Applications Received: 12.
Odds Of Winning: 8% of applicants on average receive an award each year.
Contact: See above.

PHI THETA PI HONORARY COMMERCE FRATERNITY

2103 Cortez Road
Jay, FL 32246
Phone: 904-641-9006
Fax: 904-641-9006
Email: ptpfrat@aol.com
Website: http://www.phithetapi.org

#286 • J. Spencer Borders Academic Award

Type: Scholarship. Not renewable.
Eligibility: Applicant must be a member of Phi Theta Pi in good standing, be enrolled in college level courses, and have a 3.0 GPA or better. Applicant must submit a completed application, a press release, a current picture, a transcript, and a letter of recommendation. Selection is based upon scholarship, personal goals, extracurricular activities, financial need, and general impression. This award must be used in the following years of study: • Sophomore • Junior • Senior • Masters
Deadline: December 31.
Award Amount: $ 1,500.
Number Of Awards: 1.
Contact: J. Spencer Borders Academic Award

POLISH NATIONAL ALLIANCE (PNA)

Education Department
6100 North Cicero Avenue
Chicago, IL 60646
Phone: 773-286-0500, extension 312 or 387
Fax: 773-286-4118

#287 • PNA Scholarship

Type: Scholarship. Renewable.
Eligibility: Applicant must be a PNA member, a full-time student in a college or university, meet academic qualifications, and demonstrate civic involvement. This award must be used in the following years of study: • Sophomore
Deadline: April 15.
Award Amount: $ 500.
Number Of Awards: 200.
Applications Received: 450.
Odds Of Winning: 40% of applicants on average receive an award each year.
Contact: Teresa N. Abick, Vice President

PONY OF THE AMERICAS CLUB

5240 Elmwood Avenue
Indianapolis, IN 46203
Phone: 317-788-0107

#288 • Pony of the Americas Scholarship

Type: Scholarship. Renewable. Applicant must reapply for renewal.
Eligibility: Applicant must be an active participant in Pony of the Americas Club shows and activities. This award must be used in the following years of study: • Freshman • Sophomore • Junior • Senior • Masters • Doctoral • Vocational/technical
Deadline: June 1.
Award Amount: $ 500.
Number Of Awards: 2 - 4.
Applications Received: 8.
Contact: Scholarship Endowment Fund
5240 Elmwood Avenue
Indianapolis, IN 46203
Phone: 317-788-0107
Fax: 317-788-8974

PORTUGUESE CONTINENTAL UNION OF USA

899 Boylston Street
Boston, MA 02115
Phone: 617-536-2916

#289 • Portuguese Continental Union of USA Scholarship

Type: Scholarship. Not renewable.
Eligibility: Applicant must be a member in good standing for at least one year of the Portuguese Continental Union of the USA and be of good character. Selection is based upon school records, academic activities, school recommendations, statements, and test records. This award must be used in the following years of study: • Freshman • Sophomore • Junior • Senior
Deadline: February 15.
Award Amount: Varies.
Number Of Awards: Varies.
Contact: Scholarship Committee

ROTARY FOUNDATION OF ROTARY INTERNATIONAL

One Rotary Center
1560 Sherman Avenue
Evanston, IL 60201-3698
Phone: 847-866-3000
Fax: 847-328-8554
Website: http://www.rotary.org

#290 • Multi-Year Ambassadorial Scholarship

Type: Scholarship. Renewable. Award is for two or three years.
Eligibility: Applicant must be a citizen of a country in which there is a Rotary club, have completed at least two years of college course work or two years of post-secondary employment in a recognized vocation, plan to enroll in degree-seeking program/courses, and submit essay, recommendations, club endorsement, transcripts, and language ability forms. Preference is given to disabled applicants and Rotoract club members. Rotarians, Honorary Rotarians, and employees of Rotary entities are not eligible; spouses, children/grandchildren, spouses of children/grandchildren, and parents/grandparents of living Rotarians/Honorary Rotarians/Rotary employees are not eligible. Award may be used at institutions assigned by Rotary Foundation Trustees only. This award must be used in the following years of study: • Junior • Senior • Masters • Doctoral • Workers in recognized vocations
Deadline: Varies by individual Rotary Club.
Award Amount: $11,000.
Number Of Awards: Varies.
Contact: Local Rotary club

SIGMA ALPHA EPSILON (SAE)

P.O. Box 1856
Evanston, IL 60204-1856
Phone: 847-475-1856
Fax: 847-475-2250
Website: http://www.sae.net

#291 • Jones-Laurence Award

Type: Grant. Not renewable.
Eligibility: Applicant must be a member of SAE who displays the most outstanding academic achievement and excellence. Applicant must be nominated by his chapter. This award must be used in the following years of study: • Junior • Senior • Masters
Deadline: April 17.
Award Amount: $ 1,000 - $ 3,500.
Number Of Awards: 3.
Contact: Robert Parker, Coordinator of Programs
Phone: 800-233-1856, extension 223
Email: rparker@sae.net

#292 • Warren Poslusny Award for Outstanding Achievement

Type: Grant. Not renewable.
Eligibility: Applicant must be a SAE brother demonstrating fraternity and community service. Applicant must show a dedication to the highest ideals and values established by SAE. This award must be used in the following years of study: • Junior • Senior • Masters • Doctoral
Deadline: April 17.
Award Amount: $ 500.
Number Of Awards: 7 - 13.
Contact: Robert Parker, Coordinator of Programs
Phone: 800-233-1856, extension 223
Email: rparker@sae.net

#293 • G. Robert Hamrdla Award

Type: Grant. Not renewable.
Eligibility: Applicant must be an SAE member with a strong interest in 19th and 20th century history and a minimum 3.5 GPA. Preference is given to those with an interest in modern German history or the history of the two world wars. This award must be used in the following years of study: • Junior • Senior • Masters • Doctoral • Other postgraduate level
Deadline: Varies.
Award Amount: $ 2,500.
Number Of Awards: 1.
Applications Received: 6.
Odds Of Winning: 17% of applicants on average receive an award each year.
Contact: Robert Parker, Coordinator of Programs
Phone: 800-233-1856, extension 223
Email: rparker@sae.net

SIGMA ALPHA IOTA NATIONAL HEADQUARTERS

34 Wall Street, Suite 515
Ashville, NC 28801-0606
Phone: 828-251-0606
Fax: 828-251-0644
Email: nh@sai-national.org
Website: http://www.sai-national.org/

#294 • Undergraduate Scholarship

Type: Scholarship. Not renewable.
Eligibility: Applicant must be a member of Sigma Alpha Iota who is able to demonstrate financial need. This award must be used in the following years of study: • Junior • Senior
Deadline: April 15.
Award Amount: $ 500.
Number Of Awards: 10.
Contact: Ruth Sieber Johnson, National Exec. Secretary

#295 • Summer Music Scholarship

Type: Scholarship. Not renewable.

Eligibility: Applicant must be a member of Sigma Alpha Iota. One applicant from each Sigma Alpha Iota region is selected by regional faculty at Aspen, Brevard, and Tanglewood. Award must be used during the summer. This award must be used in the following years of study: • Sophomore • Junior • Senior • Masters • Doctoral • Other postgraduate level
Deadline: March 15.
Award Amount: $ 1,000.
Number Of Awards: 5.
Contact: Ruth Sieber Johnson, National Executive Secretary

SLOVENE NATIONAL BENEFIT SOCIETY

Scholarship Chairperson
247 West Allegheny Road
Imperial, PA 15126-9774
Phone: 724-695-1100
Fax: 724-695-1555
Email: snpj@snpj.com
Website: http://www.snpj.com

#296 • Slovene National Benefit Society Scholarship

Type: Scholarship. Renewable. Completion of form and copy of transcripts required for renewal.
Eligibility: Applicant must be a member of SNJP for at least two years, have a minimum $2,000 permanent life insurance with the company, maintain a minimum 2.5 GPA, be a full-time student (12 semester hours) attending an accredited college, university, or trade school, and participate in SNPJ activities during the four-year scholarship program. This award must be used in the following years of study: • Freshman • Sophomore • Junior • Senior • Masters • Doctoral • Other postgraduate level
Deadline: August 1.
Award Amount: $ 600.
Number Of Awards: 120.
Contact: National President

SLOVENIAN WOMEN'S UNION OF AMERICA

52 Oakridge Drive
Marquette, MI 49855
Email: MTurvey@aol.com

#297 • Slovenian Women's Union of America Scholarship

Type: Scholarship. Not renewable.
Eligibility: Applicant must have a three-year membership in the Slovenian Women's Union. This award must be used in the following years of study: • Freshman
Deadline: March 1.

Award Amount: $ 1,000.
Number Of Awards: 4.
Contact: Mary H. Turvey, Scholarship Program Director
Phone: 906-249-4288

SONS OF NORWAY FOUNDATION

1455 West Lake Street
Minneapolis, MN 55408
Phone: 612-827-3611 or 800-945-8851
Fax: 612-827-0658
Email: fraternal@sofn.com

#298 • Astrid G. Cates Scholarship

Type: Scholarship. Not renewable.
Eligibility: Applicant must be a current member or the child or grandchild of a current member of the Sons of Norway. Applicant must demonstrate financial need. Selection is based upon financial need, GPA, participation in school and community activities, work experience, education and career goals, and personal and school references. This award must be used in the following years of study: • Freshman • Sophomore • Junior • Senior
Deadline: March 1.
Award Amount: $ 500 - $ 750.
Number Of Awards: 6.
Applications Received: 99.
Contact: Liv Dahl, Administrative Director

#299 • Myrtle Beinbauer Scholarship

Type: Scholarship. Not renewable.
Eligibility: Applicant must be a current member, or the child or grandchild of a current member, of the Sons of Norway. Applicant must demonstrate financial need. Selection is based upon financial need, GPA, participation in school and community activities, work experience, education and career goals, and personal and school references. This award must be used in the following years of study: • Freshman • Sophomore • Junior • Senior • Masters
Deadline: March 1.
Award Amount: $ 3,000.
Number Of Awards: Varies.
Contact: Liv Dahl, Administrative Director

TAU BETA PI ASSOCIATION

P.O. Box 2697
Knoxville, TN 37901-2697
Phone: 865-546-4578
Fax: 865-546-4579
Email: tbp@tbp.org
Website: http://www.tbp.org

#300 • Tau Beta Pi Scholarship

Type: Scholarship. Not renewable.

Eligibility: Contact for details. This award must be used in the following years of study: • Senior
Field(s) Of Study: Engineering.
Deadline: January 15.
Award Amount: $ 2,000.
Number Of Awards: 9.
Applications Received: 90.
Odds Of Winning: 10% of applicants on average receive an award each year.
Contact:
Phone: 865-546-4578
Fax: 865-546-4579
Email: tbp@tbp.org

TEXAS AMERICAN LEGION AUXILIARY

Department Headquarters
709 East 10th Street
Austin, TX 78701-2699
Phone: 512-476-7278

#301 • Texas American Legion Auxiliary Scholarship

Type: Scholarship. Renewable. Recipient must reapply for renewal to retain scholarship.
Eligibility: Applicant must be sponsored by a local American Legion Auxiliary unit. Selection is based upon character, Americanism, leadership, financial need, and scholarship. This award must be used in the following years of study: • Freshman • Sophomore • Junior • Senior • Masters • Doctoral • Other postgraduate level
Deadline: March 15.
Award Amount: $ 500.
Number Of Awards: 18.
Applications Received: 825.
Contact: Education Chairman

THETA NU EPSILON SOCIETY OF 1870 - NATIONAL ALUMNI ASSOCIATION

National Alumni Scholarships
3538 Central Avenue, Suite 2A
Riverside, CA 92506
Phone: 800-863-1870
Fax: 800-863-1870
Email: tne1870@urs2.net
Website: http://www.tne.org

#302 • TNE Scholarship

Type: Scholarship. Renewable.
Eligibility: Applicant must be directly related to a present or deceased member of the Theta Nu Epsilon Society. Society requests that a donation is made sometime during the recipient's lifetime. This award must be used in the following years of study: • Freshman • Sophomore • Junior • Senior • Masters • Doctoral • Other postgraduate level

Deadline: None.
Award Amount: $ 1,000 - $10,000.
Number Of Awards: 28.
Applications Received: 28.
Odds Of Winning: 100% of applicants on average receive an award each year.
Contact: Executive Director
Phone: 800-TNE-1870

TKE EDUCATIONAL FOUNDATION

8645 Founders Road
Indianapolis, IN 46268
Phone: 317-872-6533
Fax: 317-875-8353
Email: tef@tkehq.org

#303 • Bruce B. Melchert Scholarship

Type: Scholarship. Not renewable.
Eligibility: Applicant must be a member of Tau Kappa Epsilon who is a full-time student and has a minimum cumulative 3.0 GPA. Applicant should demonstrate leadership within his chapter as a rush chairman, Prytanis, or other major office, be a leader in IFC or other campus organizations, and plan to serve people in a political or governmental service position. This award must be used in the following years of study: • Sophomore • Junior • Senior
Field(s) Of Study: Government, political science.
Deadline: May 26.
Award Amount: $ 600.
Number Of Awards: Varies.
Contact: Timothy L. Taschwer, President/CEO

#304 • William Wilson Memorial Scholarship

Type: Scholarship. Not renewable.
Eligibility: Applicant must be an initiated member of Tau Kappa Epsilon who is enrolled full time. Applicant should have demonstrated understanding of the importance of good alumni relations to the chapter and its members and excelled in the development, promotion, and execution of effective programs which have increased alumni contact, awareness, and participation in fraternity activities. This award must be used in the following years of study: • Junior • Senior
Deadline: May 26.
Award Amount: $ 850.
Number Of Awards: Varies.
Contact: Timothy L. Taschwer, President/CEO

#305 • Wallace G. McCauley Memorial Scholarship

Type: Scholarship. Not renewable.
Eligibility: Applicant must be an initiated member of Tau Kappa Epsilon who is enrolled full time. Applicant should have demonstrated understanding of

the importance of good alumni relations to the chapter and its members and excelled in the development, promotion, and execution of effective programs which have increased alumni contact, awareness, and participation in fraternity activities. This award must be used in the following years of study: • Junior • Senior
Deadline: May 26.
Award Amount: $ 900.
Number Of Awards: Varies.
Contact: Timothy L. Taschwer, President/CEO

#306 • All Teke Academic Team and John A. Courson Top Scholar Awards

Type: Scholarship. Not renewable.
Eligibility: Applicant must be an active member in good standing of Tau Kappa Epsilon, be enrolled full time, and have a minimum cumulative 3.5 GPA. Selection is based upon academic ability, leadership skills, extracurricular activities, and social responsiblity. Recipients of the All-Teke Academic Team award will automatically be considered for the John A. Courson Top Scholar Award. One member of the team will be selected for this award. This award must be used in the following years of study: • Junior • Senior
Deadline: February 25.
Award Amount: $ 300 - $ 2,000.
Number Of Awards: Varies.
Contact: Timothy L. Taschwer, President/CEO

U.S. JUNIOR CHAMBER OF COMMERCE

4 West 21st Street
Tulsa, OK 74114-1116

#307 • Baldridge Scholarship

Type: Scholarship. Not renewable.
Eligibility: Applicant must be a member, an immediate family member, or a descendent of a member of the Jaycee organization, be an U.S. citizen, demonstrate academic potential, possess leadership traits, and have financial need. SASE and $5 application fee (check or money order payable to JWMF) must be sent between July 1 and February 1. This award must be used in the following years of study: • Freshman • Sophomore • Junior • Senior • Masters • Doctoral
Deadline: March 1.
Award Amount: $ 3,000.
Number Of Awards: 1.
Applications Received: 8.
Odds Of Winning: 13% of applicants on average receive an award each year.
Contact: Jaycee War Memorial Fund (JWMF) Scholarship

UDT/SEAL ASSOCIATION

P.O. Box 5365
Virginia Beach, VA 23471
Phone: 757-363-7490
Fax: 757-363-7491
Email: udtseal@infi.net
Website: udt-seal.org

#308 • UDT/SEAL Scholarship Grant

Type: Grant. Not renewable.
Eligibility: Applicant must be the dependent of an active UDT/SEAL member and have been a member for the previous three years plus the year of application. This award must be used in the following years of study: • Freshman • Sophomore • Junior • Senior
Deadline: April 16.
Award Amount: $ 1,000.
Number Of Awards: 5.
Odds Of Winning: 70% of applicants on average receive an award each year.
Contact: Robert M. Rieve, Executive Director

UNION AND LEAGUE OF ROMANIAN SOCIETIES OF AMERICA, INC.

14512 Royal Drive
Sterling Heights, MI 48312

#309 • Union and League of Romanian Societies of America Scholarship

Type: Scholarship. Not renewable.
Eligibility: Applicant must be a member of the Union & League of Romanian Societies of America for at least two years who is accepted or enrolled in college and ranks in the top tenth of his or her secondary school class. Selection is based upon transcripts and recommendations. Recent photograph required. One $1,000 award is distributed over four years, three $500 awards are distributed over two years. This award must be used in the following years of study: • Freshman
Deadline: April 30.
Award Amount: $ 250.
Number Of Awards: 2.
Applications Received: 6.
Odds Of Winning: 20% of applicants on average receive an award each year.
Contact: Eugene S. Raica, Scholarship Chairman

WESTERN SUNBATHING ASSOCIATION, INC. (WSA)

WSA Scholarship Committee
P.O. Box 1168-107
Studio City, CA 91604
Email: info@wsanude.com
Website: http://www.wsanude.com

#310 • **Western Sunbathing Association Scholarship**

Type: Scholarship. Renewable. Reapplication required for renewal.
Eligibility: Applicant must have a minimum 2.5 GPA and must be a member or the child of a member of the Western Sunbathing Association. This award must be used in the following years of study: • Freshman • Sophomore • Junior • Senior • Masters • Doctoral
Deadline: April 1.
Award Amount: $ 1,000.
Number Of Awards: 2.
Applications Received: 7.
Odds Of Winning: 28% of applicants on average receive an award each year.
Contact: WSA Scholarship Committee

Communications

ARABIAN HORSE TRUST

12000 Zuni Street
Westminster, CO 80234-2300
Phone: 303-450-4710
Fax: 303-450-4707

#311 • **Gladys Brown Edwards Memorial Scholarship**

Type: Scholarship. Not renewable.
Eligibility: Applicant must have an ongoing interest in and commitment to Arabian horses. This award must be used in the following years of study: • Junior • Senior
Field(s) Of Study: Media communications.
Deadline: January 31.
Award Amount: $ 1,000.
Number Of Awards: 1.
Contact: Janet Kamischke, Office Manager

JOHN BAYLISS BROADCAST FOUNDATION

P.O. Box 221070
Carmel, CA 93922
Phone: 831-624-1536, extension 440
Email: baylisroast@kagan.com

#312 • **Bayliss Radio Scholarship**

Type: Scholarship. Renewable. Recipient must reapply for renewal.
Eligibility: Applicant must have a minimum 3.0 GPA and a history of radio-related activities. Applicant must be a U.S. citizen or permanent resident. Three letters of recommendation, college transcripts, and an essay on the applicant's radio broadcasting goals required. This award must be used in the following years of study: • Junior • Senior • Masters
Field(s) Of Study: Radio.
Deadline: April 30.
Award Amount: $ 5,000.
Number Of Awards: 20.
Applications Received: 75.
Odds Of Winning: 27% of applicants on average receive an award each year.
Contact: Kit H. Franke, Executive Director

KCNC-TV MEDIA SCHOLARSHIP

P.O. Box 5012
Denver, CO 80217
Phone: 303-830-6558
Fax: 303-830-6537
Website: http://www.kcncnews4.com

#313 • **News 4 Media Scholarship**

Type: Scholarship. Renewable. Recipient must reapply for renewal.
Eligibility: Applicant must be a resident of Colorado with a minimum 2.5 GPA. Finalist must have an interview. This award must be used in the following years of study: • Freshman • Sophomore • Junior • Senior
Field(s) Of Study: Communications.
Deadline: May 1.
Award Amount: $ 1,000 - $ 3,000.
Number Of Awards: 1 - 3.
Applications Received: 175.
Odds Of Winning: 1% of applicants on average receive an award each year.
Contact: Gerri Howard, Manager of Community Affairs and Special Events
P.O. Box 5021
Denver, CO 80217
Phone: 303-830-6555

NATIONAL ACADEMY OF TELEVISION ARTS AND SCIENCES - SEATTLE CHAPTER

P.O. Box 58530
Seattle, WA 98138-1530
Phone: 206-575-3444
Fax: 206-575-9490
Website: http://www.natas-seattle.com

#314 • **National Academy of Television Arts and Sciences Scholarship**

Type: Scholarship. Not renewable.
Eligibility: Preference given to TV communications majors. This award must be used in the following years of study: • Senior
Field(s) Of Study: Communications.

Deadline: in April.
Award Amount: $ 2,000.
Number Of Awards: 3.
Applications Received: 15.
Odds Of Winning: 20% of applicants on average receive an award each year.
Contact: John Coney, Scholarship Chair

PACIFIC TELECOMMUNICATIONS COUNCIL

2454 Beretania Street, Suite 302
Honolulu, HI 96826
Phone: 808-941-3789
Fax: 808-944-4874
Email: puja@ptc.org
Website: http://www.ptc.org

#315 • Essay Prize

Type: Contest. Not renewable.
Eligibility: Applicant must submit essay dealing with telecommunications issues such as economic, policy, legal, or educational issues, especially as they relate to the Asian-Pacific area. This award must be used in the following years of study: • Sophomore • Junior • Senior • Masters • Doctoral • people who graduated within the past five years
Field(s) Of Study: Broadcasting, communications, engineering, information systems, satellite communications, telecommunications.
Deadline: May 30.
Award Amount: $ 2,000.
Number Of Awards: 1 - 3.
Applications Received: 24.
Odds Of Winning: 13% of applicants on average receive an award each year.
Contact: Ms. Puja Borries, Publication and Publicity Coordinator

SACRAMENTO BEE

P.O. Box 15779
Sacramento, CA 96852
Phone: 916-321-1790
Fax: 916-321-1783
Email: rvandiest@sacbee.com
Website: http://www.sacbee.com

#316 • Minority Media Scholarship

Type: Scholarship. Not renewable.
Eligibility: Applicant must be a member of a minority group living in the Sacramento, Calif., three-county area. This award must be used in the following years of study: • Freshman • Sophomore • Junior • Senior • Masters
Field(s) Of Study: Mass communication.
Deadline: March 14.
Award Amount: $ 1,000 - $ 5,000.

Number Of Awards: 8 - 12.
Applications Received: 20.
Odds Of Winning: 50% of applicants on average receive an award each year.
Contact: Robbi Grant, Scholarship Coordinator
Phone: 916-321-1794

SOCIETY FOR TECHNICAL COMMUNICATION (STC)

901 North Stuart Street Suite 904
Arlington, VA 22203-1854
Phone: 703-522-4114
Fax: 703-522-2075
Email: stc@stc-va.org
Website: http://www.stc-va.org

#317 • STC Scholarship

Type: Scholarship. Renewable. Reapplication required for renewal.
Eligibility: Applicant must be a full-time student in a technical communication program having completed at least one full year of academic work with at least another full year to complete the degree program. Selection is based upon academic record and potential for contributing to the technical communication profession. This award must be used in the following years of study: • Sophomore • Junior • Senior • Masters • Doctoral
Field(s) Of Study: Technical communication.
Deadline: February 12.
Award Amount: $ 2,500.
Number Of Awards: 14.
Contact: STC Office

TEXAS PROFESSIONAL COMMUNICATORS

ATTN: Scholarship Director
P.O. Box 173
Denison, TX 75021-0173
Phone: 903-465-8567
Email: kcasey@tenet.edu or kcasey@texoma.net

#318 • Texas Professional Communicators Roving Scholarship

Type: Scholarship. Not renewable.
Eligibility: Applicant must be enrolled in a Texas college or university. Award may not be used at the University of Texas at Austin. This award must be used in the following years of study: • Sophomore • Junior • Senior
Field(s) Of Study: Journalism/mass communications.
Deadline: Varies.
Award Amount: $ 500.
Number Of Awards: 1.
Contact: Kay Casey, Scholarship Director

Computer Science

ARMED FORCES COMMUNICATIONS AND ELECTRONICS ASSOCIATION

ATTN: Educational Foundation
4400 Fair Lakes Court
Fairfax, VA 22033-3899
Phone: 703-631-6149
Fax: 703-631-4693
Email: scholarship@afcea
Website: http://www.afcea.org

#319 • Copernicus Foundation Computer Graphic Design Scholarship

Type: Contest. Not renewable.
Eligibility: Applicant must be a U.S. citizen enrolled at an accredited four-year institution in the U.S., and must submit one sample of original digital artwork, current transcript, application, and one letter of recommendation. This award must be used in the following years of study: • Junior • Senior
Field(s) Of Study: Computer science, graphic design.
Deadline: October 15.
Award Amount: $ 2,000.
Number Of Awards: Varies.
Contact: Norma Corrales, Administrator, Scholarships and Awards Program
Phone: 800-336-4583, extension 6149

Culinary Arts/Baking

KENTUCKY RESTAURANT ASSOCIATION

Educational Foundation
512 Executive Park
Louisville, KY 40207
Phone: 502-896-0464
Fax: 502-896-0465
Email: betsy@kyra.org
Website: http://www.kyra.org/

#320 • Kentucky Restaurant Association Scholarship

Type: Scholarship. Renewable. Personal letter, transcripts, and letter of recommendation required for renewal.
Eligibility: Applicant must be a Kentucky resident or reside within 25 miles of Kentucky borders, must have had work experience in food service, and must submit transcripts, letters of recommendation, and proof of acceptance to college food service program.
This award must be used in the following years of study:
• Freshman • Sophomore • Junior • Senior
Field(s) Of Study: Culinary arts.
Deadline: January 1; July 1.
Award Amount: $ 500 - $ 1,250.
Number Of Awards: 30.
Applications Received: 35.
Odds Of Winning: 85% of applicants on average receive an award each year.
Contact: Betsy Byrd, Director of Member Relations

#321 • Kentucky Restaurant Association Governor's Scholarship

Type: Scholarship. Renewable.
Eligibility: Applicant must be a Kentucky resident attending a Kentucky institution, must be in good academic standing, must have at least 1,000 hours of restaurant work experience over a two-year period, and must submit transcripts, essay, and proof of acceptance into college foodservice program. This award must be used in the following years of study: • Freshman • Sophomore • Junior • Senior
Field(s) Of Study: Culinary arts, food service.
Deadline: November 15.
Award Amount: $ 5,000.
Number Of Awards: Varies.
Contact: Betsy Byrd, Director of Member Relations

Cultural Studies

GERMAN ACADEMIC EXCHANGE SERVICE (DAAD)

950 Third Avenue, 19th Floor
New York, NY 10022
Phone: 212-758-3223
Fax: 212-755-5780
Email: daadny@daad.org
Website: http://www.daad.org

#322 • DAAD-Fulbright Grant for Americans

Type: Grant. Renewable.
Eligibility: Applicant should be a U.S. citizen enrolled full time in a North American university degree program or an international student who has been enrolled full time in a graduate program for more than one academic year. Award is for one year of graduate study and/or research in Germany. Preference is given to applicants under the age of 32. This award must be used in the following years of study: • Masters • Doctoral • Other postgraduate level
Deadline: Varies.
Award Amount: $15,000.
Number Of Awards: Varies.

Contact: Campus International or Fulbright Program advisor

SONS OF NORWAY FOUNDATION

1455 West Lake Street
Minneapolis, MN 55408
Phone: 612-827-3611 or 800-945-8851
Fax: 612-827-0658
Email: fraternal@sofn.com
Website: http://www.sofn.com

#323 • King Olav V Norwegian-American Heritage Fund

Type: Scholarship. Not renewable.
Eligibility: Applicant must be an American, age 18 or older, who demonstrates a sincere interest in the Norwegian heritage or a Norwegian who demonstrates an interest in American heritage. Applicant must further the study of these heritages at a recognized educational institution. Selection is based upon GPA, participation in school and community activities, work experience, education and career goals, and personal and school references. This award must be used in the following years of study: • Freshman • Sophomore • Junior • Senior • Masters • Doctoral
Field(s) Of Study: Norwegian studies.
Deadline: March 1.
Award Amount: $ 250 - $ 3,000.
Number Of Awards: 8.
Applications Received: 100.
Odds Of Winning: 8% of applicants on average receive an award each year.
Contact: Liv Dahl, Administrative Director
Phone: 800-945-8851
Fax: 612-827-0658
Email: fraternal@sofn.com

Dentistry

AMERICAN ASSOCIATION OF WOMEN DENTISTS

645 North Michigan Ave., #800
Chicago, IL 60611
Phone: 312-280-9296
Fax: 312-280-9893
Email: info@womendentists.org
Website: http://www.womandentists.org

#324 • Colgate-Palmolive Award

Type: Scholarship. Not renewable.
Eligibility: Contact for details. This award must be used in the following years of study: • Junior • Senior
Field(s) Of Study: Dentistry.

Deadline: Varies.
Award Amount: $ 500.
Number Of Awards: 10.
Contact: Sharon Gautschy, Executive Director
Email: sg@sdiweb.com

FLORIDA DENTAL HEALTH FOUNDATION, INC.

1111 East Tennessee Street
Suite 102
Tallahassee, FL 32308
Phone: 850-681-3629
Fax: 850-681-0116
Email: csoutherland@floridadental.org
Website: http://www.floridadental.org

#325 • Allied Dental Education Scholarship

Type: Scholarship. Renewable.
Eligibility: Selection based upon academics, residence, and financial need. This award must be used in the following years of study: • Sophomore
Field(s) Of Study: Dental assisting, dental hygiene, dental lab technology.
Deadline: Varies.
Award Amount: $ 100 - $ 500.
Number Of Awards: 4 - 20.
Applications Received: 5.
Odds Of Winning: 80% of applicants on average receive an award each year.
Contact: Cheri Southerland

Dietetics/Food Science/Nutrition

ASSOCIATION OF FOOD AND DRUG OFFICIALS

P.O. Box 3425
York, PA 17402
Phone: 717-757-2888
Fax: 717-755-8089
Email: afdo@blazenet.net
Website: http://www.afdo.org

#326 • AFDO Scholarship

Type: Scholarship. Not renewable.
Eligibility: Applicant must reside within the region hosting the annual conference, demonstrate a desire to serve in a career of research, regulatory work, quality control, or teaching in an area related to foods, drugs or consumer product safety, demonstrate leadership abilities, have a minimum 2.5 GPA during first two years of undergraduate study, and submit official college transcript and two letters of recommendation from faculty members. This award

must be used in the following years of study: • Junior •
Senior • Masters
Field(s) Of Study: Consumer and drug products
safety, food safety.
Deadline: February 1.
Award Amount: $ 1,000.
Number Of Awards: 3.
Contact: Denise Rooney, Executive Director

CALIFORNIA ADOLESCENT NUTRITION AND FITNESS PROGRAM

2140 Shattuck Avenue, Suite 610
Berkeley, CA 94704
Phone: 510-644-1533
Fax: 510-644-1535
Email: info@canfit.org
Website: http://www.canfit.org

#327 • Culinary Arts/Nutrition/Physical Education Scholarship

Type: Scholarship. Renewable.
Eligibility: Applicant must be an African-American,
American Indian/Alaska Native, Asian/Pacific
Islander, or Latino/Hispanic, enrolled in an approved
program at a California institution, and submit five
copies of a personal statement, two recommendations,
a 500-to-1,000-word essay, official transcripts, photo,
and application. Undergraduate applicant must have
50 semester hours completed and a minimum
cumulative 2.5 GPA. Graduate applicants must have
12-15 units completed and a minimum cumulative 3.0
GPA. This award must be used in the following years
of study: • Freshman • Sophomore • Junior • Senior •
Masters • Doctoral • Other postgraduate level
Field(s) Of Study: Culinary arts, health, nutrition.
Deadline: March 30.
Award Amount: $ 500 - $ 1,000.
Number Of Awards: Varies.
Applications Received: 14.
Odds Of Winning: 99% of applicants on average
receive an award each year.
Contact: Brenda James, Adminstrator
Phone: 800-200-3131

SCHOOL FOOD SERVICE FOUNDATION

1600 Duke Street 7th Floor
Alexandria, VA 22314
Phone: 703-739-3900
Email: sfsf@asfsa.org
Website: http://www.asfsa.org/foundation

#328 • School Food Service Foundation Graduate/Postgraduate Study Scholarship

Type: Scholarship. Renewable. Reapplication
required for renewal.
Eligibility: Contact for details. This award must be

used in the following years of study: • Masters •
Doctoral • Other postgraduate level
Field(s) Of Study: Child nutrition, dietetics,
nutrition management, school food services.
Deadline: April 15.
Award Amount: $ 500 - $ 1,000.
Number Of Awards: 5.
Applications Received: 25.
Contact: Foundation Specialist

TONY'S FOOD SERVICE

School Food Service Foundation Scholarships
700 South Washington Street
Alexandria, VA 22314
Phone: 703-739-3900
Fax: 703-739-3915
Email: sfsf@asfsa.org
Website: http://www.asfsa.org/foundation

#329 • Tony's Scholarship

Type: Scholarship. Renewable. Reapplication
required for renewal.
Eligibility: Applicant must be a member or
dependent of a member of the American School Food
Service Association (ASFSA) for at least one year.
This award must be used in the following years of
study: • Freshman • Sophomore • Junior • Senior •
Masters
Field(s) Of Study: Child-nutrition-related fields,
school food service.
Deadline: April 15.
Award Amount: $ 100 - $ 1,000.
Number Of Awards: 75.
Applications Received: 300.
Odds Of Winning: 25% of applicants on average
receive an award each year.
Contact: Scholarship Coordinator

Disability

CHAIRSCHOLARS FOUNDATION, INC.

16101 Carencia Lane
Odessa, FL 33556
Phone: 813-920-2737
Fax: 813-920-2737

#330 • Chairscholars Foundation Scholarship

Type: Scholarship. Renewable if recipient maintains a
satisfactory GPA.
Eligibility: Applicant must be severely physically
challenged and have significant financial need.
Selection is based upon GPA and community service.

This award must be used in the following years of study:
• Freshman • Sophomore
Deadline: March 15.
Award Amount: $ 5,000.
Number Of Awards: 4.
Applications Received: 150.
Odds Of Winning: 3% of applicants on average receive an award each year.
Contact: Hugo and Alicia Keim, President/Secretary

CHRISTIAN RECORD SERVICES

4444 South 52nd Street
P.O. Box 6097
Lincoln, NE 68516
Phone: 402-488-0981

#331 • Christian Record Services Scholarship

Type: Scholarship. Renewable. Reapplication required for renewal.
Eligibility: Applicant must be legally or totally blind. Selection is based upon applicant's GPA, financial need, and accomplishments. This award must be used in the following years of study: •
Freshman • Sophomore • Junior • Senior
Deadline: April 1.
Award Amount: $ 500.
Number Of Awards: 10.
Applications Received: 47.
Contact: Pennie Marshall, Treasury Secretary

EASTER SEAL SOCIETY OF IOWA, INC.

Scholarship
P.O. Box 4002
Des Moines, IA 50333
Phone: 515-289-1933
Fax: 515-289-1281
Email: essia@netins.net

#332 • Easter Seal Society of Iowa Disability Scholarships

Type: Scholarship. Not renewable.
Eligibility: Applicant must have a permanent disability, be a resident of Iowa, rank in the top two-fifths of class or have a cumulative GPA of 2.8, and demonstrate financial need. This award must be used in the following years of study: • Freshman
Deadline: March 1.
Award Amount: $ 750 - $ 1,000.
Number Of Awards: 2.
Contact: Deb Wissink, Scholarships

LIGHTHOUSE INTERNATIONAL

Career Incentive Awards
111 East 59th Street

New York, NY 10022
Phone: 212-821-9428
Fax: 212-821-9703
Email: awards@lighthouse.org
Website: http://www.lighthouse.org

#333 • Career Incentive Award

Type: Grant. Not renewable.
Eligibility: Applicant must be legally blind, reside and attend school in the northeastearn U.S., and submit application, essay, proof of U.S. citizenship, transcripts, and letters of recommendation. This award must be used in the following years of study: •
Freshman • Sophomore • Junior • Senior • Masters
Deadline: March 31.
Award Amount: $ 5,000.
Number Of Awards: 4.
Applications Received: 70.
Contact: Kelly Clark, Projects & Events Coordinator
Email: kclark@lighthouse.org

NATIONAL AMPUTATION FOUNDATION

Scholarship Program
38-40 Church Street
Malverne, NY 11565
Phone: 516-887-3600
Fax: 516-887-3667

#334 • National Amputation Foundation Scholarship

Type: Scholarship. Renewable if recipient notifies the foundation of continuing undergraduate study.
Eligibility: Applicant must be a major limb amputee enrolled in full-time undergraduate studies and must submit social security number, doctor's letter, and name and address of the college he or she is attending. This award must be used in the following years of study: • Freshman • Sophomore • Junior • Senior
Deadline: None.
Award Amount: $ 125.
Number Of Awards: 24.
Contact: Scholarship Committee

NATIONAL AMPUTEE GOLF ASSOCIATION

131 South Mallard Way
Oxnard, CA 93030
Phone: 800-633-NAGA
Fax: 630-830-2897
Email: mynusl@aol.com

#335 • National Amputee Golf Association Scholarship

Type: Scholarship. Renewable if recipient maintains a minimum "C+" grade average and submits reports.

Eligibility: Applicant must be an amputee or the child of an amputee and submit grades and a resume. This award must be used in the following years of study: • Freshman • Sophomore • Junior • Senior
Deadline: February 28.
Award Amount: $ 1,000 - $ 2,000.
Number Of Awards: 1 - 3.
Applications Received: 3.
Odds Of Winning: 100% of applicants on average receive an award each year.
Contact: Don Zommer, Midwest Trustee Scholarship Chairman
519 Orchard Pass
Bartlett, IL 60103
Phone: 630-830-2763
Fax: 630-830-2897
Email: mynusl@aol.com

NATIONAL FEDERATION OF THE BLIND (NFB)

805 Fifth Avenue
Grinnell, IA 50112
Phone: 515-236-3366

#336 • Frank Walton Horn Memorial Scholarship

Type: Scholarship. Not renewable.
Eligibility: Applicant must be legally blind and pursing a full-time course of study. Preference is given to applicants studying architecture or engineering. Selection is based upon academic excellence, service to the community, and financial need. This award must be used in the following years of study: • Freshman • Sophomore • Junior • Senior • Masters • Doctoral
Deadline: March 31.
Award Amount: $ 3,000.
Number Of Awards: 1.
Contact: Peggy Elliott, Scholarship Commitee Chairperson

#337 • Hermione Grant Calhoun Scholarship

Type: Scholarship. Renewable. Reapplication required for renewal.
Eligibility: Applicant must be a legally blind woman pursuing a full-time course of study. Selection is based upon academic excellence, service to the community, and financial need. This award must be used in the following years of study: • Freshman • Sophomore • Junior • Senior • Masters • Doctoral
Deadline: March 31.
Award Amount: $ 3,000.
Number Of Awards: 1.
Contact: Peggy Elliott, Scholarship Committee Chairperson

#338 • Howard Brown Rickard Scholarship

Type: Scholarship. Renewable. Reapplication required for renewal.
Eligibility: Applicant must be legally blind and pursuing a full-time course of study. Selection is based upon academic excellence, service to the community, and financial need. This award must be used in the following years of study: • Freshman • Sophomore • Junior • Senior • Masters • Doctoral
Field(s) Of Study: Architecture, engineering, law, medicine, natural sciences.
Deadline: March 31.
Award Amount: $ 3,000.
Number Of Awards: 1.
Contact: Peggy Elliott, Scholarship Committee Chairperson

#339 • Melva T. Owen Memorial Scholarship

Type: Scholarship. Renewable. Reapplication required for renewal.
Eligibility: Applicant must be legally blind, be pursuing a full-time course of career-oriented study, and be directed toward attaining financial independence. Majors in cultural fields, general studies, and religion are not supported. Selection is based upon academic excellence, service to the community, and financial need. This award must be used in the following years of study: • Freshman • Sophomore • Junior • Senior • Masters • Doctoral
Deadline: March 31.
Award Amount: $ 7,000.
Number Of Awards: 1.
Contact: Peggy Elliott, Chairperson

#340 • NFB Scholarship

Type: Scholarship. Renewable. Reapplication required for renewal.
Eligibility: Applicant must be legally blind and pursuing a full-time course of study. Selection is based upon academic excellence, service to the community, and financial need. This award must be used in the following years of study: • Freshman • Sophomore • Junior • Senior • Masters • Doctoral
Deadline: March 31.
Award Amount: $ 3,000 - $ 7,000.
Number Of Awards: 19.
Contact: Peggy Elliott, Scholarship Committee Chairperson

#341 • NFB Humanities Scholarship

Type: Scholarship. Renewable. Reapplication required for renewal.
Eligibility: Applicant must be legally blind and pursuing a full-time course of study. Selection is based upon academic excellence, service to the community, and financial need. This award must be used in the following years of study: • Freshman •

Sophomore • Junior • Senior • Masters • Doctoral
Field(s) Of Study: Art, English, foreign languages, history, humanities, philosophy, religion.
Deadline: March 31.
Award Amount: $ 3,000.
Number Of Awards: 1.
Contact: Peggy Elliott, Scholarship Committee Chairperson

#342 • NFB Educator of Tomorrow Award

Type: Scholarship. Renewable. Reapplication required for renewal.
Eligibility: Applicant must be legally blind. Selection is based upon academic excellence, service to the community, and financial need. This award must be used in the following years of study: • Freshman • Sophomore • Junior • Senior • Masters • Doctoral
Field(s) Of Study: Elementary, secondary, or post-secondary teaching.
Deadline: March 31.
Award Amount: $ 3,000.
Number Of Awards: 1.
Contact: Peggy Elliott, Scholarship Committee Chairperson

#343 • Kuchler-Killian Memorial Scholarship

Type: Scholarship. Renewable. Reapplication required for renewal.
Eligibility: Applicant must be legally blind and pursuing a full-time course of study. Selection is based upon academic excellence, service to the community, and financial need. This award must be used in the following years of study: • Freshman • Sophomore • Junior • Senior • Masters • Doctoral
Deadline: March 31.
Award Amount: $ 3,000.
Number Of Awards: 1.
Contact: Peggy Elliott, Scholarship Committee Chairperson

#344 • Mozelle and Willard Gold Memorial Scholarship

Type: Scholarship. Renewable. Reapplication required for renewal.
Eligibility: Applicant must be legally blind and pursuing a full-time course of study. Selection is based upon academic excellence, service to the community, and financial need. This award must be used in the following years of study: • Freshman • Sophomore • Junior • Senior • Masters • Doctoral
Deadline: March 31.
Award Amount: $ 3,000.
Number Of Awards: 1.
Contact: Peggy Elliott, Scholarship Committee Chairperson

#345 • National Federation of the Blind Computer Science Scholarship

Type: Scholarship. Renewable. Reapplication required for renewal.
Eligibility: Applicant must be legally blind and pursuing a full-time course of study. Selection is based upon academic excellence, service to the community, and financial need. This award must be used in the following years of study: • Freshman • Sophomore • Junior • Senior • Masters • Doctoral
Field(s) Of Study: Computer Science.
Deadline: March 31.
Award Amount: $ 3,000.
Number Of Awards: 1.
Contact: Peggy Elliott, Scholarship Committee Chairperson

#346 • E.U. Parker Scholarship

Type: Scholarship. Renewable. Reapplication required for renewal.
Eligibility: Applicant must be legally blind and pursuing a full-time course of study. Selection is based upon academic excellence, service to the community, and financial need. This award must be used in the following years of study: • Freshman • Sophomore • Junior • Senior • Masters • Doctoral
Deadline: March 31.
Award Amount: $ 3,000.
Number Of Awards: 1.
Contact: Peggy Elliott, Scholarship Committee Chairperson

NATIONAL FEDERATION OF THE BLIND OF COLORADO

1830 South Acoma
Denver, CO 80223-3606
Phone: 303-778-1130
Fax: 303-778-1598
Email: nfbc@nfbc.org
Website: http://www.nfbc.org

#347 • National Federation of the Blind Scholarship

Type: Scholarship. Not renewable.
Eligibility: Applicant must be legally blind and submit an essay and letters of recommendation. This award must be used in the following years of study: • Freshman • Sophomore • Junior • Senior • Masters • Doctoral • Other postgraduate level
Deadline: August 1.
Award Amount: $ 200 - $ 2,000.
Number Of Awards: 4.
Applications Received: 8.
Odds Of Winning: 50% of applicants on average receive an award each year.
Contact: Kevan Worley, Scholarship Committee Chairman

NATIONAL TOURISM FOUNDATION (NTF)

546 East Main Street
Lexington, KY 40508
Phone: 800–682-8886
Fax: 606-226-4414
Email: scudderb@mgtserv.com
Website: http://www.ntaonline.com

#348 • Tony Orlando Yellow Ribbon Scholarship

Type: Scholarship. Not renewable.
Eligibility: Applicant must have a physical or sensory disability that is verified by an accredited physician, be entering or attending any post-secondary school, have a minimum 2.5 GPA (3.0 secondary school GPA), be a resident of North America, and submit proof of enrollment, two letters of recommendation (from a tourism-related faculty member and a tourism-industry professional), resume, transcripts, and an essay. This award must be used in the following years of study: • Sophomore • Junior • Senior • Masters • Doctoral • Other postgraduate level
Field(s) Of Study: Travel/tourism.
Deadline: April 15.
Award Amount: $ 3,000.
Number Of Awards: 1.
Contact: Brooks A. Scudder, Assistant Executive Director

NORTH CAROLINA DIVISION OF VOCATIONAL REHABILITATION SERVICES

P.O. Box 26053
Raleigh, NC 27611
Phone: 919-733-3364, TDD 919-733-5924
Fax: 919-733-7968
Email: tkemp@dhr.state.nc.us

#349 • Vocational Rehabilitation Program

Type: Grant. Renewable.
Eligibility: Applicant must be a resident of North Carolina and have a mental or physical disability that is an impairment to employment. This award must be used in the following years of study: • Freshman
Deadline: Varies.
Award Amount: $ 2,500.
Number Of Awards: Varies.
Contact: See above.

#350 • Division of Vocational Rehabilitation Services

Type: Grant. Renewable.
Eligibility: Applicant must be a resident of North Carolina and have a mental or physical disability that is an impairment to employment. This award must be used in the following years of study: • Freshman
Deadline: Varies.
Award Amount: $ 2,500.
Number Of Awards: Varies.
Contact: Terry Kemp, Program Specialist

VSA

1300 Connecticut Ave., NW, Suite 700
Washington, DC 20036
Phone: 800-933-8721
Fax: 202-737-0725
Email: playwright@vsarts.org
Website: http://www.vsarts.org

#351 • Playwright Discovery Award

Type: Scholarship. Not renewable.
Eligibility: Applicant must have a disability and submit a one-act play describing the experience of living with a disability. This award must be used in the following years of study: • Freshman • Sophomore • Junior • Senior • Masters • Doctoral • Other postgraduate level
Deadline: April 30.
Award Amount: $ 500 - $ 2,500.
Number Of Awards: 2.
Applications Received: 75.
Odds Of Winning: 2% of applicants on average receive an award each year.
Contact: Elena Widder, Program Manager

WISCONSIN HIGHER EDUCATIONAL AIDS BOARD

P.O. Box 7885
Madison, WI 53707
Phone: 608-267-2206
Fax: 608-267-2808
Email: HEABmail@heab.state.wi.us
Website: http://heab.state.wi.us

#352 • Handicapped Student Grant

Type: Grant. Renewable if recipient continues to demonstrate financial need.
Eligibility: Applicant must be a Wisconsin resident with a severe or profound hearing or visual impairment and must attend a Wisconsin school or an eligible out-of-state school. Selection is based upon financial need. Applicant must submit FAFSA and grant application. This award must be used in the following years of study: • Freshman • Sophomore • Junior • Senior
Deadline: Varies.
Award Amount: $ 250 - $ 1,800.
Number Of Awards: 73.
Contact: Sandra Thomas, Program Coordinator
Phone: 608-266-0888
Email: sandy.thomas@heab.state.wi.us

Drama/Theatre

DONNA REED FOUNDATION FOR THE PERFORMING ARTS

1305 Broadway
P.O. Box 122
Denison, IA 51442
Phone: 712-263-3334
Fax: 712-263-8026
Email: info@donnareed.org
Website: http://www.frii.com/~fujii/home.html

#353 • Donna Reed Performing Arts Scholarships - National Scholarship

Type: Scholarship. Not renewable.
Eligibility: Applicant must be a citizen or permanent resident of the U.S. or one of its official territories and graduate or have graduated from high school between September 1 of the previous year and August 31 of the current year. Scholarships will be awarded in each of the following divisions: Actiing, Musical Theatre, Vocal, Instrumental, and Dance. Applicant must submit audiotape, videotape, or CD of his or her performance, depending on category. Three finalists in each division will compete at the Donna Reed National Scholarship Final Competition for maximum award. This award must be used in the following years of study: • Freshman
Deadline: March 15 (early applications); April 1 (late entries).
Award Amount: $ 500 - $ 4,000. Partial Tuition. Tuition-free scholarships to Donna Reed Performing Arts Workshop Program.
Number Of Awards: 15.
Contact: Sandy Scott, Director

Education–General

AMERICAN LEGION AUXILIARY, DEPARTMENT OF IOWA

720 Lyon Street
Des Moines, IA 50309
Phone: 515-282-7987
Fax: 515-282-7583

#354 • Harriet Hoffman Teaching Scholarship

Type: Scholarship. Not renewable.
Eligibility: Applicant must be an Iowa student attending or planning to attend an Iowa school. This award must be used in the following years of study: •

Freshman • Sophomore • Junior • Senior
Field(s) Of Study: Teaching.
Deadline: June 1.
Award Amount: $ 400.
Number Of Awards: 1.
Applications Received: 75.
Contact: Marlene Valentine, Department Secretary/Treasurer

BOCES GENESEO MIGRANT CENTER

Scholarship Coordinator
27 Lackawanna Avenue
Mt. Morris, NY 14510
Phone: 716-658-7960
Fax: 716-658-7969
Email: gmigrant@frontiernet.net
Website: http://www.migrant.net

#355 • Frank Kazmierczak Memorial Migrant Scholarship

Type: Scholarship. Not renewable.
Eligibility: Applicant must be a migrant farm worker with a recent history of migration for agricultural employment, must demonstrate academic achievement and financial need, and must submit at least two letters of recommendation, transcript, and a 300-to-500-word personal essay. This award must be used in the following years of study: • Freshman • Sophomore • Junior • Senior
Field(s) Of Study: Teacher education.
Deadline: February 1.
Award Amount: $ 1,000.
Number Of Awards: Varies.
Contact:
Phone: 800-245-5681

GENERAL FEDERATION OF WOMEN'S CLUBS OF MASSACHUSETTS (GFWC)

245 Dutton Road, Box 679
Sudbury, MA 01776-0679
Phone: 978-443-4569

#356 • Newtonville Woman's Club Scholarship

Type: Scholarship. Not renewable.
Eligibility: Applicant must attend a Massachusetts high school and submit a letter of endorsement from the president of the sponsoring GFWC of MA club in the community of legal residence, a recommendation from career counselor or high school department head, a letter stating need for financial assistance, and high school transcript. Interview is and SASE required. This award must be used in the following years of study: • Freshman
Field(s) Of Study: Teacher training.
Deadline: March 1.

Award Amount: $ 600.
Number Of Awards: 1.
Contact: Marilyn Perry, Scholarship Chairperson

ILLINOIS CONGRESS OF PARENTS AND TEACHERS

901 South Spring Street
Springfield, IL 62704
Phone: 217-528-9617

#357 • Illinois PTA Lillian E. Glover Scholarship

Type: Scholarship. Not renewable.
Eligibility: Applicant must have graduated from an Illinois public high school and have ranked in top quarter of class. This award must be used in the following years of study: • Freshman
Field(s) Of Study: Education, education-related degree program.
Deadline: March 1.
Award Amount: $ 500 - $ 1,000.
Number Of Awards: 50.
Contact: Virginia Brown, Scholarship Chairman
9012 Knoxville Road
Milan, IL 61264

#358 • Illinois PTA Continuing Education Scholarship

Type: Scholarship. Not renewable.
Eligibility: Applicant must be a past winner of the Lillian E. Glover Scholarship. This award must be used in the following years of study: • Junior • Senior
Field(s) Of Study: Education, education-related degree program.
Deadline: March 1.
Award Amount: $ 500.
Number Of Awards: 25.
Contact: Scholarship Committee

ILLINOIS STUDENT ASSISTANCE COMMISSION/CLIENT SUPPORT SERVICES

1755 Lake Cook Road
Deerfield, IL 60015-5209
Phone: 800-899-ISAC, 847 948-8550
Website: http://www.isac1.org

#359 • Robert C. Byrd Honors Scholarship

Type: Scholarship. Renewable for up to four years.
Eligibility: Applicant must be a U.S. citizen or eligible noncitizen, a legal resident of Illinois, and demonstrate outstanding academic achievement. This award must be used in the following years of study: • Freshman • Sophomore • Junior • Senior
Field(s) Of Study: Education.

Deadline: November 15.
Award Amount: $ 1,500.
Number Of Awards: 1,100.
Contact: Client Relations

MISSISSIPPI BOARD OF TRUSTEES OF STATE INSTITUTIONS OF HIGHER LEARNING

Student Financial Aid Office
3825 Ridgewood Road
Jackson, MS 39211-6453
Phone: 601-982-6663
Fax: 601-982-6527

#360 • William Winter Teacher Scholar Program

Type: Scholarship. Renewable. Minimum 2.5 GPA is required for renewal.
Eligibility: Applicant must be a Mississippi resident. This award must be used in the following years of study: • Freshman • Sophomore • Junior • Senior
Field(s) Of Study: Education.
Deadline: Varies.
Award Amount: $ 1,000 - $ 3,000.
Number Of Awards: Varies.
Contact: Mississippi Postsecondary Education Financial Assistance Board

NORTH CAROLINA STATE DEPARTMENT OF PUBLIC INSTRUCTION

Education Building
301 North Wilmington Street
Raleigh, NC 27601-2825
Phone: 919-715-1120
Fax: 919-715-1153
Website: http://www.ofps.dpi.state.nc.us/OFPS/hm/te/scholars.htm

#361 • Robert C. Byrd Honors Scholarship

Type: Scholarship. Renewable for up to four years if satisfactory academic progress and full-time enrollment are maintained.
Eligibility: Applicant must be a North Carolina resident, have a minimum 3.0 GPA and minimum combined SAT I score of 900, demonstrate outstanding academic achievement, and show promise of continued academic excellence. This award must be used in the following years of study: • Freshman
Deadline: in February.
Award Amount: $ 1,500.
Number Of Awards: 171.
Applications Received: 749.
Contact: Linda Johnson, Scholarship Coordinator, Teacher Education Section

PHI DELTA KAPPA

Eighth Street and Union Avenue
P.O. Box 789
Bloomington, IN 47402
Phone: 812-339-1156
Fax: 812-339-0018
Email: headquarters@pdkintl.org
Website: http://www.pdkintl.org

#362 • Phi Delta Kappa Scholarship Grants for Prospective Educators

Type: Grant. Not renewable.
Eligibility: Applicant must rank in top third of graduating class. Selection is based upon scholarship, recommendations, written expression, interest in teaching as a career, and school and community activities. This award must be used in the following years of study: • Freshman
Field(s) Of Study: Education.
Deadline: January 31.
Award Amount: $ 1,000 - $ 5,000.
Number Of Awards: 50 - 57.
Applications Received: 850.
Odds Of Winning: 6% of applicants on average receive an award each year.
Contact: Shari Bradley, Director of Chapter Programs

ROOTHBERT FUND

475 Riverside Drive
Suite 252
New York, NY 10115

#363 • Roothbert Fund, Inc. Scholarship

Type: Scholarship. Renewable.
Eligibility: Applicant must be primarily motivated by spiritual values. Preference given to applicant who is considering teaching as a vocation. Financial need is considered. More information is available upon request. SASE required. This award must be used in the following years of study: • Freshman • Sophomore • Junior • Senior • Masters • Doctoral
Field(s) Of Study: Teaching.
Deadline: February 1.
Award Amount: $ 2,000.
Number Of Awards: Varies.
Contact: Scholarships

STATE COLLEGE AND UNIVERSITY SYSTEMS OF WEST VIRGINIA, CENTRAL OFFICE

1018 Kanawha Boulevard, East
Suite 700
Charleston, WV 25301-2827
Phone: 304-558-4618

Fax: 304-558-4622
Email: crocket@scusco.wvnet.edu
Website: http://www.scusco.wvnet.edu/

#364 • Underwood-Smith Teacher Scholarship

Type: Scholarship. Renewable. Minimum 3.0 GPA is required for freshmen and sophomores and 3.25 GPA for juniors for renewal.
Eligibility: Applicant must be a West Virginia resident who will attend a West Virginia institution of higher education full time, seeking teacher certification at the preschool, elementary, or secondary level. Undergraduate applicant must rank in the top tenth of class, score in the top tenth statewide of those taking the ACT, or have a cumulative 3.25 GPA after successfully completing two years of course work at an approved institution. Graduate applicant must have graduated in the top tenth of college class. This award must be used in the following years of study: • Junior • Senior • Doctoral
Field(s) Of Study: Education.
Deadline: April 1.
Award Amount: $ 766 - $ 5,000.
Number Of Awards: 67.
Applications Received: 54.
Odds Of Winning: 31% of applicants on average receive an award each year.
Contact: Michelle Wicks, Scholarship Programs Coord.
Email: wicks@scusco.wvnet.edu

STATE STUDENT ASSISTANCE COMMISSION OF INDIANA

150 West Market Street, Suite 500
Indianapolis, IN 46204-2811
Phone: 317-232-2350
Fax: 317-232-3260

#365 • Robert C. Byrd Honors Scholarship

Type: Scholarship. Renewable. Satisfactory academic progress is required to retain scholarship.
Eligibility: Applicant must be an Indiana resident, have 3.0 GPA, and a minimum combined SAT I score of 1350. This award must be used in the following years of study: • Freshman
Deadline: April 24.
Award Amount: $ 1,500.
Number Of Awards: 572.
Applications Received: 1,251.
Contact: Yvonne Heflin, Dir. of Special Programs
Email: yheflin@ssaci.state.in.us

VENTURA COUNTY COMMUNITY FOUNDATION

1317 Del Norte Road, Suite 150
Camarillo, CA 93010

Phone: 805-988-0196
Fax: 805-485-5537

#366 • Wayne Bruton Memorial Scholarship

Type: Scholarship. Not renewable.
Eligibility: Applicant must be attending Ventura High School and be in pursuit of a teaching degree. This award must be used in the following years of study: • Freshman
Field(s) Of Study: Education.
Deadline: Varies.
Award Amount: $ 750.
Number Of Awards: 1.
Contact: Gail Brown, Program Officer

WISCONSIN PARENT TEACHER ASSOCIATION

4797 Hayes Road, Suite 2
Madison, WI 53704-3256
Phone: 608-244-1455

#367 • Brookmire-Hastings Scholarship

Type: Scholarship. Not renewable.
Eligibility: Contact for details. This award must be used in the following years of study: • Freshman
Field(s) Of Study: Education.
Deadline: Varies.
Award Amount: $ 1,000.
Number Of Awards: 2.
Applications Received: 370.
Odds Of Winning: Less than 1% of applicants on average receive an award each year.
Contact: High School Guidance Office

Engineering-General

AMERICAN ELECTROPLATERS AND SURFACE FINISHERS SOCIETY

ATTN: AESF Scholarship Committee
Central Florida Research Park
12644 Research Parkway
Orlando, FL 32826-3298
Phone: 407-281-6441

#368 • American Electroplaters and Surface Finishers Society Scholarship

Type: Scholarship. Renewable. Recipient must re-apply for second year.
Eligibility: Contact for details. This award must be used in the following years of study: • Junior • Senior • Masters • Doctoral • Other postgraduate level

Field(s) Of Study: Chemical engineering, chemistry, environmental engineering, material engineering, material science, metallurgical engineering, metallurgy.
Deadline: April 15.
Award Amount: $ 1,500.
Number Of Awards: Varies.
Applications Received: 74.
Contact: Scholarship Committee

AMERICAN SOCIETY OF AGRICULTURAL ENGINEERS (ASAE)

2950 Niles Road
St. Joseph, MI 49085-9659
Phone: 616-429-0300
Fax: 616-429-3852
Email: hq@asae.org

#369 • ASAE Student Engineer of the Year Scholarship

Type: Scholarship. Not renewable.
Eligibility: Applicant must be an undergraduate student member of ASAE and an active participant in a student ASAE branch organization or a comparable student professional organization. Applicant must have a minimum 3.0 GPA and must have been enrolled for at least one year in an agricultural or biological engineering program in the U.S. or Canada that is accredited by ABET or CEAB. Selection is based upon academic excellence, character and personal development, service, leadership, participation in school activities, level of financial self-support, and essay. This award must be used in the following years of study: • Sophomore • Junior • Senior
Field(s) Of Study: Agricultural engineering, biological engineering.
Deadline: January 30.
Award Amount: $ 1,000.
Number Of Awards: Varies.
Applications Received: 5.
Contact: Carol L. Flautt, Awards and Recognition
Phone: 161-428-6336
Fax: 616-429-3852
Email: flautt@asae.org

AMERICAN SOCIETY OF CERTIFIED ENGINEERING TECHNICIANS (ASCET)

P.O. Box 1348
Flowery Branch, GA 30542-0023
Phone: 770-967-9173
Fax: 770-967-8049

#370 • Small Cash Grant

Type: Grant. Not renewable.
Eligibility: Applicant must be a certified, regular, associate, or student member of ASCET, or a high

school senior in the last five months of the academic year who has passing grades. Letters of recommendation required. This award must be used in the following years of study: • Freshman • Sophomore • Junior • Senior
Field(s) Of Study: Engineering technology.
Deadline: April 1.
Award Amount: $ 100.
Number Of Awards: 4.
Applications Received: 10.
Contact: Kurt H. Schuler, General Manager

AMERICAN SOCIETY OF NAVAL ENGINEERS (ASNE)

1452 Duke Street
Alexandria, VA 22314-3458
Phone: 703-836-6727
Fax: 703-836-7491
Email: asnehq.asne@mcimail.com
Website: http://www.jhuapl.edu/asne

#371 • ASNE Scholarship

Type: Scholarship. Not renewable.
Eligibility: Applicant must be enrolled in a full-time, undergraduate or master's degree program or be a co-op student at an accredited college or university. Applicant must demonstrate or express a genuine interest in a career in naval engineering and be a U.S. citizen. Selection is based upon academic record, work history, professional promise, extracurricular activities, and recommendations. Financial need may be considered. This award must be used in the following years of study: • Senior • Masters
Field(s) Of Study: Aeronautical engineering, civil engineering, electrical/electronic engineering, marine engineering, mechanical engineering, naval architecture, ocean engineering, physical sciences.
Deadline: February 15.
Award Amount: $ 2,500 - $ 3,500.
Number Of Awards: 18.
Applications Received: 81.
Odds Of Winning: 20% of applicants on average receive an award each year.
Contact: Capt. Dennis Pignotti, USN (Ret), Operations Manager

AMERICAN WELDING SOCIETY FOUNDATION, INC. (AWS)

550 N.W. LeJeune Road
Miami, FL 33126
Phone: 800-443-9353, extension 293, 305 445-6628
Fax: 305-443-7559
Email: found@aws.org

#372 • Howard E. Adkins Memorial Scholarship

Type: Scholarship. Renewable.

Eligibility: Applicant must have a minimum 3.2 GPA in engineering (2.8 overall), be at least 18 years old, and be a U.S. citizen. Preference is given to applicants residing or attending school in Wisconsin or Kentucky. This award must be used in the following years of study: • Junior • Senior
Field(s) Of Study: Welding engineering, welding enineering technology.
Deadline: January 15.
Award Amount: $ 2,500.
Number Of Awards: 1.
Applications Received: 15.
Odds Of Winning: 6% of applicants on average receive an award each year.
Contact: Vicki Pinsky, Scholarship Coordinator
Phone: 800-443-9353, extension 461
Email: vpinsky@aws.org

#373 • Edward J. Brady Scholarship

Type: Scholarship. Renewable. Recipient must rapply for renewal.
Eligibility: Applicant must have a minimum 2.5 GPA, be at least 18 years old, be a U.S. citizen, and attend an institution in the U.S. Applicant must submit proof of financial need and a letter of reference. This award must be used in the following years of study: • Sophomore • Junior • Senior
Field(s) Of Study: Welding engineering, welding engineering technology.
Deadline: January 15.
Award Amount: $ 2,500.
Number Of Awards: 1.
Applications Received: 15.
Odds Of Winning: 6% of applicants on average receive an award each year.
Contact: Vicki Pinsky, Scholarship Coordinator
Phone: 800-443-9353, extension 461
Email: vpinsky@aws.org

#374 • Donald F. Hastings Scholarship

Type: Scholarship. Renewable. Recipient must reapply for renewal.
Eligibility: Applicant must have a minimum 2.5 GPA, be at least 18 years old, be a U.S. citizen, and attending an institution located in the U.S. Preference given to applicants residing or attending school in Ohio or Califorina. Applicant must submit proof of financial need. This award must be used in the following years of study: • Sophomore • Junior • Senior
Field(s) Of Study: Welding engineering, welding engineering technology.
Deadline: January 15.
Award Amount: $ 2,500.
Number Of Awards: 1.
Applications Received: 15.
Odds Of Winning: 6% of applicants on average receive an award each year.
Contact: Vicki Pinsky, Scholarship Coordinator

Phone: 800-443-9353, extension 461
Email: vpinsky@aws.org

#375 • Praxair International Scholarship

Type: Scholarship. Renewable. Recipient must reapply for renewal.
Eligibility: Applicant have a minimum 2.5 GPA, be at least 18 years old, be enrolled full-time, be a U.S. or Canadian citizen, and attending an institution in the U.S. or Canada. Selection based on leadership abilities. This award must be used in the following years of study: • Sophomore • Junior • Senior
Field(s) Of Study: Welding engineering, welding engineering technology.
Deadline: January 15.
Award Amount: $ 2,500.
Number Of Awards: 1.
Applications Received: 15.
Odds Of Winning: 6% of applicants on average receive an award each year.
Contact: Vicki Pinsky, Scholarship Coordinator
Phone: 800-443-9353, extension 461
Email: vpinsky@aws.org

ARMED FORCES COMMUNICATIONS AND ELECTRONICS ASSOCIATION

ATTN: Educational Foundation
4400 Fair Lakes Court
Fairfax, VA 22033-3899
Phone: 703-631-6149
Fax: 703-631-4693
Email: scholarship@afcea
Website: http://www.afcea.org

#376 • General Emmett Paige Scholarship

Type: Scholarship. Not renewable.
Eligibility: Applicant must be a U.S. citizen enrolled in an accredited four-year institution in the U.S., have a minimum 3.4 GPA, and be on active duty in or a veteran of the uniformed military services or a spouse or dependent of an active duty member or veteran, and must submit a copy of Certificate of Service, Discharge Form DD214, or Department of Defense or Coast Guard Identification Card. This award must be used in the following years of study: • Freshman • Sophomore • Junior
Field(s) Of Study: Aerospace engineering, computer science, computer engineering, electrical engineering, electronics, mathematics, physics.
Deadline: March 1.
Award Amount: $ 2,000.
Number Of Awards: Varies.
Contact: Norma Corrales, Administrator, Scholarships and Awards Program
Email: edfoundation@afcea.org

#377 • General John A. Wickham Scholarship

Type: Scholarship. Not renewable.
Eligibility: Applicant must be a U.S. citizen enrolled at an accredited four-year institution in the U.S. and have a minimum 3.4 GPA. This award must be used in the following years of study: • Junior • Senior
Field(s) Of Study: Aerospace engineering, computer engineering, computer science, electrical engineering, electronics, mathematics, physics.
Deadline: May 1.
Award Amount: $ 2,000.
Number Of Awards: Varies.
Contact: Norma Corrales, Administrator, Scholarships and Awards Program

INSTITUTE OF INDUSTRIAL ENGINEERS (IIE)

25 Technology Park/Atlanta
Norcross, GA 30092
Phone: 770-449-0460
Fax: 770-263-8532
Website: http://www.iienet.org

#378 • A.O. Putnam Memorial Scholarship

Type: Scholarship. Not renewable.
Eligibility: Applicant must be an active member of IIE, enrolled full-time, and have a minimum 3.4 GPA. Preference given to applicants who have demonstrated interest in management counsulting. This award must be used in the following years of study: • Sophomore • Junior • Senior
Deadline: November 15.
Award Amount: $ 500.
Number Of Awards: 1.
Applications Received: 25.
Odds Of Winning: 4% of applicants on average receive an award each year.
Contact: Bisi Oyeyemi, University Operations Coordinator
Phone: 770-449-0461 extension 139
Email: boyeyemi@www.ieenet.org

JOHNS HOPKINS UNIVERSITY

3400 North Charles Street
Baltimore, MD 21218
Phone: 410-516-8028
Fax: 410-516-6015
Website: http://www.jhu.edu/~finaid

#379 • Charles R. Westgate Scholarship in Engineering

Type: Scholarship. Renewable if recipient maintains a minimum 3.0 GPA and continues enrollment in the G.W.C. Whiting School of Engineering.
Eligibility: Contact for details. This award must be

used in the following years of study: • Freshman
Field(s) Of Study: Engineering.
Deadline: January 1.
Award Amount: Full-tuition. Partial Tuition. plus living expenses stipend.
Number Of Awards: 2.
Contact: Jake Talmage, Senior Assistant Director of Admissions
Phone: 410-516-8171
Fax: 410-516-6025
Email: talmage@jhu.edu

MAINE SOCIETY OF PROFESSIONAL ENGINEERS

142 Mills Road
Kennebunkport, ME   04046-5705
Phone: 207-967-3741
Fax: 207-967-3741
Email: kencam@cybertours.com

#380 • Vernon T. Swain P.E./Robert E. Chute P.E. Memorial Scholarship

Type: Scholarship. Not renewable.
Eligibility: Applicant must be a Maine resident at time of application. This award must be used in the following years of study: • Freshman
Field(s) Of Study: Engineering.
Deadline: March 15.
Award Amount: $ 1,500.
Number Of Awards: 2.
Applications Received: 2.
Contact: Kenneth W. Campbell, Secretary

NATIONAL SOCIETY OF PROFESSIONAL ENGINEERS AUXILIARIES

1420 King Street
Alexandria, VA 22314
Phone: 703-684-2800
Fax: 703-836-4875
Website: http://www.nspe.org

#381 • Virginia D. Henry Memorial Scholarship

Type: Scholarship. Not renewable.
Eligibility: Applicant must be a female U.S. citizen with a minimum 3.0 GPA, minimum SAT I scores of 500 verbal and 600 math (ACT scores of 25 English and 29 math), and must attend a school accredited by the Engineering Accreditation Commission of the Accreditation Board for Engineering and Technology. Application, essay, and official transcripts required. This award must be used in the following years of study: • Freshman
Field(s) Of Study: Engineering.
Deadline: Deadlines are set by each state chapter.

Award Amount: $ 1,000.
Number Of Awards: 1.
Contact: State Society Chapter

#382 • Paul H. Robbins Honorary Scholarship

Type: Scholarship. Renewable. Scholarship renewal report is required for recipients to receive their second-year payment.
Eligibility: Applicant must be a U.S. citizen and must demonstrate academic achievement and attend a school accredited by the Engineering Accreditation Commission of the ABET. Application, essay, and official transcripts required. This award must be used in the following years of study: • Freshman
Field(s) Of Study: Engineering.
Deadline: Deadlines are set by each state chapter.
Award Amount: $ 1,000.
Number Of Awards: 1.
Contact: State Society Chapter

SOCIETY OF MANUFACTURING ENGINEERS (SME) EDUCATION FOUNDATION

One SME Drive, P.O. Box 930
Dearborn, MI 48121
Phone: 313-271-1500, extension 1709
Fax: 313-240-6095
Email: murrdor@sme.org
Website: http://www.sme.org/foundation

#383 • Wayne Kay Co-op Scholarship

Type: Scholarship. Renewable.
Eligibility: Applicant must be a full-time undergraduate student enrolled in a North American school and working through a co-op program in a manufacturing related environment. Applicant must have completed a minimum 30 college credit hours, be seeking a career in manufacturing engineering or technology, and possess a minimum 3.5 GPA. Applicant must provide evidence of demonstrated excellence that may include a project completed for employer and must be related to manufacturing engineering or technology. Preference will be given to students enrolled at an institution with a manufacturing engineering or technology program and to those whose work experience directly relates to manufacturing engineering or closely related fields. This award must be used in the following years of study: • Sophomore • Junior • Senior
Field(s) Of Study: Manufacturing engineering or technology.
Deadline: February 1.
Award Amount: $ 2,500.
Number Of Awards: 2.
Contact: Dora Murray, Grants Coordinator
Phone: 313-271-1500, extension 1709
Email: murrdor@sme.org

SOCIETY OF PETROLEUM ENGINEERS - SAN JOAQUIN VALLEY SECTION

P.O. Box 653
Bakersfield, CA 93302
Website: http://www.sjvspe.org

#384 • Society of Petroleum Engineers - San Joaquin Valley Section Scholarship

Type: Scholarship. Not renewable.
Eligibility: Applicant must either be a resident of California, the dependent of a San Joaquin Valley Section member, or have petroleum-related work experience in the San Joaquin Valley area. This award must be used in the following years of study: • Freshman • Sophomore • Junior • Senior • Masters • Doctoral
Field(s) Of Study: Petroleum engineering or an energy-related field of study.
Deadline: March 26.
Award Amount: $ 500 - $ 1,000.
Number Of Awards: 6.
Applications Received: 11.
Odds Of Winning: 55% of applicants on average receive an award each year.
Contact: Joe Perrick, Scholarship Director
Phone: 805-322-4031

SPE FOUNDATION

14 Fairfield Drive
Brookfield, CT 06804
Phone: 203-740-5434
Fax: 203-775-8490
Website: http://www.4spe.org

#385 • SPE Foundation Scholarship

Type: Scholarship. Renewable. Recipient must maintain required GPA and reapply for renewal.
Eligibility: Applicant must demonstrate financial need and academic qualifications. Applicant must plan a career in the plastics industry. Three letters of recommendation and an essay required. Applications available from August 15 to November 15. This award must be used in the following years of study: • Freshman • Sophomore • Junior • Senior
Field(s) Of Study: Plastics engineering, polymer science.
Deadline: December 15.
Award Amount: $ 5,000.
Number Of Awards: 10.
Applications Received: 210.
Odds Of Winning: 5% of applicants on average receive an award each year.
Contact: Gail R. Bristol, Development Director

TECHNICAL MINORITY SCHOLARSHIP PROGRAM

907 Culver Rd
Rochester, NY 14609

Phone: 716-482-3887
Website: http://xerox.com/employment

#386 • Technical Minority Scholarship

Type: Scholarship. Renewable. Reapplication is required for renewal.
Eligibility: Applicant must be a minority student. This award must be used in the following years of study: • Freshman • Sophomore • Junior • Senior • Masters • Doctoral
Field(s) Of Study: Computer science, engineering, mathematics, optics, physics, science.
Deadline: September 15.
Award Amount: $ 500 - $ 5,000.
Number Of Awards: 80.
Applications Received: 1,400.
Odds Of Winning: 6% of applicants on average receive an award each year.
Contact: Jennifer Nicoletti, Account Manager
907 Culver Rd.
Rochester, NY 14609
Phone: 716-482-3887, extension 226

English/Literature/Writing

AMELIA MAGAZINE

329 East Street
Bakersfield, CA 93304-2031
Phone: 661-323-4064
Fax: 661-323-5326
Email: amelia@lightspeed.net

#387 • Amelia Student Award

Type: Contest. Not renewable.
Eligibility: Applicant may submit a short story or essay up to 1,500 words, or a poem up to 100 lines. Recipient is published in Amelia. Send SASE and $3 handling fee for writing sample of past recipient. This award must be used in the following years of study: • Freshman • Sophomore • Junior • Senior
Deadline: May 15.
Award Amount: $ 200.
Number Of Awards: 1.
Applications Received: 90.
Odds Of Winning: 1% of applicants on average receive an award each year.
Contact: Frederick A. Raborg, Jr., Editor

AIM MAGAZINE SHORT STORY CONTEST

P.O. Box 1174
Maywood, IL 60153
Phone: 773-874-6184

Fax: 206-543-2746
Website: http://www.aimmagazine.org

#388 • Short Story Contest

Type: Contest. Not renewable.
Eligibility: Applicant must submit a short story (maximum 4,000 words) with a lasting social significance. This award must be used in the following years of study: • Freshman • Sophomore • Junior • Senior • Masters
Deadline: August 15.
Award Amount: $ 100.
Number Of Awards: 1.
Contact: Myron Apilado

AYN RAND INSTITUTE

P.O. Box 6004
Department DB
Inglewood, CA 90312
Phone: 310-306-9232
Fax: 310-306-4925
Email: essay@aynrand.org
Website: http://www.aynrand.org/contests/

#389 • Atlas Shrugged Essay Competition

Type: Contest. Not renewable.
Eligibility: Applicant must enter essay contest. Essays must demonstrate an outstanding grasp of the philosophic meaning of Ayn Rand's novel *Atlas Shrugged*. More information is available on the web site. This award must be used in the following years of study: • Freshman • Sophomore • Junior • Senior • Masters
Field(s) Of Study: Business.
Deadline: February 15.
Award Amount: $ 1,000 - $ 7,500.
Number Of Awards: 6.
Contact: Sean Saulsbury, Essay Contest Coordinator

HUMANIST MAGAZINE

7 Harwood Drive
P.O. Box 1188
Amherst, NY 14226-7188
Phone: 716-839-5080 or 800-743-6646
Fax: 716-839-5079
Email: thehumanist@juno.com
Website: http://www.humanist.net

#390 • Humanist Essay Contest for Young Women and Men of North America

Type: Contest. Not renewable.
Eligibility: Applicant must be between 13 and 17 or 18 and 24 years of age and submit a typed essay of under 2,500 words. This award must be used in the following years of study: • Freshman • Sophomore • Junior • Senior • Masters • Doctoral • Other

postgraduate level • educational training
Deadline: December 1.
Award Amount: $ 100 - $ 2,000. Partial Tuition. $50 educator prize for those who inspire a winning essay.
Number Of Awards: 6 - 18.
Applications Received: 130.
Odds Of Winning: 11% of applicants on average receive an award each year.
Contact: Marian Hetherly, Contest Coordinator

NATIONAL FEDERATION OF STATE POETRY SOCIETIES (NFSPS)

908 Burlington Avenue
Fairfield, IA 52556
Phone: 515-472-7979

#391 • Edna Meudt Scholarship

Type: Contest. Not renewable.
Eligibility: Applicant must submit 10 poems (contact chairman for guidelines). This is a prize, and only open to serious poets. This award must be used in the following years of study: • Senior • Masters
Deadline: February 1.
Award Amount: Partial Tuition. Minimum award: $500 plus travel stipend, book publication.
Number Of Awards: 2.
Contact: Victor Tichy, Scholarship Chair

NIMROD INTERNATIONAL JOURNAL OF PROSE AND POETRY

600 South College Ave
Tulsa, OK 74104-3126
Phone: 918-631 3080
Fax: 918-631-3033
Email: nimrod@utulsa.edu
Website: http://www.utulsa.edu/nimrod/

#392 • Katherine Anne Porter Prize for Fiction

Type: Contest. Not renewable.
Eligibility: Contact for details. This award must be used in the following years of study: • Freshman • Sophomore • Junior • Senior • Masters • Doctoral • Other postgraduate level
Deadline: April 20.
Award Amount: $ 1,000 - $ 2,000.
Number Of Awards: 2.
Applications Received: 900.
Odds Of Winning: Less than 1% of applicants on average receive an award each year.
Contact: Awards

#393 • Pablo Neruda Prize for Poetry

Type: Contest. Not renewable.
Eligibility: Contact for details. This award must be

used in the following years of study: • Freshman • Sophomore • Junior • Senior • Masters • Doctoral • Other postgraduate level
Deadline: April 20.
Award Amount: $ 1,000 - $ 2,000.
Number Of Awards: 2.
Contact: Awards

Environmental Science

AMERICAN INDIAN SCIENCE AND ENGINEERING SOCIETY

Scholarship Coordinator
P.O. Box 9828
Albuquerque, NM 87119-9828
Phone: 505-765-1052
Fax: 505-765-5608
Email: scholarships@aises.org
Website: http://www.aises.org

#394 • EPA Tribal Lands Environmental Science Scholarship

Type: Scholarship. Renewable. Recipient must reapply for renewal.
Eligibility: Applicant must have a minimum 2.5 GPA and be enrolled full time. Summer employment at an EPA facility and/or on an Indian reservation is also offered if resources are available. This award must be used in the following years of study: • Junior • Senior • Masters • Doctoral
Field(s) Of Study: Biochemistry, biology, chemical engineering, chemistry, entomology, environmental economics, environmental science, hydrology, related environmental sciences.
Deadline: June 15.
Award Amount: $ 4,000.
Number Of Awards: 68.
Applications Received: 83.
Odds Of Winning: 82% of applicants on average receive an award each year.
Contact: Scholarship Coordinator

Fashion Design/Interior Decorating

INTERNATIONAL FURNISHINGS AND DESIGN ASSOCIATION (IFDA)

1200 19th Street, NW #300
Washington, DC 20036-2422

Phone: 202-857-1897
Fax: 202-828-6042
Email: info@ifda.com
Website: http://www.ifda.com

#395 • IFDA Educational Foundation Student Scholarship

Type: Scholarship. Renewable. Recipient must reapply to retain scholarship.
Eligibility: Applicant must be an IFDA member enrolled in a furnishing and design-related program. This award must be used in the following years of study: • Sophomore • Junior • Senior • Masters • Doctoral • Other postgraduate level
Field(s) Of Study: Design, art, graphics, and related majors.
Deadline: October 30.
Award Amount: $ 1,000.
Number Of Awards: 2.
Applications Received: 20.
Odds Of Winning: 15% of applicants on average receive an award each year.
Contact: IFDA Executive Office

#396 • Vercille Voss Student Scholarship

Type: Scholarship. Renewable. Reapplication required for renewal.
Eligibility: Applicant must be an IFDA member enrolled in a furnishings and design-related program. This award must be used in the following years of study: • Sophomore • Junior • Senior • Masters • Doctoral • Other postgraduate level
Field(s) Of Study: Art, design, graphics, and related majors.
Deadline: Varies.
Award Amount: $ 1,500.
Number Of Awards: 1.
Contact: IFDA Executive Office

#397 • Charles D. Mayo Student Scholarship

Type: Scholarship. Renewable. Reapplication required for renewal.
Eligibility: Applicant must be enrolled in a furnishings and design-related program. Open to IFDA and non-IFDA student members. This award must be used in the following years of study: • Sophomore • Junior • Senior • Masters • Doctoral • Other postgraduate level
Field(s) Of Study: Art, design, graphics, and related majors.
Deadline: Varies.
Award Amount: $ 1,000.
Number Of Awards: 1.
Contact: IFDA Executive Office

Fine Arts

GENERAL FEDERATION OF WOMEN'S CLUBS OF MASSACHUSETTS (GFWC OF MA)

245 Dutton Road, Box 679
Sudbury, MA 01776-0679
Phone: 978-443-4569

#398 • "Pennies for Art" Scholarship

Type: Scholarship. Not renewable.
Eligibility: Applicant must attend a Massachusetts high school and must submit a letter of endorsement from the president of the sponsoring GFWC of Massachusetts club in the community of legal residence, a recommendation from high school art teacher, a letter stating goals, and portfolio of three examples of original work. SASE required. This award must be used in the following years of study: • Freshman
Field(s) Of Study: Art.
Deadline: February 1.
Award Amount: $ 500.
Number Of Awards: 1 - 4.
Contact: Bett Porter, Coordinator, Arts Department
Phone: 508-238-4040

NATIONAL COWBOY HALL OF FAME

John F. and Anna Lee Stacey Scholarship Fund for Art Education
1700 Northeast 63rd Street
Oklahoma City, OK 73111
Phone: 405-478-2250

#399 • John F. and Anna Lee Stacey Scholarship

Type: Scholarship. Renewable. Recipient must reapply for renewal.
Eligibility: Applicant must be an American citizen age 18 to 35 and must submit not more than ten 35mm slides of work (painting or drawing), four letters of reference, and a personal statement. Selection is based on the work's merit, on evidence of capacity for research, and on applicant's ability to take full advantage of the scholarship. The committee will try to gain useful publicity for the recipient. Recipient must submit a brief quarterly report with 35mm slides of work and a more complete report at the termination of the scholarship. This award must be used in the following years of study: • Freshman • Sophomore • Junior • Senior • Masters • Doctoral • Other postgraduate level
Field(s) Of Study: Conservative art, drawing, painting.

Deadline: February 1.
Award Amount: $ 500 - $ 3,000.
Number Of Awards: 1 - 7.
Applications Received: 75.
Odds Of Winning: 9% of applicants on average receive an award each year.
Contact: Ed Muno, Curator of Art

NORTHERN VIRGINIA HANDCRAFTERS' GUILD, INC.

P.O. Box 332
Vienna, VA 22116

#400 • Visual Arts Scholarship

Type: Scholarship. Not renewable.
Eligibility: Applicant must be a Virginia resident living within 50 miles of Vienna, Va., and must demonstrate reasonable chance of success in planned program of study. Selection is based upon interest and demonstrated talent in some craft or art. Financial need may be considered. This award must be used in the following years of study: • Freshman
Field(s) Of Study: Art, crafts.
Deadline: April 2.
Award Amount: $ 1,200.
Number Of Awards: 2.
Applications Received: 42.
Odds Of Winning: 5% of applicants on average receive an award each year.
Contact: Marcia Lund, Scholarship Chairperson
5107 Spring Rock Court
Fairfax, VA 22032
Email: AKLund@aol.com

TELACU EDUCATION FOUNDATION

5400 East Olympic Boulevard, Suite 300
Los Angeles, CA 90022
Phone: 323-721-1655
Fax: 323-724-3372
Website: http://www.telacu.com

#401 • TELACU Arts Award

Type: Scholarship. Not renewable.
Eligibility: Applicant must come from a low-income household, be a first-generation college student, have a minimum 2.5 GPA, and must be a U.S. citizen or permanent resident and a permanent resident of unincorporated East Los Angeles, City of Los Angeles, Bell Gardens, Commerce, Huntington Park, Montebello, Monterey Park, or South Gate. This award must be used in the following years of study: • Freshman • Sophomore • Junior • Senior
Field(s) Of Study: Fine arts, music, dance, drama.
Deadline: April 1.
Award Amount: $ 1,000.
Number Of Awards: 1 - 2.

Applications Received: 10.
Odds Of Winning: 10% of applicants on average receive an award each year.
Contact: Michael E. Alvarado, Scholarship Program Dir.

Fire Science

INTERNATIONAL ASSOCIATION OF FIRE FIGHTERS

Office of the General President
1750 New York Ave, NW
Washington, DC 20006
Phone: 202-737-8484
Fax: 202-737-8418
Website: http://www.iaff.org

#402 • W.H. "Howie" McClennan Scholarship

Type: Scholarship. Renewable for up to four years if recipient maintains academic performance.
Eligibility: Applicant must be the dependent of a fire fighter who was a member of the International Association of Fire Fighters in good standing and died in the line of duty. Selection is based upon academic performance and financial need. Applicant should submit two letters of recommendation, transcripts, and statement indicating why he/she wants to continue his/her education. This award must be used in the following years of study: • Freshman • Sophomore • Junior • Senior • Masters • Doctoral • Other postgraduate level
Deadline: February 1.
Award Amount: $ 2,500.
Number Of Awards: 13.
Applications Received: 13.
Odds Of Winning: 100% of applicants on average receive an award each year.
Contact: Department of Education and Information Resources

Foreign Languages

ACTR/ACCELS

Research Scholar Program
1776 Massachusetts Avenue, NW, Suite 700
Washington, DC 20036
Phone: 202-833-7522
Fax: 202-833-7523
Email: research@actr.org
Website: http://www.actr.org

#403 • NIS Regional Languages Grant

Type: Grant. Not renewable.
Eligibility: Award is for advanced and intermediate language study in the countries of the NIS (New Independent States): Armenia, Azerbaijan, Belarus, Georgia, Kazakhstan, Kyrgyzstan, Moldova, Russia, Tajikistan, Turkmenistan, Ukraine, and Uzbekistan. Three competitions per year. This award must be used in the following years of study: • Masters • Doctoral • Other postgraduate level • Junior faculty
Field(s) Of Study: Foreign languages.
Deadline: March 1, April 1, October 15.
Award Amount: $ 2,000 - $15,030.
Number Of Awards: 2 - 10.
Applications Received: 20.
Odds Of Winning: 50% of applicants on average receive an award each year.
Contact: Graham Hettlinger or Karen Aguilera, Russian and Eurasian Programs Officers
Email: hettlinger@actr.org or aguilera@actr.org

AMERICAN TRANSLATORS ASSOCIATION

225 Reinekers Lane, Suite 590
Alexandria, VA 22314
Phone: 703-683-6100
Fax: 703-683-6122
Email: ata@atanet.org
Website: http://www.atanet.org

#404 • Student Translation Award

Type: Contest. Not renewable.
Eligibility: Applicant must be a student or group of students completing a literary translation or translation-related project. Applicant must complete a form and submit a project description that is not to exceed 250 words. The application should be accompanied by a statement of support from the faculty member who is supervising the project. This award must be used in the following years of study: • Sophomore • Junior • Senior • Masters • Doctoral • Other postgraduate level
Deadline: Varies.
Award Amount: $ 500, plus a trip to the Annual Conference.
Number Of Awards: 1.
Contact: Walter Bacak, Executive Director

GERMAN ACADEMIC EXCHANGE SERVICE (DAAD)

950 Third Avenue, 19th Floor
New York, NY 10022
Phone: 212-758-3223
Fax: 212-755-5780
Email: daadny@daad.org
Website: http://www.daad.org

#405 • Hochschulsommerkurse at German Universities Grant

Type: Grant. Not renewable.
Eligibility: Applicant must be a U.S. or Canadian student and have at least two years of college-level German or equivalent. Preference is given to applicants under age 32. Award may be used at German universities only. This award must be used in the following years of study: • Junior • Senior • Masters • Doctoral
Field(s) Of Study: German.
Deadline: January 31.
Award Amount: Partial Tuition. Full- or half-tuition plus fees and living expenses.
Number Of Awards: Varies.

INDIANA UNIVERSITY-PURDUE UNIVERSITY AT INDIANAPOLIS

425 University Boulevard
Indianapolis, IN 46202
Phone: 317-274-4595
Website: http://www.iupui.edu/

#406 • Central American Scholarship

Type: Scholarship. Not renewable.
Eligibility: Award is for study at the University of Costa Rica in San Jose. The Office of International Affairs assists students with applying directly to the University of Costa Rica, as well as with transferring credits. Students can take regular or intensive Spanish courses. Applicant must have a strong academic record and be proficient in Spanish. Recommendations from instructors required. Applicant can apply online. This award must be used in the following years of study: • Junior • Senior
Field(s) Of Study: Spanish.
Deadline: Varies.
Award Amount: $ 2,000.
Number Of Awards: 2.
Applications Received: 3.
Odds Of Winning: 66% of applicants on average receive an award each year.
Contact: Dr. Nancy Newton
Department of Foreign Languages and Cultures
Cavanaugh Hall Room 501F
Phone: 317-274-7342

Forestry

MOORESTOWN ROTARY CHARITIES, INC.

Winston E. Parker Scholarship Committee
P.O. Box 105
Moorestown, NJ 08057
Phone: 609-231-8894
Fax: 609-273-1555
Email: bob.coackley@inrange.com

#407 • Winston E. Parker Scholarship

Type: Scholarship. Renewable. Reapplication with prior year's achievements required for renewal.
Eligibility: Applicant must demonstrate interest in the field of arboretal, forestry, ornamental studies, or associated specialties. Applicant must also demonstrate financial need and submit application form. This award must be used in the following years of study: • Freshman • Sophomore • Junior • Senior • Masters • Doctoral • Other postgraduate level
Field(s) Of Study: Arboretal, forestry, ornamental horticulture, or related fields.
Deadline: February 1.
Award Amount: $ 1,000.
Number Of Awards: Varies.
Contact: Robert Coackley, Chair of Scholarship Committee
Phone: 609-231-8894
Fax: 609-273-1555
Email: bob.coackley@inrange.com

Gender/Marital Status

ASSOCIATION FOR WOMEN IN ARCHITECTURE

2550 Beverly Boulevard
Los Angeles, CA 90057
Phone: 213-389-6490
Fax: 213-389-7514
Website: http://www.awa-la.org

#408 • AWA Scholarship Awards

Type: Scholarship. Not renewable.
Eligibility: Applicant must be a woman who has already completed one year (18 units) in major and is enrolled in ensuing term. If applicant is a non-California resident, she must attend a California school. This award must be used in the following years of study: • Junior • Senior • Masters • Doctoral • Other postgraduate level
Field(s) Of Study: Architecture, engineering as applied to architecture, environmental design, interior design, landscape architecture, urban planning.
Deadline: April 27.
Award Amount: $ 500 - $ 2,500.
Number Of Awards: 3.
Applications Received: 60.
Odds Of Winning: 5% of applicants on average receive an award each year.
Contact: AWA office, website

BROOKHAVEN WOMEN IN SCIENCE

P.O. Box 183
Upton, NY 11973

#409 • Renate W. Chasman Scholarship for Women

Type: Scholarship. Not renewable.
Eligibility: Applicant must be a woman, U.S. citizen, or permanent resident alien, and a resident of Nassau County, Suffolk County, Brooklyn, or Queens (NY). Selection is based upon academic and life/career record, letters of reference, and an essay. Applicant must send self-addressed, stamped envelope with application request. This award must be used in the following years of study: • Junior • Senior • Masters
Field(s) Of Study: Engineering, mathematics, or natural sciences.
Deadline: April 1.
Award Amount: $ 2,000.
Number Of Awards: 1.
Applications Received: 12.
Odds Of Winning: 8% of applicants on average receive an award each year.
Contact: Scholarship Committee

BUSINESS AND PROFESSIONAL WOMEN'S FOUNDATION

2012 Massachusetts Avenue, NW
Washington, DC 20036
Phone: 202-293-1200
Fax: 202-861-0298
Website: http://www.bpwusa.org

#410 • BPW Career Advancement Scholarship

Type: Scholarship. Renewable. Recipient must reapply for renewal.
Eligibility: Applicant must be a woman, age 25 or older, a U.S. citizen, demonstrate critical financial need, and be officially accepted into a program of study at an accredited U.S. institution. Applicant must have a definite plan to use the training to upgrade skills for career advancement, train for a new career, or to enter or re-enter the job market. Applicant must graduate within 24 months of receiving the scholarship. Award does not cover study at the doctoral level (Ph.D.) or non-degree programs. Applicant should enclose a business size #10, self-addressed, double-stamped envelope and write "scholarship" in the upper right-hand corner of the envelope to identify requested information. Applicant can also download application from website. This award must be used in the following years of study: • Junior • Senior • Masters • Doctoral • professional degree (J.D., D.D.S., M.D.) students
Field(s) Of Study: Biological sciences, business studies, computer science, engineering, humanities, mathematics, paralegal studies, physical sciences, social science, teacher education.
Deadline: April 15.
Award Amount: $ 500 - $ 1,000.
Number Of Awards: 45.
Applications Received: 903.
Odds Of Winning: 5% of applicants on average receive an award each year.
Contact: Scholarship Administrator
Phone: 202-293-1200, extension 169

#411 • New York Life Foundation Scholarship for Women in the Health Professions

Type: Scholarship. Renewable. Recipient must reapply for renewal.
Eligibility: Applicant must be a woman, age 25 or over, a U.S. citizen, demonstrate critical financial need, and be officially accepted into a program of study at an accredited U.S. institution. Applicant must have a definite plan to use the training to upgrade skills for career advancement, train for a new career, or to enter or re-enter the job market. Applicant must graduate within 24 months from the date of the grant. Award does not cover graduate or doctoral study or non-degree programs. Applicant should enclose a business size #10, self-addressed, double-stamped envelope and write "scholarship" in the upper right-hand corner of the envelope to identify requested information. Applicant can also download application from website. This award must be used in the following years of study: • Sophomore • Junior • Senior
Field(s) Of Study: Health care.
Deadline: April 1.
Award Amount: $ 500 - $ 1,000.
Number Of Awards: 52.
Applications Received: 737.
Odds Of Winning: 7% of applicants on average receive an award each year.
Contact: Scholarship Administrator
Email: sremeika@bpwusa.org

CHARLES W. FREES, JR. EDUCATIONAL FUND

508 Coeur de Royale
Creve Coeur, MO 63141
Phone: 314-993-5982

#412 • Charles W. Frees, Jr. Scholarship

Type: Scholarship. Not renewable.
Eligibility: Applicant must be a man. This award must be used in the following years of study: • Freshman
Deadline: April 1.
Award Amount: $ 800 - $ 1,200.
Number Of Awards: 40.
Applications Received: 60.
Odds Of Winning: 67% of applicants on average

receive an award each year.
Contact: Morris Bhitz, Chairman

COMMUNITY FOUNDATION SERVING RICHMOND AND CENTRAL VIRGINIA

7325 Beaufort Springs Drive, Suite 210
Richmond, VA 23225-8470
Phone: 804-330-7400
Fax: 804-330-5992
Email: sdavis@tcfrichmond.org
Website: http://www.tcfrichmond.org

#413 • Dorothy Armstrong Community Service Scholarship

Type: Scholarship. Not renewable.
Eligibility: Applicant must be a woman, U.S. citizen, graduating from Thomas Dale High School (Va.), plan on enrolling in a two- or four-year college or university in the continental U.S., and must demonstrate academic achievement and leadership or community service. This award must be used in the following years of study: • Freshman
Deadline: March 10.
Award Amount: $ 500 - $ 5,000.
Number Of Awards: Varies.
Contact: Susan Brown Davis, Senior Program Officer
Email: sdavis@tcfrichmond.org

#414 • William Reed Baker Outstanding Senior Award

Type: Scholarship. Not renewable.
Eligibility: Applicant must be a man, U.S. citizen, graduating from Hampton High School (Va.), must plan to enroll in an accredited two- or four-year college or university in the continental U.S., and must demonstrate academic achievement, leadership or community service, and devotion to academic, community, and athletic endeavors. This award must be used in the following years of study: • Freshman
Deadline: March 10.
Award Amount: $ 500 - $ 5,000.
Number Of Awards: Varies.
Contact: Susan Brown Davis, Senior Program Officer
Email: sdavis@tcfrichmond.org

JEANNETTE RANKIN FOUNDATION

P.O. Box 6653
Athens, GA 30604
Phone: 706-208-1211
Website: http://www.wmst.unt.edu/jrf/

#415 • Jeannette Rankin Foundation Award

Type: Scholarship. Not renewable.
Eligibility: Applicant must be a woman, 35 years or older, a U.S. citizen, and accepted or enrolled in a certified program of technical/vocational training or an undergraduate program. Financial need must be demonstrated. This award must be used in the following years of study: • Sophomore • Junior • Senior • technical/vocational students
Deadline: March 1.
Award Amount: $ 1,500.
Number Of Awards: 20.
Applications Received: 900.
Odds Of Winning: 2% of applicants on average receive an award each year.
Contact: Awards Administrator

JEWISH FOUNDATION FOR EDUCATION OF WOMEN

330 West 58th Street
New York, NY 10019
Phone: 212-265-2565
Email: FdnScholar@aol.com
Website: http://www.jfew.org

#416 • Scholarship for Emigres in the Health Professions

Type: Scholarship. Renewable if recipient continues to demonstrate financial need and is a student in good standing.
Eligibility: Applicant must be a woman, an emigre from the former Soviet Republics, and live within 50 miles of New York City. This award must be used in the following years of study: • Freshman • Sophomore • Junior • Senior • Masters • Doctoral
Field(s) Of Study: Dental hygeine, dentistry, medicine, nursing, occupational therapy, pharmacy, physical therapy, physician assistant.
Deadline: February 15.
Award Amount: $ 5,000.
Number Of Awards: 48.
Contact: Scholarship Committee

NATIONAL SOCIETY OF PROFESSIONAL ENGINEERS AUXILIARIES

1420 King Street
Alexandria, VA 22314
Phone: 703-684-2800
Fax: 703-836-4875
Website: http://www.nspe.org

#417 • Auxiliary Scholarship

Type: Scholarship. Renewable. Scholarship renewal report is required for recipients to receive their second-year payment.
Eligibility: Selection is made in a three-level process: chapter, state, and national. Applicant must be a woman, a U.S. citizen, have at least a 3.0 GPA for the 10th and 11th grades, and have SAT scores of at least 500 (verbal) and 600 (math), or ACT scores of 25

(English) and 29 (math). Applicants must attend a school accredited by the Engineering Accreditation Commission of the Accreditation Board for Engineering and Technology and should submit a completed application along with an essay and transcripts. This award must be used in the following years of study: • Freshman
Field(s) Of Study: Engineering.
Deadline: Deadlines are set by each chapter, some as early as October.
Award Amount: $ 1,000.
Number Of Awards: 1.
Contact: State Society Chapter

SOCIETY OF MANUFACTURING ENGINEERS (SME) EDUCATION FOUNDATION

One SME Drive, P.O. Box 930
Dearborn, MI 48121
Phone: 313-271-1500, extension 1709
Fax: 313-240-6095
Email: murrdor@sme.org
Website: http://www.sme.org/foundation

#418 • Lucille B. Kaufman Women's Scholarship

Type: Scholarship. Renewable. Recipients may apply in succeeding years.
Eligibility: Applicant must be a woman enrolled full time in a degree program, have completed at least 30 credit hours, and maintain a minimum 3.5 GPA. Financial need is not a consideration, except when two or more applicants have equal qualifications. This award must be used in the following years of study: • Sophomore • Junior • Senior
Field(s) Of Study: Manufacturing engineering, manufacturing engineering technology.
Deadline: February 1.
Award Amount: $ 1,000.
Number Of Awards: 1.
Contact: Dora Murray, Grants Coordinator
Email: murrdor@sme.org

THE KARLA SCHERER FOUNDATION

737 North Michigan Avenue
Suite 2330
Chicago, IL 60611
Phone: 312-943-9191
Website: http://comnet.org/kschererf

#419 • Karla Scherer Foundation Scholarship

Type: Scholarship. Renewable if recipient maintains grades, focus and financial situation.
Eligibility: Applicant must be a woman. When requesting an application, she should include the name(s) of school(s) to which she is applying (or attending), the courses she plans to take, and how she intends to use her education in her chosen career. If the request meets the preliminary criteria and encloses a self-addressed stamped envelope, then an application package will be mailed. This award must be used in the following years of study: • Freshman • Sophomore • Junior • Senior • Masters • Doctoral
Field(s) Of Study: Economics, finance.
Deadline: March 1.
Award Amount: Varies.
Number Of Awards: 25.
Applications Received: 25,000.
Contact: Katherine Ross
Executive Director
Phone: 312-943-9271

WOMEN'S JEWELRY ASSOCIATION

Scholarship Committee
333B Rte. #46 West, Suite B-201
Fairfield, NJ 07004
Phone: 973-575-7190
Fax: 973-575-1445
Website: http://www.womensjewelry.org

#420 • Women's Jewelry Association Scholarship

Type: Scholarship. Not renewable.
Eligibility: Applicant must be a woman. Applicant must submit a formal application accompanied by prints or drawings of work, a personal statement, and two letters of recommendation. This award must be used in the following years of study: • Sophomore • Junior • Senior
Field(s) Of Study: Jewelry.
Deadline: May 25.
Award Amount: $ 2,500 - $ 5,000.
Number Of Awards: Varies.
Contact: Scholarship Coordinator

WOMEN'S SOUTHERN CALIFORNIA GOLF ASSOCIATION

402 West Arrow Highway, Suite 10
San Dimas, CA 91773-2715
Phone: 909-592-1281
Fax: 909-592-7542
Email: wscga@womensgolf.org
Website: http://www.womensgolf.org

#421 • Gloria Fecht Memorial Scholarship

Type: Scholarship. Renewable if recipient maintains a minimum 3.0 GPA.
Eligibility: Applicant must be a female resident of Southern California, have an interest in golf, have a minimum 3.0 GPA, enroll in an accredited four-year school, and demonstrate financial need. This award

must be used in the following years of study: •
Freshman • Sophomore • Junior • Senior • Masters •
Doctoral • Other postgraduate level
Deadline: March 1.
Award Amount: $ 1,000 - $ 3,500.
Number Of Awards: 10.
Applications Received: 75.
Odds Of Winning: 13% of applicants on average
receive an award each year.
Contact: Mary Swingle, President

WOMEN'S SPORTS FOUNDATION

Eisenhower Park
East Meadow, NY 11554
Phone: 800-227-3988
Fax: 516-542-4716
Email: wosport@aol.com
Website: http://www.womenssportsfoundation.org

#422 • Linda Riddle/SGMA Scholarship

Type: Scholarship. Not renewable.
Eligibility: Applicant must be a woman, have a
minimim 3.0 GPA, have participated in girls' high
school sports, and be interested in pursuing a career
in a sports-related field. This award must be used in
the following years of study: • Freshman
Deadline: December 10.
Award Amount: $ 1,500.
Number Of Awards: 5.
Applications Received: 476.
Odds Of Winning: 1% of applicants on average
receive an award each year.
Contact: Scholarships

WOMEN'S WESTERN GOLF FOUNDATION

Director of Scholarships
393 Ramsay Road
Deerfield, IL 60015

#423 • Women's Western Golf Foundation Scholarship

Type: Grant. Renewable. Satisfactory GPA and
financial need are required to retain scholarship.
Eligibility: Applicant must be a woman and a U.S.
citizen. Selection is based upon academic achievement,
financial need, excellence of character, and involvement
with the sport of golf. Skill or excellence in the sport of
golf is not a criterion. Applicant must request
application by March 1. This award must be used in the
following years of study: • Freshman
Deadline: April 5.
Award Amount: $ 2,000.
Number Of Awards: 19 - 20.
Applications Received: 400.
Contact: Mrs. Richard W. Willis, Dir. of Scholarships

Graphic Arts

COASTAL ADVERTISING AND MARKETING PROFESSIONALS (CAMP)

P.O. Box 1414
Myrtle Beach, SC 29578
Phone: 843-449-7121

#424 • CAMP Scholarship

Type: Scholarship. Not renewable.
Eligibility: Applicant must have a minimum 3.0
GPA. This award must be used in the following years
of study: • Junior • Senior • Masters • Doctoral
Field(s) Of Study: Art studio/advertising design,
communications, journalism, marketing, public
relations, research.
Deadline: April.
Award Amount: $ 500 - $ 1,500.
Number Of Awards: 2.
Applications Received: 15.
Odds Of Winning: 10% of applicants on average
receive an award each year.
Contact: Julie Bostian, Scholarship Chair
Phone: 843-626-7444
Email: bostian@sccoast.net

MAINE GRAPHIC ARTS ASSOCIATION (MGGA)

P.O. Box 874
Auburn, ME 04212-0874

#425 • MGAA Scholarship

Type: Scholarship. Not renewable.
Eligibility: Applicant must be accepted or enrolled at a
Maine school that is a member of the MGAA, have a
minimum "C" high school grade average, and submit
transcript and two evaluations. This award must be used
in the following years of study: • Freshman
Field(s) Of Study: Graphic arts, printing trade.
Deadline: May 15.
Award Amount: $ 150 - $ 500.
Number Of Awards: 12.
Applications Received: 12.
Odds Of Winning: 100% of applicants on average
receive an award each year.
Contact: Chairperson, Educational Need Committee

NEW ENGLAND PRINTING AND PUBLISHING COUNCIL

New England Graphic Arts Scholarships
P.O. Box 218
Norwood, MA 02062-0218
Phone: 617-389-0076, extension 246 (days)

Phone: 781-769-0007 (nights)
Fax: 617-394-9340
Email: leop@emcoprinters.com

#426 • NEGA Scholarship

Type: Scholarship. Renewable if recipient maintains a minimum 2.5 GPA.
Eligibility: Applicant must be a New England resident and must demonstrate financial need. This award must be used in the following years of study: • Freshman • Sophomore • Junior • Senior
Field(s) Of Study: Graphic arts.
Deadline: Varies.
Award Amount: $ 1,300 - $ 2,000.
Number Of Awards: 15 - 25.
Applications Received: 100.
Odds Of Winning: 20% of applicants on average receive an award each year.
Contact: Leo Phalen, Scholarship Committee Chair
Phone: 781-769-0007

PRINTING AND GRAPHIC COMMINICATIONS ASSOCIATION

Scholarship Coordinator
7 West Tower, 1333 H St., NW
Washington, DC 20005
Phone: 202-682-3001
Fax: 202-842-0980
Website: http://www.pgca.org

#427 • Washington Printing Guild Awards

Type: Scholarship. Not renewable.
Eligibility: Applicant must maintain a minimum cumulative 2.5 GPA, be a resident of the Washington D.C. metropolitan area, be a U.S. citizen, demonstrate financial need, and be recommended by a department chairperson or school counselor. This award must be used in the following years of study: • Freshman
Field(s) Of Study: Printing/graphic communication.
Deadline: February 28.
Award Amount: $ 600 - $ 1,000.
Number Of Awards: 3 - 4.
Applications Received: 31.
Odds Of Winning: 13% of applicants on average receive an award each year.
Contact: Angie Duncanson, Program Manager

History

EAST TEXAS HISTORICAL ASSOCIATION

Ottis Lock Scholarship
P.O. Box 6223, SFA Station

Nacogdoches, TX 75962
Phone: 409-468-2407
Fax: 409-468-2190
Email: amcdonald@sfasu.edu

#428 • Ottis Lock Endowment Research Grant

Type: Grant. Not renewable.
Eligibility: Applicant must submit biographical data, a general statement of the benefit and uses of the proposed research, purpose of funds, and a complete budget. Research should focus on the history of the East Texas region. This award must be used in the following years of study: • Masters • Doctoral • Other postgraduate level
Field(s) Of Study: History.
Deadline: May 1.
Award Amount: $ 1,000.
Number Of Awards: 1 - 2.
Applications Received: 4.
Contact: Archie P. McDonald, Executive Director/ Editor

MALKI MUSEUM, INC.

Monongo Indian Reservation
11-795 Fields Road
P.O. Box 578
Banning, CA 92220
Phone: 909-849-7289

#429 • Malki Museum Scholarship

Type: Scholarship. Renewable.
Eligibility: Applicant must be at least one-quarter Native American and be an enrolled member of any Southern California Reservation. This award must be used in the following years of study: • Freshman • Sophomore • Junior • Senior
Deadline: none.
Award Amount: $ 200 - $ 500.
Number Of Awards: 1.
Contact: Hazel Duro, Secretary/Receptionist

ROCK ISLAND ARSENAL MUSEUM

Richard C. Maguire Scholarship Committee
Attn: SIORI-CFM, Rock Island Arsenal
Rock Island, IL 61299

#430 • Robert C. Maguire Scholarship

Type: Scholarship. Not renewable.
Eligibility: Applicant must be a U.S. citizen and be enrolled in a master's or doctoral program in history or a related field. Selection is based upon academic merit. Applicant should include self-addressed, stamped envelope. This award must be used in the following years of study: • Masters • Doctoral • Other postgraduate level

Field(s) Of Study: History.
Deadline: March 31.
Award Amount: $ 1,000.
Number Of Awards: 1.
Applications Received: 450.
Contact: James H. Frost, Chairman
Phone: 319-391-2308

Home Economics

LORAIN COUNTY HOME ECONOMICS ASSOCIATION

Nanci Curci
4670 Washington Avenue
Lorain, OH   44052
Phone: 440-960-1940
Email: ncurci@leeca.esu.k12.oh.us

#431 • Lorain County Home Economics Scholarship

Type: Scholarship. Not renewable.
Eligibility: Applicant must be a resident of Lorain County, Ohio. This award must be used in the following years of study: • Freshman • Sophomore • Junior • Senior
Field(s) Of Study: Family/consumer science.
Deadline: March.
Award Amount: $ 300.
Number Of Awards: 2.
Applications Received: 4.
Odds Of Winning: 50% of applicants on average receive an award each year.
Contact: See above.

Horticulture/Plant Sciences

GARDEN CLUB OF AMERICA

Grosscup Scholarship Committee
11030 East Boulevard
Cleveland, OH   44106

#432 • Katharine M. Grosscup Scholarship

Type: Scholarship. Renewable. Students must request consideration and submit additional documents for renewal.
Eligibility: Applicant must have a minimum "B" grade average, be under 35 years old, and demonstrate financial need. Preference given to residents of Ohio, Pennsylvania, Indiana, Michigan, and West Virginia. This award must be used in the following years of study: • Junior • Senior • Masters
Field(s) Of Study: Horticulture and related fields.
Deadline: February 1.
Award Amount: $ 1,000 - $ 3,000.
Number Of Awards: 6 - 7.
Applications Received: 45.
Odds Of Winning: 15% of applicants on average receive an award each year.
Contact: Nancy C. Stevenson, Grosscup Scholarship Committee Chair

GOLF COURSE SUPERINTENDENTS ASSOCIATION OF AMERICA FOUNDATION

1421 Research Park Drive
Lawrence, KS   66049
Phone: 785-832-3678
Fax: 785-832-3665
Website: http://www.gcsaa.org

#433 • GSCAA Scholars

Type: Scholarship. Not renewable.
Eligibility: Applicant must have completed at least the first year of a collegiate turfgrass management program and be planning a career as a golf course superintendent. Selection is based upon academic excellence, extracurricular activities, and recommendations from college advisors and golf course superintendents or other employers. International students attending a US institution may also apply. This award must be used in the following years of study: • Sophomore • Junior • Senior
Field(s) Of Study: Botany, chemistry, forestry, golf course management, horticulture, plant science, turfgrass science.
Deadline: June 1.
Award Amount: $ 500 - $ 3,500.
Number Of Awards: 20.
Applications Received: 50.
Odds Of Winning: 40% of applicants on average receive an award each year.
Contact: Pam Smith, Scholarship Coordinator
Email: psmith@gscaa.org

#434 • Scotts Company Scholars

Type: Scholarship. Not renewable.
Eligibility: Applicant must be interested in a career in the green industry. Preference is given to students from diverse socio-economic and cultural backgrounds. This award must be used in the following years of study: • Freshman • Sophomore • Junior • Senior
Field(s) Of Study: Green industry.
Deadline: March 1.
Award Amount: $ 2,500.
Number Of Awards: 2.
Applications Received: 20.

Odds Of Winning: 10% of applicants on average receive an award each year.
Contact: Pam Smith, Director of Development
Email: psmith@gscaa.org

#435 • Student Essay Contest

Type: Contest. Not renewable.
Eligibility: Applicant must submit essay focusing on the relationship between golf courses and the environment. This award must be used in the following years of study: • Sophomore • Junior • Senior • Masters • Doctoral
Field(s) Of Study: Agronomy, turfgrass science, golf course management.
Deadline: March 31.
Award Amount: $ 400 - $ 1,000.
Number Of Awards: 3.
Applications Received: 11.
Odds Of Winning: 30% of applicants on average receive an award each year.
Contact: Pam Smith, Scholarship Coordinator
Email: psmith@gscaa.org

HORTICULTURAL RESEARCH INSTITUTE, INC.

1250 I Street, NW Suite 500
Washington, DC 20005
Phone: 202-789-2900
Fax: 202-789-1893
Email: aruden@anla.org
Website: http://www.anla.org

#436 • Timothy Bigelow Scholarship

Type: Scholarship. Not renewable.
Eligibility: Applicant must be a resident of Connecticut, Maine, Massachusetts, New Hampshire, Rhode Island, or Vermont, with a minimum 2.25 GPA (3.0 for graduate students), who is enrolled full-time in an accredited program at a two or four-year institution. This award must be used in the following years of study: • Junior • Senior • Masters • Doctoral • Other postgraduate level
Field(s) Of Study: landscape, horticulture, or related major.
Deadline: May 15.
Award Amount: $ 2,500.
Number Of Awards: 2.
Applications Received: 7.
Odds Of Winning: 28% of applicants on average receive an award each year.
Contact: Paulette McElwain, Grants Admin. Coord.

PROFESSIONAL GROUNDS MANAGEMENT SOCIETY (PGMS)

120 Cockeysville Road Suite 104
Hunt Valley, MD 21030
Phone: 410-584-9754

Email: ppgms@aol.com
Website: http://www.pgms.org

#437 • Anne Seaman PGMS Memorial Scholarship

Type: Scholarship. Renewable.
Eligibility: Contact for details. This award must be used in the following years of study: • Freshman • Sophomore • Junior • Senior
Field(s) Of Study: Agronomy, horticulture or any other grounds-management-related major.
Deadline: July 1.
Award Amount: $ 225 - $ 1,000.
Number Of Awards: 1 - 5.
Applications Received: 50.
Odds Of Winning: 10% of applicants on average receive an award each year.
Contact: Michelle Sullivan, Scholarships

WORCESTER COUNTY HORTICULTURAL SOCIETY

Tower Hill Botanic Garden
11 French Drive
P.O. Box 598
Boylston, MA 01505-0598
Phone: 508-869-6111
Fax: 508-869-0314
Email: thbg@towerhillbg.org

#438 • Worcester County Horticultural Society Scholarship

Type: Scholarship. Not renewable.
Eligibility: Applicant must be a resident of New England attending a New England school. Selection criteria includes interest in horticulture, sincerity of purpose, academic performance, and financial need. This award must be used in the following years of study: • Junior • Senior • Doctoral
Field(s) Of Study: Horticulture or related field.
Deadline: May 1.
Award Amount: $ 500 - $ 2,000.
Number Of Awards: Varies.
Applications Received: 48.
Odds Of Winning: 6% of applicants received an award.
Contact: Susanne Cayford, Administrative Assistant

Hospitality/Hospitality Administration

AMERICAN HOTEL FOUNDATION (AHF)

1201 New York Avenue, NW, Suite 600
Washington, DC 20005-3931

Phone: 202-289-3181
Fax: 202-289-3199
Email: ahf@ahma.com
Website: http://www.ahma.com/ahf.htm

#439 • American Express Scholarship

Type: Scholarship. Renewable. Recipient must reapply for renewal.
Eligibility: Applicant must currently hold a position (minimum 20 hours per week) in a hotel or motel that is a member of AH&MA, and have a minimum of 12 months hotel experience. Dependents of AH&MA-member hotel or motel employees are also eligible. This award must be used in the following years of study: • Freshman • Sophomore • Junior • Senior
Field(s) Of Study: Hospitality, lodging program.
Deadline: May 1.
Award Amount: $ 500 - $ 2,000.
Number Of Awards: 9.
Applications Received: 18.
Odds Of Winning: 50% of applicants on average receive an award each year.
Contact: Michelle Poinelli, Scholarships Program Manager

#440 • Ecolab Scholarship

Type: Scholarship. Renewable. Reapplication required for renewal.
Eligibility: Applicant must be enrolled full-time. Selection is based upon hospitality work experience, financial need, academic record, extracurricular activities, and essay. This award must be used in the following years of study: • Freshman • Sophomore • Junior • Senior
Field(s) Of Study: Hospitality, lodging.
Deadline: June 1.
Award Amount: $ 1,000.
Number Of Awards: 16.
Applications Received: 96.
Odds Of Winning: 17% of applicants on average receive an award each year.
Contact: Michelle Poinelli, Scholarships Program Manager

#441 • Hyatt Hotels Fund for Minority Lodging Management Students

Type: Scholarship. Renewable. Recipient must reapply and be re-nominated for renewal.
Eligibility: Applicant must be a minority student at a four-year university that is a member of the Council on Hotel, Restaurant, and Institutional Education. Applicant must be nominated by the dean of the university; each school may nominate one student. This award must be used in the following years of study: • Junior • Senior
Field(s) Of Study: Hotel Management.
Deadline: April 1.

Award Amount: $ 2,000.
Number Of Awards: 14.
Applications Received: 36.
Odds Of Winning: 39% of applicants on average receive an award each year.
Contact: Your Dean's Office

ASSOCIATION FOR INTERNATIONAL PRACTICAL TRAINING (AIPT)

10400 Little Patauxent Parkway, Suite 250
Columbia, MD 21044-3510
Phone: 410-997-2200
Fax: 410-992-3924
Email: aipt@aipt.org
Website: http://www.aipt.org

#442 • Robert M. Sprinkle Scholarship

Type: Scholarship. Not renewable.
Eligibility: Applicant must be accepted to the International Association for the Exchange of Students for Technical Experience program. This award must be used in the following years of study: • Sophomore • Junior • Senior • Masters • Doctoral
Field(s) Of Study: Hospitality, tourism.
Deadline: January 1.
Award Amount: $ 1,000.
Number Of Awards: 3.
Applications Received: 70.
Odds Of Winning: 4% of applicants on average receive an award each year.
Contact: Jeff Lange, Program Manager
Email: jlange@aipt.org

INTERNATIONAL FOODSERVICE EDITORIAL COUNCIL (IFEC)

P.O. Box 491
Hyde Park, NY 12538
Phone: 914-452-4345
Fax: 914-452-0532
Email: ifec@aol.com

#443 • IFEC Foodservice Communicators Scholarship

Type: Scholarship. Not renewable.
Eligibility: Applicant must demonstrate financial need and talent and training in food studies and communications arts. Selection is based upon essay, field of interest, experience, and studies. This award must be used in the following years of study: • Sophomore • Junior • Senior • Masters • Doctoral
Field(s) Of Study: Communications arts, food service, hospitality.
Deadline: March 15.
Award Amount: $ 1,000 - $ 2,000.
Number Of Awards: 2 - 5.
Applications Received: 250.

Odds Of Winning: 2% of applicants on average receive an award each year.
Contact: Carol Metz, Executive Director
P.O. Box 491
Hyde Park, NY 12538
Phone: 914-452-4345
Fax: 914-452-0532
Email: ifec@aol.com

NATIONAL RESTAURANT ASSOCIATION

Scholarship Department
250 South Wacker Drive, Suite 1400
Chicago, IL 60606
Phone: 312-715-1010
Fax: 312-715-1362
Website: http://www.restaurant.org

#444 • Undergraduate Scholarship for High School Seniors

Type: Scholarship. Not renewable.
Eligibility: Applicant must be a high school senior with a minimum 2.75 GPA and have taken at least one food service-related course with a minimum grade of "B-" and/or have performed at least 250 hours of restaurant and hospitality work experience. Applicant must have been accepted to a hospitality-related post-secondary program, either full- or part-time. This award must be used in the following years of study: • Freshman
Field(s) Of Study: Food service, hospitality.
Deadline: May 1.
Award Amount: $ 2,000.
Number Of Awards: Varies.
Contact: Dalilah Torres-Ramos, Scholarship Program Specialist
Email: dramos@foodtrain.org

Humanities

NATIONAL COUNCIL FOR GEOGRAPHIC EDUCATION

16A Leonard Hall
Indiana University of Pennsylvania
Indiana, PA 15705
Phone: 724-357-6290
Fax: 724-357-7708
Email: ncge-org@grove.iup.edu
Website: http://www.ncge.org

#445 • Women in Geography Scholarship

Type: Scholarship. Not renewable.
Eligibility: Applicant must be a woman and have a minimum 3.0 GPA (3.5 in geography courses) and

submit a written essay. This award must be used in the following years of study: • Junior • Senior • Masters • Doctoral
Field(s) Of Study: Geography education.
Deadline: April 1.
Award Amount: $ 300.
Number Of Awards: 1.
Applications Received: 4.
Odds Of Winning: 25% of applicants on average receive an award each year.
Contact: Connie McCardle

VENTURA COUNTY COMMUNITY FOUNDATION

1317 Del Norte Road, Suite 150
Camarillo, CA 93010
Phone: 805-988-0196
Fax: 805-485-5537

#446 • William Fairburn, Jr. and Cynthia Fairburn Memorial Scholarship

Type: Scholarship. Not renewable.
Eligibility: Applicant must be a graduate of a high school in Ventura County, Calif. This award must be used in the following years of study: • Freshman
Field(s) Of Study: Humanities, liberal arts, sciences.
Deadline: March 9.
Award Amount: $ 2,000.
Number Of Awards: 1.
Applications Received: 55.
Odds Of Winning: 1% of applicants on average receive an award each year.
Contact: Gail Brown, Program Director

Industrial/Manufacturing Engineering

INSTITUTE OF INDUSTRIAL ENGINEERS (IIE)

25 Technology Park/Atlanta
Norcross, GA 30092
Phone: 770-449-0460
Fax: 770-263-8532
Website: http://www.iienet.org

#447 • Dwight D. Gardner Scholarship

Type: Scholarship. Not renewable.
Eligibility: Applicant must be an active IIE member, be enrolled full time, and have a minimum 3.4 GPA. Selection is based upon scholastic ability, character, leadership, potential service to the profession, and financial need. This award must be used in the

following years of study: • Sophomore • Junior • Senior
Field(s) Of Study: Industrial engineering.
Deadline: November 15.
Award Amount: $ 2,000.
Number Of Awards: 4.
Applications Received: 55.
Odds Of Winning: 13% of applicants on average receive an award each year.
Contact: Bisi Oyeyemi, University Operations Coordinator
Phone: 770-449-0461 extension 139
Email: boyeyemi@www.llenet.org

SOCIETY OF MANUFACTURING ENGINEERS (SME) EDUCATION FOUNDATION

One SME Drive, P.O. Box 930
Dearborn, MI 48121
Phone: 313-271-1500, extension 1709
Fax: 313-240-6095
Email: murrdor@sme.org
Website: http://www.sme.org/foundation

#448 • Caterpillar Scholars Award Fund

Type: Scholarship. Renewable. Recipient must reapply for renewal.
Eligibility: Applicant must be enrolled full time in a degree program, have completed at least 30 credit hours, and maintain a minimum 3.0 GPA. Financial need is not a consideration. This award must be used in the following years of study: • Sophomore • Junior • Senior
Field(s) Of Study: Manufacturing engineering.
Deadline: February 1.
Award Amount: $ 2,000.
Number Of Awards: 5.
Contact: Dora Murray, Grants Coordinator
Phone: 313-271-1500, extension 1705
Email: murrdor@sme.org

#449 • Myrtle and Earl Walker Scholarship

Type: Scholarship. Renewable. Recipient must reapply for renewal.
Eligibility: Applicant must be enrolled full time in a degree program, have completed at least 30 credit hours, be seeking a career in manufacturing engineering or technology, and maintain a minimum 3.5 GPA. Financial need is not a consideration, except when two or more applicants have equal qualifications. This award must be used in the following years of study: • Sophomore • Junior • Senior
Field(s) Of Study: Manufacturing engineering, manufacturing engineering technology.
Deadline: February 1.
Award Amount: $ 1,000.
Number Of Awards: 20.

Contact: Dora Murray, Grants Coordinator
Phone: 313-271-1500, extension 1709
Email: murrdor@sme.org

Instrumental Music

AMERICAN RECORDER SOCIETY

P.O. Box 631
Littleton, CO 80160
Phone: 303-347-1120
Fax: 303-347-1181
Email: recorder@compuserve.com
Website: http://ourworld.compuserve.com/homepages/recorder

#450 • American Recorder Society Scholarship

Type: Scholarship. Renewable. Recipient must reapply for renewal.
Eligibility: Applicant must play the recorder and must submit an application and two letters of reference. This award must be used in the following years of study: • Freshman • Sophomore • Junior • Senior • Masters • Doctoral • Other postgraduate level
Field(s) Of Study: Recorder.
Deadline: April 15 for summer scholarships; year-round for others.
Award Amount: $ 100 - $ 350.
Number Of Awards: 4 - 6.
Applications Received: 14.
Contact: Gail Nickless, Executive Director
Email: recorder@compuserve.com

AMERICAN THEATRE ORGAN SOCIETY, INC.

9270 Reeck Road
Allen Park, MI 48101-1461
Phone: 313-383-0133
Fax: 313-383-1875
Email: dottiev@ili.net

#451 • American Theatre Organ Society, Inc. Scholarship

Type: Scholarship. Renewable. Recipient must reapply and must continue his or her study in an organ performance college program or with a professional organ teacher for renewal.
Eligibility: Applications must be submitted by the school department head (or designated representative). Applicant's name must be submitted by his or her professional theatre organ teacher. Essay required. This award must be used in the following years of study: • Freshman • Sophomore • Junior • Senior

Field(s) Of Study: Organ performance.
Deadline: April 15.
Award Amount: $ 500 - $ 1,000.
Number Of Awards: 11 - 12.
Applications Received: 25.
Contact: Dorothy Van Steenkiste, Chairperson, ATOS Scholarship Program

Insurance

SOCIETY OF ACTUARIES/CASUALTY ACTUARIAL SOCIETY

475 North Martingale Road, Suite 800
Schaumburg, IL 60173-2226
Phone: 847-706-3500
Fax: 847-706-3599
Website: http://www.soa.org

#452 • SOA/CAS Minority Scholarship

Type: Scholarship. Renewable. Recipient must reapply for renewal.
Eligibility: Selection is based upon racial/ethnic background, financial need, and academic merit. This award must be used in the following years of study: • Freshman • Sophomore • Junior • Senior
Field(s) Of Study: Actuarial science.
Deadline: May 1.
Award Amount: $ 500 - $ 1,800.
Number Of Awards: 24.
Applications Received: 60.
Odds Of Winning: 25% of applicants on average receive an award each year.
Contact: Kelly Mayo, Minority Recruiting Coordinator
Phone: 847-706-3509
Email: kmayo@soa.org

Journalism

ATLANTA PRESS CLUB

260 14th Street Northwest #300
Atlanta, GA 30318-5360
Phone: 404-57-PRESS
Fax: 404-892-2637
Website: http://www.atlpressclub.org

#453 • Atlanta Press Club Journalism Grant

Type: Scholarship. Not renewable.
Eligibility: Applicant must demonstrate interest in journalism, be attending a school in Georgia, and demonstrate financial need. Selection is also based upon academic performance. This award must be used in the following years of study: • Freshman • Sophomore • Junior • Senior • Masters • Doctoral
Field(s) Of Study: Journalism, communications.
Deadline: Varies.
Award Amount: $ 1,000.
Number Of Awards: 4.
Contact: Amal E. Bane, Executive Director
Email: abane@atlpressclub.org

GEORGIA PRESS EDUCATIONAL FOUNDATION (GPEF)

3066 Mercer University Drive, Suite 200
Atlanta, GA 30341-4137
Phone: 770-454-6776
Fax: 770-454-6778
Email: mail@gapress.org
Website: http://www.gapress.org

#454 • GPEF Scholarship

Type: Scholarship. Renewable. Recipient must reapply for renewal.
Eligibility: Applicant must be a Georgia resident and attend a state school in Georgia. This award must be used in the following years of study: • Freshman • Sophomore • Junior • Senior
Field(s) Of Study: Print journalism.
Deadline: February 1.
Award Amount: $ 1,000 - $ 1,500.
Number Of Awards: Varies.
Applications Received: 40.
Odds Of Winning: 25% of applicants on average receive an award each year.
Contact: GPEF Coordinator

JOURNALISM EDUCATION ASSOCIATION

Kedzie Hall, Room
103 Kansas State University
Manhattan, KS 66506
Phone: 785-532-5532 or 785-532-7822
Fax: 785-532-5563 or 785-532-5484
Email: jea@spub.ksu.edu
Website: http://www.jea.org/

#455 • National High School Journalist of the Year Sister Rita Jeanne Scholarship

Type: Scholarship. Not renewable.
Eligibility: Applicant must be planning to study journalism in college, be planning a career in journalism, have a minimum 3.0 GPA, and have participated in high school journalism for at least two years. This award must be used in the following years of study: • Freshman

Field(s) Of Study: Journalism, mass media.
Deadline: February 15 (state competition), March 13 (national competition).
Award Amount: $ 1,000 - $ 2,000.
Number Of Awards: 3.
Applications Received: 50.
Odds Of Winning: 10% of applicants on average receive an award each year.
Contact: Linda S. Puntney, Executive Director
Email: lindarp@ksu.edu

MIAMI INTERNATIONAL PRESS CLUB

555 NE 15th Street, Suite 25-K
Miami, FL 33132

#456 • Miami International Press Club Scholarship

Type: Scholarship. Renewable. Recipients will receive $500 in fall and $500 in spring if interest and grades continue to be good.
Eligibility: Applicant must be a South Florida resident. Talent, ability, goals, personal motivation, and financial need are all considered. This award must be used in the following years of study: • Freshman • Sophomore • Junior • Senior
Field(s) Of Study: Journalism/communications.
Deadline: June 1.
Award Amount: $ 500.
Number Of Awards: 5.
Contact: Laura Englebright, Scholarship Chair
625 Candia Avenue
Coral Gables, FL 33134
Phone: 305-444-0345

NATION INSTITUTE

33 Irving Place, Eighth Floor
New York, NY 10003
Phone: 212-209-5400
Fax: 212-982-4022
Email: info@nationinstitute.org
Website: www.thenation.com

#457 • I.F. Stone Award for Student Journalism

Type: Contest. Not renewable.
Eligibility: Applicant must be enrolled at a U.S. college or university and submit up to three articles (or series of related articles) written within the year prior to the application deadline. Articles written as part of the applicant's regular coursework are not accepted. Selection is based upon the article's excellence and its exhibition of the following characteristics: commitment to human rights and the exposure of injustice, concern for truth-telling, interest in topics ignored by mainstream media, investigative zeal, and progressive politics.

Applicants are encourage to submit a cover letter. Winning article may be published in *The Nation*. This award must be used in the following years of study: • Sophomore • Junior • Senior • Masters • Unspecified undergraduate
Deadline: June 30.
Award Amount: $ 1,000.
Number Of Awards: 1.
Contact: Peter Meyer/Richard Kim, Executive Director

NATIONAL ASSOCIATION OF BROADCASTERS

Vice President-Research & Planning
1771 N Street, NW
Washington, DC 20036-2898
Phone: 202-429-5389
Website: http://www.nab.org/research/grants.asp

#458 • Research Grants

Type: Grant. Not renewable.
Eligibility: Proposals dealing with issues currently confronting the U.S. commercial broadcast industry are required. The intent of this program is to stimulate interest in broadcast research, especially research on economic, social, or policy issues of importance to the broadcast industry. This award must be used in the following years of study: • Masters • Doctoral • Other postgraduate level • Faculty
Field(s) Of Study: Broadcast communications or related fields.
Deadline: January 28.
Award Amount: $ 5,000.
Number Of Awards: 4.
Contact: Molly Fink, Office Manager

NEW JERSEY PRESS FOUNDATION

840 Bear Tavern Road, Suite 305
West Trenton, NJ 08628-1019
Email: njpressfnd@aol.com
Website: http://www.njpa.org/foundation

#459 • NJPA Internship/Scholarship Program

Type: Scholarship. Renewable. Recipient must reapply for renewal.
Eligibility: Applicant must be interested in a newspaper career. Recipient of scholarship will receive a 10-week paid internship at a New Jersey newspaper in addition to scholarship. Applicant must have a permant home address in New Jersey. This award must be used in the following years of study: • Sophomore • Junior • Senior
Deadline: November 15.
Award Amount: $ 3,000.

Number Of Awards: 6.
Applications Received: 25.
Odds Of Winning: 24% of applicants on average receive an award each year.
Contact: Peggy Stephan, Member Services Manager
Email: pastephan@njpa.org

#460 • College Correspondent Scholarship

Type: Scholarship. Not renewable.
Eligibility: Applicant must be a resident of New Jersey and submit an article that has been published in a newspaper that is a member of the New Jersey Press Association. This award must be used in the following years of study: • Sophomore • Junior • Senior
Deadline: Varies.
Award Amount: $ 1,000.
Number Of Awards: 12.
Contact: See above.

NEW YORK FINANCIAL WRITERS ASSOCIATION

P.O. Box 20281
Greeley Square Station
New York, NY 10001-0003
Phone: 800-533-7551
Fax: 800-533-7560
Email: nyfwa@aol.com

#461 • New York Financial Writers Association Scholarship

Type: Scholarship. Not renewable.
Eligibility: Applicant must be attending a school in the New York City metropolitan area. This award must be used in the following years of study: • Junior • Senior • Masters • Doctoral
Field(s) Of Study: Financial/business journalism.
Deadline: End of February.
Award Amount: $ 3,000.
Number Of Awards: 7.
Contact: Sally Heinemann, Scholarship Chairperson
Phone: 212-372-7510

NEW YORK PRESS ASSOCIATION

ATTN: Educational Coordinator
1681 Western Avenue
Albany, NY 12203-4305
Phone: 518-464-6483
Fax: 518-464-6489
Email: nypabmf@worldnet.att.net
Website: http://www.nynewspapers.com

#462 • Grace S. Anton Scholarship

Type: Scholarship. Not renewable.
Eligibility: Applicant must be a New York resident who plans to pursue a career in print journalism. This award must be used in the following years of study: • Freshman • Sophomore • Junior • Senior
Field(s) Of Study: Journalism.
Deadline: January 15.
Award Amount: $ 5,000.
Number Of Awards: 1.
Contact: Christa Montes, Membership Services Coordinator

OREGON ASSOCIATION OF BROADCASTERS

449, 111 West Seventh Street, Suite 230
Eugene, OR 97440-0449
Phone: 541-343-2101
Fax: 541-343-0662
Website: http://www.or-broadcasters.org

#463 • Oregon Association of Broadcasters Broadcast Scholarship

Type: Scholarship. Not renewable.
Eligibility: Applicant must be an Oregon resident. Award may be used at Oregon schools only. This award must be used in the following years of study: • Freshman • Sophomore • Junior • Senior • Masters • Doctoral • Other postgraduate level
Field(s) Of Study: Broadcasting.
Deadline: March 31.
Award Amount: $ 1,000.
Number Of Awards: 6.
Applications Received: 20.
Contact: Bill Johnstone, Executive Director

PENNSYLVANIA ASSOCIATED PRESS MANAGING EDITORS

Box 638
Somerset, PA 15501

#464 • Ralph Flammino Memorial Scholarship

Type: Scholarship. Not renewable.
Eligibility: Applicant must pursue a career in print journalism, but does not have to be a journalism major. This award must be used in the following years of study: • Senior
Field(s) Of Study: Print journalism.
Deadline: Varies.
Award Amount: $ 1,500.
Number Of Awards: 1.
Contact: James Oliver, Scholarship Committee Chair
Phone: 814-444-5931
Email: jimo@dailyamerican.com

PRESS CLUB OF DALLAS FOUNDATION

400 North Olive, LB 218
Dallas, TX 75201

Phone: 214-740-9988
Fax: 214-740-9989
Email: dallaspc@aol.com

#465 • Press Club of Dallas Foundation Scholarships

Type: Scholarship. Renewable. Recipient must reapply each year.
Eligibility: Applicant must be a Texas resident, provide letter from advisor/employer, samples of work, and personal essay. This award must be used in the following years of study: • Junior • Senior • Masters
Field(s) Of Study: Journalism, mass communications, public relations.
Deadline: May 1.
Award Amount: $ 1,000 - $ 3,000.
Number Of Awards: 10.
Applications Received: 60.
Odds Of Winning: 20% of applicants on average receive an award each year.
Contact: Carol Wortham, Executive Director

QUILL AND SCROLL FOUNDATION

School of Journalism and Mass Communication
University of Iowa
Iowa City, IA 52242-1528
Phone: 319-335-5795
Fax: 319-335-5210
Email: quill-scroll@uiowa.edu
Website: http://www.uiowa.edu/~quill.sc

#466 • Edward J. Nell Memorial Journalism Scholarships

Type: Scholarship. Not renewable.
Eligibility: Applicant must be the winner of either the Yearbook Excellence Contest or the Writing/Photo Contest. This award must be used in the following years of study: • Freshman
Field(s) Of Study: Journalism.
Deadline: November 1 (yearbook contest), February 5 (writing/photo contest).
Award Amount: $ 500.
Number Of Awards: 10.
Applications Received: 100.
Odds Of Winning: 13% of applicants on average receive an award each year.
Contact: Scholarships
Email: quill-scroll@uiowa.edu

RADIO AND TELEVISION NEWS DIRECTORS FOUNDATION (RTNDF), INC.

1000 Connecticut Avenue, NW Suite 615
Washington, DC 20036
Phone: 202-467-5218

Fax: 202-223-4007
Email: danib@rtndf.org
Website: http://www.rtndf.org

#467 • Ken Kashiwahara Scholarship

Type: Scholarship. Not renewable.
Eligibility: Applicant must be enrolled at a college or university with at least one full year remaining, interested in a career in TV or radio news, and must submit resume, one to three journalistic examples not exceeding 15 minutes and an explanation of his/her role in the pieces, personal statement, and letter of reference from dean or faculty sponsor. Preference given to a minority student. This award must be used in the following years of study: • Sophomore • Junior • Senior
Field(s) Of Study: Electronic journalism.
Deadline: May 1.
Award Amount: $ 2,500. Partial Tuition. plus all-expenses paid trip to annual conference.
Number Of Awards: Varies.
Contact: Dani Browne, Awards & Events Assistant

SAN ANTONIO EXPRESS NEWS

P.O. Box 2171
San Antonio, TX 78297-2171
Phone: 210-250-3635

#468 • Elaine Noll Scholarship

Type: Scholarship. Not renewable.
Eligibility: Applicant must be a woman pursuing a career in sportswriting and a resident of the *San Antonio Express News*' 13-county circulation area in South Texas. This award must be used in the following years of study: • Sophomore • Junior • Senior • Masters • Doctoral
Field(s) Of Study: Journalism.
Deadline: Varies.
Award Amount: $ 1,000.
Number Of Awards: 1.
Contact: Joe Rust, Special Projects Coordinator

#469 • TPW Roving Scholarship

Type: Grant. Not renewable.
Eligibility: Applicant must be attending an accredited journalism program at a Texas college or university other than the University of Texas. This award must be used in the following years of study: • Sophomore • Junior • Senior
Field(s) Of Study: Journalism.
Deadline: March 15.
Award Amount: $ 500.
Number Of Awards: 1.
Applications Received: 50.
Odds Of Winning: 2% of applicants on average receive an award each year.
Contact: Kay Casey, Scholarship Director

#470 • Express News Paul Thompson Scholarship

Type: Scholarship. Not renewable.
Eligibility: Applicant must be enrolled in an accredited journalism program and live in the circulation area of the *San Antonio Express News* in Central/South Texas. This award must be used in the following years of study: • Sophomore • Junior • Senior • Masters • Doctoral
Field(s) Of Study: Print journalism.
Deadline: Varies.
Award Amount: $ 1,000.
Number Of Awards: 1.
Contact: Joe Rust, Special Projects Coordinator

SOCIETY OF PROFESSIONAL JOURNALISTS

P.O. Box 77
16 South Jackson Street
Greencastle, IN 46135
Phone: 317-653-3333

#471 • Eddy/Peck Scholarship

Type: Scholarship. Not renewable.
Eligibility: Applicant must submit writing sample, essay, and demonstrate financial need. This award must be used in the following years of study: • Junior • Senior
Field(s) Of Study: Journalism, print or broadcast communications.
Deadline: April 13.
Award Amount: $ 1,000 - $ 2,500.
Number Of Awards: 3.
Applications Received: 24.
Contact: Debra Estock, Scholarship Chairwoman
71 Kenwood Avenue
Fairfield, CT 06430

SOCIETY OF PROFESSIONAL JOURNALISTS, FORT WORTH PROFESSIONAL CHAPTER

Vice President of Scholarships
P.O. Box 3212
Fort Worth, TX 76113-3212

#472 • Texas Gridiron Scholarship

Type: Scholarship. Not renewable.
Eligibility: Selection based upon financial need, talent, and GPA. Applicants should submit transcript, two samples of published work, one sample of unedited writing, a 500-word essay on why he or she has chosen journalism as a career, and application. This award must be used in the following years of study: • Sophomore • Junior • Senior • Graduate students
Field(s) Of Study: Journalism, photojournalism, television/radio.
Deadline: April 1.

Award Amount: $ 750.
Number Of Awards: 4.
Contact: Jan Gary, Scholarship Chairwoman
Phone: 817-460-2609
Email: jgary@flash.net

Law

AMERICAN CRIMINAL JUSTICE ASSOCIATION/LAMBDA ALPHA EPSILON (ACJA/LAE)

P.O. Box 601047
Sacramento, CA 95860
Phone: 916-484-6553
Fax: 916-488-2227
Email: acjalae@aol.com
Website: http://www.acjalae.org

#473 • ACJA/LAE National Scholarship

Type: Scholarship. Not renewable.
Eligibility: Applicant must be a ACJA/LAE member in good standing and submit an original paper on an assigned theme. This award must be used in the following years of study: • Sophomore • Junior • Senior • Masters • Doctoral
Field(s) Of Study: Criminal Justice.
Deadline: December 31.
Award Amount: $ 100 - $ 400.
Number Of Awards: 9.
Applications Received: 7.
Odds Of Winning: 100% of applicants on average receive an award each year.
Contact: Karen K. Campbell, Executive Secretary

Library Science

AMERICAN ASSOCIATION OF LAW LIBRARIES

Scholarships and Grants Committee
53 West Jackson Boulevard, Suite 940
Chicago, IL 60604
Phone: 312-939-4764
Fax: 312-431-1097
Email: aallhq@aall.org
Website: http://www.aallnet.org

#474 • Law Librarians in Continuing Education Courses

Type: Scholarship. Not renewable.

Eligibility: Applicant must have a degree from an accredited library or law school and be registered in continuing education courses related to law librarianship. This award must be used in the following years of study: • Masters • Doctoral • Other postgraduate level
Field(s) Of Study: Law librarianship.
Deadline: October 1, February 1, April 1.
Award Amount: Varies.
Number Of Awards: Varies.
Contact: Membership Coordinator
Phone: 312-939-4764, extension 10
Email: membership@aall.org

Marine Science

ATLANTIC SALMON FEDERATION

P.O. Box 807
Calais, ME 04619
Phone: 506-529-4581
Fax: 506-529-4985
Email: asfres@nbnet.nb.ca
Website: http://www.asf.ca

#475 • Olin Fellowship

Type: Scholarship. Not renewable.
Eligibility: Contact for details. This award must be used in the following years of study: • Sophomore • Junior • Senior • Masters • Doctoral
Field(s) Of Study: Atlantic salmon management.
Deadline: March 15.
Award Amount: $ 1,000 - $ 3,000.
Number Of Awards: 4.
Applications Received: 10.
Contact: See above.

HOUSTON UNDERWATER CLUB, INC.

Seaspace Scholarship Committee
P.O. Box 3753
Houston, TX 77253
Website: http://www.seaspace.ycg.org

#476 • Seaspace Scholarship

Type: Scholarship. Renewable. Recipient must reapply.
Eligibility: Contact for details. This award must be used in the following years of study: • Junior • Senior • Masters • Doctoral • Other postgraduate level
Field(s) Of Study: Marine sciences.
Deadline: February 1.
Award Amount: $ 500 - $ 5,000.
Number Of Awards: 22.
Applications Received: 80.
Odds Of Winning: 25% of applicants on average

receive an award each year.
Contact: Scholarship Administrator

INTERNATIONAL WOMEN'S FISHING ASSOCIATION SCHOLARSHIP TRUST

P.O. Drawer 3125
Palm Beach, FL 33480
Phone: 813-689-2496

#477 • International Women's Fishing Association Scholarship

Type: Grant. Renewable. Progress report is required.
Eligibility: Applicant must be studying in any marine science field at a U.S. institution. Selection is based upon academic achievements, financial need, letters of recommendation, personal statement, and research proposal. This award must be used in the following years of study: • Masters • Doctoral • Other postgraduate level
Field(s) Of Study: Marine science.
Deadline: March 1.
Award Amount: $ 500 - $ 2,000.
Number Of Awards: 12.
Contact: Scholarship Trust Secretary

SEASPACE, INC.

P.O. Box 3753
Houston, TX 77253-3753
Phone: 713-467-6675
Website: http://www.seaspace.org

#478 • Seaspace Scholarship

Type: Scholarship. Not renewable.
Eligibility: Applicant must have a minimum 3.3 GPA. Financial need is considered. This award must be used in the following years of study: • Junior • Senior • Masters • Doctoral
Field(s) Of Study: Marine science.
Deadline: March 1.
Award Amount: $ 500 - $ 3,000.
Number Of Awards: 15.
Applications Received: 78.
Odds Of Winning: 20% of applicants on average receive an award each year.
Contact: Carolyn Peterson, Scholarship Coordinator

Mechanical Engineering

AMERICAN SOCIETY OF MECHANICAL ENGINEERS (ASME)

Education Services Department
Three Park Avenue

New York, NY 10016-5990
Phone: 212-591-8131
Fax: 212-591-7143
Website: http://www.asme.org/educate/aid

#479 • Solid Waste Processing Division Scholarship

Type: Scholarship. Not renewable.
Eligibility: Applicant must attend a North American college or university with an established program in solid waste management. Three scholarships (one undergraduate and two graduate) are available. This award must be used in the following years of study: • Freshman • Sophomore • Junior • Senior • Masters • Doctoral
Field(s) Of Study: Solid waste management.
Deadline: March 1.
Award Amount: $ 2,000 - $ 4,000.
Number Of Awards: 3.
Contact: Elio Manes, Solid Waste Processing Division
Phone: 212-591-7797
Email: manese@asme.org

#480 • William J. and Mary Jane E. Adams, Jr. Scholarship

Type: Scholarship. Not renewable.
Eligibility: Applicant must be an ASME student member attending a college in ASME Region IX (California, Hawaii, or Nevada). This award must be used in the following years of study: • Freshman • Sophomore • Junior • Senior • Masters
Field(s) Of Study: Mechanical engineering or related program.
Deadline: April 15.
Award Amount: $ 2,000.
Number Of Awards: 1.
Contact: Theresa Oluwanifise, Administrative Assistant
Email: oluwanifiset@asme.org

#481 • Garland Duncan Scholarship

Type: Scholarship. Not renewable.
Eligibility: Applicant must be a student member of ASME. Selection based upon character, integrity, leadership, potential contribution to the mechanical engineering profession, and scholastic ability. Financial need is considered. This award must be used in the following years of study: • Junior • Senior
Field(s) Of Study: Mechanical engineering or related program.
Deadline: April 15.
Award Amount: $ 3,000.
Number Of Awards: 1 - 2.
Contact: Theresa Oluwanifise, Administrative Assistant
Email: oluwanifiset@asme.org

#482 • F.W. "Beich" Beichley Scholarship

Type: Scholarship. Not renewable.
Eligibility: Applicant must be a student member of ASME. Selection is based upon leadership, potential contribution to the mechanical engineering profession, and scholastic ability. Financial need is considered. This award must be used in the following years of study: • Junior • Senior
Field(s) Of Study: Mechanical engineering or related program.
Deadline: April 15.
Award Amount: $ 1,500.
Number Of Awards: 1.
Contact: Theresa Oluwanifise, Administrative Assistant
Email: oluwanifiset@asme.org

#483 • Kenneth Andrew Roe Scholarship

Type: Scholarship. Not renewable.
Eligibility: Applicant must be a student member of ASME. Selection based upon leadership, potential contribution to the mechanical engineering profession, and scholastic ability. Financial need is considered. This award must be used in the following years of study: • Junior • Senior
Field(s) Of Study: Mechanical engineering or related program.
Deadline: April 15.
Award Amount: $ 8,000.
Number Of Awards: 1.
Contact: Theresa Oluwanifise, Administrative Assistant
Email: oluwanifiset@asme.org

#484 • Frank William & Dorothy Given Miller ASME Auxiliary Scholarship

Type: Scholarship. Not renewable.
Eligibility: Applicant must be a student member of ASME. Selection based upon leadership, potential contribution to the mechanical engineering profession, and scholastic ability. Financial need is considered. This award must be used in the following years of study: • Junior • Senior
Field(s) Of Study: Mechanical engineering or related program.
Deadline: April 15.
Award Amount: $ 1,500.
Number Of Awards: 2.
Contact: Theresa Oluwanifise, Administrative Assistant
Email: oluwanifset@asme.org

#485 • John and Elsa Gracik Scholarship

Type: Scholarship. Not renewable.
Eligibility: College-level applicants must be student members of ASME. Selection based upon leadership, potential contribution to the mechanical engineering profession, and scholastic ability. Financial need is

considered. This award must be used in the following years of study: • Freshman • Sophomore • Junior • Senior
Field(s) Of Study: Mechanical engineering or related program.
Deadline: April 15.
Award Amount: $ 1,500.
Number Of Awards: 18.
Contact: Theresa Oluwanifise, Admin. Assistant
Email: oluwanifiset@asme.org

#486 • Foundation Scholarship

Type: Scholarship. Not renewable.
Eligibility: Applicant must be a student member of ASME. Selection based upon leadership, potential contribution to the mechanical engineering profession, and scholastic ability. This award must be used in the following years of study: • Junior • Senior
Field(s) Of Study: Mechanical engineering.
Deadline: Varies.
Award Amount: $ 1,500.
Number Of Awards: 17.
Contact: Theresa Oluwanifise, Administrative Assistant
Email: oluwanifiset@asme.org

AMERICAN SOCIETY OF MECHANICAL ENGINEERS (ASME) AUXILIARY, INC.

Three Park Avenue
New York, NY 10016-5990
Phone: 212-591-7733
Fax: 212-591-7439
Email: infocentral@asme.org

#487 • Berna Lou Cartwright Scholarship

Type: Scholarship. Not renewable.
Eligibility: Applicant must be an ASME member and a U.S. citizen and be enrolled in a U.S. school in an ABET accredited department. Selection is based upon academic performance, character, need, and ASME participation. Send self-addressed, stamped envelope or e-mail to request application. This award must be used in the following years of study: • Senior
Field(s) Of Study: Mechanical engineering.
Deadline: February 15.
Award Amount: $ 1,500.
Number Of Awards: 1.
Contact: Susan Flanders
3556 Stevens Way
Martinez, GA 30907
Email: dsusan@aol.com

#488 • Sylvia W. Farny Scholarship

Type: Scholarship. Not renewable.
Eligibility: Applicant must be a U.S. citizen and be enrolled in a U.S. school in an ABET accredited department. Selection is based upon academic

performance, character, need, and ASME participation. Send self-addressed, stamped envelope or e-mail to request application. This award must be used in the following years of study: • Senior
Field(s) Of Study: Mechanical engineering.
Deadline: February 15.
Award Amount: $ 1,500.
Number Of Awards: Varies.
Contact: Susan Flanders
3556 Stevens Way
Martinez, GA 30907
Email: dsusan@aol.com

SOCIETY OF MANUFACTURING ENGINEERS (SME) EDUCATION FOUNDATION

One SME Drive, P.O. Box 930
Dearborn, MI 48121
Phone: 313-271-1500, extension 1709
Fax: 313-240-6095
Email: murrdor@sme.org
Website: http://www.sme.org/foundation

#489 • Wayne Kay Scholarship

Type: Scholarship. Renewable.
Eligibility: Applicant must have a minimum 3.5 GPA, be enrolled full-time, have completed a minimum of 30 college credit hours, and be seeking a career in manufacturing engineering or technology. This award must be used in the following years of study: • Freshman • Sophomore • Junior • Senior
Field(s) Of Study: manufacturing engineering, manufacturing engineering technology.
Deadline: February 1.
Award Amount: $ 2,500.
Number Of Awards: 10.
Contact: Dora Murray, Grants Coordinator
Phone: 313-271-1500, extension 1709

Medicine

AMERICAN COLLEGE OF MEDICAL PRACTICE EXECUTIVES (ACMPE)

104 Inverness Terrace East
Englewood, CO 80112-5306
Phone: 303-643-9573

#490 • Harry J. Harwick Scholarship

Type: Scholarship. Not renewable.
Eligibility: Applicant must submit a letter stating career goals and objectives, a resume showing employment history with a brief narrative describing specific employment responsibilities in the health

care field, and three letters of recommendation. Reference letters should address performance, character, potential to succeed, and need for scholarship support. Send for an application with a self-addressed, stamped, business-size envelope. This award must be used in the following years of study: • Freshman • Sophomore • Junior • Senior • Masters • Doctoral
Field(s) Of Study: Health care administration, medical group practice, medical practice management.
Deadline: June 1.
Award Amount: $ 2,000.
Number Of Awards: 1.
Contact: See above.

#491 • Richard L. Davis National Scholarship

Type: Scholarship. Not renewable.
Eligibility: Applicant must submit a letter stating career goals and objectives, a resume showing employment history with a brief narrative describing specific employment responsibilities in the health care field, and three letters of recommendation. Reference letters should address performance, character, potential to succeed, and need for scholarship support. Send for an application with a self-addressed, stamped, business-size envelope. This award must be used in the following years of study: • Freshman • Sophomore • Junior • Senior • Masters • Doctoral
Field(s) Of Study: Medical group management, medical practice management.
Deadline: June 1.
Award Amount: $ 1,500.
Number Of Awards: 1 - 2.
Contact: See above.

#492 • Ernest S. Moscatello Scholarship

Type: Scholarship. Not renewable.
Eligibility: Applicant must submit a letter stating career goals and objectives, a resume showing employment history with a brief narrative describing specific employment responsibilities in the health care field, and three letters of recommendation. Reference letters should address performance, character, potential to suceed, and need for scholarship support. Send for an application with a self-addressed, stamped, business-size envelope. This award must be used in the following years of study: • Freshman • Sophomore • Junior • Senior • Masters • Doctoral
Field(s) Of Study: Medical group management, medical practice management.
Deadline: June 1.
Award Amount: $ 500.
Number Of Awards: 1.
Contact: See above.

#493 • Edward J. Gerloff/FACMPE Scholarship

Type: Scholarship. Not renewable.
Eligibility: Applicant must submit a letter stating career goals and objectives, a resume showing employment history with a brief narrative describing specific employment responsibilities in the health care field, and three letters of recommendation. Reference letters should address performance, character, potential to succeed, and need for scholarship support. Send for an application with a self-addressed, stamped, business-size envelope. This award must be used in the following years of study: • Freshman • Sophomore • Junior • Senior • Masters • Doctoral
Field(s) Of Study: Medical group management, medical practice management.
Deadline: June 1.
Award Amount: $ 500.
Number Of Awards: Varies.
Contact: See above.

#494 • Midwest Section Scholarship

Type: Scholarship. Not renewable.
Eligibility: Applicant must reside in a Midwest section state and submit a letter stating career goals and objectives, a resume showing employment history with a brief narrative describing specific employment responsibilities in the health care field, and three letters of recommendation. Reference letters should address performance, character, potential to succeed, and need for scholarship support. Send for an application with a self-addressed, stamped, business-size envelope. This award must be used in the following years of study: • Freshman • Sophomore • Junior • Senior • Masters • Doctoral
Field(s) Of Study: Health care administration, medical group management, medical practice management.
Deadline: June 1.
Award Amount: $ 2,000.
Number Of Awards: 1 - 3.
Contact: See above.

#495 • Western Section Scholarship

Type: Scholarship. Not renewable.
Eligibility: Applicant must be an MGMA Western section member for two years. Applicant must submit a letter stating goals and objectives, a resume showing employment history with a brief narrative describing specific employment responsibilities in the health care field, and three letters of recommendation. Reference letters should address performance, character, potential to succeed, and need for scholarship support. Send for an application with a self-addressed, stamped, business-size envelope. This award must be used in the following years of study: • Sophomore • Junior • Senior • Masters • Doctoral
Field(s) Of Study: Medical practice management.

Deadline: June 1.
Award Amount: $ 2,000.
Number Of Awards: 1 - 2.
Contact: See above.

#496 • Edgar J. Saux/FACMPE Scholarship

Type: Scholarship. Not renewable.
Eligibility: Applicant must submit a letter stating career goals and objectives, an explanation of the individual's need for professional development, such as gaps in formal education or changing health care environment, and a resume showing employment history with a brief narrative describing specific employment responsibilities in the health care field. Send for an application with a self-addressed, stamped, business-size envelope. This award must be used in the following years of study: • Freshman • Sophomore • Junior • Senior • Masters • Doctoral
Field(s) Of Study: Health care administration, medical group management.
Deadline: June 1.
Award Amount: $ 1,000.
Number Of Awards: 1.
Contact: See above.

#497 • Richard L. Davis Managers' Scholarship

Type: Scholarship. Not renewable.
Eligibility: Applicant must submit a letter stating career goals and objectives, with an explanation of the individual's need for professional development such as gaps in formal education or changing health care environment, a resume showing employment history with a brief narrative describing specific employment responsibilities in the health care field, and three letters of recommendation. Reference letters should address performance, character, potential to succeed, and need for scholarship support. Send for an application with a self-addressed, stamped, business-size envelope. This award must be used in the following years of study: • Sophomore • Junior • Senior • Masters • Doctoral
Field(s) Of Study: Medical group management.
Deadline: June 1.
Award Amount: $ 1,500.
Number Of Awards: 1 - 2.
Contact: See above.

SAN PEDRO PENINSULA HOSPITAL AUXILIARY

Health Careers Committee
1300 West Seventh Street
San Pedro, CA 90732
Phone: 310-832-3311

#498 • Health Career Scholarship

Type: Scholarship. Renewable if recipient reapplies.

Eligibility: Residency requirement waived for employees of San Pedro Peninsula Hospital. This award must be used in the following years of study: • Sophomore • Junior • Senior • Masters
Field(s) Of Study: Health professions.
Deadline: November 11.
Award Amount: $ 600 - $ 1,000.
Number Of Awards: Varies.
Contact: Scholarships

SIGMA ALPHA EPSILON (SAE)

P.O. Box 1856
Evanston, IL 60204-1856
Phone: 847-475-1856
Fax: 847-475-2250
Website: http://www.sae.net

#499 • Dr. Charles A. Preuss Medical Award

Type: Grant. Not renewable.
Eligibility: Applicant must be an SAE brother who is currently attending or planning to attend medical school. Selection is based upon academic achievement, passion for the study of medical science, and financial need. This award must be used in the following years of study: • Junior • Senior • Doctoral
Field(s) Of Study: Medicine.
Deadline: April 17.
Award Amount: $ 1,000 - $ 3,500.
Number Of Awards: 1 - 3.
Odds Of Winning: 3% of applicants on average receive an award each year.
Contact: Robert Parker, Coordinator of Programs
Phone: 800-233-1856, extension 223
Email: rparker@sae.net

TEXAS AMERICAN LEGION AUXILIARY

Department Headquarters
709 East 10th Street
Austin, TX 78701-2699
Phone: 512-476-7278

#500 • Medical Field Scholarship

Type: Scholarship. Renewable. Reapplication required for renewal.
Eligibility: Applicant must be sponsored by a local American Legion Auxiliary unit. This award must be used in the following years of study: • Freshman • Sophomore • Junior • Senior • Masters • Doctoral • Other postgraduate level
Field(s) Of Study: Medical fields.
Deadline: March 15.
Award Amount: $ 500.
Number Of Awards: 16.
Applications Received: 25.
Contact: Your Local American Legion Auxiliary Unit

Military Affiliation

1ST MARINE DIVISION ASSOCIATION

14325 Willard Road, Suite 107
Chantilly, VA 20151-2110
Phone: 703-803-3195
Fax: 703-803-7114
Email: oldbreed@aol.com
Website: http://www.erols.com/oldbreed/

#501 • 1st Marine Division Association Scholarship

Type: Scholarship. Renewable. Satisfactory academic progress and full-time enrollment are required to retain scholarship.
Eligibility: Applicant must be a full-time student and the dependent of a deceased or 100% permanently disabled veteran of service with the 1st Marine Division. This award must be used in the following years of study: • Freshman • Sophomore • Junior • Senior
Deadline: Varies.
Award Amount: $ 1,400 - $ 2,000.
Number Of Awards: 48 - 72.
Contact: Col. Jerry Brown, U.S. Marines (Ret.), Chief Administrative Officer

25TH INFANTRY DIVISION ASSOCIATION (TIDA)

3930 South Bridlewood Drive
Bountiful, UT 84010
Phone: 801-292-7354
Website: http://www.25thida.com

#502 • 25th Infantry Division Association Scholarship

Type: Scholarship. Not renewable.
Eligibility: Applicant must be the child of an active TIDA member or of a TIDA member killed in action or in the line of duty. This award must be used in the following years of study: • Freshman
Deadline: April 1.
Award Amount: $ 500 - $ 1,000.
Number Of Awards: 10.
Applications Received: 34.
Odds Of Winning: 30% of applicants on average receive an award each year.
Contact: Scholarship Administrator

43RD INFANTRY DIVISION VETERANS ASSOCIATION

c/o Secretary/Treasurer
150 Lakedell Drive
East Greenwich, RI 02818-4716
Phone: 401-884-7052
Email: howbro@aol.com

#503 • 43rd Infantry Division Veterans Scholarship

Type: Scholarship. Renewable.
Eligibility: Applicant must be a member or a descendent or a spouse of a member of the 43rd Infantry Division in good standing, KIA, or died while on active duty. This award must be used in the following years of study: • Freshman • Sophomore • Junior • Senior • Masters • Doctoral • Other postgraduate level
Deadline: Varies.
Award Amount: $ 500 - $ 1,000.
Number Of Awards: 5 - 6.
Applications Received: 13.
Odds Of Winning: 38% of applicants on average receive an award each year.
Contact: Howard F. Brown, Secretary & Treasurer
Fax: howbro@aol.com

AIR FORCE AID SOCIETY

1745 Jefferson Davis Highway, Suite 202
Arlington, VA 22202
Phone: 703-607-3072 or 800-429-9475
Fax: 703-607-3022
Website: http://www.afas.org

#504 • General Henry H. Arnold Education Grant

Type: Grant. Renewable. Reapplication required.
Eligibility: Applicant must be the spouse of an Active Duty Air Force member residing stateside, surviving spouse of an Air Force member, or the dependent child of an Air Force member in one of the following categories: on active duty, Title 10 Reservist on extended active duty, retired due to length of active duty service or disability, retired Guard/Reservist who is at least 60 years of age and receiving retirement pay, or deceased while on active duty or in retired status. Applicant must have a minimum 2.0 GPA and be accepted or enrolled as a full-time undergraduate student at an accredited college, university, or vocational/trade school. Selection is based upon financial need. Minimum 2.0 GPA required. This award must be used in the following years of study: • Freshman • Sophomore • Junior • Senior
Deadline: Late March.
Award Amount: $ 1,500.
Number Of Awards: 5,000.
Applications Received: 9,000.
Odds Of Winning: 60% of applicants on average receive an award each year.
Contact: Education Assistance Department

ALASKA SEA SERVICES SCHOLARSHIP FUND

c/o US Navy League Council 55-151
P.O. Box 201510
Anchorage, AK 99520-1510

#505 • Alaska Sea Services Scholarship

Type: Scholarship. Renewable. Recipient may reapply for one additional year.
Eligibility: Applicant must be the dependent child or spouse of a regular or reserve member of the Navy, Marine Corps, or Coast Guard on active duty, retired with pay, deceased or declared missing in action, or in drilling reserve status, who is (or was at time of death or MIA status) a resident of Alaska. Applicant must be a full-time student. Selection is based upon academic ability, character, leadership, community involvement, and financial need. Self-addressed, stamped, 9-inch-by-12-inch envelope required. This award must be used in the following years of study: • Freshman • Sophomore • Junior • Senior
Deadline: April 15.
Award Amount: $ 1,000.
Number Of Awards: 4.
Applications Received: 8.
Odds Of Winning: 50% of applicants on average receive an award each year.
Contact: Alaska Sea Services Scholarship

AMERICAN LEGION - MICHIGAN

212 North Verlinden
Lansing, MI 48915
Phone: 517-371-4720
Fax: 517-371-2401
Email: info@michiganlegion.org
Website: http://www.michiganlegion.org

#506 • Brewer/Wilson Scholarship

Type: Scholarship. Renewable. Reapplication is required to retain scholarship.
Eligibility: Applicant must be the child of a military veteran. This award must be used in the following years of study: • Freshman
Deadline: February 1.
Award Amount: $ 500.
Number Of Awards: 24.
Contact: Deanna Clark, Programs Secretary

AMERICAN LEGION - OHIO

4060 Indianola Avenue
Columbus, OH 43214
Phone: 614-268-7072
Fax: 614-268-3048
Email: ohlegion@netwalk.com

#507 • American Legion - Ohio Scholarship

Type: Scholarship. Not renewable.
Eligibility: Applicant must be the descendant of a Legionnaire or military service person killed during active duty military service. This award must be used in the following years of study: • Freshman
Deadline: April 15.
Award Amount: $ 1,500.
Number Of Awards: 17.
Applications Received: 254.
Odds Of Winning: 5% of applicants on average receive an award each year.
Contact: Scholarship Committee

AMERICAN LEGION - OHIO AUXILIARY

P.O. Box 2760
Zanesville, OH 43702-2760
Phone: 740-452-2620
Email: alaoh@msmisp.com

#508 • Department President's Scholarship

Type: Scholarship. Not renewable.
Eligibility: Applicant must be the child of a living or deceased veteran who served in World War I, World War II, Korean, Vietnam, Lebanon, or Persian Gulf conflicts. Applicant must be an Ohio resident and be sponsored by an American Legion Auxiliary unit. This award must be used in the following years of study: • Freshman
Deadline: March 3.
Award Amount: $ 1,000 - $ 1,500.
Number Of Awards: 2.
Contact: Scholarship Administrator

AMERICAN LEGION - OREGON AUXILIARY

P.O. Box 1730
Wilsonville, OR 97070-1730
Phone: 503-682-3162

#509 • Department Scholarship

Type: Scholarship. Not renewable.
Eligibility: Applicant must be a resident of Oregon and the child or widow of a deceased veteran, or wife of a disabled veteran pursuing education at any accredited institution of higher education in Oregon. This award must be used in the following years of study: • Freshman • Sophomore • Junior • Senior • Masters • Doctoral
Deadline: March 15.
Award Amount: $ 1,000.
Number Of Awards: 3.
Applications Received: 125.
Odds Of Winning: 2% of applicants on average receive an award each year.
Contact: Chairman of Education

AMERICAN LEGION - PENNSYLVANIA AUXILIARY

Department Education Chairman
P.O. Box 2643
Harrisburg, PA 17105
Phone: 717-763-7545

#510 • American Legion - Pennsylvania Auxiliary Scholarship

Type: Scholarship. Not renewable.
Eligibility: Applicant must be the child of a veteran or of a deceased veteran and have financial need. Applicant must be a graduate of a Pennsylvania high school who is planning to attend a Pennsylvania institution. This award must be used in the following years of study: • Freshman
Deadline: March 1.
Award Amount: $ 600.
Number Of Awards: 2.
Applications Received: 100.
Odds Of Winning: 2% of applicants on average receive an award each year.
Contact: Education Chairman

AMERICAN LEGION AUXILIARY

P.O. Box 547917
Orlando, FL 32854-7917
Phone: 407-293-7411
Fax: 407-299-6522

#511 • American Legion Auxiliary Department Scholarship

Type: Grant. Renewable. Good scholastic record, financial need, and reapplication are required.
Eligibility: Applicant must be sponsored by an Auxiliary Unit, be the child of an honorably discharged veteran, be a Florida resident, and attend school in Florida. Application must be requested by January 1. This award must be used in the following years of study: • Freshman • Sophomore • Junior • Senior • Vocational/technical student
Deadline: January 1.
Award Amount: $ 500 - $ 1,000.
Number Of Awards: 18.
Contact: Marie Mahoney, Secretary-Treasurer

AMERICAN LEGION AUXILIARY (ALA), NATIONAL HEADQUARTERS

777 North Meridian Street, Third Floor
Indianapolis, IN 46204
Phone: 317-635-6291
Fax: 317-636-5590

#512 • National President's Scholarship

Type: Scholarship. Not renewable.

Eligibility: Applicant must be the child of a veteran who served in the U.S. Armed Forces in World War I, World War II, or the Korean, Vietnam, Panama, Granada, or Persian Gulf conflicts and have financial need. Selection is based upon character, Americanism, leadership, scholarship, and need. This award must be used in the following years of study: • Freshman
Deadline: March 10.
Award Amount: $ 2,000 - $ 2,500.
Number Of Awards: 10.
Contact: National Secretary, National Treasurer, or Accounting Manager, Scholarships

AMERICAN LEGION AUXILIARY - ALABAMA

120 North Jackson Street
Montgomery, AL 36104
Phone: 334-262-1176
Fax: 334262-9694

#513 • American Legion Auxiliary - Alabama Scholarship

Type: Scholarship. Renewable. Award is for four years; renewable if recipient submits transcript and written request by May 1.
Eligibility: Applicant must be the child or grandchild of a veteran of World War I, World War II, Korean, or Vietnam conflicts. Applicant must be an Alabama resident and attend an Alabama college. Self-addressed, stamped envelope is required to receive application. This award must be used in the following years of study: • Freshman • Sophomore • Junior • Senior
Deadline: Varies.
Award Amount: $ 850.
Number Of Awards: 37.
Contact: Debora Stephens, Secretary

AMERICAN LEGION AUXILIARY, DEPARTMENT OF MICHIGAN

American Legion Auxiliary
212 North Verlinden Avenue
Lansing, MI 48915
Phone: 517-371-4720
Fax: 517-371-2401
Email: michalaux@voyager.net
Website: http://www.michalaux.org

#514 • Nurses', Physical Therapists', and Respiratory Therapists' Scholarship

Type: Scholarship. Not renewable.
Eligibility: Applicant must be a resident of Michigan, rank in the top quarter of class, plan to attend a Michigan school, and be the child, grandchild, or great-grandchild of an American Legion member or of

someone eligible to be a member. Selection is based upon academic ability, financial need, degree of interest in the area of study, and three letters of recommendation. This award must be used in the following years of study: • Freshman
Field(s) Of Study: Nursing, physical therapy, respiratory therapy.
Deadline: March 15.
Award Amount: $ 500.
Number Of Awards: 15 - 20.
Applications Received: 80.
Odds Of Winning: 25% of applicants on average receive an award each year.
Contact: Cheryle Thompson, Scholarship Coordinator

#515 • Memorial Scholarship

Type: Scholarship. Renewable up to one year if recipient reapplies.
Eligibility: Applicant must be a woman between the ages of 16 and 21, a Michigan resident attending or planning to attend a Michigan school, who is the daughter, granddaughter, or great-granddaughter of an American Legion Member or of someone who is eligible for American Legion Membership. Selection is based upon transcripts, letters of recommendation, and financial need. This award must be used in the following years of study: • Freshman • Sophomore • Junior • Senior
Deadline: March 15.
Award Amount: $ 500.
Number Of Awards: 20 - 30.
Applications Received: 800.
Odds Of Winning: 4% of applicants on average receive an award each year.
Contact: Cheryle Thompson, Scholarship Coordinator

#516 • Scholarship for Non-Traditional Students

Type: Scholarship. Not renewable.
Eligibility: Applicant must be a Michigan resident who is the dependent of a veteran. Applicant must be a non-traditional student returning to higher education after an interruption, a degree-seeking student over age 22 attending college in Michigan for the first time, or a student over age 22 attending a Michigan vocational or trade school. Selection is based upon academic ability, character/leadership, initiative, and financial need. Transcripts or work history required. This award must be used in the following years of study: • Freshman • Sophomore • Junior • Senior
Deadline: March 15.
Award Amount: $ 500.
Number Of Awards: 1.
Applications Received: 4.
Odds Of Winning: 25% of applicants on average receive an award each year.

Contact: Cheryle Thompson, Scholarship Coordinator

AMERICAN LEGION, DEPARTMENT OF MINNESOTA

20 West 12th Street, Room 300-A
St. Paul, MN 55155-2069
Phone: 651-291-1800
Fax: 651-291-1057
Email: department@mnlegion.org
Website: http://www.mnlegion.org

#517 • Minnesota Legionnaire Insurance Trust Scholarship

Type: Scholarship. Renewable. Reapplication required for renewal.
Eligibility: Applicant must be a U.S. citizen, a resident of Minnesota, a veteran or the child or grandchild of a veteran, and must demonstrate personal responsibility. This award must be used in the following years of study: • Freshman • Sophomore • Junior • Senior • Masters • Doctoral • Other postgraduate level
Deadline: April 1.
Award Amount: $ 500.
Number Of Awards: 3.
Applications Received: 300.
Contact: Jennifer Lindemann, Program Coordinator

#518 • American Legion Memorial Scholarship

Type: Scholarship. Renewable. Reapplication required for renewal.
Eligibility: Applicant must be a child, grandchild, adopted child, or stepchild of an American Legion or American Legion Auxiliary member, must demonstrate initiative, honesty, thrift, loyalty, and financial need, and must plan to attend a Minnesota school or a school in a state with Minnesota reciprocity. This award must be used in the following years of study: • Freshman • Sophomore • Junior • Senior • Masters • Doctoral • Other postgraduate level
Deadline: April 1.
Award Amount: $ 500.
Number Of Awards: 6.
Applications Received: 300.
Odds Of Winning: 2% of applicants on average receive an award each year.
Contact: Jennifer Lindemann, Program Coordinator

AMERICAN MILITARY RETIREES ASSOCIATION, INC. ADMINISTRATIVE OFFICE

22 U.S. Oval, Suite 1200
Plattsburgh, NY 12903
Phone: 800-424-2969

Fax: 518-563-9479
Email: infoamra1973@westelcom.com
Website: http://www.amra1973.org

#519 • Sgt. Major Douglas R. Drum Memorial Scholarship

Type: Scholarship. Renewable. Reapplication required for renewal.
Eligibility: Applicant must be a current member of AMRA or the dependent, spouse, child, or grandchild of a current member. This award must be used in the following years of study: • Freshman • Sophomore • Junior • Senior • Masters • Doctoral • Other postgraduate level
Deadline: Varies.
Award Amount: $ 750.
Number Of Awards: Varies.
Contact: Kathy Dow, Committee Chairperson
1787 Route 3
Morrisonville, NY 12962
Phone: 518-561-6256

AMVETS NATIONAL HEADQUARTERS

P.O. Box 1347
Lanham, MD 20703-1347
Phone: 301-459-9600
Fax: 301-459-7924
Email: amvets@amvets.org
Website: http://www.amvets.org

#520 • AMVETS National Four-Year Scholarship

Type: Scholarship. Renewable for up to four years.
Eligibility: Applicant must be the child or grandchild of an AMVETS member or of a deceased veteran who would have been eligible for AMVETS membership, or must be an AMVETS member who is a former or current member of the U.S. Armed Forces and who has exhausted all government financial aid. Selection is based upon U.S. citizenship, academic achievement, extracurricular activities, and financial need. This award must be used in the following years of study: • Freshman
Deadline: April 15.
Award Amount: $ 1,000.
Number Of Awards: 10.
Applications Received: 1,600.
Odds Of Winning: Less than 1% of applicants on average receive an award each year.
Contact: Michell Hammond/Don Coffman, Programs Department
Email: mhammond@amvets.org

AMVETS, ILLINOIS DEPARTMENT

2200 South Sixth Street
Springfield, IL 62703

Phone: 217-528-4713
Fax: 217-528-9896
Email: amvets@warpnet.net

#521 • Illinois AMVETS Service Foundation Scholarships

Type: Scholarship. Renewable. Recipient must submit transcripts and reapply for renewal.
Eligibility: Applicant must be an Illinois high school senior who has taken the ACT. Applicant must be the unmarried child of a member of the Armed Forces or of a veteran who served after September 15, 1940, and was honorably discharged. This award must be used in the following years of study: • Freshman
Deadline: March 1.
Award Amount: $ 1,000.
Number Of Awards: 6.
Applications Received: 70.
Contact: Shanna Hughes, AMVETS State Headquarters

#522 • Post #100 Scholarship

Type: Scholarship. Not renewable.
Eligibility: Applicant must be an Illinois resident attending school in Illinois, be single, be the child of a veteran, and submit ACT scores, transcripts, rank in class, and tax forms. This award must be used in the following years of study: • Freshman
Deadline: Varies.
Award Amount: $ 500.
Number Of Awards: 1.
Contact: Shanna Hughes, Office Manager

#523 • Paul Powell Memorial Scholarship

Type: Scholarship. Renewable for up to three years.
Eligibility: Applicant must be an Illinois resident attending school in Illinois, be single, be the child of a veteran, and submit ACT scores, transcripts, rank in class, and tax forms. This award must be used in the following years of study: • Freshman
Deadline: March 1.
Award Amount: $ 1,000.
Number Of Awards: 1.
Applications Received: 500.
Contact: AMVETS, Illinois Department

#524 • Auxiliary Worchild Scholarship

Type: Scholarship. Renewable for up to three years.
Eligibility: Applicant must be an Illinois resident attending school in Illinois, be single, be the child of a veteran, and submit ACT scores, transcripts, rank in class, and tax forms. This award must be used in the following years of study: • Freshman
Deadline: Varies.
Award Amount: $ 100.
Number Of Awards: 2 - 4.
Contact: See above.

#525 • Auxiliary Memorial Scholarship

Type: Scholarship. Renewable for up to three years.
Eligibility: Applicant must be an Illinois resident attending school in Illinois, be single, be the child of a veteran, and submit ACT scores, transcripts, rank in class, and tax forms. This award must be used in the following years of study: • Freshman
Deadline: March 1.
Award Amount: $ 500.
Number Of Awards: 2 - 4.
Contact: See above.

ARKANSAS DEPARTMENT OF HIGHER EDUCATION

114 East Capitol
Little Rock, AR 72201
Phone: 501-371-2000
Fax: 501-371-2001
Email: finaid@adhe.arknet.edu
Website: http://www.adhe.arknet.edu

#526 • MIA/KIA Dependents' Scholarship

Type: Grant. Renewable for up to eight semesters if recipient maintains satisfactory academic progress.
Eligibility: Applicant must be the dependent child or spouse of a member of the Armed Forces who was declared killed in action, missing in action, or prisoner of war after 1960, and was a resident of Arkansas before entering the Armed Forces. Award may be used at Arkansas public schools only. This award must be used in the following years of study: • Freshman • Sophomore • Junior • Senior • Masters • Doctoral
Deadline: August 1.
Award Amount: Varies.
Number Of Awards: Varies.
Applications Received: 2.
Odds Of Winning: 100% of applicants on average receive an award each year.
Contact: Lillian K. Willams, Assistant Coordinator of Student Financial Aid

ARMY EMERGENCY RELIEF (AER)

200 Stovall Street
Alexandria, VA 22332-0600
Phone: 703-428-0035
Website: http://www.aerhq.org

#527 • Scholarship Program for Dependent Children of Soldiers

Type: Grant. Renewable. Recipient must maintain a minimum 2.0 GPA and reapply for renewal.
Eligibility: Applicant must be the unmarried, dependent child of a soldier on active duty, retired, or deceased while on active duty or after retirement and must be under age 22 on June 1 preceding the

school year for which the scholarship is requested. Selection is based upon financial need, academic achievements, and individual accomplishments. This award must be used in the following years of study: • Freshman • Sophomore • Junior • Senior
Deadline: March 1.
Award Amount: $ 600 - $ 1,700.
Number Of Awards: Varies.
Applications Received: 3,000.
Odds Of Winning: 80% of applicants on average receive an award each year.
Contact: Rosamond Pariseau, M.G. James Ursano Scholarship Fund
Email: rosie@aerhq.org

BLINDED VETERANS ASSOCIATION (BVA)

477 H Street, NW
Washington, DC 20001-2694
Phone: 202-371-8880
Fax: 202-371-8258

#528 • Kathern F. Gruber Scholarship

Type: Scholarship. Renewable. Reapplication is required for renewal.
Eligibility: Applicant must be the child or spouse of a legally blind veteran and must be accepted or enrolled full time at an accredited college. Selection is based upon application, transcript, three recommendations, and 300-word essay. This award must be used in the following years of study: • Freshman • Sophomore • Junior • Senior • Masters • Doctoral • Other postgraduate level • Vocational students
Deadline: April 16.
Award Amount: $ 1,000 - $ 2,000.
Number Of Awards: 16.
Applications Received: 40.
Contact: John Williams, Scholarships
477 H Street, NW
Washington, DC 20001-2694
Phone: 202-371-8880
Fax: 202-371-8258

DAUGHTERS OF THE CINCINNATI

122 East 58th Street
New York, NY 10022

#529 • Daughters of the Cincinnati Scholarship

Type: Scholarship. Renewable. Satisfactory academic performance is required to retain scholarship.
Eligibility: Applicant must be the daughter of a commissioned officer in the regular Army, Navy, Air Force, Coast Guard, or Marine Corps (active, retired, or deceased). Send parent's rank and branch of service

with request for application. Selection is based upon merit. Amount of award is based upon need. This award must be used in the following years of study: • Freshman • Sophomore • Junior • Senior
Deadline: March 15.
Award Amount: $ 500 - $ 3,000.
Number Of Awards: 10.
Contact: Scholarship Administrator

DAUGHTERS OF UNION VETERANS OF THE CIVIL WAR

503 South Walnut Street
Springfield, IL 62704-1932
Phone: 217-544-0616
Email: DUVCW@aol.com

#530 • G.A.R. Living Memorial Scholarship

Type: Scholarship. Not renewable.
Eligibility: Applicant must be a lineal descendant of a Civil War Union veteran. Selection is based upon academic standing. Requests must include a self-addressed, stamped envelope. This award must be used in the following years of study: • Senior
Deadline: February 1.
Award Amount: $ 200.
Number Of Awards: 3 - 4.
Contact: Scholarships
Phone: 217-544-0616
Email: DUVCW@aol.com

DELAWARE HIGHER EDUCATION COMMISSION

820 North French Street
Wilmington, DE 19801
Phone: 302-577-3240 or 800-292-7935
Fax: 302-577-6765
Email: mlaffey@state.de.us
Website: http://www.doe.state.de.us/high-ed/

#531 • Educational Benefits for Children of Deceased Veterans

Type: Grant. Renewable.
Eligibility: Applicant must be a Delaware resident between the ages of 16 and 24 who is the child of a deceased military veteran or state police officer who was a Delaware resident, and whose death was service related. This award must be used in the following years of study: • Freshman • Sophomore • Junior • Senior
Deadline: Three weeks prior to start of classes.
Award Amount: $ 8,500.
Number Of Awards: 2.
Applications Received: 2.
Odds Of Winning: 100% of applicants on average receive an award each year.
Contact: Maureen Laffey, Associate Director

DOLPHIN SCHOLARSHIP FOUNDATION

5040 Virginia Beach Boulevard, Suite 104 A
Virginia Beach, VA 23462
Phone: 757-671-3200
Fax: 757-671-3330

#532 • U.S. Submarine Veterans of World War II Scholarship

Type: Scholarship. Renewable. Good academic standing and reapplication are required for renewal.
Eligibility: Applicant must be the dependent child/step-child, unmarried, and under age 24 of a paid-up, regular member of U.S. Submarine Veterans of World War II. Sponsor's membership card number must accompany application request. This award must be used in the following years of study: • Freshman • Sophomore • Junior • Senior
Deadline: April 15.
Award Amount: $ 3,000.
Number Of Awards: 10.
Applications Received: 11.
Odds Of Winning: 95% of applicants on average receive an award each year.
Contact: Tomi Roeske, Scholarship Administrator
U.S. Scholarship Veterans of World War II Scholarship Program 5040 Virginia Beach Boulevard, Suite 104 A
Virginia Beach, VA 23462

#533 • Dolphin Scholarship

Type: Scholarship. Renewable. Recipient must maintain good academic standing and submit annual transcript to retain scholarship.
Eligibility: Applicant must be the child/step-child, unmarried and under 24 years of age, of a member or former member of the Submarine Force who served for at least eight years, or of a Navy member who served at least 10 years in submarine support activities. There is no minimum service requirement for Navy members who died on active duty in the Submarine Force. This award must be used in the following years of study: • Freshman • Sophomore • Junior • Senior
Deadline: April 15.
Award Amount: $ 3,000.
Number Of Awards: 39.
Applications Received: 192.
Odds Of Winning: 20% of applicants on average receive an award each year.
Contact: Tomi Roeske, Scholarship Administrator

FOUNDATION OF THE FIRST CAVALRY DIVISION ASSOCIATION

302 North Main
Copperas Cove, TX 76522-1799
Phone: 254-547-6537
Fax: 254-547-8853
Email: firstcav@vvm.com
Website: http://www.vvm.com/~firstcav

#534 • First Cavalry Division Association Scholarship

Type: Scholarship. Renewable for up to four years or a maximum amount of $2,400.
Eligibility: Applicant must be the child of a soldier who died while serving in the First Cavalry Division, during and since the Vietnam War or during Desert Storm. If the death occurred between March 1, 1980 and August 2, 1990 or after May 1, 1991, the scholarship is offered only if the deceased parent was a member of the Association and serving with the First Cavalry Division at time of death. Also eligible are the children of a soldier who has been declared 100% disabled from injuries incurred while serving with the First Cavalry Division during the Vietnam War or Desert Storm. Applicant can also be the child or grandchild of a First Cavalry Division soldier, USAF, FAC, AIE pilot, or war correspondent who served in a designated qualifying unit which was involved in the battle of the Ia Drang Valley during the period of March 19 through November 1965. Applicant must also send a self-addressed, stamped envelope, and request for additional information and application. This award must be used in the following years of study: • Freshman • Sophomore • Junior • Senior
Deadline: Varies.
Award Amount: $ 600.
Number Of Awards: 15.
Odds Of Winning: 100% of applicants on average receive an award each year.
Contact: Arthur J. Junot, Executive Director

ILLINOIS STUDENT ASSISTANCE COMMISSION/CLIENT SUPPORT SERVICES

1755 Lake Cook Road
Deerfield, IL 60015-5209
Phone: 800-899-ISAC, 847 948-8550
Website: http://www.isac1.org

#535 • Illinois Veteran Grant

Type: Grant. Renewable.
Eligibility: Applicant must be a veteran of the U.S. Armed Forces and attend an Illinois public university or community college. This award must be used in the following years of study: • Freshman • Sophomore • Junior • Senior • Masters • Doctoral • Other postgraduate level
Deadline: Varies.
Award Amount: Varies.
Number Of Awards: 15,000.
Contact: Client Relations

#536 • Illinois National Guard Grant

Type: Grant. Renewable.
Eligibility: Applicant must have proof of current service in the National Guard and attend an Illinois public school. This award must be used in the following years of study: • Freshman • Sophomore • Junior • Senior • Masters • Doctoral • Other postgraduate level
Deadline: September 15.
Award Amount: Varies.
Number Of Awards: 1,800.
Applications Received: 15,000.
Contact: Client Relations

IOWA PROGRAM FOR WAR ORPHANS, VETERANS AFFAIRS DIVISION

Iowa Commission of Veterans Affairs
700 N.W. Beaver Drive Camp Dodge #A6A
Johnston, IA 50131-1902
Phone: 515-242-5331
Fax: 515-242-5659
Email: info@icva.state.ia.us

#537 • War Orphans Educational Aid

Type: Grant. Renewable for use up to $3,000.
Eligibility: Applicant must be a child of a man or woman who died in active federal military service while serving in the armed forces or during active federal military service in the Iowa national guard, or other military components of the U.S. or as a result of service during World War I, World War II, Korean, Vietnam, or Persian Gulf conflicts, or other specified conflicts or service; contact Iowa Commission of Veterans Affairs for qualifying dates of service. Applicant must have lived in Iowa for at least two years and attend an institution in Iowa. Applicant must submit an application, birth certificate, and death certificate for deceased parent. This award must be used in the following years of study: • Freshman • Sophomore • Junior • Senior • Masters • Doctoral • Other postgraduate level
Deadline: None.
Award Amount: $ 600.
Number Of Awards: Varies.
Applications Received: 5.
Odds Of Winning: 100% of applicants on average receive an award each year.
Contact: Brian B. Bales, Executive Director

LADIES AUXILIARY TO THE VETERANS OF FOREIGN WARS, DEPARTMENT OF MAINE

c/o Mary Wallace P.O. Box 195
Mattawamkeag, ME 04459

#538 • Past National President Fran Booth Medical Scholarship

Type: Scholarship. Not renewable.
Eligibility: Applicant must be a resident of Maine

and a descendent of a Veteran of Foreign Wars or a VFW auxiliary member. Selection is based upon academic qualification, civic involvement, employment, financial need, letters of recommendation, and a personal statement. This award must be used in the following years of study: • Freshman • Sophomore • Junior • Senior • Masters • Doctoral • Other postgraduate level
Field(s) Of Study: Medicine.
Deadline: Varies.
Award Amount: $ 1,000.
Number Of Awards: 1.
Applications Received: 3.
Odds Of Winning: 33% of applicants on average receive an award each year.
Contact: Donna Gallant
3 Morning St.
Scarborough, ME 04074
Phone: 207-883-9509

MARINE CORPS TANKERS ASSOCIATION, INC.

Phil Morell, Scholarship Chairman
1112 Alpine Heights Road
Alpine, CA 91901
Phone: 619-445-8423
Fax: 619-445-8423

#539 • John Cornelius and Max English Scholarship

Type: Scholarship. Renewable. Reapplication required for renewal.
Eligibility: Applicant must be a Marine tanker, former Marine tanker, or survivor, dependent, or under legal guardianship of a Marine who served in a tank unit and is on active duty, retired, reserve, or has been honorably discharged. The Marine tanker must be a member of MCTA or plan to join. For more information, write to above address. This award must be used in the following years of study: • Freshman • Sophomore • Junior • Senior • Masters • Doctoral • Other postgraduate level
Deadline: March 15.
Award Amount: $ 1,500.
Number Of Awards: 8 - 12.
Applications Received: 35.
Odds Of Winning: 25% of applicants on average receive an award each year.
Contact: Phil Morell, Scholarship Chairman

MARYLAND HIGHER EDUCATION COMMISSION

State Scholarship Administration
16 Francis Street
Annapolis, MD 21401-1781
Phone: 410-974-5370 or 800-974-1024
Fax: 410-974-5994

Email: ssamail@mhec.state.md.us
Website: http://www.mhec.state.md.us

#540 • Edward T. Conroy Memorial Grant

Type: Grant. Renewable for up to five years full-time study or eight years part-time study.
Eligibility: Applicant must be the child of a Maryland resident who is deceased or 100% disabled as a result of military service in the U.S. Armed Forces personnel, Vietnam-era P.O.W.s, or a Maryland state or local public safety personnel. Surviving spouses and children of safety personnel are also eligible. Applicant must attend a school in Maryland. This award must be used in the following years of study: • Freshman • Sophomore • Junior • Senior • Masters • Doctoral
Deadline: July 15.
Award Amount: $ 1,976.
Number Of Awards: 54.
Applications Received: 62.
Contact: Margaret L. Crutchley, Program Administrator
Phone: 410-974-5370, extension 145

MINNESOTA DEPARTMENT OF VETERANS AFFAIRS

Veterans Service Building
St. Paul, MN 55155-2079
Phone: 612-296-2562
Email: terrence.logan@dma.state.mn.us
Website: http://www.mdva.state.mn.us

#541 • War Orphan's Scholarship

Type: Scholarship. Renewable.
Eligibility: Applicant must be a the child of a veteran who died of a service-connected disability and who was a Minnesota resident at time of entry into active duty attending an accredited school in Minnesota (other than the University of Minnesota System). Cite Minn. stat. 197.75, subd. 1. Applicant must have been a Minnesota resident for at least two years prior to application. This award must be used in the following years of study: • Freshman • Sophomore • Junior • Senior
Deadline: Varies.
Award Amount: Full tuition or partial tuition. Plus $350 per year for books, fees, and other expenses.
Number Of Awards: Varies.
Contact: See above.

MISSISSIPPI BOARD OF TRUSTEES OF STATE INSTITUTIONS OF HIGHER LEARNING

Student Financial Aid Office
3825 Ridgewood Road
Jackson, MS 39211-6453

Phone: 601-982-6663
Fax: 601-982-6527

#542 • Southeast Asia POW/MIA Scholarship

Type: Scholarship. Renewable. Award is for a maximum of eight semesters.
Eligibility: Applicant must be the child of a Mississippi veteran presently or formerly listed as MIA in Southeast Asia who has been a prisoner of a foreign government as a result of the military action against the U.S. naval vessel Pueblo. Applicant is eligible until age 23 and must be enrolled in a Mississippi public college or university. POW/MIA must have been a Mississippi resident at the time of induction into the Armed Forces and at the time he was officially listed as POW or MIA; spouse must have been a Mississippi resident for at least 10 years during her minority and at the time of the child's enrollment. This award must be used in the following years of study: • Freshman • Sophomore • Junior • Senior
Deadline: Varies.
Award Amount: Full tuition or partial tuition. Plus average cost of dorm room and required fees.
Number Of Awards: Varies.
Contact: Student Financial Aid Office

NATIONAL GUARD ASSOCIATION OF ARIZONA

5640 East McDowell Road
Phoenix, AZ 85008
Phone: 602-275-8307
Fax: 602-275-9254

#543 • National Guard Association of Arizona Scholarship

Type: Scholarship. Renewable. Reneable if recipient maintains minimum minimum "B" average and satisfactory membership.
Eligibility: Applicant must be an active member of the Arizona National Guard in good standing and take at least 12 credit hours per semester. This award must be used in the following years of study: • Freshman • Sophomore • Junior • Senior
Deadline: March 1.
Award Amount: $ 1,000.
Number Of Awards: 2.
Contact: Tom Ralph, Executive Director
Phone: 602-275-8307

NAVY LEAGUE OF THE UNITED STATES

Scholarship Program
2300 Wilson Boulevard
Arlington, VA 22201-3308
Phone: 703-528-1755

Fax: 703-528-2333
Email: nwalker@navyleague.org

#544 • Navy League Scholarship

Type: Scholarship. Not renewable.
Eligibility: Applicant must be a U.S. citizen and under age 25. Selection is based upon academic performance, extracurricular activities, and financial need. Applicant must be a direct descendant of current, former, retired, or deceased Coast Guard, Navy, Marine Corps, or Merchant Marine personnel. Preference is given to applicants planning to major in engineering or science. SASE required. This award must be used in the following years of study: • Freshman
Deadline: April 1.
Award Amount: $ 2,500.
Number Of Awards: 11.
Applications Received: 1,000.
Odds Of Winning: 1% of applicants on average receive an award each year.
Contact: Nicole Walker, Assistant Director of Human Resources/Administration
Phone: 703-528-1775
Fax: 703-528-2333
Email: nwalker@navyleague.org

NAVY SUPPLY CORPS FOUNDATION, INC.

1425 Prince Avenue
Athens, GA 30606-2205
Phone: 706-354-4111
Fax: 706-354-0334
Email: kmorris@athens.net
Website: http://www.usnscf.com

#545 • Navy Supply Corps Foundation Scholarship

Type: Scholarship. Not renewable.
Eligibility: Applicant must be the child of a Navy Supply Corps Officer (including Warrant) or associated supply enlisted ratings on active duty, in reserve status, retired-with-pay, or deceased, and have a minimum 3.0 GPA. Selection is based upon scholastic ability, character, leadership, and financial need. This award must be used in the following years of study: • Freshman • Sophomore • Junior • Senior
Deadline: April 10.
Award Amount: $ 2,500.
Number Of Awards: 60.
Applications Received: 130.
Odds Of Winning: 30% of applicants on average receive an award each year.
Contact: Kaye Morris, Administrator

NAVY-MARINE CORPS RELIEF SOCIETY

801 North Randolph Street, Suite 1228
Arlington, VA 22203

Phone: 703-696-4960
Fax: 703-696-0144

#546 • Vice Admiral E.P. Travers Scholarship

Type: Scholarship. Renewable if recipient reapplies, maintains satisfactory academic progress, and continues to have financial need.
Eligibility: Applicant must be a dependent of an active duty or retired service member or a spouse of an active duty member, have a minimum cumulative 2.0 GPA, be enrolled or accepted as a full-time undergraduate student at a postsecondary institution approved by the Department of Education, and demonstrate financial need. This award must be used in the following years of study: • Freshman • Sophomore • Junior • Senior
Deadline: March 1.
Award Amount: $ 2,000.
Number Of Awards: Varies.
Contact: Gordon Houtman, Education Specialist

#547 • Children of Deceased Service Members Scholarship

Type: Scholarship. Renewable.
Eligibility: Applicant must be a child of a Navy or Marine Corps service member who died while on active duty or in retired status. Selection is based upon financial need. This award must be used in the following years of study: • Freshman • Sophomore • Junior • Senior
Deadline: June 30.
Award Amount: $ 500 - $ 2,000.
Number Of Awards: Varies.
Contact: Gordon Houtman, Education Specialist

#548 • USS Tennessee Scholarship

Type: Scholarship. Renewable if recipient reapplies, maintains satisfactory academic progress, and continues to have financial need.
Eligibility: Applicant must be a dependent of active duty service member assigned to or previously assigned to duty aboard the USS Tennessee. This award must be used in the following years of study: • Freshman • Sophomore • Junior • Senior
Deadline: June 30.
Award Amount: $ 1,000.
Number Of Awards: Varies.
Contact: Gordan Houtman, Education Specialist

NEW MEXICO VETERANS SERVICE COMMISSION

P.O. Box 2324
Santa Fe, NM 87503
Phone: 505-827-6300
Fax: 505-827-6372
Website: http://www.state.nm.us/veterans

#549 • Vietnam Veterans Scholarship

Type: Scholarship. Renewable.
Eligibility: Applicant must be a Vietnam veteran who was a New Mexico resident at the time of entry into the service, has been awarded the Vietnam Campaign or Service Medal, and must attend a state-sponsored school in New Mexico. This award must be used in the following years of study: • Freshman • Sophomore • Junior • Senior • Masters
Deadline: Varies.
Award Amount: Varies.
Number Of Awards: 35.
Applications Received: 37.
Odds Of Winning: 99% of applicants on average receive an award each year.
Contact: Alan T. Martinez, State Benefits Manager

NEW YORK COUNCIL NAVY LEAGUE SCHOLARSHIP FUND

Intrepid Museum
One Intrepid Square Pier 86
New York, NY 10036
Phone: 212-399-4440
Fax: 212-399-4405
Email: chiefyng@aol.com

#550 • New York Council Navy League Scholarship

Type: Scholarship. Renewable. Minimum grade average of "B-" and transcripts are required to retain scholarship.
Eligibility: Applicant must be the dependent of a regular/reserve Navy, Marine Corps, or Coast Guard service member who is serving on active duty, retired with pay, or died in the line of duty or after retirement. Applicant must be a resident of Connecticut, New Jersey, or New York. This award must be used in the following years of study: • Freshman • Sophomore • Junior • Senior
Deadline: June 15.
Award Amount: $ 3,000.
Number Of Awards: 3 - 5.
Applications Received: 28.
Odds Of Winning: 18% of applicants on average receive an award each year.
Contact: Donald I. Sternberg, Executive Administrator

NORTH CAROLINA VIETNAM VETERANS, INC.

Scholarship Program
P.O. Box 10333
Raleigh, NC 27609
Phone: 919-713-4994
Email: ncvvi@juno.com
Website: http://www.ncneighbors.com/96/

#551 • North Carolina Vietnam Veterans' Scholarship

Type: Scholarship. Renewable if recipient submits new essay and maintains a minimum 2.25 GPA.
Eligibility: Applicant must be a Vietnam veteran or the spouse, child, or grandchild of a Vietnam veteran, and must reside in Wake County or one of the counties adjacent to it. This award must be used in the following years of study: • Freshman • Sophomore • Junior • Senior
Deadline: February 28.
Award Amount: $ 500.
Number Of Awards: 4 - 5.
Applications Received: 25.
Odds Of Winning: 25% of applicants on average receive an award each year.
Contact: Bud Gross, Scholarship Administrator

RED RIVER VALLEY FIGHTER PILOTS ASSOCIATION (RRVA)

P.O. Box 1551
North Fork, CA 93643
Phone: 559-877-5000
Fax: 559-877-5001
Email: afbridger@aol.com
Website: http://www.eos.net/rrva

#552 • RRVA Scholarship Grant Assistance Program

Type: Scholarship. Renewable if recipient meets requirements.
Eligibility: Applicant must be the immediate dependent of a member of the U.S. Armed Forces who is listed as KIA or MIA from any combat situtation since August 1964, the immediate dependent of a military aircrew member killed as a result of performing aircrew duties during a non-combat mission, or the immediate dependent of current and or deceased RRVA-members who were in good standing at the time of their death. Selection is based upon financial need, scholastic achievement, college entrance exams, and accomplishments in school, church, civic, and social activities. This award must be used in the following years of study: • Freshman • Sophomore • Junior • Senior • Masters • Doctoral • Other postgraduate level
Deadline: May 15.
Award Amount: $ 500 - $ 3,500.
Number Of Awards: 14 - 42.
Applications Received: 42.
Odds Of Winning: 90% of applicants on average receive an award each year.
Contact: Alexander D. Bache, Executive Director

RETIRED ENLISTED ASSOCIATION

1111 South Abilene Court
Aurora, CO 80012

Phone: 800-338-9337
Fax: 888-882-0835
Email: treahq@aol.com
Website: http://www.trea.org

#553 • TREA Memorial Foundation National Scholarship

Type: Scholarship. Not renewable.
Eligibility: Applicant must be the child or grandchild of a TREA member in good standing and be a dependent. This award must be used in the following years of study: • Freshman • Sophomore • Junior • Senior
Deadline: April 30.
Award Amount: $ 1,000.
Number Of Awards: 40.
Applications Received: 140.
Odds Of Winning: 29% of applicants on average receive an award each year.
Contact: Scholarship Support Staff

RETIRED OFFICERS ASSOCIATION (TROA)

201 North Washington Street
Alexandria, VA 22314-2529
Phone: 703-838-5816
Fax: 703-838-5819
Email: edassist@troa.org
Website: http://www.troa.org

#554 • TROA Scholarship 200

Type: Scholarship. Not renewable.
Eligibility: Applicant must be under 24 years of age and the dependent child of active duty military personnel, officer or enlisted. This award must be used in the following years of study: • Freshman • Sophomore • Junior • Senior
Deadline: Varies.
Award Amount: $ 1,000.
Number Of Awards: 200.
Applications Received: 1,600.
Odds Of Winning: 13% of applicants on average receive an award each year.
Contact: Scholarships

SECOND MARINE DIVISION ASSOCIATION

P.O. Box 8180
Camp LeJeune, NC 28547
Phone: 910-451-3167
Fax: 910-451-3167

#555 • Second Marine Division Association Memorial Scholarship

Type: Scholarship. Renewable. Minimum 2.5 GPA.

Eligibility: Applicant must be the unmarried child of a parent who served in the Second Marine Division or a unit attached to the Second Marine Division. Parents' taxable income should not exceed $42,000. This award must be used in the following years of study: • Freshman • Sophomore • Junior • Senior
Deadline: April 1.
Award Amount: $ 800 - $ 1,600.
Number Of Awards: 30.
Contact: Martin T. McNulty, Board of Trustees, SMDA Memorial Scholarship Fund
111 Brimer Rd.
Newman, GA 30263

SUBMARINE OFFICERS' WIVES CLUB

Bowfin Memorial Scholarship Committee
Lockwood Hall
Pearl Harbor, HI 96860

#556 • Bowfin Memorial Scholarship

Type: Scholarship. Renewable. Reapplication required for renewal.
Eligibility: Applicant must be a child under age 23 of submarine force personnel (active duty or retired) or be active duty or retired submarine force personnel or a spouse of an active duty, retired, or deceased submarine force personnel. Applicant or submarine sponsor must reside in Hawaii at time of application. Applicant must demonstrate academic proficiency and potential, extracurricular activity and/or community involvement, and financial need. This award must be used in the following years of study: • Freshman • Sophomore • Junior • Senior • Masters • Doctoral • Other postgraduate level • continuing education students
Deadline: Varies.
Award Amount: $ 500 - $ 2,500.
Number Of Awards: 20.
Applications Received: 25.
Odds Of Winning: 80% of applicants on average receive an award each year.
Contact: Heather Hesslink, Committee Chairperson
836 Hays Circle
Honolulu, HI 96818-3611
Phone: 808-836-6897
Email: hesslinkt001@hawaii.rr.com

SURFLANT SCHOLARSHIP FOUNDATION

1628 Pocahontas Street
Norfolk, VA 23511
Phone: 757-423-1772
Email: cnslschf@erols.com

#557 • Surflant Scholarship

Type: Scholarship. Not renewable.
Eligibility: Applicant must be a dependent child of a Navy service member who has served at least three years under the administrative control of Commander, Naval Surface Force, U.S. Atlantic Fleet Support Activities. To obtain an application, submit military sponsor's full name, rank, and social security number, list of SURFLANT duty stations, homeports, ship hull numbers and dates on board, applicant's name and social security number, and a self-addressed, stamped (55 cents) envelope. Selection is based upon academics, extracurricular activities, character, and financial need. This award must be used in the following years of study: • Freshman • Sophomore • Junior • Senior
Deadline: April 15.
Award Amount: $ 2,000.
Number Of Awards: 15.
Applications Received: 350.
Odds Of Winning: 4% of applicants on average receive an award each year.
Contact: Kathi Thomas, Administrator

TEXAS HIGHER EDUCATION COORDINATING BOARD

Student Financial Assistance
P.O. Box 12788, Capitol Station
Austin, TX 78711-2788
Phone: 512-427-6340
Website: http://www.thecb.state.tx.us

#558 • Veterans and Dependents Tuition Exemption

Type: Scholarship. Renewable.
Eligibility: Applicant must have served in the military for at least 180 days active service, been a Texas resident at the time of entrance, have been honorably discharged, be a Texas resident for at least 12 months, and have limited federal education benefits. Exemption may also apply to applicant whose parent died while in the Armed Forces or as a result of injury or illness related to military service and to children of Texas National Guard and Texas Air National Guard who died while on active duty since January 1, 1946 or as a result of service-related injuries or illness. Applicant must attend a public college or university in Texas. This award must be used in the following years of study: • Freshman • Sophomore • Junior • Senior • Masters • Doctoral • Other postgraduate level
Deadline: Varies.
Award Amount: $ 852.
Number Of Awards: 8,743.
Contact: Jane Caldwell, Director of Grants and Special Programs
Phone: 512-427-6455

UNITED STATES COAST GUARD CHIEF PETTY OFFICERS ASSOCIATION

Scholarship Chairperson
5520 G Hempstead Way
Springfield, VA 22151

#559 • Capt. Caliendo College Assistance Fund Scholarship

Type: Scholarship. Not renewable.
Eligibility: Applicant must be the dependent, unmarried child of a member or deceased member of the U.S. Coast Guard Chief Petty Officer's Association or U.S. Coast Guard Enlisted Association. Applicant must be under 24 years of age and submit an essay (500-word maximum). This award must be used in the following years of study: • Freshman • Sophomore • Junior • Senior
Deadline: March 1.
Award Amount: $ 500 - $ 1,500.
Number Of Awards: 5.
Applications Received: 50.
Odds Of Winning: 100% of applicants on average receive an award each year.
Contact: CCCAF Scholarship Committee

UNITED STATES NAVAL ACADEMY CLASS OF 1963 FOUNDATION

702 Smallwood Road
Rockville, MD 20850-2144
Email: fhilton@erols.com

#560 • United States Naval Academy Class of 1963 Foundation Scholarship

Type: Scholarship. Renewable with satisfactory academic progress.
Eligibility: Applicant must be the son or daughter of a deceased member of the U.S. Naval Academy class of 1963. This award must be used in the following years of study: • Freshman • Sophomore • Junior • Senior • Masters • Doctoral • Vocational school students
Deadline: None.
Award Amount: $ 1,000 - $ 4,000.
Number Of Awards: 6.
Applications Received: 6.
Odds Of Winning: 100% of applicants on average receive an award each year.
Contact: Frank Hilton, Chair of Scholarship Committee

WOMEN'S ARMY CORPS VETERANS ASSOCIATION

P.O. Box 5577
Fort McClellan, AL 36205
Phone: 256-820-6824

#561 • Women's Army Corps Veterans Association Scholarship

Type: Scholarship. Not renewable.
Eligibility: Applicant must be the child, grandchild, niece, or nephew of an Army service woman and must submit documentation of sponsor's military service. Applicant must have a minimum 3.0 GPA and be enrolled full time in a four-year program at an accredited university in the

U.S. Selection is based upon academic achievement, leadership ability through co-curricular activities and community involvement, biographical sketch, recommendations, and application form. This award must be used in the following years of study: • Freshman
Deadline: May 1.
Award Amount: $ 1,500.
Number Of Awards: 1.
Applications Received: 20.
Contact: Cathy Aleshire, Chair of Scholarship Committee
Phone: 256-820-6824
Email: cathya@quicklink.net

Military Science/ROTC

ARMED FORCES COMMUNICATIONS AND ELECTRONICS ASSOCIATION

ATTN: Educational Foundation
4400 Fair Lakes Court
Fairfax, VA 22033-3899
Phone: 703-631-6149
Fax: 703-631-4693
Email: scholarship@afcea
Website: http://www.afcea.org

#562 • ROTC Scholarship

Type: Scholarship. Not renewable.
Eligibility: Applicant must be a U.S. citizen enrolled in an accredited four-year institution in the U.S., be active in ROTC program and nominated by professors of military science, naval science, or aerospace studies, and must demonstrate academic excellence, good moral character, potential to serve as an officer in the U.S. Armed Forces, and financial need. This award must be used in the following years of study: • Junior • Senior
Field(s) Of Study: Aerospace engineering, computer engineering, computer science, electrical engineering, electronics, mathematics, physics.
Deadline: April 1.
Award Amount: $ 2,000.
Number Of Awards: Varies.
Contact: School's ROTC Commander

Mining/Metallurgical/Materials Engineering

MINERALS, METALS, AND MATERIALS SOCIETY (TMS)

TMS Scholarship Committee
184 Thorn Hill Road

Warrendale, PA 15086
Phone: 724-776-9000, extension 213
Fax: 724-776-3770
Website: http://www.tms.org

#563 • EPD Scholarship

Type: Scholarship. Not renewable.
Eligibility: Applicant must be enrolled full time and be a member of TMS. Preference is given to applicants who have participated in a relevant industrial co-op program. This award must be used in the following years of study: • Sophomore • Junior • Senior • Masters
Field(s) Of Study: Non-ferrous metallurgy.
Deadline: May 1.
Award Amount: $ 2,000.
Number Of Awards: 2.
Contact: Member and Educational Services Department, TMS Student Awards Program

#564 • LMD Scholarship

Type: Scholarship. Not renewable.
Eligibility: Applicant must be enrolled full time and be a member of TMS. This award must be used in the following years of study: • Junior • Senior
Field(s) Of Study: Non-ferrous metallurgy.
Deadline: May 1.
Award Amount: $ 4,000.
Number Of Awards: 3.
Contact: Member and Educational Services Department, TMS Student Awards Program

ROCKY MOUNTAIN COAL MINING INSTITUTE (RMCMI)

3000 Youngfield Street, No. 324
Lakewood, CO 80215-6553
Phone: 303-238-9099
Fax: 303-238-0509
Email: rmcmi@eni.net
Website: RMCoalMine@aol.com

#565 • RMCMI Scholarship

Type: Scholarship. Renewable if recipient maintains full-time status, has a satisfactory GPA, and is recommended by dean of college or university.
Eligibility: Applicant must be enrolled full time and be a resident of one of the RMCMI member states: Arizona, Colorado, Montana, New Mexico, North Dakota, Texas, Utah, or Wyoming. This award must be used in the following years of study: • Junior
Field(s) Of Study: Civil engineering, electrical engineering, environmental engineering, geology, mechanical engineering, metallurgy, mineral processing, mining.
Deadline: February 1.
Award Amount: $ 2,000.
Number Of Awards: 16.

Applications Received: 71.
Odds Of Winning: 21% of applicants on average receive an award each year.
Contact: Doris G. Finnie, Executive Director

Multiple Majors

AIRCRAFT ELECTRONICS ASSOCIATION (AEA) EDUCATIONAL FOUNDATION

4217 S. Hocker Drive
Independence, MO 64055
Phone: 816-373-6565
Fax: 816-478-3100
Email: info@aea.net
Website: http://www.aea.net

#566 • Plane & Pilot Magazine/GARMIN Scholarhip

Type: Scholarship. Not renewable.
Eligibility: Contact for details. This award must be used in the following years of study: • Freshman • Sophomore • Junior • Senior • Vocational/technical students
Field(s) Of Study: Aircraft repair, avionics.
Deadline: February 15.
Award Amount: $ 2,000.
Number Of Awards: 1.
Applications Received: 150.
Odds Of Winning: 1% of applicants on average receive an award each year.
Contact: Mike Adamson, AEA Educational Foundation Executive Director

ASSOCIATION OF CERTIFIED FRAUD EXAMINERS

716 West Avenue
Austin, TX 78701
Phone: 800-245-3321
Fax: 512-478-9297
Email: info@cfenet.com
Website: http://www.cfenet.com

#567 • Association of Certified Fraud Examiners

Type: Scholarship. Not renewable.
Eligibility: Applicants must submit an essay and letters of recommendation (at least one from a certified fraud examiner or an association chapter). This award must be used in the following years of study: • Sophomore • Junior • Senior • Masters • Doctoral
Field(s) Of Study: accounting, criminal justice.
Deadline: May 12.

Award Amount: $ 1,000.
Number Of Awards: 10.
Applications Received: 60.
Odds Of Winning: 17% of applicants on average receive an award each year.
Contact: Dick Carozza, Scholarship Coordinator
Email: dick@cfenet.com

EAST TEXAS HISTORICAL ASSOCIATION

Ottis Lock Scholarship
P.O. Box 6223, SFA Station
Nacogdoches, TX 75962
Phone: 409-468-2407
Fax: 409-468-2190
Email: amcdonald@sfasu.edu

#568 • Ottis Lock Endowment Scholarship

Type: Scholarship. Renewable. Reapplication and transcript required for renewal.
Eligibility: Applicant must be attending a school in East Texas. Applicant should submit application, transcript, a statement of desire, and no more than three letters of recommendation. This award must be used in the following years of study: • Freshman • Sophomore • Junior • Senior • Masters • Doctoral • Other postgraduate level
Field(s) Of Study: History, social studies.
Deadline: May 1.
Award Amount: $ 500.
Number Of Awards: 1 - 2.
Applications Received: 16.
Odds Of Winning: 13% of applicants on average receive an award each year.
Contact: Archie P. McDonald, Executive Director/Editor

NATIONAL ASSOCIATION OF WATER COMPANIES

Scholarship Committee
1725 K Street, NW, Suite 1212
Washington, DC 20006
Website: http://www.nawc.org

#569 • David L. Owens Scholarship

Type: Scholarship. Not renewable.
Eligibility: Applicant must be a U.S. citizen. Applicant should submit an essay and letters of recommendation. This award must be used in the following years of study: • Masters • Doctoral • Other postgraduate level
Field(s) Of Study: Biology, business, chemistry, environmental.
Deadline: April 1.
Award Amount: $10,000.
Number Of Awards: 1.

Applications Received: 58.
Odds Of Winning: 5% of applicants on average receive an award each year.
Contact: Betty Jean Lewis, Administration Manager/Scholarship Committee Liaison
Email: jean@nawc.com

#570 • Utilities, Inc. Scholarship

Type: Scholarship. Not renewable.
Eligibility: Applicant must be a U.S. citizen. Applicant should submit an essay and letters of recommendation. This award must be used in the following years of study: • Masters • Doctoral • Other postgraduate level
Field(s) Of Study: Biology, business, chemistry, environmental.
Deadline: April 1.
Award Amount: $ 5,000.
Number Of Awards: 1.
Applications Received: 58.
Odds Of Winning: 5% of applicants on average receive an award each year.
Contact: Betty Jean Lewis, Administration Manager/Scholarship Committee Liaison

#571 • J.J. Barr Scholarship

Type: Scholarship. Not renewable.
Eligibility: Applicant must be a U.S. citizen. Applicant should submit an essay and letters of recommendation. This award must be used in the following years of study: • Masters • Doctoral • Other postgraduate level
Field(s) Of Study: Biology, business, chemistry, environmental.
Deadline: April 1.
Award Amount: $ 5,000.
Number Of Awards: 1.
Applications Received: 58.
Odds Of Winning: 5% of applicants on average receive an award each year.
Contact: Betty Jean Lewis, Administration Manager/Scholarship Committee Liaison

TYSON FOUNDATION

2210 West Oaklawn Drive
Springdale, AR 72762-6999
Phone: 501-290-4955
Fax: 501-290-7984

#572 • Tyson Foundation Scholarship

Type: Scholarship. Renewable. Scholarship continues as long as recipient maintains application criteria.
Eligibility: Applicant must be a U.S. citizen and a permanent resident in the vicinity of a Tyson operating facility. Applicant must have a minimum 2.5 GPA, be enrolled full time at an accredited institution, must demonstrate financial need, and must

help fund award by semester or summer employment. Write for application by February 28. This award must be used in the following years of study: • Freshman • Sophomore • Junior • Senior
Field(s) Of Study: Agriculture, business, computer science, engineering, nursing.
Deadline: April 20.
Award Amount: Partial tuition. $200 to $1,800 per semester.
Number Of Awards: Varies.
Applications Received: 400.
Odds Of Winning: 25% of applicants on average receive an award each year.
Contact: Cheryl Tyson or Annetta Young

VENTURA COUNTY COMMUNITY FOUNDATION

1317 Del Norte Road, Suite 150
Camarillo, CA 93010
Phone: 805-988-0196
Fax: 805-485-5537

#573 • Parker M. and Virginia Howell Scholarship

Type: Scholarship. Renewable.
Eligibility: Applicant must be graduating from a high school in San Buenaventura, Calif., or attending Ventura Community College This award must be used in the following years of study: • Freshman • Sophomore • Junior
Field(s) Of Study: Engineering, writing.
Deadline: March 9.
Award Amount: $ 500.
Number Of Awards: 1.
Applications Received: 3.
Odds Of Winning: 33% of applicants on average receive an award each year.
Contact: Gail Brown, Program Director

Music-General

AMERICAN LEGION - KANSAS

1314 Topeka Avenue
Topeka, KS 66612
Phone: 913-232-9315

#574 • Music Scholarship

Type: Scholarship. Not renewable.
Eligibility: Scholarship must be used at an approved Kansas college or university. This award must be used in the following years of study: • Freshman • Sophomore • Junior
Field(s) Of Study: Music.

Deadline: Febuary 15.
Award Amount: $ 1,000.
Number Of Awards: 1.
Contact: Scholarship Administrator

AMERICAN SOCIETY OF COMPOSERS, AUTHORS, AND PUBLISHERS (ASCAP)

ASCAP Building, One Lincoln Plaza
New York, NY 10023
Phone: 212-621-6327
Fax: 212-621-6504
Email: frichard@ascap.com

#575 • ASCAP Foundation Morton Gould Young Composers Award

Type: Grant. Not renewable.
Eligibility: Applicant must be a U.S. citizen or permanent resident under age 30. This award must be used in the following years of study: • Freshman • Sophomore • Junior • Senior • Masters • Doctoral
Field(s) Of Study: Music composition.
Deadline: March 15.
Award Amount: $ 250 - $ 3,000.
Number Of Awards: 27.
Applications Received: 675.
Contact: Frances Richard, Vice President & Director of Concert Music

BEEM FOUNDATION FOR THE ADVANCEMENT OF MUSIC

3864 Grayburn Avenue
Los Angeles, CA 90008
Phone: 213-291-7252
Fax: 213-291-7752
Email: beem_la@primenet.com
Website: http://www.primenet.com/~beem_la/

#576 • BEEM Foundation Scholarship

Type: Scholarship. Not renewable.
Eligibility: Applicant must be under age 25, must be a member of a minority group, must reside in Los Angeles, Los Angeles County, or Southern California, must submit musical biography, transcripts, and photo, and must audition. This award must be used in the following years of study: • Freshman • Sophomore • Junior • Senior • Masters
Field(s) Of Study: Music.
Deadline: April 1.
Award Amount: $ 2,000 - $ 5,000.
Number Of Awards: 3.
Applications Received: 20.
Odds Of Winning: 15% of applicants on average receive an award each year.
Contact: Scholarship Administrator

BRIDGEWATER COLLEGE

East College Street
Bridgewater, VA 22812
Phone: 540-828-8000
Website: http://www.bridgewater.edu

#577 • Margie Ann Conner Scholarship

Type: Scholarship. Renewable. Minimum 2.0 GPA and successful audition are required to retain scholarship.
Eligibility: Applicant must be a keyboard or vocal musician. Selection is based upon audition. This award must be used in the following years of study: • Freshman
Deadline: None.
Award Amount: $ 1,000.
Number Of Awards: 2.
Contact: Dr. Jesse E. Hopkins, Jr., Chairman of Music Department
Phone: 540-828-5303
Fax: 540-828-5479

CONTEMPORARY RECORD SOCIETY

National Competition for Composers Recording
724 Winchester Road
Broomall, PA 19008
Phone: 610-544-5920
Fax: 610-544-5921
Email: crsnews@erols.com
Website: http://www.erols.com/ersnews

#578 • Contemporary Record Society Grant

Type: Contest. Not renewable.
Eligibility: Contact for details. This award must be used in the following years of study: • Freshman • Sophomore • Junior • Senior • Masters • Doctoral • Other postgraduate level
Deadline: November 11.
Award Amount: $ 800 - $ 4,500.
Number Of Awards: 1.
Applications Received: 65.
Contact: John Gusso, President

ELON COLLEGE

2700 Campus Box
Elon College, NC 27244
Phone: 800-334-8448, extension 1
Fax: 336-538-3986
Website: http://www.elon.edu

#579 • Music Scholarship

Type: Scholarship. Renewable for up to four years.
Eligibility: Selection is based upon audition and interview. Band and choral scholarships are available to music and non-music majors. This award must be

used in the following years of study: • Freshman
Field(s) Of Study: Music, music education, music performance.
Deadline: Varies.
Award Amount: $ 500 - $ 7,500.
Number Of Awards: 28.
Contact: Department of Music
Phone: 910-582-2440

GENERAL FEDERATION OF WOMEN'S CLUBS OF MASSACHUSETTS (GFWC OF MA)

245 Dutton Road, Box 679
Sudbury, MA 01776-0679
Phone: 978-443-4569

#580 • GFWC of MA Music Scholarship

Type: Scholarship. Not renewable.
Eligibility: Applicant must attend a Massachusetts high school and submit a letter of endorsement from the president of the sponsoring GFWC of Massachusetts club in the community of legal residence, recommendation from music teacher or high school principal, and high school transcript. Audition and SASE required. This award must be used in the following years of study: • Freshman
Field(s) Of Study: Instrument, music education, music therapy, piano.
Deadline: February 1.
Award Amount: $ 500.
Number Of Awards: 1 - 5.
Contact: Sally Sears-Mack, Chairperson, Music Program
Phone: 508-349-7249

JAZZ CLUB OF SARASOTA

Scholarship Committee 290 Cocoanut Avenue, Building 3
Sarasota, FL 34236
Phone: 941-366-1552
Fax: 941-366-1553
Email: sarajazzcl@aol.com
Website: http://www.jazzclubsarasota.com

#581 • Jazz Club of Sarasota Scholarship

Type: Scholarship. Renewable.
Eligibility: Applicant must submit video audition and letter of reference. High school applicant must be enrolled in Manatee or Sarasota high school. This award must be used in the following years of study: • Freshman • Sophomore • Junior • Senior • Masters • Doctoral • Other postgraduate level
Deadline: April 1.
Award Amount: $ 500 - $ 1,500.
Number Of Awards: 2 - 6.
Applications Received: 16.

Odds Of Winning: 30% of applicants on average receive an award each year.
Contact: Rod Gibson, Chair of Scholarship Committee
1705 Village Green Parkway
Bradenton, FL 34209
Phone: 941-794-1105
Email: rgibson930@aol.com

NEW YORK TRI-STATE OWNERS & OPERATORS

Valley Stream, NY 11580
Phone: 800-537-4180
Website: http://www.mcdonaldsnymetro.com

#582 • McDonald's GospelFest Music Scholarship

Type: Scholarship. Not renewable.
Eligibility: Applicant must be a resident of the New York tri-state area, have a minimum 3.0 GPA, and demonstrate financial need. Selection is based upon community service or employment. This award must be used in the following years of study: • Freshman
Field(s) Of Study: Music.
Deadline: Varies.
Award Amount: $ 1,000 - $ 5,000.
Number Of Awards: 16.
Applications Received: 68.
Odds Of Winning: 24% of applicants on average receive an award each year.
Contact: Your high school guidance counselor.

VENTURA COUNTY COMMUNITY FOUNDATION

1317 Del Norte Road, Suite 150
Camarillo, CA 93010
Phone: 805-988-0196
Fax: 805-485-5537

#583 • Bernice Barnard Music Specialist Scholarhip

Type: Scholarship. Renewable.
Eligibility: Contact for details. This award must be used in the following years of study: • Freshman • Sophomore • Junior • Senior
Field(s) Of Study: Music education, music.
Deadline: March 9.
Award Amount: $ 500 - $ 1,000.
Number Of Awards: 5.
Applications Received: 8.
Odds Of Winning: 62% of applicants on average receive an award each year.
Contact: Gail Brown, Program Director

#584 • Helen Mathilda Yunker Music Scholarship

Type: Scholarship. Not renewable.

Eligibility: Contact for details. This award must be used in the following years of study: • Freshman
Field(s) Of Study: Music.
Deadline: Varies.
Award Amount: $ 1,000.
Number Of Awards: 1.
Applications Received: 3.
Odds Of Winning: 33% of applicants on average receive an award each year.
Contact: Gail Brown, Program Director

WOMEN BAND DIRECTORS INTERNATIONAL

345 Overlook Drive
West Lafayette, IN 47906
Phone: 765-463-1738
Email: agwright@gte.net

#585 • Volkwein Memorial Scholarship

Type: Scholarship. Not renewable.
Eligibility: Applicant must be a female band member and be planning to become an active band leader. This award must be used in the following years of study: • Freshman • Sophomore • Junior • Senior • Masters • Doctoral
Field(s) Of Study: Music education.
Deadline: December 1.
Award Amount: $ 300.
Number Of Awards: 1.
Applications Received: 100.
Contact: Linda Moorhouse, WBDI President
Department of Bands School of Music Louisiana State University
Baton Rouge, LA 70803
Phone: 504-388-2384
Fax: 504-388-4693
Email: moorhous@lsu.edu

#586 • Kathryn Siphers/Patricia Garren Memorial Scholarship

Type: Scholarship. Not renewable.
Eligibility: Applicant must be a female band member, and be planning to become an active band leader. This award must be used in the following years of study: • Freshman • Sophomore • Junior • Senior • Masters • Doctoral
Field(s) Of Study: Music education.
Deadline: December 1.
Award Amount: $ 300.
Number Of Awards: 1.
Applications Received: 100.
Contact: Linda Moorhouse, WBDI President
Department of Bands School of Music Louisiana State University
Baton Rouge, LA 70803
Phone: 504-388-2384
Fax: 504-388-4693
Email: moorhous@lsu.edu

#587 • Gladys Stone Wright Scholarship

Type: Scholarship. Not renewable.
Eligibility: Applicant must be a female band member, and be planning to become an active band leader. This award must be used in the following years of study: • Freshman • Sophomore • Junior • Senior • Masters • Doctoral
Field(s) Of Study: Music education.
Deadline: December 1.
Award Amount: $ 300.
Number Of Awards: 1.
Applications Received: 100.
Contact: Linda Moorhouse, WBDI President
Department of Bands School of Music Louisiana State University
Baton Rouge, LA 70803
Phone: 504-388-2384
Fax: 504-388-4693
Email: moorhous@lsu.edu

#588 • Martha Ann Stark Memorial Scholarship

Type: Scholarship. Not renewable.
Eligibility: Applicant must be a woman who is active in her band program and plans to become a band director. This award must be used in the following years of study: • Freshman • Sophomore • Junior • Senior • Masters • Doctoral
Field(s) Of Study: Music education.
Deadline: December 1.
Award Amount: $ 300.
Number Of Awards: 1.
Applications Received: 100.
Contact: Linda Moorhouse, WBDI President
Department of Bands School of Music Louisiana State University
Baton Rouge, LA 70803
Phone: 504-388-2384
Fax: 504-388-4693
Email: moorhous@lsu.edu

National Merit

NATIONAL MERIT SCHOLARSHIP CORPORATION

1560 Sherman Avenue, Suite 200
Evanston, IL 60201

#589 • Achievement Scholarship

Type: Scholarship. Renewable if recipient maintains full-time enrollment at an accredited school and makes normal academic progress.
Eligibility: Applicant must be a black American. Applicant must take the PSAT/NMSQT and indicate on the test answer sheet that he or she wishes to compete for the Achievement Scholarship. This award must be used in the following years of study: • Freshman
Deadline: Varies.
Award Amount: $ 500 - $ 2,000.
Number Of Awards: 800.
Contact: Your High School Guidance Counselor

#590 • Merit Scholarship

Type: Scholarship. Renewable.
Eligibility: Applicant must take the PSAT/NMSQT. This award must be used in the following years of study: • Freshman
Deadline: Varies.
Award Amount: $ 500 - $10,000.
Number Of Awards: 7,600.
Contact: High School Counselor for Student Bulletin

ROBERTS WESLEYAN COLLEGE

2301 Westside Drive
Rochester, NY 14624-1997
Phone: 716-594-6150
Fax: 716-594-6036
Website: http://www.rwc.edu

#591 • National Merit Scholarship

Type: Scholarship. Renewable. Minimum 3.4 GPA required to retain scholarship.
Eligibility: Applicant must be a National Merit finalist or National Merit semifinalist. National Merit finalist receives award amount that when combined with state grant and Pell Grant equals full tuition. Semifinalist award is one-half tuition. This award must be used in the following years of study: • Freshman
Deadline: Varies.
Award Amount: Partial tuition. Maximum award: full tuition.
Number Of Awards: 3.
Contact: John Smith, Assistant Director of Financial Aid

STANLEY WORKS SCHOLARSHIP PROGRAM

76 Batterson Park Road
Farmington, CT 06032
Phone: 860-409-1247
Fax: 860-409-1287
Email: mzdun@stanleywork.com

#592 • Stanley Works National Merit Scholarship

Type: Scholarship. Renewable. Good academic and disciplinary standing required for renewal.
Eligibility: Applicant must be a U.S. citizen and the

child of a Stanley employee or retiree. This award must be used in the following years of study: • Freshman • Sophomore • Junior • Senior
Deadline: December 31.
Award Amount: $ 1,000 - $ 4,000.
Number Of Awards: 4.
Applications Received: 39.
Odds Of Winning: 10% of applicants on average receive an award each year.
Contact: Mona Zdun, HR Administrator

UNIVERSITY OF ST. THOMAS

2115 Summit Avenue
St. Paul, MN 55105
Phone: 612-962-5000
Website: http://www.stthomas.edu

#593 • National Merit Scholarship

Type: Scholarship. Renewable.
Eligibility: Contact for details. This award must be used in the following years of study: • Freshman • Sophomore • Junior • Senior
Deadline: April 1.
Award Amount: $ 2,000.
Number Of Awards: Varies.
Contact: Lisa Moriarity, Assistant Director
Phone: 651-962-6553
Fax: 651-962-6553
Email: lamoriarity@stthomas.edu

Nuclear Engineering

AMERICAN NUCLEAR SOCIETY (ANS)

555 North Kensington Avenue
LaGrange Park, IL 60526
Phone: 708-352-6611
Website: http://www.ans.org

#594 • ANS Local Section Undergraduate Scholarship

Type: Scholarship. Not renewable.
Eligibility: Contact for details. This award must be used in the following years of study: • Sophomore • Junior • Senior
Field(s) Of Study: Nuclear engineering, nuclear science, other nuclear fields.
Deadline: Varies.
Award Amount: $ 2,000.
Number Of Awards: 1.
Contact: Scholarship Coordinator

Nursing

AMERICAN ASSOCIATION OF NEUROSCIENCE NURSES

ATTN: Neuroscience Nursing Foundation
4700 West Lake Avenue
Glenview, IL 60025
Phone: 888-557-2266
Fax: 847-375-6333
Email: infoaann@aann.org
Website: http://www.aann.org

#595 • Neuroscience Nursing Foundation Research Grant

Type: Grant. Not renewable.
Eligibility: Applicant must be a registered nurse and submit an abstract of the proposed research. This award must be used in the following years of study: • Masters • Doctoral • Other postgraduate level
Field(s) Of Study: Nursing.
Deadline: November 1.
Award Amount: $ 5,000.
Number Of Awards: 8.
Contact: See above.

AMERICAN LEGION - ARIZONA AUXILIARY

4701 North 19th Avenue, Suite 100
Phoenix, AZ 85015-3727
Phone: 602-241-1080
Fax: 602-264-0029
Email: amlegauxaz@uswest.net

#596 • Past President's Parley Nurses Scholarship

Type: Scholarship. Renewable. Recipient must reapply for renewal.
Eligibility: Applicant must be a U.S. citizen, a resident of Arizona for at least one year, and attending an accredited school in Arizona. Preference is given to an immediate family member of a veteran. Applicant must submit a photograph, a personal statement, three letters of reference, and transcripts of nursing grades. Selection is based upon character, scholarship, financial need, and initiative. This award must be used in the following years of study: • Sophomore • Junior • Senior • Masters • Doctoral • Other postgraduate level
Field(s) Of Study: Registered nurse.
Deadline: May 15.
Award Amount: $ 400.
Number Of Awards: 6.
Applications Received: 12.
Odds Of Winning: 50% of applicants on average

receive an award each year.
Contact: Past President's Parley Nurses Scholarship

AMERICAN LEGION AUXILIARY, DEPARTMENT OF IOWA

720 Lyon Street
Des Moines, IA 50309
Phone: 515-282-7987
Fax: 515-282-7583

#597 • Mary Virginia McRae Nurses Scholarship

Type: Scholarship. Not renewable.
Eligibility: Applicant must be an Iowa student attending or planning to attend an Iowa school. This award must be used in the following years of study: • Freshman • Sophomore • Junior • Senior
Field(s) Of Study: Nursing.
Deadline: June 1.
Award Amount: $ 400.
Number Of Awards: 1.
Applications Received: 75.
Contact: Marlene Valentine, Department Secretary/ Treasurer

AMVETS, ILLINOIS DEPARTMENT

2200 South Sixth Street
Springfield, IL 62703
Phone: 217-528-4713
Fax: 217-528-9896
Email: amvets@warpnet.net

#598 • Sad Sack Nursing Scholarship

Type: Scholarship. Renewable. Recipient must submit transcripts and reapply for renewal.
Eligibility: Applicant must have been accepted into a nursing program. This award must be used in the following years of study: • Freshman • Junior
Field(s) Of Study: Nursing.
Deadline: March 1.
Award Amount: $ 500.
Number Of Awards: 1 - 2.
Contact: AMVETS State Headquarters

ASSOCIATION OF REHABILITATION NURSES

4700 West Lake Avenue
Glenview, IL 60025
Phone: 847-375-4710
Fax: 847-375-4777
Email: info@rehabnurse.org

#599 • B.S. Nurs. Scholarship

Type: Scholarship. Not renewable.

Eligibility: Applicant must be a member of the Association of Rehabilitation Nurses, have at least two years of experience in rehabilitation nursing and still practicing in the field, and be currently enrolled in a degree program with good standing. This award must be used in the following years of study: • Freshman • Sophomore • Junior • Senior
Field(s) Of Study: Nursing.
Deadline: June 1.
Award Amount: $ 1,000.
Number Of Awards: 1.
Applications Received: 4.
Odds Of Winning: 25% of applicants on average receive an award each year.
Contact: Angie Forbes, Administrator
Phone: 847-375-4813
Fax: 847-375-4777
Email: info@rehabnurse.org

CALIFORNIA NURSES ASSOCIATION

ATTN: Scholarship Fund
200 Franklin Street, Third Floor
Oakland, CA 94612
Phone: 510-273-2200
Fax: 510-663-2771
Email: admin@calnurses.org

#600 • Shirley Titus Memorial Scholarship

Type: Scholarship. Not renewable.
Eligibility: Contact for details. This award must be used in the following years of study: • Masters • Doctoral • Other postgraduate level
Field(s) Of Study: Nursing.
Deadline: July 30.
Award Amount: $ 1,000 - $ 1,500.
Number Of Awards: 1.
Applications Received: 7.
Odds Of Winning: 14% of applicants on average receive an award each year.
Contact: See above.

COLORADO COMMISSION ON HIGHER EDUCATION

1300 Broadway 2nd Floor
Denver, CO 80203
Phone: 303-866-2723
Fax: 303-860-9750
Website: http://www.co.us/cche_dir/hecche.html

#601 • Colorado Nursing Scholarship

Type: Scholarship. Renewable.
Eligibility: Applicant must be a Colorado resident enrolled at an eligible Colorado school, and must agree to practice nursing in Colorado one year for each year the award is received. This award must be used in the following years of study: • Freshman •

Sophomore • Junior • Senior • Masters • Doctoral
Field(s) Of Study: Nursing.
Deadline: in May.
Award Amount: Varies.
Number Of Awards: Varies.
Contact: Rita Beachem, Colorado Nursing Scholarship

CONNECTICUT LEAGUE FOR NURSING

P.O. Box 365
Wallingford, CT   06492-0365
Phone: 203-265-4248
Fax: 203-265-5311
Email: cln@chime.net
Website: http://www.ctleaguefornursing.org

#602 • Nursing Scholarship

Type: Scholarship. Not renewable.
Eligibility: Applicant must be a Connecticut resident studying at a Connecticut nursing school. This award must be used in the following years of study: • Freshman • Sophomore • Junior • Senior • Masters • Doctoral
Field(s) Of Study: Nursing.
Deadline: October 1.
Award Amount: $ 1,000.
Number Of Awards: 2.
Applications Received: 20.
Odds Of Winning: 10% of applicants on average receive an award each year.
Contact: Mary W. Hickey, R.N., M.S., Executive Director

FOUNDATION OF THE NATIONAL STUDENT NURSES' ASSOCIATION, INC.

555 West 57th Street, Suite 1327
New York, NY 10019
Phone: 212-581-2215
Fax: 212-581-2368
Email: nsna@nsna.org
Website: http://www.nsna.org

#603 • FNSNA Scholarship

Type: Scholarship. Not renewable.
Eligibility: Applicant must be enrolled at a state-approved school of nursing or pre-nursing in an associate degree, baccalaureate, diploma, generic doctorate, or generic master's program. Award cannot be used for graduate education, unless it leads to a first degree in nursing. Selection is based upon academic achievement, financial need, and involvement in student nursing organizations and community service related to health care. Graduating high school seniors are not eligible. Applicant will automatically be considered for any specialty scholarships for which he or she is eligible. This

award must be used in the following years of study: • Sophomore • Junior • Senior
Field(s) Of Study: Nursing.
Deadline: February 1.
Award Amount: $ 1,000 - $ 2,000.
Number Of Awards: 55.
Applications Received: 2,000.
Contact: Receptionist, Scholarships

MICHIGAN LEAGUE FOR NURSING

33150 Schoolcraft Road, Suite 104
Livonia, MI 48150
Phone: 734-427-1900
Fax: 734-427-0104
Email: mln@oeonline.com

#604 • Nursing Student Scholarship

Type: Scholarship. Not renewable.
Eligibility: Applicant must complete one clinical class and be enrolled in a state of Michigan school. This award must be used in the following years of study: • Freshman • Sophomore • Junior • Senior
Field(s) Of Study: Nursing.
Deadline: Varies.
Award Amount: $ 500.
Number Of Awards: Varies.
Contact: See above.

NATIONAL ASSOCIATION OF HISPANIC NURSES SCHOLARSHIPS AND AWARDS

1501 Sixteenth Street, NW
Washington, DC 20036
Phone: 202-387-2477
Fax: 202-797-4353
Email: info@nahnhq.rog
Website: http://www.incacorp.com/nahn

#605 • National Association of Hispanic Nurses Scholarship

Type: Scholarship. Not renewable.
Eligibility: Applicant must be Hispanic and demonstrate financial need. Selection is based upon academic standing, two letters of recommendation, and essay. This award must be used in the following years of study: • Freshman • Sophomore • Junior • Senior • Masters • Doctoral • Other postgraduate level
Field(s) Of Study: Nursing.
Deadline: March 31.
Award Amount: $ 1,000 - $ 2,000.
Number Of Awards: 3 - 6.
Applications Received: 10.
Odds Of Winning: 40% of applicants on average receive an award each year.
Contact: Laura Sandals, Office Manager
Phone: 202-387-2477

NURSES EDUCATIONAL FUNDS, INC.

555 West 57th Street, Suite 1327
New York, NY 10019
Phone: 212-399-1428
Fax: 212-581-2368
Email: bbnef@aol.com
Website: http://www.n-e-f.org

#606 • M. Elizabeth Carnegie Scholarship

Type: Scholarship. Not renewable.
Eligibility: Applicant must be a black registered nurse and member of a professional nursing organization, be enrolled in a doctoral program in nursing or a nursing-related field, and be a U.S. citizen or have officially declared desire to become one. Selection is based upon academic achievement and evidence of service to the profession. Applicant must submit GRE or MAT scores. Send $10 check by February 1 to cover postage and handling when requesting application. This award must be used in the following years of study: • Masters • Doctoral • Other postgraduate level
Field(s) Of Study: Nursing.
Deadline: March 1.
Award Amount: $ 2,500 - $10,000.
Number Of Awards: 1.
Contact: Barbara Butler, Scholarship Coordinator

#607 • Nurses Educational Fund Scholarship

Type: Scholarship. Not renewable.
Eligibility: Applicant must be a registered nurse and a member of a professional nursing association, be enrolled full-time in a master's or doctoral program accredited by National League for Nursing and CCNE, and be a U.S. citizen or declare official intention of becoming one. Selection is based upon academic excellence; evidence of current and future service to the nursing profession is also important. Applicant must submit GRE or MAT scores. A $10 fee to cover postage and handling is required when requesting an application. This award must be used in the following years of study: • Masters • Doctoral • Other postgraduate level
Field(s) Of Study: Nursing.
Deadline: March 1.
Award Amount: $ 2,500 - $10,000.
Number Of Awards: 16.
Contact: Barbara Butler, Scholarship Coordinator

ODD FELLOWS AND REBEKAHS NURSING SCHOLARSHIP PROGRAM

Ellen F. Washburn
22 Munsey Avenue
Livermore Falls, ME 04254
Phone: 207-897-3173

#608 • Nurses Training Scholarship

Type: Scholarship. Renewable.
Eligibility: Applicant must be pursuing an R.N. in Maine. This award must be used in the following years of study: • Freshman • Sophomore • Junior • Senior • adult R.N. students.
Field(s) Of Study: Nursing.
Deadline: April 15.
Award Amount: $ 150 - $ 400.
Number Of Awards: 20 - 30.
Applications Received: 42.
Odds Of Winning: 52% of applicants on average receive an award each year.
Contact: Ellen F. Washburn, Secretary

TEXAS HIGHER EDUCATION COORDINATING BOARD

Student Financial Assistance
P.O. Box 12788, Capitol Station
Austin, TX 78711-2788
Phone: 512-427-6340
Website: http://www.thecb.state.tx.us

#609 • Scholarship for Rural Professional or Vocational Nursing Students

Type: Scholarship. Renewable. Recipient must reapply each year. No preference is given to renewals.
Eligibility: Applicant must be a Texas resident from a rural county, enrolled at least half time in a program leading to licensure as an L.V.N. or in an associate, bachelor, or graduate degree program in professional nursing. Applicant must attend a public or independent nonprofit institution in a nonmetropolitan county in Texas. This award must be used in the following years of study: • Freshman • Sophomore • Junior • Senior • Masters • Doctoral
Field(s) Of Study: Nursing.
Deadline: July 15.
Award Amount: $ 1,500 - $ 2,500.
Number Of Awards: 36.
Contact: Jane Caldwell, Director of Grants and Special Programs
Phone: 512-427-6455

#610 • Scholarship for Rural B.S.N. or Graduate Nursing Students

Type: Scholarship. Renewable. Recipient must reapply to retain scholarship. No preference is given to renewals.
Eligibility: Applicant must be a Texas resident from a rural county enrolled at least half time in a program leading to a B.S. in nursing or graduate degree in professional nursing at any nonprofit public or independent institution in Texas. This award must be used in the following years of study: • Freshman • Sophomore • Junior • Senior • Masters • Doctoral
Field(s) Of Study: Nursing.

Deadline: July 15.
Award Amount: $ 2,471.
Number Of Awards: 17.
Contact: Jane Caldwell, Director of Grants and Special Programs

#611 • Scholarship for L.V.N.s Becoming Professional Nurses

Type: Scholarship. Renewable. Recipient must reapply for renewal. No preference is given to renewals.
Eligibility: Applicant must be a Texas resident enrolled at least half time in a program leading to an associate, bachelor, or graduate degree in professional nursing at a Texas public or independent nonprofit institution. Applicant must have been previously licensed to practice as a vocational nurse. This award must be used in the following years of study: • Freshman • Sophomore • Junior • Senior • Masters • Doctoral
Field(s) Of Study: Nursing.
Deadline: July 15.
Award Amount: $ 1,500 - $ 2,500.
Number Of Awards: 58.
Contact: Jane Caldwell, Director of Grants and Special Programs

Optometry

NEW FOCUS, INC. AND THE OPTICAL SOCIETY OF AMERICA

Optical Society of America
2010 Massachusetts Avenue, NW
Washington, DC 20036
Phone: 202-416-1420
Fax: 202-416-6134
Email: awards@osa.org
Website: http://oas.org/awards

#612 • New Focus Student Award

Type: Contest. Not renewable.
Eligibility: Applicant must present an abstract and be nominated. This award must be used in the following years of study: • Sophomore • Junior • Senior • Masters • unspecified graduate
Field(s) Of Study: Optics.
Deadline: April 9.
Award Amount: $ 2,500 - $10,000.
Number Of Awards: 8 - 9.
Applications Received: 61.
Odds Of Winning: 15% of applicants on average receive an award each year.
Contact: Kristen Washington, Awards Coordinator

Other

AIRCRAFT ELECTRONICS ASSOCIATION (AEA) EDUCATIONAL FOUNDATION

4217 S. Hocker Drive
Independence, MO 64055
Phone: 816-373-6565
Fax: 816-478-3100
Email: info@aea.net
Website: http://www.aea.net

#613 • Lowell Gaylor Memorial Scholarship

Type: Scholarship. Not renewable.
Eligibility: Contact for details. This award must be used in the following years of study: • Freshman • Sophomore • Junior • Senior
Field(s) Of Study: Aircraft repair, avionics.
Deadline: February 15.
Award Amount: $ 1,000.
Number Of Awards: 1.
Applications Received: 150.
Odds Of Winning: 1% of applicants on average receive an award each year.
Contact: Mike Adamson, AEA Educational Foundation Executive Director

#614 • Bud Glover Memorial Scholarship

Type: Scholarship. Not renewable.
Eligibility: Contact for details. This award must be used in the following years of study: • Freshman • Sophomore • Junior • Senior
Field(s) Of Study: Aircraft repair, avionics.
Deadline: February 15.
Award Amount: $ 1,000.
Number Of Awards: 1.
Applications Received: 150.
Odds Of Winning: 1% of applicants on average receive an award each year.
Contact: Mike Adamson, AEA Educational Foundation Executive Director

#615 • Field Aviation Company, Inc. Scholarship

Type: Scholarship. Not renewable.
Eligibility: Applicant must attend an accredited institution in Canada. This award must be used in the following years of study: • Freshman • Sophomore • Junior • Senior
Field(s) Of Study: Aircraft repair, avionics.
Deadline: February 15.
Award Amount: $ 1,000.
Number Of Awards: 1.
Applications Received: 150.

Odds Of Winning: 1% of applicants on average receive an award each year.
Contact: Mike Adamson, AEA Educational Foundation Executive Director

#616 • Northern Airborne Technology Scholarship

Type: Scholarship. Not renewable.
Eligibility: Applicant must attend an accredited institution in Canada. This award must be used in the following years of study: • Freshman • Sophomore • Junior • Senior
Field(s) Of Study: Aircraft repair, avionics.
Deadline: February 15.
Award Amount: $ 1,000.
Number Of Awards: 1.
Applications Received: 150.
Odds Of Winning: 1% of applicants on average receive an award each year.
Contact: Mike Adamson, AEA Educational Foundation Executive Director

#617 • B.F. Goodrich Scholarship

Type: Scholarship. Not renewable.
Eligibility: Contact for details. This award must be used in the following years of study: • Freshman • Sophomore • Junior • Senior
Field(s) Of Study: Aircraft repair, avionics.
Deadline: February 15.
Award Amount: $ 2,500.
Number Of Awards: 1.
Applications Received: 150.
Odds Of Winning: 1% of applicants on average receive an award each year.
Contact: Mike Adamson, AEA Educational Foundation Executive Director

#618 • Mid-Continent Instrument Scholarship

Type: Scholarship. Not renewable.
Eligibility: Contact for details. This award must be used in the following years of study: • Freshman • Sophomore • Junior • Senior
Field(s) Of Study: Avionics.
Deadline: February 15.
Award Amount: $ 1,000.
Number Of Awards: 1.
Applications Received: 150.
Odds Of Winning: 1% of applicants on average receive an award each year.
Contact: Mike Adamson, AEA Educational Foundation Executive Director

#619 • Dutch and Ginger Arver Scholarship

Type: Scholarship. Not renewable.
Eligibility: Contact for details. This award must be used in the following years of study: • Freshman • Sophomore • Junior • Senior

Field(s) Of Study: Avionics.
Deadline: February 15.
Award Amount: $ 1,000.
Number Of Awards: 1.
Applications Received: 150.
Odds Of Winning: 1% of applicants on average receive an award each year.
Contact: Mike Adamson, AEA Educational Foundation Executive Director

AMERICAN FOREIGN SERVICE ASSOCIATION (AFSA)

2101 E Street, NW
Washington, DC 20037
Phone: 202-338-4045
Fax: 202-338-6820
Email: dec@afsa.org
Website: http://www.afsa.org

#620 • AFSA Financial Aid Scholarship

Type: Scholarship. Renewable if recipient maintains minimum 2.0 GPA and full-time status (12 credit hours).
Eligibility: Applicant must be a dependent of a U.S. government Foreign Service employee and must complete at least 12 credit hours per semester. Applicant must attend a college in the U.S. This award must be used in the following years of study: • Freshman • Sophomore • Junior • Senior
Deadline: February 6.
Award Amount: $ 500 - $ 3,000.
Number Of Awards: 50 - 60.
Applications Received: 150.
Odds Of Winning: 40% of applicants on average receive an award each year.
Contact: Lori Dec, Scholarship Administrator
Email: dec@afsa.org

#621 • AFSA/AAFSW Merit Award

Type: Scholarship. Not renewable.
Eligibility: Applicant must be a dependent of a U.S. government Foreign Service employee (active or retired). Membership in the American Foreign Service Association (AFSA) or the Association of American Foreign Service Women (AAFSW) is required. This award must be used in the following years of study: • Freshman
Deadline: February 6.
Award Amount: $ 100 - $ 1,000.
Number Of Awards: 25 - 35.
Applications Received: 100.
Odds Of Winning: 30% of applicants on average receive an award each year.
Contact: Lori Dec, Scholarship Administrator
Email: dec@afsa.org

AMERICAN LEGION - MAINE

American Legion State Headquarters
P.O. Box 900
Waterville, ME 04901
Phone: 207-873-3229
Fax: 207-872-0501
Email: legionme@wtul.net

#622 • American Legion Children and Youth Scholarship

Type: Scholarship. Not renewable.
Eligibility: Selection is based upon financial need. Letters of recommendation and transcripts required. This award must be used in the following years of study: • Freshman • Sophomore • Junior • Senior • Masters • Doctoral • Other postgraduate level
Deadline: April 10.
Award Amount: $ 500.
Number Of Awards: 7.
Applications Received: 500.
Contact: Scholarship Administrator

CAMPUS SAFETY, HEALTH, AND ENVIRONMENTAL MANAGEMENT ASSOCIATION (CSHEMA)

1121 Spring Lake Drive
Itasca, IL 60143-3201
Phone: 630-775-2360
Fax: 630-775-2185
Email: Merrittj@NSC.org
Website: http://www.nsc.org/mem/campus.htm

#623 • CSHEMA Scholarship Award

Type: Scholarship. Not renewable.
Eligibility: Applicant must be a full-time student. Essay and transcripts required. This award must be used in the following years of study: • Freshman • Sophomore • Junior
Field(s) Of Study: Allied health, biochemistry, biology, chemistry, environmental affairs, health, medicine, nursing, safety.
Deadline: March 31.
Award Amount: $ 2,000.
Number Of Awards: 1.
Applications Received: 200.
Odds Of Winning: Less than 1% of applicants on average receive an award each year.
Contact: Judith Merritt, Manager

EF EDUCATIONAL TOURS

Global Citizen Program One Education Street
Cambridge, MA 02141
Phone: 800-637-8222
Fax: 617-619-1001
Email: scholarships@ef.com
Website: http://www.eftours.com

#624 • Global Citizen Awards

Type: Scholarship. Not renewable.
Eligibility: Applicant must be nominated by high school and must submit essay on what it means to be a global citizen. Award includes a 10-day tour of Europe. This award must be used in the following years of study: • Freshman
Deadline: February 15.
Award Amount: $ 1,000.
Number Of Awards: 12.
Applications Received: 1,500.
Contact: Scholarship Contact
Email: scholarships@ef.com

FLEET RESERVE ASSOCIATION - PEARL HARBOR/HONOLULU BRANCH 46

P.O. Box 6067
Honolulu, HI 96818
Phone: 808-422-2121
Fax: 808-423-6707
Email: secbr46@aloha.com

#625 • Branch 46 Scholarship

Type: Scholarship. Not renewable.
Eligibility: Applicant must be the child or spouse of a regular member of Branch 46, Fleet Reserve Association, in good standing as of April 1, or the child of a deceased regular member in good standing, or a member of Unit 46 whose sponsor is a regular member of Branch 46 in good standing. Selection based on scholastic merit, character, leadership, and financial need. This award must be used in the following years of study: • Freshman • Sophomore • Junior • Senior • Masters • Doctoral • Other postgraduate level
Deadline: April 15.
Award Amount: $ 1,000.
Number Of Awards: 1.
Applications Received: 4.
Odds Of Winning: 25% of applicants on average receive an award each year.
Contact: Romona Greman, Branch Secretary
Phone: 808-422-2121
Email: exdir01@aol.com

FOUNDATION OF FLEXOGRAPHIC TECHNICAL ASSOCIATION (FFTA) SCHOLARSHIP COMMITTEE

900 Marconi Avenue
Ronkonkoma, NY 11779
Phone: 631-737-6020
Fax: 631-737-6813
Website: http://www.fta-ffta.org

#626 • FFTA Scholarship Competition

Type: Scholarship. Renewable. Recipient must

reapply for renewal.
Eligibility: Applicant must have a minimum 3.0 GPA.
This award must be used in the following years of study:
• Freshman • Sophomore • Junior • Senior
Field(s) Of Study: Flexography.
Deadline: Varies.
Award Amount: $ 2,000.
Number Of Awards: 19.
Applications Received: 105.
Odds Of Winning: 31% of applicants on average
receive an award each year.
Contact: Shelley Rubin, Educational Coordinator

IOWA COLLEGE STUDENT AID COMMISSION

200 Tenth Street, Fourth Floor
Des Moines, IA   50309-3609
Phone: 515-281-3501
Fax: 515-242-5996
Email: iscac@max.state.ia.us
Website: http://www.iowacollegeaid.org

#627 • Governor Terry E. Branstad Iowa State Fair Scholarship

Type: Scholarship. Not renewable.
Eligibility: Applicant must be a graduating senior
from an Iowa high school planning to enroll in an
Iowa college or university and actively participate in
the Iowa State Fair. This award must be used in the
following years of study: • Freshman
Field(s) Of Study: Please contact for more
information.
Deadline: Varies.
Award Amount: $ 1,000.
Number Of Awards: 4.
Contact: Brenda Nicholson-Easter, Director, Special
Programs or High School Guidance Counselor
Phone: 515-242-6710
Email: brenda.easter@csac.state.ia.us

KANKAKEE COUNTY COMMUNITY SERVICES

341 North St. Joseph Avenue
P.O. Box 2216
Kankakee, IL   60901
Phone: 815-933-7883
Fax: 815-933-0635

#628 • Kankakee County Community Services Scholarship

Type: Scholarship. Renewable. Reapplication
required for renewal.
Eligibility: Applicant must be from a low-income
family and plan to attend an Illinois school. Selection
is based upon field of interest, financial need,
community involvement, and academic acheivement.

This award must be used in the following years of study:
• Freshman • Sophomore • Junior • Senior • Masters •
Doctoral • Other postgraduate level
Deadline: May 15.
Award Amount: $ 1,000 - $ 1,100.
Number Of Awards: 3.
Applications Received: 30.
Odds Of Winning: 10% of applicants on average
receive an award each year.
Contact: Carlotta Robinson, Human Services
Assistant

MCMANNIS EDUCATIONAL TRUST FUND

Executive Director
Marine Bank Trust Division
P.O. Box 8480
Erie, PA   16553
Phone: 814-871-9324

#629 • William J. and A. Haskell McMannis Educational Trust Fund Scholarship

Type: Scholarship. Not renewable.
Eligibility: Contact for details. This award must be
used in the following years of study: • Freshman •
Sophomore • Junior • Senior • Masters
Deadline: Varies.
Award Amount: $ 200 - $ 5,000.
Number Of Awards: Varies.
Contact: Your college financial aid office

MINNESOTA HIGHER EDUCATION SERVICES OFFICE DIVISION OF STUDENT FINANCIAL AID

1450 Energy Park Drive, Suite 350
St. Paul, MN   55108-5227
Phone: 800-657-3866, 651 642-0567
Email: info@heso.state.mn.us
Website: http://www.heso.state.mn.us

#630 • Post-Secondary Child Care Grant

Type: Grant. Renewable. Applicant must reapply for
renewal.
Eligibility: Applicant must be pursuing a
nonsectarian program, be a U.S. citizen or permanent
resident, meet state residency requirements, be
enrolled at least half-time, be in the first four years of
postsecondary education, must not be in default on a
student loan, must not receive AFDC, must have a
child 12 years or younger, and must meet eligible
income guidelines. This award must be used in the
following years of study: • Freshman • Sophomore •
Junior • Senior
Deadline: Varies.
Award Amount: $ 300 - $ 2,000.
Number Of Awards: 1,533.

Contact: Financial Aid Division Staff
Email: larter@heso.state.mn.us

NATIONAL AIR TRANSPORTATION FOUNDATION

4226 King Street
Alexandria, VA 22302
Phone: 703-845-9000
Fax: 703-845-8176

#631 • Pioneers of Flight Scholarship

Type: Scholarship. Renewable if recipient maintains satisfactory academic performance.
Eligibility: Contact for details. This award must be used in the following years of study: • Sophomore • Junior
Field(s) Of Study: Aviation.
Deadline: Last Friday in November.
Award Amount: $ 2,500.
Number Of Awards: 4.
Applications Received: 35.
Contact: Tracy Thompson, Manager, Administration
4226 King Street
Alexandria, VA 22303
Phone: 703-845-9000
Fax: 703-845-8176

NATIONAL QUILTING ASSOCIATION, INC. (NQA)

NQA Grant Chairperson
P.O. Box 393
Ellicott City, MD 21041
Phone: 410-461-5733
Fax: 410-461-3693
Email: nqa@erols.com
Website: http://www.his.com/~queenb/nqa

#632 • NQA Grant

Type: Grant. Renewable. Reapplication is required for renewal.
Eligibility: Applicant must submit a resume including education and experience in research and/or quiltmaking and a self-addressed, stamped envelope. Selection is based upon education, individual research on the history of quilts and quiltmakers, experimental work in quiltmaking, group quilt research projects, and outreach to the community through the art of quiltmaking. This award must be used in the following years of study: • Masters • Doctoral • Other postgraduate level
Deadline: October 15.
Award Amount: Varies.
Number Of Awards: 4.
Contact: Grant Chairperson
Phone: 410-461-5733
Email: nga@erols.com

NATIONAL TOURISM FOUNDATION (NTF)

546 East Main Street
Lexington, KY 40508
Phone: 800–682-8886
Fax: 606-226-4414
Email: scudderb@mgtserv.com
Website: http://www.ntaonline.com

#633 • Treadway Inns, Hotels, and Resorts Scholarship

Type: Scholarship. Not renewable.
Eligibility: Applicant must have a minimum 3.0 GPA. Applicants must submit a NTF scholarship application, two recommendation letters (one from a tourism-related faculty member and the other from a professional in the tourism industry), a resume, transcripts, and an essay. This award must be used in the following years of study: • Junior • Senior
Field(s) Of Study: Travel/tourism.
Deadline: April 15.
Award Amount: $ 500.
Number Of Awards: 1.
Contact: Brooks A. Scudder, Assistant Exec. Director

RECORDING FOR THE BLIND AND DYSLEXIC

20 Roszel Road
Princeton, NJ 08540-5443
Phone: 609-520-0606
Fax: 609-520-7990

#634 • Marion Huber Learning through Listening Awards

Type: Scholarship. Not renewable.
Eligibility: Applicant must have a specific learning disability, be registered with Recording for the Blind and Dyslexic for at least one year prior to application, demonstrate leadership, enterprise, and service skills, and have an overall minimum "B" grade average. This award must be used in the following years of study: • Freshman
Deadline: February 21.
Award Amount: $ 2,000 - $ 6,000.
Number Of Awards: 6.
Applications Received: 180.
Odds Of Winning: 3% of applicants on average receive an award each year.
Contact: Public Affairs Office
Phone: 800-221-4792

ROTARY FOUNDATION OF ROTARY INTERNATIONAL

One Rotary Center
1560 Sherman Avenue

Evanston, IL 60201-3698
Phone: 847-866-3000
Fax: 847-328-8554
Website: http://www.rotary.org

#635 • Academic Year Ambassadorial Scholarship

Type: Scholarship. Not renewable.
Eligibility: Applicant must be a citizen of a country in which there is a Rotary club, have completed at least two years of college course work or two years of post-secondary employment in a recognized vocation, and submit essay, recommendations, club endorsement, transcripts, and language ability forms. Preference is given to disabled applicants and Rotoract club members. Rotarians, Honorary Rotarians, and employees of Rotary entities are not eligible; spouses, children/grandchildren, spouses of children/grandchildren, and parents/grandparents of living Rotarians/Honorary Rotarians/Rotary employees are not eligible. Award may be used at institutions assigned by Rotary Foundation Trustees only. This award must be used in the following years of study: • Junior • Senior • Masters • Doctoral • Workers in recognized vocations
Deadline: varies by individual Rotary Club.
Award Amount: $11,000 - $25,000.
Number Of Awards: 1,000.
Contact: Local Rotary club

SAFE ASSOCIATION

Embry-Riddle Aeronautical University
3200 North Willow Creek Road
Prescott, AZ 86301-8662
Phone: 520-708-3765
Fax: 520-708-3893
Email: lupind@pr.erau.edu
Website: http://www.pr.erau.edu

#636 • SAFE Association Scholarship

Type: Scholarship. Not renewable.
Eligibility: Applicant must be enrolled in a program of study with an emphasis or minor relating to safety or survival. This award must be used in the following years of study: • Senior
Field(s) Of Study: Safety/survival.
Deadline: June 1.
Award Amount: $ 1,000.
Number Of Awards: 1.
Applications Received: 75.
Odds Of Winning: 1% of applicants on average receive an award each year.
Contact: Daniel A. Lupin, Director of Financial Aid

SCHOOL TO WORK FOUNDATION

303 E. Gurley Street # 506
Prescott, AZ 86301

Phone: 520-443-9941, extension 10
Fax: 520-443-9942
Email: info@stwnews.org
Website: http://www.stwnews.org

#637 • STW Foundation Individual Award

Type: Grant. Not renewable.
Eligibility: Contact for details. This award must be used in the following years of study: • Freshman • Sophomore • Junior • Senior • Masters • Doctoral • Other postgraduate level
Deadline: Varies.
Award Amount: $ 25 - $ 1,500.
Number Of Awards: 21 - 53.
Applications Received: 128.
Odds Of Winning: 41% of applicants on average receive an award each year.
Contact: Rachael Long, 501c3 Grant Administrator

TEXAS SHEEP AND GOAT RAISING AUXILIARY

Debbie McMullan
P.O. Box 516
Iraan, TX 79744
Phone: 915-639-2208

#638 • Congressional Letter Writing Contest

Type: Contest. Not renewable.
Eligibility: Applicant must write a letter on "Is Environmental Education Biased?" to the state senator and state representative from his or her district. Letter must be pro-American agriculture and pro-private property rights. This award must be used in the following years of study: • Freshman • Sophomore • Junior • Senior • Masters • Doctoral • Other postgraduate level • High school juniors
Deadline: July 31.
Award Amount: $ 500 - $ 1,000.
Number Of Awards: Varies.
Applications Received: 100.
Contact: Debbie McMullan, Chairman

TREACY COMPANY

Box 1700
Helena, MT 59624-1700

#639 • Treacy Company Scholarship

Type: Scholarship. Renewable.
Eligibility: Contact for details. This award must be used in the following years of study: • Freshman • Sophomore
Deadline: June 15.
Award Amount: $ 400.
Number Of Awards: 75.
Contact: James O'Connell, Chairman

Pharmacy

AUXILIARY TO THE SONS OF UNION VETERANS OF THE CIVIL WAR

1016 Gorman Street
Philadelphia, PA 19116
Phone: 215-673-1688
Email: marauxsuv@aol.com

#640 • National President's Scholarship

Type: Scholarship. Not renewable.
Eligibility: Preference given to members of Auxiliary or relatives of members, but not required. This award must be used in the following years of study: • Freshman • Sophomore • Junior • Senior
Deadline: January 31.
Award Amount: $ 400.
Number Of Awards: 1.
Contact: Margaret Atkinson, Past National President

NORTHWEST PHARMACISTS COALITION

P.O. Box 22975
Seattle, WA 96122
Phone: 425-746-9618

#641 • NPC Pre-Pharmacy Scholarship

Type: Scholarship. Renewable. Reapplication is required for renewal.
Eligibility: Applicant must be a Washington resident of black ethnic origin, meet community college or university requirements, and submit a written essay and transcripts. This award must be used in the following years of study: • Freshman • Sophomore • Junior
Field(s) Of Study: Pharmacy.
Deadline: May 1.
Award Amount: $ 100 - $ 1,000.
Number Of Awards: 1 - 3.
Contact: See above.

PENNSYLVANIA PHARMACISTS ASSOCIATION

508 North 3rd Street
Harrisburg, PA 17101
Phone: 215-945-5107
Fax: 215-945-2818

#642 • Pharmacists Scholarhsip

Type: Scholarship. Not renewable.
Eligibility: Applicant must be a resident of Bucks County, Pa., and demonstrate financial need. This award must be used in the following years of study: • Senior
Field(s) Of Study: Pharmacy.
Deadline: April 30.
Award Amount: $ 500.
Number Of Awards: 3 - 5.
Applications Received: 12.
Odds Of Winning: 25% of applicants on average receive an award each year.
Contact: See above.

Physical Sciences

ACIL

1629 K Street, NW
Washington, DC 20006
Phone: 202-887-5872
Fax: 202-887-0021
Email: cparr@acil.org
Website: http://www.acil.org

#643 • ACIL Scholarship

Type: Scholarship. Not renewable.
Eligibility: Awards annually rotate among four geographical divisions, Central, Eastern, Southern, and Western. Applicant must submit a resume or personal statement, two letters of recommendation, transcripts, and information on any other scholarships or grant aid that is currently being received. This award must be used in the following years of study: • Junior • Senior • Other postgraduate level
Field(s) Of Study: Biology, chemistry, engineering, environmental science, geology, physics.
Deadline: Mid-April.
Award Amount: $ 2,000.
Number Of Awards: 1 - 2.
Contact: Connie Parr, Administrative Assistant

ASPRS, THE IMAGING AND GEOSPATIAL INFORMATION SOCIETY

ASPRS Awards Program, Suite 210
5410 Grosvenor Lane
Bethesda, MD 20814-2160
Phone: 301-493-0290
Fax: 301-493-0208
Email: scholarships@asprs.org
Website: http://www.asprs.org

#644 • Space Imaging EOSAT Award for Application of Digital Landsat TM Data

Type: Scholarship. Not renewable.
Eligibility: Applicant must be enrolled full time at a college or university with image-processing facilities.

This award must be used in the following years of study:
• Sophomore • Senior • Doctoral
Field(s) Of Study: Photogrammetry, remote sensing.
Deadline: December 1.
Award Amount: Partial tuition. Grant of data valued up to $4,000.
Number Of Awards: 1.
Applications Received: 4.
Odds Of Winning: 25% of applicants on average receive an award each year.
Contact: Jesse Winch, Program Manager
Email: jwinch@asprs.org

Physical/Occupational Therapy

EASTER SEAL SOCIETY OF IOWA, INC.

Scholarship
P.O. Box 4002
Des Moines, IA 50333
Phone: 515-289-1933
Fax: 515-289-1281
Email: essia@netins.net

#645 • Easter Seal Scholarships

Type: Scholarship. Not renewable.
Eligibility: Applicant must be an Iowa resident majoring in a rehabilitation field, and must show financial need. This award must be used in the following years of study: • Sophomore • Junior • Senior • Masters • Doctoral • Other postgraduate level
Field(s) Of Study: Nursing, physical therapy, social work.
Deadline: March 1.
Award Amount: $ 1,000.
Number Of Awards: 3.
Contact: Deb Wissink, Executive Assistant

LIVING ENDOWMENT FUND, INC.

Scholarship Coordinator
P.O. Box 5127
High Point, NC 27262-5127
Phone: 336-869-2166
Fax: 336-887-8451
Email: ambucs@ambucs.com
Website: http://www.ambucs.com

#646 • AMBUCS Scholarship

Type: Scholarship. Not renewable.
Eligibility: Applicant must be a U.S. citizen. Selection is based upon financial need, commitment to local community, demonstrated academic accomplishment, compassion, integrity, and career objectives. Applicants must apply on-line only. This award must be used in the following years of study: •

Senior • Masters • Doctoral • Other postgraduate level
Field(s) Of Study: Occupational, physical, and speech and hearing.
Deadline: April 15.
Award Amount: $ 500 - $ 1,500.
Number Of Awards: 400.
Applications Received: 1,500.
Odds Of Winning: 27% of applicants on average receive an award each year.
Contact: April Quick, Scholarship Coordinator

Psychology

PARAPSYCHOLOGY FOUNDATION

228 East 71st Street
New York, NY 10021
Phone: 212-628-1550
Fax: 212-628-1559
Website: http://www.parapsychology.org

#647 • Eileen J. Garrett Scholarship

Type: Scholarship. Not renewable.
Eligibility: Applicant must have taken at least two courses and written at least one paper on parapsychology. This award must be used in the following years of study: • Freshman • Sophomore • Junior • Senior • Masters • Other postgraduate level
Field(s) Of Study: Parapsychology.
Deadline: July 15.
Award Amount: $ 3,000.
Number Of Awards: 1.
Applications Received: 200.
Contact: Michelle Whitfield

Race/Ethnicity

AMERICAN ASSOCIATION OF HISPANIC CPAS

100 North Main Street, PMB 406
San Antonio, TX 78205
Phone: 203-255-7003
Fax: 203-259-2872
Email: aahcpa@netscape.net
Website: http://www.aahcpa.org

#648 • American Association of Hispanic CPAs Scholarship

Type: Scholarship. Not renewable.
Eligibility: Applicant must be of Hispanic descent, have completed or be enrolled in at least an

intermediate accounting course, have a minimum 3.0 GPA, and submit transcripts, essay, letter of recommendation, current course schedule, and school's financial aid offer letter. Selection is based upon academic acheivement, financial need, and community involvement. This award must be used in the following years of study: • Junior • Senior • Masters • Doctoral • Other postgraduate level • College undergraduates for fifth year
Field(s) Of Study: Accounting.
Deadline: September 15.
Award Amount: $ 1,000 - $ 5,000.
Number Of Awards: 10 - 15.
Applications Received: 120.
Odds Of Winning: 13% of applicants on average receive an award each year.
Contact: Vivian M. Coto, C.P.A., Scholarships Director

AMERICAN INDIAN SCIENCE AND ENGINEERING SOCIETY

Scholarship Coordinator
P.O. Box 9828
Albuquerque, NM 87119-9828
Phone: 505-765-1052
Fax: 505-765-5608
Email: scholarships@aises.org
Website: http://www.aises.org

#649 • A.T. Anderson Memorial Scholarship

Type: Scholarship. Renewable. Recipient must reapply for renewal.
Eligibility: Applicant must be an enrolled member of a tribe with proof of tribal enrollment or certificate of Indian Blood, have a minimum 2.0 GPA, be a full-time student, and be a member of the American Indian Science and Engineering Society (membership information is included with the application). This award must be used in the following years of study: • Freshman • Sophomore • Junior • Senior • Masters • Doctoral
Field(s) Of Study: Engineering, medicine, natural resources, science.
Deadline: June 15.
Award Amount: $ 1,000 - $ 2,000.
Number Of Awards: Varies.
Contact: Scholarship Coordinator

#650 • Burlington Northern Santa Fe Foundation Scholarship

Type: Scholarship. Renewable for four years (eight semesters) or until a bachelor's degree is earned.
Eligibility: Applicant must be a Native American with proof of tribal enrollment or a certificate of Indian blood, plan to attend a four-year, accredited educational institution full time, and live in one of the states served by the Burlington Northern, Atchison,

Topeka, and Santa Fe Railway (Arizona, Colorado, Kansas, Minnesota, Montana, New Mexico, North Dakota, Oklahoma, Oregon, South Dakota, Washington, or San Bernardino County, Calif.). This award must be used in the following years of study: • Freshman
Field(s) Of Study: Business, Health Administration, Education, Science.
Deadline: March 31.
Award Amount: $ 2,500.
Number Of Awards: 5.
Contact: Scholarship Coordinator

AMERICAN PHYSICAL SOCIETY (APS)

One Physics Ellipse 4th Floor
College Park, MD 20740
Phone: 301-209-3232
Website: http://www.aps.org

#651 • APS Corporate-Sponsored Scholarship for Minority Undergraduate Students Who Major in Physics

Type: Scholarship. Renewable. Applicant must major in physics with satisfactory GPA to retain scholarship for one additional year.
Eligibility: Applicant must be a U.S. citizen of black, Hispanic, or Native American descent. This award must be used in the following years of study: • Freshman • Sophomore • Junior
Field(s) Of Study: Physics.
Deadline: Last Friday in February.
Award Amount: $ 2,000.
Number Of Awards: 26.
Contact: Arlene Modeste Knowles, Program Coordinator
One Physics Ellipse 4th Floor
College Park, MD 20740-3844
Phone: 301-209-3232
Fax: 301-209-0865
Email: knowles@aps.org

ARKANSAS DEPARTMENT OF HIGHER EDUCATION

114 East Capitol
Little Rock, AR 72201
Phone: 501-371-2000
Fax: 501-371-2001
Email: finaid@adhe.arknet.edu
Website: http://www.adhe.arknet.edu

#652 • Freshman/Sophomore Minority Grant

Type: Grant. Renewable.
Eligibility: Applicant must be Asian, African-American, or Hispanic, and attend an institution in Arkansas. This award must be used in the following

years of study: • Freshman • Sophomore
Field(s) Of Study: Education.
Deadline: Varies by institution.
Award Amount: $ 1,000.
Number Of Awards: Varies.
Applications Received: 290.
Contact: Grants

ARMSTRONG WORLD INDUSTRIES, INC.

P.O. Box 3231
Lancaster, PA 17604
Phone: 717-397-0611
Website: http://www.armstrong.com

#653 • Armstrong Multicultural Education Scholarship

Type: Scholarship. Not renewable.
Eligibility: Applicant must be a minority student (African-American, Hispanic, Asian), demonstrate financial need, academic excellence, and leadership qualities, and submit a personal statement. Applications available at financial aid offices of designated schools. This award must be used in the following years of study: • Senior
Field(s) Of Study: Accounting, business administration, engineering, management information systems.
Deadline: March 15.
Award Amount: $ 1,000 - $ 1,500.
Number Of Awards: 30 - 40.
Applications Received: 60.
Odds Of Winning: 50% of applicants on average receive an award each year.
Contact: Karen J. Harnish, Coordinator
Phone: 717-396-2212
Email: kjharnish@armstrong.com

#654 • Armstrong Foundation - National Achievement Scholarship

Type: Scholarship. Renewable.
Eligibility: Applicant must be African-American and have National Merit Achievement status. This award must be used in the following years of study: • Freshman
Deadline: Varies.
Award Amount: $ 4,000.
Number Of Awards: 2.
Contact: Karen J. Harnish, Coordinator
Phone: 717-396-2212
Email: kjharnish@armstrong.com

ASSOCIATION ON AMERICAN INDIAN AFFAIRS, INC.

Box 268
Sisseton, SD 57262

Phone: 605-698-3998
Fax: 605-698-3316

#655 • AAIA/Adolph Van Pelt Special Fund for Indian Scholarships

Type: Scholarship. Not renewable.
Eligibility: Applicant must have at least one-fourth degree Indian blood from a federally recognized tribe. Award is based upon financial need and merit. Applicant must submit certificate of enrollment and blood quantum from his or her tribe or Bureau of Indian Affairs. This award must be used in the following years of study: • Freshman • Sophomore • Junior • Senior
Deadline: August 1.
Award Amount: $ 500 - $ 800.
Number Of Awards: 14.
Applications Received: 213.
Contact: Elena Stops, Scholarship Coordinator

#656 • Emergency Aid and Health Professions Scholarship

Type: Scholarship. Not renewable.
Eligibility: Applicant must have at least one-fourth degree American Indian/Alaskan Native blood from a federally recognized tribe and demonstrate financial need. Applicant must submit certificate of enrollment and blood quantum from his or her tribe or Bureau of Indian Affairs. This award must be used in the following years of study: • Freshman • Sophomore • Junior • Senior • Masters
Deadline: Varies.
Award Amount: $ 50 - $ 300.
Number Of Awards: Varies.
Contact: Elena Stops, Scholarship Coordinator
Phone: 605-698-3998

BLACKFEET NATION

ATTN: Higher Education Program
P.O. Box 850
Browning, MT 59417
Phone: 406-338-7539
Fax: 406-338-7530
Email: bhep@3rivers.net

#657 • Blackfeet Higher Education Scholarship

Type: Scholarship. Renewable. Reapplication is required.
Eligibility: Applicant must be a member of the Blackfeet tribe. This award must be used in the following years of study: • Freshman • Sophomore • Junior • Senior
Deadline: March 1.
Award Amount: $ 3,000 - $ 3,600.
Number Of Awards: 160.
Applications Received: 404.
Odds Of Winning: 47% of applicants on average

receive an award each year.
Contact: Higher Education Program

BLACKFOOT TRIBAL EDUCATION DEPARTMENT

P.O. Box 850
Browning, MT 59417-0850

#658 • Higher Education Grant Assistance

Type: Grant. Renewable.
Eligibility: Applicant must be an enrolled member of the Blackfeet Tribe and be actively pursuing an undergraduate degree. This award must be used in the following years of study: • Freshman • Sophomore • Junior • Senior
Deadline: March 1.
Award Amount: $ 3,100. Partial tuition. Maximum award: $3,000 (single student with no dependents); $3,600 (student with three or more dependents).
Number Of Awards: 160.
Applications Received: 322.
Odds Of Winning: 47% of applicants on average receive an award each year.
Contact: Blackfeet Higher Education Program

#659 • Adult Vocational Training Grant Assistance

Type: Grant. Not renewable.
Eligibility: Applicant must be an enrolled member of a federally recognized tribe, be between 18 and 35 years of age, be in need of training to obtain reasonable and satisfactory employment, be willing to accept full-time employment as soon as possible after completion of training, and be applying for the first time. If applying for repeat assistance, applicant must be underemployed or unable to work in primary occupation due to physical or other disabilities. Priority given first to Blackfeet Tribal members residing on and near the Blackfeet reservation, then to Blackfeet members residing off the reservation, then to members of other federally recognized tribes, as funding permits, and then to second training grant applicants, as funding permits. This award must be used in the following years of study: • Freshman • Sophomore
Deadline: March 1.
Award Amount: $ 3,100.
Number Of Awards: 25.
Applications Received: 50.
Odds Of Winning: 50% of applicants on average receive an award each year.
Contact: Blackfeet Higher Education Program

CABUGAO SONS AND DAUGHTERS ASSOCIATION OF HAWAII

45-230 Pahikaua Street

Kaneohe, HI 96744
Phone: 808-247-3784

#660 • Cabugao Sons and Daughters Association of Hawaii Incentive Award for Children of Members

Type: Scholarship. Not renewable.
Eligibility: Applicant must be a child of a member of Cabugao Sons and Daughters Association of Hawaii, have a minimum 3.5 GPA, and submit recommendation and essay. This award must be used in the following years of study: • Freshman
Deadline: May 31.
Award Amount: $ 500.
Number Of Awards: 2.
Applications Received: 2.
Odds Of Winning: 100% of applicants on average receive an award each year.
Contact: See above.

CALIFORNIA CHICANO NEWS MEDIA ASSOCIATION

University of Southern California School of Journalism
3502 Watt Way, ASCGW
Los Angeles, CA 90089-0281
Phone: 213-740-5263
Fax: 213-740-8524
Email: info@ccnma.org
Website: http://www.ccnma.org

#661 • Joel Garcia Memorial Scholarship

Type: Scholarship. Renewable. Recipient must reapply for renewal.
Eligibility: Applicant must be of Latino descent, be a California resident or be attending school in California, and submit essay, reference letters, transcripts, and samples of work. Selection is based upon committment to a career in journalism, financial need, scholastic achievement, and community awareness. This award must be used in the following years of study: • Freshman • Sophomore • Junior • Senior • Masters • Doctoral
Deadline: April 3.
Award Amount: $ 500 - $ 2,000.
Number Of Awards: 20 - 25.
Applications Received: 100.
Odds Of Winning: 25% of applicants on average receive an award each year.
Contact: Julio Moran, Executive Director

CALIFORNIA TEACHERS ASSOCIATION (CTA)

1705 Murchison Drive
P.O. Box 921
Burlingame, CA 94011-0921

Phone: 650-697-1400
Email: scholarships@cta.org
Website: http://www.cta.org

#662 • Martin Luther King, Jr. Memorial Scholarship

Type: Scholarship. Renewable.
Eligibility: Applicant must be a member of an ethnic minority and a member of the student CTA, a member of the CTA, or the dependent child of a CTA member. This award must be used in the following years of study: • Freshman • Sophomore • Junior • Senior • Masters • Doctoral • Other postgraduate level
Field(s) Of Study: Education.
Deadline: March 15.
Award Amount: $ 2,000.
Number Of Awards: Varies.
Contact: Human Rights Department

CHEYENNE-ARAPAHO TRIBE

P.O. Box 38
Concho, OK 73022
Phone: 405-262-0345
Fax: 405-262-0745

#663 • Cheyenne-Arapaho Tribal Scholarship

Type: Scholarship. Renewable every semester if recipient maintains 2.0 GPA, completes 12 or more hours, and continues to demonstrate financial need.
Eligibility: Applicant must be born into tribal membership with the Cheyenne-Arapaho tribe, possess at least one-quarter Cheyenne-Arapaho blood, have a minimum 2.0 GPA, and demonstrate financial need. This award must be used in the following years of study: • Freshman • Sophomore • Junior • Senior • Masters • Doctoral
Deadline: June 1 (fall), November 1 (spring), April 1 (summer).
Award Amount: $ 100 - $ 2,000.
Number Of Awards: 80 - 130.
Applications Received: 150.
Contact: Teresa Dorsett/Wanda Miller, Director/ Administrative Assistant of Scholarships
Phone: 405-262-0345 or 800-247-4612
Fax: 405-262-0745

CHOCTAW NATION OF OKLAHOMA

Higher Education Program
Drawer 1210
Durant, OK 74702-1210
Phone: 800-522-6170 or 580-924-8280
Fax: 580-924-1267

#664 • Higher Education Grant

Type: Grant. Renewable.
Eligibility: Applicant must have CDIB membership and be able to show Choctaw descent. Applicant must be working toward a degree and demonstrate financial need. This award must be used in the following years of study: • Freshman • Sophomore • Junior • Senior • Masters • Doctoral • Other postgraduate level
Deadline: March 15.
Award Amount: $ 800.
Number Of Awards: 500.
Applications Received: 1,800.
Contact: Liz Lee, Scholarships
Email: lizlee@choctawnation.com

#665 • Higher Education Scholarship

Type: Scholarship. Renewable.
Eligibility: Applicant must have CDIB membership and be able to show Choctaw descent. Applicant must be working toward a degree and demonstrate financial need. This award must be used in the following years of study: • Freshman • Sophomore • Junior • Senior • Masters • Doctoral • Other postgraduate level
Deadline: March 15.
Award Amount: $ 1,000.
Number Of Awards: 500.
Applications Received: 1,800.
Contact: Liz Lee, Scholarships
Email: lizlee@choctawnation.com

COLORADO COMMISSION ON HIGHER EDUCATION

1300 Broadway 2nd Floor
Denver, CO 80203
Phone: 303-866-2723
Fax: 303-860-9750
Website: http://www.co.us/cche_dir/hecche.html

#666 • Colorado Diversity Grant

Type: Grant. Renewable.
Eligibility: Applicant must be a member of an underrepresented minority group and a Colorado resident enrolled at an eligible Colorado school. This award must be used in the following years of study: • Freshman • Sophomore • Junior • Senior
Deadline: Varies.
Award Amount: Varies.
Number Of Awards: Varies.
Contact: Your College Financial Aid Office

COMMUNITY FOUNDATION SERVING RICHMOND AND CENTRAL VIRGINIA

7325 Beaufort Springs Drive, Suite 210
Richmond, VA 23225-8470
Phone: 804-330-7400
Fax: 804-330-5992
Email: sdavis@tcfrichmond.org
Website: http://www.tcfrichmond.org

#667 • Hayes E. Willis Memorial Scholarship

Type: Scholarship. Not renewable.
Eligibility: Applicant must be an African-American, U.S. citizen planning to enroll in a two- or four-year college or university in the continental U.S., and must demonstrate academic achievement and leadership or community service. This award must be used in the following years of study: • Freshman
Field(s) Of Study: Health, medicine.
Deadline: March 10.
Award Amount: $ 500 - $ 5,000.
Number Of Awards: Varies.
Contact: Susan Brown Davis, Senior Program Officer
Email: sdavis@tcfrichmond.org

CONTINENTAL SOCIETY, DAUGHTERS OF INDIAN WARS

Route 2, Box 184
Locust Grove, OK 74352-9652
Phone: 918-479-5679

#668 • CSDIW Scholarship

Type: Scholarship. Renewable.
Eligibility: Applicant must be a certified Native American tribal member with a minimum 3.0 GPA who plans to work on a reservation in the field of education or social service. Selection is based upon academic ability and commitment to the study of education or social service. Financial need is considered. This award must be used in the following years of study: • Junior • Senior
Field(s) Of Study: Education, social service.
Deadline: June 15.
Award Amount: $ 1,000.
Number Of Awards: 1.
Applications Received: 150.
Odds Of Winning: Less than 1% of applicants on average receive an award each year.
Contact: Alice E. Jacobs, National Scholarship Chairman

COUNCIL ON INTERNATIONAL EDUCATIONAL EXCHANGE

Scholarship Committee
205 East 42nd Street
New York, NY 10017
Phone: 212-822-2600
Email: info@ciee.org
Website: http://www.ciee.org/study/scholarships/index.htm

#669 • Bailey Minority Scholarship

Type: Scholarship. Not renewable.
Eligibility: Applicant must be a member of an underrepresented group and be planning to study abroad at a council study center or a Direct Enrollment Program. This award must be used in the following years of study: • Sophomore • Junior • Senior
Deadline: April 1 (summer and fall), October 26 (spring).
Award Amount: $ 500.
Number Of Awards: 20.
Applications Received: 200.
Odds Of Winning: 10% of applicants on average receive an award each year.
Contact: Janet Grunwald, Executive Assistant, International Study Programs
Email: baileygrants@ciee.org

CYMEDITHAS GYMREIG: WELSH SOCIETY OF PHILADELPHIA

367 South River Street
Wilkes-Barre, PA 18702
Phone: 570-822-4871

#670 • Cymdeithas Gymreig Scholarship

Type: Scholarship. Renewable. Recipient must reapply for renewal.
Eligibility: Applicant must be of Welsh descent, participate in Welsh events, and reside or attend a school within 150 miles of Philadelphia. Applicant must attend the Philadelphia Gymarfu game for application and interview. This award must be used in the following years of study: • Freshman • Sophomore • Junior • Senior
Deadline: March 1.
Award Amount: $ 500 - $ 1,000.
Number Of Awards: 6.
Applications Received: 100.
Odds Of Winning: 6% of applicants on average receive an award each year.
Contact: The Welsh Guild
Arch Street Presbyterian Church 1724 Arch Street
Philadelphia, PA 19103

ESPERANZA, INC.

May-Dugan Multiservice Center
4115 Bridge Avenue, Room 107
Cleveland, OH 44113
Phone: 216-651-7178
Fax: 216-651-7183
Email: hope4edu@aol.com

#671 • Esperanza Scholarship

Type: Scholarship. Renewable.
Eligibility: Applicant must be Hispanic and a resident of Cuyahoga, Geauga, Lake, Lorain, Medina, Portage, or Summit Counties, Ohio, have completed high school or earned a GED, and be accepted by an accredited college or university as a full-time student.

This award must be used in the following years of study: • Freshman • Sophomore • Junior • Senior • Masters • Doctoral • Other postgraduate level
Deadline: March 1.
Award Amount: $ 500 - $ 1,500.
Number Of Awards: 53.
Applications Received: 150.
Contact: Scholarship Administrator

FINLANDIA FOUNDATION TRUST

P.O. Box 665
Solvang, CA 93464

#672 • Finlandia Foundation Trust Scholarship Exchange Program and Grants

Type: Scholarship. Renewable. Recipient must reapply to retain scholarship.
Eligibility: Applicant must be a U.S. or Finnish college student. This award must be used in the following years of study: • Freshman • Sophomore • Junior • Senior • Masters • Doctoral • Other postgraduate level
Field(s) Of Study: Finnish studies.
Deadline: February 15.
Award Amount: $ 1,000 - $ 5,000.
Number Of Awards: 40.
Odds Of Winning: 50% of applicants on average receive an award each year.
Contact: Paul D. Halme, Trustee

GEORGE BIRD GRINNELL AMERICAN INDIAN CHILDREN'S FUND

11602 Montague Court
Potomac, MD 20854
Phone: 301-424-2440
Fax: 301-424-8281

#673 • Schuyler M. Meyer, Jr. Award

Type: Scholarship. Renewable. Reapplication required for renewal.
Eligibility: Applicant must be Native American or an Alaskan Native and show proof of tribal enrollment. Selection is based upon financial need, letters of recommendation, personal statement, and transcript. This award must be used in the following years of study: • Freshman • Sophomore • Junior • Senior • Masters • Doctoral • Other postgraduate level • nontraditional students
Deadline: June 1.
Award Amount: $ 1,000.
Number Of Awards: 9.
Contact: Paula Mintzies, President

#674 • Al Qoyawayma Award

Type: Scholarship. Not renewable.
Eligibility: Applicant must be a Native American or Alaskan Native, provide proof of tribal enrollment, and demonstrate skill in any of the arts. Selection is based upon financial need, letters of recommendation, personal statement, and transcript. This award must be used in the following years of study: • Freshman • Sophomore • Junior • Senior • Masters • Doctoral • Other postgraduate level
Field(s) Of Study: Science, engineering.
Deadline: June 1.
Award Amount: $ 1,000.
Number Of Awards: 1.
Contact: Paula Mintzies, President

GREEK WOMEN'S UNIVERSITY CLUB

7223 Oak Street
River Forest, IL 60305
Phone: 708-209-1355
Fax: 708-366-1594
Email: bjavaras@aol2.com

#675 • Greek Women's University Club Scholarship

Type: Scholarship. Renewable. Recipient must reapply to renew scholarship.
Eligibility: Applicant must be a woman of Greek descent, be a U.S. citizen and a permanent resident of the Chicago metropolitan area, be enrolled full-time, and have a minimum 3.0 GPA. This award must be used in the following years of study: • Junior • Senior • Masters • Doctoral
Deadline: July 9.
Award Amount: $ 500 - $ 1,000.
Number Of Awards: 1 - 3.
Applications Received: 15.
Odds Of Winning: 20% of applicants on average receive an award each year.
Contact: Barbara Kariotis-Javaras, Artemis Spellman, Scholarship Chairpersons

HENRY SACHS FOUNDATION

90 South Cascade Avenue, Suite 1410
Colorado Springs, CO 80903
Phone: 719-633-2353
Email: sachs@frii.com
Website: http://www.frii.com/~sachs

#676 • Henry Sachs Foundation Scholarship

Type: Scholarship. Renewable. Minimum 2.5 GPA with no failing, unsatisfactory, or incomplete grades and at least 12 credit hours per term are required to retain scholarship.
Eligibility: Applicant must be black, be a Colorado resident for the past five years, and demonstrate financial need. Minimum 3.4 GPA recommended. This award must be used in the following years of study: • Freshman

Deadline: March 1.
Award Amount: $ 1,500 - $ 7,000.
Number Of Awards: 50.
Applications Received: 200.
Odds Of Winning: 25% of applicants on average receive an award each year.
Contact: Lida Harris, Scholarships

HISPANIC BUSINESS COLLEGE FUND, INC.

One Thomas Circle, NW, Suite 1000
Washington, DC 20005
Phone: 202-775-7059 or 202-296-5400
Fax: 202-775-7006 or 202-296-3774
Email: hispaniccollegefund@earthlink.net
Website: www.hispanicfund.org

#677 • Hispanic College Fund Scholarship

Type: Scholarship. Not renewable.
Eligibility: Applicant must be a U.S. citizen of Hispanic origin residing in the continental United States or Puerto Rico, have a minimum 3.0 GPA, be enrolled full time, and demonstrate financial need. Activity in the school and/or community is also considered. Applicant must submit 250-word essay and letter of recommendation. This award must be used in the following years of study: • Freshman • Sophomore • Junior • Senior
Field(s) Of Study: Academic disciplines leading to a career in business.
Deadline: April 15.
Award Amount: $ 500 - $ 5,000. Partial Tuition. plus tuition and fees.
Number Of Awards: 146.
Applications Received: 780.
Odds Of Winning: 19% of applicants on average receive an award each year.
Contact: Idalia Pena, Program Manager

HISPANIC COLLEGE FUND, INC.

One Thomas Circle, NW, Suite 375
Washington, DC 20005
Phone: 202-296-5400
Fax: 202-296-3774
Email: hispanic.fund@cwixmail.com
Website: http://www.hispanicfund.org

#678 • Hispanic College Fund Scholarship

Type: Scholarship. Not renewable.
Eligibility: Applicant must have a minimum 3.0 GPA, be of Hispanic heritage, demonstrate financial need, and submit an essay and letter of recommendation. This award must be used in the following years of study: • Freshman • Sophomore • Junior • Senior
Field(s) Of Study: Business.

Deadline: April 15.
Award Amount: $ 500 - $ 5,000.
Number Of Awards: 146.
Applications Received: 764.
Odds Of Winning: 19% of applicants on average receive an award each year.
Contact: Idalia Pena, Program Manager

HISPANIC SCHOLARSHIP FUND (HSF)

One Sansome Street, Suite 1000
San Francisco, CA 94104
Phone: 415-445-9930 or 877-HSF-INFO
Email: info@hsf.net
Website: http://www.hsf.net

#679 • Hispanic Scholarship Fund General Scholarship

Type: Scholarship. Renewable. Recipient must reapply to renew scholarship.
Eligibility: Applicant must be a U.S. citizen or permanent resident, at least one-half Hispanic, and enrolled full time in a college or university in the U.S., have a minimum 2.5 GPA, and have earned a minimum of 15 college credits from an accredited school. Selection is based upon academic achievement, personal strengths, leadership, and financial need. For application, contact financial aid office or send business (9-inch-by-four-inch) self-addressed, stamped envelope. This award must be used in the following years of study: • Sophomore • Junior • Senior • Masters
Deadline: October 15.
Award Amount: $ 1,000 - $ 7,500.
Number Of Awards: 4,500.
Applications Received: 12,000.
Odds Of Winning: 40% of applicants on average receive an award each year.
Contact: Scholarship Program Selection Committee

HOPI TRIBE GRANTS AND SCHOLARSHIP PROGRAM

P.O. Box 123
Kykotsmovi, AZ 86039
Phone: 520-734-3533 or 800-762-9630
Fax: 520-734-9575
Email: flomakema@hopi.nsn.us

#680 • BIA Higher Education/Hopi Supplemental Grant

Type: Grant. Not renewable.
Eligibility: Applicant must be an enrolled member of the Hopi Tribe. Entering freshman applicant must have a minimum 2.0 GPA or minimum composite GED score of 45%. Continuing student applicant must have a minimum 2.0 GPA. Financial need is considered. This award must be used in the following

years of study: • Freshman • Sophomore • Junior • Senior • Masters • Doctoral • Other postgraduate level
Deadline: July 31 (fall), November 30 (spring), April 30 (summer).
Award Amount: $ 2,500.
Number Of Awards: 250.
Contact: Grants Administrator

#681 • Hopi Scholarship

Type: Scholarship. Not renewable.
Eligibility: Applicant must be an enrolled member of the Hopi Tribe. Applicant who is an entering freshman must rank in top tenth of class and have a minimum composite ACT score of 21 (combined SAT I score of 930). Applicant who is an undergraduate must have a minimum 3.0 GPA. Applicant who is graduate, post graduate, or professional student must have a minimum 3.2 GPA in graduate work. This award must be used in the following years of study: • Freshman • Sophomore • Junior • Senior • Masters • Doctoral • Other postgraduate level
Deadline: July 31.
Award Amount: $ 2,000.
Number Of Awards: 200.
Contact: Scholarship Administrator

#682 • Tuition/Book Scholarship

Type: Scholarship. Not renewable.
Eligibility: Applicant must be an enrolled member of the Hopi Tribe. This award must be used in the following years of study: • Freshman • Sophomore • Junior • Senior
Deadline: July 31 (fall), November 30 (spring), April 30 (summer).
Award Amount: Full tuition or partial tuition. Plus fees and books.
Number Of Awards: Varies.
Contact: Scholarship Administrator

INDIAN HEALTH SERVICE/U.S. DEPARTMENT OF HEALTH & HUMAN SERVICE

Twinbrook Metro Plaza
12300 Twinbrook Parkway, Suite 100
Rockville, MD 20852
Phone: 301-443-6197

#683 • Health Professions Preparatory Pregraduate Scholarship

Type: Scholarship. Renewable if recipient maintains good academic standing and at least part-time status.
Eligibility: Applicant must be a member of a federally recognized American Indian or Alaskan Native tribe, be a high school graduate or equivalent in good standing at current educational institution, have the capacity to complete a health professions

course of study, and be accepted or enrolled in a health professions pregraduate baccalaureate degree program. This award must be used in the following years of study: • Freshman • Sophomore • Junior • Senior
Field(s) Of Study: Predentistry, premedicine, preosteopathy.
Deadline: Varies.
Award Amount: Comprehensive-tuition. Partial Tuition. plus cost of books, travel, and other educational expenses.
Number Of Awards: Varies.
Contact: See above.

INSTITUTE OF CHINA STUDIES

7341 North Kolimar Street
Lincolnwood, IL 60712
Phone: 708-677-0982

#684 • Institute of China Studies Scholarship

Type: Scholarship. Renewable.
Eligibility: Applicant must be a U.S. citizen of Chinese heritage who speaks Mandarin. This award must be used in the following years of study: • Freshman • Sophomore • Junior • Senior
Field(s) Of Study: China studies.
Deadline: Varies.
Award Amount: $ 500 - $ 1,000. Partial Tuition.
Number Of Awards: Varies.
Contact: Dr. Harry Kiang, Director

INTERNATIONAL ORDER OF THE KING'S DAUGHTERS AND SONS

P.O. Box 1310
Brookhaven, MS 39602
Phone: 601-883-5418

#685 • North American Indian Scholarship

Type: Scholarship. Renewable.
Eligibility: Contact for details. This award must be used in the following years of study: • Freshman • Sophomore • Junior • Senior
Deadline: April 15.
Award Amount: $ 650.
Number Of Awards: 50 - 60.
Applications Received: 1,500.
Odds Of Winning: 4% of applicants on average receive an award each year.
Contact: Mrs. T.R. McConchie, Director, North American Indian Department
4831 Kempsville Greens Parkway
Virginia Beach, VA 23462-6439
Phone: 757-474-1488

ITALIAN CATHOLIC FEDERATION

675 Hegenberger Road Suite 110
Oakland, CA 94621
Phone: 888-423-1924
Fax: 510-633-9758
Website: http://home.earthlink.net/~icf1924

#686 • Italian Catholic Federation Scholarship Program

Type: Scholarship. Renewable.
Eligibility: Applicant must be Roman Catholic, wholly or partially of Italian ancestry, have a minimum 3.0 GPA , letters of recommendation, and financial need, and participate in church and community activities. This award must be used in the following years of study: • Freshman
Deadline: March 15.
Award Amount: $ 500 - $ 1,000.
Number Of Awards: 200.
Odds Of Winning: 39% of applicants on average receive an award each year.
Contact: Scholarship Administrator

ITALIAN-AMERICAN CULTURAL SOCIETY OF OCEAN COUNTY, INC.

P.O. Box 1602
Toms River, NJ 08754
Phone: 732-797-1400
Fax: 732-797-1400

#687 • Italian-American Cultural Society of Ocean County

Type: Scholarship. Not renewable.
Eligibility: Applicant must attend a high school in Toms River, N.J., be of Italian-American ancestry, and submit a 500-word essay. Selection is based upon financial need, SAT scores, class rank, and community and school activities and services. This award must be used in the following years of study: • Freshman
Deadline: February 1.
Award Amount: $ 1,000 - $ 1,500.
Number Of Awards: 3 - 7.
Applications Received: 40.
Odds Of Winning: 18% of applicants on average receive an award each year.
Contact: Guidence Directors

KATU

P.O. Box 2
Portland, OR 97207
Phone: 503-231-4691
Website: http://katu.citysearch.com

#688 • Thomas R. Dargan Minority Scholarship

Type: Scholarship. Renewable. Recipient must reapply for renewal.
Eligibility: Applicant must be a minority U.S. citizen, have a minimum 3.0 GPA, and attend an institution in Oregon or Washington or be a permanent resident of Oregon or Washington. Selection is based upon financial need, academic achievement, personal qualities, essay, and letters of recommendation. This award must be used in the following years of study: • Sophomore • Junior • Senior
Field(s) Of Study: Broadcasting, communications.
Deadline: April 30.
Award Amount: $ 4,000.
Number Of Awards: 2.
Applications Received: 10.
Odds Of Winning: 2% of applicants on average receive an award each year.
Contact: KATU Human Resources
Phone: 503-231-3506

MAE LASLEY OSAGE SCHOLARSHIP FUND

P.O. Box 690240
Tulsa, OK 74169-0240
Phone: 918-294-1904
Fax: 918-294-0920

#689 • Osage Scholarship

Type: Scholarship. Renewable.
Eligibility: Applicant must be an Osage Indian. This award must be used in the following years of study: • Freshman • Sophomore • Junior • Senior • Masters • Doctoral • Other postgraduate level
Deadline: Varies.
Award Amount: $ 1,000.
Number Of Awards: 10 - 15.
Applications Received: 50.
Odds Of Winning: 30% of applicants on average receive an award each year.
Contact: Cathy King, Administrative Assistant/ Secretary

MENOMINEE INDIAN TRIBE OF WISCONSIN

Menominee Tribal Education Office P.O. Box 910
Keshana, WI 54135
Phone: 715-799-5118
Fax: 715-799-1364
Email: vnuske@mail.wiscnet.net

#690 • BIA (Tribal) Grant

Type: Grant. Renewable if recipient maintains a minimum 2.0 GPA.
Eligibility: Applicant must be an enrolled member of

the Menominee Indian Tribe of Wisconsin. This award must be used in the following years of study: • Freshman • Sophomore • Junior • Senior
Deadline: In March (fall), in October (spring).
Award Amount: $ 100 - $ 2,200.
Number Of Awards: 135.
Applications Received: 146.
Odds Of Winning: 90% of applicants on average receive an award each year.
Contact: Gen Tomow or Elaine Peters, Program Assistant/Education Counselor
Phone: 715-799-5118/715 799-5120

MORRIS SCHOLARSHIP FUND

Midland Building 206 Sixth Avenue, Suite 900
Des Moines, IA 50309-4015
Phone: 515-282-8192
Fax: 515-282-9117
Email: dms@assoc-mgmt.com

#691 • Morris Scholarship

Type: Scholarship. Renewable. Recipient must reapply for renewal.
Eligibility: Applicant must be an ethnic minority, as defined by the Equal Employment Opportunity Commission, with a minimum 2.5 GPA and an Iowa high school graduate and resident attending a U.S. college or university or nonresident attending an Iowa college or university. Preference given to Iowa residents attending school in Iowa. This award must be used in the following years of study: • Freshman • Sophomore • Junior • Senior • Masters • Doctoral • Other postgraduate level
Deadline: March 1.
Award Amount: $ 1,500.
Number Of Awards: 30.
Contact: Sally Goode, Student Coordinator
Email: sgoode@assoc-mgmt.com

NATIONAL ORGANIZATION OF BLACK LAW ENFORCEMENT EXECUTIVES (NOBLE)

Pamela C. Chapman
4609 Pinecrest Office Park Drive, Suite F
Alexandria, VA 22312-1442
Phone: 703-658-1529
Fax: 703-658-9479
Email: pchapman@noblenatl.org
Website: http://www.noblenatl.org

#692 • Irlet Anderson Scholarship

Type: Scholarship. Not renewable.
Eligibility: Applicant must be an African-American with a minimum 2.5 GPA and financial need. This award must be used in the following years of study: • Freshman

Field(s) Of Study: Criminal justice, law enforcement, paralegal studies.
Deadline: April 1.
Award Amount: $ 1,000.
Number Of Awards: 1.
Applications Received: 30.
Odds Of Winning: 3% of applicants on average receive an award each year.
Contact: Pamela Chapman, Project Coordinator

NATIVE AMERICAN SCHOLARSHIP FUND, INC.

8200 Mountain Road, NE, Suite 203
Albuquerque, NM 87110
Phone: 505-262-2351
Email: nasf@nasf.com
Website: http://www.nasf.com

#693 • MESBEC Scholarships

Type: Scholarship. Renewable if student maintains respectable GPA.
Eligibility: Applicant must be at least one-quarter Native American and be an enrolled member of a U.S. tribe that is federally recognized, state-recognized, or terminated, with high GPA and test scores enrolled in a college or university seeking a baccalaureate degree, master's degree, or doctoral degree. This award must be used in the following years of study: • Freshman • Sophomore • Junior • Senior • Masters • Doctoral
Field(s) Of Study: Business, computers, education, engineering, fine arts, humanities, mathematics, science, social science.
Deadline: April 15 (fall), September 15 (spring), March 15 (summer).
Award Amount: $ 500 - $ 5,000.
Number Of Awards: 171 - 200.
Applications Received: 2,000.
Odds Of Winning: 38% of applicants on average receive an award each year.
Contact: Lucille Kelley, Director of Recruitment
8200 Mountain Road, NE Suite 203
Albuquerque, NM 87110
Phone: 505-262-2351
Fax: 505-262-0534

NEW YORK TRI-STATE OWNERS & OPERATORS

Valley Stream, NY 11580
Phone: 800-537-4180
Website: http://www.mcdonaldsnymetro.com

#694 • McDonald's African American Heritage Scholarship

Type: Scholarship. Not renewable.
Eligibility: Applicant must be an African-American

living in the New York tri-state area, must have a minimum 3.0 GPA, and must demonstrate financial need. Selection is based upon community service or employment. This award must be used in the following years of study: • Freshman
Deadline: March 1.
Award Amount: $ 1,000 - $ 5,000.
Number Of Awards: 42.
Contact: Your high school guidance counselor.

#695 • RMHC/HACER Scholarship

Type: Scholarship. Not renewable.
Eligibility: Applicant must be a U.S. citizen or permanent resident with at least one parent of Hispanic heritage. This award must be used in the following years of study: • Freshman
Deadline: Varies.
Award Amount: $ 2,500 - $10,000.
Number Of Awards: 64.
Applications Received: 600.
Odds Of Winning: 11% of applicants on average receive an award each year.
Contact: Your high school guidance counselor.

OFFICE OF INDIAN EDUCATION PROGRAMS

Code 522-Room 3512
19th and C Streets, NW
Washington, DC 20240
Phone: 202-208-3478
Fax: 202-219-9583
Email: garry_martin@ios.doi.gov

#696 • BIA Higher Education Grant

Type: Grant. Renewable.
Eligibility: Contact for details. This award must be used in the following years of study: • Freshman • Sophomore • Junior • Senior
Deadline: Varies.
Award Amount: Varies.
Number Of Awards: 3,000.
Applications Received: 9,300.
Contact: Grants Administrator

POLISH WOMEN'S CIVIC CLUB

Education Committee
P.O. Box 31967
Chicago, IL 60631-0967

#697 • Polish Women's Civic Club Scholarship

Type: Scholarship. Renewable. Recipient must reapply for renewal.
Eligibility: Applicant must be a U.S. citizen or permanent resident and a resident of Illinois with at least one parent of Polish descent. Selection is based upon academic ability and financial need. Photograph and letter of recommendation required. This award must be used in the following years of study: • Sophomore • Junior • Senior • Masters • Doctoral • Other postgraduate level
Deadline: June 28.
Award Amount: $ 500 - $ 2,000.
Number Of Awards: 5.
Applications Received: 60.
Contact: Scholarship Administrator

PRESBYTERIAN CHURCH (USA)

Office of Financial Aid for Studies
100 Witherspoon Street
Louisville, KY 40202-1396
Phone: 502-569-5745
Fax: 502-569-8766
Email: TimM@ctr.pusa.org
Website: http://www.pcusa.org

#698 • Native American Education Grant

Type: Grant. Renewable.
Eligibility: Applicant must be an Alaskan Native or Native American and a U.S. citizen or permanent resident. Preference given to members of the Presbyterian Church (USA). This award must be used in the following years of study: • Freshman • Sophomore • Junior • Senior • Masters • Doctoral • Other postgraduate level
Deadline: June 1.
Award Amount: $ 200 - $ 2,500.
Number Of Awards: 100.
Contact: Maria Alvarez, Associate for Program Management
Phone: 502-569-5760

SHARE AND CARE FOUNDATION

330 Momar Drive
Ramsey, NJ 07446
Phone: 201-825-0667
Fax: 908-273-0815
Email: seth@smcdna.com

#699 • Share and Care Undergraduate Scholarship

Type: Scholarship. Renewable for four years of undergraduate study if recipient maintains a minimum 3.0 GPA and if recipient's family income continues to be $60,000 or less per year.
Eligibility: Applicant must be of Indian origin (either born in India or have at least one natural parent born in India), have a minimum combined SAT I score of 1000, and have a family income of $60,000 or less. Applicant must be enrolling at an accredited school. Applicant must submit application, transcript, copies

of parents' tax returns, and two letters of recommendation. This award must be used in the following years of study: • Freshman
Deadline: May 15.
Award Amount: $ 1,000.
Number Of Awards: 5 - 7.
Applications Received: 28.
Odds Of Winning: 25% of applicants on average receive an award each year.
Contact: Dr. Kanan S. Patrawalla, Chairperson
Share and Care Scholarship Committee
33 Overlook Road, Suite 210
Summit, NJ 07901-3570
Phone: 908-598-0390

SONS OF ITALY FOUNDATION

219 East Street, NE
Washington, DC 20002
Phone: 202-547-2900
Email: osianat@aol.com
Website: http://www.osia.org/nlg.html

#700 • Sons of Italy Foundation National Leadership Grant

Type: Scholarship. Not renewable.
Eligibility: Applicant must be of Italian heritage and be a full-time student attending or planning on attending an accredited four-year institution who has demonstrated exceptional leadership qualities and a distinguished level of scholastic achievement. This award must be used in the following years of study: • Freshman • Sophomore • Junior • Senior • Masters • Doctoral • Professional degree
Deadline: January 30.
Award Amount: $ 4,000 - $10,000.
Number Of Awards: 12.
Applications Received: 400.
Odds Of Winning: 2% of applicants on average receive an award each year.
Contact: Danielle Grauso, Scholarship Coordinator
Phone: 202-547-5106
Email: osianat@aol.com

SWISS BENEVOLENT SOCIETY OF NEW YORK

Scholarship Director
608 Fifth Avenue #309
New York, NY 10020

#701 • Pellegrini Scholarship

Type: Grant. Renewable. Reapplication required for renewal.
Eligibility: Applicant must be of Swiss descent and a permanent resident of Connecticut, Delaware, New Jersey, New York, or Pennsylvania. This award must be used in the following years of study: • Freshman •

Sophomore • Junior • Senior • Masters • Doctoral
Deadline: March 31.
Award Amount: $ 500 - $ 3,000.
Number Of Awards: 50.
Applications Received: 59.
Odds Of Winning: 81% of applicants on average receive an award each year.
Contact: Annemarie Gilman, Executive Director

#702 • Medicus Student Exchange

Type: Grant. Not renewable.
Eligibility: Applicant must be of Swiss descent, be a permanent resident of Connecticut, Delaware, New Jersey, New York, or Pennsylvania, and attend a university in Switzerland. This award must be used in the following years of study: • Masters • Doctoral • Other postgraduate level
Deadline: March 31.
Award Amount: $ 4,000 - $ 5,000.
Number Of Awards: 1 - 4.
Applications Received: 1.
Odds Of Winning: 100% of applicants on average receive an award each year.
Contact: Annemarie Gilman, Executive Director

SYNOD OF THE TRINITY (PRESBYTERIAN CHURCH USA)

ATTN: Social and Racial Justice Ministry Unit
3040 Market Street
Camp Hill, PA 17011-4599
Phone: 717-737-0421
Fax: 717-737-8211
Email: scholarships@syntrinity.org
Website: http://www.syntrin.org

#703 • Racial-Ethnic Education Scholarship

Type: Scholarship. Not renewable.
Eligibility: Applicant must be African-American, Hispanic-/Latino-American, Asian-American, or Native American. This award must be used in the following years of study: • Freshman • Sophomore • Junior • Senior • vocational school students
Deadline: Varies.
Award Amount: $ 250 - $ 600.
Number Of Awards: 309.
Applications Received: 475.
Odds Of Winning: 65% of applicants on average receive an award each year.
Contact: Synod Scholarship Programs

UNITED SOUTH & EASTERN TRIBES SCHOLARSHIP FUND

711 Stewarts Ferry Pike, Suite 100
Nashville, TN 37214
Phone: 615-872-7900
Fax: 615-872-7417

Email: uset@bellsouth.net
Website: http://oneida-nation.net/uset/

#704 • United South & Eastern Tribes Scholarship

Type: Scholarship. Not renewable.
Eligibility: Applicant must be an enrolled member of one of 23 selected tribes. This award must be used in the following years of study: • Freshman • Sophomore • Junior • Senior • Masters • Doctoral
Deadline: April 30.
Award Amount: $ 500.
Number Of Awards: 4.
Contact: Turia Enloe, Scholarship Coordinator

WISCONSIN HIGHER EDUCATIONAL AIDS BOARD

P.O. Box 7885
Madison, WI 53707
Phone: 608-267-2206
Fax: 608-267-2808
Email: HEABmail@heab.state.wi.us
Website: http://heab.state.wi.us

#705 • Minority Retention Grant

Type: Grant. Renewable if recipient continues to demonstrate financial need.
Eligibility: Applicant must be a Wisconsin resident and African-American, American Indian, Hispanic, or Southeast Asian from Laos, Cambodia, or Vietnam admitted to the U.S. after December 31, 1975, and must be attending a Wisconsin independent institution or a Wisconsin Technical College. Selection is based upon financial need. This award must be used in the following years of study: • Sophomore • Junior • Senior
Deadline: Varies.
Award Amount: $ 250 - $ 2,500.
Number Of Awards: 662.
Contact: Mary Lou Kuzdas, Minority Retention Grant
Phone: 608-267-2212
Email: mary.kuzdas@heab.state.wi.us

Radio/TV Broadcasting

CHARLES AND LUCILLE KING FAMILY FOUNDATION, INC.

366 Madison Avenue, 10th Floor
New York, NY 10017
Phone: 212-682-2913
Fax: 212-949-0728
Email: info@kingfoundation.org
Website: info@kingfoundation.org

#706 • Charles and Lucille King Family Foundation Scholarship

Type: Scholarship. Renewable if recipient maintains minimum grade average of "B".
Eligibility: Applicant must submit a personal statement, three letters of recommendation, and transcript. This award must be used in the following years of study: • Junior • Senior
Field(s) Of Study: Broadcasting, film production, television.
Deadline: April 15.
Award Amount: $ 2,500.
Number Of Awards: 20.
Applications Received: 200.
Odds Of Winning: 10% of applicants on average receive an award each year.
Contact: Karen E. Kennedy, Michael Donovan, Assistant Edcuational Director, Educational Director

RADIO AND TELEVISION NEWS DIRECTORS FOUNDATION (RTNDF), INC.

1000 Connecticut Avenue, NW
Suite 615
Washington, DC 20036
Phone: 202-467-5218
Fax: 202-223-4007
Email: danib@rtndf.org
Website: http://www.rtndf.org

#707 • Carole Simpson Scholarship

Type: Scholarship. Not renewable.
Eligibility: Applicant must be enrolled at a college or university with at least one full year remaining, interested in a career in TV or radio news, and must submit resume, one to three journalistic examples not exceeding 15 minutes and an explanation of his/her role in the pieces, personal statement, and letter of reference from dean or faculty sponsor. Preference given to a minority student. This award must be used in the following years of study: • Sophomore • Junior • Senior
Field(s) Of Study: Broadcast journalism.
Deadline: May 1.
Award Amount: $ 2,000. Partial tuition, plus all-expenses paid trip to annual conference.
Number Of Awards: 1.
Contact: Dani Browne, Awards & Events Assistant

#708 • RTNDF Undergraduate Scholarship

Type: Scholarship. Not renewable.
Eligibility: Applicant must be enrolled at a college or university with at least one full year remaining, interested in a career in TV or radio news, and must submit resume, one to three journalistic examples not exceeding 15 minutes and an explanation of his/her role in the pieces, personal statement, and letter of reference from dean or faculty sponsor. This award

must be used in the following years of study: •
Sophomore • Junior • Senior
Field(s) Of Study: Broadcast journalism.
Deadline: May 1.
Award Amount: $ 1,000. Partial tuition, plus all-
expenses paid trip to annual conference.
Number Of Awards: 9.
Contact: Dani Browne, Awards & Events Assistant

#709 • Len Allen Award of Merit

Type: Scholarship. Not renewable.
Eligibility: Applicant must be enrolled at a college or
university with at least one full year remaining,
interested in a career in radio newsroom management,
and must submit resume, one-page essay, personal
statement, and letter of reference from dean or faculty
sponsor. This award must be used in the following
years of study: • Sophomore • Junior • Senior •
Masters • Doctoral
Field(s) Of Study: Broadcast journalism.
Deadline: May 1.
Award Amount: $ 2,000. Partial tuition, plus all-
expenses paid trip to annual conference.
Number Of Awards: 1.
Contact: Dani Browne, Awards & Events Assistant

#710 • Ed Bradley Scholarship

Type: Scholarship. Not renewable.
Eligibility: Applicant must be enrolled at a college or
university with at least one full year remaining,
interested in a career in TV or radio news, and must
submit resume, one to three journalistic examples not
exceeding 15 minutes and an explanation of his/her
role in the pieces, personal statement, and letter of
reference from dean or faculty sponsor. Preference
given to a minority student. This award must be used
in the following years of study: • Sophomore • Junior
• Senior
Field(s) Of Study: Broadcast journalism.
Deadline: May 1.
Award Amount: $ 5,000. Partial tuition, plus all-
expenses paid trip to annual conference.
Number Of Awards: 1.
Contact: Dani Browne, Awards & Events Assistant

#711 • RTNDA President's Award for Television News Management

Type: Scholarship. Not renewable.
Eligibility: Applicant must want a career in television
news management, be enrolled at a college or
university with at least one full year remaining, and
must submit resume, one-page essay, personal
statement, and letter of reference from dean or faculty
sponsor. This award must be used in the following
years of study: • Sophomore • Junior • Senior •
Masters • Doctoral
Field(s) Of Study: Electronic journalism.
Deadline: May 1.

Award Amount: $ 2,000. Partial tuition, plus all-
expenses paid trip to annual conference.
Number Of Awards: 1.
Contact: Dani Browne, Awards & Events Assistant

Real Estate

ILLINOIS REAL ESTATE EDUCATIONAL FOUNDATION

3180 Adloff Lane
P.O. Box 19451
Springfield, IL 62794
Phone: 217-529-2600
Fax: 217-529-3904
Email: bhale@iar.org

#712 • Thomas F. Seay Scholarship

Type: Scholarship. Renewable.
Eligibility: Applicant must be enrolled in a real
estate-related program and have a minimum 3.5 GPA.
This award must be used in the following years of
study: • Sophomore • Junior • Senior • Masters •
Doctoral • Other postgraduate level
Field(s) Of Study: Real estate.
Deadline: April 1.
Award Amount: $ 2,000.
Number Of Awards: 1.
Contact: Barbara Hale, Meeting and Program Liaison

#713 • Academic Scholarship

Type: Scholarship. Renewable.
Eligibility: Applicant must be enrolled in a real
estate-related field at a school in Illinois. This award
must be used in the following years of study: •
Sophomore • Junior • Senior • Masters • Doctoral •
Other postgraduate level
Field(s) Of Study: Real estate.
Deadline: April 1.
Award Amount: $ 1,000.
Number Of Awards: 6.
Contact: Barbara Hale, Meeting and Program Liaison

INSTITUTE OF REAL ESTATE MANAGEMENT (IREM) FOUNDATION

Attn: Brooker Scholarship
430 N. Michigan Avenue
Chicago, IL 60611-4090
Phone: 312-329-6008
Fax: 312-329-6039
Website: http://www.irem.org/

#714 • George M. Brooker Collegiate Scholarship for Minorities

Type: Scholarship. Not renewable.
Eligibility: Applicant must be a member of a minority group and a U.S. citizen. Applicant must have a minimum GPA of 3.0 on 4.0 scale within their major and must have completed two courses in real estate or indicate an intent to complete such courses. Recipients must maintain a minimum 3.0 GPA for the academic year for which the award applies or the scholarship may be revoked. Three letters of recommendation and essay (500 words maximum) required. This award must be used in the following years of study: • Junior • Senior • Masters
Field(s) Of Study: Business, real estate.
Deadline: March 15.
Award Amount: $ 1,000 - $ 2,500.
Number Of Awards: 3.
Applications Received: 10.
Contact: Ann Arnott, IREM Foundation

JOHN C. STANINGER MEMORIAL FOUNDATION

c/o Northeast Florida Association of Realtors, Inc.
3949 Atlantic Boulevard
Jacksonville, FL 32207
Phone: 904-396-1323
Fax: 904-398-8025

#715 • Real Estate Scholarship Fund

Type: Scholarship. Not renewable.
Eligibility: Contact for details. This award must be used in the following years of study: • Freshman • Sophomore • Junior • Senior
Field(s) Of Study: Real estate.
Deadline: Varies.
Award Amount: $ 500 - $ 1,000.
Number Of Awards: 3 - 7.
Applications Received: 204.
Odds Of Winning: 1% of applicants on average receive an award each year.
Contact: Celeta McClamma, Committee Liaison

Religion/Theology/Philosophy

CATHOLIC KNIGHTS OF AMERICA (CKA)

ATTN: Fraternal Affairs Department
3525 Hampton Avenue
St. Louis, MO 63139-1980
Phone: 314-351-1029
Fax: 314-351-9937
Email: ckoa@ckoa.com
Website: http://ckoa.com

#716 • CKA Seminarian Scholarsip

Type: Scholarship. Renewable. Recipient must maintain eligibility and make a written request.
Eligibility: Applicant must be enrolled as an undergraduate student majoring in seminarian studies or a related field. Applicant must provide an essay on why he wishes to become a priest, a recommendation from his parish and signature of Bishop with application. This award must be used in the following years of study: • Sophomore • Junior • Senior
Field(s) Of Study: Seminarian.
Deadline: May 1.
Award Amount: $ 250.
Number Of Awards: 6 - 12.
Contact: Christina Kenawell, Fraternal Coordinator
Phone: 314-351-1029
Email: ckoa@ckoa.com

ORDER OF DAUGHTERS OF THE KING

101 Weatherstone Drive, Suite 870
Woodstock, GA 30188
Phone: 770-517-8552
Website: http://www.dok-national.org

#717 • Master's Fund Grant

Type: Grant. Renewable if recipient continues study.
Eligibility: Applicant must be preparing for Christian service. Preference given for graduate study. This award must be used in the following years of study: • Masters • Doctoral • Other postgraduate level
Deadline: March 1.
Award Amount: $ 500 - $ 700.
Number Of Awards: 50.
Applications Received: 55.
Odds Of Winning: 90% of applicants on average receive an award each year.
Contact: Grant Administrator

Religious Affiliation

BETHESDA LUTHERAN HOMES AND SERVICES, INC.

National Christian Resource Center
700 Hoffmann Drive
Watertown, WI 53094
Phone: 800-369-4636, extension 416
Fax: 920-261-8441
Email: ncrc@blhs.org
Website: http://www.blhs.org

#718 • Mental Retardation Scholastic Achievement Scholarship

Type: Scholarship. Not renewable.

Eligibility: Applicant must be an active communicant member of the Lutheran Church, have a minimum 3.0 GPA, have completed 100 hours of work with people with mental retardation, and have career plans in the field of mental retardation. Applicant must submit three official transcripts and three copies each of four letters of recommendation (one from pastor) and an essay. This award must be used in the following years of study: • Junior • Senior • Masters • Doctoral • Other postgraduate level
Deadline: March 15.
Award Amount: $ 1,000.
Number Of Awards: 1 - 5.
Applications Received: 6.
Contact: Thomas Heuer, Coordinator of Outreach Programs and Services
Email: theuer@blhs.org

#719 • Nursing Scholastic Achievement Scholarship

Type: Scholarship. Not renewable.
Eligibility: Applicant must be an active communicant member of the Lutheran Church, have a minimum 3.0 GPA, have completed a minimum 100 hours of work with people with mental retardation, and submit three official transcripts and three copies each of four letters of recommendation (one from pastor) and essay stating career objectives. This award must be used in the following years of study: • Sophomore • Junior • Senior • Masters • Doctoral • Other postgraduate level
Field(s) Of Study: Nursing.
Deadline: March 15.
Award Amount: $ 1,000.
Number Of Awards: 1 - 5.
Applications Received: 2.
Contact: Thomas Heuer, Coordinator
Email: theuer@blhs.org

CHAVERIM OF DELAWARE VALLEY, INC.

9357 Hoff Street
Philadelphia, PA 19115-4706
Phone: 215-676-6769
Email: w3slf@juno.com

#720 • Ed Ludin K2UK Memorial Scholarship

Type: Scholarship. Renewable. Recipient must reapply to retain scholarship.
Eligibility: Applicant must be of the Judaic Faith and must hold and submit a copy of an amateur radio license. Selection is based upon academic achievements and financial need. This award must be used in the following years of study: • Freshman • Sophomore • Junior • Senior • Masters • Doctoral • Other postgraduate level • technical school students
Deadline: June 1.

Award Amount: $ 1,000.
Number Of Awards: 1.
Applications Received: 10.
Contact: Sylvia Soble W3SLF, Scholarship

FREEDOM FROM RELIGION FOUNDATION

P.O. Box 750
Madison, WI 53701
Phone: 608-256-8900
Email: ffrf@mailbag.com
Website: http://www.ffrf.org

#721 • Blanche Fern Memorial Award

Type: Contest. Not renewable.
Eligibility: Applicant must be a graduating college-bound high school senior and must submit a three- to four-page, typed, double-spaced essay on "Rejecting Religion" and a paragraph biography. For further information, send a business-size self-addressed, stamped envelope with inquiry. This award must be used in the following years of study: • Freshman
Deadline: July 15.
Award Amount: $ 250 - $ 1,000.
Number Of Awards: 3.
Contact: Anne Gaylor, Foundation President

#722 • Rosamond M. Austin Memorial Award

Type: Contest. Not renewable.
Eligibility: Applicant must attend a high school in Austin, Texas and plan to enroll in college. Applicant must write essay on the topic of "Rejecting Religion" and submit a paragraph biography. For more information, send a business-size, self-addressed, stamped envelope with inquiry. This award must be used in the following years of study: • Freshman
Deadline: July 15.
Award Amount: $ 250 - $ 1,000.
Number Of Awards: 3.
Contact: Anne Gaylor, Foundation President

#723 • Phyllis Stevens Grams Memorial Award

Type: Contest. Not renewable.
Eligibility: Applicant must submit a five-to-six-page typed, double-spaced essay (with an original title) on the topic of "The Experiences That Made Me A Freethinker (Atheist/Agnostic." Paragraph biography also required. For more information, send a business-size self-addressed, stamped envelope with inquiry. This award must be used in the following years of study: • Sophomore • Junior • Senior • Masters
Deadline: July 15.
Award Amount: $ 250 - $ 1,000.
Number Of Awards: 3.
Contact: Anne Gaylor, Foundation President

GENERAL COMMISSION ON ARCHIVES AND HISTORY, THE UNITED METHODIST CHURCH

P.O. Box 127
Madison, NJ 07940-2230
Phone: 973-408-3189
Fax: 973-408-3909
Website: http://www.gcah.org

#724 • Racial/Ethnic History Research Grant

Type: Grant. Not renewable.
Eligibility: Award is for research into the history and heritage of ethnic groups in the American United Methodist tradition. This award must be used in the following years of study: • Masters • Doctoral • Other postgraduate level
Deadline: December 31.
Award Amount: $ 750 - $ 1,500.
Number Of Awards: 1 - 2.
Contact: Tasha Whitton, Administrative Assistant
Email: nwhitton@gcah.org

#725 • Women in United Methodist History Research Grant

Type: Grant. Not renewable.
Eligibility: Award provides seed money for research projects relating specifically to the history of women in The United Methodist Church or its antecedents. This award must be used in the following years of study: • Masters • Doctoral • Other postgraduate level
Deadline: December 31.
Award Amount: $ 500 - $ 1,000.
Number Of Awards: 1 - 2.
Contact: Tasha Whitton, Administrative Assistant
Email: nwhitton@gcah.org

#726 • Women in United Methodist History Writing Award

Type: Contest. Not renewable.
Eligibility: Applicant must submit an original manuscript, no longer than 20 pages, on the history of women in the United Methodist Church or its antecedents. This award must be used in the following years of study: • Masters • Doctoral • Other postgraduate level
Deadline: May 1.
Award Amount: $ 250.
Number Of Awards: 1.
Contact: Tasha Whitton, Administrative Assistant
Email: nwhitton@gcah.org

HEBREW IMMIGRANT AID SOCIETY

Attention: Scholarship Program
333 Seventh Avenue
New York, NY 10001-5004
Phone: 212-613-1358

#727 • Hebrew Immigrant Aid Society Scholarship

Type: Scholarship. Renewable.
Eligibility: Applicant must have attended at least two semesters at an American high school or college. Applicant or his or her parent must be a Hebrew Immigrant Aid Society-assisted refugee who immigrated to the U.S. during or after 1985. Selection is based upon academic excellence, financial need, and community activity, especially that performed within the Jewish community. This award must be used in the following years of study: • Freshman • Sophomore • Junior • Senior • Masters • Doctoral • Other postgraduate level
Deadline: March 15.
Award Amount: $ 1,500.
Number Of Awards: 114.
Applications Received: 600.
Odds Of Winning: 19% of applicants on average receive an award each year.
Contact: Phoebe Lewis, Scholarship Coordinator
Phone: 212-613-1358 or 212-613-1357

JEWISH SOCIAL SERVICE AGENCY

6123 Montrose Road
Rockville, MD 20852
Phone: 301-881-3700
Fax: 301-770-8741

#728 • Max and Emmy Dreyfuss Jewish Undergraduate Scholarship

Type: Scholarship. Renewable. Recipient must reapply for renewal.
Eligibility: Applicant must be Jewish, be under age 30, and be a resident of the Washington, D.C., metropolitan area. Selection is based upon financial need. Preference is given to refugees. This award must be used in the following years of study: • Freshman • Sophomore • Junior • Senior
Deadline: May 30.
Award Amount: $ 1,500 - $ 3,500.
Number Of Awards: Varies.
Contact: Linda Platt, Scholarship and Loan Coordinator
Phone: 301-881-3700, extension 757

#729 • Morton A. Gibson Memorial Scholarship

Type: Scholarship. Not renewable.
Eligibility: Applicant must be a Jewish resident of the Washington, D.C., metropolitain area who has performed significant volunteer service for the local Jewish community or with a Jewish organization. Selection is based upon volunteer service, academics, and need. This award must be used in the following years of study: • Freshman
Deadline: May 30.

Award Amount: $ 2,500.
Number Of Awards: 2.
Contact: Linda Platt, Scholarship and Loan Coord.
Phone: 301-881-3700, extension 757

JEWISH VOCATIONAL SERVICE (L.A.)

5700 Wilshire Boulevard
Los Angeles, CA 90036
Phone: 213-761-8888
Fax: 213-761-8850
Email: jvsla@aol.com

#730 • JVS Jewish Community Scholarship Fund

Type: Scholarship. Renewable.
Eligibility: Applicant must be a member of the Jewish faith, be a permanent resident of Los Angeles County, be a U.S. citizen or have permanent residence status, demonstrate financial need, and submit personal statement. Preference is given to students of California schools. This award must be used in the following years of study: • Sophomore • Junior • Senior • Masters • Doctoral • Other postgraduate level • vocational training
Deadline: April 15.
Award Amount: Varies.
Number Of Awards: 79.
Applications Received: 500.
Contact: Jeanie Gaynor, Scholarship Administrator
Phone: 213-761-8888, extension 122

KNIGHTS OF COLUMBUS

P.O. Box 1670
Department of Scholarships
New Haven, CT 06507-0901
Phone: 203-772-2130, extension 332
Fax: 203-772-2696

#731 • Pro Deo and Pro Patria Scholarships

Type: Scholarship. Renewable. Satisfactory academic performance required to retain scholarship.
Eligibility: Applicant must be a member or the child of a member of the Knights of Columbus or Columbian Squires and must be attending a Catholic college. Selection is based upon academic excellence. Transcripts, test scores, autobiography, and recommendation required. This award must be used in the following years of study: • Freshman
Deadline: March 1.
Award Amount: $ 1,500.
Number Of Awards: 50.
Applications Received: 500.
Odds Of Winning: 10% of applicants on average receive an award each year.
Contact: Rev. Donald Barry, S.J., Director of Scholarship Aid

LIGHTS OF THE JEWISH SPECIAL NEEDS SOCIETY

Sylvia Ehrlich 9036 Watsonia Court
St. Louis, MO 63132
Phone: 314-993-6640

#732 • Lights of Jewish Special Needs Society Scholarship

Type: Grant. Renewable. Recipient must reapply for renewal.
Eligibility: Applicant must be Jewish and attending an institution in Missouri. Applicant should submit a transcript, two letters of reference (one from a teacher and one from a rabbi or employer), and financial statement. This award must be used in the following years of study: • Freshman • Sophomore • Junior • Senior • Masters • Doctoral • Other postgraduate level
Deadline: May 31.
Award Amount: $ 300 - $ 1,000.
Number Of Awards: 16.
Applications Received: 16.
Odds Of Winning: 100% of applicants on average receive an award each year.
Contact: Sylvia Ehrlich, Chairperson

PRESBYTERIAN CHURCH (USA)

Office of Financial Aid for Studies
100 Witherspoon Street
Louisville, KY 40202-1396
Phone: 502-569-5745
Fax: 502-569-8766
Email: TimM@ctr.pusa.org
Website: http://www.pcusa.org

#733 • Appalachian Scholarship

Type: Scholarship. Renewable.
Eligibility: Applicant must be a member of the Presbyterian Church (USA), be a U.S. citizen or permanent resident living in the Appalachia region, and demonstrate financial need. Nontraditional students with no previous college experience are encouraged to apply. This award must be used in the following years of study: • Freshman • Sophomore • Junior • Senior
Deadline: July 1.
Award Amount: $ 100 - $ 1,500.
Number Of Awards: 200.
Contact: Maria Alvarez, Associate for Program Management
Phone: 502-569-5760

#734 • Student Opportunity Scholarship

Type: Scholarship. Renewable.
Eligibility: Applicant must be African-American, Alaskan Native, Asian-American, Hispanic-American, or Native American, be a member of the Presbyterian

Church (USA), be a U.S. citizen or permanent resident, and demonstrate financial need. This award must be used in the following years of study: • Freshman • Sophomore • Junior • Senior
Deadline: April 1.
Award Amount: $ 100 - $ 1,400.
Number Of Awards: 200.
Contact: Maria Alvarez, Associate for Program Management
Phone: 502-569-5760

ROSE AND JOSEPH SOKOL SCHOLARSHIP FUND

Dorothy S. Kipnis
118 Chadwick Drive
Charleston, SC 29407
Phone: 843-766-4766

#735 • Rose and Joseph Sokol Scholarship

Type: Scholarship. Renewable if recipient maintains good grades and continues to demonstrate financial need.
Eligibility: Applicant must be a Jewish resident of South Carolina who demonstrates financial need. Application should consist of information about applicant and his/her family and copy of family's most recent tax return. This award must be used in the following years of study: • Freshman • Sophomore • Junior • Senior
Deadline: November 15.
Award Amount: $ 500.
Number Of Awards: 1.
Contact: Frances Sokol Halio
1308 Winchester Drive
Charleston, SC 29407
Phone: 843-766-0708

SYNOD OF THE TRINITY (PRESBYTERIAN CHURCH USA)

ATTN: Social and Racial Justice Ministry Unit
3040 Market Street
Camp Hill, PA 17011-4599
Phone: 717-737-0421
Fax: 717-737-8211
Email: scholarships@syntrinity.org

#736 • Synod of the Trinity Education Scholarship

Type: Scholarship. Not renewable.
Eligibility: Applicant must be a Presbyterian attending a Presbyterian school. This award must be used in the following years of study: • Freshman • Sophomore • Junior • Senior • vocational school students
Deadline: Varies.
Award Amount: $ 250 - $ 600.

Number Of Awards: 309.
Applications Received: 475.
Odds Of Winning: 65% of applicants on average receive an award each year.
Contact: Synod Scholarship Programs

Respiratory Therapy

AMERICAN RESPIRATORY CARE FOUNDATION

11030 Ables Lane
Dallas, TX 75229-4593
Phone: 972-243-2272
Fax: 972-484-2720
Email: info@aarc.org
Website: http://www.aarc.org

#737 • Morton B. Duggan Memorial Education Recognition Award

Type: Scholarship. Renewable. Recipients must reapply for renewal.
Eligibility: Applicant must have a minimum 3.0 GPA, be enrolled full-time in an accredited respiratory therapy program, be a U.S. citizen or legal resident, submit an original essay on some aspect of respiratory care, and submit letters of recommendation. Preference is given to Georgia and South Carolina residents. This award must be used in the following years of study: • Freshman • Sophomore • Junior • Senior • Masters • Doctoral
Field(s) Of Study: Respiratory therapy.
Deadline: June 30.
Award Amount: $ 1,000.
Number Of Awards: 1.
Contact: Norma Hernandez, Educational Awards Coordinator

#738 • NBRC/AMP Robert M. Lawrence, M.D., Education Recognition Award

Type: Scholarship. Renewable. Reapplication is required for renewal.
Eligibility: Applicant must have a minimum 3.0 GPA, be enrolled in an accredited respiratory therapy program leading to a bachelor's degree, demonstrate U.S. citizenship or legal residency, and submit an original referenced paper and an essay describing how the award will assist the applicant. This award must be used in the following years of study: • Senior
Field(s) Of Study: Respiratory therapy.
Deadline: June 30.
Award Amount: $ 2,500.
Number Of Awards: 1.
Contact: Norma Hernandez, Educational Awards Coordinator

#739 • NBRC/AMP William W. Burgin, Jr., M.D., Education Recognition Award

Type: Scholarship. Renewable. Reapplication is required for renewal.
Eligibility: Applicant must have a minimum 3.0 GPA, be enrolled in an accredited respiratory therapy program leading to an associate degree, demonstrate U.S. citizenship or legal residency, and submit an original referenced paper and an essay describing how the award will assist the applicant. This award must be used in the following years of study: • Sophomore
Field(s) Of Study: Respiratory therapy.
Deadline: June 30.
Award Amount: $ 2,500.
Number Of Awards: 1.
Contact: Norma Hernandez, Educational Awards Coordinator

#740 • Jimmy A. Young Memorial Educational Recognition Award

Type: Scholarship. Renewable. Reapplication is required for renewal.
Eligibility: Applicant must have a minimum 3.0 GPA, demonstrate U.S. citizenship or legal residency and enrollment in an accredited respiratory care program, and submit letters of reference and an original referenced paper on some aspect of respiratory care. Preference is given to minority applicants. This award must be used in the following years of study: • Freshman • Sophomore • Junior • Senior • Masters • Doctoral
Field(s) Of Study: Respiratory therapy.
Deadline: June 30.
Award Amount: $ 1,000.
Number Of Awards: 1.
Contact: Norma Hernandez, Educational Awards Coordinator

Sciences-General

AMERICAN CHEMICAL SOCIETY (ACS)

1155 16th Street, NW
Washington, DC 20036

#741 • ACS/Bayer Scholars Program

Type: Scholarship. Renewable.
Eligibility: Applicant must be African-American, Hispanic/Latino, or American Indian, a U.S. citizen or permanent resident, and a full-time student in a four-year program at an accredited school in or near one of the following locations: Berkeley, Calif.; West Haven, Conn.; Shawnee, Kans.; Fitchburg and Wilmington, Mass.; Kansas City, Miss.; Morristown and Ridgefield Park, N.J.; Tarrytown, N.Y.; Addyston, Ohio; Myerstown and Pittsburgh, Pa.; Goose Creek, S.C.; Baytown and Orange, Texas; Middletown, Va.; or New Martinsville, W.Va. This award must be used in the following years of study: • Freshman • Sophomore • Junior
Field(s) Of Study: Biochemistry, chemical engineering, chemistry.
Deadline: Varies.
Award Amount: $ 2,500.
Number Of Awards: 75.
Contact: Robert J. Hughes, Program Manager
Phone: 202-872-6048 or 800-227-5558
Fax: 202-776-8003

AMERICAN CONCRETE INSTITUTE

ATTN: Concrete Research and Education Foundation
P.O. Box 9094
Farmington Hills, MI 48333-9094
Phone: 248-848-3713
Fax: 248-848-3720
Email: dlepping@aci-int.org

#742 • Peter D. Courtois Concrete Construction Scholarship

Type: Scholarship. Not renewable.
Eligibility: Applicant must be studying concrete construction, be enrolled for at least six credit hours per semester, and must submit transcripts, recommendations, and an essay. This award must be used in the following years of study: • Senior
Field(s) Of Study: Construction, engineering, technology, concrete-related fields.
Deadline: January 14.
Award Amount: $ 1,000.
Number Of Awards: 2.
Contact: Dot Lepping, Scholarship Coordinator

INTERNATIONAL SOCIETY FOR OPTICAL ENGINEERING (SPIE)

SPIE Scholarship Committee
P.O. Box 10
Bellingham, WA 98227-0010
Phone: 360-676-3290
Fax: 360-647-1445
Email: spie@spie.org
Website: http://www.spie.org

#743 • Educational Scholarships & Grants in Optical Science & Engineering

Type: Scholarship. Not renewable.
Eligibility: Selection is based upon the long-range contribution the applicant could make to optics and optical engineering. This award must be used in the following years of study: • Freshman • Sophomore • Junior • Senior • Masters • Doctoral • Other

postgraduate level
Field(s) Of Study: Aerospace science/sensing, automation/product engineering, biomedical optics, chemistry/biology, electronic imaging, fiber optics, laser/source technologies, microelectronic/optoelectronic devices, optical physics, optical science/engineering, signal/image processing.
Deadline: March 31.
Award Amount: $ 1,000 - $10,000.
Number Of Awards: 20 - 85.
Applications Received: 242.
Odds Of Winning: 35% of applicants on average receive an award each year.
Contact: Groot Gregory, Scholarship Committee Chair
Email: pascale@spie.org

Speech/Forensics

AMERICAN LEGION - HAWAII

612 McCully Street
Honolulu, HI 96826
Phone: 808-946-6383
Fax: 808-947-3957
Email: aldepthi@gte.com

#744 • Oratorical Contest

Type: Contest. Not renewable.
Eligibility: Applicant must give an oration of the Constitution of the United States. This award must be used in the following years of study: • Freshman
Deadline: January.
Award Amount: $ 50 - $ 300.
Number Of Awards: Varies.
Applications Received: 6.
Odds Of Winning: 100% of applicants on average receive an award each year.
Contact: Oratorical Contest Chairman

AMERICAN LEGION - KANSAS

1314 Topeka Avenue
Topeka, KS 66612
Phone: 913-232-9315

#745 • Oratorical Contest Scholarship

Type: Scholarship. Not renewable.
Eligibility: Contact for details. This award must be used in the following years of study: • Freshman
Deadline: Varies.
Award Amount: $ 150 - $ 1,500.
Number Of Awards: 4.
Contact: Scholarship Administrator

AMERICAN LEGION - MICHIGAN

212 North Verlinden
Lansing, MI 48915
Phone: 517-371-4720
Fax: 517-371-2401
Email: info@michiganlegion.org
Website: http://www.michiganlegion.org

#746 • Oratorical Contest Scholarship

Type: Scholarship. Not renewable.
Eligibility: Applicant must be a finalist in the oratorical contest. This award must be used in the following years of study: • Freshman
Deadline: February.
Award Amount: $ 600 - $ 1,000.
Number Of Awards: 5.
Contact: Deanna Clark, Programs Secretary

AMERICAN LEGION - NORTH DAKOTA

Education and Scholarship Program
P.O. Box 2666
Fargo, ND 58108
Phone: 701-293-3120
Fax: 701-293-9951
Email: adjutant@ndlegion.org
Website: http://www.ndlegion.org

#747 • North Dakota American Legion High School Oratorical Contest

Type: Contest. Not renewable.
Eligibility: Applicant must be a student in a North Dakota high school and compete in an oratorical contest. This award must be used in the following years of study: • Freshman
Deadline: In fall semester.
Award Amount: $ 100 - $ 1,900.
Number Of Awards: 10 - 30.
Applications Received: 28.
Odds Of Winning: 100% of applicants on average receive an award each year.
Contact: Teri Anderson, Programs Assistant

AMERICAN LEGION - SOUTH CAROLINA

P.O. Box 11355
Columbia, SC 29211
Phone: 803-799-1992
Fax: 803-771-9831

#748 • Oratorical Contest Scholarship

Type: Scholarship. Renewable.
Eligibility: Applicant must compete in and win the High School Oratorical Contest. This award must be used in the following years of study: • Freshman
Deadline: None.

Award Amount: $ 500 - $ 1,600.
Number Of Awards: 5.
Contact: Jim Hawk, Department Adjutant

AMERICAN LEGION - TENNESSEE

State Headquarters 215 Eighth Avenue, North
Nashville, TN 37203
Phone: 615-254-0568
Fax: 615-255-1551

#749 • Oratorical Contest Scholarship of Tennessee

Type: Contest. Not renewable.
Eligibility: Applicant must attend high school in
Tennessee. Contestant must speak eight to 10 minutes
on some phase of the U.S. Constitution, emphasizing
the attendant duties and obligations of a citizen to
our government. This award must be used in the
following years of study: • Freshman
Deadline: January 15.
Award Amount: $ 1,500 - $ 5,000.
Number Of Awards: 3.
Applications Received: 61.
Odds Of Winning: 5% of applicants on average
receive an award each year.
Contact: A. Mike Hammer, Department Adjutant

AMERICAN LEGION - TEXAS

Department of Texas
P.O. Box 789
Austin, TX 78767
Phone: 512-472-4138
Email: txlegion@txlegion.org
Website: http://www.txlegion.org

#750 • Oratorical Contest Scholarship

Type: Contest. Not renewable.
Eligibility: Applicant must be a Texas resident,
current high school student, be sponsored by an
American Legion post, and compete in the state
oratorical contest. This award must be used in the
following years of study: • Freshman
Deadline: November.
Award Amount: $ 250 - $ 1,000.
Number Of Awards: 4.
Contact: James P. Heath, Dept. Oratorical Chairman

AMERICAN LEGION, DEPARTMENT OF MINNESOTA

20 West 12th Street, Room 300-A
St. Paul, MN 55155-2069
Phone: 651-291-1800
Fax: 651-291-1057
Email: department@mnlegion.org
Website: http://www.mnlegion.org

#751 • High School Oratorical Contest

Type: Scholarship. Not renewable.
Eligibility: Applicant must be a U.S. citizen or
permanent resident under the age of 20. This award
must be used in the following years of study: •
Freshman
Deadline: Varies.
Award Amount: $ 500 - $ 1,200.
Number Of Awards: Varies.
Contact: See above.

State/Country of Residence

AIRCRAFT ELECTRONICS ASSOCIATION (AEA) EDUCATIONAL FOUNDATION

4217 S. Hocker Drive
Independence, MO 64055
Phone: 816-373-6565
Fax: 816-478-3100
Email: info@aea.net
Website: http://www.aea.net

#752 • Monte Mitchell Global Scholarship

Type: Scholarship. Not renewable.
Eligibility: Applicant must be a European student
studying at an accredited school in the U.S. or
Europe. This award must be used in the following
years of study: • Freshman • Sophomore • Junior •
Senior
Field(s) Of Study: Aircraft repair, aviation
maintenance technology, avionics.
Deadline: February 15.
Award Amount: $ 1,000.
Number Of Awards: 1.
Applications Received: 150.
Odds Of Winning: 1% of applicants on average
receive an award each year.
Contact: Mike Adamson, AEA Educational
Foundation Executive Director

ALABAMA STATE DEPARTMENT OF EDUCATION

Instructional Services Division
Gordon Persons Building
50 North Ripley Street
Montgomery, AL 36130
Phone: 334-242-8249
Fax: 334-242-2475

#753 • Alabama Scholarship for Dependents of Blind Parents

Type: Scholarship. Renewable.

Eligibility: Applicant must come from a family in which the head of the family is blind and whose family income is insufficient to provide educational benefits. Applicant must be an Alabama resident, applying to or enrolled at an Alabama institution, and must apply within two years of high school graduation. This award must be used in the following years of study: • Freshman • Sophomore • Junior • Senior
Deadline: Varies.
Award Amount: Full tuition or partial tuition. Plus fees.
Number Of Awards: Varies.
Contact: Terry Longest, Administrator, Blind Assistance
Phone: 334-242-8114
Fax: 334-242-9192

ALBUQUERQUE COMMUNITY FOUNDATION (ACF)

P.O. Box 36960
Albuquerque, NM 87176-6960
Phone: 505-883-6240
Email: acf@albuquerquefoundation.org
Website: http://www.albuquerquefoundation.org

#754 • Sussman-Miller Educational Assistance Award

Type: Scholarship. Renewable. Recipient must maintain a 2.5 GPA, remain a New Mexico resident, and demonstrate continued financial need.
Eligibility: Applicant must be a resident of New Mexico and have a minimum 3.0 GPA (high school) or 2.5 GPA (college). Applicants must submit a resume, statement of goals and unusual circumstances, offical transcripts, academy references, and proof of financial need. This award must be used in the following years of study: • Freshman • Sophomore • Junior • Senior
Deadline: July 7.
Award Amount: $ 1,000 - $ 6,500.
Number Of Awards: 35.
Applications Received: 168.
Odds Of Winning: 20% of applicants on average receive an award each year.
Contact: Nancy Johnson, Program Manager
Email: njohnson@albuquerquefoundation.org

AMERICAN LEGION - ALASKA

519 West Eighth Avenue, Suite 208
Anchorage, AK 99501
Phone: 907-278-8598
Fax: 907-278-0041
Email: legion@anch.net

#755 • American Legion - Alaska Scholarship

Type: Scholarship. Not renewable.

Eligibility: Applicant must be a resident of Alaska and have a minimum 2.5 to 3.7 GPA. This award must be used in the following years of study: • Freshman
Deadline: February 15.
Award Amount: $ 500.
Number Of Awards: 3.
Applications Received: 3.
Contact: Bill Frederick, Western District Scholarship Chair
1760 Muldoon Circle, Apartment 1
Anchorage, AK 99504
Phone: 907-276-8211
Fax: 907-258-0756
Email: legionl@anch.net

AMERICAN LEGION - ARIZONA AUXILIARY

4701 North 19th Avenue, Suite 100
Phoenix, AZ 85015-3727
Phone: 602-241-1080
Fax: 602-264-0029
Email: amlegauxaz@uswest.net

#756 • Past President's Parley Scholarship Assistance in Health Care Occupations

Type: Scholarship. Renewable. Recipient must reapply for renewal.
Eligibility: Applicant must be enrolled in a health care occupations program, be a U.S. citizen, a resident of Arizona for at least one year, and attending an accredited Arizona school. Preference is given to an immediate family member of a veteran. Applicant must submit a photograph, statement giving resaons for choosing a career in health care, three letters of reference, and transcripts. Selection is based upon character, scholarship, financial need, and initiative. This award must be used in the following years of study: • Freshman • Sophomore • Junior • Senior • Masters • Doctoral • Other postgraduate level
Deadline: May 15.
Award Amount: $ 300.
Number Of Awards: 6.
Applications Received: 10.
Odds Of Winning: 50% of applicants on average receive an award each year.
Contact: Past President's Parley Scholarship Assistance in Health Care Occupations

AMERICAN LEGION - VIRGINIA AUXILIARY

Department Secretary-Treasurer
1805 Chantilly Street
Richmond, VA 23230
Phone: 804-355-6410
Fax: 804-353-5246

#757 • Dr. Kate Waller Barrett Grant

Type: Scholarship. Not renewable.
Eligibility: Applicant must be the son or daughter of a veteran or Auxiliary member, a high school senior or graduate of a high school in Virginia, and a Virginia resident who demonstrates financial need. This award must be used in the following years of study: • Freshman
Deadline: March 15.
Award Amount: $ 1,000.
Number Of Awards: 1.
Applications Received: 100.
Contact: Margaret Dellinger, Education Chairman
417 Park Street, SE
Vienna, VA 22180
Phone: 703-255-2918

AMERICAN LEGION AUXILIARY, DEPARTMENT OF IOWA

720 Lyon Street
Des Moines, IA 50309
Phone: 515-282-7987
Fax: 515-282-7583

#758 • American Legion Auxiliary, Department of Iowa Scholarship

Type: Scholarship. Not renewable.
Eligibility: Applicant must be an Iowa student attending or planning to attend an Iowa school. This award must be used in the following years of study: • Freshman • Sophomore • Junior • Senior
Deadline: June 1.
Award Amount: $ 300.
Number Of Awards: 1.
Applications Received: 100.
Contact: Marlene Valentine, Department Secretary/ Treasurer

AMERICAN LEGION AUXILIARY, DEPARTMENT OF MICHIGAN

American Legion Auxiliary
212 North Verlinden Avenue
Lansing, MI 48915
Phone: 517-371-4720
Fax: 517-371-2401
Email: michalaux@voyager.net
Website: http://www.michalaux.org

#759 • National President Scholarship

Type: Scholarship. Not renewable.
Eligibility: Applicant must be a resident of Michigan, the son or daughter of a veteran, a high school senior, have spent at least 50 hours doing community service, and submit four letters of recommendation, verification of military service of parent, official transcripts, ACT or SAT I scores, and a 1,000-word essay. This award must be used in the following years of study: • Freshman
Deadline: March 10.
Award Amount: $ 1,000 - $ 2,500.
Number Of Awards: 15.
Contact: Cheryle Thompson, Scholarship Coordinator

AMERICAN SOCIETY OF TRAVEL AGENTS (ASTA) FOUNDATION, INC.

1101 King Street
Alexandria, VA 22314
Phone: 703-739-2782
Fax: 703-684-8319
Email: astasysop@astanet.com
Website: http://www.astanet.com

#760 • Rocky Mountain Chapter Estey Scholarship

Type: Scholarship. Renewable. Recipient must reapply to retain scholarship.
Eligibility: Applicant must submit letter describing proposed use of the award and letter of recommendation from an officer of the ASTA Rocky Mountain Chapter. This award must be used in the following years of study: • Freshman • travel agents seeking further industry-specific training
Field(s) Of Study: Travel/tourism.
Deadline: None.
Award Amount: $ 100 - $ 750.
Number Of Awards: Varies.
Contact: Myriam Lechuga or Mary Kate Koehl, Scholarships

AMVETS, ILLINOIS DEPARTMENT

2200 South Sixth Street
Springfield, IL 62703
Phone: 217-528-4713
Fax: 217-528-9896
Email: amvets@warpnet.net

#761 • Musical or Recreational Therapy Scholarship

Type: Scholarship. Renewable for up to three years.
Eligibility: Applicant must be an Illinois resident attending school in Illinois, be entering the field of music, be single, and submit ACT scores, transcripts, rank in class, and tax forms. This award must be used in the following years of study: • Freshman
Field(s) Of Study: Music therapy, recreational therapy.
Deadline: March 1.
Award Amount: $ 500.
Number Of Awards: 1.
Contact: See above.

ARKANSAS DEPARTMENT OF HIGHER EDUCATION

114 East Capitol
Little Rock, AR 72201
Phone: 501-371-2000
Fax: 501-371-2001
Email: finaid@adhe.arknet.edu
Website: http://www.adhe.arknet.edu

#762 • Arkansas Governor's Scholars Award

Type: Scholarship. Renewable if minimum 3.0 GPA is maintained and 24 credit hours per year are taken.
Eligibility: Applicant must be an Arkansas resident and have a minimum combined SAT I score of 1100 (composite ACT score of 27) or a minimum 3.6 GPA, and demonstrate leadership abilities. Applicants with minimum combined SAT I score of 1410 (composite ACT score of 32) or who are National Merit finalists automatically qualify for award. Recipients must attend an approved Arkansas institution. This award must be used in the following years of study: • Freshman
Deadline: March 1.
Award Amount: $ 4,000. Full tuition or partial tuition, plus mandatory fees, room, and board.
Number Of Awards: 100.
Applications Received: 2,400.
Odds Of Winning: 9% of applicants on average receive an award each year.
Contact: Melissa Goff, Manager of Student Financial Aid
Phone: 501-371-2050
Email: melissag@adhe.arknet.edu

#763 • Arkansas Academic Challenge Scholarship

Type: Scholarship. Renewable if minimum 2.5 GPA is maintained and 24 credit hours per year are taken.
Eligibility: Applicant must have completed the precollegiate core curriculum recommended by the Arkansas Higher Education Coordinating Board, have a minimum composite ACT score of 19, and have a minimum 2.5 GPA in the core curriculum. Applicant must be an Arkansas resident, attend an approved Arkansas school, be a U.S. citizen, and demonstrate financial need. This award must be used in the following years of study: • Freshman
Deadline: October 1.
Award Amount: $ 2,500.
Number Of Awards: 4,673.
Applications Received: 6,567.
Odds Of Winning: 71% of applicants on average receive an award each year.
Contact: Elyse Price, Assistant Coordinator of Student Financial Aid

#764 • Law Enforcement Officers Dependents' Scholarship

Type: Grant. Renewable for up to eight semesters.
Eligibility: Applicant must be a resident of Arkansas who is the dependent child or spouse (who has not remarried) of a person who was killed or permanently disabled in the line of duty as law enforcement officers in the State of Arkansas or certain Highway and Transportation Department employees. Applicant must be under 23 years of age (except for spouses). Award may be used at Arkansas public postsecondary institutions only. This award must be used in the following years of study: • Freshman • Sophomore • Junior • Senior
Deadline: August 1.
Award Amount: Varies.
Number Of Awards: Varies.
Applications Received: 22.
Odds Of Winning: 100% of applicants on average receive an award each year.
Contact: Assistant Coordinator of Student Financial Aid

ARKANSAS SINGLE PARENT SCHOLARSHIP FUND

614 East Emma, Suite 119
Springdale, AR 72764
Phone: 501-927-1402
Fax: 501-751-1110
Email: rnesson@jtlshop.jonesnet.org
Website: http://scholarships-ar-us.org/aspsf.htm or http://www.aspsf.org

#765 • Arkansas Single Parent Scholarship

Type: Scholarship. Renewable if applicant remains a resident of Arkansas and a single parent with custody and continues to demonstrate financial need.
Eligibility: Applicant must be an Arkansas resident, have custody of a child or children under 18, and demonstrate financial need. Graduate students are not eligible. This award must be used in the following years of study: • Freshman • Sophomore • Junior • Senior • Technical program students, job certification
Deadline: in spring, summer, and winter.
Award Amount: $ 250 - $ 600.
Number Of Awards: 860.
Contact: Ralph Nesson, ASPSF Director

BOETTCHER FOUNDATION

600 17th Street
Suite 2210 South
Denver, CO 80202-5422
Phone: 303-285-6207
Email: scholarships@boettcherfoundation.org
Website: http://www.boettcherfoundation.org

#766 • Boettcher Foundation Scholarship

Type: Scholarship. Renewable if recipient maintains a minimum 3.0 GPA.
Eligibility: Applicant must have resided in Colorado during junior and senior year of high school and be attending an institution in Colorado. Applicant must be a U.S. citizen, rank in the top 5% of class, and have a minimum combined SAT I score of 1200 (composite ACT score of 27). Applicant must see his/her high school counselor for an application. This award must be used in the following years of study: • Freshman • Sophomore • Junior • Senior
Deadline: December 1.
Award Amount: Full-tuition. Partial Tuition. plus living stipend, book stipend.
Number Of Awards: 40.
Applications Received: 900.
Odds Of Winning: 4% of applicants on average receive an award each year.
Contact: Katie Kramer, Director of Scholars Program

C.G. FULLER FOUNDATION

c/o Bank of America
P.O. Box 448
Columbia, SC 29202
Phone: 803-255-7385

#767 • C.G. Fuller Foundation Scholarship

Type: Scholarship. Renewable if minimum 3.0 GPA is maintained.
Eligibility: Applicant must have a minimum combined SAT I score of 1100, be a South Carolina resident attending a South Carolina college or university, and demonstrate financial need. Family income may not exceed $60,000. This award must be used in the following years of study: • Freshman
Deadline: April 15.
Award Amount: $ 2,000.
Number Of Awards: 15.
Odds Of Winning: 15% of applicants on average receive an award each year.
Contact: Rebecca Simpson, Relationship Associate

CALIFORNIA MASONIC FOUNDATION

1111 California Street
San Francisco, CA 94108
Phone: 415-292-9196
Website: http://www.mhcsf.org/foundation

#768 • California Masonic Foundation Scholarship

Type: Scholarship. Renewable if recipient reapplies, maintains minimum 3.0 GPA, and continues to show financial need.
Eligibility: Applicant must be a U.S. citizen, a California resident for at least one year, demonstrate financial need, and have a minimum 3.0 GPA. This award must be used in the following years of study: • Freshman
Deadline: March 15.
Award Amount: $ 2,500 - $10,400.
Number Of Awards: 185.
Applications Received: 1,200.
Odds Of Winning: 5% of applicants on average receive an award each year.
Contact: Judy Liang, Coordinator
Phone: 415-292-9196

CALIFORNIA STUDENT AID COMMISSION

P.O. Box 419027
Rancho Cordova, CA 95741-9027
Phone: 916-526-7590
Fax: 916-526-8002
Email: custsvcs@csac.ca.gov
Website: http://www.csac.ca.gov

#769 • Robert C. Byrd Honors Scholarship

Type: Scholarship. Renewable for up to four years if funding is available.
Eligibility: Applicant must be a legal resident of California and be nominated by his/her high school. Applicant must have graduated from high school during the previous year, plan to enroll in a U.S. public or private nonprofit postsecondary institution, and plan to file a Selective Service Registration Status statement. Selection is based solely upon merit. This award must be used in the following years of study: • Freshman
Deadline: April 30.
Award Amount: $ 1,500.
Number Of Awards: 770.
Applications Received: 1,500.
Odds Of Winning: 15% of applicants on average receive an award each year.
Contact: High School Robert C. Byrd Scholarship Coordinator/Special Programs
Phone: 916-526-8276
Fax: 916-526-7977

#770 • Law Enforcement Personnel Dependents Scholarship

Type: Scholarship. Renewable for up to four years.
Eligibility: Applicant must be a dependent or spouse of a California peace officer, Department of Corrections employee, Youth Authority employee, or full-time firefighter who has been killed or totally disabled in the line of duty. This award must be used in the following years of study: • Freshman • Sophomore • Junior • Senior • Masters • Doctoral
Deadline: None.
Award Amount: $ 100 - $ 9,420.
Number Of Awards: 5.

Applications Received: 5.
Contact: Grant Services Division

COLORADO COMMISSION ON HIGHER EDUCATION

1300 Broadway, 2nd Floor
Denver, CO 80203
Phone: 303-866-2723
Fax: 303-860-9750
Website: http://www.co.us/cche_dir/hecche.html

#771 • Colorado Part-Time Grant/ Scholarship

Type: Grant. Renewable.
Eligibility: Applicant must be a Colorado resident enrolled part-time at an eligible Colorado school. This award must be used in the following years of study: • Freshman • Sophomore • Junior • Senior
Deadline: Varies.
Award Amount: $ 5,000.
Number Of Awards: Varies.
Contact: College financial aid office

#772 • Colorado Student Grant

Type: Grant. Renewable.
Eligibility: Applicant must be a Colorado resident enrolled at an eligible Colorado school. Financial need is required. This award must be used in the following years of study: • Freshman • Sophomore • Junior • Senior
Deadline: Varies.
Award Amount: $ 5,000.
Number Of Awards: Varies.
Contact: College financial aid office

DAVIS-ROBERTS SCHOLARSHIP FUND, INC.

c/o Gary Skillern
P.O. Box 20645
Cheyenne, WY 82003
Phone: 307-632-0491

#773 • Davis-Roberts Scholarship

Type: Scholarship. Not renewable.
Eligibility: Applicant must be a Wyoming resident and a member of DeMolay or Jobs Daughters. This award must be used in the following years of study: • Freshman • Sophomore • Junior • Senior
Deadline: June 15.
Award Amount: $ 300 - $ 1,000.
Number Of Awards: 3 - 10.
Applications Received: 15.
Contact: See above.

DELAWARE HIGHER EDUCATION COMMISSION

820 North French Street
Wilmington, DE 19801
Phone: 302-577-3240 or 800-292-7935
Fax: 302-577-6765
Email: mlaffey@state.de.us
Website: http://www.doe.state.de.us/high-ed/

#774 • Scholarship Incentive Program

Type: Grant. Not renewable.
Eligibility: Applicant must have a minimum 2.5 GPA, demonstrate financial need, and be enrolled full-time in an institution in Delaware or Pennsylvania. This award must be used in the following years of study: • Freshman • Sophomore • Junior • Senior • Masters • Doctoral
Deadline: April 15.
Award Amount: $ 700 - $ 2,200.
Number Of Awards: 1,200.
Applications Received: 11,000.
Odds Of Winning: 10% of applicants on average receive an award each year.
Contact: Maureen Laffey, Associate Director

#775 • Diamond State Scholarship

Type: Scholarship. Renewable if recipient maintains a minimum 3.0 GPA.
Eligibility: Applicant must be a Delaware resident enrolled as a full-time student. This award must be used in the following years of study: • Freshman
Deadline: March 31.
Award Amount: $ 1,250.
Number Of Awards: 50.
Applications Received: 250.
Odds Of Winning: 16% of applicants on average receive an award each year.
Contact: Maureen Laffey, Associate Director

#776 • Governor's Workforce Development Grant

Type: Grant. Not renewable.
Eligibility: Applicant must be an employed Delaware resident over 18 years old. Selection is based upon need. Award may be used at Delaware schools only. This award must be used in the following years of study: • Freshman • Sophomore • Junior • Senior
Deadline: prior to add/drop.
Award Amount: $ 1,000.
Number Of Awards: 150.
Applications Received: 175.
Odds Of Winning: 85% of applicants on average receive an award each year.
Contact: Maureen Laffey, Associate Director

#777 • Robert C. Byrd Scholarship

Type: Scholarship. Renewable if recipient maintains

satisfactory academic progress.
Eligibility: Applicant must be a Delaware resident, rank in the top quarter of class, have a minimum combined SAT I score of 1200 (composite ACT score of 27), and be enrolled as a full-time student. This award must be used in the following years of study: • Freshman
Deadline: March 31.
Award Amount: $ 1,500.
Number Of Awards: 16.
Applications Received: 250.
Odds Of Winning: 5% of applicants on average receive an award each year.
Contact: Maureen Laffey, Associate Director

FLORIDA LEADER MAGAZINE

P.O. Box 14081
Gainesville, FL 32604-2081
Phone: 352-373-6907
Fax: 352-373-8120
Email: oxendine@csi.com
Website: http://www.floridaleader.com\soty

#778 • Florida College Student of the Year Award

Type: Scholarship. Not renewable.
Eligibility: Applicant must be a Florida college student attending a college in Florida. Selection is based upon academic achievement, campus and community involvement, and financial self-reliance. This award must be used in the following years of study: • Junior • Senior • Masters • Doctoral • Other postgraduate level
Deadline: February 1.
Award Amount: $ 750 - $ 1,500.
Number Of Awards: 20.
Applications Received: 171.
Odds Of Winning: 12% of applicants on average receive an award each year.
Contact: See above.

GENERAL FEDERATION OF WOMEN'S CLUBS OF MASSACHUSETTS (GFWC OF MA)

245 Dutton Road, Box 679
Sudbury, MA 01776-0679
Phone: 978-443-4569

#779 • International Affairs Scholarship

Type: Scholarship. Renewable. Reapplication is required for renewal.
Eligibility: Applicant must be a legal resident of Massachusetts and submit a letter of endorsement from the president of the sponsoring GFWC of Massachusetts club in the community of legal residence, college transcript, personal statement, and

a recommendation from the department head of major. SASE required. This award must be used in the following years of study: • Junior • Senior • Masters • Doctoral
Deadline: March 1.
Award Amount: $ 500.
Number Of Awards: 1 - 2.
Contact: Marian Holbrook, Coordinator of International Affairs
Phone: 413-498-2081

HIGHER EDUCATION SERVICES CORPORATION

99 Washington Avenue
Albany, NY 12255
Phone: 518-473-7087
Fax: 518-474-2839
Website: http://www.hesc.com

#780 • Vietnam Veterans Tuition Award/ Persian Gulf Veterans Tuition Award

Type: Scholarship. Renewable. Award is available for up to five years.
Eligibility: Applicant must be enrolled in an undergraduate program in a New York degree-granting institution or vocational school and must have served in the U.S. Armed Forces in Indochina between January 1, 1963, and May 7, 1975 (dishonorable discharge not eligible). Applicant must have resided in New York on April 20, 1984, or at the time of entry into service and resume residency by September 1 of the year of application. Selection is based solely upon documenting and meeting eligibility requirements. Applicant must also have applied for Tuition Assistance Program and Pell Grant awards. Applicant must have served in hostilities begining August 2, 1990 (for Persian Gulf Veterans Tuition Award only). This award must be used in the following years of study: • Freshman • Sophomore • Junior • Senior
Deadline: May 1.
Award Amount: $ 500 - $ 1,000.
Number Of Awards: Varies.
Contact: New York State Higher Education Services Corporation

#781 • Memorial Scholarship for Children and Spouses of Deceased Police Officers and Firefighters

Type: Scholarship. Renewable for up to five years.
Eligibility: Applicant must be the child or spouse of a police officer, firefighter, or volunteer firefighter and a New York resident attending a New York school at the start of the term for which payment is requested. Parent must have died as a result of injury sustained in the line of duty. Award is actual tuition cost or SUNY undergraduate tuition, whichever is less. This award must be used in the following years

of study: • Freshman • Sophomore • Junior • Senior
Deadline: May 1.
Award Amount: Varies.
Number Of Awards: Varies.
Contact: New York State Higher Education Services Corporation

IDAHO STATE BOARD OF EDUCATION

Len B. Jordan Building, Room 307
P.O. Box 83720
Boise, ID 83720-0037
Phone: 208-334-2270
Fax: 208-334-2632
Email: csmith@osbe.state.id.us

#782 • State of Idaho Scholarship

Type: Scholarship. Renewable. Automatically renewed if recipient maintains a satisfactory GPA.
Eligibility: Applicant must take the ACT and be an Idaho resident planning to enroll full time in an academic or vocational program at an Idaho college or university. Selection is based upon academic merit; 25% of initial awards are given to vocational students. This award must be used in the following years of study: • Freshman
Deadline: December 31.
Award Amount: $ 2,750.
Number Of Awards: 25.
Applications Received: 700.
Odds Of Winning: 3% of applicants on average receive an award each year.
Contact: Caryl Smith, Scholarship Assistant
Email: csmith@osbe.state.id.us

#783 • Governor's Challenge Scholarship

Type: Scholarship. Renewable.
Eligibility: Applicant must be an Idaho resident interested in pursuing a vocational/technical program in Idaho, demonstrate a commitment to public service through essay, and submit transcripts and letters of recommendation. This award must be used in the following years of study: • Freshman
Field(s) Of Study: Vocational/technical.
Deadline: December 31.
Award Amount: $ 3,000.
Number Of Awards: 20.
Applications Received: 125.
Odds Of Winning: 16% of applicants on average receive an award each year.
Contact: Caryl Smith, Scholarship Assistant

ILLINOIS AMVETS SCHOLARSHIP PROGRAM

Illinois Amvets State Headquarters
2200 Sixth Street
Springfield, IL 62703

Phone: 217-528-4713
Fax: 217-528-9896

#784 • Illinois Amvets Service Foundation Scholarship

Type: Scholarship. Renewable.
Eligibility: Applicant must be an Illinois high school senior, unmarried, have taken the ACT, and be the child of a veteran who has served or is presently serving in the military. This award must be used in the following years of study: • Freshman
Deadline: March 1.
Award Amount: $ 1,000.
Number Of Awards: 30.
Applications Received: 700.
Contact: Shanna Hughes, Office Manager
Email: offmgr@amvets.com

ILLINOIS DEPARTMENT OF CHILDREN AND FAMILY SERVICES

406 East Monroe Street #50
Springfield, IL 62701
Phone: 217-785-1172
Fax: 217-524-2101

#785 • Department of Children & Family Services Scholarship

Type: Scholarship. Renewable if recipient continues to maintain at least 12 credits per semester.
Eligibility: Applicant must be a ward (or former ward) of the State of Illinois who has been adopted or is in a subsidized guardianship and who has graduated from an accredited high school. This award must be used in the following years of study: • Freshman
Deadline: 2nd Monday in March.
Award Amount: $ 2,250.
Number Of Awards: 24 - 48.
Applications Received: 89.
Contact: Patricia James Davis, Public Service Administrator

ILLINOIS STUDENT ASSISTANCE COMMISSION/CLIENT SUPPORT SERVICES

1755 Lake Cook Road
Deerfield, IL 60015-5209
Phone: 800-899-ISAC or 847-948-8550
Website: http://www.isac1.org

#786 • Merit Recognition Scholarship

Type: Scholarship. Not renewable.
Eligibility: Applicant must be a U.S. citizen or eligible noncitizen, a resident of Illinois, and rank in the top 5% of class at end of seventh semester.

Applicant must attend an approved Illinois postsecondary institution as an undergraduate on at least a half-time basis, comply with Selective Service (draft) registration requirements, and claim the award within one year of high school graduation. This award must be used in the following years of study: • Freshman
Deadline: Varies.
Award Amount: $ 1,000.
Number Of Awards: 2,200.
Contact: Client Relations

#787 • Monetary Award

Type: Grant. Not renewable.
Eligibility: Applicant must be an Illinois resident, attend an Illinois school, have financial need, and complete FAFSA. This award must be used in the following years of study: • Freshman • Sophomore • Junior • Senior
Deadline: October 1 (new students); June 1 (continuing students).
Award Amount: $ 300 - $ 4,120.
Number Of Awards: 13,000.
Applications Received: 40,000.
Odds Of Winning: 32% of applicants on average receive an award each year.
Contact: Client Relations

IOWA COLLEGE STUDENT AID COMMISSION

200 Tenth Street Fourth Floor
Des Moines, IA 50309-3609
Phone: 515-281-3501
Fax: 515-242-5996
Email: iscac@max.state.ia.us
Website: http://www.iowacollegeaid.org

#788 • Iowa Tuition Grant

Type: Grant. Renewable up to four years.
Eligibility: Applicant must be an Iowa resident, a U.S. citizen, permanent resident, or refugee, and attend an eligible Iowa school. FAFSA required. This award must be used in the following years of study: • Freshman • Sophomore • Junior • Senior
Deadline: June 1 (priority).
Award Amount: $ 3,900.
Number Of Awards: Varies.
Contact: Julie Leeper, Grants Director
Phone: 515-242-6703
Email: julie.leeper@csac.state.ia.us

#789 • Iowa Grants

Type: Grant. Renewable up to four years.
Eligibility: Applicant must be an Iowa resident, a U.S. citizen, permanent resident, or refugee, and attend an eligible Iowa school. Selection is based upon need. FAFSA required. This award must be used in the following years of study: • Freshman •

Sophomore • Junior • Senior
Deadline: Varies.
Award Amount: $ 1,000.
Number Of Awards: Varies.
Contact: Julie Leeper, Grants Director
Phone: 515-242-6703
Email: julie.leeper@csac.state.ia.us

JAMES F. BYRNES FOUNDATION

P.O. Box 9596
Columbia, SC 29290-9596
Phone: 803-254-9325
Fax: 803-254-9354
Email: jfbfsc@usit.net
Website: http://www.byrnesscholars.org

#790 • James F. Byrnes Scholarship

Type: Scholarship. Renewable if recipient maintains a minimum 2.0 GPA and participates in activities.
Eligibility: Applicant must be a South Carolina resident with one deceased parent. This award must be used in the following years of study: • Freshman • Sophomore • Junior
Deadline: February 15.
Award Amount: $ 2,750.
Number Of Awards: 20.
Applications Received: 204.
Odds Of Winning: 10% of applicants on average receive an award each year.
Contact: Barbara R. Kirk, Executive Secretary

LATIN AMERICAN EDUCATIONAL FOUNDATION

Pena Business Plaza
930 West Seventh Avenue
Denver, CO 80204
Phone: 303-446-0541
Fax: 303-446-0526
Email: laef@uswest.net
Website: http://www.laef.org

#791 • LAEF Scholarship

Type: Scholarship. Renewable.
Eligibility: Applicant must be a Colorado resident with a minimum 2.5 GPA who is either Hispanic or active in the Hispanic community. This award must be used in the following years of study: • Freshman • Sophomore • Junior • Senior • Masters • Doctoral • Technical students
Deadline: February 15.
Award Amount: $ 500 - $ 3,000.
Number Of Awards: Varies.
Applications Received: 133.
Odds Of Winning: 50% of applicants on average receive an award each year.
Contact: Scholarship Administrator

LEE-JACKSON FOUNDATION

P.O. Box 8121
Charlottesville, VA 22906
Phone: 804-977-1861
Website: http://www.bitlink.com/leejackson

#792 • Lee Jackson Foundation Scholarship

Type: Scholarship. Not renewable.
Eligibility: Applicant must submit an essay on the career, character, or some other aspect of the lives of General Robert E. Lee, or General "Stonewall" Jackson, or both. Applicant must be attend a secondary school in Virginia, and plan on attending an accredited college or university in the U.S. This award must be used in the following years of study: • Freshman
Deadline: December 17.
Award Amount: $ 1,000 - $10,000.
Number Of Awards: 27.
Applications Received: 1,100.
Odds Of Winning: 2% of applicants on average receive an award each year.
Contact: Stephanie Leech, Foundation Administrator

LOUISIANA OFFICE OF STUDENT FINANCIAL ASSISTANCE

P.O. Box 91202
Baton Rouge, LA 70821-9202
Phone: 800-259-5626
Fax: 225-922-1089
Website: http://www.osfa.state.la.us

#793 • TOPS - Performance Award

Type: Scholarship. Renewable up to four years if recipient remains continuously enrolled in school, has a minimum of 24 credit hours per year, maintains a minimum 3.0 GPA, and maintains steady academic progress.
Eligibility: Applicant must be a Louisiana resident or the child of parents who have been Louisiana residents for at least two years prior to graduation and be graduating from a public or state-approved private high school, have 16.5 units of core curriculum courses in high school, a minimum 3.5 GPA, and minimum composite ACT score of 23. Applicant must submit FAFSA. Alternate eligibility requirements for home-schooled applicants and Louisiana applicants from out-of-state high schools. Award may be used at Louisiana public schools and LAICU schools only. This award must be used in the following years of study: • Freshman
Deadline: April 15 (priority), July 1 (final).
Award Amount: Partial tuition. Maximum award: Full tuition plus $400.
Number Of Awards: Varies.
Contact: Public Information and Communication
Phone: 800-259-5626, extension 1012

Fax: 225-922-0790
Email: custserv@osfa.state.la.us

#794 • TOPS - Opportunity Award

Type: Scholarship. Renewable up to four years if recipient remains continuously enrolled in school, has a minimum of 24 credit hours per year, maintains a minimum 2.3 GPA after 24 credit hours, a minimum 2.5 GPA after 48 credit hours, and maintains steady academic progress.
Eligibility: Applicant must be a Louisiana resident or the child of parents who have been Louisiana residents for at least two years prior to graduation and be graduating from a public or state-approved private high school, have 16.5 units of core curriculum courses in high school, a minimum 2.5 GPA, and minimum composite ACT score equalling the prior year's national average. Applicant must submit FAFSA. Alternate eligibility requirements for home-schooled applicants and Louisiana applicants from out-of-state high schools. Award may be used at Louisiana public schools and LAICU schools only. This award must be used in the following years of study: • Freshman
Deadline: April 15 (priority), July 1 (final).
Award Amount: Full tuition. Partial tuition (at LAICU schools). Plus some fees.
Number Of Awards: 13,200.
Applications Received: 25,400.
Odds Of Winning: 52% of applicants on average receive an award each year.
Contact: Public Information and Communication
Phone: 800-259-5626, extension 1012
Fax: 225-922-0790
Email: custserv@osfa.state.la.us

#795 • TOPS - Honors Award

Type: Scholarship. Renewable up to four years if recipient remains continuously enrolled in school, has a minimum of 24 credit hours per year, maintains a minimum 3.0 GPA, and maintains steady academic progress.
Eligibility: Applicant must be a Louisiana resident or the child of parents who have been Louisiana residents for at least two years prior to graduation and be graduating from a public or state-approved private high school, have 16.5 units of core curriculum courses in high school, a minimum 3.5 GPA, and minimum composite ACT score of 27. Applicant must submit FAFSA. Alternate eligibility requirements for home-schooled applicants and Louisiana applicants from out-of-state high schools. Award may be used at Louisiana public schools and LAICU schools only. This award must be used in the following years of study: • Freshman
Deadline: April 15 (priority), July 1 (final).
Award Amount: Partial tuition. Maximum award: Full tuition plus $800.
Number Of Awards: Varies.

Contact: Public Information and Communication
Phone: 800-259-5626, extension 1012
Fax: 225-922-0790
Email: custserv@osfa.state.la.us

#796 • TOPS - Tech Award

Type: Scholarship. Renewable. Award is renewable up to two years if recipient remains continuously enrolled full-time and maintains a minimum 2.5 GPA.
Eligibility: Applicant must be a Louisiana resident or the child of parents who have been Louisiana residents for at least two years prior to graduation and be graduating from a public or state-approved private high school, have 16.5 units of tech core courses in high school, a minimum 2.5 GPA, and minimum composite ACT score of 19. Applicant must submit FAFSA. Applicant must plan to enroll in an applied associate, certificate, or non-academic degree program. Alternate eligibility requirements for home-schooled applicants and Louisiana applicants from out-of-state high schools. Award may be used at Louisiana public technical schools only. This award must be used in the following years of study: • Freshman
Deadline: April 15 (priority), July 1 (final).
Award Amount: Varies.
Number Of Awards: Varies.
Contact: Public Information and Communication
Phone: 800-259-5626, extension 1012
Fax: 225-922-0790
Email: custserv@osfa.state.la.us

LOUISIANA STATE DEPARTMENT OF EDUCATION

PO Box 94064
Baton Rouge, LA 70804
Phone: 504-342-2098
Fax: 504-342-3432
Email: ptrisler@mail.doe.state.la.us

#797 • Robert C. Byrd Honors Scholarship

Type: Scholarship. Renewable if recipient remains in good standing and maintains full-time status.
Eligibility: Applicant must be a U.S. citizen and Louisiana resident, graduate from a Louisiana high school, and have a minimum 3.5 GPA and minimum composite ACT score of 23 after seven semesters. Applicant must demonstrate outstanding academic achievement and promise of continuous of achievement. This award must be used in the following years of study: • Freshman
Deadline: in March.
Award Amount: $ 1,500.
Number Of Awards: 116.
Applications Received: 800.
Contact: Phyllis Trisler, Scholarship Coordinator

MAINE CAMPGROUND OWNERS ASSOCIATION (MECOA)

655 Main Street
Lewiston, ME 04240
Phone: 207-782-5874
Fax: 207-782-4497
Email: info@campmaine.com
Website: http://www.campmaine.com

#798 • MECOA Scholarship

Type: Scholarship. Renewable. Recipient must reapply for renewal.
Eligibility: Applicant must be a Maine resident. Selection is based upon academic record, letters of recommendation, and financial need. This award must be used in the following years of study: • Sophomore • Junior • Senior
Field(s) Of Study: Outdoor recreation.
Deadline: April 1.
Award Amount: $ 500.
Number Of Awards: 1.
Applications Received: 10.
Odds Of Winning: 10% of applicants on average receive an award each year.
Contact: Daniel Billings, Executive Director

MAINE DEPARTMENT OF AGRICULTURE, FOOD, AND RURAL RESOURCES

ATTN: Rural Rehabilitation Fund Scholarship Committee
28 State House Station
Augusta, ME 04333-0028
Phone: 207-287-7628
Fax: 207-287-7548
Email: Rod.McCormick@state.me.us

#799 • Maine Rural Rehabilitation Fund Scholarship

Type: Scholarship. Renewable upon approval of selection committee.
Eligibility: Applicant must be a Maine resident, be enrolled or planning to enroll as a full-time student, demonstrate unmet financial need, and meet at least one of the following qualifications: Be a member of a family in which at least half of the family's gross income for the past year has been derived from farm/woodswork occupation; be the child of a deceased or physically disabled farm operator/woodsworker; be an FFA member in good standing planning to pursue a career in agriculture/woodswork. Applicants currently enrolled in college must have a minimum 2.7 cumulative GPA or a minimum 3.0 GPA for the current term. This award must be used in the following years of study: • Freshman • Sophomore • Junior • Senior • vocational and trade school programs

Deadline: June 15.
Award Amount: $ 1,000.
Number Of Awards: 16 - 22.
Applications Received: 45.
Contact: Rod McCormick, Research Associate

MAINE EDUCATION ASSISTANCE DIVISION

Teachers for Maine Program State House Station #119
Augusta, ME   04333
Phone: 800-228-3734 (in Maine) or 207-623-3263
Fax: 207-626-8208
Email: info@famemaine.com
Website: http://www.famemaine.com

#800 • Maine Student Incentive Scholarship

Type: Grant. Not renewable.
Eligibility: Applicant must be a Maine resident attending an eligible school in a state with a reciprocal agreement. This award must be used in the following years of study: • Freshman • Sophomore • Junior • Senior
Deadline: May 1.
Award Amount: $ 250 - $ 1,000.
Number Of Awards: 9,200.
Odds Of Winning: 50% of applicants on average receive an award each year.
Contact: Scholarship Administrator

MAINE EDUCATION SERVICES FOUNDATION

P.O. Box 549
Augusta, ME   04332
Phone: 207-623-2600
Fax: 207-623-1493
Website: http://www.mesfoundation.com

#801 • Maine Legislature Memorial Scholarship

Type: Scholarship. Not renewable.
Eligibility: Applicant must be enrolled in a Maine school. Selection is based upon academic ability, extracurricular activities, and talents. Essay and letters of recommendation required. This award must be used in the following years of study: • Freshman • Sophomore • Junior • Senior • Masters • Doctoral • Other postgraduate level
Deadline: March 26.
Award Amount: $ 500.
Number Of Awards: 16.
Contact: Betty Ryder, Scheduling Coordinator
Phone: 207-623-2600, extension 645
Email: eryder@mesfoundation.com

#802 • Royal Arch Masonic Scholarship

Type: Scholarship. Renewable.
Eligibility: Applicant must be a graduate of a Maine high school, must be nominated by his or her high school, and must remain chem-free. Selection is based upon academic ability, financial need, extracurricular activities, and talents. Essay and letters of recommendation required. This award must be used in the following years of study: • Freshman
Deadline: March 26.
Award Amount: $ 500 - $ 1,500.
Number Of Awards: Varies.
Contact: Betty Ryder, Scheduling Coordinator
Phone: 207-623-2600, extension 645
Fax: 207-623-1493
Email: eryder@mesfoundation.com

#803 • Maine Chamber and Business Alliance Scholarship

Type: Scholarship. Not renewable.
Eligibility: Applicant must be a Maine resident attending a Maine school. Selection is based upon academic ability, extracurricular activities, and financial need. Essay and letters of recommendation required. This award must be used in the following years of study: • Freshman
Field(s) Of Study: Business, technical.
Deadline: March 26.
Award Amount: $ 1,000.
Number Of Awards: 2.
Contact: Betty Ryder, Scheduling Coordinator
Phone: 207-623-2600, extension 645
Email: eryder@mesfoundation.com

MAINE STATE SOCIETY OF WASHINGTON, D.C., FOUNDATION, INC.

3508 Wilson Street
Fairfax, VA   22030-2936

#804 • Maine State Society of Washington D.C. Foundation Inc. Scholarship

Type: Scholarship. Not renewable.
Eligibility: Applicant must be under age 23, have been born in or have been a legal resident of the state of Maine for at least four years or have at least one parent who whas born in or who has been a legal resident for at least four years, and be enrolled for a minimum of 14 semester hours at a four-year nonprofit college or university in Maine. Applicant must have a minimum 3.0 GPA and submit "student copy" of college transcript and a handwritten composition (500-word maximum) containing background information on applicant's qualifications for scholarship. SASE required. This award must be used in the following years of study: • Sophomore • Junior • Senior
Deadline: April 1.
Award Amount: $ 1,000.

Number Of Awards: 2.
Applications Received: 40.
Odds Of Winning: 5% of applicants on average receive an award each year.
Contact: Scholarship Administrator

MARION D. AND EVA S. PEEPLES FOUNDATION

18 West Jefferson Street
Franklin, IN 46131
Phone: 317-738-2213
Fax: 317-736-7220

#805 • Peeples Foundation Trust Scholarship

Type: Scholarship. Renewable if recipient provides transcripts each semester.
Eligibility: Applicant must be a resident of Indiana, demonstrate academic achievement and financial need. Recommendations required. This award must be used in the following years of study: • Freshman • Sophomore • Junior • Senior
Field(s) Of Study: Dietetics, industrial arts teaching, nursing.
Deadline: March 1.
Award Amount: $ 500 - $ 3,500.
Number Of Awards: Varies.
Applications Received: 100.
Contact: Teresa Mankin, Scholarship Coordinator
Email: teresam@iquest.net

MARYLAND HIGHER EDUCATION COMMISSION

State Scholarship Administration
16 Francis Street
Annapolis, MD 21401-1781
Phone: 410-974-5370 or 800-974-1024
Fax: 410-974-5994
Email: ssamail@mhec.state.md.us
Website: http://www.mhec.state.md.us

#806 • Distinguished Scholar

Type: Scholarship. Renewable if recipient maintains Maryland residency, is enrolled full-time, and maintains a minimum 3.0 GPA.
Eligibility: Applicant must be a Maryland resident, National Merit finalist, National Achievement finalist, demonstrate superior academic achievement (minimum 3.7 GPA), or demonstrate superior talent in the arts. Applicant must be nominated by high school during second semester of junior year. Award may be used at Maryland schools only. This award must be used in the following years of study: • Freshman • Sophomore • Junior • Senior
Deadline: in March.
Award Amount: $ 3,000.

Number Of Awards: 350.
Applications Received: 3,500.
Odds Of Winning: 10% of applicants on average receive an award each year.
Contact: Program Administrator
Phone: 410-974-5370, extension 168

#807 • Senatorial Scholarship

Type: Grant. Renewable. Automatically renewed for three years if recipient continues to meet eligibility requirements.
Eligibility: Applicant must be a Maryland resident who is a full-time or part-time student. Applicant should contact his or her state senator for additional information. Award may be used at Maryland schools only unless applicant is enrolled in a major not offered at any Maryland school. This award must be used in the following years of study: • Freshman • Sophomore • Junior • Senior • Masters • Doctoral
Deadline: March 1.
Award Amount: $ 400 - $ 2,000.
Number Of Awards: 7,088.
Contact: Program Specialist

#808 • Delegate Scholarship

Type: Scholarship. Renewable. Reapplication is required to retain scholarship.
Eligibility: Applicant must be a Maryland resident, a full- or part-time student, and must contact all three delegates in his/her state legislative district for application instructions. Award may be used at Maryland schools only unless applicant is enrolled in a major not offered at any Maryland school. This award must be used in the following years of study: • Freshman • Sophomore • Junior • Senior • Masters • Doctoral
Deadline: Varies.
Award Amount: $ 200. Full tuition or partial tuition, plus fees.
Number Of Awards: 2,600.
Contact: Program Specialist

#809 • Guaranteed Access Grant

Type: Grant. Renewable. Award is renewable up to six additional semesters if minimum 2.0 GPA is maintained.
Eligibility: Applicant must be a Maryland resident, be a full-time student, and have a minimum 2.5 GPA. Award may by used at Maryland schools only. Selection is based upon financial need. This award must be used in the following years of study: • Freshman
Deadline: March 1 (FAFSA & SSA).
Award Amount: $ 400 - $ 8,700.
Number Of Awards: Varies.
Contact: Program Specialist

MARYLAND STATE SCHOLARSHIP ADMINISTRATION

The Jeffrey Building
16 Francis Street
Annapolis, MD 21401
Phone: 410-974-5370
Fax: 410-974-5994
Email: ssamail@mhec.state.md-us
Website: http://www.mhec.state.md.us

#810 • Professional School Scholarship

Type: Scholarship. Renewable up to three years.
Eligibility: Applicant must be a Maryland resident, attand a Maryland school, and demonstrate financial need. This award must be used in the following years of study: • Freshman • Sophomore • Junior • Senior • Masters
Field(s) Of Study: Dentistry, law, medicine, nursing, pharmacy, social work.
Deadline: March 1.
Award Amount: $ 200 - $ 1,000.
Number Of Awards: Varies.
Contact: Scholarship Administrator

MASONIC GRAND LODGE CHARITIES OF RHODE ISLAND

222 Taunton Avenue
East Providence, RI 02914-4556
Phone: 401-435-4650

#811 • Masonic Grand Lodge Charities of Rhode Island Scholarship

Type: Scholarship. Renewable. Reapplication required for renewal.
Eligibility: Applicant must be a Rhode Island resident for at least five years or the child or grandchild of a Rhode Island Mason. This award must be used in the following years of study: • Freshman • Sophomore • Junior • Senior
Deadline: April 18.
Award Amount: $ 750 - $ 3,500.
Number Of Awards: 100 - 185.
Applications Received: 215.
Odds Of Winning: 88% of applicants on average receive an award each year.
Contact: Masonic Grand Lodge Charities of Rhode Island

MASSACHUSETTS OFFICE OF STUDENT FINANCIAL ASSISTANCE

330 Stuart Street
Boston, MA 02116
Phone: 617-727-9420
Fax: 617-727-0667

#812 • Massgrant

Type: Grant. Renewable. Recipient must file FAFSA for renewal.
Eligibility: Applicant must be a resident of Massachusetts, enrolled full time, in good academic standing, and demonstrate financial need. This award must be used in the following years of study: • Freshman • Sophomore • Junior • Senior
Deadline: May 1.
Award Amount: $ 250 - $ 2,500.
Number Of Awards: 34,000.
Contact: Dr. Clantha McCurdy, Director

MINNESOTA HIGHER EDUCATION SERVICES OFFICE DIVISION OF STUDENT FINANCIAL AID

1450 Energy Park Drive, Suite 350
St. Paul, MN 55108-5227
Phone: 800-657-3866, 651 642-0567
Email: info@heso.state.mn.us
Website: http://www.heso.state.mn.us

#813 • Minnesota State Grant

Type: Grant. Renewable. Applicant must reapply and demonstrate need for renewal.
Eligibility: Applicant must show need, be a U.S. citizen or permanent resident, meet state residency requirements, be in first four years of postsecondary education, not be in default on a student loan, and be current in child support obligation. This award must be used in the following years of study: • Freshman • Sophomore • Junior • Senior
Deadline: June 30.
Award Amount: $ 100 - $ 7,089.
Number Of Awards: 60,000.
Contact: Grants Staff

#814 • Public Safety Officers Survivor Grant

Type: Grant. Renewable. Reapplication is required for renewal for each academic term.
Eligibility: Applicant must be the dependent child under age 23 or the surviving spouse of a public safety officer who was killed in the line of duty on or after January 1, 1973. Applicant must also be a U.S. citizen or permanent resident, meet state residency requirements, be enrolled at least half time, be in the first four years of postsecondary education, and must not be in default on a student loan. This award must be used in the following years of study: • Freshman • Sophomore • Junior • Senior
Deadline: last day of classes.
Award Amount: $ 3,419.
Number Of Awards: 9.
Applications Received: 9.
Odds Of Winning: 100% of applicants on average receive an award each year.

Contact: Brenda Larter, Program Assistant
Email: larter@heso.state.mn.us

MISSISSIPPI BOARD OF TRUSTEES OF STATE INSTITUTIONS OF HIGHER LEARNING

Student Financial Aid Office
3825 Ridgewood Road
Jackson, MS 39211-6453
Phone: 601-982-6663
Fax: 601-982-6527

#815 • Law Enforcement Officers and Fireman Scholarship

Type: Scholarship. Renewable. Awarded for a maximum of eight semesters.
Eligibility: Applicant must be the spouse or child of a full-time Mississippi law enforcement officer or firefighter who was fatally injured or totally disabled from injuries that occured in the line of duty. Applicant must attend a Mississippi public college or university. Children are eligible until age 23. This award must be used in the following years of study: • Freshman • Sophomore • Junior • Senior
Deadline: Varies.
Award Amount: Full-tuition. Partial Tuition. plus required fees and average cost of dorm room.
Number Of Awards: Varies.
Contact: Student Financial Aid Office

MISSOURI DEPARTMENT OF ELEMENTARY AND SECONDARY EDUCATION

P.O. Box 480
Jefferson City, MO 65102
Phone: 573-751-1668
Fax: 573-526-3580
Email: jboeckma@mail.dese.state.mo.us

#816 • Robert C. Byrd Honors Scholarship

Type: Scholarship. Renewable up to three years if recipient remains in good standing.
Eligibility: Applicant must be a resident of Missouri, rank in the top tenth of class, score in the top 10% on the ACT, and file with the school a statement certifying registration with the Selective Service. This award must be used in the following years of study: • Freshman
Deadline: April 15.
Award Amount: $ 1,500.
Number Of Awards: 126.
Applications Received: 1,000.
Odds Of Winning: 12% of applicants on average receive an award each year.
Contact: Janet Goeller, Director of Teacher Recruitment & Retention

NATIONAL ASSOCIATION OF WATER COMPANIES-NEW JERSEY CHAPTER

600 South Avenue
Westfield, NJ 07090
Phone: 908-654-9122
Fax: 908-232-2719

#817 • National Association of Water Companies-New Jersey Chapter Scholarship

Type: Scholarship. Not renewable.
Eligibility: Applicant must be a U.S. citizen, a New Jersey resident for at least five years, and pursuing a degree at a New Jersey college or university. Applicant must have a minimum 3.0 GPA and be pursuing a professional career in the water utility industry or any field related to it, with an interest in investor-owned water companies/industry. This award must be used in the following years of study: • Sophomore • Junior • Senior • Masters • Doctoral • Other postgraduate level
Field(s) Of Study: Biology, business, chemistry, communication, computer science, engineering, environmental sciences, law, natural resource management.
Deadline: April 1.
Award Amount: $ 2,500.
Number Of Awards: 2.
Contact: Gail P. Brady, NAWC-NJ Scholarship Committee Chairperson

NATIONAL TOURISM FOUNDATION (NTF)

546 East Main Street
Lexington, KY 40508
Phone: 800-682-8886
Fax: 606-226-4414
Email: scudderb@mgtserv.com
Website: http://www.ntaonline.com

#818 • State Scholarships

Type: Scholarship. Not renewable.
Eligibility: Applicant must be a resident of Alaska, California, Connecticut, Florida, Michigan, Minnesota, Mississippi, Montana, Nebraska, New Jersey, North Carolina, Ohio, Oklahoma, or Wyoming. This award must be used in the following years of study: • Junior • Senior
Field(s) Of Study: Travel/tourism.
Deadline: April 15.
Award Amount: $ 500 - $ 1,000.
Number Of Awards: 19.
Contact: Brooks A. Scudder, Assistant Exec. Director

NEVADA DEPARTMENT OF EDUCATION

700 East Fifth Street
Carson City, NV 89701

Phone: 775-687-9200
Fax: 775-687-9101
Website: http://www.nsn.k12.nv.us/nvdoe

#819 • Robert C. Byrd Honors Scholarship Program

Type: Scholarship. Renewable for up to four years of undergraduate study if recipient continues to meet eligibility requirements.
Eligibility: Applicant must be a resident of Nevada, be a Nevada High School Scholars Program recipient, and file a Statement of Selective Service Registration Status. Selection is based upon unweighted GPA and SAT I or ACT scores. This award must be used in the following years of study: • Freshman • Sophomore • Junior • Senior
Deadline: Varies.
Award Amount: $ 1,500.
Number Of Awards: 40.
Contact: Phyllis Furlong, Program Coordinator
Phone: 775-687-9228
Email: pfurlong@nsn.k12.nv.us

NEW HAMPSHIRE POSTSECONDARY EDUCATION COMMISSION

Student Financial Assistance Coordinator
2 Industrial Park Drive
Concord, NH 03301-8512
Phone: 603-271-2555
Fax: 603-271-2696
Website: http://www.state.nh.us/postsecondary

#820 • New Hampshire Incentive Program

Type: Grant. Renewable.
Eligibility: Applicant must be a New Hampshire resident, have a minimum 2.0 GPA, attend a NEASC-accredited New England school, and demonstrate financial need. This award must be used in the following years of study: • Freshman • Sophomore • Junior • Senior
Deadline: May 1.
Award Amount: $ 225 - $ 1,000.
Number Of Awards: 1,348.
Applications Received: 27,000.
Contact: Judith A. Knapp, Student Financial Aid Coordinator
Email: jknapp@nhsa.state.nh.us

NEW JERSEY HIGHER EDUCATION AND ASSISTANCE AUTHORITY

Four Quakerbridge Plaza CN 540
Trenton, NJ 08625
Phone: 609-588-3226
Fax: 609-588-2228
Website: http://www.state.nj/us/treasury/osa

#821 • Educational Opportunity Fund Grant

Type: Grant. Renewable. Satisfactory academic progress and financial need are required to retain scholarship.
Eligibility: Applicant must be from an educationally disadvantaged background and demonstrate financial need. Applicant must be a full-time, matriculated student at a New Jersey college or university and be a resident of New Jersey for at least 12 consecutive months. This award must be used in the following years of study: • Freshman • Sophomore • Junior • Senior • Doctoral
Deadline: October 1, March 1 (spring).
Award Amount: $ 200 - $ 2,100.
Number Of Awards: Varies.
Contact: Leah Fletcher, Assistant Director, Student Information Services
Phone: 609-584-4350
Fax: 609-588-2228
Email: lfletche@osa.state.nj.us

#822 • Edward J. Bloustein Distinguished Scholars

Type: Scholarship. Renewable. Satisfactory academic progress is required to retain scholarship.
Eligibility: Applicant must be (and have been for the previous 12 consecutive months) a New Jersey resident planning to attend a New Jersey college or university full time and be nominated for the award by high school based upon GPA, class rank, and SAT I scores. Additional scholarships will be provided to applicants from the state's urban and economically distressed areas based upon class rank and GPA. This award must be used in the following years of study: • Freshman • Sophomore • Junior • Senior
Deadline: March 1.
Award Amount: $ 4,549.
Number Of Awards: Varies.
Contact: Leah Fletcher, Assistant Director, Student Information Services
Phone: 609-584-4350
Fax: 609-588-2228
Email: lfletche@osa.state.nj.us

#823 • Tuition Aid Grant

Type: Grant. Renewable. Satisfactory academic progress and financial need are required to retain scholarship.
Eligibility: Applicant must be or intend to be a full-time undergraduate at a New Jersey college or university, demonstrate financial need, and must have lived in New Jersey for at least 12 consecutive months. Grant amount is based upon applicant's need and college choice. This award must be used in the following years of study: • Freshman • Sophomore • Junior • Senior
Deadline: October 1.
Award Amount: $ 824 - $ 6,052.

Number Of Awards: Varies.
Contact: Leah Fletcher, Assistant Director, Student Information Services
Phone: 609-584-4350
Email: lfletche@osa.state.nj.us

NEW YORK STATE EDUCATION DEPARTMENT

Bureau of HEOP/DATEA/Scholarships
Room 1071 EBA
Albany, NY 12230
Phone: 518-486-1319
Fax: 518-486-5341

#824 • Robert C. Byrd Honors Scholarship Program

Type: Scholarship. Renewable.
Eligibility: Applicant must be a legal resident of New York state and a senior in high school with a grade average of 96 and minimum combined SAT I score of 1250 or a student earning a GED diploma by the end of February. This award must be used in the following years of study: • Freshman
Deadline: in February.
Award Amount: $ 1,500.
Number Of Awards: 412.
Contact: Harold Rutherford, Associate in Higher Education

NORTH CAROLINA BAR ASSOCIATION

P.O. Box 3688
Cary, NC 27519
Phone: 919-677-0561
Fax: 919-677-0761
Email: jtfount@mail.barlinc.org
Website: http://www.barlinc.org/

#825 • North Carolina Bar Association Scholarship

Type: Scholarship. Renewable up to a maximum of $8,000 over four years if recipient reapplies.
Eligibility: Applicant must be the child of a North Carolina law enforcement officer who was killed or permanently disabled in the line of duty and must apply prior to age 27. Selection is based upon financial need and merit. This award must be used in the following years of study: • Freshman • Sophomore • Junior • Senior • Masters • Doctoral
Deadline: April 1.
Award Amount: $ 2,000.
Number Of Awards: Varies.
Contact: Jacquelyn Terrell-Fountain, Assistant Director of Sections and Divisions

OKLAHOMA STATE REGENTS FOR HIGHER EDUCATION

500 Education Building
State Capitol Complex
Oklahoma City, OK 73105
Phone: 405-524-9100
Fax: 405-524-9230

#826 • Academic Scholars Program

Type: Scholarship. Renewable. Minimum 3.25 GPA and full-time enrollment are required to retain scholarship.
Eligibility: Applicant must be an Oklahoma resident at or above the 99.5 percentile on ACT or SAT I, or be a resident or nonresident that is one of the following: National Merit scholar or finalist, National Achievement scholar or finalist, National Hispanic scholar or honorable mention awardee, or Presidential scholar. This award must be used in the following years of study: • Freshman • Junior
Deadline: mid-August.
Award Amount: $ 3,500 - $ 5,500.
Number Of Awards: 350.
Applications Received: 410.
Odds Of Winning: 96% of applicants on average receive an award each year.
Contact: Dawn Scott, Research Analyst

OREGON AFL-CIO

2110 State Street
Salem, OR 97301
Phone: 503-585-6320

#827 • Oregon AFL-CIO May Darling-Asat. Williams-Northwest Labor Press Scholarship

Type: Contest. Not renewable.
Eligibility: Applicant must be a graduating senior from an accredited Oregon high school in the year that the written scholarship exam is given. Selection is based upon superior performance on the written labor history exam, financial need, high school GPA, and an interview by a panel of professionals. Applicant must plan to attend a certified trade school. This award must be used in the following years of study: • Freshman
Deadline: March 1.
Award Amount: $ 850 - $ 3,000.
Number Of Awards: 4.
Contact: Arthur Stern Kunis, Research and Education Director
Phone: 503-585-6320
Fax: 503-585-1668
Email: askbeany@compuserve.com

STATE/COUNTRY OF RESIDENCE

PACD AUXILIARY

Blair County Conservation District
1407 Blair Street
Holidaysburg, PA 16648
Phone: 814-696-0877
Fax: 814-696-9981

#828 • PACD Auxiliary Scholarship

Type: Scholarship. Not renewable.
Eligibility: Applicant must be a resident of
Pennsylvania. Applicant must provide a resume and
statement of need. This award must be used in the
following years of study: • Senior • Masters • Second-
year of associate degree
Field(s) Of Study: Agriculture, conservation,
environmental.
Deadline: June 30.
Award Amount: $ 500.
Number Of Awards: 1.
Applications Received: 30.
Odds Of Winning: 3% of applicants on average
receive an award each year.
Contact: Donna Fisher, Manager, Margaret Angle,
Clerk
Phone: 814-696-0877
Fax: 814-696-9981

PARRETT SCHOLARSHIP FOUNDATION

c/o U.S. Bank of Washington, Trustee
P.O. Box 720
Seattle, WA 98111-0720
Phone: 206-344-3691

#829 • Arthur and Doreen A. Parrett Scholarship

Type: Scholarship. Not renewable.
Eligibility: Applicant must be a resident of
Washington state enrolled full-time in an accredited
institution. This award must be used in the following
years of study: • Sophomore • Junior • Senior • Other
postgraduate level
Field(s) Of Study: Engineering, dentistry, medicine,
science.
Deadline: July 31.
Award Amount: $ 1,000 - $ 3,000.
Number Of Awards: 15 - 20.
Contact: See above.

PINE TREE STATE 4-H CLUB FOUNDATION

c/o University of Maine
5717 Corbett Hall
Orono, ME 04469-5717
Phone: 207-581-3739

#830 • 4-H Postsecondary Scholarship

Type: Scholarship. Not renewable.
Eligibility: Applicant must be a 4-H member and be
a Maine high school student in high academic
standing who is entering a post-secondary institution
within one year of graduation. Applicant must submit
application form, transcript, and other materials. This
award must be used in the following years of study: •
Freshman
Deadline: Varies.
Award Amount: $ 1,000.
Number Of Awards: 4 - 6.
Contact: Annie Brown, Assistant

PORTUGUESE FOUNDATION (CONNECTICUT)

86 New Park Avenue
Hartford, CT 06106
Phone: 860-236-5514
Fax: 860-236-5514
Website: http://www.pfict.org

#831 • Portuguese Foundation (Connecticut) Scholarship

Type: Scholarship. Renewable. Recipient must
reapply to renew scholarship.
Eligibility: Applicant must be of Portuguese descent
and be a resident of Connecticut. Applicant must
submit essay on his or her needs and a description of
roots. This award must be used in the following years
of study: • Freshman • Sophomore • Junior • Senior •
Masters • Doctoral • Other postgraduate level
Deadline: March 1.
Award Amount: $ 1,000 - $ 2,500.
Number Of Awards: 3 - 8.
Applications Received: 65.
Contact: Gabriel R. Serrano
Phone: 860-236-5514

RHODE ISLAND HIGHER EDUCATION ASSISTANCE AUTHORITY

560 Jefferson Boulevard
Warwick, RI 02886
Phone: 401-736-1100
Fax: 401-732-3541
Website: http://www.riheaa.org

#832 • Rhode Island State Grant

Type: Grant. Renewable. Recipient must maintain
satisfactory academic progress, financial need, and
residency to retain scholarship.
Eligibility: Applicant must be a Rhode Island
resident, a U.S. citizen or eligible noncitizen,
demonstrate financial need, and file FAFSA.
Applicant must be enrolled at least part time in a
degree or certificate program. This award must be

used in the following years of study: • Freshman • Sophomore • Junior • Senior
Deadline: January 1-March 1.
Award Amount: $ 250 - $ 750.
Number Of Awards: 10,000.
Applications Received: 37,338.
Odds Of Winning: 27% of applicants on average receive an award each year.
Contact: Mary Ann Welch, Director of Program Administration
Email: mawelch@riheaa.org

SELBY FOUNDATION

1800 Second Street, Suite 750
Sarasota, FL 34236
Phone: 941-957-0442
Fax: 941-957-3135

#833 • Selby Direct Scholarship

Type: Scholarship. Not renewable.
Eligibility: Applicant must be a resident of Charlotte, DeSoto, Manatee, or Sarasota counties in Florida. This award must be used in the following years of study: • Freshman • Sophomore • Junior • Senior
Deadline: March 1.
Award Amount: $ 1,000 - $ 5,000.
Number Of Awards: 10.
Contact: Jan Noah, Scholarship Coordinator

SHAWNEE STATE UNIVERSITY (SSU)

940 Second Street
Portsmouth, OH 45662-4344
Phone: 740-355-2237
Fax: 740-355-2435
Website: http://www.shawnee.edu

#834 • Development Foundation Diversity Scholarship

Type: Scholarship. Not renewable.
Eligibility: Applicant cannot be a resident of Ohio or have attended high school in Ohio. Applicant must have a minimum 3.0 GPA and preference is given to minorities. This award must be used in the following years of study: • Freshman
Deadline: Varies.
Award Amount: Partial tuition. Variable awards.
Number Of Awards: 2.
Contact: Debra Atkinson, Financial Aid Department
940 Second St.
Portsmouth, OH 45662
Phone: 740-355-2237
Fax: 740-335-2435
Email: datkinson@shawnee.edu

SOUTH DAKOTA DEPARTMENT OF EDUCATION AND CULTURAL AFFAIRS

Office of the Secretary
700 Governors Drive
Pierre, SD 57501-2291
Phone: 605-773-5669
Fax: 605-773-6139
Website: http://www.state.sd.us/deca

#835 • Robert Byrd Honors Scholarship

Type: Scholarship. Renewable if recipient continues to maintain satisfactory progress.
Eligibility: Applicant must be a South Dakota resident, have at least a 3.5 GPA, and an ACT score of atleast 24. This award must be used in the following years of study: • Freshman
Deadline: May 1.
Award Amount: $ 1,500.
Number Of Awards: 20.
Applications Received: 300.
Odds Of Winning: 7% of applicants on average receive an award each year.
Contact: Roxie Thielen, Financial Aid Administrator
Phone: 605-773-5669
Email: roxie.thielen@state.sd.us

SOUTH DAKOTA, DEPARTMENT OF EDUCATION AND CULTURAL AFFAIRS

700 Governors Drive
Pierre, SD 57501-2291
Phone: 605-773-5669
Fax: 605-773-6139
Website: http://www.state.sd.us/deca/

#836 • Robert C. Byrd Honors Scholarship

Type: Scholarship. Renewable if recipient maintains satisfactory progress.
Eligibility: Applicant must be a South Dakota resident. Selection is based upon GPA and standardized test scores. This award must be used in the following years of study: • Freshman
Deadline: May 1.
Award Amount: $ 1,500.
Number Of Awards: 20.
Applications Received: 300.
Contact: Roxie Thielen, Financial Aid Administrator
Email: roxie.thielen@state.sd.us

STATE COLLEGE AND UNIVERSITY SYSTEMS OF WEST VIRGINIA, CENTRAL OFFICE

1018 Kanawha Boulevard, East
Suite 700
Charleston, WV 25301-2827
Phone: 304-558-4618

Fax: 304-558-4622
Email: crocket@scusco.wvnet.edu
Website: http://www.scusco.wvnet.edu/

#837 • West Virginia Higher Education Grant

Type: Grant. Renewable. Reapplication, financial need, and satisfactory academic performance are required for renewal.
Eligibility: Applicant must demonstrate financial need, meet academic qualifications, be a U.S. citizen, have been a resident of the state of West Virginia for at least one year, and enroll as a full-time undergraduate student at an approved educational institution. This award must be used in the following years of study: • Freshman • Sophomore • Junior • Senior
Deadline: March 1.
Award Amount: $ 350 - $ 2,446.
Number Of Awards: 9,100.
Applications Received: 55,000.
Odds Of Winning: 6% of applicants on average receive an award each year.
Contact: Robert E. Long, Grant Program Coordinator
Phone: 304-558-4614 or 888-825-5707
Fax: 304-558-4622
Email: long@scusco.wvnet.edu

#838 • Robert C. Byrd Honors Scholarship

Type: Scholarship. Renewable. Satisfactory academic progress is required to retain scholarship.
Eligibility: Applicant must be a high school graduate enrolled at a non profit, degree-granting institution of higher education and must demonstrate outstanding academic achievement and show promise of continued achievement. Students apply for this award through high school counselors. This award must be used in the following years of study: • Freshman • Sophomore • Junior • Senior
Deadline: March 15.
Award Amount: $ 1,500.
Number Of Awards: 170.
Applications Received: 178.
Odds Of Winning: 22% of applicants on average receive an award each year.
Contact: Michelle Wicks, Scholarship Programs Coordinator
Email: wicks@scusco.wvnet.edu

TEXAS HIGHER EDUCATION COORDINATING BOARD

Student Financial Assistance
P.O. Box 12788, Capitol Station
Austin, TX 78711-2788
Phone: 512-427-6340
Website: http://www.thecb.state.tx.us

#839 • Good Neighbor Scholarship

Type: Scholarship. Renewable. Recipient must reapply for renewal.
Eligibility: Applicant must be a native-born citizen and resident from another nation of the American hemisphere, certified by native country, and scholastically qualified for admission to a public college or university in Texas. This award must be used in the following years of study: • Freshman • Sophomore • Junior • Senior • Masters • Doctoral
Deadline: March 15.
Award Amount: $ 4,452.
Number Of Awards: 257.
Contact: Gustavo O. DeLeon, Assistant Director of Grant Programs

#840 • Children of Disabled Firemen and Peace Officers Tuition Exemption

Type: Scholarship. Renewable.
Eligibility: Applicant must be the child of a deceased or disabled fireman, peace officer, custodial employee of the Department of Conservation, or game warden who died or was disabled in the line of duty while serving Texas. Applicant must apply prior to 21st birthday and attend a public college or university in Texas. This award must be used in the following years of study: • Freshman • Sophomore • Junior • Senior
Deadline: Varies.
Award Amount: $ 1,377.
Number Of Awards: 74.
Contact: Sharon W. Cobb, Assistant Commissioner for Student Services

#841 • Robert C. Byrd Honors Scholarship

Type: Scholarship. Renewable when funds are available.
Eligibility: Selection is based upon GPA, class rank, and test scores. Financial need is not considered. Each Texas high school is allowed to nominate three candidates. This award must be used in the following years of study: • Freshman
Deadline: March 15.
Award Amount: $ 1,098.
Number Of Awards: 1,583.
Contact: Gustavo DeLeon, Assistant Director of Grant Programs

#842 • Early High School Graduation Scholarship

Type: Scholarship. Renewable.
Eligibility: Applicant must be a resident of Texas who completed the requirements for graduation from a public high school in no more than 36 consecutive months. This award must be used in the following years of study: • Freshman • Sophomore • Junior • Senior • Masters • Doctoral • Other postgraduate level
Deadline: Varies.
Award Amount: $ 349.

Number Of Awards: 4,105.
Contact: Scholarship Administrator

#843 • Texas Tuition Assistance Grant

Type: Grant. Renewable. Recipient must reapply and maintain a minimum 2.5 GPA for renewal.
Eligibility: Applicant must be a resident of Texas enrolled full time in a school in Texas. Applicant must have a minimum grade average of 80 and can not have been convicted of a felony or a crime involving "moral turpitude." This award must be used in the following years of study: • Sophomore • Junior • Senior
Deadline: Varies.
Award Amount: $ 908.
Number Of Awards: 5,668.
Contact: Grants Administrator

#844 • Texas New Horizons Scholarship

Type: Scholarship. Renewable. Recipient must reapply for renewal.
Eligibility: Applicant must be a resident of Texas and attending a public school in Texas. This award must be used in the following years of study: • Sophomore • Junior • Senior • Masters
Deadline: Varies.
Award Amount: $ 630.
Number Of Awards: 2,321.
Contact: College financial aid office

#845 • Texas Grant

Type: Grant. Renewable.
Eligibility: Applicant must be a Texas resident enrolled at least three-fourth time, have graduated from a U.S. high school in December 1998 or later, and must demonstrate financial need. This award must be used in the following years of study: • Freshman • Sophomore
Deadline: Varies.
Award Amount: Partial tuition and fees.
Number Of Awards: Varies.
Contact: Grants Administrator

TOWNSHIP OFFICIALS OF ILLINOIS

Scholarship Program
408 South Fifth Street
Springfield, IL 62701
Phone: 217-744-2212
Fax: 217-744-7419
Email: bryantoi@fgi.net
Website: http://www.toi.org

#846 • Township Officials of Illinois Scholarship

Type: Scholarship. Not renewable.
Eligibility: Applicant must be graduating from an Illinois high school with a minimum grade average of "B," must demonstrate an active interest in school activities or in local government/community service, and must submit letter of recommendation, transcripts, and a 500-word original essay. Applicant must attend an Illinois four-year or junior college. This award must be used in the following years of study: • Freshman
Deadline: March 1.
Award Amount: $ 2,000.
Number Of Awards: 6.
Applications Received: 200.
Odds Of Winning: 3% of applicants on average receive an award each year.
Contact: Bryan E. Smith, Executive Director

TY COBB FOUNDATION

P.O. Box 725
Forest Park, GA 30298
Email: tycobb@mindspring.com

#847 • Ty Cobb Scholarship

Type: Scholarship. Renewable. Minimum "B" grade average for 45 quarter or 30 semester hours is required to retain scholarship. Satisfactory academic progress is required for professional degree students to retain scholarship.
Eligibility: Applicant must demonstrate financial need and be a resident of Georgia. Applicant must submit application, reason for requesting financial assistance, recommendation, and transcript. This award must be used in the following years of study: • Sophomore • Junior • Senior • Medical and dental professional degrees
Deadline: June 15.
Award Amount: $ 2,000 - $ 3,000.
Number Of Awards: 250.
Applications Received: 1,000.
Contact: Rosie C. Atkins, Secretary

UNIVERSITY OF CENTRAL OKLAHOMA

100 North University
Edmond, OK 73034
Phone: 405-974-2727
Fax: 405-974-5420
Website: http://www.ucok.edu

#848 • Merit Scholarship - Tuition Waiver

Type: Scholarship. Renewable. Reapplication is required for renewal.
Eligibility: Applicant must be an Oklahoma resident enrolled for a minimum of six hours. Freshman applicant must have a minimum composite ACT score of 22; upperclass student must have a minimum 3.25 GPA. This award must be used in the following years of study: • Freshman • Sophomore • Junior •

Senior • Masters • Doctoral
Deadline: March 1.
Award Amount: $ 262 - $ 1,500.
Number Of Awards: 400.
Contact: Stacy Meldrum, Scholarship Coordinator

VERMONT STUDENT ASSISTANCE CORPORATION (VSAC)

Champlain Mill
P.O. Box 2000
Winooski, VT 05404
Phone: 800-642-3177 (in state) or 802-655-9602
Fax: 802-654-3765
Email: info@vsac.org
Website: http://www.vsac.org

#849 • Vermont Part-Time Grant

Type: Grant. Renewable. Recipient must reapply for renewal.
Eligibility: Applicant must be a Vermont resident who is enrolled in fewer than 12 credit hours per semester and does not have a bachelor's degree. Selection is based upon financial need. This award must be used in the following years of study: • Sophomore • Junior • Senior
Deadline: None.
Award Amount: $ 250 - $ 5,100.
Number Of Awards: 2,600.
Applications Received: 4,718.
Odds Of Winning: 55% of applicants on average receive an award each year.
Contact: Grant Department

WASHINGTON CROSSING FOUNDATION

6934 North Radcliffe Street
Bristol, PA 19007
Phone: 215-949-8841
Website: http://www.gwcf.org

#850 • Washington Crossing Foundation Scholarship

Type: Scholarship. Renewable. Recipient must maintain career goals and meet school's requirements to retain scholarship.
Eligibility: Applicant must be a U.S. citizen with a career interest in government service. Awards greater than $2,000 are paid over a four-year period. This award must be used in the following years of study: • Freshman
Field(s) Of Study: Government service.
Deadline: January 1.
Award Amount: $ 1,000 - $10,000.
Number Of Awards: 6.
Applications Received: 1,500.
Odds Of Winning: Less than 1% of applicants on

average receive an award each year.
Contact: Eugene C. Fish, Esq., Vice Chairman of the Board

WASHINGTON GAS

Public Affairs Office
1100 H Street, NW
Washington, DC 20080
Phone: 202-624-6758
Fax: 202-624-6221

#851 • Washington Gas Scholarship

Type: Scholarship. Not renewable.
Eligibility: Applicant must be a resident of Washington, D.C., have a minimum 3.0 GPA, and demonstrate community involvement. This award must be used in the following years of study: • Freshman
Field(s) Of Study: Accounting, business, computer science, engineering, marketing, mathematics, non-biolgocial science, or any other business- or science-related area.
Deadline: February 20.
Award Amount: $ 1,000.
Number Of Awards: 16.
Contact: Scholarship Coordinator
Phone: 202-624-6791

WATERVILLE BUSINESS & PROFESSIONAL WOMEN'S CLUBS

Myra Chaloult
P.O. Box 585
Waterville, ME 04903
Phone: 207-465-2162

#852 • Pearl Ramsey Memorial Nursing Scholarship

Type: Scholarship. Not renewable.
Eligibility: Applicant must be a resident of Kennebec County, Maine. Selection is based upon financial need, school and civic involvement, and GPA. Applicant must submit two letters of recommendation and a short essay on why scholarship is needed and what goals are hoped to be achieved. Send a self-addressed, stamped envelope for application. This award must be used in the following years of study: • Freshman • Sophomore • Junior • Senior
Field(s) Of Study: Medical related.
Deadline: April 20.
Award Amount: $ 200.
Number Of Awards: 1.
Applications Received: 6.
Odds Of Winning: 16% of applicants on average receive an award each year.
Contact: Myra Chaloult, Scholarship Chairperson

WISCONSIN HIGHER EDUCATIONAL AIDS BOARD

P.O. Box 7885
Madison, WI 53707
Phone: 608-267-2206
Fax: 608-267-2808
Email: HEABmail@heab.state.wi.us
Website: http://heab.state.wi.us

#853 • Talent Incentive Program Grant

Type: Grant. Renewable if recipient continues to demonstrate financial need.
Eligibility: Applicant must be a Wisconsin resident attending a Wisconsin college or university at least half-time. Selection is based upon financial need. Applicant must submit FAFSA and be nominated by the Student Financial Aid Department or WEOP. This award must be used in the following years of study: • Freshman • Sophomore • Junior • Senior
Deadline: Varies.
Award Amount: $ 600 - $ 1,800.
Number Of Awards: 4,408.
Contact: John Whitt, Program Coordinator
Phone: 608-266-1665
Email: john.whitt@heab.state.wi.us

Transportation/Traffic Management

AMERICAN SOCIETY OF TRAVEL AGENTS (ASTA) FOUNDATION, INC.

1101 King Street
Alexandria, VA 22314
Phone: 703-739-2782
Fax: 703-684-8319
Email: astasysop@astanet.com
Website: http://www.astanet.com

#854 • Healy Scholarship

Type: Scholarship. Renewable. Reapplication is required for renewal.
Eligibility: Applicant must submit a 500-word essay on suggested improvements in the travel industry. Send a self-addressed, stamped envelope for information and application. This award must be used in the following years of study: • Sophomore • Junior • Senior • Masters
Field(s) Of Study: Travel, tourism.
Deadline: July 23.
Award Amount: $ 2,000.
Number Of Awards: 1.
Applications Received: 5.
Contact: Myriam Lechuga or Mary Kate Koehl

#855 • Joseph R. Stone Scholarship

Type: Scholarship. Renewable. Reapplication is required for renewal.
Eligibility: Applicant must be the child of a travel industry employee and submit a 500-word essay on career goals. Send a self-addressed, stamped envelope for information and application. This award must be used in the following years of study: • Freshman • Sophomore • Junior • Senior
Field(s) Of Study: Travel, tourism.
Deadline: July 28.
Award Amount: $ 2,400.
Number Of Awards: 3.
Contact: Myriam Lechuga or Mary Kate Koehl, Scholarships

#856 • Holland-America Line Westours, Inc. Scholarship

Type: Scholarship. Renewable. Reapplication is required for renewal.
Eligibility: Applicant must submit a 500-word essay on the future of the cruise industry. Send a self-addressed, stamped envelope for information and application. This award must be used in the following years of study: • Freshman • Sophomore • Junior • Senior • Masters • Doctoral • Proprietary travel schools
Field(s) Of Study: Tourism, travel.
Deadline: July 28.
Award Amount: $ 3,000.
Number Of Awards: 2.
Applications Received: 40.
Contact: Myriam Lechuga or Mary Kate Koehl, Scholarships

#857 • Air Travel Card Grant

Type: Grant. Renewable. Recipient must reapply for renewal.
Eligibility: Applicant must submit career goals and a 500-word essay on the importance and challenges of managing business travel. Send a self-addressed, stamped envelope for information and application. This award must be used in the following years of study: • Freshman • Sophomore • Junior • Senior
Field(s) Of Study: Business travel management, tourism, travel.
Deadline: July 28.
Award Amount: $ 3,000.
Number Of Awards: 1.
Applications Received: 50.
Contact: Myriam Lechuga or Mary Kate Koehl, Scholarships

#858 • Arizona Chapter Gold

Type: Scholarship. Renewable. Reapplication is required for renewal.
Eligibility: Applicant must be enrolled at an accredited four-year college in the state of Arizona

and submit a 500-word essay. Send a self-addressed, stamped envelope for information. This award must be used in the following years of study: • Sophomore • Junior • Senior
Field(s) Of Study: Travel, tourism.
Deadline: July 28.
Award Amount: $ 3,000.
Number Of Awards: 1.
Contact: Myriam Lechuga or Mary Kate Koehl, Scholarships

#859 • Northern California/Richard Epping Scholarship

Type: Scholarship. Renewable. Reapplication is required for renewal.
Eligibility: Applicant must apply to a school located in California or Northern Nevada, be a permanent resident of either Northern California or Northern Nevada, and submit a 500-word essay on "Why I Desire a Profession in the Travel and Tourism Industry." Send a self-addressed, stamped envelope for information and application. This award must be used in the following years of study: • Freshman • Sophomore • Junior • Senior • proprietary travel school
Field(s) Of Study: Travel, tourism.
Deadline: July 28.
Award Amount: $ 2,000.
Number Of Awards: 1.
Contact: Myriam Lechuga or Mary Kate Koehl, Scholarships

#860 • Alaska Airlines Scholarship

Type: Scholarship. Renewable. Reapplication is required for renewal.
Eligibility: Applicant must submit a 500-word essay on career goals. Send a self-addressed, stamped envelope for information and application. This award must be used in the following years of study: • Freshman • Sophomore • Junior • Senior • Masters
Field(s) Of Study: Travel, tourism.
Deadline: July 28.
Award Amount: $ 2,000.
Number Of Awards: 1.
Contact: Myriam Lechuga or Mary Kate Koehl, Scholarships

#861 • Southern California Chapter/ Pleasant Hawaiian Holidays Scholarship

Type: Scholarship. Renewable. Reapplication is required for renewal.
Eligibility: Applicant must submit a 500-word essay on "My Goals in the Travel Industry." One award is reserved for an applicant attending school in Southern California. Send a self-addressed, stamped envelope for information and application. This award must be used in the following years of study: • Freshman • Sophomore • Junior • Senior

Field(s) Of Study: Travel, tourism.
Deadline: July 28.
Award Amount: $ 1,500.
Number Of Awards: 2.
Contact: Myriam Lechuga or Mary Kate Koehl, Scholarships

#862 • American Express Travel Scholarship

Type: Scholarship. Renewable. Reapplication is required for renewal.
Eligibility: Applicant must submit a 500-word essay. Send a self-addressed, stamped envelope for information and application. This award must be used in the following years of study: • Freshman • Sophomore • Junior • Senior • Proprietary travel school
Field(s) Of Study: Tourism, travel.
Deadline: July 28.
Award Amount: $ 2,500.
Number Of Awards: 1.
Contact: Myriam Lechuga or Mary Kate Koehl, Scholarships

ARTBA

ARTBA Student Paper Competition
1010 Massachusetts Avenue, NW
Washington, DC 20001
Phone: 202-289-4434
Fax: 202-289-4435
Website: http://www.artba.org

#863 • Student Paper Competition - Undergraduate Level

Type: Contest. Not renewable.
Eligibility: Appliant must submit (via ARTBA faculty member) four copies of a paper not to exceed 3,000 words, addressing transportation problems and focusing on an issue affecting transportation infrastructure system/construction industry. Papers must be typed and double-spaced, must include a 300-word (maximum) abstract, and must have a member's endorsement. Selection is based upon merits, content, relevance, composition, presentation, and originality of paper. This award must be used in the following years of study: • Junior • Senior
Deadline: November 30.
Award Amount: $ 500.
Number Of Awards: 1.
Applications Received: 4.
Odds Of Winning: 25% of applicants on average receive an award each year.
Contact: William Buechner, Manager of Education Division

NATIONAL TOURISM FOUNDATION (NTF)

546 East Main Street
Lexington, KY 40508
Phone: 800-682-8886
Fax: 606-226-4414
Email: scudderb@mgtserv.com
Website: http://www.ntaonline.com

#864 • H. Neil Mecaskey Scholarship

Type: Scholarship. Not renewable.
Eligibility: Applicant must have a minimum 3.0 GPA. Applicants must submit a NTF scholarship application, two recommendation letters (one from a tourism-related faculty member and the other from a professional in the tourism industry), a resume, transcripts, and an essay. This award must be used in the following years of study: • Junior • Senior
Field(s) Of Study: Travel/tourism.
Deadline: April 15.
Award Amount: $ 500.
Number Of Awards: 1.
Contact: Brooks A. Scudder, Assistant Executive Director

#865 • Louise Dessureault Memorial Scholarship

Type: Scholarship. Not renewable.
Eligibility: Applicant must have a minimum 3.0 GPA. Applicant must submit a NTF scholarship application, two recommendation letters (one from a tourism-related faculty member and the other from a professional in the tourism industry), a resume, college transcripts, and an essay. This award must be used in the following years of study: • Junior • Senior
Field(s) Of Study: Travel/tourism.
Deadline: April 15.
Award Amount: $ 500.
Number Of Awards: 1.
Contact: Brooks A. Scudder, Assistant Executive Director

TRANSPORTATION CLUBS INTERNATIONAL (TCI) SCHOLARSHIP

P.O. Box 52
Arabi, LA 70032
Phone: 504-278-1107
Fax: 504-278-1110
Website: http://www.transclubsintl.org

#866 • Charlotte Woods Memorial Scholarship

Type: Scholarship. Not renewable.
Eligibility: Applicant must be a TCI member or the dependent of a member. Selection is based upon scholastic ability, potential, professional interest, character, and financial need. This award must be used in the following years of study: • Sophomore • Junior • Senior • Masters • Doctoral
Field(s) Of Study: Logistics, traffic management, transportation.
Deadline: April 30.
Award Amount: $ 1,000.
Number Of Awards: 1.
Applications Received: 3.
Contact: Gay Fielding

#867 • Fred A. Hooper Memorial Scholarship

Type: Scholarship. Not renewable.
Eligibility: Selection is based upon scholastic ability, potential, professional interest, character, and financial need. This award must be used in the following years of study: • Sophomore • Junior • Senior • Masters • Doctoral
Field(s) Of Study: Logistics, traffic management, transportation.
Deadline: April 30.
Award Amount: $ 1,500.
Number Of Awards: Varies.
Applications Received: 26.
Contact: Gay Fielding

#868 • Texas Transportation Scholarship

Type: Scholarship. Not renewable.
Eligibility: Applicant must have been enrolled in a school in Texas during some phase of education (elementary, secondary, or high school). Selection is based upon scholastic ability, potential, professional interest, character, and financial need. This award must be used in the following years of study: • Sophomore • Junior • Senior • Masters • Doctoral
Field(s) Of Study: Logistics, traffic management, transportation.
Deadline: April 30.
Award Amount: $ 1,000.
Number Of Awards: Varies.
Applications Received: 7.
Contact: Gay Fielding

TRUCKLOAD CARRIERS ASSOCIATION

ATTN: Director of Operations
2200 Mill Road
Alexandria, VA 22314
Phone: 703-838-1950
Fax: 703-836-6610
Email: csimpson@truckload.org
Website: http://www.truckload.org

#869 • TCA Scholarship

Type: Scholarship. Renewable. Reapplication and exceptional grades required for renewal.
Eligibility: Applicant must be an employee or related

to an employee of a trucking company. This award must be used in the following years of study: • Junior • Senior
Field(s) Of Study: Business and transportation.
Deadline: May 15.
Award Amount: $ 2,000.
Number Of Awards: 9 - 12.
Applications Received: 125.
Odds Of Winning: 10% of applicants on average receive an award each year.
Contact: Cynthia Simpson, Director of Operations

WYOMING TRUCKING ASSOCIATION

Box 1909
Casper, WY 82602-1909
Phone: 307-234-1579
Fax: 307-234-7082
Email: WYTRUCK@aol.com

#870 • Wyoming Trucking Association Trust Fund Scholarship

Type: Scholarship. Not renewable.
Eligibility: Applicant must be a Wyoming high school graduate, be enrolled at a Wyoming university, community college, or approved trade school, and plan to pursue a course of study leading to a career in the highway transportation industry. This award must be used in the following years of study: • Freshman • Sophomore • Junior • Senior
Field(s) Of Study: Accounting, business management, computer skills, diesel mechanics, office procedures/management, safety, sales management, truck driving.
Deadline: March 3.
Award Amount: $ 250 - $ 2,300.
Number Of Awards: 4 - 10.
Applications Received: 35.
Contact: Kathy Cundall, Adminstrative Assistant

Union Affiliation

AIR LINE PILOTS ASSOCIATION

1625 Massachusetts Avenue, NW
Washington, DC 20036
Phone: 202-797-4050
Fax: 202-797-4052

#871 • Air Line Pilots Association Scholarship

Type: Scholarship. Renewable for up to four years if minimum 3.0 GPA is maintained.
Eligibility: Applicant must be the child of a medically retired, long-term disabled, or deceased

pilot member of the Air Line Pilots Association, must be enrolled or planning to enroll in a baccalaureate program, and must submit transcripts. This award must be used in the following years of study: • Freshman • Sophomore • Junior • Senior
Deadline: April 1.
Award Amount: $ 3,000.
Number Of Awards: 1.
Contact: Jan Redden, Scholarship Program Monitor

AMERICAN FEDERATION OF GRAIN MILLERS (AFGM) INTERNATIONAL UNION

ATTN: International Scholarship Program
4949 Olson Memorial Highway
Minneapolis, MN 55422-5199
Phone: 612-545-0211
Fax: 612-545-5489

#872 • Bakery, Confectionary, Tobacco Workers and Grain Millers (BCTGM) Scholarship Competition

Type: Contest. Not renewable.
Eligibility: Applicant must be a member, employee, or child of a member or employee of the BCTGM or AFGM international unions. Applicant must submit an application proving eligibility, a personal profile, an academic report, and an essay on a specific topic. This award must be used in the following years of study: • Freshman • Sophomore • Junior • Senior • Recignized technical or vocational post-secondary schools
Deadline: March 31.
Award Amount: $ 1,000.
Number Of Awards: 20.
Contact: BCTGM International Union, Scholarship Program
10401 Connecticut Ave
Kensington, MD 20895-3961
Phone: 301-933-8600
Fax: 301-946-8452

GRAPHIC COMMUNICATIONS INTERNATIONAL UNION (GCIU)

1900 L Street, NW
Washington, DC 20036
Phone: 202-462-1400
Fax: 202-721-0641

#873 • A.J. DeAndrade Scholarship

Type: Scholarship. Renewable for up to four years if recipient submits transcripts each year.
Eligibility: Applicant must be a high school senior graduating in January or June of current year or a recent graduate with less than one-half year of college by September 1. Applicant must be the dependent of a

member of the Graphic Communications International Union with continuous membership for at least one year prior to October 1. Standardized test scores and biographical essay are required. This award must be used in the following years of study: • Freshman

Deadline: February 16 (priority), April 14 (final).
Award Amount: $ 500.
Number Of Awards: 10.
Applications Received: 225.
Odds Of Winning: 4% of applicants on average receive an award each year.
Contact: Gerald Deneau, Secretary-Treasurer/ Scholarship Administration

INTERNATIONAL UNION OF ELECTRONIC, ELECTRICAL, SALARIED, MACHINE AND FURNITURE WORKERS (IUE)

1126 16th Street, NW
Department of Social Action
Washington, DC 20036-4866

#874 • William H. Bywater Scholarship

Type: Scholarship. Not renewable.
Eligibility: Applicant must be the child of an IUE local union elected official and submit class rank, GPA, SAT I or ACT scores, copy of W-2 form, short statement of interest and goals, and three recommendations. Selection is based upon academic record, character, leadership ability, and a desire to improve and move ahead. This award must be used in the following years of study: • Freshman • Sophomore • Junior • Senior
Deadline: April 15.
Award Amount: $ 3,000.
Number Of Awards: 1.
Contact: Gloria T. Johnson, Department of Social Action

#875 • James B. Carey Scholarship

Type: Scholarship. Not renewable.
Eligibility: Applicant must be the child of an IUE member and submit class rank, GPA, SAT I or ACT scores, copy of W-2 form, short statement of interest and goals, and three recommendations. Selection is based upon academic record, character, leadership ability, and a desire to improve and move ahead. This award must be used in the following years of study: • Freshman • Sophomore • Junior • Senior
Deadline: April 15.
Award Amount: $ 1,000.
Number Of Awards: 9.
Contact: Gloria T. Johnson, Director Department of Social Action

#876 • David J. Fitzmaurice Scholarship

Type: Scholarship. Not renewable.
Eligibility: Applicant must be the child of an IUE member and submit class rank, GPA, SAT I or ACT scores, copy of W-2 form, short statement of interest and goals, and three recommendations. Selection is based upon academic record, character, leadership ability, and a desire to improve and move ahead. This award must be used in the following years of study: • Freshman • Sophomore • Junior • Senior
Field(s) Of Study: Engineering.
Deadline: April 15.
Award Amount: $ 2,000.
Number Of Awards: 1.
Contact: Gloria T. Johnson, Director

NATIONAL ALLIANCE OF POSTAL AND FEDERAL EMPLOYEES (NAPFE)

1628 11th Street, NW
Washington, DC 20001
Phone: 202-939-6325
Fax: 202-939-6389
Email: naple@patriot.net
Website: http://www.napfe.com

#877 • Ashby B. Carter Memorial Scholarship

Type: Scholarship. Not renewable.
Eligibility: Applicant must be the child or legal dependent of a NAPFE member. This award must be used in the following years of study: • Freshman
Deadline: April 1.
Award Amount: $ 1,900 - $ 5,000.
Number Of Awards: 6.
Applications Received: 80.
Odds Of Winning: 8% of applicants on average receive an award each year.
Contact: Wilbur Duncan, Secretary
Email: wduncan@patriot.net

RICHARD F. WALSH/ALFRED W. DiTOLLA FOUNDATION

1515 Broadway, Suite 601
New York, NY 10036
Phone: 212-730-1770
Fax: 212-730-7809

#878 • Richard F. Walsh/Alfred W. DiTolla Scholarship

Type: Scholarship. Renewable for up to four years.
Eligibility: Applicant must be attending a four-year school, be the son or daughter of a member of good standing of the International Alliance of Theatrical Stage Employes and Moving Picture Technicians, Artists, and Allied Crafts of the United States and

Canada. Applicant must submit a letter of recommendation from a teacher or a clergyman. This award must be used in the following years of study: • Freshman
Deadline: December 31.
Award Amount: $ 1,750.
Number Of Awards: 2.
Applications Received: 150.
Odds Of Winning: 1% of applicants on average receive an award each year.
Contact: Colleen Paul, Office Administrator

SCHOOL FOOD SERVICE FOUNDATION

1600 Duke Street, 7th Floor
Alexandria, VA 22314
Phone: 703-739-3900
Email: sfsf@asfsa.org
Website: http://www.asfsa.org/foundation

#879 • School Food Service Foundation Scholarship

Type: Scholarship. Renewable. Reapplication, satisfactory academic progress, financial need, and potential required to retain scholarship.
Eligibility: Applicant must be a member or the child of a member of the American School Food Service Association, planning to pursue a career in food service, and have a minimum 2.7 GPA. This award must be used in the following years of study: • Freshman • Sophomore • Junior • Senior • Masters • Doctoral
Field(s) Of Study: Dietetics, food science, food service management, nutrition.
Deadline: April 15.
Award Amount: $ 100 - $ 1,000.
Number Of Awards: 131.
Odds Of Winning: 90% of applicants on average receive an award each year.
Contact: Foundation Coordinator

#880 • Schwan's Food Service Scholarship

Type: Scholarship. Renewable. Reapplication is required for renewal.
Eligibility: Applicant must be a member or the child of a member of the American School Food Service Association (ASFSA). Selection is based upon essay and two recommendations. This award must be used in the following years of study: • Freshman • Sophomore • Junior • Senior • Masters • Doctoral
Field(s) Of Study: Nutrition/food science, school food service.
Deadline: April 15.
Award Amount: $ 100 - $ 1,000.
Number Of Awards: 50 - 100.
Applications Received: 120.
Odds Of Winning: 90% of applicants on average receive an award each year.
Contact: Foundation Specialist

SCREEN ACTORS GUILD FOUNDATION

5757 Wilshire Boulevard
Los Angeles, CA 90036-3600
Phone: 323-549-6610

#881 • John L. Dales Scholarship

Type: Scholarship. Renewable. Recipient must reapply for renewal.
Eligibility: Applicant for the regular scholarship must be a member or the child of a member of the Screen Actors Guild. Applicant for the transitional scholarship must be a Screen Actors Guild member who needs financial assistance to change careers. This award must be used in the following years of study: • Freshman • Sophomore • Junior • Senior • Masters • Doctoral • Other postgraduate level
Deadline: March 15.
Award Amount: $ 4,000.
Number Of Awards: 30.
Applications Received: 65.
Odds Of Winning: 46% of applicants on average receive an award each year.
Contact: Joan Hanson, Program Administrator
Phone: 323-549-6603

TWO/TEN INTERNATIONAL FOOTWEAR FOUNDATION

1466 Main Street
Waltham, MA 02451-1623
Phone: 800-346-3210

#882 • Two/Ten International Footwear Foundation College Scholarship

Type: Scholarship. Renewable. Satisfactory academic progress and financial need are required to retain scholarship.
Eligibility: Applicant's parent must have worked in the footwear, leather, or allied industries for at least one year, or the applicant must have worked for a minimum of 500 hours in those industries in the year before the scholarship will be used. Selection is based upon academic achievement, personal promise, and financial need. Applicant must be enrolled full time. This award must be used in the following years of study: • Freshman • Sophomore • Junior • Senior
Deadline: January 15.
Award Amount: $ 200 - $ 2,000.
Number Of Awards: 194.
Applications Received: 540.
Odds Of Winning: 44% of applicants on average receive an award each year.
Contact: Catherine M. Nelson, Scholarship Director

UNION OF NEEDLETRADES, INDUSTRIAL, AND TEXTILE EMPLOYEES (UNITE!)

National Scholarship Award Program
Education & Mobilization Department
1710 Broadway, 2nd Floor
New York, NY 10019
Phone: 212-265-7000
Website: http://www.uniteunion.org/whatisunite/
directory.html

#883 • UNITE! National Scholarship Award

Type: Scholarship. Renewable.
Eligibility: Applicant must be the child of a member in good standing of UNITE. This award must be used in the following years of study: • Freshman
Deadline: June 30.
Award Amount: $ 325.
Number Of Awards: Varies.
Applications Received: 250.
Contact: Myra Garcia, Administrative Assistant
Phone: 212-265-7000, extension 224

UNITED FOOD AND COMMERCIAL WORKERS (UFCW) INTERNATIONAL UNION

Education Office
1775 K Street, NW
Washington, DC 20006
Phone: 202-223-3111

#884 • UFCW International Union Scholarship

Type: Scholarship. Renewable. Transcript and verification of enrollment must be sent to retain scholarship.
Eligibility: Applicant must be an UFCW union member in good standing for at least one year prior to December 31, or be the child of a member and be under age 20 on March 15. This award must be used in the following years of study: • Freshman • Sophomore • Junior • Senior
Deadline: December 31 (preliminary), March 15 (application).
Award Amount: $ 1,000.
Number Of Awards: 7.
Odds Of Winning: Less than 1% of applicants on average receive an award each year.
Contact: Education Office

UTILITY WORKERS UNION OF AMERICA

815 16th Street, NW
Washington, DC 20006

Phone: 202-347-8105
Fax: 202-347-4872

#885 • Utility Workers Union of America Scholarship

Type: Scholarship. Renewable. Satisfactory academic progress is required to retain scholarship.
Eligibility: Applicant must be the child of a member of the Utility Workers Union of America. Selection is made by the National Merit Scholarship Corp. This award must be used in the following years of study: • Freshman
Deadline: January 1 of junior year.
Award Amount: $ 500 - $ 2,000.
Number Of Awards: 2.
Applications Received: 67.
Contact: Donald E. Wightman, National President

Vocational/Technical

AIRCRAFT ELECTRONICS ASSOCIATION (AEA) EDUCATIONAL FOUNDATION

4217 S. Hocker Drive
Independence, MO 64055
Phone: 816-373-6565
Fax: 816-478-3100
Email: info@aea.net
Website: http://www.aea.net

#886 • David Arver Memorial Scholarship

Type: Scholarship. Not renewable.
Eligibility: Applicant must attend an accredited vocational/technical school in Illinois, Indiana, Iowa, Kansas, Michigan, Minnesota, Missouri, Nebraska, North Dakota, South Dakota, or Wisconsin. This award must be used in the following years of study: • Freshman • Sophomore • Junior • Senior
Field(s) Of Study: Aircraft repair, avionics.
Deadline: February 15.
Award Amount: $ 1,000.
Number Of Awards: 1.
Applications Received: 150.
Odds Of Winning: 1% of applicants on average receive an award each year.
Contact: Mike Adamson, AEA Educational Foundation Executive Director

AMERICAN LEGION AUXILIARY, DEPARTMENT OF NEBRASKA

Department Headquarters
P.O. Box 5227
Lincoln, NE 68505

#887 • Vocational/Technical Scholarship

Type: Scholarship. Not renewable.
Eligibility: Applicant must plan to enroll in a vocational or technical school and must be connected to a veteran. This award must be used in the following years of study: • Freshman
Deadline: in April.
Award Amount: $ 200 - $ 300.
Number Of Awards: 10 - 15.
Applications Received: 70.
Odds Of Winning: 20% of applicants on average receive an award each year.
Contact: See above.

AMERICAN WELDING SOCIETY FOUNDATION, INC. (AWS)

550 N.W. LeJeune Road
Miami, FL 33126
Phone: 800-443-9353, extension 293 or 305-445-6628
Fax: 305-443-7559
Email: found@aws.org

#888 • John C. Lincoln Memorial Scholarhip

Type: Scholarship. Renewable. Recipient must reapply for renewal.
Eligibility: Applicant must have a minimum 2.5 GPA, be at least 18 years old, be a U.S. citizen, and attend an institution in the U.S. Applicant must submit proof of finanical aid, two letters of reference, biography, and transcript. Preference given to applicants residing or attending school in Arizona or Ohio. This award must be used in the following years of study: • Sophomore • Junior • Senior
Field(s) Of Study: Welding engineering, welding engineering technology.
Deadline: February 1.
Award Amount: $ 2,500.
Number Of Awards: 1.
Contact: Vicky Pinsky, Scholarship Coordinator
Phone: 800-443-9353, extension 461
Email: vpinsky@aws.org

IOWA COLLEGE STUDENT AID COMMISSION

200 Tenth Street, Fourth Floor
Des Moines, IA 50309-3609
Phone: 515-281-3501
Fax: 515-242-5996
Email: iscac@max.state.ia.us
Website: http://www.iowacollegeaid.org

#889 • Iowa Vocational-Technical Tuition Grant

Type: Grant. Renewable for up to two years.
Eligibility: Applicant must be an Iowa resident, a U.S. citizen, permanent resident, or refugee, and attend an eligible Iowa vocational-technical school. FAFSA required. This award must be used in the following years of study: • Freshman
Field(s) Of Study: Vocational/technical.
Deadline: June 1 (priority).
Award Amount: $ 650.
Number Of Awards: Varies.
Contact: Julie Leeper, Grants Director, State Student Aid Programs
Phone: 515-242-6703
Email: julie.leeper.csac.state.ia.us

MARYLAND ASSOCIATION OF PRIVATE CAREER SCHOOLS

584 Bellerive Drive, Suite 3D
Annapolis, MD 21401
Phone: 410-974-4473
Fax: 410-757-3809
Email: mapcs@mdassn.com

#890 • Maryland Association of Private Career Schools Scholarship

Type: Scholarship. Not renewable.
Eligibility: Applicant must be a Maryland high school graduate planning to attend a private career school in Maryland. Selection is based upon academic qualifications. This award must be used in the following years of study: • Freshman
Field(s) Of Study: Vocational/technical.
Deadline: April 2.
Award Amount: $ 500 - $ 5,000.
Number Of Awards: 60.
Applications Received: 120.
Odds Of Winning: 50% of applicants on average receive an award each year.
Contact: Sharon Jonkel, Executive Assistant

Voice

ACADEMY OF VOCAL ARTS

1920 Spruce Street
Philadelphia, PA 19103
Phone: 215-735-1685
Fax: 215-732-2189
Email: info@avaopera.com
Website: http://www.avaopera.com

#891 • Gifted Opera Singers' Scholarship

Type: Scholarship. Renewable.
Eligibility: Applicant must be an unusually gifted opera singer with potential for a career in opera and with at least two years or equivalent of college music

and opera-oriented training. Male applicants must be age 30 or under; female applicants must be age 28 or under. Preference is given to applicants with a college degree. This award must be used in the following years of study: • Junior • Senior • Masters • Doctoral • Other postgraduate level
Field(s) Of Study: Opera studies, voice.
Deadline: in January.
Award Amount: Varies.
Number Of Awards: 8 - 10.
Applications Received: 150.
Contact: Val Starr, Admissions Director

GENERAL FEDERATION OF WOMEN'S CLUBS OF MASSACHUSETTS (GFWC OF MA)

245 Dutton Road, Box 679
Sudbury, MA 01776-0679
Phone: 978-443-4569

#892 • Dorchester Woman's Club Scholarship

Type: Scholarship. Not renewable.
Eligibility: Applicant must attend an accredited four-year college, university, or school of music, submit a letter of endorsement from the president of the sponsoring GFWC of Massachusetts club in the community of legal residence, a recommendation from college department head or music professor, a letter stating reasons for financial assistance, and transcript. Audition is and SASE required. This award must be used in the following years of study: • Sophomore • Junior • Senior
Field(s) Of Study: Voice.
Deadline: February 1.
Award Amount: $ 500.
Number Of Awards: 1.
Contact: Sally Sears-Mack, Chairperson
Phone: 508-349-7249

Wildlife Resources/Management

ROCKY MOUNTAIN ELK FOUNDATION

RMEF Conservation Education Department
P.O. Box 8249
Missoula, MT 59807
Phone: 406-523-4500
Fax: 406-523-4550
Email: jodi@rmef.org
Website: http://www.rmef.org

#893 • Wildlife Leadership Awards

Type: Scholarship. Not renewable.
Eligibility: Applicant must have at least one semester or two quarters remaining in degree program. Applicant must submit application with essay and two recommendation letters. This award must be used in the following years of study: • Junior • Senior
Field(s) Of Study: Wildlife biology, wildlife management.
Deadline: March 1.
Award Amount: $ 2,000.
Number Of Awards: 10.
Applications Received: 36.
Odds Of Winning: 27% of applicants on average receive an award each year.
Contact: Jodi Bishop, Conservation Education Projects Manager

21 Indexes To The Scholarships

1. General Category Index

Language/Literature/Humanities

Cultural Studies
DAAD-Fulbright Grant for Americans #322
King Olav V Norwegian-American Heritage Fund #323

English/Literature/Writing
Amelia Student Award #387
Atlas Shrugged Essay Competition #389
Edna Meudt Scholarship #391
Humanist Essay Contest for Young Women and Men of North America #390
Katherine Anne Porter Prize for Fiction #392
Pablo Neruda Prize for Poetry #393
Short Story Contest #388

Foreign Languages
Central American Scholarship #406
Hochschulsommerkurse at German Universities Grant #405
NIS Regional Languages Grant #403
Student Translation Award #404

History
Malki Museum Scholarship #429
Ottis Lock Endowment Research Grant #428
Robert C. Maguire Scholarship #430

Humanities
William Fairburn, Jr. and Cynthia Fairburn Memorial Scholarship #446
Women in Geography Scholarship #445

Religion/Theology/Philosophy
CKA Seminarian Scholarsip #716
Master's Fund Grant #717

Medicine/Nursing

Dentistry
Allied Dental Education Scholarship #325
Colgate-Palmolive Award #324

Medicine
Dr. Charles A. Preuss Medical Award #499
Edgar J. Saux/FACMPE Scholarship #496
Edward J. Gerloff/FACMPE Scholarship #493
Ernest S. Moscatello Scholarship #492

Harry J. Harwick Scholarship #490
Health Career Scholarship #498
Medical Field Scholarship #500
Midwest Section Scholarship #494
Richard L. Davis Managers' Scholarship #497
Richard L. Davis National Scholarship #491
Western Section Scholarship #495

Nursing
B.S. Nurs. Scholarship #599
Colorado Nursing Scholarship #601
FNSNA Scholarship #603
M. Elizabeth Carnegie Scholarship #606
Mary Virginia McRae Nurses Scholarship #597
National Association of Hispanic Nurses Scholarship #605
Neuroscience Nursing Foundation Research Grant #595
Nurses Educational Fund Scholarship #607
Nurses Training Scholarship #608
Nursing Scholarship #602
Nursing Student Scholarship #604
Past President's Parley Nurses Scholarship #596
Sad Sack Nursing Scholarship #598
Scholarship for L.V.N.s Becoming Professional Nurses #611
Scholarship for Rural B.S.N. or Graduate Nursing Students #610
Scholarship for Rural Professional or Vocational Nursing Students #609
Shirley Titus Memorial Scholarship #600

Optometry
New Focus Student Award #612

Other/Miscellaneous

Academic/Leadership Ability
ABFSE Scholarship #1
Academic Excellence Scholarship #62
Academic Merit Award #33
Academic Merit Scholarship #52
Academic Recognition Scholarship #36
Alphonso Deal Scholarship #43
Arkansas Student Assistance Grant #2
Associated Builders and Contractors Scholarship #15

Barry M. Goldwater Scholarship and Excellence in Education Program #3
Baruch Incentive Grant #9
CHSSC Scholarship #8
Coca-Cola Scholarship #10
CollegeNET Scholarship #11
Colorado Student Incentive Grant #12
Dean's Award #61
Dean's Scholarship #45
Dean's Scholarship #46
Dean's Scholarship #6
Easley National Scholarship #38
Eddie G. Robinson Foundation High School Senior Scholarship #17
Edmund F. Maxwell Scholarship #18
Educational Communications Scholarship #19
Elks National Foundation Most Valuable Student Award #20
Eric and Bette Friedheim Scholarship #44
FACT Continuing Education Scholarship #23
Friendship One Flight Training Scholarship #16
Gough Family Scholarship #25
Grant Program for Descendents of Police, Fire, or Correctional Officers #31
Helping Outstanding Pupils Educationally (HOPE) Scholarship #24
Higher Education License Plate Program (HELP) #29
Honored Scholars and Artists Program #40
Honors Fellow Scholarship #21
Illinois College Savings Bond Bonus Incentive Grant #30
Illinois Incentive for Access #27
Isabella Cannon Leadership Fellows Scholarship #22
Jaycee War Memorial Fund Scholarship (JWMF) #55
John F. Kennedy University Scholarship #32
Laura Duval Toomey Saticoy Poinsettia Club Scholarship #59
Manpower Foundation Scholarship #34
Mark Smith Neale II "Cross of Life" Scholarship #14
Masonic Range Science Scholarship #49
Miss Outstanding Teenager #37
NAAS II National Scholarship #39
National Honor Society Scholarship #41
National Youth of the Year Scholarship #5
Olin L. Livesey Scholarship #47

Principal's Leadership Award #42
Public Employees Public Service Scholarship #48
Raymond F. Burmester Endowment for Scholastic Achievement #13
Regents Professional Opportunity Scholarship #7
Sage Scholarship #57
Salik Omar Shah Scholarship #58
Sam Walton Community Scholarship #60
SDRA Scholarship #50
Shaw-Worth Memorial Scholarship #26
St. David's Society of the State of New York Scholarship #51
Student to Student Program of Matching Grants #28
TELACU/Cesar Chavez Award #53
U.S. Jaycee War Memorial Fund Scholarship #54
Vicky Howard Community Service Award #56
Walter and Dorothy Ross Memorial Scholarship #4
Wilson Grant #35

Athletic Ability
AWSEF Scholarship #102
Billy Welu Memorial Scholarship #106
FINA/*Dallas Morning News* All-State Scholar-Athlete Team Scholarship #103
John Jowdy Scholarship #107
New Jersey State Golf Association (NJSGA) Caddie Scholarship #104
Peter A. McKernan Scholarship #105
United States Ski and Snowboard Team Foundation Scholarship #108

Automotive Studies
Charles V. Hagler Memorial Scholarship #109
Dr. Dorothy M. Ross Scholarship #111
John E. Echlin Memorial Scholarship #113
Ken Krum-Bud Kouts Memorial Scholarship #112
Larry H. Averill Memorial Scholarship #110
Specialty Equipment Market Association Fund #115
TRW Foundation Scholarship #114

Business/Corporate/Professional Affiliation
AIL/Lawrence Bankowski AFGWU Scholarship Award #127

American Airlines/AMR Management Club Merit Scholarship #125

American Airlines/AMR Management Club Community/Leadership Scholarship #126

Armstrong Foundation Award #128

Baptist Life Association Scholarship Grant #129

BECU Foundation Scholarship #131

Biomet Foundation Scholarship #130

Butler Manufacturing Company Foundation Scholarship #132

Clara Abbott Foundation Educational Grant Program #133

DCAT Scholarship #134

Duke Energy Scholars Program #135

Employee Dependent Scholarship #153

FEEA Scholarship #136

Gerber Foundation Scholarship #150

Horace Mann Scholarship #137

Hormel Foods Scholarship #138

John P. Burke Memorial Scholarship #147

Johnson Controls, Inc. Foundation Scholarship #139

Kohler, Co. College Scholarship #140

L.O. Barnes Scholarship #154

Mary Macey Scholarship #157

Maytag Scholarship Program #141

New Hampshire Food Industry Scholarship #144

Palmer J. Hermunslie Scholarship #142

Pitney-Bowes Scholarship #145

Rahr Foundation Scholarship #146

Saticoy Lemon Association Employee Scholarhip #155

Sid Richardson Memorial Fund Scholarship #148

Stone Foundation Scholarship #149

Tuition Exchange Scholarship #151

Ultramar Diamond Shamrock Scholarship #152

Washington Post Thomas Ewing Memorial Education Grant #156

Wm. C. Doherty Scholarship #143

City/County of Residence

AAF Scholarship #161

Almanor Scholarship #167

Cental Virginia Scholarship #170

Charles K. Gose Scholarship #198

Charles Walton Peace Essay Contest #196

ChemFirst Foundation Scholarship #166

Christopher Gray and George Chancellor Memorial Scholarships #175

Dollars for Scholars #172

Donna Reed Performing Arts Scholarships - Crawford County Scholarship #177

Frederic Scott Reed Scholarship #176

Gary W. Chism Memorial Award #199

General Scholarship #197

George E. Andrews Scholarship #165

George J. Record School Foundation Scholarship #179

H.T. Ewald Scholarship #180

Hatton Lovejoy Scholarship #178

Hauss-Helms Foundation, Inc. Scholarship #181

Italian American Chamber of Commerce Scholarship #182

Jacob Rassen Memorial Scholarship Fund #184

James B. Simmons Memorial Scholarship #160

Jean Weber Memorial Scholarship #200

Joseph H. Jones, Sr., Scholarship #174

Kristin Elaine Dickerson Scholarship #171

Lawrence Conservation District Scholarship #187

Leonard H. Bulkeley Scholarship #189

Marin County American Revolution Bicentennial Scholarship #190

Marin County American Revolution Bicentennial Scholarship #164

Matthew Anthony Grappone Memorial Scholarship #173

McDonald's Golden Arches Scholarship #193

Mercer Silas Bailey Memorial Scholarship #162

Nellie Martin Carman Scholarship #192

Phoenix Scholarship #194

Rosalie Tilles Scholarship Award #195

Rozsi & Jeno Zisovich Jewish Studies Scholarship Fund to Teach the Holocaust #186

Stanley Olson Youth Scholarship #185

Thomas E. Sharpe Memorial Scholarship #191

Together We Can Scholarship #168

Trust Scholarship #188

Vivienne Camp College Scholarship #183

Walter and Virginia Nord Scholarship #169

World of Expressions Scholarship #163

Club Affiliation

A.R.A. Scholarship #208

Abe & Esther Hagiwara Student Aid Award #262

ACJA/LAE National Student Paper Competition #213

Adele Filene Travel Award #232

ADVA Scholarship Fund #210

Aiko Susanna Tashiro Hiratsuka Memorial Scholarship #263

Albert M. Lappin Scholarship #214

Alice Yuriko Endo Memorial Scholarship #254

All Teke Academic Team and John A. Courson Top Scholar Awards #306

American Legion Robert E. David Scholarship #216

Angus Foundation Scholarship #211

AQHYA Scholarship #220

Arby's/Big Brothers Big Sisters of America Scholarship #224

Arizona Chapter Dependent/ Employee Membership Scholarship #222

Association of the Sons of Poland Achievement Award #223

Astrid G. Cates Scholarship #298

Baldridge Scholarship #307

Becky Briggs Memorial Scholarship #230

Bruce B. Melchert Scholarship #303

CASE Scholarship #277

Catholic Aid Association College Tuition Scholarship #228

Catholic Workman College Scholarship #229

Charles W. and Annette Hill Scholarship #215

Children and Youth Scholarship #217

Claude and Ina Brey Memorial Endowment Fund Scholarship #270

CTA Scholarship for Members #227

Danish Sisterhood of America Scholarship #233

David Birenbaum Scholarship #212

Deaf Scholarship #278

Dean's List Scholarship #267

Del-Mar-Va Council, Inc. Boy Scouts of America Educational Scholarship #225

Delta Gamma Foundation Scholarship #234

Delta Phi Epsilon Scholarship #235

Dr. Thomas T. Yatabe Memorial Scholarship #261

Eagle Scout Scholarship #279

Eastern Orthodox Committee on Scouting Scholarship #236

Federation Life Insurance of America Scholarship #238

First Catholic Slovak Ladies Association Scholarship #239

G. Robert Hamrdla Award #293

GCSAA Legacy Awards #240

Girl Scout Achievement Award #219

Gongoro Nakamura Memorial Scholarship #249

Henry & Chiyo Kuwahara Memorial Scholarship for Entering Freshmen #246

Henry & Chiyo Kuwahara Memorial Scholarship for Undergraduates #257

International Symposium on Superalloys Scholarship #273

J. Keith Brimacombe Presidential Scholarship #271

J. Spencer Borders Academic Award #286

Jones-Laurence Award #291

Kenji Kasai Memorial Scholarship #245

Kirtland Kiwanis Memorial Scholarship #265

Kyataro & Yasuo Abiko Memorial Scholarship #243

Lee Tarbox Scholarship #209

LIT Scholarship for Excellence #268

Mari & James Michener Scholarship #259

Masao & Sumako Itano Memorial Scholarship #244

Matthews & Swift Educational Trust Scholarship #266

Melvin R. Green Scholarship #221

Menominee Tribal Higher Education/Adult Vocational Grant #269

Mitchell-Beall Scholarship #274

Mitsuyuki Yonemura Memorial Scholarship #253

Mr. & Mrs. Takashi Moriuchi Scholarship #248

Mr. & Mrs. Uyesugi Memorial Scholarship #252

Multi-Year Ambassadorial Scholarship #290

Myrtle Beinbauer Scholarship #299

NABA National Scholarship Program #275

National Beta Club Scholarship #276

National Woman's Relief Corps
   Scholarship #280
NELA Scholarship Contest
   #281
Nichols Scholarship #226
Nobuko R. Kodama Fong
   Memorial Scholarship #255
Parents Without Partners
   Scholarship #282
Patricia & Gail Ishimoto
   Memorial Scholarship #242
Phi Sigma Iota Scholarship
   #283
PNA Scholarship #287
Pony of the Americas
   Scholarship #288
Portuguese Continental Union
   of USA Scholarship #289
Richard C. Todd & Claude P.
   Todd Tripod Scholarship
   #285
Saburo Kido Memorial
   Scholarship #256
Sam S. Kuwahara Memorial
   Scholarship for Entering
   Freshmen #247
Sam S. Kuwahara Memorial
   Scholarship for
   Undergraduates #258
Scholarship Program #264
Slovene National Benefit
   Society Scholarship #296
Slovenian Women's Union of
   America Scholarship #297
SMD Scholarship #272
South Park Japanese
   Community Scholarship
   #251
Spirit of Youth Scholarship
   #218
Stella Blum Research Grant
   #231
Summer Music Scholarship
   #295
Tau Beta Pi Scholarship #300
Texas American Legion
   Auxiliary Scholarship #301
TNE Scholarship #302
UDT/SEAL Scholarship Grant
   #308
Undergraduate Scholarship
   #294
Union and League of
   Romanian Societies of
   America Scholarship #309
Wallace G. McCauley
   Memorial Scholarship #305
Warren Poslusny Award for
   Outstanding Achievement
   #292
Wenderoth Undergraduate
   Scholarship #284
Western Sunbathing Association
   Scholarship #310
William Wilson Memorial
   Scholarship #304
Yoshiko Tanaka Memorial
   Scholarship #260
Youth Activity Grant #237
Youth Scholarship Fund of
   IBHA, Inc. #241

Yutaka Nakazawa Memorial
   Scholarship #250

Culinary Arts/Baking
Kentucky Restaurant
   Association Governor's
   Scholarship #321
Kentucky Restaurant
   Association Scholarship
   #320

Disability
Career Incentive Award #333
Chairscholars Foundation
   Scholarship #330
Christian Record Services
   Scholarship #331
Division of Vocational
   Rehabilitation Services
   #350
E.U. Parker Scholarship #346
Easter Seal Society of Iowa
   Disability Scholarships
   #332
Frank Walton Horn Memorial
   Scholarship #336
Handicapped Student Grant
   #352
Hermione Grant Calhoun
   Scholarship #337
Howard Brown Rickard
   Scholarship #338
Kuchler-Killian Memorial
   Scholarship #343
Melva T. Owen Memorial
   Scholarship #339
Mozelle and Willard Gold
   Memorial Scholarship #344
National Amputation
   Foundation Scholarship
   #334
National Amputee Golf
   Association Scholarship
   #335
National Federation of the Blind
   Computer Science
   Scholarship #345
National Federation of the Blind
   Scholarship #347
NFB Educator of Tomorrow
   Award #342
NFB Humanities Scholarship
   #341
NFB Scholarship #340
Playwright Discovery Award
   #351
Tony Orlando Yellow Ribbon
   Scholarship #348
Vocational Rehabilitation
   Program #349

Gender/Marital Status
Auxiliary Scholarship #417
AWA Scholarship Awards #408
BPW Career Advancement
   Scholarship #410
Charles W. Frees, Jr.
   Scholarship #412
Dorothy Armstrong
   Community Service
   Scholarship #413
Gloria Fecht Memorial
   Scholarship #421

Jeannette Rankin Foundation
   Award #415
Karla Scherer Foundation
   Scholarship #419
Linda Riddle/SGMA
   Scholarship #422
Lucille B. Kaufman Women's
   Scholarship #418
New York Life Foundation
   Scholarship for Women in
   the Health Professions #411
Renate W. Chasman
   Scholarship for Women
   #409
Scholarship for Emigres in the
   Health Professions #416
William Reed Baker
   Outstanding Senior Award
   #414
Women's Jewelry Association
   Scholarship #420
Women's Western Golf
   Foundation Scholarship
   #423

Military Affiliation
1st Marine Division Association
   Scholarship #501
25th Infantry Division
   Association Scholarship
   #502
43rd Infantry Division Veterans
   Scholarship #503
Alaska Sea Services Scholarship
   #505
American Legion - Ohio
   Scholarship #507
American Legion -
   Pennsylvania Auxiliary
   Scholarship #510
American Legion Auxiliary -
   Alabama Scholarship #513
American Legion Auxiliary
   Department Scholarship
   #511
American Legion Memorial
   Scholarship #518
AMVETS National Four-Year
   Scholarship #520
Auxiliary Memorial
   Scholarship #525
Auxiliary Worchild Scholarship
   #524
Bowfin Memorial Scholarship
   #556
Brewer/Wilson Scholarship
   #506
Capt. Caliendo College
   Assistance Fund Scholarship
   #559
Children of Deceased Service
   Members Scholarship #547
Daughters of the Cincinnati
   Scholarship #529
Department President's
   Scholarship #508
Department Scholarship #509
Dolphin Scholarship #533
Educational Benefits for
   Children of Deceased
   Veterans #531

Edward T. Conroy Memorial
   Grant #540
First Cavalry Division
   Association Scholarship
   #534
G.A.R. Living Memorial
   Scholarship #530
General Henry H. Arnold
   Education Grant #504
Illinois AMVETS Service
   Foundation Scholarships
   #521
Illinois National Guard Grant
   #536
Illinois Veteran Grant #535
John Cornelius and Max
   English Scholarship #539
Kathern F. Gruber Scholarship
   #528
Memorial Scholarship #515
MIA/KIA Dependents'
   Scholarship #526
Minnesota Legionnaire
   Insurance Trust Scholarship
   #517
National Guard Association of
   Arizona Scholarship #543
National President's Scholarship
   #512
Navy League Scholarship #544
Navy Supply Corps Foundation
   Scholarship #545
New York Council Navy
   League Scholarship #550
North Carolina Vietnam
   Veterans' Scholarship #551
Nurses', Physical Therapists',
   and Respiratory Therapists'
   Scholarship #514
Past National President Fran
   Booth Medical Scholarship
   #538
Paul Powell Memorial
   Scholarship #523
Post #100 Scholarship #522
RRVA Scholarship Grant
   Assistance Program #552
Scholarship for Non-Traditional
   Students #516
Scholarship Program for
   Dependent Children of
   Soldiers #527
Second Marine Division
   Association Memorial
   Scholarship #555
Sgt. Major Douglas R. Drum
   Memorial Scholarship #519
Southeast Asia POW/MIA
   Scholarship #542
Surflant Scholarship #557
TREA Memorial Foundation
   National Scholarship #553
TROA Scholarship 200 #554
U.S. Submarine Veterans of
   World War II Scholarship
   #532
United States Naval Academy
   Class of 1963 Foundation
   Scholarship #560
USS Tennessee Scholarship
   #548

Davis-Roberts Scholarship #773

Delegate Scholarship #808

Department of Children & Family Services Scholarship #785

Development Foundation Diversity Scholarship #834

Diamond State Scholarship #775

Distinguished Scholar #806

Dr. Kate Waller Barrett Grant #757

Early High School Graduation Scholarship #842

Educational Opportunity Fund Grant #821

Edward J. Bloustein Distinguished Scholars #822

Florida College Student of the Year Award #778

Good Neighbor Scholarship #839

Governor's Challenge Scholarship #783

Governor's Workforce Development Grant #776

Guaranteed Access Grant #809

Illinois Amvets Service Foundation Scholarship #784

International Affairs Scholarship #779

Iowa Grants #789

Iowa Tuition Grant #788

James F. Byrnes Scholarship #790

LAEF Scholarship #791

Law Enforcement Officers and Fireman Scholarship #815

Law Enforcement Officers Dependents' Scholarship #764

Law Enforcement Personnel Dependents Scholarship #770

Lee Jackson Foundation Scholarship #792

Maine Chamber and Business Alliance Scholarship #803

Maine Legislature Memorial Scholarship #801

Maine Rural Rehabilitation Fund Scholarship #799

Maine State Society of Washington D.C. Foundation Inc. Scholarship #804

Maine Student Incentive Scholarship #800

Masonic Grand Lodge Charities of Rhode Island Scholarship #811

Massgrant #812

MECOA Scholarship #798

Memorial Scholarship for Children and Spouses of Deceased Police Officers and Firefighters #781

Merit Recognition Scholarship #786

Merit Scholarship - Tuition Waiver #848

Minnesota State Grant #813

Monetary Award #787

Monte Mitchell Global Scholarship #752

Musical or Recreational Therapy Scholarship #761

National Association of Water Companies-New Jersey Chapter Scholarship #817

National President Scholarship #759

New Hampshire Incentive Program #820

North Carolina Bar Association Scholarship #825

Oregon AFL-CIO May Darling-Asat. Williams-Northwest Labor Press Scholarship #827

PACD Auxiliary Scholarship #828

Past President's Parley Scholarship Assistance in Health Care Occupations #756

Pearl Ramsey Memorial Nursing Scholarship #852

Peeples Foundation Trust Scholarship #805

Portuguese Foundation (Connecticut) Scholarship #831

Professional School Scholarship #810

Public Safety Officers Survivor Grant #814

Rhode Island State Grant #832

Robert Byrd Honors Scholarship #835

Robert C. Byrd Honors Scholarship #769

Robert C. Byrd Honors Scholarship #838

Robert C. Byrd Honors Scholarship #841

Robert C. Byrd Honors Scholarship #816

Robert C. Byrd Honors Scholarship #797

Robert C. Byrd Honors Scholarship #836

Robert C. Byrd Honors Scholarship Program #824

Robert C. Byrd Honors Scholarship Program #819

Robert C. Byrd Scholarship #777

Rocky Mountain Chapter Estey Scholarship #760

Royal Arch Masonic Scholarship #802

Scholarship Incentive Program #774

Selby Direct Scholarship #833

Senatorial Scholarship #807

State of Idaho Scholarship #782

State Scholarships #818

Sussman-Miller Educational Assistance Award #754

Talent Incentive Program Grant #853

Texas Grant #845

Texas New Horizons Scholarship #844

Texas Tuition Assistance Grant #843

TOPS - Honors Award #795

TOPS - Opportunity Award #794

TOPS - Performance Award #793

TOPS - Tech Award #796

Township Officials of Illinois Scholarship #846

Tuition Aid Grant #823

Ty Cobb Scholarship #847

Vermont Part-Time Grant #849

Vietnam Veterans Tuition Award/Persian Gulf Veterans Tuition Award #780

Washington Crossing Foundation Scholarship #850

Washington Gas Scholarship #851

West Virginia Higher Education Grant #837

Union Affiliation

A.J. DeAndrade Scholarship #873

Air Line Pilots Association Scholarship #871

Ashby B. Carter Memorial Scholarship #877

Bakery, Confectionary, Tobacco Workers and Grain Millers (BCTGM) Scholarship Competition #872

David J. Fitzmaurice Scholarship #876

James B. Carey Scholarship #875

John L. Dales Scholarship #881

Richard F. Walsh/Alfred W. DiTolla Scholarship #878

School Food Service Foundation Scholarship #879

Schwan's Food Service Scholarship #880

Two/Ten International Footwear Foundation College Scholarship #882

UFCW International Union Scholarship #884

UNITE! National Scholarship Award #883

Utility Workers Union of America Scholarship #885

William H. Bywater Scholarship #874

Vocational/Technical

David Arver Memorial Scholarship #886

Iowa Vocational-Technical Tuition Grant #889

John C. Lincoln Memorial Scholarhip #888

Maryland Association of Private Career Schools Scholarship #890

Vocational/Technical Scholarship #887

Science/Mathematics

Biology

Kathleen S. Anderson Award #116

Chemistry

ACS Scholars Program #158

ACS/PPG Scholars Plus Program #159

Environmental Science

EPA Tribal Lands Environmental Science Scholarship #394

Marine Science

International Women's Fishing Association Scholarship #477

Olin Fellowship #475

Seaspace Scholarship #478

Seaspace Scholarship #476

Physical Sciences

ACIL Scholarship #643

Space Imaging EOSAT Award for Application of Digital Landsat TM Data #644

Sciences-General

ACS/Bayer Scholars Program #741

Educational Scholarships & Grants in Optical Science & Engineering #743

Peter D. Courtois Concrete Construction Scholarship #742

Social Science/ Political Science/Law

Home Economics

Lorain County Home Economics Scholarship #431

Law

ACJA/LAE National Scholarship #473

Military Science/ROTC

ROTC Scholarship #562

Psychology

Eileen J. Garrett Scholarship #647

2. Race/ Ethnicity Index

3. Religious Affiliation Index

Protestant

Appalachian Scholarship #733
George J. Record School
Foundation Scholarship
#179
Mental Retardation Scholastic
Achievement Scholarship
#718
Native American Education
Grant #698
Nursing Scholastic
Achievement Scholarship
#719
Racial/Ethnic History Research
Grant #724
Student Opportunity
Scholarship #734
Synod of the Trinity Education
Scholarship #736
Women in United Methodist
History Research Grant
#725
Women in United Methodist
History Writing Award #726

Roman Catholic

Italian Catholic Federation
Scholarship Program #686
Pro Deo and Pro Patria
Scholarships #731

4. Athletics Index

Athletics

Mark Smith Neale II "Cross of
Life" Scholarship #14
William Reed Baker
Outstanding Senior Award
#414

Bowling

Billy Welu Memorial
Scholarship #106
John Jowdy Scholarship #107

Golf

Gloria Fecht Memorial
Scholarship #421
John P. Burke Memorial
Scholarship #147
Women's Western Golf
Foundation Scholarship
#423

United States Ski and Snowboard Team

United States Ski and
Snowboard Team
Foundation Scholarship
#108

Varsity Sports

FINA Dallas Morning News
All-State Scholar-Athlete
Team Scholarship #103

Water Skiing

AWSEF Scholarship #102

5. State/ Country of Residence Index

Alabama

Alabama Scholarship for
Dependents of Blind Parents
#753
American Legion Auxiliary -
Alabama Scholarship #513

Alaska

Alaska Sea Services Scholarship
#505
American Legion - Alaska
Scholarship #755
State Scholarships #818
Western Section Scholarship
#495

All Except Iowa

Morris Scholarship #691

All Except Ohio

Development Foundation
Diversity Scholarship #834

Appalachia

Appalachian Scholarship #733

Arizona

Arizona Chapter Dependent/
Employee Membership
Scholarship #222
Arizona Chapter Gold #858

Burlington Northern Santa Fe
Foundation Scholarship
#650
John C. Lincoln Memorial
Scholarhip #888
Past President's Parley Nurses
Scholarship #596
Past President's Parley
Scholarship Assistance in
Health Care Occupations
#756
RMCMI Scholarship #565
Western Section Scholarship
#495

Arkansas

Arkansas Academic Challenge
Scholarship #763
Arkansas Governor's Scholars
Award #762
Arkansas Single Parent
Scholarship #765
Law Enforcement Officers
Dependents' Scholarship
#764
MIA/KIA Dependents'
Scholarship #526

California

California Masonic Foundation
Scholarship #768
Donald F. Hastings Scholarship
#374
Joel Garcia Memorial
Scholarship #661
Law Enforcement Personnel
Dependents Scholarship
#770
Malki Museum Scholarship
#429
Marin County American
Revolution Bicentennial
Scholarship #190
Robert C. Byrd Honors
Scholarship #769
Society of Petroleum Engineers
- San Joaquin Valley Section
Scholarship #384
State Scholarships #818
Western Section Scholarship
#495
William J. and Mary Jane E.
Adams, Jr. Scholarship #480

Canada

King Olav V Norwegian-
American Heritage Fund
#323

Colorado

Boettcher Foundation
Scholarship #766
Burlington Northern Santa Fe
Foundation Scholarship
#650
Colorado Diversity Grant #666
Colorado Nursing Scholarship
#601

Colorado Part-Time Grant/
Scholarship #771
Colorado Student Grant #772
Henry Sachs Foundation
Scholarship #676
LAEF Scholarship #791
News 4 Media Scholarship
#313
RMCMI Scholarship #565
Western Section Scholarship
#495

Connecticut

Medicus Student Exchange
#702
NEGA Scholarship #426
New York Council Navy
League Scholarship #550
Nursing Scholarship #602
Pellegrini Scholarship #701
State Scholarships #818
Timothy Bigelow Scholarship
#436

Countries with Rotary Clubs

Academic Year Ambassadorial
Scholarship #635
Multi-Year Ambassadorial
Scholarship #290

Delaware

Diamond State Scholarship
#775
Educational Benefits for
Children of Deceased
Veterans #531
Governor's Workforce
Development Grant #776
Medicus Student Exchange
#702
Pellegrini Scholarship #701
Robert C. Byrd Scholarship
#777

Eastern U.S.

Alice Yuriko Endo Memorial
Scholarship #254

Europe

Monte Mitchell Global
Scholarship #752

Finland

Finlandia Foundation Trust
Scholarship Exchange
Program and Grants #672

Florida

American Legion Auxiliary
Department Scholarship
#511
Florida College Student of the
Year Award #778

Selby Direct Scholarship #833
State Scholarships #818

Former Soviet Republics

Scholarship for Emigres in the Health Professions #416

Georgia

Constance L. Lloyd/ACMPE Scholarship #88
GPEF Scholarship #454
Morton B. Duggan Memorial Education Recognition Award #737
Ty Cobb Scholarship #847

Hawaii

Fukunaga Foundation Scholarship #123
Miss Outstanding Teenager #37
Western Section Scholarship #495
William J. and Mary Jane E. Adams, Jr. Scholarship #480

Idaho

Governor's Challenge Scholarship #783
Miss Outstanding Teenager #37
State of Idaho Scholarship #782
Western Section Scholarship #495

Illinois

Academic Scholarship #713
Auxiliary Memorial Scholarship #525
Auxiliary Worchild Scholarship #524
Illinois Amvets Service Foundation Scholarship #784
Illinois AMVETS Service Foundation Scholarships #521
Illinois Incentive for Access #27
Merit Recognition Scholarship #786
Midwest Section Scholarship #494
Monetary Award #787
Musical or Recreational Therapy Scholarship #761
Paul Powell Memorial Scholarship #523
Polish Women's Civic Club Scholarship #697
Post #100 Scholarship #522
Robert C. Byrd Honors Scholarship #359
Township Officials of Illinois Scholarship #846

Indiana

Katharine M. Grosscup Scholarship #432
Midwest Section Scholarship #494
Peeples Foundation Trust Scholarship #805
Robert C. Byrd Honors Scholarship #365

Iowa

American Legion Auxiliary, Department of Iowa Scholarship #758
Easter Seal Scholarships #645
Easter Seal Society of Iowa Disability Scholarships #332
Harriet Hoffman Teaching Scholarship #354
Iowa Grants #789
Iowa Tuition Grant #788
Iowa Vocational-Technical Tuition Grant #889
Mary Virginia McRae Nurses Scholarship #597
Midwest Section Scholarship #494
Morris Scholarship #691
War Orphans Educational Aid #537

Kansas

Burlington Northern Santa Fe Foundation Scholarship #650
Oratorical Contest Scholarship #745

Kentucky

Howard E. Adkins Memorial Scholarship #372
Kentucky Restaurant Association Governor's Scholarship #321
Kentucky Restaurant Association Scholarship #320

Louisiana

Robert C. Byrd Honors Scholarship #797
TOPS - Honors Award #795
TOPS - Opportunity Award #794
TOPS - Performance Award #793
TOPS - Tech Award #796

Maine

4-H Postsecondary Scholarship #830
Maine Chamber and Business Alliance Scholarship #803
Maine Legislature Memorial Scholarship #801
Maine State Society of Washington, D.C., Foundation, Inc. Scholarship #804
Maine Student Incentive Scholarship #800
MECOA Scholarship #798
NEGA Scholarship #426
Nurses Training Scholarship #608
Past National President Fran Booth Medical Scholarship #538
Peter A. McKernan Scholarship #105
Royal Arch Masonic Scholarship #802
Timothy Bigelow Scholarship #436
Vernon T. Swain P.E./Robert E. Chute P.E. Memorial Scholarship #380

Maryland

Delegate Scholarship #808
Distinguished Scholar #806
Edward T. Conroy Memorial Grant #540
Guaranteed Access Grant #809
Maryland Association of Certified Public Accountants Educational Foundation Scholarship #66
Maryland Association of Private Career Schools Scholarship #890
Professional School Scholarship #810
Senatorial Scholarship #807

Massachusetts

"Pennies for Art" Scholarship #398
Dorchester Woman's Club Scholarship #892
GFWC of MA Music Scholarship #580
International Affairs Scholarship #779
Massgrant #812
NEGA Scholarship #426
Newtonville Woman's Club Scholarship #356
Timothy Bigelow Scholarship #436

Michigan

Katharine M. Grosscup Scholarship #432
Memorial Scholarship #515
Midwest Section Scholarship #494
National President Scholarship #759
Nurses', Physical Therapists', and Respiratory Therapists' Scholarship #514
Nursing Student Scholarship #604

Scholarship for Non-Traditional Students #516
State Scholarships #818

Minnesota

American Legion Memorial Scholarship #518
Burlington Northern Santa Fe Foundation Scholarship #650
Midwest Section Scholarship #494
Minnesota Legionnaire Insurance Trust Scholarship #517
Minnesota State Grant #813
Post-Secondary Child Care Grant #630
Public Safety Officers Survivor Grant #814
State Scholarships #818
War Orphan's Scholarship #541

Mississippi

Law Enforcement Officers and Fireman Scholarship #815
Southeast Asia POW/MIA Scholarship #542
State Scholarships #818
William Winter Teacher Scholar Program #360

Missouri

Lights of Jewish Special Needs Society Scholarship #732
Robert C. Byrd Honors Scholarship #816
Rosalie Tilles Scholarship Award #195

Montana

Burlington Northern Santa Fe Foundation Scholarship #650
Miss Outstanding Teenager #37
RMCMI Scholarship #565
State Scholarships #818
Western Section Scholarship #495

Nebraska

Midwest Section Scholarship #494
Nebraska Space Grant and EPSCOR College and Fellowship Program #74
State Scholarships #818

Nevada

Miss Outstanding Teenager #37
Robert C. Byrd Honors Scholarship Program #819
Western Section Scholarship #495
William J. and Mary Jane E. Adams, Jr. Scholarship #480

New England

NEGA Scholarship #426
Worcester County Horticultural Society Scholarship #438

New Hampshire

NEGA Scholarship #426
New Hampshire Incentive Program #820
Timothy Bigelow Scholarship #436

New Jersey

College Correspondent Scholarship #460
Educational Opportunity Fund Grant #821
Edward J. Bloustein Distinguished Scholars #822
Medicus Student Exchange #702
National Association of Water Companies-New Jersey Chapter Scholarship #817
New York Council Navy League Scholarship #550
NJPA Internship/Scholarship Program #459
Pellegrini Scholarship #701
State Scholarships #818
Tuition Aid Grant #823

New Mexico

Burlington Northern Santa Fe Foundation Scholarship #650
RMCMI Scholarship #565
Sussman-Miller Educational Assistance Award #754
Vietnam Veterans Scholarship #549
Western Section Scholarship #495

New York

Grace S. Anton Scholarship #462
Medicus Student Exchange #702
Memorial Scholarship for Children and Spouses of Deceased Police Officers and Firefighters #781
New York Council Navy League Scholarship #550
Pellegrini Scholarship #701
Robert C. Byrd Honors Scholarship Program #824
State Scholarships #818
Vietnam Veterans Tuition Award/Persian Gulf Veterans Tuition Award #780

North America

Tony Orlando Yellow Ribbon Scholarship #348

North Carolina

American Society of Highway Engineers - Carolina Triangle Section Scholarship #202
Division of Vocational Rehabilitation Services #350
North Carolina Bar Association Scholarship #825
Robert C. Byrd Honors Scholarship #361
State Scholarships #818
Vocational Rehabilitation Program #349

North Dakota

Burlington Northern Santa Fe Foundation Scholarship #650
Midwest Section Scholarship #494
North Dakota American Legion High School Oratorical Contest #747
Rocky Mountain Coal Mining Institute (RMCMI) Scholarship #565

Northern California

Northern California/Richard Epping Scholarship #859

Northern Nevada

Northern California/Richard Epping Scholarship #859

Norway

King Olav V Norwegian-American Heritage Fund #323

Ohio

Department President's Scholarship #508
Donald F. Hastings Scholarship #374
John C. Lincoln Memorial Scholarhip #888
Katharine M. Grosscup Scholarship #432
Kirtland Kiwanis Memorial Scholarship #265
Midwest Section Scholarship #494
State Scholarships #818

Oklahoma

Academic Scholars Program #826
Burlington Northern Santa Fe Foundation Scholarship #650
Cheyenne-Arapaho Tribal Scholarship #663

Merit Scholarship - Tuition Waiver #848
State Scholarships #818

Oregon

Burlington Northern Santa Fe Foundation Scholarship #650
Department Scholarship #509
Oregon AFL-CIO May Darling-Asat. Williams-Northwest Labor Press Scholarship #827
Oregon Association of Broadcasters Broadcast Scholarship #463
Thomas R. Dargan Minority Scholarship #688
Western Section Scholarship #495

Pacific Northwest Region

Nobuko R. Kodama Fong Memorial Scholarship #255

Pennsylvania

American Legion - Pennsylvania Auxiliary Scholarship #510
Cymdeithas Gymreig Scholarship #670
Katharine M. Grosscup Scholarship #432
Medicus Student Exchange #702
PACD Auxiliary Scholarship #828
Pellegrini Scholarship #701
Professional Pilot, Aviation Management, Aviation Technology Scholarship #72

Puerto Rico

Hispanic College Fund Scholarship #677

Rhode Island

Masonic Grand Lodge Charities of Rhode Island Scholarship #811
NEGA Scholarship #426
Rhode Island State Grant #832
Timothy Bigelow Scholarship #436

South Carolina

C.G. Fuller Foundation Scholarship #767
James F. Byrnes Scholarship #790
Morton B. Duggan Memorial Education Recognition Award #737
Rose and Joseph Sokol Scholarship #735

South Dakota

Burlington Northern Santa Fe Foundation Scholarship #650
Midwest Section Scholarship #494
Robert Byrd Honors Scholarship #835
Robert C. Byrd Honors Scholarship #836

South Florida

Miami International Press Club Scholarship #456

Southern California

BEEM Foundation Scholarship #576
Gloria Fecht Memorial Scholarship #421
Golden State Minority Foundation Scholarship #120

Tennessee

Oratorical Contest Scholarship of Tennessee #749

Texas

Amarillo Area Foundation Scholarship #161
Children of Disabled Firemen and Peace Officers Tuition Exemption #840
Early High School Graduation Scholarship #842
FINA/*Dallas Morning News* All-State Scholar-Athlete Team Scholarship #103
Oratorical Contest Scholarship #750
Press Club of Dallas Foundation Scholarships #465
RMCMI Scholarship #565
Robert C. Byrd Honors Scholarship #841
Scholarship for L.V.N.s Becoming Professional Nurses #611
Scholarship for Rural B.S.N. or Graduate Nursing Students #610
Scholarship for Rural Professional or Vocational Nursing Students #609
Texas Grant #845
Texas New Horizons Scholarship #844
Texas Professional Communicators Roving Scholarship #318
Texas Transportation Scholarship #868
Texas Tuition Assistance Grant #843
TPW Roving Scholarship #469

6. Union Affiliation Index

7. Misc. Criteria Index

Child of a Blind Parent

Alabama Scholarship for Dependents of Blind Parents #753

Kathern F. Gruber Scholarship #528

Child of a Deceased Or Physically Disabled Parent

Maine Rural Rehabilitation Fund Scholarship #799

Child of a Single Parent

Nobuko R. Kodama Fong Memorial Scholarship #255

Community Involvement

Alaska Sea Services Scholarship #505

American Association of Hispanic CPAs Scholarship #648

Kankakee County Community Services Scholarship #628

Sam Walton Community Scholarship #60

Community Service

Becky Briggs Memorial Scholarship #230

Cental Virginia Scholarship #170

Christopher Gray and George Chancellor Memorial Scholarships #175

Dollars for Scholars #172

Dorothy Armstrong Community Service Scholarship #413

Frederic Scott Reed Scholarship #176

Hayes E. Willis Memorial Scholarship #667

Joseph H. Jones, Sr., Scholarship #174

Kristin Elaine Dickerson Scholarship #171

Lori Ann Robinson Memorial Scholarship #119

Mark Smith Neale II "Cross of Life" Scholarship #14

Matthew Anthony Grappone Memorial Scholarship #173

McDonald's African American Heritage Scholarship #694

McDonald's Golden Arches Scholarship #193

McDonald's GospelFest Music Scholarship #582

National President Scholarship #759

Raymond F. Burmester Endowment for Scholastic Achievement #13

Township Officials of Illinois Scholarship #846

Vicky Howard Community Service Award #56

Warren Poslusny Award for Outstanding Achievement #292

William Reed Baker Outstanding Senior Award #414

Deceased Parent

James F. Byrnes Scholarship #790

Drug-free

Eddie G. Robinson Foundation High School Senior Scholarship #17

Engineering Accreditation Comm. of the Accreditation Board for Engineering/Tech.

Auxiliary Scholarship #417

Paul H. Robbins Honorary Scholarship #382

Virginia D. Henry Memorial Scholarship #381

Essay

A.J. DeAndrade Scholarship #873

Bakery, Confectionary, Tobacco Workers and Grain Millers (BCTGM) Scholarship Competition #872

Capt. Caliendo College Assistance Fund Scholarship #559

Ecolab Scholarship #440

Eddie G. Robinson Foundation High School Senior Scholarship #17

Eric and Bette Friedheim Scholarship #44

H. Neil Mecaskey Scholarship #864

Louise Dessureault Memorial Scholarship #865

Mitchell-Beall Scholarship #274

Tony Orlando Yellow Ribbon Scholarship #348

Treadway Inns, Hotels, and Resorts Scholarship #633

Wenderoth Undergraduate Scholarship #284

Essay Contest

Bakery, Confectionary, Tobacco Workers and Grain Millers (BCTGM) Scholarship Competition #872

Capt. Caliendo College Assistance Fund Scholarship #559

I.F. Stone Award for Student Journalism #457

Student Paper Competition - Undergraduate Level #863

Wenderoth Undergraduate Scholarship #284

Extracurricular Activities

Ecolab Scholarship #440

J. Spencer Borders Academic Award #286

RRVA Scholarship Grant Assistance Program #552

Township Officials of Illinois Scholarship #846

Financial Need

Abe & Esther Hagiwara Student Aid Award #262

Al Qoyawayma Award #674

Alabama Scholarship for Dependents of Blind Parents #753

Alaska Sea Services Scholarship #505

Allied Dental Education Scholarship #325

American Association of Hispanic CPAs Scholarship #648

American Legion Children and Youth Scholarship #622

American Legion Memorial Scholarship #518

AMVETS National Four-Year Scholarship #520

Arkansas Academic Challenge Scholarship #763

Arkansas Student Assistance Grant #2

Armstrong Multicultural Education Scholarship #653

Atlanta Press Club Journalism Grant #453

AWSEF Scholarship #102

Baldridge Scholarship #307

Baptist Life Association Scholarship Grant #129

Bowfin Memorial Scholarship #556

Butler Manufacturing Company Foundation Scholarship #132

Charles V. Hagler Memorial Scholarship #109

Christopher Gray and George Chancellor Memorial Scholarships #175

Clara Abbott Foundation Educational Grant Program #133

Colorado Student Grant #772

CSDIW Scholarship #668

Dollars for Scholars #172

Dr. Charles A. Preuss Medical Award #499

Dr. Dorothy M. Ross Scholarship #111

Easter Seal Scholarships #645

Easter Seal Society of Iowa Disability Scholarships #332

Ecolab Scholarship #440

Edmund F. Maxwell Scholarship #18

First Catholic Slovak Ladies Association Scholarship #239

FNSNA Scholarship #603

Frank Kazmierczak Memorial Migrant Scholarship #355

Fukunaga Foundation Scholarship #123

General Henry H. Arnold Education Grant #504

General Scholarship #197

Gloria and Joseph Mattera National Scholarship for Migrant Children #77

Gloria Fecht Memorial Scholarship #421

Handicapped Student Grant #352

Hispanic College Fund Scholarship #678

Hispanic College Fund Scholarship #677

J. Spencer Borders Academic Award #286

Jaycee War Memorial Fund Scholarship (JWMF) #55

John E. Echlin Memorial Scholarship #113

John F. Kennedy University Scholarship #32

Kankakee County Community Services Scholarship #628

Ken Krum-Bud Kouts Memorial Scholarship #112

Larry H. Averill Memorial Scholarship #110

Maryland Association of Certified Public Accountants Educational Foundation Scholarship #66

Massgrant #812

McDonald's African American Heritage Scholarship #694

McDonald's Golden Arches Scholarship #193

McDonald's GospelFest Music Scholarship #582

Memorial Scholarship #515

Migrant Farmworker Baccalaureate Scholarship #76

Minority Retention Grant #705

National President's Scholarship #512

NEGA Scholarship #426

New Jersey State Golf Association (NJSGA) Caddie Scholarship #104

Nurses', Physical Therapists', and Respiratory Therapists' Scholarship #514

Past National President Fran Booth Medical Scholarship #538

Past President's Parley Nurses Scholarship #596

Past President's Parley Scholarship Assistance in Health Care Occupations #756

Peeples Foundation Trust Scholarship #805

Peeples Promise Scholarship #121

Polish Women's Civic Club Scholarship #697

Professional School Scholarship #810

Rhode Island State Grant #832

Rose and Joseph Sokol Scholarship #735

ROTC Scholarship #562

Royal Arch Masonic Scholarship #802

Rozsi & Jeno Zisovich Jewish Studies Scholarship Fund to Teach the Holocaust #186

RRVA Scholarship Grant Assistance Program #552

Scholarship for Non-Traditional Students #516

Scholarship Incentive Program #774

Schuyler M. Meyer, Jr. Award #673

Sid Richardson Memorial Fund Scholarship #148

SOA/CAS Minority Scholarship #452

Stanley Olson Youth Scholarship #185

Sussman-Miller Educational Assistance Award #754

Talent Incentive Program Grant #853

Texas American Legion Auxiliary Scholarship #301

Texas Grant #845

TRW Foundation Scholarship #114

Undergraduate Scholarship #294

Vivienne Camp College Scholarship #183

W.H. "Howie" McClennan Scholarship #402

First-Generation College Student

TELACU Arts Award #401

TELACU/Cesar Chavez Award #53

Full-Time Student

AFSA Financial Aid Scholarship #620

Charles V. Hagler Memorial Scholarship #109

Dr. Dorothy M. Ross Scholarship #111

Esperanza Scholarship #671

Golden State Minority Foundation Scholarship #120

Health Careers Scholarship #95

Hispanic College Fund Scholarship #677

John E. Echlin Memorial Scholarship #113

Johnson Controls, Inc. Foundation Scholarship #139

Ken Krum-Bud Kouts Memorial Scholarship #112

Larry H. Averill Memorial Scholarship #110

Massgrant #812

National Amputation Foundation Scholarship #334

TRW Foundation Scholarship #114

Vice Admiral E.P. Travers Scholarship #546

Wayne Kay Co-op Scholarship #383

Girl Scout Gold Award

Girl Scout Achievement Award #219

High School Student

Charles Walton Peace Essay Contest #196

Educational Communications Scholarship #19

High School Oratorical Contest #751

Humanitarian Parolee

Coca-Cola Scholarship #10

International Study

Global Citizen Awards #624

Leadership

AFDO Scholarship #326

Alaska Sea Services Scholarship #505

Baldridge Scholarship #307

Becky Briggs Memorial Scholarship #230

Cental Virginia Scholarship #170

Christopher Gray and George Chancellor Memorial Scholarships #175

Dollars for Scholars #172

Dorothy Armstrong Community Service Scholarship #413

Frederic Scott Reed Scholarship #176

Hayes E. Willis Memorial Scholarship #667

Jaycee War Memorial Fund Scholarship (JWMF) #55

Joseph H. Jones, Sr., Scholarship #174

Kristin Elaine Dickerson Scholarship #171

Lori Ann Robinson Memorial Scholarship #119

Marion Huber Learning through Listening Awards #634

Mark Smith Neale II "Cross of Life" Scholarship #14

Matthew Anthony Grappone Memorial Scholarship #173

National President's Scholarship #512

New Jersey State Golf Association (NJSGA) Caddie Scholarship #104

Raymond F. Burmester Endowment for Scholastic Achievement #13

William Reed Baker Outstanding Senior Award #414

Letter Carrier

Wm. C. Doherty Scholarship #143

Local Government Service

Township Officials of Illinois Scholarship #846

Mandarin

Institute of China Studies Scholarship #684

Merit Scholarship

Coca-Cola Scholarship #10

NASA Federal Credit Union

Mitchell-Beall Scholarship #274

Need-Based

Katharine M. Grosscup Scholarship #432

Nevada High School Scholars Program

Robert C. Byrd Honors Scholarship Program #819

Nomination

Jones-Laurence Award #291

New Focus Student Award #612

Non-Traditional Student

Scholarship for Non-Traditional Students #516

Outdoorsman

Mark Smith Neale II "Cross of Life" Scholarship #14

Parents

L.O. Barnes Scholarship #154

Part-Time Student

Colorado Part-Time Grant/ Scholarship #771

Safety/Survival

SAFE Association Scholarship #636

School Involvement

Becky Briggs Memorial Scholarship #230

Single Parent

Arkansas Single Parent Scholarship #765

Thomas Scholarship #93

Technical Program

Governor's Challenge Scholarship #783

Iowa Vocational-Technical Tuition Grant #889

Jeannette Rankin Foundation Award #415

Maryland Association of Private Career Schools Scholarship #890

Technology Program

Maine Chamber and Business Alliance Scholarship #803

Temporary Resident

Coca-Cola Scholarship #10

U.S. College/ University

I.F. Stone Award for Student Journalism #457

Vocational Program

Governor's Challenge Scholarship #783

Iowa Vocational-Technical Tuition Grant #889

Jeannette Rankin Foundation Award #415

Maryland Association of Private Career Schools Scholarship #890

Scholarship for Non-Traditional Students #516

Wards of Illinois

Department of Children & Family Services Scholarship #785

Worship

Mark Smith Neale II "Cross of Life" Scholarship #14

8. Academic Record Index

Academic Ability

Alaska Sea Services Scholarship #505

Bakery, Confectionary, Tobacco Workers and Grain Millers (BCTGM) Scholarship Competition #872

Polish Women's Civic Club Scholarship #697

Academic Achievement

4-H Postsecondary Scholarship #830

Abraham Mitchell Business Scholarship #124

American Association of Hispanic CPAs Scholarship #648

AMVETS National Four-Year Scholarship #520

Becky Briggs Memorial Scholarship #230

Cental Virginia Scholarship #170

Christopher Gray and George Chancellor Memorial Scholarships #175

Coca-Cola Scholarship #10

Danish Sisterhood of America Scholarship #233

Dollars for Scholars #172

Dorothy Armstrong Community Service Scholarship #413

Dr. Charles A. Preuss Medical Award #499

FNSNA Scholarship #603

Frank Kazmierczak Memorial Migrant Scholarship #355

Frederic Scott Reed Scholarship #176

Hayes E. Willis Memorial Scholarship #667

Joel Garcia Memorial Scholarship #661

Jones-Laurence Award #291

Joseph H. Jones, Sr., Scholarship #174

Kankakee County Community Services Scholarship #628

Kentucky Restaurant Association Governor's Scholarship #321

Kristin Elaine Dickerson Scholarship #171

Lori Ann Robinson Memorial Scholarship #119

Mark Smith Neale II "Cross of Life" Scholarship #14

Matthew Anthony Grappone Memorial Scholarship #173

Migrant Farmworker Baccalaureate Scholarship #76

New Jersey State Golf Association (NJSGA) Caddie Scholarship #104

Paul H. Robbins Honorary Scholarship #382

Peeples Foundation Trust Scholarship #805

Raymond F. Burmester Endowment for Scholastic Achievement #13

RRVA Scholarship Grant Assistance Program #552

Sid Richardson Memorial Fund Scholarship #148

W.H. "Howie" McClennan Scholarship #402

William Reed Baker Outstanding Senior Award #414

Wilson Grant #35

Academic Excellence

Armstrong Multicultural Education Scholarship #653

Jones-Laurence Award #291

ROTC Scholarship #562

Academic Merit

Past National President Fran Booth Medical Scholarship #538

Sam Walton Community Scholarship #60

Academic Promise

Baldridge Scholarship #307

Gloria and Joseph Mattera National Scholarship for Migrant Children #77

Jaycee War Memorial Fund Scholarship (JWMF) #55

ACT Score 19

Arkansas Academic Challenge Scholarship #763

TOPS - Tech Award #796

ACT Score 21

Dean's Scholarship #45

Dean's Scholarship #6

Hopi Scholarship #681

Robert C. Byrd Scholarship #777

ACT Score 22

Merit Scholarship - Tuition Waiver #848

ACT Score 23

Abraham Mitchell Business Scholarship #124

Horace Mann Scholarship #137

Robert C. Byrd Honors Scholarship #797

TOPS - Performance Award #793

ACT Score 24

Robert Byrd Honors Scholarship #835

ACT Score 25

Dean's Scholarship #46

ACT Score 27

Arkansas Governor's Scholars Award #762

Boettcher Foundation Scholarship #766

TOPS - Honors Award #795

ACT Score 32

Arkansas Governor's Scholars Award #762

ACT English Score 25

Auxiliary Scholarship #417

Virginia D. Henry Memorial Scholarship #381

ACT Math Score 29

Auxiliary Scholarship #417

Virginia D. Henry Memorial Scholarship #381

Class Rank Top 5%

Boettcher Foundation Scholarship #766

Elks National Foundation Most Valuable Student Award #20

Merit Recognition Scholarship #786

Class Rank Top 10%

FINA/*Dallas Morning News* All-State Scholar-Athlete Team Scholarship #103

Hopi Scholarship #681

Kohler, Co. College Scholarship #140

Robert C. Byrd Honors Scholarship #816

Underwood-Smith Teacher Scholarship #364

Union and League of Romanian Societies of America Scholarship #309

Class Rank Top 20%

Principal's Leadership Award #42

Class Rank Top 30%

Johnson Controls, Inc. Foundation Scholarship #139

Class Rank Top 33%

George E. Andrews Scholarship #165

Phi Delta Kappa Scholarship Grants for Prospective Educators #362

Pitney-Bowes Scholarship #145

Class Rank Top 35%

LIT Scholarship for Excellence #268

Class Rank Top 40%

Easter Seal Society of Iowa Disability Scholarships #332

Class Rank Top 50%

Hauss-Helms Foundation, Inc. Scholarship #181

GPA 2.0

A.T. Anderson Memorial Scholarship #649

AFSA Financial Aid Scholarship #620

BIA Higher Education/Hopi Supplemental Grant #680

Butler Manufacturing Company Foundation Scholarship #132

Cheyenne-Arapaho Tribal Scholarship #663

Easley National Scholarship #38

General Henry H. Arnold Education Grant #504

Hauss-Helms Foundation, Inc. Scholarship #181

Margie Ann Conner Scholarship #577

MGAA Scholarship #425

New Hampshire Incentive Program #820

Olin L. Livesey Scholarship #47

Peter A. McKernan Scholarship #105

Thomas E. Sharpe Memorial Scholarship #191

Vice Admiral E.P. Travers Scholarship #546

GPA 2.25

Timothy Bigelow Scholarship #436

GPA 2.5

AFDO Scholarship #326
Arkansas Academic Challenge Scholarship #763
Billy Welu Memorial Scholarship #106
Culinary Arts/Nutrition/ Physical Education Scholarship #327
Donald F. Hastings Scholarship #374
Edward J. Brady Scholarship #373
EPA Tribal Lands Environmental Science Scholarship #394
Guaranteed Access Grant #809
Irlet Anderson Scholarship #692
John C. Lincoln Memorial Scholarhip #888
John Jowdy Scholarship #107
Kirtland Kiwanis Memorial Scholarship #265
LAEF Scholarship #791
Mexican American Grocers Association Foundation Scholarship #122
Morris Scholarship #691
NABA National Scholarship Program #275
News 4 Media Scholarship #313
Nichols Scholarship #226
Scholarship Incentive Program #774
Slovene National Benefit Society Scholarship #296
Suburban Hospital Scholarship #98
Sussman-Miller Educational Assistance Award #754
TELACU Arts Award #401
TELACU/Cesar Chavez Award #53
Tony Orlando Yellow Ribbon Scholarship #348
TOPS - Opportunity Award #794
TOPS - Tech Award #796
Tyson Foundation Scholarship #572
Washington Printing Guild Awards #427
Western Sunbathing Association Scholarship #310

GPA 2.5 to 3.7

American Legion - Alaska Scholarship #755

GPA 2.7

Maine Rural Rehabilitation Fund Scholarship #799

School Food Service Foundation Scholarship #879

GPA 2.75

Undergraduate Scholarship for High School Seniors #444

GPA 2.8

Dean's Award #61
Easter Seal Society of Iowa Disability Scholarships #332

GPA 3.0

AACC Undergraduate Scholarships #75
ACS Scholars Program #158
AIAA Undergraduate Scholarship #71
Air Line Pilots Association Scholarship #871
American Association of Hispanic CPAs Scholarship #648
ASAE Student Engineer of the Year Scholarship #369
ASWA Scholarship #63
Auxiliary Scholarship #417
Barry M. Goldwater Scholarship and Excellence in Education Program #3
Bayliss Radio Scholarship #312
California Masonic Foundation Scholarship #768
CAMP Scholarship #424
Caterpillar Scholars Award Fund #448
Charles R. Westgate Scholarship in Engineering #379
CHSSC Scholarship #8
Coca-Cola Scholarship #10
CSDIW Scholarship #668
Culinary Arts/Nutrition/ Physical Education Scholarship #327
Dean's Scholarship #45
Dean's Scholarship #6
Development Foundation Diversity Scholarship #834
Diamond State Scholarship #775
Duke Energy Scholars Program #135
Eric and Bette Friedheim Scholarship #44
Excellence in Accounting Scholarship #68
Express News Paul Thompson Scholarship #470
FFTA Scholarship Competition #626
Fukunaga Foundation Scholarship #123
General Scholarship #197
George M. Brooker Collegiate Scholarship for Minorities #714

Gloria Fecht Memorial Scholarship #421
Golden State Minority Foundation Scholarship #120
Greek Women's University Club Scholarship #675
H. Neil Mecaskey Scholarship #864
Helping Outstanding Pupils Educationally (HOPE) Scholarship #24
Hispanic College Fund Scholarship #678
Hispanic College Fund Scholarship #677
Hopi Scholarship #681
Horace Mann Scholarship #137
Italian Catholic Federation Scholarship Program #686
J. Spencer Borders Academic Award #286
Jacob Rassen Memorial Scholarship Fund #184
Jimmy A. Young Memorial Educational Recognition Award #740
Linda Riddle/SGMA Scholarship #422
LIT Scholarship for Excellence #268
Louise Dessureault Memorial Scholarship #865
Maine Rural Rehabilitation Fund Scholarship #799
Maine State Society of Washington D.C. Foundation Inc. Scholarship #804
Manpower Foundation Scholarship #34
MAPA Safety Foundation Scholarship #73
Maryland Association of Certified Public Accountants Educational Foundation Scholarship #66
McDonald's African American Heritage Scholarship #694
McDonald's Golden Arches Scholarship #193
McDonald's GospelFest Music Scholarship #582
Mental Retardation Scholastic Achievement Scholarship #718
Miss Outstanding Teenager #37
Morton B. Duggan Memorial Education Recognition Award #737
NAAS II National Scholarship #39
National AMBUCS Scholarship for Therapists #87
National Association of Water Companies-New Jersey Chapter Scholarship #817
National High School Journalist of the Year Sister Rita Jeanne Scholarship #455

Navy Supply Corps Foundation Scholarship #545
NBRC/AMP Robert M. Lawrence, M.D., Education Recognition Award #738
NBRC/AMP William W. Burgin, Jr., M.D., Education Recognition Award #739
Nellie Martin Carman Scholarship #192
Nursing Scholastic Achievement Scholarship #719
Robert C. Byrd Honors Scholarship #365
Robert C. Byrd Honors Scholarship #361
Rozsi & Jeno Zisovich Jewish Studies Scholarship Fund to Teach the Holocaust #186
Seaspace Scholarship #478
Stanley Olson Youth Scholarship #185
Sussman-Miller Educational Assistance Award #754
Thomas R. Dargan Minority Scholarship #688
Timothy Bigelow Scholarship #436
Tony Orlando Yellow Ribbon Scholarship #348
Treadway Inns, Hotels, and Resorts Scholarship #633
Virginia D. Henry Memorial Scholarship #381
Vivienne Camp College Scholarship #183
Washington Gas Scholarship #851
Women in Geography Scholarship #445
Women's Army Corps Veterans Association Scholarship #561

GPA 3.2

Hopi Scholarship #681
Underwood-Smith Teacher Scholarship #364

GPA 3.25

Academic Recognition Scholarship #36
Merit Scholarship - Tuition Waiver #848

GPA 3.3

Dean's Scholarship #46

GPA 3.4

A.O. Putnam Memorial Scholarship #378
Dwight D. Gardner Scholarship #447
General Emmett Paige Scholarship #376
General John A. Wickham Scholarship #377

9. Citizenship Index

10. Specific High School Index

11. Business Corporate Professional Affiliation Index

American Airlines/AMR Management Club Community/Leadership Scholarship #126

Armstrong World Industries, Inc.

Armstrong Foundation Award #128

Automotive Recyclers Association

A.R.A. Scholarship #208

Automotive Replacement Parts Industry

Charles V. Hagler Memorial Scholarship #109
Dr. Dorothy M. Ross Scholarship #111
John E. Echlin Memorial Scholarship #113
Ken Krum-Bud Kouts Memorial Scholarship #112
Larry H. Averill Memorial Scholarship #110
TRW Foundation #114

Baptist Life Association

Baptist Life Association Scholarship Grant #129

Bass Brothers Enterprises, Inc.

Sid Richardson Memorial Fund Scholarship #148

Bass Enterprises Production Company

Sid Richardson Memorial Fund Scholarship #148

Boeing Employees' Credit Union

BECU Foundation Scholarship #131

Butler Manufacturing Company

Butler Manufacturing Company Foundation Scholarship #132

Child of Abbott Laboratories Employee/Retiree

Clara Abbott Foundation Educational Grant Program #133

Child of an Agriculture Worker

Ventura County Agriculture Scholarship #86

Child of U.S. Public School, College, or University Employee

Horace Mann Scholarship #137

Child/Spouse of Deceased Police Officer/Firefigher

Memorial Scholarship for Children and Spouses of Deceased Police Officers and Firefighters #781

City Center Development Company

Sid Richardson Memorial Fund Scholarship #148

Coca-Cola Bottling Company

Coca-Cola Scholarship #10

Construction

Student Paper Competition - Undergraduate Level #863

Correctional Officer

Grant Program for Descendents of Police, Fire, or Correctional Officers #31

Deceased State Police Officer

Educational Benefits for Children of Deceased Veterans #531

Department of Conservation

Children of Disabled Firemen and Peace Officers Tuition Exemption #840

Department of Corrections

Law Enforcement Personnel Dependents Scholarship #770

Dependent of Fire Fighter

W.H. "Howie" McClennan Scholarship #402

Dependent of U.S. Government Foreign Service Employee

AFSA Financial Aid Scholarship #620

Drug/Chemical/Allied Trades Association

DCAT Scholarship #134

Duke Energy

Duke Energy Scholars #135

Farming

Maine Rural Rehabilitation Fund Scholarship #799

Federal Government

FEEA Scholarship #136

Fire Fighter

Children of Disabled Firemen and Peace Officers Tuition Exemption #840
Grant Program for Descendents of Police, Fire, or Correctional Officers #31
Law Enforcement Personnel Dependents Scholarship #770
Matthews & Swift Educational Trust Scholarship #266

Footwear Industry

Two/Ten International Footwear Foundation College Scholarship #882

Game Warden

Children of Disabled Firemen and Peace Officers Tuition Exemption #840

Gerber Products

Gerber Foundation Scholarship #150

Golf Course

John P. Burke Memorial Scholarship #147

Grocery Industry

Mary Macey Scholarship #157

Hormel Foods Corporation

Hormel Foods Scholarship #138

Johnson Controls, Inc.

Johnson Controls, Inc. Foundation Scholarship #139

Kohler

Kohler, Co. College Scholarship #140

Law Enforcement Officers

Law Enforcement Officers Dependents' Scholarship #764
North Carolina Bar Association Scholarship #825

Leapartners, L.P.

Sid Richardson Memorial Fund Scholarship #148

Leather Industry

Two/Ten International Footwear Foundation College Scholarship #882

Manpower

Manpower Foundation Scholarship #34

Maytag Corporation

Maytag Scholarship Program #141

Medtronic, Inc.

Palmer J. Hermunslie Scholarship #142

Migrant Worker

Frank Kazmierczak Memorial Migrant Scholarship #355
Gloria and Joseph Mattera National Scholarship for Migrant Children #77
Migrant Farmworker Baccalaureate Scholarship #76

New Hampshire Food Industry

New Hampshire Food Industry Scholarship #144

Peace Officer

Children of Disabled Firemen and Peace Officers Tuition Exemption #840
Law Enforcement Personnel Dependents Scholarship #770

Perry R. Bass, Inc.

Sid Richardson Memorial Fund Scholarship #148

Pitney-Bowes

Pitney-Bowes Scholarship #145

Police Officer

Grant Program for Descendents of Police, Fire, or Correctional Officers #31
Matthews & Swift Educational Trust Scholarship #266

Rahr Malting Company

Rahr Foundation Scholarship #146

Richardson Aviation

Sid Richardson Memorial Fund Scholarship #148

Richardson Oils, Inc.

Sid Richardson Memorial Fund Scholarship #148

Richardson Products Company

Sid Richardson Memorial Fund Scholarship #148

San Jose Cattle Company

Sid Richardson Memorial Fund Scholarship #148

Saticoy Lemon Association

Saticoy Lemon Association Employee Scholarhip #155

Sid Richardson Carbon Company

Sid Richardson Memorial Fund Scholarship #148

Sid Richardson Gasoline Company

Sid Richardson Memorial Fund Scholarship #148

Sid W. Richardson Foundation

Sid Richardson Memorial Fund Scholarship #148

SRGC Aviation, Inc.

Sid Richardson Memorial Fund Scholarship #148

Stanley

Stanley Works National Merit Scholarship #592

Stone Container Corporation

Stone Foundation Scholarship #149

The Biomet Foundation, Inc.

Biomet Foundation Scholarship #130

Transportation Industry

Student Paper Competition - Undergraduate Level #863

Travel Industry

Joseph R. Stone Scholarship #855
Rocky Mountain Chapter Estey Scholarship #760

Trucking Company

TCA Scholarship #869

Ultramar Diamond Shamrock Corporation

Ultramar Diamond Shamrock Scholarship #152

Union Pacific Railroad

Employee Dependent Scholarship #153

USAirways

L.O. Barnes Scholarship #154

Washington Post

Washington Post Thomas Ewing Memorial Education Grant #156

Woodswork

Maine Rural Rehabilitation Fund Scholarship #799

Youth Authority

Law Enforcement Personnel Dependents Scholarship #770

12. City/ County of Residence Index

Allen County (OH)

General Scholarship #197
Hauss-Helms Foundation, Inc. Scholarship #181

Armstrong County (TX)

AAF Scholarship #161

Ashtabula County (OH)

George J. Record School Foundation Scholarship #179

Auglaize County (OH)

Hauss-Helms Foundation, Inc. Scholarship #181

Austin (TX)

Rosamond M. Austin Memorial Award #722

Bell Gardens (CA)

TELACU Arts Award #401
TELACU/Cesar Chavez Award #53

Beloit (WI)

George E. Andrews Scholarship #165

Briscoe County (TX)

AAF Scholarship #161

Brooklyn (NY)

Renate W. Chasman Scholarship for Women #409

Bucks County (PA)

Pharmacists Scholarhsip #642

Carson County (TX)

AAF Scholarship #161

Castro County (TX)

AAF Scholarship #161

Charles City (VA)

Joseph H. Jones, Sr., Scholarship #174

Charlotte County (FL)

Selby Direct Scholarship #833

Chattanooga (TN)

Together We Can Scholarship #168

Chicago (IL)

Greek Women's University Club Scholarship #675

Childress County (TX)

AAF Scholarship #161

Collingsworth County (TX)

AAF Scholarship #161

Commerce (CA)

TELACU Arts Award #401
TELACU/Cesar Chavez Award #53

Cook County (IL)

Italian American Chamber of Commerce Scholarship #182

Crawford County (IA)

Donna Reed Performing Arts Scholarships - Crawford County Scholarship #177

Cuyahoga County (OH)

Esperanza Scholarship #671

Dallam County (TX)

AAF Scholarship #161

Dallas-Fort Worth (TX)

American Airlines/AMR Management Club Merit Scholarship #125
American Airlines/AMR Management Club Community/Leadership Scholarship #126

Dayton (OH)

ChemFirst Foundation Scholarship #166

Deaf Smith County (TX)

AAF Scholarship #161

DeSoto County (FL)

Selby Direct Scholarship #833

Donley County (TX)

AAF Scholarship #161

DuPage County (IL)

Italian American Chamber of Commerce Scholarship #182

East Los Angeles (CA)

TELACU Arts Award #401
TELACU/Cesar Chavez Award #53

Fredericksburg (VA)

Christopher Gray and George Chancellor Memorial Scholarships #175

Geauga County (OH)

Esperanza Scholarship #671

Goochland County (VA)

Frederic Scott Reed Scholarship #176

Gray County (TX)

AAF Scholarship #161

Hall County (TX)

AAF Scholarship #161

Hamilton County (TN)

Together We Can Scholarship #168

Hanover County (VA)

Kristin Elaine Dickerson Scholarship #171
Matthew Anthony Grappone Memorial Scholarship #173

Hansford County (TX)

AAF Scholarship #161

Harbor City (CA)

Health Career Scholarship #498

Hartley County (TX)

AAF Scholarship #161

Hayward (CA)

ChemFirst Foundation Scholarship #166

Heathsville (VA)

Dollars for Scholars #172

Hemphill County (TX)

AAF Scholarship #161

Huntington Park (CA)

TELACU Arts Award #401
TELACU/Cesar Chavez Award #53

Hutchinson County (TX)

AAF Scholarship #161

Jackson (MS)

ChemFirst Foundation Scholarship #166

Kane County (IL)

Italian American Chamber of Commerce Scholarship #182

Kennebec County (ME)

Pearl Ramsey Memorial Nursing Scholarship #852

King County (WA)

Nellie Martin Carman Scholarship #192

Lake County (IL)

Italian American Chamber of Commerce Scholarship #182

Lake County (OH)

Esperanza Scholarship #671

Lawrence County (PA)

Lawrence Conservation District Scholarship #187

Lipscomb County (TX)

AAF Scholarship #161

Livingston County (MI)

Phoenix Scholarship #194

Lomita (CA)

Health Career Scholarship #498

Lorain County (OH)

Esperanza Scholarship #671
Lorain County Home Economics Scholarship #431

Los Angeles (CA)

BEEM Foundation Scholarship #576
TELACU Arts Award #401
TELACU/Cesar Chavez Award #53

Los Angeles County (CA)

BEEM Foundation Scholarship #576
JVS Jewich Community Scholarship Fund #730

Manatee County (FL)

Selby Direct Scholarship #833

Marin County (CA)

Jacob Rassen Memorial Scholarship Fund #184
Marin County American Revolution Bicentennial Scholarship #190
Marin County American Revolution Bicentennial Scholarship #164
Rozsi & Jeno Zisovich Jewish Studies Scholarship Fund to Teach the Holocaust #186
Stanley Olson Youth Scholarship #185
Vivienne Camp College Scholarship #183

McHenry County (IL)

Italian American Chamber of Commerce Scholarship #182

Medina County (OH)

Esperanza Scholarship #671

Merrifield (VA)

Visual Arts Scholarship #400

Metropolitan Detroit (MI)

H.T. Ewald Scholarship #180

Metropolitan Richmond (VA)

Cental Virginia Scholarship #170

Middlesex County (NJ)

FSCD Scholarship #79
Munch & Clark Scholarship #78

Mississippi Gulf Coast

ChemFirst Foundation Scholarship #166

Monmouth County (NJ)

FSCD Scholarship #79
Munch & Clark Scholarship #78

Montebello (CA)

TELACU Arts Award #401

TELACU/Cesar Chavez Award #53

Monterey Park (CA)

TELACU Arts Award #401
TELACU/Cesar Chavez Award #53

Moore County (TX)

AAF Scholarship #161

Mount Vernon (NY)

Thomas E. Sharpe Memorial Scholarship #191

Nassau County (NY)

Renate W. Chasman Scholarship for Women #409

New London (CT)

Leonard H. Bulkeley Scholarship #189

New York (NY)

McDonald's African American Heritage Scholarship #694
McDonald's Golden Arches Scholarship #193
McDonald's GospelFest Music Scholarship #582
World of Expressions Scholarship #163

New York City Metropolitan Area (NY)

McDonald's African American Heritage Scholarship #694
McDonald's Golden Arches Scholarship #193
McDonald's GospelFest Music Scholarship #582
Scholarship for Emigres in the Health Professions #416

Ochiltree County (TX)

AAF Scholarship #161

Oldham County (TX)

AAF Scholarship #161

Palos Verdes (CA)

Health Career Scholarship #498

Parmer County (TX)

AAF Scholarship #161

Paulding County (OH)

General Scholarship #197

Philadelphia (PA)

Cymdeithas Gymreig Scholarship #670

Pierce County (WA)

Nellie Martin Carman Scholarship #192

Portage County (OH)

Esperanza Scholarship #671

Potter County (TX)

AAF Scholarship #161

Queens (NY)

Renate W. Chasman Scholarship for Women #409

Randall County (TX)

AAF Scholarship #161

Roberts County (TX)

AAF Scholarship #161

Sacramento (CA)

Minority Media Scholarship #316

San Antonio Express News' Circulation Area (TX)

Express News Paul Thompson Scholarship #470

San Bernardino County (CA)

Burlington Northern Santa Fe Foundation Scholarship #650

San Buenaventura (CA)

Parker M. and Virginia Howell Scholarship #573

San Francisco (CA)

Jacob Rassen Memorial Scholarship Fund #184
Rozsi & Jeno Zisovich Jewish Studies Scholarship Fund to Teach the Holocaust #186
Stanley Olson Youth Scholarship #185
Vivienne Camp College Scholarship #183

San Mateo County (CA)

Jacob Rassen Memorial Scholarship Fund #184

Rozsi & Jeno Zisovich Jewish Studies Scholarship Fund to Teach the Holocaust #186
Stanley Olson Youth Scholarship #185
Vivienne Camp College Scholarship #183

San Pedro (CA)

Health Career Scholarship #498

Santa Clara County (CA)

Charles Walton Peace Essay Contest #196
Jacob Rassen Memorial Scholarship Fund #184
Rozsi & Jeno Zisovich Jewish Studies Scholarship Fund to Teach the Holocaust #186
Stanley Olson Youth Scholarship #185
Vivienne Camp College Scholarship #183

Sarasota County (FL)

Selby Direct Scholarship #833

Sherman County (TX)

AAF Scholarship #161

Snohomish County (WA)

Nellie Martin Carman Scholarship #192

Sonoma County (CA)

Jacob Rassen Memorial Scholarship Fund #184
Rozsi & Jeno Zisovich Jewish Studies Scholarship Fund to Teach the Holocaust #186
Stanley Olson Youth Scholarship #185
Vivienne Camp College Scholarship #183

South Gate (CA)

TELACU Arts Award #401
TELACU/Cesar Chavez Award #53

South Texas

Elaine Noll Scholarship #468

St. Louis (MO)

Rosalie Tilles Scholarship Award #195

St. Louis County (MO)

Rosalie Tilles Scholarship Award #195

Suffolk County (NY)

Renate W. Chasman Scholarship for Women #409

Summit County (OH)

Esperanza Scholarship #671

Swisher County (TX)

AAF Scholarship #161

Toms River (NJ)

Italian-American Cultural Society of Ocean County #687

Troup County (GA)

Hatton Lovejoy Scholarship #178

Tyrone (PA)

ChemFirst Foundation Scholarship #166

Van Wert County (OH)

General Scholarship #197

Ventura County (CA)

Gary W. Chism Memorial Award #199
Laura Duval Toomey Saticoy Poinsettia Club Scholarship #59
Milton McKevett Teague Scholarship #85

Vicinity of Tyson Operating Facility

Tyson Foundation Scholarship #572

Wake County (NC)

North Carolina Vietnam Veterans' Scholarship #551

Washington Metropolitan Area (DC)

Max and Emmy Dreyfuss Jewish Undergraduate Scholarship #728
Morton A. Gibson Memorial Scholarship #729
Suburban Hospital Scholarship #98
Washington Printing Guild Awards #427

Wheeler County (TX)

AAF Scholarship #161

Will County (IL)

Italian American Chamber of Commerce Scholarship #182

Williamson County (TX)

Trust Scholarship #188

Wilmington (CA)

Health Career Scholarship #498

13. Club Affiliation Index

4-H

4-H Postsecondary Scholarship #830

Aircraft Electronics Asssociation

Lee Tarbox Scholarship #209

Americal Division Veterans Association

ADVA Scholarship Fund #210

American Angus Association

Angus Foundation Scholarship #211

American Association of Bioanalysts

David Birenbaum Scholarship #212

American Criminal Justice Association/ Lambda Alpha Epsilon

ACJA/LAE National Scholarship #473
ACJA/LAE National Student Paper Competition #213

American Flint Glass Workers Union

AIL/Lawrence Bankowski AFGWU Scholarship Award #127

American Health Information Management Association (AHIMA)

Aspen Scholarship #90
Foundation of Research & Education in Health Information Management Scholarship #91

American Indian Science & Engineering Society

A.T. Anderson Memorial Scholarship #649

American Legion

Albert M. Lappin Scholarship #214
American Legion Memorial Scholarship #518
Charles W. and Annette Hill Scholarship #215
Children and Youth Scholarship #217
High School Oratorical Contest #751
Oratorical Contest Scholarship #750

American Legion – South Carolina

American Legion Robert E. David Scholarship #216

American Legion Auxiliary

Albert M. Lappin Scholarship #214
Department President's Scholarship #508
Dr. Kate Waller Barrett Grant #757
Medical Field Scholarship #500
Spirit of Youth Scholarship #218
Texas American Legion Auxiliary Scholarship #301

American Military Retirees Association, Inc. (AMRA)

Sgt. Major Douglas R. Drum Memorial Scholarship #519

American Quarter Horse Youth Association (AQHYA)

AQHYA Scholarship #220

American School Food Service Association

Schwan's Food Service #880

Tony's Scholarship #329

American Society of Agricultural Engineers

ASAE Student Engineer of the Year Scholarship #369

American Society of Certified Engineering Technicians (ASCET)

Small Cash Grant #370

American Society of Mechanical Engineers

Berna Lou Cartwright Scholarship #487
F.W. "Beich" Beichley Scholarship #482
Frank William & Dorothy Given Miller ASME Auxiliary Scholarship #484
Garland Duncan Scholarship #481
John and Elsa Gracik Scholarship #485
Kenneth Andrew Roe Scholarship #483
William J. and Mary Jane E. Adams, Jr. Scholarship #480

American Society of Travel Agents

Arizona Chapter Dependent/ Employee Membership Scholarship #222

American Water Ski Association

AWSEF Scholarship #102

American Water Ski Educational Foundation

AWSEF Scholarship #102

ASME

Foundation Scholarship #486

Associated Builders and Contractors, Inc. (ABC)

ABC Scholarship #15

Association of the Sons of Poland

Association of the Sons of Poland Achievement Award #223

Auxiliary to the Grand Army of the Republic

National Woman's Relief Corps Scholarship #280

B.P.O. Elks of the U.S.A.

Elks National Foundation Most Valuable Student Award #20

Beta Sigma Phi

Walter and Dorothy Ross Memorial Scholarship #4

Big Brothers

Arby's/Big Brothers Big Sisters of America Scholarship #224

Big Sisters

Arby's/Big Brothers Big Sisters of America Scholarship #224

Boy Scouts of America

Del-Mar-Va Council, Inc. Boy Scouts of America Educational Scholarship #225
Eagle Scout Scholarship #279
Eastern Orthodox Committee on Scouting Scholarship #236

Boys and Girls Club

National Youth of the Year Scholarship #5

Boys and Girls Clubs of Chicago

Nichols Scholarship #226

California Teachers Association (CTA)

CTA Scholarship for Members #227
Martin Luther King, Jr. Memorial Scholarship #662

Catholic Aid Association

Catholic Aid Association College Tuition Scholarship #228

Catholic Workman

Catholic Workman College Scholarship #229

Columbian Squires

Pro Deo and Pro Patria Scholarships #731

Costume Society of America

Adele Filene Travel Award #232
Stella Blum Research Grant #231

Danish Sisterhood of America

Danish Sisterhood of America Scholarship #233

Del-Mar-Va Council

Del-Mar-Va Council, Inc. Boy Scouts of America Educational Scholarship #225

Delta Gamma

Delta Gamma Foundation Scholarship #234

Delta Phi Epsilon

Delta Phi Epsilon Scholarship #235

DeMolay

Davis-Roberts Scholarship #773

Descendant of American Legion Member

Charles W. and Annette Hill Scholarship #215

Federation of American Consumers and Travelers

FACT Continuing Education Scholarship #23

First Catholic Slovak Ladies Association

First Catholic Slovak Ladies Association Scholarship #239

Fourth Degree Kansas Grange

Claude and Ina Brey Memorial Endowment Fund Scholarship #270

Future Farmers of America (FFA)

Maine Rural Rehabilitation Fund Scholarship #799

General Federation of Women's Clubs of Massachusetts

"Pennies for Art" Scholarship #398

Dorchester Woman's Club Scholarship #892

GFWC of MA Music Scholarship #580

International Affairs Scholarship #779

Newtonville Woman's Club Scholarship #356

Girl Scouts of America

Eastern Orthodox Committee on Scouting Scholarship #236

Girl Scout Achievement Award #219

Golf Course Superintendents Association of America

GCSAA Legacy Awards #240

Institute of Industrial Engineers

A.O. Putnam Memorial Scholarship #378

Dwight D. Gardner Scholarship #447

International Assoc. for the Exchange of Students for Technical Experience

Robert M. Sprinkle Scholarship #442

International Association of Fire Fighters

W.H. "Howie" McClennan Scholarship #402

International Buckskin Horse Association

Youth Scholarship Fund of IBHA, Inc. #241

International Furnishings and Design Association

IFDA Educational Foundation Student Scholarship #395

Vercille Voss Student Scholarship #396

Japanese American Citizens League

Abe & Esther Hagiwara Student Aid Award #262

Aiko Susanna Tashiro Hiratsuka Memorial Scholarship #263

Alice Yuriko Endo Memorial Scholarship #254

Dr. Thomas T. Yatabe Memorial Scholarship #261

Gongoro Nakamura Memorial Scholarship #249

Henry & Chiyo Kuwahara Memorial Scholarship for Entering Freshmen #246

Henry & Chiyo Kuwahara Memorial Scholarship for Undergraduates #257

Kenji Kasai Memorial Scholarship #245

Kyataro & Yasuo Abiko Memorial Scholarship #243

Mari & James Michener Scholarship #259

Masao & Sumako Itano Memorial Scholarship #244

Mitsuyuki Yonemura Memorial Scholarship #253

Mr. & Mrs. Takashi Moriuchi Scholarship #248

Mr. & Mrs. Uyesugi Memorial Scholarship #252

Nobuko R. Kodama Fong Memorial Scholarship #255

Patricia & Gail Ishimoto Memorial Scholarship #242

Saburo Kido Memorial Scholarship #256

Sam S. Kuwahara Memorial Scholarship for Entering Freshmen #247

Sam S. Kuwahara Memorial Scholarship for Undergraduates #258

South Park Japanese Community Scholarship #251

Yoshiko Tanaka Memorial Scholarship #260

Yutaka Nakazawa Memorial Scholarship #250

Jaycee

Baldridge Scholarship #307

Scholarship Program #264

Job's Daughters

Davis-Roberts Scholarship #773

Knights of Columbus

Matthews & Swift Educational Trust Scholarship #266

Pro Deo and Pro Patria Scholarships #731

Lambda Alpha

Dean's List Scholarship #267

Lambda Iota Tau (LIT)

LIT Scholarship for Excellence #268

Marine Corps Tankers Association

John Cornelius and Max English Scholarship #539

Masons

Masonic Grand Lodge Charities of Rhode Island Scholarship #811

Menominee Indian Tribe

Menominee Tribal Higher Education/Adult Vocational Grant #269

Minerals/Metals/ Materials Society

EPD Scholarship #563

International Symposium on Superalloys Scholarship #273

J. Keith Brimacombe Presidential Scholarship #271

LMD Scholarship #564

SMD Scholarship #272

Mooney Aircraft Pilot Association

MAPA Safety Foundation Scholarship #73

National Association of Black Accountants, Inc. (NABA)

NABA National Scholarship Program #275

National Association of Soil and Water Conservation Districts (NACD)

Masonic Range Science Scholarship #49

National Beta Club

National Beta Club Scholarship #276

National Court Reporters Association

CASE Scholarship #277

National Fraternal Society of the Deaf

Deaf Scholarship #278

National Honor Society

National Honor Society Scholarship #41

National Roofing Contractors Association

Roofing Industry Scholarship/ Grant #207

National Society of Public Accountants

NSA Scholarship Award #67

National Woman's Relief Corps

National Woman's Relief Corps Scholarship #280

New Hampshire Grocer's Association (NHGA)

New Hampshire Food Industry Scholarship #144

New Jersey State Golf Association (NJSGA)

New Jersey State Golf Association (NJSGA) Caddie Scholarship #104

Northeastern Loggers' Association

NELA Scholarship Contest #281

Parents Without Partners

Parents Without Partners Scholarship #282

Phi Sigma Iota

Phi Sigma Iota Scholarship #283

Phi Sigma Kappa

Wenderoth Undergraduate Scholarship #284

Phi Sigma Pi

Richard C. Todd & Claude P. Todd Tripod Scholarship #285

Phi Theta Pi

J. Spencer Borders Academic Award #286

Polish National Alliance (PNA)

PNA Scholarship #287

Pony of the Americas Club

Pony of the Americas Scholarship #288

Portuguese Continental Union of the USA

Portuguese Continental Union of USA Scholarship #289

Recording for the Blind and Dyslexic

Marion Huber Learning through Listening Awards #634

Red River Valley Fighter Pilots Association

RRVA Scholarship Grant Assistance Program #552

Retired Enlisted Association

TREA Memorial Foundation National Scholarship #553

Rhode Island Golf Association

John P. Burke Memorial Scholarship #147

Rotary

Becky Briggs Memorial Scholarship #230

Sigma Alpha Epsilon

Dr. Charles A. Preuss Medical Award #499
G. Robert Hamrdla Award #293
Jones-Laurence Award #291
Warren Poslusny Award for Outstanding Achievement #292

Sigma Alpha Iota

Summer Music Scholarship #295
Undergraduate Scholarship #294

Slovene National Benefit Society

Slovene National Benefit Society Scholarship #296

Society for Range Management (SRM)

Masonic Range Science Scholarship #49

Society of Manufacturing Engineers

Wayne Kay Scholarship #489

Sons of Norway

Astrid G. Cates Scholarship #298
Myrtle Beinbauer Scholarship #299

Student California Teachers Association (SCTA)

Martin Luther King, Jr. Memorial Scholarship #662

Tau Beta Pi

Tau Beta Pi Scholarship #300

Tau Kappa Epsilon

All Teke Academic Team and John A. Courson Top Scholar Awards #306
Bruce B. Melchert Scholarship #303
Wallace G. McCauley Memorial Scholarship #305
William Wilson Memorial Scholarship #304

The Retired Officers Association

TROA Scholarship 200 #554

Theta Nu Epsilon

TNE Scholarship #302

Theta Nu Epsilon Society

TNE Scholarship #302

Transportation Clubs International

Charlotte Woods Memorial Scholarship #866

Tuition Exchange

Tuition Exchange Scholarship #151

UDT/SEAL Association

UDT/SEAL Scholarship Grant #308

Union & League of Romanian Societies of America

Union and League of Romanian Societies of America Scholarship #309

Western Sunbathers Association

Western Sunbathing Association Scholarship #310

14. Gender/ Marital Status Index

Men

Charles W. Frees, Jr. Scholarship #412
CKA Seminarian Scholarsip #716
Dr. Charles A. Preuss Medical Award #499
Eagle Scout Scholarship #279
G. Robert Hamrdla Award #293
Jones-Laurence Award #291
Warren Poslusny Award for Outstanding Achievement #292
William Reed Baker Outstanding Senior Award #414

Unmarried

Auxiliary Memorial Scholarship #525
Auxiliary Worchild Scholarship #524
Capt. Caliendo College Assistance Fund Scholarship #559
CKA Seminarian Scholarsip #716
Illinois Amvets Service Foundation Scholarship #784
Miss Outstanding Teenager #37
Musical or Recreational Therapy Scholarship #761
Paul Powell Memorial Scholarship #523
Post #100 Scholarship #522
Scholarship Program for Dependent Children of Soldiers #527

Second Marine Division Association Memorial Scholarship #555
U.S. Submarine Veterans of World War II Scholarship #532

Women

American Society of Woman Accountants Scholarship #64
ASWA Scholarship #63
Auxiliary Scholarship #417
AWA Scholarship Awards #408
BPW Career Advancement Scholarship #410
Constance L. Lloyd/ACMPE Scholarship #88
Daughters of the Cincinnati Scholarship #529
Dorothy Armstrong Community Service Scholarship #413
Elaine Noll Scholarship #468
Gladys Stone Wright Scholarship #587
Greek Women's University Club Scholarship #675
Hermione Grant Calhoun Scholarship #337
Jeannette Rankin Foundation Award #415
Karla Scherer Foundation Scholarship #419
Kathryn Siphers/Patricia Garren Memorial Scholarship #586
Linda Riddle/SGMA Scholarship #422
Lucille B. Kaufman Women's Scholarship #418
Martha Ann Stark Memorial Scholarship #588
Memorial Scholarship #515
Miss Outstanding Teenager #37
New York Life Foundation Scholarship for Women in the Health Professions #411
Renate W. Chasman Scholarship for Women #409
Scholarship for Emigres in the Health Professions #416
Virginia D. Henry Memorial Scholarship #381
Volkwein Memorial Scholarship #585
Women in Geography Scholarship #445
Women's Jewelry Association Scholarship #420
Women's Western Golf Foundation Scholarship #423

Margie Ann Conner
Scholarship #577
Music Scholarship #579
Summer Music Scholarship
#295
World of Expressions
Scholarship #163

Music Composition

Phoenix Scholarship #194

Music Performance

Gifted Opera Singers'
Scholarship #891
Music Scholarship #579
Phoenix Scholarship #194

New Media

World of Expressions
Scholarship #163

Oratorical

Oratorical Contest #744

Ornithology

Kathleen S. Anderson Award
#116

Painting

Phoenix Scholarship #194

Public Service

Public Employees Public
Service Scholarship #48

Recorder

American Recorder Society
Scholarship #450

Sculpture

Phoenix Scholarship #194

Singing

Gifted Opera Singers'
Scholarship #891
Margie Ann Conner
Scholarship #577
Phoenix Scholarship #194

Speech

Gongoro Nakamura Memorial
Scholarship #249

Telecommunications

Essay Prize #315

Writing

Amelia Student Award #387
Blanche Fern Memorial Award
#721

Charles Walton Peace Essay
Contest #196
Phyllis Stevens Grams
Memorial Award #723
Rosamond M. Austin Memorial
Award #722

17. Military Affiliation Index

1st Marine Divison

1st Marine Division Association
Scholarship #501

25th Infantry Division Association

25th Infantry Division
Association Scholarship #502

43rd Infantry Division

43rd Infantry Division Veterans
Scholarship #503

Air Force

Daughters of the Cincinnati
Scholarship #529
General Henry H. Arnold
Education Grant #504

American Legion

American Legion Children and
Youth Scholarship #622
Memorial Scholarship #515
Minnesota Legionnaire Insurance
Trust Scholarship #517
Nurses', Physical Therapists',
and Respiratory Therapists'
Scholarship #514

AMVETS

AMVETS National Four-Year
Scholarship #520

Arizona National Guard

National Guard Association of
Arizona Scholarship #543

Armed Forces

AMVETS National Four-Year
Scholarship #520
Illinois AMVETS Service
Foundation Scholarships
#521

Illinois Veteran Grant #535
Matthews & Swift Educational
Trust Scholarship #266
MIA/KIA Dependents'
Scholarship #526
RRVA Scholarship Grant
Assistance Program #552

Army

Daughters of the Cincinnati
Scholarship #529
Scholarship Program for
Dependent Children of
Soldiers #527

Child of a Service Member Missing in Action

RRVA Scholarship Grant
Assistance Program #552

Child of Deceased Service Member

Children of Deceased Service
Members Scholarship #547
RRVA Scholarship Grant
Assistance Program #552

Child of Military Personnel

TROA Scholarship 200 #554

Child of Military Veteran

American Legion Auxiliary
Department Scholarship #511
Brewer/Wilson Scholarship #506

Child of Veteran

Auxiliary Memorial
Scholarship #525
Auxiliary Worchild Scholarship
#524
National President Scholarship
#759
National President's Scholarship
#512
Paul Powell Memorial
Scholarship #523
Post #100 Scholarship #522
War Orphans Educational Aid
#537

Child/Grandchild of AMVETS Member

AMVETS National Four-Year
Scholarship #520

Child/Grandchild of Deceased Veteran

AMVETS National Four-Year
Scholarship #520

Child/Grandchild/ Spouse of Vietnam Veteran

North Carolina Vietnam
Veterans' Scholarship #551

Child/Spouse of Disabled Veteran

Kathern F. Gruber Scholarship
#528

Child/Spouse of Veteran

Kathern F. Gruber Scholarship
#528

Civil War Veteran

G.A.R. Living Memorial
Scholarship #530

Coast Guard

Alaska Sea Services Scholarship
#505
Capt. Caliendo College
Assistance Fund Scholarship
#559
Daughters of the Cincinnati
Scholarship #529
New York Council Navy
League Scholarship #550

Coast Guard Reserve

Alaska Sea Services Scholarship
#505

Deceased or Disabled Veteran

Edward T. Conroy Memorial
Grant #540

Deceased Veteran

American Legion -
Pennsylvania Auxiliary
Scholarship #510
Educational Benefits for
Children of Deceased
Veterans #531
War Orphans Educational Aid
#537

Dependent of a Marine Tanker

John Cornelius and Max
English Scholarship #539

Dependent of Active Duty Personnel of the USS Tennessee

USS Tennessee Scholarship
#548

Dependent of Active Duty/Retired Service Member

Alaska Sea Services Scholarship #505

Vice Admiral E.P. Travers Scholarship #546

Dependent of Deceased Active Duty/Retired Service Member

Alaska Sea Services Scholarship #505

Children of Deceased Service Members Scholarship #547

Descendent of Veteran of Foreign Wars or Auxilary Member

Past National President Fran Booth Medical Scholarship #538

Disabled Veteran

1st Marine Division Association Scholarship #501

First Cavalry Division Association

First Cavalry Division Association Scholarship #534

Fleet Reserve Association

Branch 46 Scholarship #625

KIA

Alaska Sea Services Scholarship #505

MIA/KIA Dependents' Scholarship #526

RRVA Scholarship Grant Assistance Program #552

Legionnaire

American Legion - Ohio Scholarship #507

Marine

Alaska Sea Services Scholarship #505

Marine Corps

Alaska Sea Services Scholarship #505

Daughters of the Cincinnati Scholarship #529

John Cornelius and Max English Scholarship #539

Navy League Scholarship #544

New York Council Navy League Scholarship #550

MIA

Alaska Sea Services Scholarship #505

MIA/KIA Dependents' Scholarship #526

RRVA Scholarship Grant Assistance Program #552

Southeast Asia POW/MIA Scholarship #542

Military

Illinois Amvets Service Foundation Scholarship #784

Sgt. Major Douglas R. Drum Memorial Scholarship #519

Military Aviation

RRVA Scholarship Grant Assistance Program #552

National Guard

Illinois National Guard Grant #536

Navy

Alaska Sea Services Scholarship #505

Daughters of the Cincinnati Scholarship #529

Navy League Scholarship #544

New York Council Navy League Scholarship #550

Surflant Scholarship #557

Navy (U.S.N.A. Class of 1963)

United States Naval Academy Class of 1963 Foundation Scholarship #560

Navy Supply Corps

Navy Supply Corps Foundation Scholarship #545

Persian Gulf Veteran

Vietnam Veterans Tuition Award/Persian Gulf Veterans Tuition Award #780

POW/ MIA/ KIA Dependents' Scholarship #526

Southeast Asia POW/MIA Scholarship #542

Relative in Marine Corps

Alaska Sea Services Scholarship #505

ROTC

ROTC Scholarship #562

Second Marine Division

Second Marine Division Association Memorial Scholarship #555

Service Medal

Vietnam Veterans Scholarship #549

Spouse of Active Duty Service Member

Vice Admiral E.P. Travers Scholarship #546

Spouse of Blind Veteran

Kathern F. Gruber Scholarship #528

Spouse of Military Veteran

Kathern F. Gruber Scholarship #528

Submarine Force

Bowfin Memorial Scholarship #556

Dolphin Scholarship #533

U.S. Submarine Veterans of World War II Scholarship #532

SURFLANT

Surflant Scholarship #557

U.S. Coast Guard Chief Petty Officers Association

Capt. Caliendo College Assistance Fund Scholarship #559

U.S. Coast Guard Enlisted Association

Capt. Caliendo College Assistance Fund Scholarship #559

U.S. Submarine Veterans of WW II

U.S. Submarine Veterans of World War II Scholarship #532

Uniformed Military Services

General Emmett Paige Scholarship #376

Veteran

1st Marine Division Association Scholarship #501

American Legion - Pennsylvania Auxiliary Scholarship #510

American Legion Auxiliary - Alabama Scholarship #513

American Legion Auxiliary Department Scholarship #511

American Legion Memorial Scholarship #518

AMVETS National Four-Year Scholarship #520

Department President's Scholarship #508

Department Scholarship #509

Dr. Kate Waller Barrett Grant #757

Illinois Veteran Grant #535

Memorial Scholarship #515

Minnesota Legionnaire Insurance Trust Scholarship #517

National President's Scholarship #512

Nurses', Physical Therapists', and Respiratory Therapists' Scholarship #514

Past President's Parley Scholarship Assistance in Health Care Occupations #756

Scholarship for Non-Traditional Students #516

Veterans and Dependents Tuition Exemption #558

Vietnam Veterans Scholarship #549

Vocational/Technical Scholarship #887

War Orphan's Scholarship #541

Vietnam Campaign Medal

Vietnam Veterans Scholarship #549

Vietnam Veteran

North Carolina Vietnam Veterans' Scholarship #551

Vietnam Veterans Scholarship #549

Vietnam Veterans Tuition Award/Persian Gulf Veterans Tuition Award #780

War Veteran

War Orphans Educational Aid #537

18. National Merit Status Index

National Achievement

Armstrong Foundation -
National Achievement
Scholarship #654

National Achievement Finalist

Academic Scholars Program
#826
Distinguished Scholar #806

National Achievement Scholar

Academic Scholars Program
#826

National Hispanic Scholar

Academic Scholars Program
#826

National Merit

Armstrong Foundation -
National Achievement
Scholarship #654
National Merit Scholarship #591
National Merit Scholarship #593

National Merit Finalist

Academic Scholars Program
#826
Arkansas Governor's Scholars
Award #762
Distinguished Scholar #806
Employee Dependent
Scholarship #153
National Merit Scholarship #591

National Merit Scholar

Academic Scholars Program
#826
Armstrong Foundation Award
#128

National Merit Semifinalist

National Merit Scholarship #591

Presidential Scholar

Academic Scholars Program
#826

Tips For Using The Major & Field Of Study Index

One of the last but most important indexes is the Major and Field of Study Index, which begins on the following page. Here are some tips for making the most of this index:

Think broadly about your major and how it can be applied to scholarships. For example, if you are a history major specializing in American history, look for scholarships not only for history but also for social studies, liberal arts, and American history.

If you don't yet know what your major will be, don't think that you have to lock yourself into scholarships in only one area. For example, if you show promise in both English and Government and could see yourself headed into either academic area, look for scholarships in both areas. Just don't be too liberal about applying for scholarships in academic areas in which you have minimal interest. You will waste the time of both you and the selection committee.

If you have a double major, remember to look for scholarships in both fields.

Many scholarships are designed to reward or give preference to students studying certain disciplines. But you should remember that if you are undecided or a high school senior entering college, you may only need to express an interest in the major or field of study to qualify.

Don't rule out a scholarship simply because it lists a specific field of study. Check with the scholarship organization to see if you must officially declare the major to apply. Sometimes just showing your intention to select the major or even your intention to minor in a particular area is enough.

Colleges also refer to various majors differently. The index that appears on the next page uses the standard classification of majors as outlined by the Department of Education. However, keep in mind that your school may name its majors differently. Harvard, for example, doesn't offer an undergraduate "Business" degree. This does not mean that a business-oriented, economics-major student at Harvard can't make a case for applying to a business scholarship.

Give yourself a little latitude when deciding if you should apply to a particular scholarship listed under a specific major. Be sure to check with the scholarship organization directly if you think you can make a case for yourself even if you have not technically declared that specific major.

19. Major & Field Of Study Index

Auto/Automotive Mechanic/Technician

Charles V. Hagler Memorial Scholarship #109
Dr. Dorothy M. Ross Scholarship #111
John E. Echlin Memorial Scholarship #113
Ken Krum-Bud Kouts Memorial Scholarship #112
Larry H. Averill Memorial Scholarship #110
SEMA Scholarship Fund #115
TRW Foundation Scholarship #114

Aviation and Airway Science

Friendship One Flight Training Scholarship #16
Half to Full-time Student Scholarship #69
MAPA Safety Foundation Scholarship #73
Nebraska Space Grant and EPSCOR College and Fellowship Program #74
Pioneers of Flight Scholarship #631
Professional Pilot, Aviation Management, Aviation Technology Scholarship #72

Aviation Management

Professional Pilot, Aviation Management, Aviation Technology Scholarship #72

Aviation Systems and Avionics Main. Technologist/ Technician

B.F. Goodrich Scholarship #617
Bud Glover Memorial Scholarship #614
David Arver Memorial Scholarship #886
Dutch and Ginger Arver Scholarship #619
Field Aviation Company, Inc. Scholarship #615
Garmin Scholarship #70
Lee Tarbox Scholarship #209
Lowell Gaylor Memorial Scholarship #613
Mid-Continent Instrument Scholarship #618
Monte Mitchell Global Scholarship #752
Northern Airborne Technology Scholarship #616
Plane & Pilot Magazine/ GARMIN Scholarship #566
Professional Pilot, Aviation Management, Aviation Technology Scholarship #72

Biochemistry

ACS/Bayer Scholars Program #741
CSHEMA Scholarship Award #623
EPA Tribal Lands Environmental Science Scholarship #394

Bioengineering and Biomedical Engineering

ASAE Student Engineer of the Year Scholarship #369

Biological and Physical Sciences

BPW Career Advancement Scholarship #410

Biology, General

ACIL Scholarship #643
CSHEMA Scholarship Award #623
David L. Owens Scholarship #569
EPA Tribal Lands Environmental Science Scholarship #394
J.J. Barr Scholarship #571
Kathleen S. Anderson Award #116
National Association of Water Companies-New Jersey Chapter Scholarship #817
Renate W. Chasman Scholarship for Women #409
Utilities, Inc. Scholarship #570

Botany, General

GSCAA Scholars #433

Broadcast Journalism

Carole Simpson Scholarship #707
Charles and Lucille King Family Foundation Scholarship #706
Ed Bradley Scholarship #710
Eddy/Peck Scholarship #471
Len Allen Award of Merit #709
Oregon Association of Broadcasters Broadcast Scholarship #463
Research Grants #458
RTNDF Undergraduate Scholarship #708
Thomas R. Dargan Minority Scholarship #688

Business Administration and Management, General

Burlington Northern Santa Fe Foundation Scholarship #650

David L. Owens Scholarship #569
Fukunaga Foundation Scholarship #123
George M. Brooker Collegiate Scholarship for Minorities #714
Golden State Minority Foundation Scholarship #120
Hispanic College Fund Scholarship #677
J.J. Barr Scholarship #571
James A. Turner, Jr. Scholarship #118
Lori Ann Robinson Memorial Scholarship #119
Maine Chamber and Business Alliance Scholarship #803
MESBEC Scholarships #693
Mexican American Grocers Association Foundation Scholarship #122
NABA National Scholarship Program #275
National Association of Water Companies-New Jersey Chapter Scholarship #817
Tyson Foundation Scholarship #572
Utilities, Inc. Scholarship #570
Wyoming Trucking Association Trust Fund Scholarship #870

Business Administration and Management, Other

BPW Career Advancement Scholarship #410
Edgar J. Saux/FACMPE Scholarship #496
Edward J. Gerloff/FACMPE Scholarship #493
Ernest S. Moscatello Scholarship #492
Harry J. Harwick Scholarship #490
Midwest Section Scholarship #494
Richard L. Davis Managers' Scholarship #497
Richard L. Davis National Scholarship #491
SDRA Scholarship #50

Business, General

Atlas Shrugged Essay Competition #389
Gary W. Chism Memorial Award #199
Hispanic College Fund Scholarship #677
New York Financial Writers Association Scholarship #461
TCA Scholarship #869
Washington Gas Scholarship #851

Cartography

Space Imaging EOSAT Award for Application of Digital Landsat TM Data #644

Chemical Engineering

ACS/Bayer Scholars Program #741
American Electroplaters and Surface Finishers Society Scholarship #368
EPA Tribal Lands Environmental Science Scholarship #394

Chemistry, General

ACIL Scholarship #643
ACS Scholars Program #158
ACS/Bayer Scholars Program #741
CSHEMA Scholarship Award #623
David L. Owens Scholarship #569
EPA Tribal Lands Environmental Science Scholarship #394
GSCAA Scholars #433
J.J. Barr Scholarship #571
National Association of Water Companies-New Jersey Chapter Scholarship #817
Renate W. Chasman Scholarship for Women #409
Utilities, Inc. Scholarship #570

Chemistry, Other

American Electroplaters and Surface Finishers Society Scholarship #368

Child Growth, Care and Development Studies

School Food Service Foundation Graduate/ Postgraduate Study Scholarship #328

Chinese Language and Literature

Institute of China Studies Scholarship #684

Civil Engineering, General

AGC Education and Research Foundation Undergraduate Scholarship #204
American Society of Highway Engineers - Carolina Triangle Section Scholarship #202
ASDSO Scholarship #205

ASNE Scholarship #371
Associated Builders and
Contractors Scholarship #15
Peter D. Courtois Concrete
Construction Scholarship #201
RMCMI Scholarship #565

Communications Technology/ Technicians, Other

Essay Prize #315

Communications, General

Atlanta Press Club Journalism
Grant #453
CAMP Scholarship #424
Gladys Brown Edwards
Memorial Scholarship #311
IFEC Foodservice
Communicators Scholarship
#443
Miami International Press Club
Scholarship #456
National Academy of Television
Arts and Sciences
Scholarship #314
National Association of Water
Companies-New Jersey
Chapter Scholarship #817
News 4 Media Scholarship #313
Research Grants #458
Thomas R. Dargan Minority
Scholarship #688

Communications, Other

STC Scholarship #317

Computer Engineering

General Emmett Paige
Scholarship #376
General John A. Wickham
Scholarship #377
ROTC Scholarship #562

Computer Science

BPW Career Advancement
Scholarship #410
Copernicus Foundation
Computer Graphic Design
Scholarship #319
General Emmett Paige
Scholarship #376
General John A. Wickham
Scholarship #377
MESBEC Scholarships #693
National Association of Water
Companies-New Jersey
Chapter Scholarship #817
National Federation of the Blind
Computer Science
Scholarship #345
ROTC Scholarship #562
Technical Minority Scholarship
#386

Tyson Foundation Scholarship
#572
Washington Gas Scholarship
#851
Wyoming Trucking Association
Trust Fund Scholarship
#870

Conservation and Renewable Natural Resources, Other

FSCD Scholarship #79
Lawrence Conservation District
Scholarship #187
Munch & Clark Scholarship
#78
PACD Auxiliary Scholarship
#828

Construction and Building Finishers and Managers, Other

Associated Builders and
Contractors Scholarship #15

Construction Trades, Other

Peter D. Courtois Concrete
Construction Scholarship
#742

Construction/Building Tech./Technician

AGC Education and Research
Foundation Undergraduate
Scholarship #204
Associated Builders and
Contractors Scholarship #15
NAWIC Founders' Scholarship
Foundation #206
Peter D. Courtois Concrete
Construction Scholarship
#201

Court Reporter

CASE Scholarship #277

Criminal Justice Studies

ACJA/LAE National
Scholarship #473
ACJA/LAE National Student
Paper Competition #213
Association of Certified Fraud
Examiners #567
Irlet Anderson Scholarship #692

Crop Production Operations and Management

AACC Undergraduate
Scholarships #75

Culinary Arts and Related Services, Other

Culinary Arts/Nutrition/
Physical Education
Scholarship #327
Kentucky Restaurant
Association Governor's
Scholarship #321
Kentucky Restaurant
Association Scholarship
#320

Culinary Arts/Chef Training

Kentucky Restaurant
Association Governor's
Scholarship #321
Kentucky Restaurant
Association Scholarship
#320

Dairy Science

McCullough Scholarship #100

Dance

Donna Reed Performing Arts
Scholarships - Crawford
County Scholarship #177
Donna Reed Performing Arts
Scholarships - National
Scholarship #353
TELACU Arts Award #401

Dental Assistant

Allied Dental Education
Scholarship #325

Dental Hygienist

Allied Dental Education
Scholarship #325
Scholarship for Emigres in the
Health Professions #416

Dental Laboratory Technician

Allied Dental Education
Scholarship #325

Dentistry (D.D.S., D.M.D.)

Arthur and Doreen A. Parrett
Scholarship #829
Colgate-Palmolive Award #324
Health Careers Scholarship #95
Professional School Scholarship
#96
Professional School Scholarship
#810
Scholarship for Emigres in the
Health Professions #416
Ty Cobb Scholarship #847

Design and Applied Arts, Other

Charles D. Mayo Student
Scholarship #397
IFDA Educational Foundation
Student Scholarship #395
Vercille Voss Student
Scholarship #396

Design and Visual Communications

Charles D. Mayo Student
Scholarship #397
Vercille Voss Student
Scholarship #396

Diesel Engine Mechanic and Repairer

Wyoming Trucking Association
Trust Fund Scholarship
#870

Dietetics/Human Nutritional Services

School Food Service
Foundation Graduate/
Postgraduate Study
Scholarship #328
School Food Service
Foundation Scholarship
#879
Tony's Scholarship #329

Drama/Theater Arts, General

Aiko Susanna Tashiro Hiratsuka
Memorial Scholarship #263
Donna Reed Performing Arts
Scholarships - Crawford
County Scholarship #177
Donna Reed Performing Arts
Scholarships - National
Scholarship #353
TELACU Arts Award #401

Dramatic/Theater Arts and Stagecraft, Other

Aiko Susanna Tashiro Hiratsuka
Memorial Scholarship #263

Drawing

John F. and Anna Lee Stacey
Scholarship #399

Earth and Planetary Sciences

A.T. Anderson Memorial
Scholarship #649
Arthur and Doreen A. Parrett
Scholarship #829

Barry M. Goldwater Scholarship and Excellence in Education Program #3
BPW Career Advancement Scholarship #410
Burlington Northern Santa Fe Foundation Scholarship #650
Howard Brown Rickard Scholarship #338
MESBEC Scholarships #693
Navy League Scholarship #544
Technical Minority Scholarship #386
William Fairburn, Jr. and Cynthia Fairburn Memorial Scholarship #446

Economics, General

Golden State Minority Foundation Scholarship #120
Karla Scherer Foundation Scholarship #419
Lori Ann Robinson Memorial Scholarship #119
NABA National Scholarship Program #275

Education, General

Brookmire-Hastings Scholarship #367
Burlington Northern Santa Fe Foundation Scholarship #650
CSDIW Scholarship #668
Freshman/Sophomore Minority Grant #652
Harriet Hoffman Teaching Scholarship #354
Illinois PTA Continuing Education Scholarship #358
Illinois PTA Lillian E. Glover Scholarship #357
Lawrence Conservation District Scholarship #187
Martin Luther King, Jr. Memorial Scholarship #662
MESBEC Scholarships #693
Newtonville Woman's Club Scholarship #356
NFB Educator of Tomorrow Award #342
Phi Delta Kappa Scholarship Grants for Prospective Educators #362
Robert C. Byrd Honors Scholarship #365
Robert C. Byrd Honors Scholarship #361
Robert C. Byrd Honors Scholarship #359
Underwood-Smith Teacher Scholarship #364
Wayne Bruton Memorial Scholarship #366
William Winter Teacher Scholar Program #360
Women in Geography Scholarship #445

Education, Other

Lawrence Conservation District Scholarship #187

Electrical and Electronic Engineering/ Technicians, Other

ASNE Scholarship #371

Electrical, Electronics and Communication Engineering

General Emmett Paige Scholarship #376
General John A. Wickham Scholarship #377
RMCMI Scholarship #565
ROTC Scholarship #562

Elementary Teacher Education

NFB Educator of Tomorrow Award #342

Engineering Design

Peter D. Courtois Concrete Construction Scholarship #201

Engineering, General

A.T. Anderson Memorial Scholarship #649
ACIL Scholarship #643
AIAA Undergraduate Scholarship #71
Arthur and Doreen A. Parrett Scholarship #829
Auxiliary Scholarship #417
Barry M. Goldwater Scholarship and Excellence in Education Program #3
BPW Career Advancement Scholarship #410
Charles R. Westgate Scholarship in Engineering #379
David J. Fitzmaurice Scholarship #876
F.W. "Beich" Beichley Scholarship #482
Frank Walton Horn Memorial Scholarship #336
Frank William & Dorothy Given Miller ASME Auxiliary Scholarship #484
Garland Duncan Scholarship #481
Howard Brown Rickard Scholarship #338
International Symposium on Superalloys Scholarship #273

J. Keith Brimacombe Presidential Scholarship #271
John and Elsa Gracik Scholarship #485
Kenneth Andrew Roe Scholarship #483
Melvin R. Green Scholarship #221
MESBEC Scholarships #693
National Association of Water Companies-New Jersey Chapter Scholarship #817
Navy League Scholarship #544
Parker M. and Virginia Howell Scholarship #573
Paul H. Robbins Honorary Scholarship #382
Peter D. Courtois Concrete Construction Scholarship #742
Renate W. Chasman Scholarship for Women #409
Technical Minority Scholarship #386
Tyson Foundation Scholarship #572
Vernon T. Swain P.E./Robert E. Chute P.E. Memorial Scholarship #380
Virginia D. Henry Memorial Scholarship #381
Washington Gas Scholarship #851
Wayne Kay Co-op Scholarship #383

Engineering, Other

ASNE Scholarship #371
Donald F. Hastings Scholarship #374
Edward J. Brady Scholarship #373
Howard E. Adkins Memorial Scholarship #372
John C. Lincoln Memorial Scholarhip #888
Ken Krum-Bud Kouts Memorial Scholarship #112
Larry H. Averill Memorial Scholarship #110
Praxair International Scholarship #375

Engineering/ Industrial Management

Caterpillar Scholars Award Fund #448
Dwight D. Gardner Scholarship #447
Lucille B. Kaufman Women's Scholarship #418
Myrtle and Earl Walker Scholarship #449

Engineering-Related Technology/ Technician, General

Essay Prize #315

Engineering-Related Technology/ Technicians, Other

Peter D. Courtois Concrete Construction Scholarship #742
Small Cash Grant #370

English Creative Writing

Amelia Student Award #387
Blanche Fern Memorial Award #721
Katherine Anne Porter Prize for Fiction #392
Pablo Neruda Prize for Poetry #393
Parker M. and Virginia Howell Scholarship #573
Phyllis Stevens Grams Memorial Award #723
Rosamond M. Austin Memorial Award #722

English Language and Literature, General

LIT Scholarship for Excellence #268
NFB Humanities Scholarship #341

Entomology

EPA Tribal Lands Environmental Science Scholarship #394

Environmental and Pollution Control Tech./Technician

Solid Waste Processing Division Scholarship #479

Environmental Science/Studies

ACIL Scholarship #643
David L. Owens Scholarship #569
EPA Tribal Lands Environmental Science Scholarship #394
FSCD Scholarship #79
J.J. Barr Scholarship #571
Lawrence Conservation District Scholarship #187
Munch & Clark Scholarship #78

National Association of Water Companies-New Jersey Chapter Scholarship #817
PACD Auxiliary Scholarship #828
Utilities, Inc. Scholarship #570

Environmental/ Environmental Health Engineering

American Electroplaters and Surface Finishers Society Scholarship #368

Ethnic and Cultural Studies, Other

Finlandia Foundation Trust Scholarship Exchange Program and Grants #672
King Olav V Norwegian-American Heritage Fund #323
NIS Regional Languages Grant #403
St. David's Society of the State of New York Scholarship #51

European History

Rozsi & Jeno Zisovich Jewish Studies Scholarship Fund to Teach the Holocaust #186

European Studies

Rozsi & Jeno Zisovich Jewish Studies Scholarship Fund to Teach the Holocaust #186

Experimental Psychology

Eileen J. Garrett Scholarship #647

Family/Consumer Resource Management, Other

AFDO Scholarship #326

Fashion Design and Illustration

Adele Filene Travel Award #232
Stella Blum Research Grant #231

Film/Cinema Studies

Charles and Lucille King Family Foundation Scholarship #706

Finance, General

Karla Scherer Foundation Scholarship #419

Lori Ann Robinson Memorial Scholarship #119
NABA National Scholarship Program #275

Fine Arts and Art Studies, Other

MESBEC Scholarships #693

Fishing and Fisheries Sciences and Management

Olin Fellowship #475

Food and Beverage/ Restaurant Operations Manager

Kentucky Restaurant Association Governor's Scholarship #321
Kentucky Restaurant Association Scholarship #320

Food Caterer

Kentucky Restaurant Association Governor's Scholarship #321
Kentucky Restaurant Association Scholarship #320
School Food Service Foundation Graduate/ Postgraduate Study Scholarship #328

Food Products Retailing and Wholesaling Operations

School Food Service Foundation Graduate/ Postgraduate Study Scholarship #328

Food Sales Operations

School Food Service Foundation Graduate/ Postgraduate Study Scholarship #328

Food Sciences and Technology

IFEC Foodservice Communicators Scholarship #443
School Food Service Foundation Graduate/ Postgraduate Study Scholarship #328
School Food Service Foundation Scholarship #879

Food Systems Administration

AFDO Scholarship #326
School Food Service Foundation Graduate/ Postgraduate Study Scholarship #328
School Food Service Foundation Scholarship #879
Schwan's Food Service Scholarship #880
Tony's Scholarship #329
Undergraduate Scholarship for High School Seniors #444

Foods and Nutrition Science

AFDO Scholarship #326
School Food Service Foundation Graduate/ Postgraduate Study Scholarship #328
Schwan's Food Service Scholarship #880
Tony's Scholarship #329

Foods and Nutrition Studies, General

School Food Service Foundation Graduate/ Postgraduate Study Scholarship #328
Tony's Scholarship #329

Foreign Language Interpretation and Translation

Student Translation Award #404

Foreign Languages and Literatures, General

NFB Humanities Scholarship #341
NIS Regional Languages Grant #403
Phi Sigma Iota Scholarship #283

Forestry, General

GSCAA Scholars #433
Lawrence Conservation District Scholarship #187

Funeral Services and Mortuary Science

ABFSE Scholarship #1

Geography

Space Imaging EOSAT Award for Application of Digital Landsat TM Data #644

Women in Geography Scholarship #445

Geology

ACIL Scholarship #643
ASDSO Scholarship #205
RMCMI Scholarship #565

Geotechnical Engineering

ASDSO Scholarship #205

German Language and Literature

Hochschulsommerkurse at German Universities Grant #405

Graphic and Printing Equipment Operator, General

MGAA Scholarship #425

Graphic Design, Commercial Art and Illustration

Charles D. Mayo Student Scholarship #397
Copernicus Foundation Computer Graphic Design Scholarship #319
IFDA Educational Foundation Student Scholarship #395
MGAA Scholarship #425
NEGA Scholarship #426
Vercille Voss Student Scholarship #396

Health and Medical Preparatory Programs, Other

Health Professions Preparatory Pregraduate Scholarship #683

Health Professions and Related Sciences, Other

Anthony Scholarship #89
CSHEMA Scholarship Award #623
Culinary Arts/Nutrition/ Physical Education Scholarship #327
Eileen J. Garrett Scholarship #647
Foundation of Research & Education in Health Information Management Scholarship #91
Hayes E. Willis Memorial Scholarship #667
Pearl Ramsey Memorial Nursing Scholarship #852

Professional School Scholarship #810
Smart Scholarship #92
Thomas Scholarship #93
Transcript Scholarship #94

Health System/Health Services Administration

Burlington Northern Santa Fe Foundation Scholarship #650
Constance L. Lloyd/ACMPE Scholarship #88
Edgar J. Saux/FACMPE Scholarship #496
Harry J. Harwick Scholarship #490
Midwest Section Scholarship #494
New York Life Foundation Scholarship for Women in the Health Professions #411
Past President's Parley Scholarship Assistance in Health Care Occupations #756

History, General

G. Robert Hamrdla Award #293
NFB Humanities Scholarship #341
Ottis Lock Endowment Scholarship #568
Robert C. Maguire Scholarship #430

History, Other

NIS Regional Languages Grant #403

Home Economics, General

Lorain County Home Economics Scholarship #431

Horticulture Science

Anne Seaman PGMS Memorial Scholarship #437
GSCAA Scholars #433
Timothy Bigelow Scholarship #436
Worcester County Horticultural Society Scholarship #438

Hospitality Services Management, Other

American Express Scholarship #439
Ecolab Scholarship #440
IFEC Foodservice Communicators Scholarship #443

Hospitality/Administration Management

Kentucky Restaurant Association Governor's Scholarship #321

Kentucky Restaurant Association Scholarship #320
Undergraduate Scholarship for High School Seniors #444

Hotel/Motel and Restaurant Management

American Express Scholarship #439
Ecolab Scholarship #440
Hyatt Hotels Fund for Minority Lodging Management Students #441
Kentucky Restaurant Association Governor's Scholarship #321
Kentucky Restaurant Association Scholarship #320

Humanities/Humanistic Studies

BPW Career Advancement Scholarship #410
CHSSC Scholarship #8
Eileen J. Garrett Scholarship #647
MESBEC Scholarships #693
NFB Humanities Scholarship #341
Stanley Olson Youth Scholarship #185
William Fairburn, Jr. and Cynthia Fairburn Memorial Scholarship #446

Hydraulic Technology/Technician

ASDSO Scholarship #205

Information Sciences and Systems

Essay Prize #315

Insurance and Risk Management

Golden State Minority Foundation Scholarship #120

Interior Design

AWA Scholarship Awards #408
Charles D. Mayo Student Scholarship #397

IFDA Educational Foundation Student Scholarship #395
Vercille Voss Student Scholarship #396

International Relations and Affairs

Yoshiko Tanaka Memorial Scholarship #260

Japanese Language and Literature

Yoshiko Tanaka Memorial Scholarship #260

Jewish/Judaic Studies

Rozsi & Jeno Zisovich Jewish Studies Scholarship Fund to Teach the Holocaust #186

Journalism

Atlanta Press Club Journalism Grant #453
CAMP Scholarship #424
Eddy/Peck Scholarship #471
Edward J. Nell Memorial Journalism Scholarships #466
Elaine Noll Scholarship #468
Express News Paul Thompson Scholarship #470
GPEF Scholarship #454
Grace S. Anton Scholarship #462
I.F. Stone Award for Student Journalism #457
Joel Garcia Memorial Scholarship #661
Ken Kashiwahara Scholarship #467
Kyataro & Yasuo Abiko Memorial Scholarship #243
Miami International Press Club Scholarship #456
National High School Journalist of the Year Sister Rita Jeanne Scholarship #455
Press Club of Dallas Foundation Scholarships #465
Ralph Flammino Memorial Scholarship #464
RTNDA President's Award for Television News Management #711
Texas Gridiron Scholarship #472
Texas Professional Communicators Roving Scholarship #318
TPW Roving Scholarship #469

Journalism and Mass Communication, Other

Kyataro & Yasuo Abiko Memorial Scholarship #243
McCullough Scholarship #100

Texas Professional Communicators Roving Scholarship #318

Landscape Architecture

AWA Scholarship Awards #408
Timothy Bigelow Scholarship #436

Law (LL.B., J.D.)

Howard Brown Rickard Scholarship #338
National Association of Water Companies-New Jersey Chapter Scholarship #817
Professional School Scholarship #96
Professional School Scholarship #810

Law and Legal Studies, Other

Law Librarians in Continuing Education Courses #474
Professional School Scholarship #810

Law Enforcement/Police Science

Irlet Anderson Scholarship #692

Liberal Arts and Sciences/Liberal Studies

William Fairburn, Jr. and Cynthia Fairburn Memorial Scholarship #446

Library Science/Librarianship

Law Librarians in Continuing Education Courses #474

Logistics and Materials Management

Charlotte Woods Memorial Scholarship #866
Fred A. Hooper Memorial Scholarship #867

Management Science

Donald W. Fogarty International Student Paper Competition #117

Marine Science/Merchant Marine Officer

ASNE Scholarship #371

International Women's Fishing Association Scholarship #477
Seaspace Scholarship #478
Seaspace Scholarship #476

Marketing Management and Research, Other

Washington Gas Scholarship #851
Wyoming Trucking Association Trust Fund Scholarship #870

Marketing Research

CAMP Scholarship #424

Mass Communications

Eddy/Peck Scholarship #471
Joel Garcia Memorial Scholarship #661
Minority Media Scholarship #316
Press Club of Dallas Foundation Scholarships #465
Texas Professional Communicators Roving Scholarship #318

Material Engineering

American Electroplaters and Surface Finishers Society Scholarship #368
SMD Scholarship #272
SPE Foundation Scholarship #385

Materials Science

American Electroplaters and Surface Finishers Society Scholarship #368
International Symposium on Superalloys Scholarship #273
J. Keith Brimacombe Presidential Scholarship #271
SMD Scholarship #272

Mathematics

Barry M. Goldwater Scholarship and Excellence in Education Program #3
BPW Career Advancement Scholarship #410
General Emmett Paige Scholarship #376
General John A. Wickham Scholarship #377
MESBEC Scholarships #693
Nebraska Space Grant and EPSCOR College and Fellowship Program #74
Renate W. Chasman Scholarship for Women #409

ROTC Scholarship #562
SOA/CAS Minority Scholarship #452
Technical Minority Scholarship #386
Washington Gas Scholarship #851

Mechanical Engineering

ASNE Scholarship #371
Berna Lou Cartwright Scholarship #487
F.W. "Beich" Beichley Scholarship #482
Foundation Scholarship #486
Frank William & Dorothy Given Miller ASME Auxiliary Scholarship #484
Garland Duncan Scholarship #481
John and Elsa Gracik Scholarship #485
Kenneth Andrew Roe Scholarship #483
Melvin R. Green Scholarship #221
RMCMI Scholarship #565
William J. and Mary Jane E. Adams, Jr. Scholarship #480

Medical Clinical Sciences (M.S., Ph.D.)

Medical Field Scholarship #500

Medical Office Management

Edward J. Gerloff/FACMPE Scholarship #493
Ernest S. Moscatello Scholarship #492
Harry J. Harwick Scholarship #490
Midwest Section Scholarship #494
Richard L. Davis National Scholarship #491
Western Section Scholarship #495

Medical Radiologic Technology

Suburban Hospital Scholarship #98

Medical Technology

Health Careers Scholarship #95
Suburban Hospital Scholarship #98

Medicine (M.D.)

Arthur and Doreen A. Parrett Scholarship #829
CSHEMA Scholarship Award #623

Dr. Charles A. Preuss Medical Award #499
Edgar J. Saux/FACMPE Scholarship #496
Edward J. Gerloff/FACMPE Scholarship #493
Ernest S. Moscatello Scholarship #492
Gary W. Chism Memorial Award #199
Harry J. Harwick Scholarship #490
Health Careers Scholarship #95
Howard Brown Rickard Scholarship #338
Medical Field Scholarship #500
Midwest Section Scholarship #494
Past National President Fran Booth Medical Scholarship #538
Professional School Scholarship #96
Professional School Scholarship #810
Richard L. Davis Managers' Scholarship #497
Richard L. Davis National Scholarship #491
Scholarship for Emigres in the Health Professions #416
Ty Cobb Scholarship #847

Metal and Jewelry Arts

Women's Jewelry Association Scholarship #420

Metallurgical Engineering

American Electroplaters and Surface Finishers Society Scholarship #368

Metallurgy

American Electroplaters and Surface Finishers Society Scholarship #368
EPD Scholarship #563
International Symposium on Superalloys Scholarship #273
J. Keith Brimacombe Presidential Scholarship #271
LMD Scholarship #564
RMCMI Scholarship #565
SMD Scholarship #272

Mining and Mineral Engineering

International Symposium on Superalloys Scholarship #273
J. Keith Brimacombe Presidential Scholarship #271
RMCMI Scholarship #565

Music - General Performance

American Recorder Society Scholarship #450
BEEM Foundation Scholarship #576
Donna Reed Performing Arts Scholarships - Crawford County Scholarship #177
Donna Reed Performing Arts Scholarships - National Scholarship #353
GFWC of MA Music Scholarship #580
Music Scholarship #579

Music - Piano and Organ Performance

American Theatre Organ Society, Inc. Scholarship #451
GFWC of MA Music Scholarship #580

Music - Voice and Choral/Opera Performance

Donna Reed Performing Arts Scholarships - Crawford County Scholarship #177
Donna Reed Performing Arts Scholarships - National Scholarship #353
Dorchester Woman's Club Scholarship #892
Gifted Opera Singers' Scholarship #891

Music Teacher Education

Bernice Barnard Music Specialist Scholarhip #583
GFWC of MA Music Scholarship #580
Gladys Stone Wright Scholarship #587
Kathryn Siphers/Patricia Garren Memorial Scholarship #586
Music Scholarship #579
Volkwein Memorial Scholarship #585

Music Theory and Composition

ASCAP Foundation Morton Gould Young Composers Award #575

Music Therapy

GFWC of MA Music Scholarship #580
Musical or Recreational Therapy Scholarship #761

Music, General

Aiko Susanna Tashiro Hiratsuka Memorial Scholarship #263
Bernice Barnard Music Specialist Scholarhip #583
Helen Mathilda Yunker Music Scholarship #584
McDonald's GospelFest Music Scholarship #582
Music Scholarship #574
Music Scholarship #579
TELACU Arts Award #401

Music, Other

Aiko Susanna Tashiro Hiratsuka Memorial Scholarship #263

Natural Resources Conservation, General

A.T. Anderson Memorial Scholarship #649

Natural Resources Management and Policy

National Association of Water Companies-New Jersey Chapter Scholarship #817
Wildlife Leadership Awards #893

Naval Architecture and Marine Engineering

ASNE Scholarship #371

Nuclear Engineering

ANS Local Undergraduate Scholarship #594

Nuclear Physics

ANS Local Section Undergraduate Scholarship #594

Nursing (R.N. Training)

B.S. Nurs. Scholarship #599
Colorado Nursing Scholarship #601
FNSNA Scholarship #603
Nurses Training Scholarship #608
Nurses', Physical Therapists', and Respiratory Therapists' Scholarship #514
Nursing Scholarship #602
Past President's Parley Nurses Scholarship #596
Shirley Titus Memorial Scholarship #600

Nursing Administration (Post-R.N.)

Shirley Titus Memorial Scholarship #600

Nursing Anesthetist (Post-R.N.)

Shirley Titus Memorial Scholarship #600

Nursing Midwifery (Post-R.N.)

Shirley Titus Memorial Scholarship #600

Nursing Science (Post-R.N.)

Shirley Titus Memorial Scholarship #600

Nursing, Adult Health (Post-R.N.)

Shirley Titus Memorial Scholarship #600

Nursing, Family Practice (Post-R.N.)

Shirley Titus Memorial Scholarship #600

Nursing, Maternal/Child Health (Post-R.N.)

Shirley Titus Memorial Scholarship #600

Nursing, Other

CSHEMA Scholarship Award #623
Easter Seal Scholarships #645
FNSNA Scholarship #603
Health Careers Scholarship #95
M. Elizabeth Carnegie Scholarship #606
Mary Virginia McRae Nurses Scholarship #597
National Association of Hispanic Nurses Scholarship #605
Neuroscience Nursing Foundation Research Grant #595
Nurses Educational Fund Scholarship #607
Nursing Scholarship #602
Nursing Scholastic Achievement Scholarship #719
Nursing Student Scholarship #604
Professional School Scholarship #96
Professional School Scholarship #810
Sad Sack Nursing Scholarship #598
Scholarship for Emigres in the Health Professions #416
Scholarship for L.V.N.s Becoming Professional Nurses #611

Scholarship for Rural B.S.N. or Graduate Nursing Students #610
Scholarship for Rural Professional or Vocational Nursing Students #609
Shirley Titus Memorial Scholarship #600
Suburban Hospital Scholarship #98
Tyson Foundation Scholarship #572

Nursing, Pediatric (Post-R.N.)

Shirley Titus Memorial Scholarship #600

Nursing, Psychiatric/Mental Health (Post-R.N.)

Shirley Titus Memorial Scholarship #600

Nursing, Public Health (Post-R.N.)

Shirley Titus Memorial Scholarship #600

Nursing, Surgical (Post-R.N.)

Shirley Titus Memorial Scholarship #600

Nutritional Sciences

Culinary Arts/Nutrition/Physical Education Scholarship #327
School Food Service Foundation Graduate/Postgraduate Study Scholarship #328
School Food Service Foundation Scholarship #879
Tony's Scholarship #329

Occupational Safety and Health Technology

Wyoming Trucking Association Trust Fund Scholarship #870

Occupational Therapy

AMBUCS Scholarship #646
Easter Seal Scholarships #645
Health Careers Scholarship #95
National AMBUCS Scholarship for Therapists #87
Scholarship for Emigres in the Health Professions #416
Suburban Hospital Scholarship #98

Ocean Engineering

ASNE Scholarship #371

Oceanography

EPA Tribal Lands Environmental Science Scholarship #394

Office Supervision and Management

Wyoming Trucking Association Trust Fund Scholarship #870

Optics

Educational Scholarships & Grants in Optical Science & Engineering #743
New Focus Student Award #612
Technical Minority Scholarship #386

Painting

John F. and Anna Lee Stacey Scholarship #399

Paralegal/Legal Assistant

BPW Career Advancement Scholarship #410
Irlet Anderson Scholarship #692

Petroleum Engineering

Society of Petroleum Engineers - San Joaquin Valley Section Scholarship #384

Pharmacy (B. Pharm., Pharm.D.)

Professional School Scholarship #810

Pharmacy Administration and Pharmaceutics

NPC Pre-Pharmacy Scholarship #641

Pharmacy, Other

AFDO Scholarship #326
Health Careers Scholarship #95
Pharmacists Scholarhsip #642
Professional School Scholarship #96
Scholarship for Emigres in the Health Professions #416

Philosophy

NFB Humanities Scholarship #341

Photography

Space Imaging EOSAT Award for Application of Digital Landsat TM Data #644
Texas Gridiron Scholarship #472

Physical Sciences, General

A.T. Anderson Memorial Scholarship #649
Arthur and Doreen A. Parrett Scholarship #829
ASNE Scholarship #371
BPW Career Advancement Scholarship #410
Burlington Northern Santa Fe Foundation Scholarship #650
MESBEC Scholarships #693
Navy League Scholarship #544
Nebraska Space Grant and EPSCOR College and Fellowship Program #74
Technical Minority Scholarship #386
William Fairburn, Jr. and Cynthia Fairburn Memorial Scholarship #446

Physical Therapy

AMBUCS Scholarship #646
Easter Seal Scholarships #645
Health Careers Scholarship #95
National AMBUCS Scholarship for Therapists #87
Nurses', Physical Therapists', and Respiratory Therapists' Scholarship #514
Scholarship for Emigres in the Health Professions #416
Suburban Hospital Scholarship #98

Physical Therapy Assistant

Suburban Hospital Scholarship #98

Physician Assistant

Scholarship for Emigres in the Health Professions #416
Suburban Hospital Scholarship #98

Physics, General

ACIL Scholarship #643
APS Corporate-Sponsored Scholarship for Minority Undergraduate Students Who Major in Physics #651
General Emmett Paige Scholarship #376
General John A. Wickham Scholarship #377

Renate W. Chasman Scholarship for Women #409
ROTC Scholarship #562
Technical Minority Scholarship #386

Plant Sciences, General

GSCAA Scholars #433

Plastics Technology/ Technician

SPE Foundation Scholarship #385

Political Science and Government, Other

Bruce B. Melchert Scholarship #303
Washington Crossing Foundation Scholarship #850

Political Science, General

Bruce B. Melchert Scholarship #303

Polymer Chemistry

SPE Foundation Scholarship #385

Pre-Dentistry Studies

Health Professions Preparatory Pregraduate Scholarship #683

Pre-Medicine Studies

Health Professions Preparatory Pregraduate Scholarship #683

Pre-Pharmacy Studies

Health Professions Preparatory Pregraduate Scholarship #683

Printmaking

FFTA Scholarship Competition #626

Psychology, Other

Eileen J. Garrett Scholarship #647

Public Administration

Golden State Minority Foundation Scholarship #120

Public Administration and Services, Other

Alice Yuriko Endo Memorial Scholarship #254

Public Relations and Organizational Communications

CAMP Scholarship #424
Press Club of Dallas Foundation Scholarships #465

Quality Control and Safety Technology/ Technicians, Other

Wyoming Trucking Association Trust Fund Scholarship #870

Radio and Television Broadcasting

Bayliss Radio Scholarship #312
Charles and Lucille King Family Foundation Scholarship #706
National Academy of Television Arts and Sciences Scholarship #314
Texas Gridiron Scholarship #472

Range Science and Management

Masonic Range Science Scholarship #49

Real Estate

Academic Scholarship #713
George M. Brooker Collegiate Scholarship for Minorities #714
Real Estate Scholarship Fund #715
Thomas F. Seay Scholarship #712

Recreational Therapy

Musical or Recreational Therapy Scholarship #761
National AMBUCS Scholarship for Therapists #87

Religion/Religious Studies

CKA Seminarian Scholarsip #716
NFB Humanities Scholarship #341

Respiratory Therapy Technician

Jimmy A. Young Memorial Educational Recognition Award #740

Morton B. Duggan Memorial Education Recognition Award #737
NBRC/AMP Robert M. Lawrence, M.D., Education Recognition Award #738
NBRC/AMP William W. Burgin, Jr., M.D., Education Recognition Award #739
Nurses', Physical Therapists', and Respiratory Therapists' Scholarship #514
Suburban Hospital Scholarship #98

Russian Language and Literature

NIS Regional Languages Grant #403

Scandinavian Area Studies

King Olav V Norwegian-American Heritage Fund #323

Science Technology/ Technicians, Other

Washington Gas Scholarship #851

Security and Loss Prevention Services

CSHEMA Scholarship Award #623

Social Sciences and History, Other

BPW Career Advancement Scholarship #410
CHSSC Scholarship #8

Social Sciences, General

Alice Yuriko Endo Memorial Scholarship #254
Arthur and Doreen A. Parrett Scholarship #829
BPW Career Advancement Scholarship #410
Burlington Northern Santa Fe Foundation Scholarship #650
MESBEC Scholarships #693
Navy League Scholarship #544
Technical Minority Scholarship #386
William Fairburn, Jr. and Cynthia Fairburn Memorial Scholarship #446

Social Studies Teacher Education

Ottis Lock Endowment Scholarship #568

Social Work

Alice Yuriko Endo Memorial Scholarship #254
CSDIW Scholarship #668
Easter Seal Scholarships #645
Professional School Scholarship #96
Professional School Scholarship #810

Speech-Language Pathology

National AMBUCS Scholarship for Therapists #87

Speech-Language Pathology and Audiology

AMBUCS Scholarship #646

Teacher Education, Multiple Levels

BPW Career Advancement Scholarship #410
Frank Kazmierczak Memorial Migrant Scholarship #355
Roothbert Fund, Inc. Scholarship #363

Theological and Ministerial Studies, Other

CKA Seminarian Scholarsip #716

Theological Studies and Religious Vocations, Other

CKA Seminarian Scholarsip #716

Theology/Theological Studies

CKA Seminarian Scholarsip #716

Toxicology

EPA Tribal Lands Environmental Science Scholarship #394

Transportation and Highway Engineering

American Society of Highway Engineers - Carolina Triangle Section Scholarship #202
Charlotte Woods Memorial Scholarship #866
Fred A. Hooper Memorial Scholarship #867

TCA Scholarship #869
Texas Transportation Scholarship #868

Transportation and Materials Moving Workers, Other

Wyoming Trucking Association Trust Fund Scholarship #870

Travel-Tourism Management

Air Travel Card Grant #857
Alaska Airlines Scholarship #860
American Express Travel Scholarship #862
Arizona Chapter Gold #858
Eric and Bette Friedheim Scholarship #44
H. Neil Mecaskey Scholarship #864
Healy Scholarship #854
Holland-America Line Westours, Inc. Scholarship #856
Joseph R. Stone Scholarship #855
Louise Dessureault Memorial Scholarship #865
Northern California/Richard Epping Scholarship #859
Rocky Mountain Chapter Estey Scholarship #760
Southern California Chapter/ Pleasant Hawaiian Holidays Scholarship #861
State Scholarships #818
Tony Orlando Yellow Ribbon Scholarship #348
Treadway Inns, Hotels, and Resorts Scholarship #633

Truck, Bus and Other Commercial Vehicle Operator

TCA Scholarship #869
Wyoming Trucking Association Trust Fund Scholarship #870

Turf Management

GCSAA Legacy Awards #240
GSCAA Scholars #433
Scotts Company Scholars #434
Student Essay Contest #435

Urban Affairs/Studies

AWA Scholarship Awards #408

Water Resources Engineering

John C. Robbins Scholarship #203

Welder/Welding Technologist

Donald F. Hastings Scholarship #374
Edward J. Brady Scholarship #373
Howard E. Adkins Memorial Scholarship #372
John C. Lincoln Memorial Scholarhip #888
Praxair International Scholarship #375

Wildlife and Wildlands Management

Wildlife Leadership Awards #893

20. Top 200 Scholarships By Award Size

(Note: We have included all information provided by the sponsors. Not all provide their average award size. Also, some award more money in total but in smaller award sizes to more winners. This ranking is composed of the top 200 largest maximum awards given to an individual.)

Academic Year Ambassadorial Scholarship #635
Maximum award amount: **$25,000**
Minimum award amount: **$11,000**

Horace Mann Scholarship #137
Maximum award amount: **$25,000**
Minimum award amount: **$1,000**
Number of applications received each year: **11,000**

Coca-Cola Scholarship #10
Maximum award amount: **$20,000**
Minimum award amount: **$4,000**
Number of applications received each year: **137,000**

NIS Regional Languages Grant #403
Maximum award amount: **$15,030**
Average award amount: **$8,515**
Minimum award amount: **$2,000**
Number of applications received each year: **20**

Clara Abbott Foundation Educational Grant Program #133
Maximum award amount: **$13,000**
Average award amount: **$3,200**
Minimum award amount: **$1,100**
Number of applications received each year: **4,100**

California Masonic Foundation Scholarship #768
Maximum award amount: **$10,400**
Average award amount: **$2,500**
Minimum award amount: **$2,500**
Number of applications received each year: **1,200**

Academic Merit Award #33
Maximum award amount: **$10,000**
Minimum award amount: **$3,000**

CollegeNET Scholarship #11
Maximum award amount: **$10,000**
Minimum award amount: **$1,000**

Dean's Scholarship #46
Maximum award amount: **$10,000**
Average award amount: **$7,950**
Minimum award amount: **$4,000**
Number of applications received each year: **1,400**

Easley National Scholarship #38
Maximum award amount: **$10,000**
Minimum award amount: **$200**

Educational Scholarships & Grants in Optical Science & Engineering #743
Maximum award amount: **$10,000**
Minimum award amount: **$1,000**
Number of applications received each year: **242**

FACT Continuing Education Scholarship #23
Maximum award amount: **$10,000**
Minimum award amount: **$2,500**
Number of applications received each year: **750**

Lee Jackson Foundation Scholarship #792
Maximum award amount: **$10,000**
Minimum award amount: **$1,000**
Number of applications received each year: **1,100**

M. Elizabeth Carnegie Scholarship #606
Maximum award amount: **$10,000**
Minimum award amount: **$2,500**

Merit Scholarship #590
Maximum award amount: **$10,000**
Minimum award amount: **$500**

Miss Outstanding Teenager #37
Maximum award amount: **$10,000**
Average award amount: **$2,500**
Minimum award amount: **$500**
Number of applications received each year: **200**

New Focus Student Award #612
Maximum award amount: **$10,000**
Minimum award amount: **$2,500**
Number of applications received each year: **61**

Nurses Educational Fund Scholarship #607
Maximum award amount: **$10,000**
Minimum award amount: **$2,500**

Olin L. Livesey Scholarship #47
Maximum award amount: **$10,000**
Average award amount: **$1,000**
Minimum award amount: **$100**
Number of applications received each year: **67,473**

RMHC/HACER Scholarship #695
Maximum award amount: **$10,000**
Minimum award amount: **$2,500**
Number of applications received each year: **600**

Sons of Italy Foundation National Leadership Grant #700
Maximum award amount: **$10,000**
Average award amount: **$4,000**
Minimum award amount: **$4,000**
Number of applications received each year: **400**

TNE Scholarship #302
Maximum award amount: **$10,000**
Average award amount: **$5,000**
Minimum award amount: **$1,000**
Number of applications received each year: **28**

Washington Crossing Foundation Scholarship #850
Maximum award amount: **$10,000**
Minimum award amount: **$1,000**
Number of applications received each year: **1,500**

World of Expressions Scholarship #163
Maximum award amount: **$10,000**
Minimum award amount: **$500**
Number of applications received each year: **2,363**

Law Enforcement Personnel Dependents Scholarship #770
Maximum award amount: **$9,420**
Minimum award amount: **$100**
Number of applications received each year: **5**

Guaranteed Access Grant #809
Maximum award amount: $8,700
Minimum award amount: $400

Educational Benefits for Children of Deceased Veterans #531
Maximum award amount: $8,500
Number of applications received each year: 2

Abraham Mitchell Business Scholarship #124
Maximum award amount: $8,000

Kenneth Andrew Roe Scholarship #483
Maximum award amount: $8,000

National Youth of the Year Scholarship #5
Maximum award amount: $8,000
Minimum award amount: $2,000
Number of applications received each year: 750

Atlas Shrugged Essay Competition #389
Maximum award amount: $7,500
Minimum award amount: $1,000

Barry M. Goldwater Scholarship and Excellence in Education Program #3
Maximum award amount: $7,500
Number of applications received each year: 1,200

Elks National Foundation Most Valuable Student Award #20
Maximum award amount: $7,500
Average award amount: $1,000
Minimum award amount: $1,000

Hispanic Scholarship Fund General Scholarship #679
Maximum award amount: $7,500
Average award amount: $2,000
Minimum award amount: $1,000
Number of applications received each year: 12,000

Music Scholarship #579
Maximum award amount: $7,500
Minimum award amount: $500

Nebraska Space Grant and EPSCOR College and Fellowship #74
Maximum award amount: $7,500
Minimum award amount: $250

Minnesota State Grant #813
Maximum award amount: $7,089
Average award amount: $1,700
Minimum award amount: $100

Henry Sachs Foundation Scholarship #676
Maximum award amount: $7,000
Average award amount: $4,000
Minimum award amount: $1,500
Number of applications received each year: 200

NFB Scholarship #340
Maximum award amount: $7,000
Minimum award amount: $3,000

Wilson Grant #35
Maximum award amount: $7,000
Minimum award amount: $2,000

Public Safety Officers Survivor Grant #814
Maximum award amount: $6,748
Average award amount: $3,419
Number of applications received each year: 9

Sussman-Miller Educational Assistance Award #754
Maximum award amount: $6,500
Minimum award amount: $1,000
Number of applications received each year: 168

Tuition Aid Grant #823
Maximum award amount: $6,052
Minimum award amount: $824

AGC Education and Research Foundation Undergraduate Scholarship #204
Maximum award amount: $6,000
Average award amount: $1,500
Minimum award amount: $1,500

Marion Huber Learning through Listening Awards #634
Maximum award amount: $6,000
Minimum award amount: $2,000
Number of applications received each year: 180

NABA National Scholarship Program #275
Maximum award amount: $6,000
Number of applications received each year: 120

National AMBUCS Scholarship for Therapists #87
Maximum award amount: $6,000
Minimum award amount: $500
Number of applications received each year: 1,600

Sid Richardson Memorial Fund Scholarship #148
Maximum award amount: $6,000
Average award amount: $2,815
Minimum award amount: $1,000
Number of applications received each year: 62

UAL Scholarship #83
Maximum award amount: $6,000
Average award amount: $2,500
Minimum award amount: $1,000
Number of applications received each year: 35

Academic Scholars Program #826
Maximum award amount: $5,500
Average award amount: $4,000
Minimum award amount: $3,500
Number of applications received each year: 410

Vermont Part-Time Grant #849
Maximum award amount: $5,100
Average award amount: $384
Minimum award amount: $250
Number of applications received each year: 4,718

Abe & Esther Hagiwara Student Aid Award #262
Maximum award amount: $5,000
Minimum award amount: $1,000

Aiko Susanna Tashiro Hiratsuka Memorial Scholarship #263
Maximum award amount: $5,000
Minimum award amount: $1,000

Alice Yuriko Endo Memorial Scholarship #254
Maximum award amount: $5,000
Minimum award amount: $1,000

American Association of Hispanic CPAs Scholarship #648
Maximum award amount: $5,000
Average award amount: $1,000
Minimum award amount: $1,000
Number of applications received each year: 120

Arby's/Big Brothers Big Sisters of America Scholarship #224
Maximum award amount: $5,000

ASDSO Scholarship #205
Maximum award amount: $5,000
Average award amount: $2,500
Number of applications received each year: 50

Ashby B. Carter Memorial Scholarship #877
Maximum award amount: $5,000
Minimum award amount: $1,900
Number of applications received each year: 80

Bayliss Radio Scholarship #312
Maximum award amount: $5,000
Number of applications received each year: 75

Becky Briggs Memorial Scholarship #230
Maximum award amount: $5,000
Minimum award amount: $500

BEEM Foundation Scholarship #576
Maximum award amount: $5,000
Minimum award amount: $2,000
Number of applications received each year: 20

Cental Virginia Scholarship #170
Maximum award amount: $5,000
Minimum award amount: $500

Christopher Gray and George Chancellor Memorial Scholarships #175
Maximum award amount: $5,000
Minimum award amount: $500

Colorado Part-Time Grant/Scholarship #771
Maximum award amount: $5,000

Colorado Student Grant #772
Maximum award amount: $5,000

Dollars for Scholars #172
Maximum award amount: $5,000
Minimum award amount: $500

Dorothy Armstrong Community Service Scholarship #413
Maximum award amount: $5,000
Minimum award amount: $500

Dr. Thomas T. Yatabe Memorial Scholarship #261
Maximum award amount: $5,000
Minimum award amount: $1,000

Duke Energy Scholars Program #135
Maximum award amount: $5,000
Minimum award amount: $1,000

Eagle Scout Scholarship #279
Maximum award amount: $5,000
Minimum award amount: $1,000
Number of applications received each year: 1,500

Ed Bradley Scholarship #710
Maximum award amount: $5,000

Finlandia Foundation Trust Scholarship Exchange Program and Grants #672
Maximum award amount: $5,000
Average award amount: $2,500
Minimum award amount: $1,000

Foundation of Research & Education in Health Information Management Scholarship #91
Maximum award amount: $5,000
Minimum award amount: $1,000

Frederic Scott Reed Scholarship #176
Maximum award amount: $5,000
Minimum award amount: $500

Friendship One Flight Training Scholarship #16
Maximum award amount: $5,000
Minimum award amount: $2,500

Gongoro Nakamura Memorial Scholarship #249
Maximum award amount: $5,000
Minimum award amount: $1,000

Grace S. Anton Scholarship #462
Maximum award amount: $5,000

Hauss-Helms Foundation, Inc. Scholarship #181
Maximum award amount: $5,000
Minimum award amount: $400

Hayes E. Willis Memorial Scholarship #667
Maximum award amount: $5,000
Minimum award amount: $500

Henry & Chiyo Kuwahara Memorial Scholarship for Entering Freshmen #246
Maximum award amount: $5,000
Minimum award amount: $1,000

Henry & Chiyo Kuwahara Memorial Scholarship for Undergraduates #257
Maximum award amount: $5,000
Minimum award amount: $1,000

Hispanic College Fund Scholarship #678
Maximum award amount: $5,000
Average award amount: $2,000
Minimum award amount: $500
Number of applications received each year: 764

Hispanic College Fund Scholarship #677
Maximum award amount: $5,000
Average award amount: $2,000
Minimum award amount: $500
Number of applications received each year: 780

Honored Scholars and Artists Program #40
Maximum award amount: $5,000
Average award amount: $2,000
Minimum award amount: $1,000
Number of applications received each year: 7,000

Honors Fellow Scholarship #21
Maximum award amount: $5,000
Minimum award amount: $2,000
Number of applications received each year: 258

J.J. Barr Scholarship #571
Maximum award amount: $5,000
Number of applications received each year: 58

Joseph H. Jones, Sr. Scholarship #174
Maximum award amount: $5,000
Minimum award amount: $500

Kenji Kasai Memorial Scholarship #245
Maximum award amount: **$5,000**
Minimum award amount: **$1,000**

Kristin Elaine Dickerson Scholarship #171
Maximum award amount: **$5,000**
Minimum award amount: **$500**

Kyataro & Yasuo Abiko Memorial Scholarship #243
Maximum award amount: **$5,000**
Minimum award amount: **$1,000**

Lori Ann Robinson Memorial Scholarship #119
Maximum award amount: **$5,000**
Minimum award amount: **$500**

Mari & James Michener Scholarship #259
Maximum award amount: **$5,000**
Minimum award amount: **$1,000**

Mark Smith Neale II "Cross of Life" Scholarship #14
Maximum award amount: **$5,000**
Minimum award amount: **$500**

Maryland Association of Private Career Schools Scholarship #890
Maximum award amount: **$5,000**
Average award amount: **$1,000**
Minimum award amount: **$500**
Number of applications received each year: **120**

Masao & Sumako Itano Memorial Scholarship #244
Maximum award amount: **$5,000**
Minimum award amount: **$1,000**

Matthew Anthony Grappone Memorial Scholarship #173
Maximum award amount: **$5,000**
Minimum award amount: **$500**

McDonald's African American Heritage Scholarship #694
Maximum award amount: **$5,000**
Minimum award amount: **$1,000**

McDonald's Golden Arches Scholarship #193
Maximum award amount: **$5,000**
Minimum award amount: **$1,000**
Number of applications received each year: **1,800**

McDonald's GospelFest Music Scholarship #582
Maximum award amount: **$5,000**
Minimum award amount: **$1,000**
Number of applications received each year: **68**

Medicus Student Exchange #702
Maximum award amount: **$5,000**
Minimum award amount: **$4,000**
Number of applications received each year: **1**

MESBEC Scholarships #693
Maximum award amount: **$5,000**
Minimum award amount: **$500**
Number of applications received each year: **2,000**

Minority Media Scholarship #316
Maximum award amount: **$5,000**
Average award amount: **$2,500**
Number of applications received each year: **20**

Mitchell-Beall Scholarship #274
Maximum award amount: **$5,000**
Minimum award amount: **$1,000**

Mitsuyuki Yonemura Memorial Scholarship #253
Maximum award amount: **$5,000**
Minimum award amount: **$1,000**

Mr. & Mrs. Takashi Moriuchi Scholarship #248
Maximum award amount: **$5,000**
Minimum award amount: **$1,000**

Mr. & Mrs. Uyesugi Memorial Scholarship #252
Maximum award amount: **$5,000**
Minimum award amount: **$1,000**

Neuroscience Nursing Foundation Research Grant #595
Maximum award amount: **$5,000**

Nobuko R. Kodama Fong Memorial Scholarship #255
Maximum award amount: **$5,000**
Minimum award amount: **$1,000**

Oratorical Contest Scholarship of Tennessee #749
Maximum award amount: **$5,000**
Average award amount: **$2,500**
Minimum award amount: **$1,500**
Number of applications received each year: **61**

Patricia & Gail Ishimoto Memorial Scholarship #242
Maximum award amount: **$5,000**
Minimum award amount: **$1,000**

Phi Delta Kappa Scholarship Grants for Prospective Educators #362
Maximum award amount: **$5,000**
Minimum award amount: **$1,000**
Number of applications received each year: **850**

Raymond F. Burmester Endowment for Scholastic Achievement #13
Maximum award amount: **$5,000**
Minimum award amount: **$500**

Regents Professional Opportunity Scholarship #7
Maximum award amount: **$5,000**
Minimum award amount: **$1,000**
Number of applications received each year: **2,000**

Saburo Kido Memorial Scholarship #256
Maximum award amount: **$5,000**
Minimum award amount: **$1,000**

Sam S. Kuwahara Memorial Scholarship for Entering Freshmen #247
Maximum award amount: **$5,000**
Minimum award amount: **$1,000**

Sam S. Kuwahara Memorial Scholarship for Undergraduates #258
Maximum award amount: **$5,000**
Minimum award amount: **$1,000**

Scholarship Program #264
Maximum award amount: **$5,000**
Minimum award amount: **$1,000**

Seaspace Scholarship #476
Maximum award amount: **$5,000**
Average award amount: **$2,000**
Minimum award amount: **$500**
Number of applications received each year: **80**

Selby Direct Scholarship #833
Maximum award amount: **$5,000**
Average award amount: **$2,500**
Minimum award amount: **$1,000**

South Park Japanese Community Scholarship #251
Maximum award amount: **$5,000**
Minimum award amount: **$1,000**

SPE Foundation Scholarship #385
Maximum award amount: **$5,000**
Number of applications received each year: **210**

Suburban Hospital Scholarship #98
Maximum award amount: **$5,000**

Technical Minority Scholarship #386
Maximum award amount: **$5,000**
Minimum award amount: **$500**
Number of applications received each year: **1,400**

U.S. Jaycee War Memorial Fund Scholarship #54
Maximum award amount: **$5,000**
Average award amount: **$1,000**
Number of applications received each year: **3,800**

Underwood-Smith Teacher Scholarship #364
Maximum award amount: **$5,000**
Average award amount: **$4,024**
Number of applications received each year: **54**

William J. and A. Haskell McMannis Educational Trust Fund Scholarship #629
Maximum award amount: **$5,000**
Minimum award amount: **$200**

William Reed Baker Outstanding Senior Award #414
Maximum award amount: **$5,000**
Minimum award amount: **$500**

Women's Jewelry Association Scholarship #420
Maximum award amount: **$5,000**
Minimum award amount: **$2,500**

Yoshiko Tanaka Memorial Scholarship #260
Maximum award amount: **$5,000**
Minimum award amount: **$1,000**

Yutaka Nakazawa Memorial Scholarship #250
Maximum award amount: **$5,000**
Minimum award amount: **$1,000**

Edward T. Conroy Memorial Grant #540
Maximum award amount: **$4,939**
Average award amount: **$1,976**
Number of applications received each year: **62**

Edward J. Bloustein Distinguished Scholars #822
Maximum award amount: **$4,549**

ASWA Scholarship #63
Maximum award amount: **$4,500**
Minimum award amount: **$2,000**
Number of applications received each year: **53**

Contemporary Record Society Grant #578
Maximum award amount: **$4,500**
Average award amount: **$1,200**
Minimum award amount: **$800**
Number of applications received each year: **65**

Vivienne Camp College Scholarship #183
Maximum award amount: **$4,350**

Monetary Award #787
Maximum award amount: **$4,120**
Average award amount: **$2,700**
Minimum award amount: **$300**
Number of applications received each year: **40,000**

Arkansas Governor's Scholars Award #762
Maximum award amount: **$4,000**
Number of applications received each year: **2,400**

Armstrong Foundation Award #128
Maximum award amount: **$4,000**
Minimum award amount: **$2,000**
Number of applications received each year: **100**

Donna Reed Performing Arts Scholarships - National Scholarship #353
Maximum award amount: **$4,000**
Minimum award amount: **$500**

FINA/*Dallas Morning News* All-State Scholar-Athlete Team Scholarship #103
Maximum award amount: **$4,000**
Minimum award amount: **$500**
Number of applications received each year: **2,500**

Solid Waste Processing Division Scholarship #479
Maximum award amount: **$4,000**
Minimum award amount: **$2,000**

Stanley Works National Merit Scholarship #592
Maximum award amount: **$4,000**
Minimum award amount: **$1,000**
Number of applications received each year: **39**

United States Naval Academy Class of 1963 Foundation Scholarship #560
Maximum award amount: **$4,000**
Average award amount: **$1,000**
Minimum award amount: **$1,000**
Number of applications received each year: **6**

Iowa Tuition Grant #788
Maximum award amount: **$3,900**

Blackfeet Higher Education Scholarship #657
Maximum award amount: **$3,600**
Minimum award amount: **$3,000**
Number of applications received each year: **404**

Academic Recognition Scholarship #36
Maximum award amount: **$3,500**
Average award amount: **$1,446**
Minimum award amount: **$500**
Number of applications received each year: **943**

ASNE Scholarship #371
Maximum award amount: **$3,500**
Average award amount: **$3,000**
Minimum award amount: **$2,500**
Number of applications received each year: **81**

Dr. Charles A. Preuss Medical Award #499
Maximum award amount: **$3,500**
Average award amount: **$2,000**
Minimum award amount: **$1,000**

Edmund F. Maxwell Scholarship #18
Maximum award amount: $3,500
Minimum award amount: $900
Number of applications received each year: **180**

Gloria Fecht Memorial Scholarship #421
Maximum award amount: $3,500
Minimum award amount: $1,000
Number of applications received each year: **75**

GSCAA Scholars #433
Maximum award amount: $3,500
Average award amount: $2,500
Number of applications received each year: **50**

Jones-Laurence Award #291
Maximum award amount: $3,500
Minimum award amount: $1,000

Marin County American Revolution Bicentennial Scholarship #190
Maximum award amount: $3,500
Minimum award amount: $500

Marin County American Revolution Bicentennial Scholarship #164
Maximum award amount: $3,500
Minimum award amount: $500
Number of applications received each year: **125**

Masonic Grand Lodge Charities of Rhode Island Scholarship #811
Maximum award amount: $3,500
Minimum award amount: $750
Number of applications received each year: **215**

Max and Emmy Dreyfuss Jewish Undergraduate Scholarship #728
Maximum award amount: $3,500
Average award amount: $2,000
Minimum award amount: $1,500

Peeples Foundation Trust Scholarship #805
Maximum award amount: $3,500
Minimum award amount: $500
Number of applications received each year: **100**

RRVA Scholarship Grant Assistance Program #552
Maximum award amount: $3,500
Minimum award amount: $500
Number of applications received each year: **42**

ADVA Scholarship Fund #210
Maximum award amount: $3,000
Average award amount: $2,000
Minimum award amount: $1,000
Number of applications received each year: **19**

AFSA Financial Aid Scholarship #620
Maximum award amount: $3,000
Average award amount: $1,800
Minimum award amount: $500
Number of applications received each year: **150**

Arthur and Doreen A. Parrett Scholarship #829
Maximum award amount: $3,000
Minimum award amount: $1,000

ASCAP Foundation Morton Gould Young Composers Award #575
Maximum award amount: $3,000
Minimum award amount: $250
Number of applications received each year: **675**

Baldridge Scholarship #307
Maximum award amount: $3,000
Number of applications received each year: **8**

Daughters of the Cincinnati Scholarship #529
Maximum award amount: $3,000
Minimum award amount: $500

Distinguished Scholar #806
Maximum award amount: $3,000
Number of applications received each year: **3500**

Eileen J. Garrett Scholarship #647
Maximum award amount: $3,000
Number of applications received each year: **200**

Garland Duncan Scholarship #481
Maximum award amount: $3,000

General Scholarship #197
Maximum award amount: $3,000
Average award amount: $1,100
Minimum award amount: $350
Number of applications received each year: **300**

George J. Record School Foundation Scholarship #179
Maximum award amount: $3,000
Average award amount: $2,500
Minimum award amount: $500
Number of applications received each year: **50**

Hormel Foods Scholarship #138
Maximum award amount: $3,000
Minimum award amount: $750

John F. and Anna Lee Stacey Scholarship #399
Maximum award amount: $3,000
Average award amount: $2,000
Minimum award amount: $500
Number of applications received each year: **75**

Katharine M. Grosscup Scholarship #432
Maximum award amount: $3,000
Average award amount: $2,000
Minimum award amount: $1,000
Number of applications received each year: **45**

King Olav V Norwegian-American Heritage Fund #323
Maximum award amount: $3,000
Average award amount: $1,000
Minimum award amount: $250
Number of applications received each year: **100**

LAEF Scholarship #791
Maximum award amount: $3,000
Minimum award amount: $500
Number of applications received each year: **133**

Melvin R. Green Scholarship #221
Maximum award amount: $3,000

Milton McKevett Teague Scholarship #85
Maximum award amount: $3,000
Average award amount: $2,500
Number of applications received each year: **5**

NAAS II National Scholarship #39
Maximum award amount: $3,000
Minimum award amount: $1,000

News 4 Media Scholarship #313
Maximum award amount: **$3,000**
Minimum award amount: **$1,000**
Number of applications received each year: **175**

Olin Fellowship #475
Maximum award amount: **$3,000**
Average award amount: **$1,500**
Minimum award amount: **$1,000**
Number of applications received each year: **10**

Oregon AFL-CIO May Darling-Asat. Williams-Northwest Labor Press Scholarship #827
Maximum award amount: **$3,000**
Minimum award amount: **$850**

Palmer J. Hermunslie Scholarship #142
Maximum award amount: **$3,000**
Minimum award amount: **$500**
Number of applications received each year: **150**

Pellegrini Scholarship #701
Maximum award amount: **$3,000**
Minimum award amount: **$500**
Number of applications received each year: **59**

Press Club of Dallas Foundation Scholarships #465
Maximum award amount: **$3,000**
Average award amount: **$1,000**
Minimum award amount: **$1,000**
Number of applications received each year: **60**

Seaspace Scholarship #478
Maximum award amount: **$3,000**
Average award amount: **$2,000**
Minimum award amount: **$500**
Number of applications received each year: **78**

Ty Cobb Scholarship #847
Maximum award amount: **$3,000**
Average award amount: **$2,500**
Minimum award amount: **$2,000**
Number of applications received each year: **1,000**

William Winter Teacher Scholar Program #360
Maximum award amount: **$3,000**
Minimum award amount: **$1,000**

James F. Byrnes Scholarship #790
Maximum award amount: **$2,750**
Number of applications received each year: **204**

Together We Can Scholarship #168
Maximum award amount: **$2,660**
Minimum award amount: **$1,330**
Number of applications received each year: **150**

ACS Scholars Program #158
Maximum award amount: **$2,500**
Minimum award amount: **$600**
Number of applications received each year: **1,000**

ACS/Bayer Scholars Program #741
Maximum award amount: **$2,500**

AIA Minority/Disadvantaged Scholarship Program #101
Maximum award amount: **$2,500**
Minimum award amount: **$500**
Number of applications received each year: **135**

Angus Foundation Scholarship #211
Maximum award amount: **$2,500**
Minimum award amount: **$1,000**
Number of applications received each year: **70**

AWA Scholarship Awards #408
Maximum award amount: **$2,500**
Average award amount: **$1,500**
Minimum award amount: **$500**
Number of applications received each year: **60**

B.F. Goodrich Scholarship #617
Maximum award amount: **$2,500**
Number of applications received each year: **150**

BIA Higher Education/Hopi Supplemental Grant #680
Maximum award amount: **$2,500**

Bowfin Memorial Scholarship #556
Maximum award amount: **$2,500**
Average award amount: **$1,000**
Minimum award amount: **$500**
Number of applications received each year: **25**

Eddy/Peck Scholarship #471
Maximum award amount: **$2,500**
Minimum award amount: **$1,000**
Number of applications received each year: **24**

G. Robert Hamrdla Award #293
Maximum award amount: **$2,500**
Number of applications received each year: **6**

George M. Brooker Collegiate Scholarship for Minorities #714
Maximum award amount: **$2,500**
Minimum award amount: **$1,000**
Number of applications received each year: **10**

Half to Full-time Student Scholarship #69
Maximum award amount: **$2,500**
Average award amount: **$2,000**
Minimum award amount: **$1,500**
Number of applications received each year: **350**

21. Top 100 Scholarships With The Best Odds Of Winning

(Note: This ranking is based on data supplied by the awarding organizations. Not all provide complete data, including the percentage of applicants who receive an award.)

ACJA/LAE National Scholarship #473
100% of applicants received an award.
7 applications received.
$400 maximum awarded to each winner.
$200 average awarded to each winner.
$100 minimum awarded to each winner.

ACJA/LAE National Student Paper Competition #213
100% of applicants received an award.
6 applications received.
$150 maximum awarded to each winner.
$100 average awarded to each winner.
$50 minimum awarded to each winner.

Association of the Sons of Poland Achievement Award #223
100% of applicants received an award.
16 applications received.
$50 average awarded to each winner.

Cabugao Sons and Daughters Association of Hawaii Incentive Award for Children of Members #660
100% of applicants received an award.
2 applications received.
$500 average awarded to each winner.

Calavo Scholarship #84
100% of applicants received an award.
1 application received.
$625 average awarded to each winner.

Capt. Caliendo College Assistance Fund Scholarship #559
100% of applicants received an award.
50 applications received.
$1,500 maximum awarded to each winner.
$500 minimum awarded to each winner.

ChemFirst Foundation Scholarship #166
100% of applicants received an award.
23 applications received.
$1,300 average awarded to each winner.

Educational Benefits for Children of Deceased Veterans #531
100% of applicants received an award.
2 applications received.
$8,500 maximum awarded to each winner.

Federation Life Insurance of America Scholarship #238
100% of applicants received an award.
22 applications received.
$350 minimum awarded to each winner.

First Cavalry Division Association Scholarship #534
100% of applicants received an award.
$600 average awarded to each winner.

Law Enforcement Officers Dependents' Scholarship #764
100% of applicants received an award.
22 applications received.

Lights of Jewish Special Needs Society Scholarship #732
100% of applicants received an award.
16 applications received.
$1,000 maximum awarded to each winner.
$556 average awarded to each winner.
$300 minimum awarded to each winner.

Medicus Student Exchange #702
100% of applicants received an award.
1 applications received.
$5,000 maximum awarded to each winner.
$4,000 minimum awarded to each winner.

MGAA Scholarship #425
100% of applicants received an award.
12 applications received.
$500 maximum awarded to each winner.
$200 average awarded to each winner.
$150 minimum awarded to each winner.

MIA/KIA Dependents' Scholarship #526
100% of applicants received an award.
2 applications received.

National Amputee Golf Association Scholarship #335
100% of applicants received an award.
3 applications received.
$2,000 maximum awarded to each winner.
$1,000 minimum awarded to each winner.

North Dakota American Legion High School Oratorical Contest #747
100% of applicants received an award.
28 applications received.
$1,900 maximum awarded to each winner.
$200 average awarded to each winner.
$100 minimum awarded to each winner.

Oratorical Contest #744
100% of applicants received an award.
6 applications received.
$300 maximum awarded to each winner.
$50 minimum awarded to each winner.

Public Safety Officers Survivor Grant #814
100% of applicants received an award.
9 applications received.
$6,748 maximum awarded to each winner.
$3,419 average awarded to each winner.

TNE Scholarship #302
100% of applicants received an award.
28 applications received.
$10,000 maximum awarded to each winner.
$5,000 average awarded to each winner.
$1,000 minimum awarded to each winner.

United States Naval Academy Class of 1963 Foundation Scholarship #560
100% of applicants received an award.
6 applications received.
$4,000 maximum awarded to each winner.
$1,000 average awarded to each winner.
$1,000 minimum awarded to each winner.

W.H. "Howie" McClennan Scholarship #402
100% of applicants received an award.
13 applications received.
$2,500 average awarded to each winner.

War Orphans Educational Aid #537
100% of applicants received an award.
5 applications received.
$600 maximum awarded to each winner.

Culinary Arts/Nutrition/Physical Education Scholarship #327
99% of applicants received an award.
14 applications received.
$1,000 maximum awarded to each winner.
$500 minimum awarded to each winner.

Vietnam Veterans Scholarship #549
99% of applicants received an award.
37 applications received.

United States Ski and Snowboard Team Foundation Scholarship #108
98% of applicants received an award.
33 applications received.
$2,000 maximum awarded to each winner.
$1,000 average awarded to each winner.

Academic Scholars Program #826
96% of applicants received an award.
410 applications received.
$5,500 maximum awarded to each winner.
$4,000 average awarded to each winner.
$3,500 minimum awarded to each winner.

Almanor Scholarship #167
95% of applicants received an award.
50 applications received.
$2,400 maximum awarded to each winner.
$1,800 minimum awarded to each winner.

U.S. Submarine Veterans of World War II Scholarship #532
95% of applicants received an award.
11 applications received.
$3,000 minimum awarded to each winner.

BIA (Tribal) Grant #690
90% of applicants received an award.
146 applications received.
$2,200 maximum awarded to each winner.
$2,200 average awarded to each winner.
$100 minimum awarded to each winner.

General Scholarship #197
90% of applicants received an award.
300 applications received.
$3,000 maximum awarded to each winner.
$1,100 average awarded to each winner.
$350 minimum awarded to each winner.

Master's Fund Grant #717
90% of applicants received an award.
55 applications received.
$700 maximum awarded to each winner.
$500 minimum awarded to each winner.

RRVA Scholarship Grant Assistance Program #552
90% of applicants received an award.
42 applications received.
$3,500 maximum awarded to each winner.
$500 minimum awarded to each winner.

School Food Service Foundation Scholarship #879
90% of applicants received an award.
$1,000 maximum awarded to each winner.
$500 average awarded to each winner.
$100 minimum awarded to each winner.

Schwan's Food Service Scholarship #880
90% of applicants received an award.
120 applications received.
$1,000 maximum awarded to each winner.
$500 average awarded to each winner.
$100 minimum awarded to each winner.

Masonic Grand Lodge Charities of Rhode Island Scholarship #811
88% of applicants received an award.
215 applications received.
$3,500 maximum awarded to each winner.
$750 minimum awarded to each winner.

Governor's Workforce Development Grant #776
85% of applicants received an award.
175 applications received.
$1,500 maximum awarded to each winner.
$1,000 average awarded to each winner.

Kentucky Restaurant Association Scholarship #320
85% of applicants received an award.
35 applications received.
$1,250 maximum awarded to each winner.
$1,000 average awarded to each winner.
$500 minimum awarded to each winner.

EPA Tribal Lands Environmental Science Scholarship #394
82% of applicants received an award.
83 applications received.
$4,000 average awarded to each winner.

Pellegrini Scholarship #701
81% of applicants received an award.
59 applications received.
$3,000 maximum awarded to each winner.
$500 minimum awarded to each winner.

Allied Dental Education Scholarship #325
80% of applicants received an award.
5 applications received.
$500 maximum awarded to each winner.
$300 average awarded to each winner.
$100 minimum awarded to each winner.

Bowfin Memorial Scholarship #556
80% of applicants received an award.
25 applications received.
$2,500 maximum awarded to each winner.
$1,000 average awarded to each winner.
$500 minimum awarded to each winner.

Scholarship Program for Dependent Children of Soldiers #527
80% of applicants received an award.
3,000 applications received.
$1,700 maximum awarded to each winner.
$900 average awarded to each winner.
$600 minimum awarded to each winner.

Washington Post Thomas Ewing Memorial Education Grant #156
80% of applicants received an award.
$2,000 maximum awarded to each winner.
$1,000 average awarded to each winner.
$1,000 minimum awarded to each winner.

Catholic Aid Association College Tuition Scholarship #228
75% of applicants received an award.
200 applications received.
$500 maximum awarded to each winner.
$300 minimum awarded to each winner.

Excellence in Accounting Scholarship #68
75% of applicants received an award.
100 applications received.
$1,500 average awarded to each winner.

Leonard H. Bulkeley Scholarship #189
75% of applicants received an award.
80 applications received.
$1,000 maximum awarded to each winner.

Youth Scholarship Fund of IBHA, Inc. #241
75% of applicants received an award.
12 applications received.
$1,500 maximum awarded to each winner.
$500 minimum awarded to each winner.

Arkansas Academic Challenge Scholarship #763
71% of applicants received an award.
6,567 applications received.
$2,500 average awarded to each winner.

UDT/SEAL Scholarship Grant #308
70% of applicants received an award.
$1,000 average awarded to each winner.

Gerber Foundation Scholarship #150
68% of applicants received an award.
48 applications received.
$1,500 average awarded to each winner.

Charles W. Frees, Jr. Scholarship #412
67% of applicants received an award.
60 applications received.
$1,200 maximum awarded to each winner.
$1,000 average awarded to each winner.
$800 minimum awarded to each winner.

Central American Scholarship #406
66% of applicants received an award.
3 applications received.
$2,000 average awarded to each winner.

National Woman's Relief Corps Scholarship #280
66% of applicants received an award.
12 applications received.
$350 maximum awarded to each winner.
$200 minimum awarded to each winner.

Saticoy Lemon Association Employee Scholarhip #155
66% of applicants received an award.
3 applications received.
$600 average awarded to each winner.

Racial-Ethnic Education Scholarship #703
65% of applicants received an award.
475 applications received.
$600 maximum awarded to each winner.
$250 minimum awarded to each winner.

Synod of the Trinity Education Scholarship #736
65% of applicants received an award.
475 applications received.
$600 maximum awarded to each winner.
$250 minimum awarded to each winner.

Bernice Barnard Music Specialist Scholarhip #583
62% of applicants received an award.
8 applications received.
$1,000 maximum awarded to each winner.
$500 minimum awarded to each winner.

General Henry H. Arnold Education Grant #504
60% of applicants received an award.
9,000 applications received.
$1,500 average awarded to each winner.

Phoenix Scholarship #194
60% of applicants received an award.
12 applications received.
$1,000 maximum awarded to each winner.
$100 minimum awarded to each winner.

Maryland Association of Certified Public Accountants Educational Foundation Scholarship #66
58% of applicants received an award.
40 applications received.
$1,000 average awarded to each winner.

Society of Petroleum Engineers - San Joaquin Valley Section Scholarship #384
55% of applicants received an award.
11 applications received.
$1,000 maximum awarded to each winner.
$500 minimum awarded to each winner.

Vermont Part-Time Grant #849
55% of applicants received an award.
4,718 applications received.
$5,100 maximum awarded to each winner.
$384 average awarded to each winner.
$250 minimum awarded to each winner.

Nurses Training Scholarship #608
52% of applicants received an award.
42 applications received.
$400 maximum awarded to each winner.
$200 average awarded to each winner.
$150 minimum awarded to each winner.

TOPS - Opportunity Award #794
52% of applicants received an award.
25,400 applications received.

AACC Undergraduate Scholarships #75
50% of applicants received an award.
33 applications received.
$2,000 maximum awarded to each winner.
$1,000 minimum awarded to each winner.

ABFSE Scholarship #1
50% of applicants received an award.
100 applications received.
$500 maximum awarded to each winner.
$250 average awarded to each winner.
$250 minimum awarded to each winner.

Adult Vocational Training Grant Assistance #659
50% of applicants received an award.
50 applications received.
$3,100 average awarded to each winner.

Alaska Sea Services Scholarship #505
50% of applicants received an award.
8 applications received.
$1,000 maximum awarded to each winner.

American Express Scholarship #439
50% of applicants received an award.
18 applications received.
$2,000 maximum awarded to each winner.
$500 minimum awarded to each winner.

Armstrong Multicultural Education Scholarship #653
50% of applicants received an award.
60 applications received.
$1,500 maximum awarded to each winner.
$1,000 minimum awarded to each winner.

Baruch Incentive Grant #9
50% of applicants received an award.
$1,000 maximum awarded to each winner.
$500 minimum awarded to each winner.

Charles Walton Peace Essay Contest #196
50% of applicants received an award.
30 applications received.
$1,000 maximum awarded to each winner.
$25 minimum awarded to each winner.

Delta Gamma Foundation Scholarship #234
50% of applicants received an award.
$1,000 average awarded to each winner.

Finlandia Foundation Trust Scholarship Exchange Program and Grants #672
50% of applicants received an award.
$5,000 maximum awarded to each winner.
$2,500 average awarded to each winner.
$1,000 minimum awarded to each winner.

Jacob Rassen Memorial Scholarship Fund #184
50% of applicants received an award.
$1,900 maximum awarded to each winner.

LAEF Scholarship #791
50% of applicants received an award.
133 applications received.
$3,000 maximum awarded to each winner.
$500 minimum awarded to each winner.

Lawrence Conservation District Scholarship #187
50% of applicants received an award.
2 applications received.
$500 maximum awarded to each winner.

Lorain County Home Economics Scholarship #431
50% of applicants received an award.
4 applications received.
$300 average awarded to each winner.

Maine Student Incentive Scholarship #800
50% of applicants received an award.
$1,000 maximum awarded to each winner.
$250 minimum awarded to each winner.

Maryland Association of Private Career Schools Scholarship #890
50% of applicants received an award.
120 applications received.
$5,000 maximum awarded to each winner.
$1,000 average awarded to each winner.
$500 minimum awarded to each winner.

Minority Media Scholarship #316
50% of applicants received an award.
20 applications received.
$5,000 maximum awarded to each winner.

$2,500 average awarded to each winner.
$1,000 minimum awarded to each winner.

National Federation of the Blind Scholarship #347
50% of applicants received an award.
8 applications received.
$2,000 maximum awarded to each winner.
$500 average awarded to each winner.
$200 minimum awarded to each winner.

Nebraska Space Grant and EPSCOR College and Fellowship Program #74
50% of applicants received an award.
$7,500 maximum awarded to each winner.
$250 minimum awarded to each winner.

NIS Regional Languages Grant #403
50% of applicants received an award.
20 applications received.
$15,030 maximum awarded to each winner.
$8,515 average awarded to each winner.
$2,000 minimum awarded to each winner.

Past President's Parley Nurses Scholarship #596
50% of applicants received an award.
12 applications received.
$400 maximum awarded to each winner.

Past President's Parley Scholarship Assistance in Health Care Occupations #756
50% of applicants received an award.
10 applications received.
$300 maximum awarded to each winner.

Blackfeet Higher Education Scholarship #657
47% of applicants received an award.
404 applications received.
$3,600 maximum awarded to each winner.
$3,000 minimum awarded to each winner.

Higher Education Grant Assistance #658
47% of applicants received an award.
322 applications received.
$3,100 average awarded to each winner.

John L. Dales Scholarship #881
46% of applicants received an award.
65 applications received.
$4,000 average awarded to each winner.

Two/Ten International Footwear Foundation College Scholarship #882
44% of applicants received an award.
540 applications received.
$2,000 maximum awarded to each winner.
$1,055 average awarded to each winner.
$200 minimum awarded to each winner.

Illinois Incentive for Access #27
41% of applicants received an award.
46,000 applications received.
$500 maximum awarded to each winner.

STW Foundation Individual Award #637
41% of applicants received an award.
128 applications received.
$1,500 maximum awarded to each winner.
$500 average awarded to each winner.
$25 minimum awarded to each winner.

AFSA Financial Aid Scholarship #620
40% of applicants received an award.
150 applications received.
$3,000 maximum awarded to each winner.
$1,800 average awarded to each winner.
$500 minimum awarded to each winner.

Biomet Foundation Scholarship #130
40% of applicants received an award.
25 applications received.
$2,000 average awarded to each winner.

First Catholic Slovak Ladies Association Scholarship #239
40% of applicants received an award.
200 applications received.
$1,000 average awarded to each winner.

GSCAA Scholars #433
40% of applicants received an award.
50 applications received.
$3,500 maximum awarded to each winner.
$2,500 average awarded to each winner.
$500 minimum awarded to each winner.

Hispanic Scholarship Fund General Scholarship #679
40% of applicants received an award.
12,000 applications received.
$7,500 maximum awarded to each winner.
$2,000 average awarded to each winner.
$1,000 minimum awarded to each winner.

Milton McKevett Teague Scholarship #85
40% of applicants received an award.
5 applications received.
$3,000 maximum awarded to each winner.
$2,500 average awarded to each winner.

National Association of Hispanic Nurses Scholarship #605
40% of applicants received an award.
10 applications received.
$2,000 maximum awarded to each winner.
$1,000 average awarded to each winner.
$1,000 minimum awarded to each winner.

Appendix A: Glossary

Academic year: Time period a school uses to compute an amount of study. For example, many schools define an academic year as the fall and spring semester or three quarters.

Accrual date: Date in which interest charges start to accumulate on the loan balance.

Accrued interest: Interest that is added to a loan amount.

AmeriCorps: Provides full-time educational awards for working in community service.

Amortize: To repay a debt by periodic or installment payments.

Borrower: Student or parent who receives a loan.

Byrd Program: Robert C. Byrd Honors Scholarship Program, which is based on academic achievement and promise of future academic achievement. Administered by the state agencies for public elementary and secondary schools.

Campus-based aid: Financial aid programs in which the government provides a fixed annual allowance to the colleges, which in turn award the funds. Campus-based aid programs include Federal Supplemental Educational Opportunity Grants (FSEOGs), Federal Perkins Loans, and Federal Work-Study.

Capitalization or compounding interest: The accrual, or addition, of interest to the loan principal by a lender before a borrower starts repaying the loan. Capitalization increases the total outstanding balance due and the monthly minimum payments. It can be avoided by paying the accrued interest.

Citizen or eligible non-citizen: Status to be eligible for federal financial aid. Includes: U.S. citizens, U.S. nationals, or U.S. permanent residents who have an I-151, I-551, or I-551C. Or, who have an Arrival-Departure Record (I-94) from the U.S. Immigration and Naturalization Service designating their status as Refugee, Asylum Granted, Indefinite Parole and/or Humanitarian Parole, Cuban-Haitian Entrant Status Pending, or Conditional Entrant (if issued before April 1, 1980).

Consolidation Loans: Allow students and parents to consolidate a number of federal financial aid loans into a single loan to simplify repayment. This allows the borrowers to make one payment per month and in some cases obtain a lower interest rate. All of the federal loans described in this book can be consolidated.

Cooperative education: A program in which students alternate between periods of full-time study and full-time work, usually in a field related to their studies. Under this program, students usually take five years to complete an undergraduate degree.

Co-signer: A person other than the borrower who is responsible for repaying a loan if the borrower does not pay.

Cost Of Attendance (COA): The cost of attending your college or university for one year, including tuition and other fees, room and board, transportation, books and other supplies, and personal expenses. This amount is used in the formula to determine your financial need.

Default: Failure to repay a loan according to the loan terms.

Deferment: Temporary postponement of payments on your loan due to special circumstances.

Delinquent: Failure to make a loan payment on time.

Department of Education (DOE, ED, DE, or USED): The government agency that directs federal financial aid programs.

Dependency status: To establish eligibility and need, students are either considered dependent on their parents for financial contribution or independent of their parents for financial contribution. You are independent if one of the following is true:
  ● You were born before January 1, 1977 (for the 2000-2001 school year).
  ● You're married.
  ● You're enrolled in a graduate or professional degree program.
  ● You have legal dependents other than a spouse.

- You're an orphan or ward of the court.
- You're a veteran of the U.S. Armed Forces.

Direct Stafford Loans: Federal financial aid loan program available through the William D. Ford Federal Direct Loan Program. The U.S. government is the direct lender. Loans must be repaid over a time period that is generally 10 years or less but that can be extended to as many as 30 years.

Disbursement: The distribution of funds from a lender to a borrower. For federal loans, the money is released to your school.

Disclosure statement: A declaration of the total amount of a loan, including the interest and any additional fees.

Education IRA: Individual retirement account that allows you to accumulate interest tax-free and to withdraw money without penalty for education expenses of you, your spouse, child, or grandchild.

Eligible non-citizen: Non-U.S. citizen who is eligible for Federal financial aid. Eligible non-citizens include U.S. permanent residents who have an I-151, I-551, or I-551C. Or, have an Arrival-Departure Record (I-94) from the U.S. Immigration and Naturalization Service designating status as Refugee, Asylum Granted, Indefinite Parole and/or Humanitarian Parole, Cuban-Haitian Entrant Status Pending, or Conditional Entrant (if issued before April 1, 1980).

Enrollment status: Your standing as a student, either full time or part time. In most cases, to be eligible for federal financial aid, you must be enrolled at least half-time.

Entrance and exit interviews: Informational meetings that borrowers must attend before the release of loan funds and before leaving the school.

Expected Family Contribution (EFC): Based on a formula established by the U.S. Congress, the amount that your family and you are expected to contribute to your education. This amount is used in the formula to determine your financial need.

FAFSA Express: Software version of the Free Application for Federal Student Aid (FAFSA) available to download from the Internet at www.ed.gov or by diskette by calling 800-801-0576.

FAFSA on the Web: Online version of the Free Application for Federal Student Aid (FAFSA) available at www.fafsa.ed.gov.

Federal methodology: The formulas by which the government determines students' eligibility for federal financial aid programs.

Federal Pell Grants: Need-based grants that do not need to be repaid awarded by the government for undergraduate and post-baccalaureate teacher certification students.

Federal Perkins Loans: Low-interest loans for undergraduate and graduate students with extreme financial need. Your school provides the loan from funds provided by the government and its own funds. You must repay the loan.

Federal Supplemental Educational Opportunity Grants (FSEOGs): Grants for undergraduates with the most financial need, i.e., the lowest Expected Family Contributions. FSEOG Grants do not need to be repaid. Based on financial need, other aid you receive, and availability of funds at your school. Priority is given to those who receive Federal Pell Grants.

Federal work-study: Money you earn the old-fashioned way—by working. Provides jobs for undergraduate and graduate students with financial need allowing them to earn money while attending school. Generally, you will work for your school on campus or for a nonprofit organization or public agency if you work off campus.

FFEL Stafford Loans: Loans available through the Federal Family Education Loan Program. Lenders are banks, credit unions, or other participating lenders. Loans must be repaid within 10 years.

Financial aid: Financial support for students or parents to assist with paying for educational expenses. Financial aid can consist of loans, grants, work-study, or scholarships. It can assist with tuition, fees and books and sometimes with other costs such as room and board, travel expenses, and research expenses.

Financial aid administrator (FAA): An employee of your college's financial aid office who uses the information you provide to determine your financial need and to develop a corresponding financial aid package.

Financial aid award letter: Letter students receive from their colleges' financial aid office outlining their official financial aid package. Usually the letter is accompanied by information about the terms and conditions of the financial aid offered and the factors taken into consideration when determining the package.

Financial aid package: The total amount of financial aid, including federal and nonfederal aid, a student receives.

Financial need: Cost Of Attendance – Expected Family Contribution = Financial Need. The Financial aid administrator (FAA) at your school will use this formula to calculate if you have financial need. If you do, he or she will try to develop a corresponding financial aid package.

Fixed interest rate: A loan in which the interest rate does not change for the term of the loan.

Forbearance: A limited and temporary postponement or reduction of your payments if you are unable to meet your repayment schedule and are not eligible for a deferment. These circumstances may include poor health, serving in a medical or dental internship or residency, or if the payments exceed 20 percent of your monthly gross income

Free Application for Federal Student Aid (FAFSA): Form from the Department of Education that you need to complete to apply for federal financial aid. The FAFSA requests information about your family's financial status that is used to determine your Estimated Family Contribution (EFC). See Appendix B for information on where to obtain the form.

General Education Development (GED) Certificate: A certificate for passing a high school equivalency test.

Gift aid: Financial aid such as grants or scholarships that does not have to be repaid.

Grants: Money with no strings attached–meaning you don't have to pay it back. This is like hitting the financial aid jackpot. Grants are given by the government, state agencies, and colleges.

Guaranty Agency: The organization that administers the FFEL Program for your school.

Hope tax credit: Tuition tax credits of up to $1,500 in 2001. The credit is subtracted from your income tax on a dollar-for-dollar basis and can be used for the first two years of school. Qualified expenses that can be credited include tuition and related fees, minus any tax-free grants or scholarships received.

In-school status: Standing in which student borrowers are either attending school at least half-time or are in a loan grace period.

Interest: A charge for a loan, usually a percentage of the amount borrowed.

Internship: Student jobs that provide training in a related academic field, typically part-time during the school year or part-time or full-time during the summer. Internships may be paid or unpaid.

Lifetime Learning tax credit: Tuition tax credits of up to $1,000. The credit is subtracted from your income tax on a dollar-for-dollar basis. The Lifetime Learning credit can be used for any postsecondary education including graduate school. Qualified expenses that can be credited include tuition and related fees, minus any tax-free grants or scholarships received.

Loans: Money you borrow and are required to pay back with interest. In most cases the terms are more generous than other types of loans such as home or auto loans.

Need-based: Financial aid that is based on financial need.

PLUS Loans: Loans for parents with good credit histories to pay for their dependent undergraduate students who are enrolled at least half time. Available through both the Direct PLUS Loan and FFEL PLUS Loan Program. Not based on financial need.

Post-secondary: Educational programs attended after high school including colleges, universities, and vocational or technical schools.

Prepaid tuition plan: A savings program that guarantees to increase in value in correspondence with the increase in college tuition. For example, if a parent purchases shares that are worth one year of tuition now, the plan will guarantee that the shares will be worth one year of tuition in the future even though tuition rates will have changed.

Principal: The debt amount upon which interest is calculated.

PROFILE (CSS/Financial Aid PROFILE): Financial aid application service managed by the College Board and used by about 450 colleges and 350 scholarship programs.

Promissory note: The legal document you sign when you get a student loan.

Renewable: Financial aid awards that may be renewed for more than one term, i.e., for more than one year. Some require that applicants re-apply; others require that applicants maintain a certain level of academic achievement.

Renewal Free Application for Federal Student Aid (Renewal FAFSA): Form to complete to apply for federal financial aid if you've previously applied. Most students who have applied before are eligible to use this form, pre-filled with information from the previous year.

Repayment period: The time in which borrowers repay a loan.

State-sponsored tuition plans: These plans allow you to save for tuition and room and board. You do not pay taxes until you withdraw the money.

Statement of educational purpose: Legal agreement in which students state that they will only use financial aid for educational costs.

Student Aid Report (SAR): Report generated by the Department of Education from the information you provide in the Free Application for Federal Student Aid (FAFSA). This report provides your Expected Family Contribution (EFC), which is used by your college or university to develop a financial aid package.

Subsidized Stafford Loans: Based on financial need. The government subsidizes interest payments so that you are not charged interest before you begin repayment or in approved periods of deferment.

Transcript: A document that lists students' coursework and grades.

Tuition: The charge or fee for instruction at a college or university. Typically it does not include expenses for room and board, travel to and from the campus, and other necessary living and personal expenses.

Unsubsidized Stafford Loans: Not based on financial need. You are charged interest from the time the loan is disbursed until it is paid off.

Variable interest: Interest rate that fluctuates over time.

Work-study: See Federal work-study.

Appendix B: Resource Guide

SuperCollege, LLC
4546 B10 El Camino Real #281
Los Altos, CA 94022
Phone: 650-618-2221
Email: supercollege@supercollege.com
www.supercollege.com
Our publishing company, which focuses on helping students get into and pay for college. Please visit our website, www.supercollege.com, to search a free database of thousands of scholarships, get more financial aid and scholarship tips and strategies, and enter our SuperCollege.com scholarship.

Access America For Students
400 Maryland Ave., SW
ROB-3, ROOM 4004
Washington, DC 20202-5132
Email: contact@students.gov
www.students.gov: From the U.S. Department of Education, a directory of government websites for planning and paying for your education. Also contains resources for finding a job, registering for the Selective Service, and applying to be a Peace Corps volunteer.

America's Learning Exchange
Phone: 877-348-0502
Phone: 877-348-0501(TTY)
Email: helpme@alx.org
www.alx.org: Resources for career exploration, career tools, career testing and assessment, work-study programs.

Corporation for National Service
1201 New York Avenue, NW
Washington, DC 20525
Phone: 800-942-2677
Email: webmaster@cns.gov
www.cns.gov or www.americorps.org
Public service resources including information on AmeriCorps, a federal program in which you can volunteer for one year and receive a modest living allowance, health insurance, student loan deferment, training, and a $4,725 education award to help pay for college, grad school, vocational training, or to pay off student loans. If you serve part time, you'll get a portion of that amount.

College Board
www.collegeboard.org
On the website, the makers of the SAT and PSAT offer financial aid calculators, a scholarship search, and articles on financial aid.

IRS
Phone: 800-829-1040
www.irs.gov
Information on higher-education income tax credits and tax implications of financial aid awards.

National Association of Intercollegiate Athletics
6120 S. Yale Avenue
Suite 1450
Tulsa, OK 74136
Phone: 918-494-8828
www.naia.org
Information on eligibility requirements and financial aid for student-athletes.

National Collegiate Athletic Association (NCAA)
700 W. Washington Avenue
P.O. Box 6222
Indianapolis, IN 46206-6222
Phone: 317-917-6222
Fax: 317-917-6888
www.ncaa.org
Information on eligibility requirements and directory of schools that award scholarships for athletics.

National Junior College Athletic Association
PO Box 7305
Colorado Springs, CO 80933-7305
Phone: 719-590-9788
Fax: 719-590-7324
www.njcaa.org
Information on scholarships and awards for student-athletes and individuals based on performance, service, merit, or achievement.

National Small College Athletic Association
113 East Bow Street
Franklin, NH 03235
Phone: 603-934-4152
www.thenscaa.com
Information for student-athletes and directory of member schools that award financial aid for athletics.

Sallie Mae
Phone: 888-2-SALLIE or 800-239-4269
Email: college.answer@slma.com.
www.salliemae.com: Contains a financial aid glossary, information on lenders, financial aid calculators, and financial aid 101.

U.S. Department of Education & Federal Financial Aid
Federal Student Aid Information Center
P.O. Box 84
Washington, DC 20044-0084
Phone: 800-4-FED-AID (800-433-3243) toll-free, TTY 800-730-8913, or 319-337-5665 for international callers

The Federal Student Aid Information Center can help you with:
● Completing the FAFSA.
● Making corrections to your SAR.
● Questions about eligibility.
● Questions about the federal financial aid process.
● Providing you with free federal financial aid publications.

Consolidated Loans
Phone: The Loan Origination Center's Consolidation Department, 800-557-7392 or TTY 800-557-7395

Direct Loan Servicing Center
Phone: 800-848-0979 or TDD 800-848-0983 (Telecommunications Device for the Deaf)

Estimated Family Contribution (EFC)
www.ifap.ed.gov/csb_html/efcform.htm: Worksheets that show how to calculate EFC.

FAFSA
Phone: For general information and help on the FAFSA, checking the status of your FAFSA, requesting a copy of your Student Aid Report (SAR), and ordering the FAFSA on computer disk, 800-801-0576 or 319-337-5665 for international callers.

www.ed.gov: Includes information on completing the FAFSA, federal aid program eligibility, descriptions, and deadlines, tips on reducing costs, tax cuts for education, and online versions of two informative guides, *Funding Your Education* and *The Student Guide*.

www.fafsa.ed.gov: To download the FAFSA on the Internet.

Veteran Benefits
Phone: 888-GI-BILL-1 (888-442-4551)
www.gibill.va.gov: Information on educational programs for veterans and dependents.

Appendix C: State Agencies For Student Financial Assistance

Contact your state agency for student financial assistance for more information on state-funded financial aid programs, such as the Robert C. Byrd Honors Scholarship Program, which is based on academic achievement and promise of future academic achievement.

Alabama	334-242-2276	South Carolina	803-734-1200
Alaska	907-465-6741	South Dakota	605-773-3134
Arizona	602-229-2591	Tennessee	800-342-1663
Arkansas	800-547-8839	Texas	800-242-3062
California	916-526-7590	Utah	800-418-8757
Colorado	303-866-2723	Vermont	800-642-3177
Connecticut	860-947-1855	Virginia	804-786-1690
Delaware	800-292-7935	Washington	360-753-7850
District of Columbia	202-727-3688	West Virginia	888-825-5707
Florida	888-827-2004	Wisconsin	608-267-2944
Georgia	800-776-6878	Wyoming	307-777-7763
Hawaii	800-956-8213	Guam	671-475-0457
Idaho	208-334-2270	Northern Mariana Islands	670-234-6128
Illinois	800-899-4722	Puerto Rico	800-724-7100
Indiana	317-232-2350	Republic of Palau	680-488-2471
Iowa	515-281-3501	Virgin Islands	340-774-4546
Kansas	785-296-3517		
Kentucky	800-928-8926		
Louisiana	800-259-5626	Source: *Funding Your Education, 2000-2001* from
Maine	800-228-3734	the Department of Education.
Maryland	410-974-5370		
Massachusetts	617-727-1205		
Michigan	888-447-2687		
Minnesota	800-657-3866		
Mississippi	601-982-6663		
Missouri	800-473-6757		
Montana	800-537-7508		
Nebraska	402-471-2847		
Nevada	775-687-9200		
New Hampshire	603-271-2555		
New Jersey	800-792-8670		
New Mexico	800-279-9777		
New York	800-642-6234		
North Carolina	800-234-6400		
North Dakota	701-328-4114		
Ohio	888-833-1133		
Oklahoma	405-858-4356		
Oregon	800-452-8807		
Pennsylvania	800-692-7435		
Rhode Island	800-922-9855		

Index

Attention Students & Parents:
Win $$$ From The SuperCollege.com Scholarship

From the proceeds of our book sales, we award two scholarships each year:

For students: We reward high school and college undergraduates who excel in both academics and extracurriculars.

For parents: We offer the only scholarship of its kind for parents who support their children with college admissions or financial aid.

These scholarships are a part of the ongoing mission of SuperCollege.com to help students get into and pay for the college of their dreams. The awards range from $500 to $2,500.

To enter, please visit www.supercollege.com. Only online applications are accepted.

Get What You Need To Get Into & Pay For College!

We invite you to visit our website at **www.supercollege.com** to:

- Enter the SuperCollege.com Scholarship, the only scholarship of its kind for both students and parents.

- Find more scholarships that match your background in the free database of thousands of awards.

- Learn more tips and strategies on financial aid, scholarships, and college admissions.

- Use the SuperCollege MatchMaker to find colleges that fit you.

- Connect with other students who understand what you are going through and can offer helpful advice.

- Get advice for parents on how you can help your child get into and pay for any college.

- Ask questions of the authors.

About The Authors

Harvard graduates Gen S. Tanabe and Kelly Y. Tanabe are the founders of SuperCollege.com and the award-winning authors of the books *Get Into Any College: Secrets Of Harvard Students* and *Get Free Cash For College: Scholarship Secrets Of Harvard Students.*

Together, Gen and Kelly were accepted to every school to which they applied: all of the Ivy League colleges plus other prestigious universities including Stanford, Berkeley, Duke, and Rice. They earned over $100,000 in merit-based scholarships and left Harvard debt-free and their parents guilt-free.

The husband and wife team have spent the past six years researching college admissions and financial aid to develop the SuperCollege.com website and their books, which draw on the knowledge and experiences of other students at top colleges.

Gen and Kelly lecture at high schools across the country and write the "Ask The SuperCollege.com Experts" column syndicated in over 200 local and school newspapers nationwide.

They have made dozens of appearances on television and radio programs and have served as expert sources for respected publications including *USA Today*, the *New York Daily News*, the *San Jose Mercury News*, the *Richmond Times Dispatch*, and the *Chronicle of Higher Education.*

Gen grew up in Waialua, Hawaii. Between eating banana-flavored shave ice and basking in the sun, he was president of the Student Council, captain of the Speech Team, and a member of the tennis team. A graduate of Waialua High School, he was the first student from his school to be accepted at Harvard. In college, Gen was chair of the Eliot House Committee and graduated *magna cum laude* with a degree in both History and East Asian Studies.

Kelly attended Whitney High School, a nationally ranked public high school in her hometown of Cerritos, California. She was the editor of the school newspaper, assistant editor of the yearbook, and founder of a public service club to promote literacy. In college, she was the co-director of the HAND public service program and the brave co-leader of a Brownie Troop. She graduated *magna cum laude* with a degree in Sociology.

The Tanabes approach college admissions and financial aid from a practical, hands-on point of view. Drawing on the collective knowledge and experiences of students at America's top colleges, they provide real strategies students can use to increase their chances of getting into their dream school and paying for their education.

Gen, Kelly, and their dog Sushi live in Palo Alto, California.